Encyclopedia of Modern Christian Politics

ENCYCLOPEDIA OF
MODERN CHRISTIAN POLITICS

Volume 2, L–Z

Edited by
Roy P. Domenico and Mark Y. Hanley

GREENWOOD PRESS
Westport, Connecticut • London

Library of Congress Cataloging-in-Publication Data

Encyclopedia of modern Christian politics / edited by Roy P. Domenico and Mark Y. Hanley.

      p. cm.

  Includes bibliographical references and index.

  ISBN 0–313–33889–2 (v. 1 : alk. paper) — ISBN 0–313–33890–6 (v. 2 : alk. paper) — ISBN 0–313–32362–3 (set) 1. Christianity and politics—History—Encyclopedias. I. Domenico, Roy Palmer. II. Hanley, Mark Y.

BR115.P7E58   2006

320.008´27—dc22   2006015695

British Library Cataloguing in Publication Data is available.

Library of Congress Catalog Card Number: 2006015695
ISBN: 0–313–32362–3 (set)
     0–313–33889–2 (vol. 1)
     0–313–33890–6 (vol. 2)

First published in 2006

Greenwood Press, 88 Post Road West, Westport, CT 06881
An imprint of Greenwood Publishing Group, Inc.
www.greenwood.com

Printed in the United States of America

The paper used in this book complies with the Permanent Paper Standard issued by the National Information Standards Organization (Z39.48–1984).

10 9 8 7 6 5 4 3 2 1

Contents

List of Entries

L

LABOR MOVEMENT, BELGIAN CHRISTIAN.
In almost every industrialized country, the labor union movements that arose in the late nineteenth and early twentieth centuries were socialist or secular in their political stance. Belgium provides perhaps the most interesting counterexample to this pattern. The Belgian labor movement has long been divided between a largely socialist federation and a Catholic-inspired one.

Indeed, Belgium is the only country in the world where, since the 1950s, the Catholic federation is larger than its neutral or socialist rival. Social scientists sometimes argue that religious movements are the product of delayed economic development. Yet, after Britain, Belgium was the first European country to industrialize, and it has long been one of the most urbanized countries in the world as well. Interestingly, Belgium also had nearly the highest rate of unionization in the world for much of the twentieth century.

The Catholic labor unions, however, did not arise because socialism was weak. Around 1900, Belgium had what was considered one of the strongest socialist movements in the world. But it emphasized electoral politics rather than union organizing. The neglect of unionism by the socialists provided an opening for the Catholics. Initially, however, Belgian social

Catholics were as conservative as Catholics elsewhere in Europe. They tried to revive the medieval guilds and wanted "mixed unions" of employers and workers. None of these succeeded. What drove Catholic leaders to create real labor unions was the fear of socialist anticlericalism. If socialist unions were the only alternative for Catholic workers, and if socialist leaders preached against the church, then more and more Catholic workers would be lost to the church. As Emile Vandervelde, long-time leader of the Socialist Party, proclaimed on May Day 1891, "Christian holidays are those of a world that is dying, May Day is that of a world being born."

Despite the revulsion against anticlericalism and the fear of socialism, Catholic unionism would have remained weak but for the decisive action of a few leaders in Ghent in 1891. Arthur Verhaegen, an upper-class Catholic architect, convinced a number of neutral (that is, nonsocialist) unions in Ghent to ally with a group of Catholic workers' clubs and launch a genuine working-class movement as an alternative to socialism. The Catholics in Ghent in the 1890s under Verhaegen's leadership created mutual insurance societies, consumer cooperatives, women's groups, and political clubs, all united into a dynamic federation. As Verhaegen himself put it, "We have to borrow something from the socialists in Ghent, the cooperation they get from a well-disciplined army."

By 1904, under the leadership of Dominican father Georges-Celas Rutten, the Ghent Catholic unions provided the base of a national Christian labor movement. By 1914, after Germany, which had almost ten times more people, Belgium had the largest Christian union movement in Europe, with 102,177 Catholic unionists to 126,745 socialist unionists. While socialist union membership skyrocketed after World War I to 689,000, it then drifted downward. Meanwhile, the Catholic unions doggedly recruited members until, in 1935, 545,000 socialist unionists faced 297,000 Catholic unionists. This pattern of faster growth continued until 1960, when there were 800,000 Catholic unionists to 770,000 socialists.

The Catholic movement succeeded, first, by emphasizing a pragmatic kind of reformism that appealed to many workers, especially in small towns and the countryside. It rejected nationalization of industry, called for pro-family policies, and encouraged the government to provide services through the unions, mutual insurance societies, and other nongovernmental organizations, a policy that is known as *liberté subsidiée*, "subsidized liberty." Secondly, Catholic unions appealed to Flemish, that is, Dutch-speaking workers in northern Belgium, whom the French speakers who dominated the socialist party often saw as backward. The Belgian Christian unions have always had 80 percent of their membership in Flanders, which has about 55 percent of the country's population. Thirdly, the Catholic unions won support, even in secular French-speaking communities, from committed Catholics. In Seraing, a tough coal and steel town in French-speaking southern Belgium, many of the Christian unionists in the 1930s had previously belonged to the dominant socialist or communist unions and had relatives who opposed their decision to join the rival union.

The Catholic union movement in Belgium combined a core of Christian beliefs and practices with a pragmatic drive to recruit members. Violence was always rejected, strikes were officially a means of last resort, and Catholic priests counseled unions and urged members to send their children to religious schools. But individual members were always able to join without a public adherence to the church. According to Jesuit father Joseph Arendt, a leading activist and intellectual of the Christian union federation, "no personal declaration of faith, let alone membership in a political party" was required of members.

Christian unionism was stronger among textile workers because the movement as a whole began in Ghent, in Flanders, where the textile industry was based. It was weaker among coal miners, who were concentrated in French-speaking southern Belgium. On the other hand, these distinctive patterns were not inevitable. From the 1880s to 1900, socialist unions dominated the textile unions in Flanders. In the late 1890s in Ghent, where almost 70 percent of the Flemish textile industry was concentrated, there were 5,446 socialist textile workers, and only 1,582 Christian unionists. Through relentless organizing, Christian textile unions nearly caught up with the socialists, closing the gap between the two movements in Ghent and actually out-organizing them outside the city, where the industry was expanding most rapidly. In the 1940s to 1960s, as the coal mines in southern Belgium shut down, new ones opened in Flanders, in the Kempen region of the province of Limburg. Catholic unions emerged as the dominant movement in these mines.

The illusion created by separate histories of the Catholic and socialist movements is that they developed with minimal connections between them. In fact, Christian and socialist unions always cooperated with each other, right from the earliest days of their coexistence. That they also fought each other, accused each other of bad faith, blamed the failure of strikes or negotiations on each other, and claimed to ignore each other should not obscure the tremendously important cases of cooperation. In most strikes in industries where both movements were strong, rival unions planned strategy behind the scenes together and supported their own members on strike. In the strike wave of 1936 in which 600,000 workers went on strike across Belgium, socialist and Catholic union leaders went on the radio together to announce a settlement and tell their members to return to work.

Belgium influenced the rise of Catholic unionism across Europe. Dutch Catholic unions were heavily concentrated in the southern provinces of Limburg and Noord-Brabant, right across the border from Flanders, and had numerous ties with the stronger Belgian unions. Besides Paris, the core of French Catholic unions was the *departement* of the Nord, right on the Belgian border, many of whose workers were Belgian immigrants or commuters. At one point in the 1930s, Belgian Catholic and socialist unions and French Catholic unions even collaborated against French communist unions. The **Young Christian Workers,** Jeunesse Ouvrière Chrétien/Katholieke Arbeider Jeugd (JOC/KAJ), began in Belgium, spread throughout western Europe, and provided a critical boost to Christian unionism in the 1920s to the 1950s. Belgian Catholic union leaders have long been leaders in the international Christian union movement, the offices of which were in Belgium for much of its history.

Bibliography. Arendt, Joseph. *La nature, l'organisation, et le programme des syndicats ouvriers chrétiens.* Brussels, Belgium: A. Dewitt, 1926. Gerard, Emmanuel, and Paul Wynants, eds. *Histoire du mouvement ouvrier chrétien en Belgique.* Leuven, Belgium: Leuven University Press, 1994. Pasture, Patrick. "Diverging Paths: The Development of Christian Labour Organisations in France, the Netherlands, and Belgium Since 1944." *Revue d'histoire ecclesiatique* 89 (1): 66–67. Strikwerda, Carl. *A House Divided: Catholics, Socialists, and Flemish Nationalists in Nineteenth Century Belgium.* Lanham, MD: Rowman & Littlefield, 1997. Strikwerda, Carl. "Labor History." In *The Encyclopedia of Historians and Historical Writing,* ed. Kelly Boyd. London: Fitzroy Dearborn, 1999. Van Kersbergen, Kees. *Social Capitalism: A Study of Christian Democracy and the Welfare State.* London: Routledge, 1995.

Carl Strikwerda

LACORDAIRE, JEAN BAPTISTE HENRI (1802–1861). Lacordaire was a French Dominican preacher and pioneer liberal Catholic. His father was a surgeon who died when his son was four. Raised with his three brothers by his mother in very difficult circumstances, he began the study of law at Dijon in 1819 and continued it in Paris. While earning a reputation for his brilliance at the bar, however, he rediscovered his faith and entered the seminary. Ordained a priest in 1827, he observed how the church's union with the dying old regime had earned it the hatred of the people.

Totally discouraged, he prepared to sail for the New World, where he believed the church was free and uncontaminated by gross hypocrisy; but before leaving, he paid a visit to **Félicité de Lamennais.** The visit with "the only great man in the Church of France" made an enormous impression on Lacordaire. In the meantime the July Revolution of 1830 toppled the reactionary Bourbon monarchy. And when Lacordaire heard that Lamennais was starting a daily newspaper to advance the cause of liberal Catholicism, he abandoned his plans for New York and joined in the venture, as did Count **Charles Montalembert.**

The three called this first Catholic daily, *L'Avenir* (The Future), a paper that claimed to be integrally Catholic both in its total loyalty to the pope and in its commitment to liberalism. *L'Avenir,* however, was far ahead of the church at this juncture and soon had more than its share of enemies. An ill-conceived journey to Rome to solicit Pope **Gregory XVI**'s endorsement proved a disaster, as it only succeeded in securing his condemnation of liberal Catholicism.

Lacordaire submitted with much less anguish than did his friend Montalembert. But as one of the band of notorious liberal innovators, he faced the suspicions of the hierarchy, including those of the archbishop of Paris, Monsignor Henri de Quelen. However, de Quelen was in a bind to secure a suitable preacher for the Notre Dame Lenten Conferences of 1836, so he offered the pulpit to Lacordaire.

His success was astonishing. Although many in the audience were skeptics and deists and wary of the clergy, they listened with increasing interest to a priest so fully involved in the struggles of the time. The crowds swelled until police barriers were necessary. Lacordaire's Notre Dame Conferences, in fact, proved to be one of the most dramatic events of nineteenth-century church history.

Still liberal, Lacordaire welcomed the Revolution of 1848 and tried to rally Catholic support for it in *L'Ère Nouvelle* (The New Era), the newspaper he published with two friends, **Antoine-Frédéric Ozanam** and Abbé Maret. They also wanted to shake their fellow Catholics out of their complacency at the deplorable state of the workers. Lacordaire won a seat in the Constituent Assembly but was soon disillusioned by the disorder and the deal making and realized he was not cut out for political office.

He continued to speak out, however, and called Louis Napoleon's coup d'état of 1851 "an irreparable disaster." The sight of his fellow Catholics in tow to a shameless dictator greatly depressed him. Later in a sermon in Saint Roch Church he bravely admonished the emperor in pointed, scarcely veiled, allusions. Lacordaire was

hence barred from pulpits in Paris, but despite all this, he remained firm in his conviction that the church would eventually emerge as a true champion of human freedom in a world increasingly divided between despots and despotic masses. He devoted the rest of his life to writing, running a boys' school, and working on behalf of the Dominican Order, which against all odds he had been able to restore in France.

Bibliography. Sheppard, Lancelot. *Lacordaire.* London: Burns & Oates, 1964. Spencer, P. *Politics of Belief in Nineteenth Century France.* London: Faber & Faber, 1951.

Thomas Bokenkotter

LAHAYE, TIM (b. 1926). Baptist minister, author, and one of the earliest leaders of the Christian Right in the 1980s, LaHaye was born in Detroit, Michigan. In 1948, right out of seminary and while an undergraduate at Bob Jones University, he took a position as pastor of a Baptist church in Pumpkintown, South Carolina. He graduated from Bob Jones University in 1950 and moved to a Baptist church in Minneapolis. From 1956 until 1981, LaHaye was senior pastor of Scott Memorial Baptist Church in El Cajon, California. During these decades, he founded two Christian high schools and Christian Heritage College, as well as helping develop the Institute for Creation Research.

In 1979, LaHaye cofounded Concerned Women for America with his wife, Beverly. This group was created to counter feminism and the women's rights movement. He was present at the birth of the **Moral Majority** in 1980. In 1981, he cofounded and served as the first president of the Council for National Policy (CNP), a secretive conservative public policy think tank. In 1983, LaHaye created the American Coalition for Traditional Values (ACTV) to assist in registering religious conservatives for President **Ronald**

Reagan's 1984 reelection campaign. The group was an umbrella organization that included most of the other Christian Right organizations. Members of its executive committee included many other leaders of Christian Right organizations including **Jerry Falwell,** Rex Humbard, D. James Kennedy, Charles Stanley, Bill Bright, and Don Wildmon. To prepare for the 1986 congressional elections, LaHaye moved ACTV's headquarters to Washington, D.C., in 1984. After an investigative reporter uncovered details about financial support from Reverend Sun Myung Moon's Unification Church in 1986, he closed ACTV.

LaHaye explained his motivation for participating in politics as part of his attack on the religion of humanism. He saw humanism as a threat to the ability of the United States to serve as a missionary outlet to the rest of the world. LaHaye noted, "80 to 85 percent of the world's missionaries, technology for preaching the Gospel, and money for world missions comes from America. If the atheistic, amoral, one-world humanists succeed in enslaving our country, that missionary outlet will eventually be terminated" (1980, 222–223). He also expressed concern that the children of America have "access to the truth, rather than the heresies of humanism."

LaHaye served as national cochairman of Jack Kemp's campaign for the Republican presidential nomination. He resigned from that position in 1987 after a reporter published excerpts from one of LaHaye's books in which the minister referred to Catholicism as a false religion that gives man and woman a false sense of security and keeps them from seeking salvation. He maintained a low public profile after his political activities, taking a position as an assistant pastor at a Baptist church in Rockville, Maryland.

In 1995, he reemerged in the public eye as an author with the publication of *Left Behind,* the first in a series of popular books examining the world after the Rapture. The books were the result of a partnership, with LaHaye providing a sketch of the plot, which was completed by coauthor Jerry Jenkins. The series installment published in 2001 sold three million copies, and all the books were listed on the *New York Times* best-sellers list. Besides the *Left Behind* series, LaHaye has been an author or coauthor of nonfiction books on theology, self-help, and psychology.

Bibliography. Boston, Rob. *"Left Behind." Church and State,* February 2002, 8–13. LaHaye, Tim. *The Battle for the Mind.* Old Tappen, NJ: Fleming H. Revell, 1980. Moen, Matthew C. *The Transformation of the Christian Right.* Tuscaloosa: University of Alabama Press, 1992. Oldfield, Duane M. *The Right and the Righteous: The Christian Right Confronts the Republican Party.* Lanham, MD: Rowman & Littlefield, 1996.

John David Rausch, Jr.

LAMENNAIS, FÉLICITÉ ROBERT DE (1782–1854). A Roman Catholic priest and social reformer, Lamennais founded the French liberal Catholic movement. He was educated by his uncle, who encouraged him to read widely, especially in Rousseau and the works of the freethinkers. He suffered an eclipse of faith, but the experience of a failed romance helped to lead him back to the church, and he found a focus for his life in religion. Lamennais began an intense study of the Bible and fathers of the church as well as contemporary philosophers and theologians. This bore fruit in several works that reflected a fervent ultramontane or pro-papal version of church history.

After much inner turmoil he was ordained a priest and began a literary career of political and social criticism that would put him in the center of French life for several decades. His *Essay on Indifference* was an attack on the Voltairean rationalism of the eighteenth century and propounded an anti-Lockean thesis that held religion to be the essential cement of every society known to history. He espoused the doctrine of traditionalism, which held that the basic truths for a moral life, such as the existence of God, immortality, and the need for redemption, derive from a primitive revelation and are transmitted through a so-called *sens commun* (common agreement) and clearly and authoritatively preserved only in the Catholic Church.

After encouragement through a personal audience with Pope **Leo XII,** Lamennais launched a campaign against the dominant Gallicanism that he believed enslaved the church to an irreligious government. His remedy was an ultramontane polity that would greatly increase the power of the pope. In this perspective he saw the need for separation of church and state but was hesitant to accept all the freedoms advocated by the liberals. Two things led him to embrace the complete liberal position: the example of the acceptance by Belgian Catholics of liberal ideology, which provided a model, he thought, for France; and a recent act of the French ministers of education, who took away the bishops' control of the primary schools, revealing an intention to subjugate the church to the state. He expounded his program of a liberal Catholicism in his 1829 book *The Progress of the Revolution and the War against the Church.*

Lamennais' writings soon attracted a number of brilliant young men, including Victor Hugo, Alphonse Lamartine, and Alfred de Vigny, to his scholarly retreat at La Chesnaie in Brittany. His plan was to make it a kind of think tank for the regeneration of the church and ready it for combat with the Enlightenment. Two of those who came—**Jean Baptiste Lacordaire** and Comte **Charles de Montalembert**— would soon form with him a dynamic team. Lacordaire was a young priest ordained in 1827 who was disillusioned

with the servile state of the church and its mediocre clergy. He had sought out Lamennais and rallied with great enthusiasm to his vision of a liberal church reconciled with the new world being born. The aristocratic Montalembert was the scion of a family with a lineage stretching back to the dim medieval past, a scholarly layman much affected by the romanticism of the era and passionate in his enthusiasm for the church.

To carry on their campaign for a liberal Catholicism they published a daily newspaper, *L'Avenir* (The Future), which soon won international acclaim. It called for complete religious liberty, freedom of education, freedom of the press, freedom of association, decentralization, and universal suffrage. In his promotion of democracy and church-state separation, Lamennais moved a half-century ahead of his time in Europe. He thought Catholicism would prove to be an invaluable ally of liberalism, for he was convinced that the atomized individuals of classical liberalism would never prevail over the tendency of the strong to oppress the weak. But he saw the church as able to counter this tendency of oppression by its mission to uphold the principles of justice.

It was soon apparent that Lamennais and company were too far ahead of the French church. The bishops especially had many reasons for rejecting his project of a liberal Catholicism. These included their memory of the recent persecution of the church by the liberals during the Revolution and their fear of opening the floodgates to the forces of impiety and unbelief. There was also the suspicion that separation from the state would leave the church without financial support, since there was no tradition of free-will offerings by the people. Finally the bishops were disturbed by Lamennais and company's spirit of insubordination and incitement to the laity to take independent action. The bishops' denunciations of *L'Avenir* caused a drop in subscriptions, and the paper was soon in the red.

As defenders of the papacy, Lamennais and his followers thought they could secure papal support, which might reverse the situation. Lamennais, after all, was the chief ultramontane voice in France. But it was a most unrealistic idea because **Gregory XVI** was an arch reactionary faced with a revolution that threatened to topple his throne. The trip of the three to Rome to petition him hence proved a disaster and only succeeded in triggering a disastrous condemnation of liberal Catholicism by Gregory in the encyclical *Mirari vos* in 1832. Lamennais' dream of a liberal Catholicism collapsed. The three submitted and returned home, but their enemies were not satisfied and kept up a vicious campaign of rumors and denunciations of the intrepid team and demanded an explicit renunciation of their errors. Finally the exhausted Lamennais caved in and signed a simple and unqualified act of submission. But he suffered revulsion and began to question his Catholic faith. He also feared that people might think he had sold out to the despots who trampled down the people across Europe. To silence such suspicions, he published *Paroles d'un croyant* (Words of a Believer), which created a sensation all over Europe. The pope condemned it in his encyclical *Singulari nos* as a "book small in size but immense in perversity." Lamennais' two collaborators eventually broke with him and made their submission. But Lamennais adamantly refused to submit. He was never formally excommunicated, and no definite date can be given for his actual break with the church, but his book *Affaires de Rome* (1836) registered the rupture. He predicted the end of Catholicism but believed that Christianity, which inspired much that is best in European history and culture, would live on.

He settled in Paris and devoted himself to the cause of the poor. His support of radical causes and advocacy of revolution landed him in prison for a year in 1840. There he worked on his *Esquisse d'une philosophie* (An Outline of Philosophy). Vaguely socialist, he never belonged to any socialist party and rejected Marx's invitation to collaborate with him on a journalistic project. Lamennais remained profoundly religious and believed in the importance of faith in God and the need for personal spiritual renewal as the basis of social renewal.

All three erstwhile friends were elected to the Constituent Assembly that emerged from the Revolution of 1848. Lamennais took his seat on the extreme left only a few rows away from Lacordaire, whom he totally ignored. In his last illness Lamennais asked to be buried in the middle of the poor, without a church service. His grave was marked simply with a paper scribbled with the words "Félicité Robert de La Mennais."

The withdrawal of Lamennais from his church was one of the greatest blows suffered by the church in modern times. At a time when the Catholic intellect was at a low point, the church could ill afford to lose such a prophetic genius, a priest who foresaw the triumph of democracy, the emergence of the lay state and the huge importance that the problem of poverty would assume.

Bibliography. Finlay, James. *The Liberal Who Failed.* Washington DC: Corpus, 1968. Roe, W. G. *Lamennais and England.* Oxford: Oxford University Press, 1966. Vidler, Alec. *Prophecy and Papacy.* New York: Charles Scribner's Sons, 1954.

Thomas Bokenkotter

LAND LEAGUE (IRELAND). The Land League is also known as the Irish National Land League. It was founded in 1879 to help resolve the conflict over land ownership that had plagued rural life in Ireland since the mid-eighteenth century. The immediate cause of the establishment of the Land League in 1879 was a series of failed crops and falling grain prices, which led to fears of a recurrence of the famine years of the late 1840s. While ostensibly peaceful, and under the presidency of the leader of the Home Rule movement, **Charles Stewart Parnell,** the movement rapidly degenerated into the agrarian violence associated with land conflicts in Ireland, which resulted in the period of 1879 to 1882 (when the league was abolished) also being known as the Land War. The pressure it brought on the British government, along with the increased demand for local autonomy known as home rule, led to a series of Land Acts which led to a resolution of the issue by 1905 and the creation of a peasant proprietorship.

The tenant farmers and their supporters in the Land League were overwhelmingly Catholic. The landowners and their supporters were predominantly Protestant. The roots of the conflict between the two groups was also ethnic, since the tenant farmers were Irish and the majority of landlords were descended from English settlers of the seventeenth and eighteenth centuries. The Land League and its predecessors of both public and secret societies seeking redress over land issues represented one of the three demands of Irish Catholic society in the nineteenth century. These were the establishment of a separate Irish identity; the resolution of the land question; and the demand for a separate legislature, or home rule, for Ireland.

The relationship between members of the Irish Catholic community was much more complex than the popular image of a "priest-ridden people" would indicate. The alliance, if you wish, between the tenant farmers and the Catholic Church in the aftermath of the Great Famine of the 1840s led to a widespread acceptance of the church's dominant role in matters of education and the maintenance of a strong, if rigid, morality to support the preservation of the family unit and family land. The

church along with emigration also played a major role in the preservation of the family holdings by supporting vocations to the priesthood and religious life.

Irish identity was linked closely to Catholicism. It was not only a matter of faith but also of culture. All this was reinforced in this period by the church community's need for both reinforcement of a morality to hold together the land and also the community through what has become known as the Devotional Revolution, which linked the members of the community to the church and to each other. Yet at the same time the land issue indicates the limits of the control and dominance of the clergy and hierarchy in Irish life. The church strongly condemned the use of force and of secret societies associated with agrarian unrest. The hierarchy often found itself following the people on issues of land. This was certainly the case on support for the Land League and its activities, which were strong within the community even though much of the hierarchy opposed it.

Bibliography. Clark, Samuel. *Social Origins of the Irish Land War.* Princeton, NJ: Princeton University Press, 1979.

Gretchen M. MacMillan

LA PIRA, GIORGIO (1904–1977). La Pira was one of the leading figures of the Italian **Christian Democracy**'s left wing, serving in the nation's postwar Constituent Assembly and national government and as mayor of Florence. Even in this last role, La Pira, a Third Order Dominican, was a model of lay asceticism, living across the street from the Dominican church of San Marco, decorated with its famous Fra Angelico frescoes and where Savonarola based himself in the fifteenth century.

La Pira was born in Pozzallo, Sicily, and lived for a time in Messina and Turin before he transferred to Florence in 1926 and took a position as a university professor of

Roman law. His antifascist credentials were established in his articles for a Florentine review, *Frontespizio,* and a short-lived review, *Principi,* that La Pira published for a few months in 1939 until it was banned by the authorities. After Italy's collapse in World War II and German occupation of the north in September 1943, La Pira eluded arrest in Florence and made it to Rome, where he was given shelter on the grounds of the Cathedral of St. John Lateran.

After the war, La Pira joined fellow Christian Democrats **Amintore Fanfani** and Giuseppe Lazzati in a group that came to be known as the "little professors" (*professorini*), under **Giuseppe Dossetti**'s leadership, which formed a left-leaning faction of the Christian Democracy. He wrote for *Cronache sociali,* the journal most associated with the group, and in which La Pira published one of his key works, *In attesa della povera gente,* which insisted on adherence to the Christian obligation of work and housing for all. As

the cold war developed, a rift opened between the Dossetti group and the DC's centrist followers of **Alcide De Gasperi** over adherence to the Atlantic Alliance, a debate that ended with the victory of the De Gasperi faction at the 1949 Venice party congress. Dossetti retired from public life for awhile, but Fanfani and La Pira continued as party activists.

It was during his terms as mayor of Florence (1951–1958 and 1961–1964) that La Pira forged his greatest legacy. He was instrumental in the construction of low-cost housing and intervened in labor disputes, most famously to prevent the 1954 closing of the Pignone manufacturing works by Franco Marinotti. La Pira joined strikers at Mass and had his friend Fanfani hold Marinotti's passport until the question was resolved. After La Pira said that the Holy Spirit had come to him in a dream with a plan, the mayor convinced the Italian state energy corporation, ENI, to buy and save the plant.

Mayor of Florence Giorgio La Pira talking to workers during an election campaign in an industrial section of Florence, 1956. © Time Life Pictures / Getty Images

La Pira also worked on the international level in pursuit of peace and understanding among nations, what he called the "path of Isaiah." As mayor, for example, he engineered conferences such as those on "Peace and Christian Civilization" (beginning in 1952) and the Mediterranean Colloquia in 1958. His most celebrated endeavor was an ill-fated 1965 mission to North Vietnam in search of an end to the war there.

Pope **John Paul II** launched La Pira's beatification and on the twenty-seventh anniversary of the mayor's death (shortly before his own) praised him in Florence's Santa Maria dei Fiori Cathedral as a man "of great intellectual and moral energies, empowered and refined in the daily exercise of study, reflection, asceticism and prayer."

Bibliography. Doni, Rodolfo. *Giorgio La Pira: Profeta di dialogo e di pace.* Milan: Paoline, 2004. Fondazione La Pira, et al. *La Pira oggi: Atti del 1º Convegno di studi sul messaggio di Giorgio La Pira nella presente epoca storica, Firenze, 4–5-6–7 Novembre 1981.* Florence: Cultura editrice, 1983. Miller, James Edward. *Politics in a Museum: Governing Postwar Florence.* Westport, CT: Praeger, 2002.

Roy P. Domenico

LATAPIÉ, EUGENIO VEGAS (1907–1985). Latapié gave life and consistency to a vein of Spanish traditionalist thought that advocated values for, as he saw it, the resurrection of the ruined body of Spanish society and the foundation for a restored and pure Spanish monarchy. His work led to the foundation before the civil war of the clerical/monarchist review *Acción Española* with a small group of intellectuals who would aim to provide a more solid ideological (both religious and sociopolitical) basis to the uprising of 1936.

Latapié was born in Irun to a modest family, with a military father and a school teacher mother. They moved to Santander, where he spent his youth. He was raised in the environment of a traditional Catholic family of an evident Ignatian spirituality, which contributed to his introspective temperament and interest in serious discussion. Latapié grew interested in the causes of the masses' revolution and prepared himself for political life by going into law school, which he did at Oviedo, and later receiving his doctorate at Madrid. He developed an admiration for **Nocedal**'s integralism and became familiar with the works of **Donoso Cortés, Menendez y Pelayo, Vásquez de Mella** and sixteenth-century Spanish theologians and jurists.

While a doctoral student in Madrid, he also became constant reader of *L'Action Française* and of **Charles Maurras**'s thought, basing his politics on two fundamental points: the defense of a traditional Catholicism and fidelity to monarchial legitimacy. In 1931, while working toward his doctorate in Madrid, he met the traditionalist thinker Ramiro Maetzu y Whitney who proposed the creation of the magazine *Acción Española.* Latapié became one of the guiding lights of the new review which soon served as one of the pillars of Spanish traditionalist thought and gathered around it a group of like-minded intellectuals.

During the civil war, **Francisco Franco** included Latapié on his first National Council in October 1937 although the intellectual's reluctance to compromise eventually led him to break with the Caudillo over his lack of enthusiasm in the prompt restoration of the Spanish monarchy. By March of the following year, Franco removed Latapié from the council.

Later, Latapié published his most important books, the respected *Consideraciones sobre la democracia sine ira et studio* (1965) and his *Escritos Politicos* (1959) which was a frontal attack on democratic liberal ideology founded in Rousseau's thought, promoting in its place the traditional concept of power in one person but assisted with the advice of wise counselors.

Bibliography. Raúl Morodo, *Orígenes ideológicos del franquismo: Acción Española* Madrid: Alianza, 1985.

Fernando Murillo Rubiera

LA TOUR DU PIN, CHARLES HUMBERT RENÉ (1834–1924). The French Catholic Social philosopher La Tour du Pin was descended from an illustrious military family and began his own career as an officer with service in campaigns in the Crimea, Italy, and Algeria. Taken prisoner in the war of 1870, he was interned at Aix-La-Chapelle, where he formed a friendship with **Alfred de Mun,** a fellow officer. After studying a commentary on Pope **Pius IX**'s *Syllabus of Errors* by the Catholic scholar Emile Keller, both men agreed that individualist and rationalist liberalism was the main source of social injustice and a cause of class conflict.

Shocked by the savagery of the worker rebellion in the Commune of 1871, they developed a project to bring together workers and employers. This took the form of Workers Clubs, or Oeuvre des Cercles, where the workers could get counseling and material help and also meet employers in relaxed surroundings. At its height, the Cercles numbered some fifty thousand workers before giving way in the 1880s to more dynamic and innovative Social Catholic movements such as De Mun's own ACJF (Association of Catholic Youth).

La Tour Du Pin was a strong advocate of corporativism, a system of state organization much favored by the Austrian Social Catholics under Karl von Vogelsang (1818–1890). It was based on representation by vocational groups or corporations, such as farmers, mechanics, or factory workers. In La Tour du Pin's view, a three-tiered arrangement would be typical, so that a factory "corporation" would comprise the first level, a regional mixed commission or union consisting of half employers and half employees of the same industry would compose the second level, and a "corporative senate" elected by the mixed unions would represent "the organized people" at the national level. Unlike a liberal parliamentary regime, the chosen delegates would represent not individuals but vocational groups.

People of the same occupation would elect regional delegates, who would formulate the platform of the regional "estates." They in turn would elect their own delegates to the National Assembly who would be empowered with a specified mandate. At the top of the structure would be some form of monarchy. This model of society was called organic since it was based on the natural grouping of members according to the economic role they played. In other words it saw society ordered on the analogy of the body (*corpus*), whose members each contribute, but in diverse ways, to the well-being of the whole.

La Tour du Pin was an active participant in the Fribourg Union, which prepared the way for Pope **Leo XIII**'s encyclical *Rerum novarum.* He assisted De Mun, who as a member of the French National Assembly called for such measures as a living wage, improved working conditions, shorter workdays, old-age pensions, and sickness and unemployment insurance. One of La Tour du Pin's closest followers was Henri Lorin, founder of the *Semaines sociales de France,* an influential annual week of study for Social Catholics. Like many monarchist Catholics, he could not accept Leo XIII's *Ralliement,* which drastically revised the *Syllabus of Errors* and urged French Catholics to accept the French Republic. The decline of the Cercles also isolated him, and he turned to **Action Française,** a right-wing movement later condemned by the pope.

La Tour du Pin played a significant role in the 1880s and 1890s in the awakening of the Catholic Social conscience. He remained staunchly antiliberal and a leading exponent of corporativism, a political theory that was later unfairly discountenanced by being confused with fascism.

Bibliography. Misner, Paul. *Social Catholicism in Europe.* New York: Crossroad, 1991.

Thomas Bokenkotter

LAURIER, SIR WILFRID (1841–1919). Laurier, prime minister of Canada (1896–1911), was a committed advocate of religious toleration and fervent opponent of clerical interference in partisan politics.

Born near Montreal and educated in the classics by Catholic priests at Collège de l'Assomption, Laurier studied Law at McGill University, Montreal, and was called to the bar in 1864. While a student, he became an enthusiastic member of the Institut Canadien, a political club of advanced liberals with strong anticlerical and republican views. He later joined the law offices of leading liberal politicians and made a name for himself by writing for radical newspapers.

In 1871, when many ultramontane bishops and priests in French Canada were ferociously attacking the Liberal Party and refusing the sacraments to its adherents, Laurier was elected as a Liberal, first to the Provincial Legislature of Quebec, and then in 1874 to the federal House of Commons, where he would remain a member for an unprecedented forty-five years.

For over twenty of these years, as he gradually rose from the back benches to the ministry of internal revenue, which he held briefly (1877–1878), and eventually to the leadership of the opposition Liberal Party in 1887, Laurier consistently sought compromise on questions relating both to the relations of church and state and to the bicultural entente between French Canadian Catholics and Anglophone, mostly Protestant, Canadians. One of the highlights of these years was his famous speech on liberalism delivered on June 20, 1877, at the Institut Canadien in Quebec City. In this he set himself at once against both the attempt of the pro-clerical wing of the Conservatives to form a Catholic party and the extremists among the Liberals who sought to deny members of the clergy the right to take part in political affairs. He drew a clear distinction between the doctrinaire anticlericalism prevalent on the Continent and the reforming liberalism of the British tradition. The speech led at first to a marshalling of ultramontane forces against him, but gradually the combination of Laurier's political skills and undoubted personal magnetism—"he had affinities with both Machiavelli and Sir Galahad," one of his associates later declared—began to thaw the cold antagonism between Conservative ultramontane leaders and liberal politicians.

In 1885 the execution of the Metis leader Louis Riel provoked violent outbursts between Catholic French Canadian nationalists, who supported him, and Britannic, especially Orange, groups across the rest of Canada, who demanded the death penalty. Laurier's moving plea for clemency emphasized the need for toleration. During the six-year crisis over denominational schools in Manitoba, another bitter question that pitted ultramontane against liberal and brought the Catholic clergy actively into the general election of 1896, he so strongly urged moderation and compromise that he emerged as the only political leader able to effect a national reconciliation.

After he became prime minister he appealed to Pope **Leo XIII.** Monsignor (later Cardinal) **Merry del Val** was dispatched to investigate, recommending in the end, as Laurier wished, that a permanent Apostolic Delegation be established in Ottawa to monitor clerical activity in politics. In June 1899 Archbishop (later Cardinal) Diomede Falconio was appointed as such. Since then, no anticlerical ever attained public office in Canada, nor have

Catholic clerics ever interfered again significantly in partisan politics.

During Laurier's fifteen consecutive years as prime minister (an unrivalled record in Canada's political history) and during his last eight years as leader of the opposition, he never ceased working, as he put it, "to promote unity and harmony and amity between the diverse elements of this country." Troubling religious issues arose again, especially about denominational schools in Saskatchewan and Alberta in 1905, and about the language rights of Franco-Ontarioan Catholics in 1912. Each time he urged understanding in reaching agreements. In the eyes of many Canadians, these did not always completely redress the wrongs inflicted by both sides, but to him, they were an honorable, if not a necessary, compromise.

In the end Laurier was defeated on other issues. The questions of reciprocity, or free trade, with the United States, and the creation of a Canadian Navy independent of the British brought down his government. Conscription for service overseas during World War I split his party. Still, he remained to the end true to his personal ideals. As he expressed in a speech at St. John's, Quebec, in 1911, "I have had before me as a pillar of fire by night and a pillar of cloud by day a policy of true Canadianism, of moderation, of conciliation."

Bibliography. LaPierre, Laurier L. *Sir Wilfrid Laurier and the Romance of Canada.* Toronto: Stoddart, 1996. Schull, Joseph. *Laurier: The First Canadian.* Toronto: MacMillan, 1965. Skelton, Oscar D. *Life and Letters of Sir Wilfrid Laurier.* 2 vols. Toronto: McClelland & Stewart, 1921.

Jacques Monet

LEAGUE OF CHRISTIAN TRADE UNIONS OF GERMANY. In 1894, coal miners in the Ruhr Valley founded the first enduring "Christian" trade union for workers offended by the anticlericalism of the socialist unions. Within five years, their example inspired enough imitation in other trades to allow the formation of the League of Christian Trade Unions of Germany (Gesamtverband der christlichen Gewerkschaften Deutschlands).

The delegates to its founding congress in Mainz agreed unanimously that their unions should be "interconfessional" (i.e., open to both Catholics and Protestants) and "stand on the foundation of Christianity." They were nonpartisan but sought legislative reforms "on the basis of the existing social order." They promised to raise only reasonable demands of employers but proclaimed their resolve to back up those demands with strikes if necessary. The Catholic Social movement had created a favorable climate for this initiative, but Lutheran pastors who demonstrated social activism faced the threat of harsh disciplinary action. Recruitment among Protestant workers suffered further when Social Democrats, Protestant employers, and liberal politicians alike denounced the Christian unions as tools of the ultramontanist clergy.

Even among Catholics, moreover, a strident faction of so-called integralists appealed repeatedly to the Vatican to condemn interconfessional unions, and the league's chair, Adam Stegerwald, was compelled to wage an impassioned struggle to gain respect for the right of elected union leaders to set their own course, independent of clerical tutelage. Under the circumstances, it was surprising that the league grew to a membership of 351,000 in 1912, 1.1 million in 1920, and 659,000 in 1930, but it never became more than one-sixth as large as the socialist labor federation.

After 1919 it became more difficult to answer the question of why a good Christian could not join a socialist trade union as the Social Democrats of the Weimar Republic renounced anticlericalism. Stegerwald emphasized nationalism to maintain a distinctive identity for the league and promote recruitment among Protestants. He forged a close alliance with a militantly nationalist white-collar union, sought to organize Protestant farm workers in East Elbia, and promoted political coalitions between the **Center Party** and the German Nationalist People's Party. This strategy sowed confusion in the movement as German nationalism evolved in a radical, antidemocratic direction. Many of the groups with which Stegerwald tried to cooperate were eventually swept up in the Nazi current, but the core membership of the league defended democracy vigorously in the last years of the Weimar Republic.

After Hitler ordered the brutal suppression of all trade unions in 1933, most veterans of the league concluded in sorrow that divisions within the labor movement had gravely weakened the Weimar Republic. After 1945 they resolved to join with socialist colleagues in today's unified German Labor Federation, although they retained a distinctive political identity in the **Christian Democratic Union.** This development was possible because of the resolute anticommunism of Germany's Social Democratic labor leaders, but the original program of the League of Christian Trade Unions continued to exert great influence in France, Italy, and other countries where communists played a dominant role in trade unionism.

Bibliography. Brose, Eric Dorn. *Christian Labor and the Politics of Frustration in Imperial Germany.* Washington, DC: Catholic University of America Press, 1985. Patch, William. *Christian Trade Unions in the Weimar Republic, 1918–1933: The Failure of "Corporate Pluralism."* New Haven, CT: Yale University Press, 1985.

William Patch

LEFEBVRE, MARCEL (1905–1991). The man who personifies the Catholic integralist movement in the twentieth century, Cardinal Lefebvre was born in Lille, France, into a family of eight children, five of whom became priests or nuns. He was ordained in 1929, after study at the French Seminary in Rome. Although most teachers there followed **Charles Maurras**'s doctrine, Lefebvre never really was a royalist nor paid much attention to politics. Ordained in 1929, he belonged to the Congregation of the Holy Spirit and became a missionary in Gabon, then in Senegal until 1962, where he became archbishop of Dakar.

Around 1949–1950, he joined the Cité Catholique, a French movement in the antimodernist ideology of La Sapinière. He wrote the foreword to *Pour qu'Il règne,* the master work of Jean Ousset, the Cité's founder. Lefebvre later opposed the changes introduced by the Second Vatican Council, an attitude that explains his "exile" as the archbishop of the small city of Tulle in 1962. It is not clear whether he signed the "Dignitatis Humanae" and "Gaudium et Spes" declarations or not, but he wrote that the 1964 declaration on relations with Judaism was "inopportune." He rejected liturgical reform, religious freedom, and ecumenism. With two Brazilian bishops, Proença Sigaud and Castro Mayer, he founded Coetus Internationalis Patrum, which acted as a lobby against the Council.

At this time, he remained within the Catholic Church and was even the superior of his congregation. He resigned in 1968 and was authorized by the Vatican to set up his own Fraternity of St. Pius X, headquartered in Ecône, Switzerland. The first step in his separation from the church was a 1968 manifesto, signed by 150 (mostly French) priests, the "Vademecum of the Faithful Catholic." It was followed, on November 21, 1974, by a statement in which he "refused to follow Rome in the neo-modernist and neo-Protestant trend which clearly manifested itself during Vatican II." Consequently, his fraternity was deprived of its canonical agreement in May 1975, and in July 1976, he was suspended *a divinis* after having ordained thirteen priests.

The political content of Lefebvre's thinking became obvious when, in August 1976, during a sermon, he cited the Argentine dictatorship of General Videla as an example of a Catholic regime. But it was only in April 1985 that he endorsed the policies of the French extreme-right Front National. All attempts to bring him back to the fold failed because he refused to recognize the validity of the New Mass, even as a counterpart for being authorized to use the St. Pius V *Ordo*. The aging Lefebvre was anxious to appoint a successor. On June 30, 1988, he consecrated four bishops, a decision that led to his excommunication. However, his fraternity survived him and remains the only Catholic integralist movement of some significance.

Bishop Lefebvre died on March 25, 1991. He was neither a theologian nor a theoretician; his ideas were simply those of the *Syllabus* of Pope **Pius IX**. His ideological trilogy included staunch anticommunism, belief in the conspiracy theory of the Freemasons and the Jews, and opposition to democracy. Rather than a spiritual leader, he became, under the circumstances, the figurehead of a movement that is rooted in the nineteenth-century counterrevolutionary school of thought.

Bibliography. Ternisien, Xavier. *L'Extrême droite et l'Église.* Paris: Brepols, 1997.

Jean-Yves Camus

LÉGER, PAUL-EMILE (1904–1991). Roman Catholic cardinal and humanitarian, Leger was born in Valleyfield, near Montreal, Quebec. He studied for the priesthood at the Grand Séminaire in Montreal, where he was ordained in 1929 before entering the Sulpician Fathers at Issy-les-Moulineaux, near Paris. He then took a degree in canon law at the Institut Catholique. He taught the subject at the Séminaire Saint-Sulpice and, in 1933, was sent to Fukuoka, near Nagasaki, to found a seminary for the training of Japanese priests.

Léger returned in 1939 to Canada, where, after serving as vicar-general of the diocese of Valleyfield (1940–1947), he was appointed rector of the Pontifical Canadian College in Rome. While there, he worked closely with Monsignor Giovanni Battista Montini (later, Pope **Paul VI**), whose influence helped him negotiate the return to the Canadian Sulpicians of their college building, which that had been confiscated during the war by the Italian government. Moved by the distress of the children in Rome's industrial and war-ravaged suburbs, he almost single-handedly organized appeals back in Canada, which in 1948 and 1949 delivered to Vatican charities some twenty-six thousand crates of clothing, medicine, and school supplies as well as 150 barrels of cod liver oil. On March 26, 1950, he was appointed archbishop of Montreal and in January 1953 was elevated to the College of Cardinals by Pope **Pius XII**.

Cardinal Léger became extraordinarily popular in Montreal, with a growing reputation there and across Canada as a charismatic leader who remained independent of politicians and whose devotion and energy seemed exclusively directed toward helping the poor. An eloquent and gifted orator with a theatrical talent to inspire people, he gave over five thousand major sermons, homilies, and speeches during his years as archbishop (1950–1967). Almost daily, his public activities and statements made headlines that won wide support for his causes.

By the early 1960s, his authority in the Canadian church was undisputed. Without the prestige of his leadership during Quebec's Quiet Revolution, which consisted essentially of transferring the province's educational, health, and social institutions from the clerical control of the Catholic church to that of the provincial government, church and state might well have become mired in sterile opposition: the church a stumbling block against political and social reform, and the government and lay politicians entrenched in anticlericalism.

Léger's pastoral activity fell into two very distinct approaches. At first he was authoritarian and princely, traditional and suspicious of change, but after the death of his parents in 1957, he became increasingly accessible, unusually attentive to the needs and opinions of laymen and women and increasingly conciliatory and unassuming in his ways of dealing with people, policies, and problems.

At the Second Vatican Council (1962–1965), Cardinal Léger played a leading, sometimes decisive, role in the progressive wing, especially in discussions on the questions of religious freedom, the ministry of the laity, marriage, ecumenism, and interfaith dialogue. After the last session on December 8, 1965, he was chosen along with cardinals Alfrink of Utrecht, Koening of Vienna, and Sunens of Malines to deliver the Council's Four Messages to the Laity and to the Nations.

In December 1967, Léger resigned as archbishop of Montreal to become a missionary among lepers and handicapped children at Etang-Ebé, near Yaoundé in Cameroon. He began some forty projects there, and with the help of his brother Jules, Canada's undersecretary of state and later governor-general, he won the Canadian government's support for African, especially francophone, development. In failing health, he returned permanently in 1979 to Montreal, where he continued very successfully to raise funds for three foundations he began—Fame Pereo, Cardinal Léger and His Works, and the Jules and Paul-Emile Léger Foundation—which continued after his death to support both his African projects and several new humanitarian works he initiated in Haiti, India, and Thailand.

Cardinal Léger was a Companion of the Order of Canada and a recipient of, among many other honors, the Pearson Peace Prize.

Bibliography. *Canadian Who's Who.* Toronto Press, 1910–. Goulet, Emilius. *Les Prêtres de Saint-Sulpice au Canada.* Saint-Foy, Canada: Presses de l'Université Laval, 1992. Le Blanc, Jean. *Dictionnaire biographique des évêques catholiques du Canada.* Montreal: Wilson & Lafleur, 2002.

Jacques Monet

LELAND, JOHN (1754–1841). A Baptist elder and itinerant preacher, Leland effectively advocated for the disestablishment of religion in Virginia and the New England states during the Revolutionary and post-Revolutionary years. As the first party competition heated up in the 1790s, he emerged as a spokesman on behalf of the Jeffersonian Republicans against their Federalist opponents. He also harmonized the dissenting Protestant tradition with the Enlightenment liberalism of Thomas Jefferson at the levels of both ideological content and rhetorical style.

Born in Grafton, Massachusetts, Leland experienced conversion at the age of twenty. He soon embarked on a life of preaching, in which he logged thousands of miles of itinerancy and delivered some 8,000 sermons. A theological independent, Leland had no use for creeds or systems of belief, unlike his fellow New England Baptist, the orthodox Calvinist Isaac Backus. Above all, Leland stood for the rights of the individual conscience to render correct judgments in matters of religion (or politics).

In 1777 Leland moved to Virginia, where he resided for 15 years. A popular preacher, he itinerated as far south as Georgia. The Virginia Baptists had run afoul of the colony's law that required preachers to obtain licenses, so Leland worked for the complete disestablishment of the Anglican Church. In that struggle he allied with

Thomas Jefferson and James Madison and helped organize Baptist petitioning in favor of disestablishment, which was achieved in 1786. He probably influenced Madison to accept the idea that the U.S. Constitution should be amended to include the establishment clause of the First Amendment. In 1790 Leland also tried, albeit unsuccessfully, to get the Virginia Baptists to take a stand against slavery as another denial of the Revolution's natural rights philosophy.

Leland returned to New England in 1791. During a three-month stay in Connecticut, he attacked the state's certificate system, by which dissenters were required to file certificates with their local town clerks in order to avoid having to pay tax in support of the established Congregational church. Once again, Leland called for disestablishment and a free market of ideas in religion. "It is error, and error alone, that needs human support," he stated that year, "and whenever men fly to the law or sword to protect their system of religion, and force it upon others, it is evident that they have something in their system that will not bear the light, and stand upon the basis of truth" (*Writings*, 185).

By February 1792 Leland had settled in Cheshire, Massachusetts, where he would spend most of the rest of his life. He protested the similar Massachusetts religious establishment and became a committed Republican partisan, even sitting in the Massachusetts legislature from 1811 to 1812. Publishing widely in pamphlets and newspapers, Leland blended plain Jeffersonian language about natural rights and limited government with mocking attacks on the Congregational clergy. "What may we not expect," he declared in 1801, "under the auspices of heaven, while JEFFERSON presides, with *Madison* in state by his side. Now the greatest orbit in America is occupied by the brightest orb: but, sirs, expect to see religious

bigots, like cashiered officers, and displaced statesmen, growl and gnaw their galling bands, and, like a yelping mastiff, bark at the moon, whose rising they cannot prevent" (*Writings*, 255). Nothing epitomized either Leland's partisan fervor or his knack for publicity better than his delivery to the White House on January 1, 1802, of a 1,235-pound cheese that the farmers of Cheshire had produced in honor of President Jefferson and his support for religious freedom.

Leland lived long enough to become a devoted follower also of Andrew Jackson. In 1830 he joined the Jacksonians in opposing the efforts of evangelical petitioners to halt the transportation of mail on Sundays. His dogged independence, however, put him out of step with other Baptists late in life. As the denomination was becoming more respectable by the second quarter of the nineteenth century, Baptists followed the Congregationalists in organizing institutions for missions, publication, and ministerial education. From all of these endeavors, John Leland dissented, maintaining the independent stance that characterized his whole life.

Bibliography. Butterfield, L. H. "Elder John Leland, Jeffersonian Itinerant." *Proceedings of the American Antiquarian Society* 62 (October 1952): 155–42. Greene, L. F., ed. *The Writings of the Late Elder John Leland, including Some Events in his Life, Written by Himself, with Additional Sketches, &c.* New York: G. W. Wood, 1845.

Jonathan D. Sassi

LEMIRE, JULES AUGUSTE (1853–1928). Ordained in 1878, the abbé Lemire was elected to the Chamber of Deputies in 1893 as the representative of Hazebrouck, a northern town in a Flemish region of France, of which he was also elected mayor in 1914, retaining both positions until his death in 1928. One of the *abbés democrats,* who thought that the church needed to reach out to the people and adapt itself to the times, Lemire was a pioneer of Christian democracy in France. He sought to apply the teachings of **Leo XIII**'s *Rerum novarum* on social questions through his support for retirement schemes for workers, trade unions, mutual aid societies, and assistance for the elderly, and he was instrumental in obtaining legislation banning night work for children and protecting young female workers. He also campaigned against the death penalty.

Lemire was a solid believer in the reconciliation of the Catholic Church and its members with the French Republic and even supported the secular school program of the French Third Republic, which many other Catholics felt threatened the church. He came out in favor of the separation of the church and state in 1905, arguing that neutral secularism was not the same as anticlericalism, and that the church would be better off freed from the impositions of the state. His position on many of these great debates of his time was unusual for Catholics and earned him much opposition from within the mainstream traditionalist, conservative French Catholic society as well as from the church hierarchy.

This was most true after 1910, when he had several confrontations with his bishop, leading to his suspension on January 10, 1914. He was reinstated in 1916 and given permission to stand again in the elections of 1919, with the support of Pope **Benedict XV.** He did not consider that his electoral mandate made him a representative of the church (rather, he stood as an individual), and he always claimed personal autonomy from the absolutist nature of church authorities (including his own bishops). He did feel, however, that as a Christian and as a priest he had a duty to be a missionary for his faith, and to bring it to the population through outreach organizations and pastoral initiatives on the part of the clergy.

Lemire is best known for his creation and support for the "workers" gardens program (*jardins ouvriers*), which involved securing small allotments of land for working-class families often living in overcrowded conditions in the cities. They would be able to use these plots of land to grow food, thereby reducing pressure on small incomes as well as promoting self-help among the workers. He also founded the Hearth, Home, and Corner of Earth League (La Ligue du Coin de Terre et du Foyer) and had links with the Sillon of **Marc Sangnier** and other social Catholic organizations of his time. As first a priest and then a representative of French Flanders, he also learned the Flemish language and supported Flemish cultural activities in his region.

Bibliography. Mayeur, Jean-Marie. *L'Abbé Lemire 1853–1928: Un prêtre démocrate.* Paris: Casterman, 1968.

Timothy Baycroft

LEO XIII [GIOACCHINO RAFFAELE LUIGI PECCI] (1810–1903). Gioacchino Pecci had a long career in the papal service as a priest, archbishop, nuncio, cardinal, and pope. Confounding the prognosticators—who expected his pontificate to be a brief, transitional interlude—Leo XIII sat as pope for a full quarter-century (1878–1903). An immensely respected figure in his own day, Leo's pontificate is considered one of the most significant of modern times—the era of the church's first significant rapprochement with the modern world following the pontificate of **Pius IX** (1846–78).

Born in Carpineto (in Latium, southeast of Rome) to a noble family of modest means, Pecci graduated with a degree in theology and civil law from the University of the Sapienza, Rome, in 1837. He was ordained that same year and immediately entered the papal service under Pope **Gregory XVI.** His first appointments were in the administration of the Papal States. As governor—first in Benevento (1838–41), then in Perugia (1841–43)—Pecci proved himself an able administrator. He stood firmly against the anticlericals and liberals while enhancing the church's (and his own) reputation among the populace through his administration of justice, sponsorship of public works, and financial assistance to peasant landholders.

Appointed titular archbishop of Damietta in 1843, Pecci was sent to Belgium that same year as papal nuncio. This was his first—and, as it turned out, his only—extended posting outside the Italian peninsula, and it was in Belgium that he gained firsthand exposure to the great movements—industrialization, urbanization, trade unionism, and parliamentarism—that were already transforming life in much of Europe in the nineteenth century. Three years in Belgium also afforded Pecci the opportunity to assert the authority of Rome in a state headed by a Protestant king with a mixed population of Protestants and Catholics. Pecci's diplomatic skills were sorely tested upon the outbreak of a dispute over education that pitted the Belgian episcopate and leading Catholic politicians against the government. Pecci's open opposition to the government's project led King Leopold I to ask Rome for Pecci's recall, a request that was duly confirmed in May 1846; Pecci was returned to Perugia by Gregory, this time as bishop.

Pecci's tenure in Perugia was to last for the duration of the pontificate of Gregory's successor, Pius IX (1846–1878). It was in this era of heightened tension between church and state in the Italian peninsula that Pecci developed the outlook that would come to mark his own pontificate. Even as Pius IX openly denounced all things modern—notably in the *Syllabus* of 1864—Pecci, all the while, was quietly formulating an alternative approach to the great issues of the day. His subtle divergence from Rome was perhaps, in part, both cause and effect of his thirty-year stay in Perugia. Named a cardinal in 1853, he was not recalled to Rome, suspected as he was by some members of the curia of harboring liberal sentiments. The collapse of papal rule in central Italy in 1859–1860—against which Pecci spoke out unambiguously—served to confirm him in his belief that the church must not simply reject the modern world outright. In his pastoral letters of 1874–1877, Pecci proposed that Rome's loss of temporal power should allow the church to focus on its spiritual mission in contemporary society and to develop an approach to the great issues of the day within the parameters of traditional church teachings.

Recalled to Rome as camerlengo in 1877, Pecci was elected pope on the third ballot at the conclave of February 1878 and took the name Leo XIII. Over the course of his long pontificate, Leo disappointed both the progressives, who called for a repudiation of Pius IX's legacy, and the conservatives, whose animus against the modern world was unshaken. But the contrast between Leo and Pius was as much one of style as it was one of substance. Whereas Pius was inflexible, opinionated, willful, and condemnatory, Leo was given to compromise, conciliation, compassion, and understanding.

Leo used his spiritual authority and the power centralized in the curia to undertake an ambitious and wide-ranging diplomacy, one of the goals of which was to compensate for the church's loss of the temporal power. He was a very political pope in that he understood well that Rome could use the nunciature and national episcopates to seek to influence both Catholics and governments in an age of secularism and nationalism. He successfully worked for a compromise to halt the Kulturkampf in Germany, warned Belgian Catholics away from political extremism, promoted the *Ralliement* in France, and undertook to improve relations with Russia on behalf of the czar's Roman Catholic subjects. At the same time—and particularly in regard to Italian affairs—on many issues Leo confirmed the positions taken up by his predecessor. He maintained Pius IX's intransigent position on the Roman Question, insisted on the recovery of the Papal States, and maintained the prohibition on Catholic participation in elections in Italy.

In his many encyclical letters and epistles, Leo addressed all the major social and political issues of his day. He confirmed Pius IX's condemnation of socialism and communism (*Quod apostolici muneris,* 1878), sanctioned Christian liberty against secular license (*Libertas praestantissimum,* 1888), distinguished between temporal and spiritual power (*Immortale Dei,* 1885), addressed the obligations of citizenship in the secular state (*Sapientiae christianae,* 1890), and reiterated the modern papacy's condemnation of slavery (*In plurimis,* 1888). Time and again, Leo returned to the question of the relations between church and state, urging Catholics to accept the legitimacy of existing institutions and to defend Catholic interests by entering fully into the life of society. In one of his last encyclicals, *Graves de communi* (1901), Leo addressed the emerging Christian democratic movement, embracing the term "Christian democracy" but draining it of political significance by defining it as "beneficent Christian action in behalf of the people."

Leo's most important statement on the social question was the encyclical *Rerum novarum* (1891), in which he examined the conditions of modern labor and set out the obligations of employers, workers, and the state in the emerging wage economy. Rejecting both socialism (which denied the legitimacy of private property) and economic liberalism (which treated the worker as a factor of production), Leo emphasized the dignity of the worker as a human being and his right to a just wage, the obligation of the state to intervene in economic affairs to prevent exploitation of the worker, and the right of workers to form trade unions. Leo argued that adherence to such guidelines would not only serve to protect the worker and dignify his labor but would help to improve class relations. Thus were laid the essential principles of modern Social Catholicism—and, thereby, the most significant legacy of the pontificate of Leo XIII.

Bibliography. Chadwick, Owen. *A History of the Popes, 1830–1914.* Oxford: Clarendon Press, 1998. Gargan, Edward T., ed. *Leo XIII and the Modern World.* New York: Sheed & Ward, 1961. Launay, Marcel. *La papauté à l'aube du XXe siècle: Léon XIII et Pie X, 1878–1914.* Paris: Éditions du Cerf, 1997. Lupi, Maria. *Il clero a Perugia durante l'episcopato di Gioacchino Pecci, 1846–1878, tra Stato pontificio e Stato unitario.* Rome: Herder, 1998. Prudhomme, Claude. *Stratégie missionnaire du Saint-Siège sous Léon XIII, 1878–1903: centralisation romaine et défis culturels.* Rome: École française de Rome, 1994.

Ramesh J. Rajballie

LE PLAY, PIERRE-GUILLAME-FRÉDÉRIC (1806–1882). A French economist and social theorist, Le Play was born in Calvados and began his studies at the College of Havre, and then the College St. Louis in Paris. He studied chemistry, metallurgy, and mining and held a particular interest in the relationship among mining, labor, and social institutions, which he developed during a tour of Rhine Provinces in 1829. He later became secretary of the Annales de Mines and was appointed a professor in the School of Mines in 1840.

In his early research, Le Play displayed special interest in issues of labor and social reform. He contrasted modern ways with feudal systems of authority, where stability, family, and community were overriding concerns. Essential to social stability and prosperity, he felt, was religion—a point that became foundational for his later work. Le Play's research method was not only empirical, in its concern with statistics, but also ethnographic, in that much of his research data was gathered during interviews and meetings with a wide range of laborers, merchants, and peasants.

In 1855, Le Play was appointed a councilor of state and some nine years later published a work expounding his understanding of the principles necessary for social prosperity entitled "Reformé social en France, déduite de l'observation comparée des européens." A profusion of works followed in the next two decades in which Le Play examined the family and various aspects of social reform. Le Play's vision was characterized by a deep suspicion of human nature, which has led some Catholic commentators to conclude that much of Le Play's social vision was intended to counteract the effects of original sin. Because human institutions, like individual human beings themselves, are subject to corruption, the foundation of society must be "the Moral Law." In his writings, Le Play identified the Ten Commandments as the foundation for that moral law upon which society must stand. Organized religion and public worship were also necessary features of any stable social order. Le Play argued, furthermore, for unrestricted inheritance in order to maintain the integrity of the family over time. He promoted a decentralized state government and an educational system free from state control. Throughout his work, Le Play emphasized the power of local custom and tradition over state efforts to prescribe particular social ends.

Toward the end of his life, and most certainly after his death, Le Play realized a significant influence on Catholic Social thought in its resistance to theories developed during the French Revolution. Commentators, however, are rather skeptical of assimilating Le Play too quickly into the ambit of Catholic theorizing about society. While it is reported that he did become a "practicing Catholic" in the years immediately preceding his death, some of his key points might be considered challenging to Catholic orthodoxy. He was certainly more interested in the implicit social theory of the Decalogue than in the New Testament. As Michael Z. Brooke observes (118), God for Le Play was a sanction for the moral law, rather than a personal entity with which one could commune. With specific regard to Catholicism, Le Play also raised questions over celibacy's effect on the family and criticized the structure of the Catholic Church in France. For these reasons, it is difficult to classify Le Play himself as a Catholic Social theorist if what this implies is conformity with institutional Catholic orthodoxy. Nonetheless, Le Play's influence on Catholic Social thought is significant and undeniable.

Bibliography. Brooke, Michael Z., *Le Play: Engineer and Social Scientist.* London: Longman, 1970.

Mathew N. Schmalz

LÉVESQUE, GEORGES-HENRI (1909–2000). Lévesque is considered by many historians the father of the Canadian Quiet Revolution (1960–1970), during which Quebec underwent radical social and political changes. When this young Dominican came back from Europe in 1932, following a study journey in Belgium and France (with fathers Delos, Rutten, Foliet, and others), the Canadian Jesuits were interpreting the Catholic Social doctrine in the perspective of corporatism, French Canadian nationalism, and clericalism. The Dominicans, for their part, were inspired by a more liberal philosophy. This opposition lead to continuous frictions and, sometimes, to open conflicts.

Yet when Lévesque founded the École des Sciences Sociales at Laval University (1938), he received the support of nationalists like **Lionel Groulx** and partisans of the corporatist regime like father J. P. Archambault. But in the aftermaths of the war, when the review *Esprit* began to be the crossroads of a new definition of Catholic political philosophy, Lévesque was driven away from his old friendships.

In 1949–1951, he was appointed commissioner of the Royal Commission on National Development in the Arts, Letters and Sciences. The commission's report sanctioned interference of the federal government in the provincial jurisdictional sphere of education. At a time when the Duplessis government was struggling to assert and safeguard provincial autonomy, this report was deemed an act of war. Tensions did not cool down when Lévesque declared that Canada and not Quebec was French Canadians' country and that nationalism was a xenophobic and reactionary ideology contrary to the teaching of true Catholicism.

In 1948, the Asbestos Strike shook the province. Lévesque and his students pleaded in favor of the exploited working class. The church's right wing, fearful of whatever could be related to state interventionism, denounced the École as a "hive of leftists."

In 1945–1947, as director of the Conseil Supérieur de la Coopération, Lévesque signed a series of articles on the subject of secularization of cooperatives. Since this could be conceived as a first step toward the secularization of the entire province (whether of the Catholic unions, the educational system, or the health-care institutions), he was again accused of being an instrument of the Anglophone Protestant majority.

Lévesque won two trials in Rome conducted by the conservative forces of the Quebec clergy. In 1955, he was coerced by the university to resign as dean of the Faculté des Sciences Sociales. However, his contribution persisted through his former students, who were to eventually hold influential positions at every level of power.

Bibliography. Georges-Henri Lévesque. *Souvenances.* 3 vols. Montréal: La Presse, 1983.

Jean-Philippe Warren

LICHTENBERG, BERNHARD (1875–1943). A German priest known for his resistance to the Nazi regime, Lichtenberg was born in the Silesian village of Ohlau, Germany (today's Olawa, Poland). After receiving his high school diploma in 1895, he studied theology and philosophy in Innsbruck and Breslau and became a Catholic priest in 1899.

First he served at St. Jakobus Church in Neisse, Germany (today's Nysa, Poland), and after a few months he was called to minister at St. Mauritius Church in the Friedrichsberg district of Berlin. In 1913 Lichtenberg took over Herz Jesu Parish in Berlin-Charlottenburg, one of the largest parishes in Berlin. In 1932 he was offered the position as priest at Berlin's St. Hedwig Cathedral. Since Lichtenberg openly criticized the Nazi regime, the Gestapo (Secret State Police) searched his apartment in 1933 but did not find any incriminating evidence. During vespers on November 9, 1938, the night of the *Kristallnacht,* Lichtenberg urged his congregation to pray for non-Aryan Christians and for Jews, who suffered persecution. He later became head of a Catholic charity that supported non-Aryan Christians and Jews in the German Reich. Lichtenberg's organization assisted numerous persecuted Germans to emigrate to other countries.

In 1941, he filed a formal complaint to Germany's surgeon general, harshly critical of the Nazis' euthanasia program. As a consequence, he was arrested and sentenced to two years in prison. Before his release he informed Bishop Preysing of his intention to serve as counselor in the Jewish ghetto of Litzmannstadt (today's Lodz, Poland). However, Lichtenberg never arrived in the ghetto, since the Gestapo arrested him again shortly after his release and took him to the concentration camp of Dachau. Lichtenberg suffered from heart and kidney disease, he was frequently hospitalized, and his health had dramatically deteriorated during his first time in prison. He died en route to Dachau. Lichtenberg was first buried at the St. Hedwig Cemetery, and in 1965, his remains were placed in the vaults of St. Hedwig's Cathedral. In 1994 Pope **John Paul II** officially acknowledged Lichtenberg as a blessed martyr.

Bibliography. Persch, Martin. "Lichtenberg, Bernhard." In *Biographisch-Bibliographisches Kirchenlexikon,* ed. Friedrich Wilhelm Bautz. Herzberg, Germany: Bautz, 1993 Spicer, Kevin. "Last Years of a Resister in the Diocese of Berlin: Bernhard Lichtenberg's Conflict with Karl Adam and His Fateful Imprisonment." *Church History* 70 (June 2001): 248–70.

Gregor Thuswaldner

LIÉNART, ACHILLE (1884–1973). Named the third bishop of the Diocese of Lille, created in 1914 to cater to the working-class industrial region of the north of France, Liénart was, at forty-four, the nation's youngest bishop. Made a cardinal less than two years later, he lived through the great crises of the twentieth century.

A chaplain during the First World War, he was made chevalier of the French Legion of Honor for his courage and devotion. He earned the nickname the "workers' bishop" and also the "red bishop" for his keen pastoral interest in helping the workers of his diocese, going so far as to defend strikers. When criticized for a contribution to a strike support fund in the town of Halluin in 1929, he replied that it was an instance of charity. Trained in the tradition of Social Catholicism, resolutely devoted to the humble and exploited, and later in the 1950s a supporter of the initiatives of the worker-priests, he was at the same time fervently anti-Marxist.

Lille suffered greatly during the Second World War, and Cardinal Liénart, like many veterans of the Great War, was a supporter of Marshal **Philippe Pétain.** He believed that his own responsibility was to remain at his post during the difficult times, devoting himself to pastoral concerns within the forbidden zone, passing over the most difficult questions concerning the persecution of the Jews and collaboration with the Nazis with ambiguity and silence. Always suspicious of the Marxism of the Resistance, he nevertheless emerged from the war with relatively little loss of prestige or authority.

Cardinal Liénart maintained an active interest in the affairs of the people of his diocese, while at the same time taking on several national and international responsibilities, including the leadership of the French Assembly of Cardinals and Archbishops. Throughout his career he sought to encourage participation and dialogue at all levels, from actively promoting the development of the Action Catholique movement in the 1930s to becoming one of the most vocal advocates at the forefront of the reforms made to the church during the Second Vatican Council in the 1960s. He was also interested in reaching out to Christians around the world, in ecumenism, and in developing friendly relations with both Judaism and Islam, in the context of the Algerian War.

Bibliography. Masson, Catherine. *Le Cardinal Liénart: Évêque de Lille 1928–1968.* Paris: Éditions du Cerf, 2001.

Timothy Baycroft

LINCOLN, ABRAHAM (1809–1865). The sixteenth president of the United States (1861–1865), Lincoln never affiliated with a church and never formally declared allegiance to Christian orthodoxy. In his successful congressional campaign under the Illinois Whig banner in 1846, he was compelled to defend himself from charges of religious infidelity. Yet from such an unlikely foundation, Lincoln assigned meaning and historical significance to the Civil War that marked his presidency, using biblical models of divine intervention and retribution more powerful than those employed by any other American chief executive. Historians have traced Lincoln's elusive spiritual journey not only to reconstruct his personal beliefs, but also to better understand the broader religious impulse that has historically shaped Americans' sense of national purpose.

Born near Hodgenville, Kentucky, in 1809 to Thomas and Nancy Hanks Lincoln, Abraham's childhood was disrupted early by his mother's death shortly after the family's move to Indiana in 1816. Thomas married Sarah Bush Johnston in 1819, a decision that helped stabilize Abraham's adolescent years, which centered on farming, hard labor, and barely a year of formal schooling. When Thomas moved the family a third time to Illinois in 1830, young Lincoln found opportunity to escape the agricultural lifestyle he despised. By 1836, he was a licensed lawyer in Springfield and a rising star in state-level politics under the Whig Party banner. His marriage to Mary Todd in 1842 gave him a partner equally committed to his political career, and by 1847 he was serving in Washington, D.C., as an Illinois congressman. While he chose not to seek reelection, his deep commitment to stopping the spread of slavery compelled him back to the political platform in the 1850s as a stalwart of the new Republican Party. In 1860, he accepted that party's presidential nomination and ultimately the nation's electoral nod that put him in the White House. Eleven Southern states registered their contempt for that decision in a secession movement that ultimately led to war.

Although Lincoln grew up amid the spiritual turbulence of the Second Great Awakening, evangelical Christianity's impact on his religious outlook was limited at best. His letters and formal writings contain virtually no mention of Christ, and he appears to have had little interest in a systematic evangelical understanding of personal sin, salvation, and judgment. On the other hand, he rejected deistic conceptions of a distant and impersonal God. Keenly aware that sparring with proponents of either extreme served none of his ample political ambitions, Lincoln counted silence on doctrinal details to be the wisest course. Indeed, his friend and law partner William Herndon cautioned against drawing sweeping conclusions about Lincoln's spiritual predispositions from particular speeches or documents. "Lincoln was very politic," Herndon noted, "and a very shrewd man in some particulars. When he was talking to a Christian, he adapted himself to the Christian. When he spoke to or joked with one of his own kind, he was indecently vulgar."

Political posturing aside, Lincoln's deep fascination with biblical models of God's providential interest in human affairs significantly shaped what scholars have variously described as his political pragmatism, passivity, and optimistic fatalism. Early in his political career, Lincoln developed an interest in the "doctrine of necessity," a conviction that human action is either stayed or encouraged by a higher power. "I claim not to have controlled events," he bluntly declared in 1864 in a letter to Albert Hodges, "but confess plainly that events have controlled me." As the Civil War progressed, Lincoln increasingly drew upon Judeo-Christian understanding to develop a political outlook guided by four essential principles. First, biblical models of divine intervention in human affairs provided assurance that a broader controlling force in the universe overlay the chaos and uncertainties of war. Secondly, the war itself affirmed humanity's sinful nature, shared guilt, and collective vulnerability to divine judgment. Third, Lincoln viewed himself as an instrument of God but without messianic credentials, prophetic discernment, or the capacity to promise

Americans a future millennium of perfect peace and prosperity. Finally, he abandoned these disclaimers on one essential point: Americans as an "almost chosen people" had a sacred and certain responsibility to preserve the Union as an indispensable agent of republican liberty.

In his brief "Meditation on the Divine Will" (1862), Lincoln conceded that God's controlling power was guided by a perfect righteousness imperfectly understood by humankind. In great contests," he explained, "each party claims to act in accordance with the will of God. Both may be, and one must be wrong. . . . In the present civil war it is quite possible that God's purpose is something different from the purpose of either party—and yet the human instrumentalities, working just as they do, are of the best adaptation to effect His purpose." The Almighty, he believed, assigned victory or defeat to either side at a time of his own choosing, irrespective of how his

Abraham Lincoln, 1864. Courtesy of the Library of Congress

human instruments might hope to dictate outcomes.

Lincoln also deferred to God as the ultimate judge of humankind. The same biblical understanding that compelled him to declare Southern clerical apologists for slavery to be without spiritual merit also led him to admonish Northern evangelicals who too easily claimed the mantle of holiness. Southerners who exploited slave labor engaged in common thievery, Lincoln believed, and surely "contemned [sic] and insulted God and His church." Divine principles, however, also required the North to admit its own historical complicity in supporting the slave institution. In his second inaugural address, arguably the most powerful use of religious language by any American president, Lincoln warned that "it may seem strange that any men should dare to ask a just God's assistance in wringing their bread from the sweat of the men's faces; but let us judge not that we be not judged. . . . The Almighty has His own purposes."

This reluctance to align either side with absolute good or evil was an act of restraint consistent with Lincoln's assessment of his own role in the conflict. Despite his belief that the divine will would be achieved through human instrumentality, he never sanctified his own political or military decisions. In Lincoln's mind, human agency would always be reigned by human limitations. While many nineteenth-century evangelicals measured progress toward a Christian millennium of peace and prosperity, Lincoln rested in the hope of compromise solutions and partial victories. The divine will simply lay beyond full human understanding. From Christianity, then, Lincoln learned to act with boldness and humility. Surely God wanted "some great good to follow this mighty convulsion," he told the Quaker Eliza P. Gurney, but "erring mortals may not accurately perceive [it] in advance."

On two fundamental issues—slavery and republican liberty—Lincoln's usual caution gave way to a brace of moral and political certainties: Slavery was utterly inconsistent with divine principles, and American republicanism was the seedbed of freedom for all humanity. That God had allowed American slavery to develop merely indulged the human capacity to make immoral decisions. Conversely, the rise of American republicanism gave vital political expression to God's enduring commitment to human freedom and to the Union as visible evidence of the Creator's promise that human effort could expand that freedom. To be sure, Lincoln's respect for law, constitutional precedent, and military necessities compelled him toward compromise measures, but he acted out of conviction that every effort to preserve the Union gave freedom a wider berth. At the dedication of the Gettysburg cemetery in 1863, Lincoln called attention to lives sacrificed in order to press Americans toward a "new birth of freedom," ultimately with global consequences. "In *giving* freedom to the slave, we *assure* freedom to the *free*—honorable alike in what we give, and what we preserve. We shall nobly save, or meanly lose, the last best, hope of earth."

It has often been said that Lincoln's real faith was narrowly political, and that preserving the Union, not eliminating slavery or improving the lot of black Americans, ruled his actions. One moves closer to the mark, however, in recognizing that Lincoln held individual freedom as the wellspring of all human progress. He simply could not conceive of advancing that cause without the Union or while slavery remained unchallenged. Consequently, any attempt to order Lincoln's commitments obscures the fundamental unity of his political vision. As for clarifying particular forms and outcomes of racial equality in America, Lincoln's vision disappointed Republican Radicals, who plotted a faster, more radical path to racial justice as the war drew to a close in 1865. Still, his magnanimity toward Southerners, zeal for national unity, and cautious optimism as to the future of the freedmen and women did not reveal a moral failure of nerve, as some critics argue. By placing final judgments and outcomes under the divine prerogative, Lincoln reaffirmed the core of a faith long in the making.

Bibliography. Basler, Roy P., ed. *The Collected Works of Abraham Lincoln.* New Brunswick, NJ: Rutgers University Press, 1953–55. Donald, David Herbert. *Lincoln.* New York: Simon & Schuster, 1996. Fornieri, Joseph R. *Abraham Lincoln's Political Faith.* Dekalb: Northern Illinois University Press, 2005. Herndon, William H., and Jesse W. Weik. *Herndon's Life of Lincoln.* New York: Da Capo Press, 1983.

Mark Y. Hanley

LOPEZ BRU, CLAUDIO (1853–1925). In 1883, Bru became the second Marquess of Comillas after the death of the first marquess, who had made a fortune in Cuba thanks to astute investments in shipping, banking, railroads, tobacco, and the slave trade. A very pious man under the influence of the priest-poet Jacinto Verdaguer and members of the Jesuit order, Lopez Bru paid for the construction of the Pontifical Seminary in his father's birthplace, Comillas, which became the Catholic university of that name. The marquess was also inspired by **Leo XIII's** 1891 social encyclical, *Rerum novarum,* and in 1894, he organized with his own company ships a massive pilgrimage to Rome by Spanish workers to see the pope. The energy and resources of Lopez Bru were crucial to the creation in 1894 of the Spanish Catholic Action, of which he remained vice president until his death.

Lopez Bru's political and organizational activities practically coincide with the Restoration period (1875–1923) in Spanish history, a time of a liberal parliamentary monarchy based in electoral manipulation and stagnant social reforms. Many social and political groups felt excluded from Spain's political process and developed attitudes toward the regime that varied from middle-class radical anticlericalism to violent anarcho-syndicalism among workers and peasants.

A man of conservative and elitist convictions, the marquess considered Pope Leo's new social doctrine to be the best alternative to counteract those critical and destabilizing forces. His leadership and social connections enabled him to garner support for his reform projects among the elites of the Restoration. His markedly paternalistic attitude, however, limited the appeal of Catholic labor organizations among workers and peasants while at the same time creating hostility among progressive and left-wing groups, who saw social reform as their own political domain. At the same time, other less traditional Catholic social reformers, such as fathers Antonio Vicent, Gabriel Palau, Maximiliano Arboleya, and José Gafo, were often criticized and even ostracized by the church. Until his death, Lopez Bru continued to be very active in charities and relief organizations. In 1948, his cause of beatification was opened.

Bibliography. Benavides Gomez, Domingo. *El fracaso social del catolicismo español, Arboleya-Martínez.* Barcelona: Nova Terra, 1973.

Antonio Cazorla Sanchez

LOVEJOY, ELIJAH PARISH (1802–1837). Lovejoy was a Presbyterian minister, newspaper editor, and an early martyr in the antislavery movement. Born in Albion, Maine, he was the son of a Congregational clergyman. He graduated from Waterville (now Colby) College in 1826, taught school for a year in New England, and then moved to St. Louis, where he continued teaching and began editing a local newspaper.

Following a conversion experience, under the preaching of an antislavery evangelist, Lovejoy returned in 1832 to the east, where he attended Princeton Seminary and was licensed to preach by the Philadelphia Presbytery in 1833. He returned to St. Louis and became the editor of a Presbyterian weekly, the *St. Louis Observer,* the first Protestant newspaper to be published west of the Mississippi River. The paper's editorial policy was moderate at first but eventually became strident in its attacks on intemperance, Catholics, Baptists, and other religious groups with whom Lovejoy disagreed. The paper then moved against slavery, calling initially for gradual emancipation but then siding with the **abolitionists** in their demand for immediate emancipation. Lovejoy became increasingly unwelcome in St. Louis, the leading city in a slave state. In 1836 he moved his paper to Alton, Illinois, twenty-five miles up the Mississippi River from St. Louis.

Illinois was a free state, and Lovejoy hoped for a more conciliatory atmosphere. It was not to be. On three occasions mobs destroyed his presses. The greater the opposition, the more certain Lovejoy became of the rightness of his convictions that slavery was a monstrous evil. On November 7, 1837, another new press arrived in Alton and was placed in a warehouse where it was protected by Lovejoy and those who shared his goals. That night an armed mob stormed the warehouse. At first the mob was repelled by those inside. The attackers then attempted to burn down the warehouse. Lovejoy ran outside, where he attempted to extinguish the fires. He was soon killed by gunfire.

No one was ever convicted for the shooting of Lovejoy, although there were numerous witnesses. Nevertheless, as Paul Simon has written, "No one event up to that time had mobilized antislavery like the death of Lovejoy" (153).

342 Lubbers, Rudolphus "Ruud" Franciscus Marie

Bibliography. Simon, Paul. *Freedom's Champion: Elijah Lovejoy.* Foreword by Clarence Page. Carbondale: Southern Illinois University Press, 1994.

David B. Chesebrough

LUBBERS, RUDOLPHUS "RUUD" FRANCISCUS MARIE (b. 1939). A Christian democratic politician and prime minister of the Netherlands, Lubbers, the son of a Catholic entrepreneur, was born in Rotterdam. He studied at the Jesuit's Canisius College in Nijmegen and at the former Dutch Economic Academy, now Erasmus University, in Rotterdam. Finishing his studies in 1962, he anticipated a scientific career, but circumstances compelled him to take over management of the family's firm in 1963. His entrepreneurial activities and his Christian understanding of politics and economic pushed him early in life into public life.

Already in 1964, Lubbers became chairman of the Christian Association of Young Employers and joined the Dutch Catholic People's Party (KVP). Later he took over the presidency of the Catholic Association of Metalworkers Employers and was appointed to the board of the Dutch Christian Employer's Association. From 1973 to1977, Lubbers served as the minister for economic affairs in the Den Uyl cabinet. He worked for the consolidation of the Catholic parties that became the **Christian Democratic Appeal** (CDA), serving as its first vice chairman and, in the autumn of 1978, as the leader of the CDA's parliamentary group. In 1982, 1986, and 1989, he was elected prime minister.

In 1994, after a crushing defeat in the elections that after seventy years put the CDA into opposition, Lubbers finished his political career and devoted his life to academic tasks. He taught "Globalization and Lasting Development" as professor at the university of Tilburg and as guest professor at the John F. Kennedy School of Government at Harvard University. He was vice chairman of the Independent World Commission on the Oceans and chairman of the Institute for Globalization and Lasting Development (GLOBUS) in Tilburg. In November 1999 Lubbers was elected international president of the World Wildlife Fund (WWF) and at the beginning of 2001 succeeded Sadako Ogata as the United Nations high commissioner for refugees, a position in which he advocated for a refugee- and asylum-friendly atmosphere in the industrial nations of the northern hemisphere. However, charged with sexual molestation by a female colleague, a charge he denied, he resigned on February 21, 2005.

As Dutch prime minister, Lubbers enforced the social rebuilding of the polder's system with globalization in the background. For this he enforced the transformation to private ownership and the deregulation of the economy. A convinced Europeanist, he also championed the North Atlantic Treaty Organization and better Euro-American relations. In 1990, for example, his cabinet called for Dutch participation in the Gulf War. Differences with the German chancellor **Helmut Kohl** resulted mainly from Lubbers's disapproval of the German reunification. To Lubbers's insistence that the Dutch had a say in the union, Germany's foreign minister Hans-Dietrich Genscher retorted, "You are not part of the game." Lubbers's negative attitude toward German reunification and his difficult relationship with Kohl later became detrimental to his career. His bid for the presidency of the European Union was unsuccessful, while Kohl promoted Luxemburg's Jacques Santer. The office of NATO's general secretary was also refused to him.

Bibliography. Ammerlaan, Robbert. *Afscheid van Rudd Lubbers.* Baarn, Netherlands: Uitgeverij Anthos, 1994.

Helmut Rönz

LUEGER, KARL (1844–1910). The Christian Social deputy to the Austrian parliament and mayor of Vienna, where he was born and raised, Lueger studied law at the University of Vienna and worked for several law firms between 1867 and 1874. During these years he joined the Liberalen Landstrasser Bürgerclub (Citizens' Club of the Landstrasse) and quickly advanced as its second secretary. Having defended his dissertation in 1874, Lueger opened his own law firm and remained politically active.

In 1875 he took on the position as a municipal councilor for the second curia from Vienna's third district. He served as a liberal politician in the city council but grew more and more weary of liberalism. Finally, he turned away from his party and was drawn to Karl Freiherr von Vogelsang's conservative Catholic organization, United Christians. In September 1888 Vogelsang renamed his organization **Christian Social Party** and declared Lueger its new political leader. Lueger was elected to the Landtag (parliament) of Lower Austria in 1890. In this position he harshly criticized corruption, the free press, and liberalism and propagated Catholicism. Pope **Leo XIII**'s encyclical *Rerum novarum* (1891) had a lasting impact on the party's agenda, as it set forth a genuine Catholic vision of social reform.

In 1895 the Christian Social Party won the elections, and Lueger was nominated as mayor of Vienna. His demagogic rhetoric, however, prompted Emperor Franz Joseph to block Lueger's accession to the position. After a two year struggle, though, the emperor eventually gave in and Lueger was officially elected as Vienna's new mayor.

Unlike other anti-Semitic politicians of his time, such as Georg Ritter von Schönerer, Lueger remained a monarchist. His anti-Jewish rhetoric certainly influenced a new generation of anti-Semites, such as Adolf Hitler, who spent several

Bürgermeister von Wien, ca. 1900. © National Library of Vienna

years in Lueger's Vienna. In *Mein Kampf* Hitler mentions Lueger as "the greatest German mayor of all times" (Geehr, 14). However, Lueger's anti-Semitism was more religious and economic than racial. Surprisingly, some of his friends were actually Jewish. When he was told about this discrepancy, he famously replied: "I decide who is a Jew!" (Geehr, 16). Lueger was not just a demagogic politician; he also left a positive mark on the city. Under him, Vienna became fully modernized, the public transportation system was expanded, and hospitals and schools were built. Lueger remained in office until his death in 1910.

Bibliography. Brown, Karin Brinkman. *Karl Lueger, the Liberal Years: Democracy, Municipal Reform, and Struggle for Power in the Vienna City Council 1875–1882.* London: Taylor & Francis, 1987. Geehr, Richard S. *Karl Lueger: Mayor of Fin de Siècle Vienna.* Detroit, MI: Wayne State University Press, 1990.

Gregor Thuswaldner

M

MACAULAY, THOMAS BABINGTON (1800–1859). Macaulay, later Lord Macaulay, is often regarded as the quintessential Victorian, convinced as to the inevitable progress of civilization, especially under the beneficent influence of the British constitution. The son of Zachary Macaulay, a leading figure in the **Clapham Sect** of evangelical Anglicans, Macaulay was shaped by the rigorous morality of his family but shed all outward signs of piety. After joining the Whig party, he gained a seat in Parliament and was a government minister; he served on the Supreme Council of India, where he took part in reforming the law code. A renowned literary critic and orator, he also wrote an unfinished five-volume *History of England* expounding the so-called Whig interpretation, which portrays the rise of liberal democracy as ordained by reason and historical circumstance.

Following a precocious childhood, Macaulay entered Cambridge University, where he was drawn to journalism and the debating society. His father, however, believed that he was wasting his time reading novels and pressured him to withdraw from one student periodical on account of its frivolous tone. As the protégé of a powerful Whig politician, Macaulay became a contributor to the *Edinburgh Review* while still at university. His first article, echoing the abolitionist sentiments of his father, attacked not only slave-holding itself but also the idea that the West Indian colonies were profitable. Macaulay's early views were influenced by the writings of the Scottish school of philosophical history and also by those of the more radical Utilitarians. In the late 1820s, however, he deliberately distanced himself from utilitarianism, criticizing the work of James Mill as excessively logical and divorced from historical context, points that struck home even with John Stuart Mill, the author's own son.

In the political arena, Macaulay made his name as a prominent spokesman for the Whig party during the debate over parliamentary reform in 1830–1832. There is controversy as to the degree to which he embraced liberal democratic ideals. In one view, Macaulay's sympathy for the enemies of King Charles I signals a genuine identification with the "heritage of Cromwell and the Roundheads" (Clive, 89, 95); according to another, freedom from any partisan loyalty was characteristic of his entire career (Hamburger, 149–50). His eloquent advocacy of extending the franchise and leaving open the question of the secret ballot was based in large part on his fear of violent revolution, abetted by the discontent of the middle class. But he never supported universal suffrage. For

Thomas Macaulay. Courtesy of the Library of Congress

him, politics was above all the art of averting instability and factionalism, which could jeopardize the peaceful unfolding of progress in the social, economic, and artistic spheres. The version of seventeenth-century English revolution that he advanced in his *History,* which sold over 140,000 copies (Hamburger, 163), offered salutary warnings to politically minded readers in his own day.

Macaulay's religious views remain a mystery, perhaps as he intended. He could be seen as one of the first influential Victorians to believe that a public confessional stance was irrelevant to political life. He condemned the exclusion of Jews from Parliament as simply unreasonable. Although he deplored many traditional practices of the Indians as immoral and superstitious, he did not share the missionaries' enthusiasm for religious conversion as the answer. More significantly, Macaulay confessed that he was uninterested in deep metaphysical questions. **William Gladstone,** a stern judge, accu-

rately observed that Macaulay failed to make Christian dogma the central pillar of his intellect; Macaulay probably revealed himself more clearly by his private admission that he "always hated confessors—Protestant as Catholic"(Clive, 248). The historian and politician belonged to a generation for whom evangelicalism was still a hereditary faith but no longer a personal creed.

Bibliography. Clive, John. *Macaulay: The Shaping of the Historian.* New York: Vintage, 1975. Hamburger, Joseph. *Macaulay and the Whig Tradition.* Chicago: Chicago University Press, 1976.

John D. Ramsbottom

MACKINNON, COLIN FRANCIS (1810–1879). A Roman Catholic priest, bishop, and educator, MacKinnon was born in Williams Point, Nova Scotia, Canada, into a Highland Scottish family that immigrated to Antigonish County in 1791. He attended grammar schools at Grand Narrows and at East Bay, Cape Breton, Nova Scotia. From 1829 to1837 he studied for the priesthood at the Urban College, Rome, where he was also awarded the PhD and doctor of divinity He was ordained priest in 1837 at the Propaganda. Upon returning to his native diocese, he was assigned as the first pastor of St. Andrews, where he remained until he was appointed second bishop of the Diocese of Arichat in 1852. While at that post, he established St. Andrews Grammar School in 1838 with an annual government subsidy. MacKinnon was very concerned about the status of Roman Catholics in the diocese since they had no real influence. The social, economic, religious, and political power lay firmly in the hands of the Anglican establishment in Halifax. As a result, he founded St. Francis Xavier's College on July 20, 1853, in Arichat, which was the seat of the diocese. Through MacKinnon's petitioning of the legislature, St. Francis Xavier's College obtained full degree-granting status in 1866. He was also able to acquire an annual grant. Undoubtedly, his brother, John, aided him immensely, as the latter was a member of the legislative assembly and executive for over twenty years. MacKinnon believed that the Roman Catholics were equally permitted to as much public monies for education as were the other denominations in the province. Also, MacKinnon set the plans in motion for the construction of the large St. Ninian's Cathedral in 1866. Due to the poor nature of the economy, the cathedral was not completed until 1874. The pressure of this undertaking detrimentally affected MacKinnon's mental and physical health. As a result he became incompetent, and his resignation was forced by his Halifax superior in July 1877. He died two years later from a stroke. MacKinnon was a man of vision who was greatly loved by his people. His greatest achievement was undoubtedly the promotion of education for Roman Catholics in northeastern Nova Scotia.

Bibliography. A. A. Johnston Collection, Diocesan Historian, Antigonish Diocesan Archives, Antigonish, Nova Scotia. Johnston, A. A. *Antigonish Diocese Priests and Bishops, 1786–1925.* Ed. Kathleen M. MacKenzie. Antigonish, NS: Casket, 1994. Johnston, A. A. *A History of the Catholic Church in Eastern Nova Scotia.* 2 vols. Antigonish, NS: St. Francis Xavier Press, 1960, 1971. William X. Edwards Collection, St. Francis Xavier Archives, Antigonish, Nova Scotia.

Kathleen M. MacKenzie

MADIRAN, JEAN. *See* Arfel, Jean-Louis

MAISTRE, JOSEPH DE (1753–1821). Although a government official all his adult life, serving in judicial and diplomatic positions, Count Joseph de Maistre's significance for modern Christian politics lies primarily in his influence as a writer. Born in Chambéry at a time when Savoy was a province of the Kingdom of Piedmont-Sardinia, and always a subject of that northern Italian monarchy, Maistre was nevertheless thoroughly French in language and culture, and it was in France that his apologetics for monarchy, Catholicism, and the papacy were most influential.

Educated by the Jesuits and in the local *collège,* Maistre earned his law degrees from the University of Turin. Like his father, he served in the Senate of Savoy (a high law court equivalent to a French parlement), and was named a senator in 1788. Following the French invasion of Savoy in 1792, Maistre fled Chambéry and served as a Piedmontese diplomat in Lausanne (1793–1797) and St. Petersburg (1803–1817). His later legal career included service as regent (head of the court system) in Sardinia (1800–1803) and regent of Piedmont-Sardinia (1818–1821).

A sympathetic observer of developments in France in the years immediately preceding the Revolution, Maistre had looked to the magistrates of the French parlements as the natural leaders of moderate reform. Initially enthusiastic about reform possibilities, he was soon disillusioned by the news from Versailles. He opposed the "leveling" implied in the joining together of the three orders of clergy, nobility, and third estate and predicted it would lead to a "deluge of evils." By the time a French army invaded Savoy in September of 1792, Maistre's intellectual opposition of the Revolution and its philosophy was firmly fixed. He fled to Piedmont and then settled in Lausanne, where he served as Piedmontese consul and began to write against the Revolution.

Maistre's *Letters of a Savoyard Royalist,* published in 1793 for clandestine circulation in French-occupied Savoy, revealed the dilemma of a purely political royalism in an age of democratic revolution. While he complained that political loyalty was becoming a matter of calculation rather than an instinct as it had once been, his own appeal was precisely to enlightened self-interest. He asked his readers to judge the old monarchy on its record and exhorted his fellow Savoyards to "love your sovereign as you love *order* with all the strength of your intelligence." This was the very rationalism that had repudiated the old order.

Maistre quickly abandoned a purely political analysis in favor of a religious and providential interpretation of events. His *Considerations on France,* which appeared in early 1797, announced Maistre's new theological explanation of the French Revolution and established his reputation as a major defender of throne and altar. Maistre gave cosmic significance to the Revolution by proclaiming that never had the role of Providence in human affairs been more palpable. Construing what was happening as both a divine punishment and as providentially ordained means for the regeneration of France, Maistre was able to condemn the Revolution and the ideas it embodied and, at the same time, treat it as a necessary prelude to the restoration of the Bourbon monarchy. The political dilemma of the Savoyard royalist had found its resolution in a religious vision of redemption.

It was Maistre's stress on the antireligious character of the Revolution, what he called its "satanic quality," that appears to have resonated with French Catholic royalists for much of the nineteenth century. This theme sustained their adamant hostility to the Revolution, to the Enlightenment ideas that Maistre condemned for having spawned the Revolution, and to the Jacobin heritage that they associated with republicanism.

Maistre had read Edmund Burke's *Reflections on the Revolution in France* soon after that work appeared in 1790, and he shared Burke's emotional reaction against the violence, "immorality," and "atheism" of the Revolution. Maistre's work echoed Burkean themes, including reverence for established institutions, distrust of innovation, and defense of prejudice, aristocracy, and an established church. Maistre differed from Burke primarily in his providentialism, and in his defense of Roman Catholicism and papal authority.

Maistre's later works, *An Essay on the Generative Principle of Political Constitutions* (1814), *The Pope* (1817), *St. Petersburg Dialogues* (1821), and *An Examination of the Philosophy of Bacon* (not published until 1836), reveal a gradual shift in emphasis from politics to fundamental philosophical and theological issues. A major theorist of the Counter-Enlightenment, Maistre's writings stimulated such thinkers as Saint-Simon, Auguste Comte, and **Charles Maurras** and inspired generations of French royalists and ultramontane Catholics.

Bibliography. Lebrun, Richard A. *Joseph de Maistre: An Intellectual Militant.* Kingston, ON: McGill-Queen's University Press, 1988. Lebrun, Richard. Joseph de Maistre Homepage. www.umanitoba.ca/faculties/arts/history/maistre.html. Maistre, Joseph de. *Considerations on France.* Ed. and trans. Richard A. Lebrun. Introduction by Isaiah Berlin. Cambridge: Cambridge University Press, 1994.

Richard A. Lebrun

MAKARIOS III. *See* Mouskos, Michael

MAKRAKIS, APOSTOLOS (1831–1905). Makrakis was a Greek Orthodox lay theologian active throughout the second half of the nineteenth century who divided his time among Athens, Constantinople, and the island of Syros. A gifted preacher and writer, he directed his ambitious polemics toward Cartesian philosophy, Freemasonry (as a form of atheism), the official Orthodox Church, and the Greek king and the state.

Apostolos founded a philosophical and educational system based on his belief that man consists of body, heart, and soul and that Christ was perfected in the face of

John the Baptist. To advance his ideas, he established the School of Logos, the John the Theologian Society, the pan-Hellenic political society of Constantine the Great, and the Plato Society. His efforts secured a faithful following of priests, students, and fellow activists until his death.

Makrakis was educated at the Great School of the Race in Constantinople and soon developed a fierce antipapal rhetoric. Spending two years in Paris as a tutor to the sons of a Constantinople banker, in 1863 he wrote a polemic against Ernest Renan's *Life of Jesus*. On his return to Athens, he delivered university lectures on Plato's *Politics,* on the glory of a Christian Greek nation and, in May 1866, more than twenty open speeches in Athens' central Omonoia Square on the Greek national liberation struggle. His public attacks (and related books in 1867 and 1868) against Freemasons provoked the first governmental reactions. In a celebrated trial for disrespect to King George I in 1867, Makrakis was proved innocent after an impressive plea. With the birth of the king's son, Makrakis gave another series of speeches on the relationship of the newborn prince and the national symbolism of his baptism.

In 1868 Makrakis established his own newspaper, *Logos,* and from 1876 to 1879 taught at his own School of Logos. After accusing three bishops of simony and being censured by the Holy Synod for compromising the standards of the Gospels, his school was closed. Makrakis was accused of introducing controversies to the canon and was sent to prison in 1879. From prison, Makrakis ran without success to represent Attica in Parliament. On his release, he resumed his preaching until he was again called to court in 1881 and sentenced for heresy and subversion of religion.

During a speech in 1885, an assassination attempt was made on him. From then onward, accusations abounded that his attacks on clergy, king, and state were made for personal gain. In 1894, after a long period of extensive preaching throughout the whole country, Makrakis received a considerable yet inadequate seven thousand votes as candidate for minister. Between 1895 and 1899 he prepared his full interpretation of the New Testament and a new polemic against Freemasonry. In 1901, he founded the Plato Society, although this movement virtually dissolved after his death.

Makrakis, partly a victim of the caste character of the relations between church and state in Greece, has remained a symbol of Orthodox militancy and populism, as well as of antipapal and anti-Masonic fervor. Contemporary and Orthodox readings of his works continue to illustrate aspects of his inspired and original Christian thinking.

Bibliography. Balanos, Dimitrios. *Apostolos Makrakis, 1831–1905.* Thessaloníki, Greece: 1920. Diomedes-Kyriakos, Anastasios. *Geschichte der orientalischen Kirchen von 1453–1898.* Hildesheim, Germany: Gerstenberg, 1975. Kalafatis, Athanasios "Religiosité et protestation sociale: Les adeptes de Apostolos Makrakis dans le Péloponnese du Nordouest." *Historica* 18–19 (1993):113–42. Papadopoulos, Chrysostomos. *Apostolos Makrakis.* Ed. Grigoris Papamichail. Athens: Phoinikos, 1939. Synodinos, Polykarpos. "Biography of Apostolos Makrakis." *Nea Sion* 3 (1906): 486–93, 618–35.

Lia Yoka

MALAN, DANIEL FRANÇOIS (1874–1959). D. F. Malan, South African Afrikaner clergyman and politician, was the first premier of the Herenigde Nasionale Party (HNP), later known as the National Party. He developed and then introduced apartheid as state policy after the party's election victory in 1948.

Born on the farm Allesverloren, near Riebeeck West, in what was then Cape Colony, he attended the local school with his later political opponent, General Jan Christiaan Smuts. After he graduated from Victoria College (later Stellenbosch University) with teaching credentials in 1895, he decided to enter the ministry of the Dutch Reformed Church (DRC), simultaneously working on a master's degree in philosophy and a theological degree. While traveling abroad, he represented South Africa at the World Student Christian Association meeting in Denmark.

Returning to South Africa in 1905, he was ordained and appointed to the famed Dutch Reformed Klipkerk in Heidelberg, Tranvaal (the former Zuid Afrikaansche Republiek). He subsequently served numerous congregations (Montagu, Graaf-Reinett) before undertaking a tour of DRC congregations in the Rhodesias and Belgian Congo. He founded numerous Afrikaner cultural organizations, including the critically important Zuid-Afrikaansche Akademie voor Taal, Letteren en Kunst (South African Academy for Language, Literature, and Art). In 1915 he left the pastorate to edit a new newspaper, *De Burger,* to support the newly formed National Party.

For Malan, embracing the Afrikaner people's struggle to attain nationhood meant resisting British imperialism and cultural Anglicization. He became a member of Parliament, representing Calvinia (Cape) and was appointed minister for interior affairs, education, and public health. In 1919 he was a member of the Afrikaner delegation to the Versailles Peace Conference, seeking the restoration of the Old Afrikaner Republics of the South African Republic and the Orange Free State. Strongly supporting state tolerance of religious differences, he nonetheless included religious language in the Union constitution and passed legislation enabling Afrikaans to replace Dutch as an official language. He also successfully replaced the British Union Jack with a South African flag (1928). Despite reversals due to the party's

anti-British and pro-German stance in the late 1930s, his party won a narrow victory in 1948 on a platform advocating separation, or apartheid, of the different racial groups.

Thus in 1949, Malan promoted passage of the Prohibition of Mixed Marriages Act, beginning a series of apartheid measures. The Immorality Act outlawed interracial sexual relations, and the Population Registration Act required state registration of all citizens by race. The Group Areas Act was the first of a series of laws establishing racially defined residential and business areas, while the Bantu Education Act mandated segregated schools. A 1957 act to prohibit interracial worship was defeated in the face of intense political and ecclesiastical pressure from the English churches. Such apartheid was the result of a fusion of Protestant missionary principles (for example, sending the Gospel to each people in their own language) and the sphere theology of the nineteenth-century Dutch theologian and politician **Abraham Kuyper,** in which different segments of human society are regarded as partly autonomous. Apartheid is in effect an application of this, together with strands of German romanticism, along racial lines. Malan's political philosophy, stressing the separateness of peoples, stood in stark contrast to the integrationalist (though still paternalistic and racist) approach expressed in the holism of General Smuts. Malan unexpectedly announced his resignation from politics in 1956 and died two years later while finishing his biography on his farm, Môrewag, near Stellenbosch.

Bibliography. Booyen, B. "Daniel François Malan" *Dictionary of South African Biography.* Vol. 3. Pretoria, South Africa: Human Sciences Research Council, 1977. Malan, Daniel François. *Afrikaner Volkseenheid en My Ervarings op die Pad Daarheen.* Cape Town, South Africa: Nasionale Boekhandel Beperk, 1959.

Iain S. Maclean

MALINES CONGRESS. The Malines Congress was a meeting of Belgian Catholic leaders in 1863 in the city of Malines, or Mechelen, as it is known in Dutch. The congress, followed by subsequent congresses in Mechelen in 1864 and 1867, helped create what was probably the first Catholic political organization in continental Europe. It also led to some of the first large lay organizations of Social Catholicism, efforts by Catholics to help the lower classes. The Belgian organizations helped inspire similar Catholic political and social organizations in Germany, the Netherlands, France, Switzerland, and Italy. The Malines Congress was an important landmark in the development of church-state relations. It marked a halfway point between the so-called alliance of throne and altar that characterized Catholic church-state relations up to the early nineteenth century and the pluralism and Christian democratic politics that began in the late nineteenth century.

The congress was called by Cardinal Sterkyx, the archbishop of Malines. The archbishopric of Malines was not only the seat of the Belgian primate among the bishops but was the largest in the country and included the country's two largest cities, Brussels and Antwerp. Sterkyx hoped to help Belgian Catholic leaders deal with a new policy of anticlericalism against the church by liberals, who had taken control of the Belgian government in elections in 1857.

The Kingdom of Belgium had been allowed to emerge as an independent state in 1831 by the Great Powers, in particular Britain and France, after the country revolted from Dutch rule. Independence was supported by an unusual coalition of Belgian liberals and Catholics. The liberals saw the Dutch king as arbitrary, while Catholics feared that rule by the Protestant Dutch would undermine the church's position. Belgium was, and is, almost completely Catholic, but the church had suffered greatly under Austrian, French, and Dutch rule from 1780 to 1830. The liberal and Catholic leaders who allied to write a new constitution in 1830–1831 were known as Unionists. "Unionism" meant that Belgium had liberal freedoms of the press, assembly, and religion and a limited constitutional monarchy. But the Belgian constitution allowed the Catholic Church to receive government subsidies and maintain its de facto control of social welfare, education, and parishes.

Although denounced by the pope, the constitution was accepted by the bishops in 1831. Shrewdly, and, as later events proved, correctly, they gambled that the church could thrive under the Unionist constitution as though it were an established church. Progressive Catholic writers such as **Félicité de Lammenais** in France praised the Belgian constitution as a model of how the church could thrive in a liberal political system.

The Congress of Malines was convoked to deal with the breakdown of the Unionist compromise. Beginning with the second Rogier government in 1857, Belgian liberals had adopted anticlerical measures to limit the church's control over education and social welfare and to exert state control over regular clergy and the creation of new parishes. The liberals already in 1846 had adopted the British system of political clubs, a kind of proto-political party. Catholics, meanwhile, had been content to participate in elections and Parliament as a very loose group of like-minded individuals. Bishops and priests had generally tried to avoid political involvement.

Simultaneously, Catholics faced the challenge of poverty and industrialization. Belgium was the first country in the world to industrialize after Britain. A large population of rural weavers and spinners, squeezed nearly to starvation by the potato famine and crop failures of the 1840s, flocked to the cities. The traditional charity by parishes was inadequate. Meanwhile, the liberals pursued a policy of laissez-faire and did little to help social problems.

The Malines Congress of 1863 helped Catholics form a new policy of political involvement and social activism. In politics, they were able to defend the church by claiming to defend the constitution. At the same time, Catholic leaders rejected the arguments of conservative Catholics, known as ultramontanes, or pro-papalists, who rejected electoral politics and constitutional government altogether. Cardinal Sterkyx's *Lettres sur la Constitution,* published in 1864, stated the position of the Congress in favor of Catholic political action in a liberal state. In social work, the Congress attacked the liberals' neglect and called for activism by Catholics to minister to the poor.

The Federation of Constitutional Conservative Associations (*Fédération des Associations Constitutionnelles Conservatrices*), founded in 1864, and the Federation of Catholic Clubs (*Fédération des Cercles Catholiques*), founded in 1868, both grew out of the Malines Congresses. After years of collaboration, the two federations merged in 1879. They were not true political parties. No single political program united the members of the federations. The federations, however, brought Catholic politicians together and formed the basis for a true Catholic party by the 1890s. Similarly, the congress inspired the creation in 1867 of the Belgian Federation of Catholic Workers Clubs (*Fédération des Cercles Ouvriers Catholiques Belges/Bond der Belgische Katholieke Werkmanskringen*), which organized charitable work for industrial populations.

Bibliography. Maier, Hans. *Revolution and the Church: The Early History of Christian Democracy, 1789–1907.* Notre Dame, IN: University of Notre Dame, 1969. Misner, Paul. *Social Catholicism in Europe: From the Onset of Industrialization to the First World War.* New York: Crossroads, 1991.

Carl Strikwerda

MALLINCKRODT, HERMANN VON (1821–1874). Among the most important German Catholic political figures of the nineteenth century and a founder of the **Center Party,** Hermann von Mallinckrodt was greatly influenced by the strong faith of his mother and sisters. He began studying law in Berlin in 1838 and finished his studies in Bonn four years later.

From an early age, Mallinckrodt expressed an admiration for Prussia as well as an interest in the relationship between church and state, which was the topic of his *Examensarbeit.* Between 1842 and 1849, he held a variety of positions within the Prussian state. After passing his final exams in 1849, Mallinckrodt became government assessor, which took him to Minden, Erfurt, Stralsund, and Frankfurt an der Oder during the 1850s. The German revolutions of 1848–1849 influenced his conservative political outlook, and upon entering politics in the early 1850s, he quickly became known as a staunch defender of the rights of the monarch and the church. Most of his political efforts during the 1850s centered on protecting and strengthening the role of the church in society, particularly in education, as well as reforming the administrative and electoral system of the Prussian state.

Together with the brothers August and Peter Reichensperger, Mallinckrodt founded what would in 1859 become known as the Center Party. The three led the Catholic faction in the Prussian parliament and fought diligently to protect the interests of the Catholic Church in the predominantly Protestant Prussian state.

During the 1860s, Mallinckrodt cemented his role as one of the leading Catholic politicians, and his increasing cooperation with **Ludwig Windthorst** provided the Center Party with a firmer organizational structure. Due to his ambivalence toward democracy, he supported Otto von Bismarck in the Iron Chancellor's conflict with the Prussian parliament between

1862 and 1866. Although Mallinckrodt supported Bismarck in the face of liberal and progressive demands for more participatory politics, he opposed the Prussian wars against Denmark and Austria in 1864 and 1866. In regard to the German question, Mallinckrodt was hesitant about a quick unification, as he resisted the centralizing tendencies that he believed were inevitable once Germany unified. Between 1866 and 1870, he worked closely with Windthorst to establish the political program that later constituted the basis of the Center Party that operated in the Second Empire after its unification. A brilliant orator, Mallinckrodt became known as one of the strongest opponents of Bismarck and his minister of education and cultural affairs, Adalbert Falk, during the *Kulturkampf*. After long suffering from ill health, Mallinckrodt died in 1874 while still one of the most formidable politicians of the Second German Empire.

Bibliography. Anderson, Margaret Lavinia. *Windthorst: A Political Biography.* Oxford: Clarendon Press, 1981. Pfülf, Otto. *Hermann von Mallinckrodt. Die Geschichte seines Lebens.* Freiburg, Germany: Herdersche Verlagshandlung, 1901.

Pontus Hiort

MANNING, HENRY EDWARD (1808–1892). Cardinal Manning, a Roman Catholic convert contemporary of **John Henry Cardinal Newman,** became the second archbishop of Westminster after the reinstatement of the Roman hierarchy in England in 1850. In an unavoidable and striking contrast to Newman, he is known for his active support for the declaration of the dogma of papal infallibility in Vatican I and for an active life of pastoral work and involvement in secular politics and social projects on behalf of the largely poor and Irish Catholic population in England. Manning's authoritarian personality was famously libeled by Lytton Strachey in *Emiment Victorians* (1918), which remains the most widely read biographical sketch, but his contributions to the development of Catholic Social teaching and his ecclesiological reflections on infallibility justify continued interest in this figure whom thousands mourned in the streets on his death in 1892.

Henry Manning was born the son of a banker and attended Oxford, where his oratorical skills seemed to presage a political career, but he also experienced an evangelical conversion while at Oxford, and after his father's bank failed he was ordained as an Anglican priest. Although he was on the fringes of the Oxford movement, in correspondence with John Henry Newman, and a friend of **William Gladstone,** he nevertheless maintained a High Church position on the maintenance of the establishment. In an early volume of sermons, *The Unity of the Church* (1842), he contended that the argument for the sacramental character of the church and apostolic succession from antiquity and tradition put forward by Tractarians remained rooted in the great Protestant principle of private judgment merely clothed with historical scholarship.

One can see a coherent line from these early Anglican writings on the abiding presence of the Holy Spirit in Christ's Church to Manning's position in later life on papal infallibility. His famous dictum on "sectarian catholicity" was succinctly put: "Ritualism is private judgment in gorgeous raiment." His hope of finding within the Church of England a principle of unity and certainty for religious truth was shattered by the celebrated Hampden and Gorham cases, in which the civil authority overruled the church and gave pastoral and teaching positions to heterodox candidates. For Manning, this subordination of the sovereignty of Christ's Mystical Body to the expedients of secular concerns vitiated the Church of England's claim to speak the truth with the unified and infallible voice of the Holy Spirit.

Manning was influenced further by a reading of the Spanish Tridentine theologian Melchior Cano, renowned for his revival of interest in the patristic tradition and his elaboration of the sources of theological truth and the validity of the argument from authority. Persuaded by these voices, Manning joined with the Roman Catholic Church in 1851, and in the wake of his speedy ordination as a priest, he worked closely with Cardinal Wiseman, to whose see he succeeded in 1865.

As a cardinal he devoted his greatest energies to the Catholic education of poor London children, but he was also indefatigable in his support for the Irish Home Rule movement, the temperance movement, the trade unions' efforts to secure a minimum wage, rent control and housing reform commissions, and many other projects in aid of the poor. Most famously he single-handedly mediated a conclusion of the great London dock workers' strike in 1889. From his position in the curia, he supported the American James Cardinal Gibbons of Baltimore in his struggle to avoid a condemnation of the Knights of Labor in order to maintain good relations between the hierarchy and Catholic workers. His considerations on the problems of labor may have contributed to **Leo XIII**'s encyclical *Rerum novarum.*

Manning's support for the declaration of the dogma of papal infallibility was the natural outgrowth of his prescient ecclesiastical concern for the liberty of the church vis-à-vis the state in an era of rising nationalism. His ultramontane concern to maintain the temporal power of the papacy as a bolster to its sovereignty should be seen in light of these concerns. These hopes proved unavailing, however, and were regardless never as essential as his far-from-narrow theological understanding of infallibility. Manning clearly recognized the parameters of papal infallibility, as can

be seen in his dissent from Leo XIII's condemnation of Irish civil disobedience, and forcefully affirmed in the great social movements of the day some sparks of the continuous action of the Holy Spirit in earthly works of charity (cf. *England and Christendom,* 1867). In his light, Manning could be considered as much a theologian of Vatican II as of Vatican I.

Bibliography. Gray, Robert, *Cardinal Manning: A Biography.* London: Weidenfield & Nicolson, 1985. Newsome, David. *The Convert Cardinals: John Henry Newman and Henry Edward Manning.* London: John Murray, 1993. Pereiro, James. *Cardinal Manning: An Intellectual Biography.* Oxford: Oxford University Press, 1998.

Susan Hanssen

MANNIX, DANIEL (1864–1963). Roman Catholic archbishop of Melbourne, Australia, Mannix was a principal guide of Irish Catholicism and a defender of nonviolent policies. He was born in County Cork, Ireland, and was educated at the Mercy Sister School and the Christian Brothers in Charleville. Mannix studied for the priesthood at St. Patrick's College at Maynooth, County Kildare, and following ordination in 1890 became a professor of theology. He was appointed chair of moral theology in 1895. As president of what was then Maynooth College from 1903 to 1912, he welcomed a royal visit by King George V and Queen Mary in 1911.

Mannix arrived in Melbourne in 1913 as coadjutor (assistant with right of succession) to Archbishop T. Carr. Without delay, his reputation increased in the State of Victoria when he campaigned against the laborite government of W. M. Hughes and the national conscription referendum. During the First World War, the pacifism of the new archbishop of Melbourne was uncompromising and not very popular among the partisans of the empire. He vigorously denounced the brutality of the Easter Rising in Dublin (1916), but his sympathy for **Sinn Fein** and Irish nationalism during wartime elicited sharp criticism from many quarters. During peacetime, Mannix dedicated himself to several causes, including an independent Catholic educational system and republicanism in Ireland. Increasingly, the Communist Party of Australia (CPA) became his favorite enemy.

According to Mannix, Communism remained the chief menace to the church. Significantly, he supported in the early 1930s the initiative of the Labor dissident Joseph Lyons to create the United Australia Party (UAP). Later, he encouraged **Bartholomew Santamaria**'s anticommunist crusade and was prominent in the secretive foundation of the Catholic Social Studies Movement (CSSM) in 1941. During the cold war, Mannix played a key role in the Australian political arena. When disputes over communist influence in the Australian Labor Party ultimate split the group in 1955, Mannix openly supported Santamaria's lay activism and the formation of the anticommunist Democratic Labor Party (DLP).

Despite the various turns of his political activism, Mannix remained popular in Melbourne. When he died in 1963, a crowd of 200,000 persons joined the funeral ceremony. Recently, a nine-foot-high bronze statue of Daniel Mannix was dedicated in the forecourt of St. Patrick's Cathedral.

Bibliography. Brennan, Niall. *Dr. Mannix.* Adelaide, Australia: Rigby, 1964. O'Farrell, Patrick. *The Catholic Church and Community.* West Melbourne, Australia: NSW Press, 1992.

Jérôme Dorvidal

MARCHAND, JEAN (1918–1988). Marchand, the feisty Canadian union leader, anti-separatist campaigner, cabinet minister, and social justice advocate, was a very important and prominent figure in Quebec politics during the time of the Quiet Revolution (*Le Révolution Tranquille*).

Born into a family of modest means in Champlain, Quebec, he worked his way through the School of Social Sciences at Laval University under the tutelage of the great social thinker and philosopher Fr. **Georges-Henri Lévesque,** OP. From the 1940s through to the 1960s he remained strongly associated with the Confédération des Travailleurs Catholiques du Canada, rising from organizer to secretary-general to the president.

A product of Catholic schools, Marchand noted at one point that "the Catholic syndicates are the only unions that have a chance of doing any good in Quebec. They cannot be accused of Communism or enmity to French Canadian nationalism."

Inspired by the social teaching of the Roman Catholic Church—**Leo XIII**'s *Rerum novarum* (1891) and **Pius XI**'s *Quadragesimo anno* (1931)—the work of the Catholic unions, and his own well-grounded teaching in Thomism, Marchand, like his compatriot **Pierre Elliott Trudeau,** fought on the side of the workers in the infamous Asbestos Strike of 1949. He was persuaded that the myopic nationalism, corrupt business practices, and ultramontanist clericalism characteristic of the Quebec of Maurice Duplessis had to be resisted. He worked hard for the liberalization of Quebec institutions and social thinking that became known as the province's Quiet Revolution, or radical internal transformation, of the late 1950s and early 1960s.

In 1965, along with Trudeau and the distinguished Catholic journalist and activist **Gérard Pelletier,** he aligned himself with the Quebec federalists and found himself identified for the rest of his personal and political career as one of the "Three Wise Men." Marchand held six cabinet portfolios throughout the Trudeau years and then resigned in 1976 to run in the Quebec provincial election against the emerging separatist *Parti Québécois.* Subsequently appointed to the Senate, he was elected speaker in March of 1980, played an important role in the debates over the reform and repatriation of the constitution, and served as the president of the Canadian Transport Commission.

An accomplished public speaker, combative labor leader, passionate defender of the rights of working-class Quebecers, and intellectually pugilistic lieutenant to the more cerebral Pierre Elliott Trudeau, Marchand marshaled his strengths and passion to serve the cause of a wider federalism, of a more liberal Quebec, and of a more economically secure and prosperous working class, and he remained to the end an inspiring Catholic leader in an increasing de-Catholicized Quebec. At the time of his death at the age of sixty-nine, he was a nationally respected conciliator and politician possessed of the common touch.

Bibliography. Behiels, N.D. "Marchand, Jean." *The Canadian Encyclopedia.* Edmonton, AB: Hurtig, 1988.

Michael W. Higgins

MARINA, JUSTINIAN (1901–1977). Marina was a fiercely contested figure whose leadership of the Orthodox Church in Romania for three decades coincided with the advance of communist power in Romania. Justinian Marina had been a country priest who came to the notice of the communists in 1944 when he shielded the future leader of Romania, Gheorghe Gheorghiu-Dej (1901–1965), after his prison escape.

In 1930 Marina had published a pamphlet entitled *Cooperation and Christianity,* which showed his commitment to social justice. His lightning rise from ordinary priest to patriarch of the Orthodox Church occurred from 1945 to 1948 and paralleled the communist seizure of power. In 1948 Orthodoxy was stripped of its title as "the dominant church," and the land it owned became the property of the state. But the communist repudiation

of the West provided common ground with a church long suspicious of Western intervention in Romania.

In 1948, the Orthodox Church hailed the dissolution of the Uniate Church, the churches and congregations of which were transferred to the Orthodox Church. There is scant evidence that Justinian and his fellow bishops actively defended the several hundred Orthodox priests imprisoned in the 1950s and the much larger number of Christians imprisoned and killed. Critics argue that Justinian became the tool of a regime that never faltered in its belief that religion was an instrument for the exploitation of the masses and must wither away. Supporters say that the main Romanian church was in better shape than any other in the communist bloc (excepting Poland's Catholics) by the time of Justinian's death in 1977. He managed to protect the monasteries from persecution at least until the end of the 1950s, and he left ten thousand parishes adequately staffed with plentiful candidates for the priesthood in seminaries.

But the Orthodox defense that communism was part of God's plan and the submissive reaction of the church was in accord with God's intentions, is treated with disdain by anticommunist intellectuals. They believe its vigor would have been affirmed more clearly through resistance, despite the inevitable price in repression and hardship, rather than by playing the role of the confessional arm of an irreligious state.

Bibliography. Durandin, Catherine. *Histoire des Roumains.* Paris: Fayard, 1995.

Tom Gallagher

MARITAIN, JACQUES (1882–1973). Maritain was a French Catholic philosopher whose intellectual, political, and spiritual influence extended from Europe to the Americas and beyond. A leading exponent of the philosophy of Saint

Thomas Aquinas, he drew on the Thomistic heritage of integrating faith and reason to engage the most pressing social and political issues of his time. His writings and lectures on natural law, personalist democracy, and human rights made a particular impact after the Second World War, most notably in the United Nations Universal Declaration of Human Rights (1948), which he played a crucial role in drafting. Pope **Paul VI** also credited Maritain with helping to provide the philosophical foundation for the Second Vatican Council (1962–65).

Maritain was born in Paris in 1882 into the *haute bourgeoisie.* His father practiced law, and his Protestant mother was the intellectually gifted daughter of Jules Favre, one of the Third Republic's founders. In 1901, while studying philosophy and natural sciences at the Sorbonne, he met his future wife, a daughter of Russian Jewish immigrants named Raïssa Oumansoff. The prevailing scientism and relativism at the Sorbonne left the couple in such despair that they planned to commit suicide if they could not find a true sense of meaning in their lives. Their desperation abated when they followed friend and poet **Charles Péguy**'s advice and attended the lectures of Henri Bergson at the Collège de France. Bergson's emphasis on intuitive knowledge helped inspire the Maritains—they married in 1904—to embrace a spiritual path that would lead them to the mystic Léon Bloy and their 1906 conversion to Catholicism.

The converted philosopher began teaching at the Lycée Stanislaus in 1912 and in 1914 assumed a professorship at the Institut Catholique de Paris, where he taught until 1939. By the 1920s, Maritain—who published *Antimoderne* in 1922—came to be associated with the reactionary **Action Française** movement. Though he disdained founder **Charles Maurras**'s positivism and anti-Semitism, he became philosophy editor of the affiliated publication *La revue universelle,* where he maintained

a friendship with Maurras disciple Henri Massis until after Pope **Pius XI**'s condemnation of the Action Française. Maritain's *Une opinion sur Charles Maurras et les devoirs des catholiques* (1926) underlined his fidelity to the church and earned him undying resentment on the French Right.

Though Maritain advocated "the primacy of the spiritual," the 1930s saw anything but political detachment and a return to pure speculative philosophy on his part. As a prominent "liberal Catholic" voice (thusly labeled after the break with Maurras) he joined **Emmanuel Mounier** in launching the review *Esprit* in 1932. Maritain and Mounier advocated a "personalism" to counteract the materialist, dehumanizing tendencies of Marxist revolution on one hand and capitalist plutocracy on the other, though Maritain found Mounier's flirtation with quasi-fascist Third Force movements disconcerting. Maritain's own philosophical development

Jacques Maritain, c. 1951. Courtesy of the University of Notre Dame Archives

was evidenced by his 1936 work *Humanisme intégrale.*

Maritain offended many French Catholics beginning in 1936 by denouncing **Francisco Franco** during the Spanish civil war, giving his rightist enemies new cause not only to attack him at home but also to lobby unsuccessfully in Rome for the condemnation of his philosophical works. In 1939 Maritain left for what would become, due to World War II, an extended stay in North America. He was lecturing in Toronto in 1940, the year France fell to the Nazis. After moving to New York he became a rallying figure for the French exile community, also contributing weekly radio broadcasts to his compatriots in occupied France. His 1942 *The Rights of Man and Natural Law (Les droits de l'homme et la loi naturelle)* expressed a Christian-democratic resistance to the high tide of totalitarianism.

From 1944 until 1948 Maritain served as France's ambassador to the Holy See and helped write a United Nations human rights declaration, which embodied many of the ideas about democratic freedoms and the dignity of the human being expressed in his 1947 book *The Person and The Common Good (La personne et le bien commun). Man and the State* (1951) appeared after Maritain returned to teaching at Princeton. Upon Raïssa's death in 1960 he went to live in Toulouse with a religious order, the Little Brothers of Jesus. Though honored at the close of the Second Vatican Council, Maritain surprised many longtime admirers by criticizing the liberalization of the church in his 1966 book *The Peasant of the Garonne (Le paysan de la Garonne).* Later taking monastic vows, he died in 1973 and was buried beside his wife in Kolbsheim, Alsace.

Bibliography. Allard, Jean-Louis, and Pierre Germain, eds. *Répertoire bibliographique sur la vie et l'oeuvre de Jacques et Raïssa Maritain.* Ottawa, ON: Éditions de l'Université d'Ottawa, 1994. DiJoseph, John. *Jacques Maritain and the Moral Foundations of Democracy.* Lanham, MD: Rowman & Littlefield, 1996. Doering, Bernard E. *Jacques Maritain and the French Catholic Intellectuals.* Notre Dame, IN: Notre Dame University Press, 1983. Fuller, Timothy, and John P. Hittinger. *Reassessing the Liberal State: Reading Maritain's Man and the State.* Washington, DC: American Maritain Association/Catholic University of America Press, 2001. Schall, James V. *Jacques Maritain: The Philosopher in Society.* Lanham, MD: Rowman & Littlefield, 1998.

Richard Francis Crane

MARSHALL, JOHN ROSS (1912–1988). Jack Marshall was a leading conservative politician in New Zealand for twenty-five years, serving in successive National Party governments. Born in Wellington, New Zealand, Marshall was raised in an active Presbyterian home and underwent a personal conversion in 1926. An important formative influence was his involvement in the New Zealand Bible Class movement, which began in his own church, St. John's Presbyterian, Wellington, and became a major socializing and training ground for three generations of Christian youth.

Marshall trained as a lawyer and, after military service in World War II, was elected to Parliament in 1946. Few Christian politicians in New Zealand at this time trumpeted their faith from the podium. Marshall was no exception, preferring to let his lifelong interest in Christian organizations such as the Bible Society be evidence enough of his commitment. Nevertheless, it is clear that his faith was a key factor in his political life. Although as a young man he was attracted to Christian socialism, Marshall came to espouse a sophisticated form of Christian liberalism, which recognized at once both the value of individuals and their "want of original righteousness" (Marshall, 304–5). This approach guided him throughout his career. It led him to take part in modifying the welfare state set up by the first Labour government (1935–1949) and in limiting the powers of labor unions. On the other hand, he also promoted tighter censorship of indecent materials and sought greater state administration of the health system. In 1949 he became a cabinet minister in the conservative government of Sydney Holland. Under Holland (1949–1957), and later as deputy to Keith Holyoake (1960–1971), Marshall was often assigned difficult and complex portfolios.

In the 1960s, New Zealand's trade position was threatened by successive attempts by Great Britain to enter the European Economic Community. Marshall led diplomatic efforts to delay and to soften the impact on an economy then largely dependent on the British market. Holyoake stepped down early in 1972, and Marshall became prime minister. Significant shifts were underway in New Zealand political life, however, and Marshall's government was heavily defeated in the election later that year. Always diplomatic and polite in public (he was dubbed "gentleman Jack" by the electorate), Marshall found the more confrontational style of the 1970s unappealing. He retired from Parliament in 1975. In the remaining years of his life he continued and expanded his associations with Christian and other community groups.

Bibliography. Marshall, John. *Memoirs.* 2 vols. Auckland, NZ: Collins, 1983–1989.

Martin Sutherland

MARTY, MARTIN E. (b. 1928). Minister, professor, administrator, and editor but probably best known as a cultural historian of modern Christianity, Marty has examined the intersection of religion and politics in America in several prominent works.

Ordained in 1952 as a pastor in the Missouri Synod of the Lutheran Church, Marty is also a distinguished emeritus professor at the University of Chicago; senior editor for the *Christian Century;* founder of the Park Ridge Center for the Study of Health, Faith, and Ethics; and director for the Pew Charitable Trust's Public Religion Project, the Academy of Arts and Sciences' Fundamentalism Project, and the University of Chicago's Martin Marty Center. A recipient of the National Humanities Medal, the National Book Award, and Medal of American Academy of Arts and Sciences, Marty has written over fifty books and five thousand articles that range from personal reflections on aspects of Christian faith to the problems and complexities required in sustaining a public moral discourse in a religiously pluralistic America.

Born in West Point, Nebraska, Marty enrolled in 1942 at Concordia College in Milwaukee, Wisconsin, as preparation for a ministerial vocation in the Lutheran Church. He completed his seminary education in 1952 at Concordia in St. Louis, Missouri. He was assigned to River Forest, a suburb of Chicago, instead of London, as a disciplinary measure for his having invented a theologian as a hoax and published writing about him. In 1956, Marty finished his doctoral thesis, *The Uses of Infidelity,* at the University of Chicago. He served parishes in the west and northwest suburbs of Chicago before joining the faculty at University of Chicago in 1963.

The underlying theme for most of Marty's writing is the public role of religion in the politics and culture of America. In *Righteous Empire: The Protestant Experience in America* (1970), he traces the attempt of white English-speaking Protestants to create a virtual empire of beliefs and values in America, only to fail when confronted with internal divisions and external events such as immigration, urbanization, and intellectual secularism. In *Pilgrims in Their Own Land* (1984), Marty examines the role of public religion in providing a stable moral framework for the American state, and in his three-volume *Modern American Religions* (1986, 1991, 1996), he examines the political consequences—immigration restriction, labor relations, government welfare, pacifism—of sectarian disagreements about "core-culture" Protestantism in America. Marty seeks to dispel both totalist and tribalist thinking in America, the former seeking to impose a national identity to the exclusion of cultural difference, and the latter favoring cultural absolutism at the expense of a national narrative. He explores this cultural absolutism in *The One and the Many: America's Struggle for the Common Good* (1997). In these and other works, Marty advocates a greater openness to religion in both politics and education, believing that religious values and perspectives would enrich the public dialogue between secular and religious ideas, movements, and institutions in America.

Bibliography. Dolan, Jay P., and James P. Wind, eds. *New Dimensions in American Religious History: Essays in Honor of Martin E. Marty.* Grand Rapids, MI: William B. Eerdmans, 1993. Marty, Martin E. "The Provincial, the Parochial, the Public." *Contemporary Authors* 194 (2001): 258–82. Zoba, Wendy Murray. "A Sense of Place." *Christian Century* (October 2002): 20–28.

Lee Trepanier

MARX, WILHELM (1863–1946). Marx, a leading German Catholic politician and jurist, was the son of a primary school teacher in Cologne's Catholic milieu. In 1881, he passed his final examination at the venerable Marzellengymnasium and afterwards studied law in Bonn until 1884. There, he joined the Catholic Student's Association Arminia within the *Kartellverband* (KV), the breeding ground for twentieth-century leaders in the churches, politic circles, and associations. The experience left a deep impression on his thought.

The young Marx devoted himself to politics. Between 1899 and 1904 he was chairman of the **Center Party** (*Zentrum*) in Elberfeld, and between 1907 and 1919 in Düsseldorf. At the same time he was vice chairman of the Rhenish Zentrum party from 1906 to 1919. Within the wide network of Catholic associations and clubs, he took many honorary offices. In 1911, he launched the Catholic Schools Association and served as its chairman until 1933. He became general director in 1919, and from 1921 until 1933, he served as chairman of the **People's Union for the Catholic Germany** (*Volksverein*). In Augsburg in 1910 and in Freiburg in 1929 he was president of the Assembly of German Catholics. From 1899 to 1921, Marx was a member of the Prussian Chamber of Deputies and in 1919–1920 of the Prussian Constituent Assembly. From 1910 to 1932 he belonged to the German Reichstag and led the Zentrum parliamentary group. He also served as the party's chairman and headed four cabinets.

In 1925, at the top of his career, Marx was twice candidate for Reich president, first on March 29 for Zentrum and again on April 26 for the Weimar Coalition. He lost by a narrow margin to Paul von Hindenburg. Also in 1925, he served as Reich minister of justice and minister for the occupied territories. Marx again headed the government as Reich chancellor in two cabinets between 1926 and 1928. After the failure of his fourth cabinet, Marx resigned in 1928 as his party's chairman and vacated his mandate in 1932. Marx was brought down by the Social Democrat Philipp Scheidemann's revelation of the secret cooperation of the Reichswehr and Red Army. From 1933 until his death in 1946, Marx lived in seclusion in Bonn.

In the early years of his political career, Marx mainly built up a reputation as an expert in school politics and in the conflict about denominational schools. Beyond that, he succeeded in home and foreign politics in a difficult time. His first two cabinets witnessed the settlement of the Ruhr conflict and the end to inflation. Germany's first significant postwar economic boosts resulted from his rigid conservative policy of savings and order. Marx was also noted for uniting Germany's democratic parties and, in foreign affairs, for his reliance on the brilliant diplomat, Gustav Stresemann. The Dawes Plan and Germany's entry into the League of Nations took place under Marx.

Because of his integrity, personal modesty, and independence, Marx was proposed for many important offices by his party and nation. His political vision was based on the obligations of an active Christ. He therefore was, as Baden's president Willi Hellpach noted, the "ideal type of a Zentrum politician."

Bibliography. Hehl, Ulrich von. *Wilhelm Marx 1863–1946: Eine politische Biographie.* Mainz, Germany: Matthias-Grünewald-Verlag, 1987.

Helmut Rönz

Wilhelm Marx. Courtesy of the Library of Congress

MÁSPERO, EMILIO (1927–2000). Born in Santa Fe, Argentina, a child of Italian immigrants, Emilio Máspero became a labor leader and educator whose audacity strengthened the rise of trade unionism as a social force throughout Latin America. Inspired by Catholic faith, he believed that a Christian trade union movement offered the best path toward workers' rights. When he died at seventy-two in Caracas, Venezuela, his vision as general secretary of the Central Latino Americana de Trabajadores (CLAT) and vice president of the World Confederation of Labor (WCL) had shaped the development of Latin American trade unionism for half a century.

Máspero received a short formal education. By force of necessity he joined the labor force at twelve, first working in a hotel, a textile factory, and in the metallurgical industry. His early connection to the **Young Christian Workers** movement (JOC) formed his knowledge of Christian trade unions. He was elected president of the Argentine branch of the JOC and became its representative for all of South America in 1952.

In 1955, Máspero was instrumental in the founding of the *Asociación Sindical Argentina* (ASA), a group informed by humanist and Christian principles. His protest against coercive labor policies culminated in a prison sentence for having organized a strike. Forced into exile, he spent a year among Christian worker circles in Europe.

By 1960, Máspero had gained experience in leadership positions with the Confederación Latino Americana de Sindicalistas Cristianas (CLASC, later CLAT) and became its first permanent organizer in Latin America. Working from Caracas, Venezuela, he held the office of executive secretary for the Caribbean area of the CLASC and gained the secretary general's office in 1966. As a leader and educator, Máspero is best known for defending Latin American autonomy, his central concern to the end of his life.

Bibliography. Hawkins, Carroll. *Two Democratic Labor Leaders in Conflict.* Lexington, MA: D. C. Heath, 1973.

Jadwiga E. Pieper Mooney

MASTERMAN, CHARLES FREDERICK GURNEY (1874–1927). A British politician and journalist, Masterman is considered the quintessential "New Liberal" politician and man of letters. He served in David Lloyd George's cabinet from 1909 to 1914 and helped to guide the National Insurance Bill of 1911 through Parliament. His book *The Condition of England* (1909) contributed to the new social scientific approach to political philosophy, and his *New Liberalism* (1920) unsuccessfully tried to prolong the life of the Liberal party, embracing both traditional liberalism and the development of social welfare policy.

Masterman was raised in the Wesleyan tradition. At Cambridge University, he was influenced by the Lux Mundi group as he moved into High Anglican circles. He lived briefly at a university settlement house and then moved into a flat in Camberwell Road, a poor district of London, living the life of social worker/social scientist for ten years. Masterman served on the district's board of guardians, as literary editor for the Liberal *Daily News,* and as member of Parliament while living in his workman's flat. Scurrying back and forth from Fleet Street or Parliament to Camberwell Road, Masterman acquired a reputation as a slovenly journalist activist on behalf of the poor. During this time, Masterman wrote a number of social panoramic books—*The Heart of the Empire* (1901), *From the Abyss* (1902) and *In Peril of Change* (1905)—that

are striking for the lack of sympathy with the poor that they reveal. The individual, the eccentric neighbor, the unusual personality never appears in his account of the poor, although he lived in a five-story block of flats for eight years. Masterman describes only the multitude or crowd. After marrying into a well-connected political family and landing a position in the cabinet, Masterman was attacked by his old Liberal journalist friends **Hilaire Belloc** and the brothers **Cecil and Gilbert Chesterton** for his pessimism about democracy—a pessimism they considered rooted in an evangelical sense of the depravity of humankind and the world.

Bibliography. David, Edward. "The New Liberalism of C.F.G. Masterman." In *Essays in Anti-Labour History: Responses to the Rise of Labour in Britain,* ed. Kenneth D. Brown. London: Macmillan, 1974. Masterman, Lucy. *C.F.G. Masterman: A Biography.* London: Frank Cass, 1939.

Susan E. Hanssen

MAURICE, JOHN FREDERICK DENISON (1805–1872). Anglican theologian and a founder of Christian Socialism, Maurice was born the son of a Unitarian minister in Normanston, Suffolk, England. He entered Trinity College, Cambridge (1823), though it was then impossible for any but members of the established church to obtain a degree. He then migrated to Trinity Hall to study civil law before going to London, where he devoted himself to literary work, edited literary journals, revised his religious opinions, and ultimately found direction in a decision to take a further university course and seek Anglican orders.

Entering Exeter College, Oxford, he took a second class in classics (1831) and was ordained in 1834. He was elected professor of English history and literature at King's College, Cambridge, in 1840 and was appointed professor of divinity in 1846.

Maurice's reputation as a theologian was enhanced with the publication of his book *The Kingdom of Christ* (1838), in which he held the church to be a united body that transcended the diversity and partiality of individual men, factions, and sects. That view aroused the suspicions of orthodox Anglicans. Their misgivings were intensified when he joined **Charles Kingsley,** J. M. Ludlow, and others to found the Christian Socialist movement in 1848. This group hoped to vindicate for "the Kingdom of Christ" its "true authority over the realms of industry and trade," and "to christianize Socialism and to socialize Christianity." The theology and ideology of Christian Socialism were mainly Maurician, exposed in his numerous publications (under the pseudonym "A Clergyman"), such as *Politics for the People* (1848), *Tractsby Christian Socialism* (1850), *Tracts on Christian Socialism* (1850), and *The Christian Socialist* (1850–1851). He also played the key role in the Society for Promoting Working Men's Associations during the early 1850s. Because his Christian Socialism was more educative and ethical than political, he withdrew from the movement.

Maurice later helped to found Queen's College for the education of women (1848) and the Working Men's College (1854). As organizer and first principal of the latter, he strongly supported the abolition of university tests. His denial of the eternity of hell in *Theological Essays* (1853) fueled on-going conflict with church leaders, but he nevertheless completed his career as professor of moral philosophy at Cambridge (1866–1872). Those who knew him best were deeply impressed with the spirituality of his character. While he presented himself as a man of peace, his life was marked by a series of conflicts.

Bibliography. McClain, Frank Mauldin. *Maurice: Man and Moralist.* London: SPCK, 1972.

Irina Novichenko

MAURRAS, CHARLES (1868–1952). It has been said of Maurras, one of the most influential thinkers in the lives of several generations of French Catholics, that he was Catholic without being Christian! He admired the historic role of the Roman Catholic Church in preserving classical culture and providing the model of order and stability for the once-barbarian masses of Europe, but early in his life he lost his faith and returned to the church only in his last few years after a period of imprisonment by the post-Vichy French authorities.

Maurras certainly had nothing but disdain for the prophetic Jewish vision of a united humanity under the fatherhood of God, a disdain he expressed most notably in his repudiation of the Magnificat of the Blessed Virgin Mary in the Gospel of Luke (or some scholars would say, of St. Elizabeth), where she upheld the poor and scorned the rich and the mighty. Maurras shared with Nietzsche, whether he had read him or not, the view that Christianity as it was in the beginning was a religion fit only for slaves. Most remarkable was the fact that this nonbelieving layman became for all intents and purposes almost a doctor of the church. There had been laymen before, like **Louis Veuillot** in the nineteenth century, who were so highly considered among Catholics, but never before a nonbeliever, even an avowed atheist, like Maurras. His prestige and influence over bourgeois Catholics in France was enormous over most of the period from the Dreyfus Affair to 1945.

Maurras's integral nationalism had its origin in the outbreak of the Dreyfus Affair. Never really concerned with whether Dreyfus had actually been guilty of espionage for the enemy, Maurras was convinced that any attempt to defend Dreyfus was to place the national security of France in danger. As a result he came to believe that Dreyfus's guilt was a necessary article of faith, repeating in essence the argument of

Caiaphas in the Gospel of John that it was necessary for one man (Jesus) to die for the welfare of the nation. The irony of a pro-Catholic intellectual advocating ritual murder never registered among the bourgeois Catholics who took Maurras's vigorous defense of the hierarchical church to their bosom. Maurras defended the perjury of Colonel Henry, who had forged Dreyfus's signature in order to condemn him, as an innocent patriot whose "holy lie" was necessary for the welfare of the nation.

Maurras used the thought of Auguste Comte, stripped of its universalism, to construct a defense of nationalism and of the state over the individual that was close to Fascism if not Fascism *tout court*. Few Catholics were willing to see the incompatibilities between this secular political philosophy and Christian faith. Even Pope **Pius X** delayed a projected condemnation of Maurras and his **Action Française** organization for political reasons. Although Maurras and his movement were condemned in 1926, many Catholic ecclesiastics found ways of mitigating the church's official opposition, and on the eve of World War II **Pius XII** lifted the ban on Maurras.

Maurras, while not believing in the Gospels, which he called the work of "four obscure Jews," greatly prized the church's appropriation of Aristotle and of much of classical culture. He claimed to be a monarchist, but his monarchism was in truth less concerned with a king than with the destruction of the Third Republic, less involved with political forms than with the exaltation of the state above all concern for individual rights. He also prized the historic antipathy of the church toward the Jews, and anti-Semitism was one of the chief features of his movement, something that certainly did not put off the Catholic establishment in France at all.

The actual role Maurras and his Action Française played in French life was to reconcile the elites and the church around a "Voltairean" appreciation of the value of religion to social harmony and stability. There might be no God, but he and his church were needed to keep the masses in line. Thus Maurras performed a valuable service to the bourgeois elites of France, while his appropriation of Catholicism did only harm to the faith's ability to be a popular force among the French people. He can be called a "Christian" politician only in the sense that he used the church and the faith for reactionary purposes, and the church and its faithful were for many decades perfectly willing to be led by him.

Maurras saw the defeat of his beloved France in 1940 at the hands of Nazi Germany and the coming to power of the conservative Marshal **Philippe Pétain** and his entourage, men heavily influenced by Maurrasian ideas about the state, the Jews, and the republic, as providential, as a chance to replace the republic with a new political and social order. During the Vichy regime and the German occupation of France his followers were split over their political stance; some rallied to General **Charles de Gaulle,** while most supported Marshal Pétain. Very few were direct collaborators with the Germans or the French Fascists who supported them, but Maurras was very comfortable with the anti-Jewish legislation of the Vichy state. At the liberation he was placed on trial and condemned to prison, in his eyes the "revenge of Dreyfus." He might have returned to the church before his death, but he never repudiated the essential doctrines of integral nationalism and anti-Semitism and never ceased to have a following among French Catholics, despite its considerable diminution when French Catholics were forced to come to terms with their own anti-Semitism during the German deportations and largely turned away from it.

Maurras is now an embarrassment for French Catholics, but one who exemplifies the destructive consequences of bigotry and racism.

Bibliography. Doering, Bernard E. *Jacques Maritain and the French Catholic Intellectuals.* Notre Dame, IN: University of Notre Dame Press, 1983. Nguyen, Victor. *Aux origines de l'Action Française: Intelligence et politique vers 1900.* Paris: Fayard, 1991. Nolte, Ernst. *Three Faces of Fascism: Action Française, Italian Fascism, National Socialism.* New York: Holt, Rinehart and Winston, 1966. Poulat, Emile. *Église contre bourgeoisie: Introduction au devenir du catholicism actuel.* Tournai, Belgium: Casterman, 1977. Ravitch, Norman. *The Catholic Church and the French Nation, 1589–1989.* London: Routledge, 1990. Sutton, Michael. *Nationalism, Positivism and Catholicism: The Politics of Charles Maurras and French Catholics, 1890–1914.* Cambridge: Cambridge University Press, 1982. Weber, Eugen. *Action Française: Royalism and Reaction in Twentieth-Century France.* Stanford, CA: Stanford University Press, 1962.

Norman Ravitch

MAYNARD, FARNHAM EDWARD (1882–1964). Born the son of an English surgeon, Maynard served as vicar of the St. Peter's Eastern Hill, Melbourne (1926–1964); Australian delegate to the World Council of Churches; review editor of the *Australian Church Quarterly* (1929–1950); and intermittently as editor of *Defender: The Journal of the Australian Church Union.*

Maynard was strongly influenced by the Christian Social Union founded by **Henry Scott Holland.** Without waiting for his nomination as vicar of the St. Peter's Eastern Hill (a Melbourne Anglican church notorious for tolerating the diffusion of politically oriented sermons), Maynard defended the strike of British seamen (1925) from the pulpit of Brisbane's All Saints Church. Advocating the compatibility between Christianity and socialist theories, Maynard's texts, such as *Economics and the Kingdom of God* (1929), *Fair Hearing for Socialism* (1944) and *Religion and Revolution* (1947), publicized anti-capitalist and anti-imperialist ideas.

Determinedly antifascist during World War II, Maynard operated as chairman of the Australia-Soviet Friendship League (1945), a significant nod to the new Australian peace movement in the immediate postwar era. At this time considered by the Australian government services as a fellow traveler, he engendered further controversy through his personal participation in the 1952 Peking Peace Conference at the height of the Korean War. In St. Peter's Church, a mirror of Melbourne's religious culture, Maynard affirmed during his ministry a distinct Anglo-Catholic identity and determined to spread the word each Sunday with an ever-increasing audience. Furthermore, he exploited review opportunities for the *Australian Church Quarterly,* as well as radio broadcasts, for promoting an intense exchange over religious conviction between liberal Anglicans and intellectuals. With a radicalism that attracted a considerable variety of people, Maynard was well appreciated, particularly within the homosexual community for his open-mindedness and his nonjudgmental behavior, an attitude that helped to improve tolerance among the Melbourne citizenry. Not without a certain paradox, he justified on many occasions his personal attachment to doctrinal conservatism and revealed a reverential penchant for the Anglican traditional liturgy. Continuity remained for him a precept expressed too in his last manuscript, written in 1963, *The Continuity of the Church of England: The Story of the Kings and Popes in the Sixteenth Century.*

Bibliography. Gibson, Ralph, Merz Kurt, and F. E. Maynard. *A Fair Hearing for Socialism.* Melbourne, Australia: Fraser and Morphett, 1944. Holden, Colin, ed. *Anglo-Catholicism in Melbourne: Papers to Mark the 150th Anniversary of St. Peter's Eastern Hill 1846–1996.* Parkville, Australia: University of Melbourne, Department of History, 1997.

Jérôme Dorvidal

MAZZINI, GIUSEPPE (1805–1872). The patriot celebrated by future generations as the "soul" of modern Italy was a controversial and often vilified figure in his time. His most bitter critics were to be found in the Catholic camp that opposed the movement for Italian independence and unity, and he in turn lashed out against them as enemies of true religion and corruptors of the people. True religion was something very dear to Mazzini, as dear as love of country, and in his mind inseparable from it.

Mazzini's religious sentiment is traceable to the influence of the home on the child. He was born in Genoa to a family of what today would be described as the upper-middle class, and his father, Giacomo Mazzini, was a respected medical doctor and university professor. His mother, Maria Drago Mazzini, was a well-educated woman who took a keen interest in the education and upbringing of her only son and continued to champion him and his causes for as long as she lived. The father's early association with Jacobin revolutionaries was not in evidence by the time that the son was born, for by then Giacomo had turned away from revolution and embraced the Catholic Church with all its rituals. The mother's religiosity was of a different and more spiritual kind. Her devotion aimed less at respecting the forms and more at capturing the essence of the Christian spirit. Such an attitude was not without political implications. Through her and the private tutors that she chose, Jansenist ideas may have influenced the son and instilled in him that love of liberty and those republican principles inherent in Jansenist doctrine, to which he adhered in his adult life.

Giuseppe Mazzini's political career began when he was a student at the University of Genoa, from which he graduated in 1827 with a law degree. It continued when he joined the secretive *Carboneria* to conspire and fight for Italian independence and unity. Arrested in 1830 but released for lack of credible evidence, in January 1831 he left for France, settling in the port city of Marseilles, which became the headquarters of his own movement. Giovine Italia (Young Italy), the society that he founded in July 1831, called on the youth of Italy to conspire and take up arms against tyrants, and to reach out to the people who needed their help and guidance. The "apostles" who answered the call were to be prepared for martyrdom; their blood would nurture the tree of liberty.

Young Italy fought for Italian political independence and for the spiritual renewal of the Italian people, two goals that were inseparable in Mazzini's mind. The emphasis on spiritual renewal gave Mazzini's movement a religious character that set it apart from patriotic movements that were secularly inspired. He looked to Rome to provide the inspiration, but it was the *Roma del Popolo* (Rome of the People), not the Rome of the popes, that would provide the inspiration. Like his contemporary and one-time follower **Vincenzo Gioberti,** Mazzini believed in the primacy of the Italian people, but he saw that primacy as being rooted in the republican traditions of Italy's medieval communes and the democratic spirit of the people rather than the universal role of the papacy. Mazzini enjoyed a brief opportunity at political leadership for a few months, beginning in March 1849, when he arrived in the revolutionary Roman Republic. He quickly became the republic's dominant figure, although the experiment soon collapsed when a citizen's army under Giuseppe Garibaldi crumbled, after brave resistance, before the more professional French army.

Religious faith proved to be a powerful consolation and an encouragement to persevere in moments of crisis, of which there were many in Mazzini's life. The repeated failure of his conspiracies, imprisonment and death of close friends, attacks on his ideas and character, difficulties of exile, and the crises of confidence that might have overwhelmed a less fervent patriot merely confirmed Mazzini's confidence in his mission. More than once in life, Mazzini invoked Martin Luther's historic phrase: "Here I stand, so help me God." He might fail personally, but the cause could not be defeated, for it was nothing less than the cause of progress, and progress, according to Mazzini, was the law of God. Mazzini's religious faith approached Protestantism in some of its doctrines, including rejection of papal authority, direct approach to scripture, and appeal to individual conscience. But Mazzini explicitly refused to be known as a Protestant and believed that the Catholic Church was inherently superior to the Protestant denominations because of the spirit of universality that dominated it. What the church needed was democratic reform. A general council of believers in place of the papacy's absolute monarchy would make the Catholic Church democratic and responsive to the spiritual and material needs of the faithful. Politics and religion came together in Mazzini's mind. He was neither Catholic nor Protestant, he said, but a believer "convinced that the spirit of religion must dominate the new Italy and the new Young Europe."

Young Europe was another Mazzinian society, this one founded in Switzerland in April 1834 after the clamorous failure of an attempt to stir up revolution in Italy. Young Europe may have been more influential than Young Italy, for it inspired a new generation of patriots who thought in terms of cooperation across national lines and hoped that the revolution would lead to a federation of independent, democratic European republics. Mazzini thus has a strong claim to being not only the pioneer of Italian independence, but also of European democracy and unity.

He lived long enough to see the patriotic movements of his youth become the nationalist movements of his old age. He himself did not always resist the nationalist temptation, as when he claimed for Italy territories that were not inhabited solely by Italian-speaking populations or invoked the need for a general European war that would test the national resolve of a people. But he rejected the label of nationalist for himself and his ideas, despite the isolated expressions of national pride that came from the pen of an embittered old man. Mazzini, after all, had witnessed Italy unified as a monarchy rather than as the republic of his dreams and most of his followers deserting him to join the monarchist camp. Nevertheless, there was a spirit of solidarity that animated his social philosophy. It brought him to a position that can be described, perhaps anachronistically, as social democratic. Just as people of different nationalities should join in a European union of free nations, so should people of different classes come together in the spirit of mutual assistance. This was the "associational" philosophy that Mazzini invoked to combat socialism, which he saw as based on class resentments and a materialist philosophy that left no room for spiritual values. Thus, in the name of a religiosity that defies classification, Mazzini ended his life fighting against monarchy on one side, and socialism on the other.

Bibliography. Mack Smith, Denis. *Mazzini.* New Haven, CT: Yale University Press, 1994. Sarti, Roland. *Mazzini: A Life for the Religion of Politics.* Westport, CT: Praeger, 1997.

Roland Sarti

MAZZOLARI, PRIMO (1890–1959). An anticonformist Italian priest and prolific writer, Mazzolari was primarily concerned with the problem of how to keep his allegiance to the Catholic Church and at the same time reconcile human behavior with divine purpose.

Influenced by modernism, with a historicist and immanentist approach to theological issues, during his seminary studies Mazzolari briefly assisted Italian emigrants in Switzerland in 1914. Following the outbreak of World War I, he advocated Italy's entry into the conflict and subsequently served as an army chaplain. Yet the war experience turned Mazzolari into a pacifist who would later campaign for Italians' right to conscience as a basis for objecting to military service. He blamed his interventionist past on Catholic theologians who had distinguished between just and unjust wars instead of stressing that all wars were "useless slaughters."

Back at his parish in Bozzolo, in the province of Mantua, Mazzolari took issue with fascism even before Benito Mussolini's 1922 rise to power and participated in the Resistance against the Nazis, even though he refused to carry weapons. Although he dreamed of a Catholic postwar reconstruction for Italy, Mazzolari became the critical conscience of the **Christian Democracy.** In order to voice his concerns, he contributed to the Christian Democrat weekly *Democrazia* from 1945 to 1948 and founded his own fortnightly, *Adesso,* in 1949. *Adesso*'s willingness to dialogue with the Left and its pacifist stance during the cold war placed Mazzolari at odds with the more traditionalist Catholic hierarchy. He was barred from preaching outside his diocese and prevented from publishing his writings without ecclesiastical scrutiny in 1951. **John XXIII**'s papacy provided a more suitable framework for Mazzolari's activities and ideals, but he died just a few months after Angelo Roncalli became pope.

Bibliography. Bergamaschi, Aldo. *Presenza di Mazzolari: Un contestatore per tutte le stagioni.* Bologna, Italy: Edizioni Dehoniane, 1986.

Stefano Luconi

MCGEE, THOMAS D'ARCY (1825–1868). Born in Ireland, McGee was an editor and politician sensitive to Irish, American, and Canadian political tides. He attended a Catholic Hedge School and lived and worked in his native land, the United States, and Canada.

The Irish in Montreal were 20 percent of the population and needed a newspaper to promote their political agenda—especially separate schools for Canada West. The Irish were unhappy with the city's sole English-language Catholic newspaper, *True Witness,* which they saw as an instrument of Bishop Ignace Bourget, who was no friend of Irish aspirations. Catholic and Protestant Irish raised $2,000 in 1857 and invited McGee from the United States to found an Irish Canadian newspaper that espoused a "new nationality" of railway construction, immigration, and protective tariff to unite Canadian people into a federal compact.

The following year McGee ran in the federal election with A.A. Dorion and Luther Holton. They ran as Liberals, captured the Irish vote, and defeated the Tories. For McGee, the choice to run for the Liberals was easy, as they were associated with reform and labor, and the Tories with the Orange Lodge. McGee went on to expand his influence to Canada West by gaining the support of the St. Patrick societies and the Toronto-based *Canadian Freeman.*

McGee encouraged the Irish to vote Reform and promised them that legislation would be prepared for a Catholic school system. In the election of 1861 McGee brought out the Irish vote, and a Catholic school bill was introduced into the Canadian Assembly. McGee rallied the Reform Party to support it while the leader George Brown was on the sidelines. After a snap by-election, George Brown returned to the Assembly, and the Catholic school bill was scuttled. Brown triumphed, and McGee, disillusioned, withdrew from government.

In the 1863 election, McGee ran as an independent and campaigned with the Conservatives. John A. Macdonald's government came to power, and McGee won a cabinet post. As part of the Great Coalition, he attended the Charlottetown and Quebec Conferences on Confederation. At Quebec he proposed that the education rights of religious minorities be respected, and they were written into the British North America Act.

McGee wanted Irish Canadians to focus on the Canadian issues of "new nationality." After the Fenian invasions of 1866, he asked for the death penalty for Fenian prisoners. This stance initiated McGee's political downfall, and in the election of 1867, McGee barely defeated his opponent.

In Ottawa, McGee was shot on April 7, 1868, and James Patrick Whelan was convicted. McGee's sudden death at the age of forty-three left a political vacuum within the Irish Canadian leadership. For a time Thomas D'Arcy McGee had united the Protestant and Catholic Irish, but after his death Irish Canadians no longer voted as a bloc. Beginning his career as a visionary Irish republican, McGee completed his career by embracing the Canadian national policy. He was the most exciting Irish Canadian politician of the 1860s.

Bibliography. O'Driscoll, Robert, and Lorna Reynolds, eds. *The Untold Story: The Irish in Canada.* 2 vols. Toronto: Celtic Arts of Canada, 1988.

Terence J. Fay

MEDA, FILIPPO (1869–1939). An Italian Catholic journalist and politician, Meda was an active lecturer to Catholic associations, heavily involved in the electoral mobilization of Catholics at a municipal level, and an important figure in the umbrella organization of the Italian Catholic movement, the *Opera dei Congressi.*

Meda earned degrees in literature from the University of Milan (1891) and in law from Genoa (1892). A prolific writer, he worked for the Vatican news organ, the *Osservatore Cattolico,* and later for the Catholic *Unione,* which he edited for several years until it became *L'Italia* in 1911. In addition, he wrote for Catholic reviews, most notably *Nuova Antologia, La Rassegna Nazionale, Vita e Pensiero,* and *Civitas,* of which he was founder.

Meda accepted the unification of Italy, and the consequent loss by the popes of their temporal power in the former Papal States, with a pragmatism that did not go down well in more intransigent Catholic circles in Italy. As far as national politics was concerned, he accepted the *Non expedit,* the papal decree forbidding Italian Catholics to be either candidates or voters in parliamentary elections, espousing a policy of "preparation in abstention." In 1909 he was one of the first Catholics to be elected to the Italian parliament, after **Pius X** had gently relaxed the *Non expedit.*

Though initially a neutralist, he supported Italian intervention in the First World War in May 1915, and between 1915 and 1919, he played a key role in Italian politics as finance minister, symbolizing Catholic support for the war effort, despite the disapproval of the Vatican. He introduced a bill to reform the system of income tax in Italy. The bill was lost, but its essential principles were implemented by his successor in November 1919. In that same month, Meda was reelected as a parliamentary deputy for the new Catholic **Italian Popular Party** (*Partito Popolare Italiano,* PPI) and took his place close to the centrist position of its secretary, Fr. **Luigi Sturzo.** He was wary of Guido Miglioli and the "socialistoide" Left but proclaimed the party to be "aconfessional," that is rejecting the demands of the Right that the party should be more openly Catholic, serving the interests of the church. Meda became the effective parliamentary leader of the party in the absence of Sturzo, who, as a priest, could not hold national political office.

Meda's importance in Italian politics in the early 1920s, however, is chiefly negative: he thrice declined the king's invitation to form a government, on the grounds that he needed to devote more time to the practice of his profession—the law. His refusals to serve as prime minister notably diminished the influence of the PPI, which had become the second largest party in the Chamber of Deputies after the Socialists, and undoubtedly contributed to the weakening of parliamentary government in Italy, which in turn led to the triumph of Fascism in October 1922.

By this time, Meda was increasingly at odds with his party colleagues, and he effectively broke with the party in 1923 over whether to collaborate with the new Fascist government or not, preferring, like some of the more fascist-leaning of Catholic politicians, to wait and see if the government could bring order and peace to Italy out of the postwar chaos. He did not represent himself for election in 1924 and retired entirely from politics into the practice of law.

Bibliography. Molony, John N. *The Emergence of Political Catholicism in Italy: Partito Popolare, 1919–1926.* London: Croom Helm, 1977. Traniello, F., and Campanini, G., eds. *Dizionario Storico del Movimento Cattolico in Italia, 1860–1980.* Vols. 1 and 2. Torino, Italy: Marietti, 1982.

John F. Pollard

MENDES MACIEL, ANTÔNIO VICENTE. *See* Conselheiro, Antônio

MENENDEZ Y PELAYO, MARCELINO (1856–1912). Menendez y Pelayo was born in Santander (Cantabria, Spain) on November 3, 1856, and died in the same city on May 13, 1912. After high school in Santander he attended the University of Barcelona and the University of Madrid

and earned his licentiate at Valladolid and his doctorate at Madrid. In 1878 he assumed the chair of Spanish literature at the Central University of Madrid and two years later began the publication of *Historia de los heterodoxos españoles,* a three-volume study of Spain's history in relation to the Catholic Church. The fame earned by this endeavor brought commissions for many other works on the history of aesthetics and Spanish literature. After twenty years of teaching, he became director of Spain's National Library and, in 1909, director of the Academy of History. At first he identified with the militant Catholic and reactionary Carlist movement but later joined the more moderate Catholic Union and collaborated with the Conservative Party of Antonio Cánovas del Castillo. Carlists subsequently considered him a traitor, and **Ramón Nocedal** led an attack on him in the pages of *El Siglo Futuro.* Menendez y Pelayo felt that Catholic unity gave Spain its identity, and at the end of his life he delivered a heart-rending lament: "Today we are witnessing the slow suicide of a people," a despair that is a proof against those who maintain that there are two Menendez y Pelayos. Our author neither wished to return to the sixteenth century, nor did he wish to make a political agenda of his revelation of Spanish identity. He did suggest, it is true, the theme of the "the two Spains," but **Ángel Herrera** comments that there was a third Spain, one at the same time both traditional and progressive, of which Menendez y Pelayo, himself, was a symbol.

Bibliography. Capestany, Edward J. *Menendez y Pelayo y su Obra.* Buenos Aires, Argentina: Depalma, 1981.

Edward J. Capestany

MEOUCHI, PAUL (1894–1975). Patriarch of the Lebanon-based Maronite Church, Meouchi rigorously defended the right of

Christians to remain in the Middle East. Born in Jezzine, in South Lebanon, he completed his studies in Lebanon and was ordained priest in Rome in December 1917. Meouchi then left for the United States of America, where he stayed for fourteen years.

In June 1955, Pope **Pius XII** appointed him as Maronite patriarch. Meouchi attended the Second Vatican Council and became the first Maronite clergyman to become a cardinal of the church. During Vatican II, Meouchi strongly defended the right of patriarchs to discourage the emigration of Christians from the region. In 1962 Patriarch Meouchi visited the Maronite community in the United States and dedicated the Maronite Seminary in Washington, D.C.

The reign of Patriarch Meouchi was affected by the situation at all levels of political engagement. As the Middle East became affected by cold war politics and the resulting tensions in the region, Meouchi´s concern was to maintain unity within his community, promote reconciliation among the Lebanese, and reach out to the Arab and Muslim communities in Lebanon and the Arab countries. Meouchi stood in opposition to the then-president of Lebanon Camille Chamoun´s pro-U.S. and anti-Egyptian president Gamal Abdel-Nasser stand. Sympathetic to pro-Arab nationalism, Meouchi's position has led some government supporters and critics in the Maronite community to assign him the epithet "Mohammad Meouchi."

Bibliography. Kerr, David A. "The Temporal Authority of the Maronite Patriarchate, 1920–1958: A Study in the Relationship of Religion and Secular Power." PhD diss., St. Anthony's College, University of Oxford, 1973. Salibi, Kamal. *Modern History of Lebanon.* New York: Caravan Books, 1997.

George Emile Irani

MERRY DEL VAL, RAFAEL (1865–1930).

Rafael Merry del Val was born in London of a Spanish father and an English mother. He studied in England, Belgium, and at the Pontifical Scots College in Rome and the Academy of Noble Ecclesiastics, the training ground for curial officials and Vatican diplomats, and was ordained in 1888. He rose rapidly in the Roman Curia, despite a desire for a role as a simple pastor of souls. Postings in Berlin, Vienna, and Canada, where he was apostolic delegate, were followed by his appointment as archbishop and president of the academy in 1899. He served on the commission that advised **Leo XIII** to declare Anglican orders "null and void," and in 1903 he was one of the candidates for the succession to Cardinal Vaughan at Westminster.

Following the death of Leo XIII, Merry Del Val was elected secretary of the conclave. It was he who allegedly persuaded the tearfully reluctant Giuseppe Cardinal Sarto to accept election as Pope **Pius X.** His confidence and linguistic skills led Pius to appoint him secretary of state in October 1903 and cardinal in November. His tenure was marked by the severing of relations by France following President Loubet's controversial visit to the Italian king in 1904. It has been argued that most of the policies pursued by Merry Del Val as secretary of state were really those of the pope rather than his own. Whatever the case, the papacy was more diplomatically isolated at the end of his tenure of office than it had been since 1878.

After the election of **Benedict XV** in September 1914, Merry Del Val became secretary of the Holy Office. He died in Rome in 1930, and a process for his beatification was opened in 1953 without positive results.

Bibliography. Cenci, P. *Il Cardinale Raffaele Merry Del Val.* Rome-Turin: L.I.C.E., Berenti, 1933.

John F. Pollard

METTERNICH, KLEMENS VON (1773–1859).

Prince Metternich served as the Austrian foreign minister during most of the early nineteenth century. The architect of the Congress of Vienna in 1815, he sought to reestablish peace in Europe in the wake of the Napoleonic Wars. One of the ways he did this was to promote the influence of the Roman papacy.

Metternich was appointed foreign minister in 1809 at a time when the power of the papacy was in question. Following the French Revolution of 1789, revolutionaries had unleashed a dechristianization campaign in traditionally Roman Catholic France, and Napoleon's armies had conquered many of the Papal States in Italy. Austria remained the only major Roman Catholic power in Europe, but even here the system of church-state relations known as Josephinism had largely replaced papal authority with that of the emperor. As a result, the state had come to control the Austrian church. For instance, some 10 percent of the edicts issued by Emperor Joseph II (r. 1780–1790), after whom the system was named, regulated the details of church life.

The Congress of Vienna brought an end to the Napoleonic Wars and the revolutionary ideals that had launched them. Metternich, who emerged as the main architect of the peace, was dedicated to reestablishing the political order of Europe as it had existed before 1789. His ideology of conservatism was in many ways secular, yet he saw in a revived papacy a bulwark against the return of revolutionary ideologies such as liberalism, nationalism, and socialism. He was inspired by a doctrine called ultramontanism, which, formulated in the wake of the French Revolution by **Joseph de Maistre** and other Roman Catholic intellectuals, assigned the papacy the leading place in the life of the church.

Metternich thus set about the restoration of papal influence at the Congress, insisting, for instance, that the territories of the Papal States be restored. He also formed a lasting relationship with the papal legate **Ercole Cardinal Consalvi,** an alliance that ultimately reversed the long estrangement between Vienna and Rome resulting from Josephinism. In subsequent years, he used his power as Europe's leading statesman to advance papal interests. In 1819 he helped persuade Emperor Francis I (r. 1792–1835) of Austria to moderate his claims to the right to appoint the important archbishop of Salzburg, creating a victory for the papacy. In Italy, Metternich succeeded in forging a policy of support for the papacy in the face of the rising nationalist movement called the *Risorgimento,* a commitment that would bear fruit in the second half of the nineteenth century when Italian political unification was completed. Metternich himself was forced to resign from government in 1848 in the face of new revolutionary disturbances, and he died in retirement in 1859.

Bibliography. Palmer, Alan. *Metternich.* New York: Harper & Row, 1972. Reinerman, Alan J. *Austria and the Papacy in the Age of Metternich.* Washington, DC: Catholic University of America Press, 1979.

John Strickland

MEXICAN CATHOLIC ACTION (ACCIÓN CATÓLICA MEXICANA). Mexican Catholic organizers at the end of the nineteenth century took as their model Western European Catholic Action organizations, following their pattern of division by age and sex to organize laypeople in religious education and social action programs while deterring radical socialist mobilization. Prior to and at the beginning of Mexico's armed revolution (1910–1917), several political, civic, and social groups formed the foundations of Catholic social action in Mexico: the Knights of Columbus (*Caballeros de Colón*), first established in Mexico in 1905; the **National Catholic Party** (*Partido Católico Nacional,* PCN), founded in 1911; the *Unión de Damas Católicas Mexicanas* (UDCM, Union of Mexican Catholic Ladies); and the *Asociación Católica de la Juventud Mexicana* (ACJM, Association of Mexican Catholic Youth, for young and unmarried

Catholic men), founded in 1912, as well as labor unions, rural cooperatives, mutual aid societies, student groups, study circles, and devotional societies.

Pope Pius XI's encyclical to Mexican Catholics, *Paterna sane sollicitudo* (1926), encouraged organizing the laity in passive resistance as preferable to the armed resistance sparked by the government's enforcement of anticlerical provisions of the 1917 constitution. The encyclical offered Western European Catholic Action organizations as models but also recommended Catholic Action as a concept that lent itself to and encouraged adaptation to local circumstances. At the close of the **Cristero** Rebellion (1926–1929), Pius XI reminded Mexican Catholic leaders of the encyclical's recommendations and added another: to make Mexico a leader of Catholic Action in Latin America by implementing a strong nationwide organization. The reputation of groups like the ACJM had been damaged, both in the eyes of the Mexican government, as many members had supported or joined the rebellion, and in those of the church hierarchy, which had found itself unable to direct all Catholics' actions in protest of the revolutionary government's policies. Still, the Mexican church hierarchy drew on the ACJM, UDCM, and other existing Catholic associations to create the ACM in 1929.

The director of the **Mexican Social Secretariat** (*Secretariado Social Mexicano,* SSM) and several other clerical and lay representatives drew up statutes for the new organization, dividing it into four main sections: the Unión de Católicos Mexicanos (UCM) for men married or over thirty-five; the UFCM, reorganized from the UDCM, for women married or over thirty-five; the ACJM, purged of its ties to the Cristeros, for young single men; and the JCFM for young single women (unchanged from its founding in 1926). The SSM supervised the organization of the central committees of each branch of the ACM, based

in Mexico City; organized the *Comisión Central de Instrucción Religiosa* (CCIR, Central Commission for Religious Instruction) to coordinate religious education projects in conjunction with the clergy and the ACM; and began to develop training courses for clergy, lay leaders, and diocesan and parochial groups to continue their work under the conditions of post-Cristero Mexico, plus propaganda, reading materials, and fundraising campaigns for these organizations.

The ACM's Central Council (*Junta Central*), comprised of representatives from each branch and advised by an ecclesiastical assistant (a priest appointed by the Mexican Episcopate, or in other cases, the local bishop), was to study problems and methods at a national level and to exist as a resource for consultation by regional and local committees. On the next level, the diocesan councils (*Juntas Diocesanas*), also composed of representatives of each group and ecclesiastical assistants, was to promote the ACM in the dioceses and stimulate the development of its branch organizations and auxiliaries in Mexico's numerous parishes. The diocesan councils would also maintain closer contact with the central council than could each parish council (*Consejo Parroquial*) and would supervise the parochial groups under the general leadership of the Junta Central. Individual diocesan and parish councils were given latitude to create ancillary secretariats, commissions, auxiliaries, and technical groups within the ACM as necessary in order to address local problems. The ACM's hierarchical, centralized scheme of organization was offered as a model for Catholic Action groups across Latin America by the mid-1930s.

The ACM was not homogenous. Although initially more a middle- and upper-class phenomenon, the movement extended sufficiently to working-class and rural Mexicans to build a wider base, particularly in central and central-western dioceses. In the 1930s and 1940s, some diocesan groups gathered tens of thousands of members from many parishes, while others barely managed to pull together several dozen in the diocesan seat. Some tried to continue progressive programs (worker and childhood education, support for Catholic workers, charity projects, etc.) that had been carried out before the Mexican Revolution, while others concentrated their efforts on opposing socialism, communism, and the radical reforms of the Mexican Revolutionary government, including its socialist education project, programs of land expropriation and redistribution, and explicitly antireligious organizations of urban workers and rural farmers. Females consistently outnumbered males, as the UFCM and JCFM consistently formed the largest part of parish, diocesan, and national membership.

Catholic Action's education campaigns proved to be its most effective. The organization's policy of careful study and training of lay leaders to promote harmony within the church and its social groups attracted little notice, but its goal to catechize the masses and encourage religious education clashed with laws passed in the 1920s and 1930s. The church insisted that Catholics had the right to open schools and that it had the right to ensure that the curricula of both Catholic and public schools were morally sound. At the behest of the church hierarchy, ACM activists worked alongside parish priests, and often in the place of priests in exile or who were unable to work openly, encouraging Catholics to join campaigns in "defense" of their church and their families. These actions weakened the church's post-1929 claim to be law abiding and to encourage its adherents to do the same. Nevertheless, lay Catholic associations like the ACM were the key to the church's survival and growth through the revolutionary period. They enjoyed some success—in particular, the socialist education project was moribund by 1940, and other anticlerical laws, while

not struck down or modified until the end of the twentieth century, gradually were enforced less frequently, allowing priests and nuns to circulate; Catholic schools, hospitals, and other institutions to open; and religious celebrations to be held in public spaces.

Through the 1950s, membership in the four principle sections of the ACM continued to grow. The ACM established new specialized sections such as the Student and Professional Movement (*Movimiento Estudantil y Profesional*), Women Nurses of Catholic Action (*Movimiento de Enfermeras de Acción Católica*), and the Catholic Worker Youth (*Juventud Obrera Católica*) and expanded its charitable and educational programs. Some scholars link early twentieth-century Catholic Social Action movements to the social movements of basismo and liberation theology that developed in Latin America after the Second Vatican Council and the 1968 meeting of the Latin American Bishops' Conference in Medellín, Colombia. For Mexico, Catholic Action was an important step in between— lay activism provided a continuity of sustained Catholic social action through periods of government repression. The ACM also provided opportunities for the laity to gain a more profound education in the church's social and spiritual undertakings and to design and participate in them. The ACM diminished in size from the 1960s onward, as groups founded during and since the Vatican II conference that blended ages, sexes, and occupations came to be more popular. However, the organization continues its activities to this day, though its membership is fewer in number and more advanced in age.

Bibliography. Azpiazu, Joaquín. *Manual de la Acción Católica.* Madrid: Editorial Razón y Fe, 1930. Barranco V., Bernardo. "Posiciones políticas en la historia de la Acción Católica Mexicana." In *El pensamiento social de los católicos mexicanos,* ed. Roberto Blancarte. Mexico City: Fondo de Cultura Económica, 1996. Blancarte, Roberto. *Historia de la Iglesia católica en*

México. Mexico City: El Colegio Mexiquense y el Fondo de Cultura Económica, 1992. Ceballos Ramírez, Manuel. *El catolicismo social: Un tercero en discordia.* Mexico City: El Colegio de México, 1991. Dario Miranda, Miguel. "Seis Años de Actividades del Secretariado Social Mexicano, 1925–1931." *Archivo Histórico del Secretariado Social Mexicano, Carpeta Episcopado–Informes, 1924–1931,* 1931. García Ugarte, Marta Eugenia. "Movimientos Católicos Internacionales: Comunión y Liberación y Opus Dei." In *El pensamiento social de los católicos mexicanos,* ed. Roberto Blancarte. Mexico City: Fondo de Cultura Económica, 1996. Hanson, Randall S. "'The Day of Ideals': Catholic Social Action in the Age of the Mexican Revolution, 1867–1929." PhD diss., Indiana University–Bloomington, 1994. Komonchak, Joseph A. "Returning from Exile: Catholic Theology in the 1930s." In *The Twentieth Century: A Theological Overview,* ed. Gregory Baum. Maryknoll, NY: Orbis, 1999. Romero de Solís, José Miguel. *El Aguijon del Espíritu: Historia Contemporánea de la Iglesia en México (1895–1990).* Mexico City: Instituto Mexicano de Doctrina Social Cristiana, 1994. Schell, Patience A. *Church and State Education in Revolutionary Mexico City.* Tucson: University of Arizona Press, 2003.

Kristina A. Boylan

MEXICAN SOCIAL SECRETARIAT [SECRETARIADO SOCIAL MEXICANO] (MEXICO).

After Mexico's armed revolution (1910–1917), Catholic activists revived social action organizations dating from the late 1800s. The Mexican Episcopate coordinated them under an umbrella organization, the *Secretariado Social Mexicano* (SSM, Mexican Social Secretariat) in 1920. Father Alfredo Méndez Medina, SJ, the first director, used his re-interpretation of medieval Catholic corporatism (with religious bodies and faith-based social and civic organizations essential to the body politic) to model the SSM on contemporary European Catholic social action organizations and on an assessment of the recent failures of civil society and of the Church: the false calm of Porfirio Díaz's dictatorship (1876–1911); the radical, revolutionary movements resulting from pressures from rural poverty and repressive working conditions; the negative reactions and civil war following General Victoriano Huerta's coup, supported by some elite Catholic leaders; and the increasing use of class war rhetoric in politics and labor organizing. The SSM's purposes were to research social problems and to promote action that would restore *La Paz Social* (Social Peace, the SSM's periodical).

Though placed under a permanent committee of clergy's supervision of, the Mexican Episcopate did not intend for them to direct the SSM exclusively. Rather, its design allowed for lay participation and leadership. The SSM sponsored and drew leaders from the growing Acción Católica Mexicana (**Mexican Catholic Action**), study circles, mutual aid societies, credit unions, and rural cooperatives. Méndez Medina prioritized Catholic labor organizing, evidenced by the SSM's support for the *Confederación Nacional Católica del Trabajo* (CNCT, National Confederation of Catholic Labor, fd.1922). Some Catholic leaders intended for the CNCT to bring a confessional, anti-socialist aspect to labor organizing, but Mendez Medina believed Catholic Social thought could aid the struggle for better working conditions and wages. In 1924, the Jesuit Superior General of Mexico ordered Méndez Medina to resign, probably because of his militancy. The Mexican Episcopate named in his stead Father Miguel Darío Miranda, who focused more on pious associations and activity than on social issues. Nevertheless, for the next two years the SSM promoted CNCT and peasant association projects alongside those of Catholic Action.

The escalation of tensions between the state and Catholics that resulted in the **Cristero** Rebellion (1926–1929) curtailed the activities of the SSM and other Catholic organizations. The SSM fell under government suspicion, as it had worked with the Liga Nacional Defensora de la Libertad Religiosa (National League for the Defense of Religious Freedom), a lay, Catholic organization that engaged in armed opposition. In 1928, government agents searched the SSM headquarters, seized materials, and arrested several staff members, after which the SSM all but ceased activity. Given the Mexican government renewed efforts to enforce the 1917 constitution's prohibitions on confessional organization in politics, labor, and education, Catholic leaders placed more emphasis on lay, social groups like the ACM. Reconstituted in 1929 and still led by Miranda, the SSM placed the ACM at its core and supported and other lay, Catholic organizations where they existed, and documented restrictions on religious and social activity where hostilities were greater. The SSM also coordinated the Organización Nacional de Instrucción Religiosa (National Organization for Religious Instruction), a catechism program that relied on lay instructors and organizers, given the reduced ability of clergy and women religious to work in public.

In 1936, pope **Pius XI** named Miranda Bishop of Tulancingo. The Mexican Episcopate designated Father Rafael Dávila Vilchis, ecclesiastical advisor to the Central Committee of the *Unión Femenina Católica Mexicana* (Mexican Catholic Women's Union, the largest branch of the ACM), as director of both the SSM and the entire ACM. Dávila Vilchis led the organizations through the gradual calming of church-state tensions at that time, and then oversaw their separation in 1946. The ACM would concentrate more on personal piety and education, while the SSM again would focus on social organization. Enthusiasm came from participant priests like Pedro Velásquez, who were able to return from study and work in Europe given the church-state detente and who were influenced

by organizations like the Belgian, labor-oriented *Jeunesse Ouvrière Chrétienne* (in Spanish, *Juventud Obrera Cristiana;* **Young Christian Workers**, JOC, fd.1925). The SSM again established co-operatives and mutual aid societies, as well as Mexican JOC chapters and schools of social work and domestic science, work which continued through the 1950s.

Faced with social conflicts like disputes over the content of universal textbooks and growing disillusionment with the one-party state, Velásquez and others identified the SSM's function of fomenting lay organization as necessary for Mexican society as well as for its own mission. In the mid-1960s the SSM promoted the study of the Second Vatican Council documents among its constituent associations, and soon after encouraged the study of those of the Conference of Latin American Bishops. The SSM also established diocesan social secretariats to increase lay participation, and supported the *Centro Nacional de Misiones a los Indigenas* (National Center for Missions to the Indigenous), founded by the Mexican Episcopate to consolidate missionary work in the 1950s, and which also placed growing emphasis on organizing in the 1960s.

The SSM consistently claimed to heed the direction and leadership of the church hierarchy, but also increasingly emphasized its lay identity. In the late 1960s, participants in the diocesan and local organizations as well as SSM leaders in Mexico City called for autonomy from the Mexican Episcopate's directorship. The SSM's opposition to government repression of student and popular protests in 1968 and 1971, which went beyond the episcopates' public statements, strengthened this inclination. Conservative episcopate members tried to rein in the SSM after Pedro Velázquez's death in 1970. However, his brother, Manuel Velázquez, was appointed interim director, and continued to argue for the SSM's independence, envisioning its conversion into an "autonomous, ecclesial center of research and social action" that would serve the Church without being bound to its hierarchical leadership (Escondrilla Valdez, 129). The SSM issued a declaration to this effect in late 1970, and the organization acquired its independent juridical identity in 1971. Pastoral letters issued by the Mexican Episcopate in 1973 further clarified the end of the SSM's official ties to the church hierarchy. Since 1973, the SSM, directed by Manuel Velázquez, has continued to promote social and spiritual education and action throughout Mexico.

Bibliography. Escontrilla Valdez, Hugo Armando. "El Secretariado Social Mexicano: Los orígenes de la autonomía, 1965–1973." MA thesis, Institución de Investigaciones Dr. Jose Maria Luis Mora, 2000. Fazio, Carlos. *Algunos aportes del Secretariado Social Mexicano en la transición a la democracia.* Mexico City: Academia Mexicana de Derechos Humanos, 1997. Hanson, Randall S. "'The Day of Ideals': Catholic Social Action in the Age of the Mexican Revolution, 1867–1929." PhD diss., Indiana University–Bloomington, 1994. Pacheco Hinojosa, María Martha. "Presencia de la Iglesia Católica en la Sociedad Mexicana (1958–1973). Estudio de dos casos: Secretariado Social Mexicano, Conferencia de Organizaciones Nacionales." PhD diss., Universidad Nacional Autonoma de México, 1997. Quirk, Robert E. *The Mexican Revolution and the Catholic Church, 1910–1929.* Bloomington and London: Indiana University Press, 1973. Velázquez, Manuel H. *Pedro Velázquez, H.: Apostol de la justicia, Vida y Pensamiento.* Mexico City: Secretariado Social Mexicano, AC, 1978.

Kristina A. Boylan

MILANI, DON LORENZO (1923–1967). From the late 1950s until his death in 1967 at the age of forty-four, Milani gained notoriety as a leading figure on the anticapitalist Catholic Left in Italy. An author and teacher, he lamented the deep malaise in society that followed the overthrow of communal and spiritual values by consumerist individualism. His ideas inspired many on the Marxist Left to view him as their ideal interlocutor in the Catholic world.

Born in Florence into a wealthy and cultivated family, Milani began life without even a hint of the church career that awaited him. He came from two long lines of atheists and agnostics. His father, who had a university degree in chemistry, and his Jewish mother kept intact the family's traditional disinterest regarding religion. Milani indifferently pursued a classical education in Milan, where the family relocated in 1930. He did not attend the university. Instead he returned to Florence to study painting.

In 1943 at age twenty, Milani shocked his family with the announcement that he was converting to Catholicism. Something even more shocking than his conversion lay in store for the Milani family when he entered the seminary later that year. He became an ordained priest on July 13, 1947. He had turned to the church in stages, impelled by a feeling of emptiness that religion alone seemed to assuage in him.

Don Milani spent the next seven years as an assistant chaplain in San Donato, near Florence. Appalled by the ignorance and illiteracy of the young people in his working-class parish, he opened a night school. At the same time he publicly commented on the anti-Christian character of the socioeconomic system that exploited the poor. His radical ideas made him numerous enemies among churchmen and local Christian Democratic politicians.

Under pressure to reassign Don Milani, the church in 1954 sent the thirty-one-year-old priest on an exile assignment to the parish of Sant' Andrea in Barbiana in the hills northeast of Florence. An even more impoverished and backward place than San Donato, Barbiana deepened his commitment to the cause of the poor. He set up yet another school, with the same consequence that had befallen him in San Donato: critics within the church and local Christian Democrats complained about the exclusively political character of his ministry.

Don Milani replied to his detractors in *Esperienze pastorali* (1958)—the only book that he ever would complete. In this indictment of the church for failing to live up to the values of the New Testament, he charged that during Benito Mussolini's Fascist dictatorship the papacy had lost its moral compass. Even now the Catholic Church continued to stand with the powerful and wealthy, not with Christ and the poor. To authentic church doctrine, he professed the most fervent devotion, but the conformist Catholic culture of Christian Democratic Italy repelled him. The church responded to this book by demanding to have it withdrawn from sale and by prohibiting re-publication or translation.

Controversy continued to swirl around Don Milani and gained in intensity. His health began to fail in 1960 with the onset of Hodgkin's disease. This aggressive cancer inexorably destroyed his body, but he fought energetically for his beliefs until the end. Accused in 1965 by some military chaplains of encouraging young men to disobey the draft law, he was too ill to appear in court to answer their charges. Instead he wrote *"Lettera ai giudici"* (Letter to the Judges), which revealed the large influence on his Catholic thinking of Gandhi and the principles of nonviolence. The case against him was dismissed on February 15, 1966.

Six weeks before Don Milani's death on June 26, 1967, *Lettera a una professoressa* (Letter to a School Mistress) appeared. The work of his students at Barbiana, this book created a sensation in its strident call for a complete overhaul of Italy's class-ridden school system. It remains one of the most representative left-wing books of the late 1960s, when Italy was descending into the period of severe social contestation that preceded and overlapped the Red Brigade reign of terror.

Bibliography. Pecorini, Giorgio. *Don Milani! Chi era costui?* 2nd ed. Milan: Baldini & Castoldi, 1998. Riccioni, Gianfranco, ed. *Lorenzo Milani: Scritti.* Florence: Luciano Manzuoli, 1982.

Richard Drake

MINDSZENTY, JÓSEF (1892–1975). Born into a humble village family in the town of Mindszent, western Hungary, Jósef Mindszenty became a leading Catholic voice against Nazi Germany and an uncompromising opponent of Soviet communism.

He was ordained a Catholic priest in 1915. After two years as an assistant pastor, he was transferred to the city of Zalaegerszeg, where he remained until 1944. Mindszenty served as a teacher and parish priest. Subsequently he became archdeacon (1921), titular abbot of Porno (1924), papal prelate (1937), bishop of Veszprém (1944), archbishop of Esztergom, and the prince primate of Hungary (1945). In 1946 Pope **Pius XII** also named him a cardinal.

József Mindszenty was a conservative nationalist and a monarchist who supported Hungary's territorial revisionism and the restoration of the Habsburg dynasty. He thus openly disagreed with Admiral Nicholas Horthy's regency in Hungary (1920–1944). During the 1930s, Mindszenty opposed Hungary's rightward turn and wished to counteract the spread of National Socialism through the establishment of a Catholic People's Party, which never materialized. After becoming the bishop of Veszprém, Mindszenty joined his fellow bishops to protest the persecution of the Jews. His philo-Semitic and anti-Nazi stance resulted in his 1944 arrest by the Arrow Cross regime (October 1944–March 1945).

Although openly anti-Nazi, Mindszenty was equally anticommunist and anti-Soviet. He also possessed an unyielding personality that made it impossible for him to negotiate and to compromise on certain issues. He was convinced that as Hungary's prince primate, he was the primary source of legitimacy and constitutionalism in a period of political interregnum.

In 1946, Mindszenty protested against the establishment of a Hungarian republic, as well as against the expulsion of the nation's German minorities. At the same time he spoke against the persecution of the Hungarian minorities in Czechoslovakia, Romania, and Yugoslavia. He likewise protested against communist-inspired laws depriving the Catholic Church of its rights and privileges, as well as against the dissolution of religious organizations, the elimination of obligatory teaching of religion, and the nationalization of Catholic schools and related social and cultural institutions.

Rejecting the communist takeover of Hungary's government, and expressing his views in pastoral letters, Mindszenty was arrested for treason in 1948, tortured, and then sentenced to life imprisonment. He remained in prison and then under house arrest until 1956, when Hungary's revolutionary government ordered his release. Upon reassuming his post as Hungary's primate, Mindszenty delivered a major address to the nation, in which he demanded free elections, establishment of a constitutional government, social justice, and the freedom of religion.

Following the Soviet military intervention in 1956, Mindszenty sought political asylum at the United States Embassy, where he remained for fifteen years. He was able to leave Hungary only in 1971. After a brief visit to Rome, he settled in Vienna, from where he made several protracted tours, visiting the Hungarian diaspora throughout the world, including the United States

in 1974. Although Cardinal Mindszenty never broke with Rome, he was displeased with the Vatican's policy of compromising with the Communist world.

Following his death, Mindszenty was buried in Mariazell, Austria, but after the collapse of communism, his remains were reinterred among his predecessors in Esztergom.

Bibliography. Mindszenty, József Cardinal. *Memoirs.* New York: Macmillan, 1974. Vecsey, Joseph, and Phyllis Schlafly. *Mindszenty the Man.* St. Louis, MO: Cardinal Mindszenty Foundation, 1972.

Steven Béla Várdy

MOLTMANN, JÜRGEN (b. 1926). Currently professor emeritus of theology at Tübingen University (Germany), Moltmann is one of the most important political theologians of the late twentieth century. His so-called theology of hope captured the imagination of the global church, inspiring several generations to work for peace and justice in the world. The suffering of humanity has always been an important theme for Moltmann because of his own experiences of suffering as a young German soldier and prisoner of war in World War II, as well as his empathy with the suffering of the Jewish people during the Shoah.

With Johann B. Metz and Jan M. Lochman, he participated in the Christian-Marxist dialogues in Germany in the 1960s. The Marxist influence on Moltmann's theology lies primarily in his left-wing Hegelianism, his praxis orientation, and his internalization of an ethics of social transformation of all dimensions of human reality, including the socioeconomic conditions of the poor and the environmental conditions of the earth. Moltmann saw Marx's functional critique of religion as a challenge to the church to prophetically embody its deepest impulse for justice.

Moltmann's interpretation of Marx was influenced by the radical Christian socialism that was mediated to him through **Karl Barth,** as well as **Leonhard Ragaz,** Hermann Kutter, **Christoph Blumhardt,** and Eduard Heimann. Following in the footsteps of Barth and the religious socialists, Moltmann argues that living the Gospel of Jesus Christ includes prophetically confronting sites of systemic sin and injustice. While this pietist stream of religious socialism shaped Moltmann's religious matrix, Marxist thinker Ernst Bloch's apocalyptic philosophy of hope provided Moltmann with a philosophical frame that linked the human struggle for justice with a historic horizon of hope.

In 1964, Moltmann published *Theology of Hope,* in which he argued that Christian theology was fundamentally eschatological and politically radical. The book was well received in Germany and led to Moltmann's international notoriety. *Theology of Hope* played an important role in the early development of Latin American liberation theology.

In 1967, Moltmann was appointed professor of theology at the University of Tübingen, where he retired in 1994. His books have been numerous and translated into many languages. His early trilogy, *Theology of Hope* (1964), *The Crucified God* (1972), and *The Church in the Power of the Spirit* (1979), provides a foundational logic for his project. The first two works consider the death and resurrection of Jesus Christ, forming a dialectic that is synthesized by his doctrine of the Holy Spirit presented in the third work. As his theology developed, the Holy Spirit continued to play a prominent role in his thinking.

Moltmann then turned to a six-volume systematic theology entitled *Contributions to Christian Theology,* which included *Trinity and the Kingdom of God* (1980), *God in Creation* (Gifford Lectures 1985), *The Way of Jesus Christ* (1989), *The Spirit of Life* (1991), *The Coming of God: Christian Eschatology* (1995), and *Experiences in Theology* (1999). In these works he developed doctrines of the social Trinity, creation based on eco-justice, Jesus Christ as a fellow human on the way, the Holy Spirit as the spirit of life, and transformational eschatology.

One of the important ways that Moltmann helped to mobilize Christian theologians to engage public life was through his editing of different theological journals. Moltmann was coeditor of the *Deutsch-Poinshe Helfte* (1959–1968) and worked for reconciliation between Poland and Germany. For twenty years he served as a member of the Faith and Order Committee of the World Council of Churches (1963–1983). During this time, Moltmann helped the ecumenical movement shift its emphasis from the church to the world. He was editor of the journal *Evangelische Theologie,* and from 1979 to 1994 one of the directors of the Catholic journal *Concilium.* Moltmann's editorial work demonstrated his commitment to justice, ecumenical generosity, and reconciliation of communities divided by race, culture, nationality, and religion.

One of his most important contributions to political theology is his notion of the kingdom of God. Moltmann views the kingdom of God as a reign of love, justice, and peace that cannot be identified with the church. History and the world are the primary horizon of eschatological hope. Thus, the church's outreach must always be intended *for* the world. Throughout his life Moltmann and his wife, Elisabeth Wendel, have pursued global justice through a variety of feminist and liberationist struggles. His trajectory for the reconstruction and reconstitution of a progressive global political theology remains a vital and radical theological stream for early twenty-first-century theology.

Bibliography. Moltmann, Jürgen. *The Crucified God: The Cross of Christ as the Foundation and Criticism of Christian Theology.* Trans. R.

A. Wilson and John Bowden. New York: Harper & Row, 1974. Moltmann, Jürgen. *God in Creation: A New Theology of Creation and the Spirit of God.* Trans. Margaret Kohl. Minneapolis, MN: Fortress Press, 1993. Moltmann, Jürgen. *Theology of Hope: On the Ground and the Implications of a Christian Eschatology.* Trans. James W. Leitch. New York: Harper & Row, 1967.

Peter G. Heltzel

MONOD, WILFRED (1867–1943). Together with Élie Gounelle, Monod belonged to the moderate liberal, though splintered, branch of the Reformed Church in France, and he worked to unite the two factions, the *Union des Églises Réformées Évangéliques* and the *Églises Réformées Unies.* The merger of both unions into the Union des Églises Réformées on October 24, 1906, at the Synod of Paris was essentially the result of his work.

Born in Paris, Monod was descended from a famous Reformed Protestant family. After theological studies, he became a pastor of the Reformed Church of France. In 1909, he became professor for practical theology at the *Faculté Libre de Théologie de Paris,* and in 1912 president of the *Union des Églises Réformées de France,* founded in 1907. Monod, who was marked by mystical religiousness, aimed to establish a socially reforming apostolate.

In 1904, Monod also took the initiative to establish a federation of Protestant churches, the Fédération Protestante de France. This project was delayed by four years when the French National Assembly divided state and church in 1905, and by disputes among the Reformed churches. In November 1909, however, the first general assembly of the *Fédération Protestante de France* finally met in Nîmes. Monod's ecumenical engagement showed in the fact that he was among the leading personalities of the World Alliance for Promoting International Friendship through the Churches, and of the Life and Work Movement. Monod was a close friend of the movement's founder, Swedish pastor, religious scientist, and archbishop of Uppsala, Nathan Söderblom.

After 1918, Monod engaged in intense discussions over German war guilt in ecumenical forums. Despite his own religious-social and international orientation, here he represented the hard nationalist position of his government. He demanded that the Germans declare the invasion of Belgium inexcusable and accept the peace conditions of the Treaty of Versailles as just expiation for their barbaric deeds. In 1923, Monod founded the tertiarian order *Tiers Ordre Protestante des Veilleurs,* a Franciscan order for Protestant laypersons. In connection with this work, Monod became a speaker of the liturgical movement in France.

At the beginning of the 1930s, Monod campaigned among the churches to support the League of Nations, which he wanted to infuse with the Christian soul of a spiritual church federation. He called for radical structural changes in the churches to fulfill the Gospel mission, namely to end class struggle, war, and interchurch disputes. Friedrich Heiler rightly defined Monod as a "harbinger of a social and ecumenical Christianity."

Bibliography. Besier, G. *Krieg, Frieden, Abrüstung.* Göttingen, Germany: Vandenhoeck & Ruprecht, 1982. Monod, W. *Après la journée, 1867–1937: Souvenirs et visions.* Paris: B. Grasset, 1938.

Gerhard Besier

MONTALEMBERT, CHARLES RENÉ FORBES (1810–1870). Montalembert was a historian and leader of the French liberal Catholic party. The scion of a family with a medieval aristocratic lineage, Montalembert spent his boyhood in England, where his father, le Comte Marc-René, had landed in 1792 in flight from the Revolution. Returning to the Continent in 1819, he enrolled in the Collège Ste. Barbe and distinguished himself by his brilliance and also by a piety most unusual among his school fellows at the time.

The death of a beloved sister devastated him and intensified his feelings of alienation from a bleak universe. Like many young people at the time, he turned away from the dry rationalism of the eighteenth century and turned to the romantic spirit celebrated in the writings of **René Chateaubriand** and Sir Walter Scott with their medieval lore and intimations of mystery and strangeness. A young man of passionate enthusiasms, Montalembert's deepest passion was for the church, whose glory, as he said, he loved more than life itself.

On a trip to Ireland he heard about the start of a French Catholic daily newspaper called *L'Avenir,* the slogan of which was "God and Liberty." As he said in a letter, he foresaw that once the church was disengaged from its alliance with political power, it would recover its liberty and primal energy. He hurried back to France and was welcomed by **Félicité Lamennais** to join the staff of the paper. Together with **Jean Baptiste Henri Lacordaire,** a young priest, the three men set out to show that a Catholic could be thoroughly loyal to Rome and thoroughly liberal in commitment to the expansion of the human rights advocated by the French Revolution. In the course of their campaign for a liberal Catholicism, Montalembert joined Lacordaire in opening a free school for poor children in Paris. Arrested by the police for this illegal action, he was put on trial. At this point, his father died, and Montalembert inherited his title. Hence the trial had to be held in the House of Peers, where he demonstrated his great oratorical talent, though he still lost the case and paid the fine.

When their enterprise came to grief with the condemnation of liberal Catholicism by Pope **Gregory XVI,** Montalembert had to make a painful decision—whether to remain on the side of Lamennais, who ultimately refused to submit to the pope's condemnation, or join Lacordaire in making his submission. He chose the latter course, but the break with Lamennais was terribly wrenching and made even more so by his realization that Lamennais was losing the faith.

Montalembert, nevertheless, remained faithful to his basic liberal convictions, including belief in a parliamentary system on the British model with strong limitations on the central government. He therefore considered the Revolution of 1848 a disaster, a catastrophe that alienated him from Lacordaire, whom he called "a golden tongue demagogue" for supporting it.

Montalembert was nonetheless elected to the Constitutent Assemby and joined his two erstwhile friends there. As a member of the Chamber of Deputies from 1848 to 1857 and leader of the 250 Catholic deputies, he spoke eloquently in defense of the church with a voice as "penetrating as a sword" and impressing even the skeptics with his sincerity.

In the negotiations between the Catholics and the reactionary Party of Order, Montalembert showed both the narrow limits of his liberalism and his inability to rise above his class prejudices. Frightened by the looming specter of communism, he turned his back on the workers whose rights he had earlier championed. With this stance, he won the favor of the dominant bourgeoisie and helped to fix French Catholicism in a long-lasting political and social conservatism and opened up a chasm between the French church and the workers that still endures. He even lent valuable support to the arch reactionary Louis Napoleon, who in the coup d'état of 1851 took power as a virtual dictator. But Montalembert repented of his folly, and as leader of the liberal Catholic party he opposed the dominant Catholic ultramontanes (favoring greater papal power) led by the brilliant lay Catholic journalist **Louis Veuillot.**

At the behest of the Belgian Raffaele Cardinal Sterckx, Montalembert delivered a rousing speech at the 1863 **Malines Congress,** calling for a Catholic liberalism and a "free church in a free state." Though applauded vigorously by the cardinal, it ironically helped to trigger **Pius IX**'s *Syllabus of Errors,* which excoriated the leading liberal ideas. He spent his declining years at his desk, one fruit of this being his study *Monks of the West.* Disconsolate at the definition of papal infallibility by the Vatican Council (1870–1871), which he thought "erected an idol in the Vatican," Montalembert still never wavered in his faith in the church and died in her bosom.

Bibliography. Aspinwall, Bernard. "Montalembert and Idolatry." *Downside Review* 89 (1971): 158. Bokenkotter, Thomas. *Church and Revolution.* New York: Doubleday, 1998. O'Connell, Marvin. "Montalembert at Mechlin: A Reprise of 1830." *Journal of Church and State* 36 (Autumn 1984): 515–36.

Thomas Bokenkotter

MORAL MAJORITY (UNITED STATES). The Moral Majority is a religious and political grassroots movement of Protestant evangelicals, conservative Roman Catholics, and Mormons. Galvanized by what they regarded as the steady secularization of American society resulting in the destruction of traditional family values, and led by Rev. **Jerry Falwell,** the group burst onto the national political scene in 1980 and was credited with helping elect **Ronald Reagan.**

Regarded at the moment of its 1979 appearance as a new political player, the Moral Majority in fact represented a resurgence of political activism rooted in the nineteenth-century Protestant moral worldview, a reformist impulse illustrated by evangelists such as **Charles A. Finney.** This battle on behalf of the kingdom of God fought to eradicate slavery, establish prohibition, and combat the moral evils that many Protestants associated with urbanization.

Derailed in the early twentieth century by the widespread acceptance of Darwinism, however, the rise of critical biblical scholarship, the increasing religious diversity of America, and by the 1925 Scopes Trial, a significant subset of American evangelicalism created an enclave mentality. Reform gave way to revivalism emphasizing personal salvation, separatism eschewing association with "the world," and an eschatology positing an inevitable worsening of conditions preceding the return of Christ. Following the end of World War II, these evangelicals constructed a subculture—a network of publishing houses, Bible and liberal arts colleges, mission agencies, youth ministries, and radio networks all geared toward the salvation of souls.

With the end of the war and the subsequent rise in cold war tensions, fear of Communist subversion at home, and the social changes set in motion by the war, the evangelical political reawakening soon occurred. Evangelist **Billy Graham,** the postwar face of American evangelicalism, began to speak of the likelihood of nuclear annihilation at the hands of the Communists. The rising postwar popularity of Billy James Hargis's Christian Crusade and Fred Schwartz's Christian Anti-Communist Crusade reflected this reawakening.

The events and movements of the 1960s—the rise of the youth counterculture and its assault on traditional sexual mores, the domestic turmoil induced by the Vietnam War, and what these evangelicals saw as an attack upon patriotism by the antiwar movement—accelerated evangelical awareness and anger. Equally troubling was the unrest associated with the civil rights movement, the rise of an assertive feminism that called into question their conception of God's plan for family structure, and a Supreme Court actively attempting, in their view, to undermine public morality by ruling in 1962 and 1963 that organized public school prayer and Bible reading was unconstitutional. The downward trend continued into the early 1970s as the equal rights amendment (ERA)—seen as another assault upon traditional God-given gender roles—seemed destined for ratification, and the 1973 Supreme Court decision in *Roe v. Wade* gave legal protection to abortion. The *Roe* decision not only deepened conservative evangelical militancy, but it also inspired political cooperation between evangelicals and Roman Catholics.

Ironically, evangelical opposition to the administration of the first self-proclaimed "born-again" president, **Jimmy Carter,** fully reawakened a subculture feeling exiled in its own land and now determined to get it back. Although the peanut farmer from Georgia garnered 58 percent of the evangelical vote in 1976, doubts about Carter's spiritual credentials quickly gathered. Carter gave an interview to *Playboy,* articulated a vague position on abortion, and enthusiastically supported the ERA. Under Carter's watch, the Internal Revenue Service announced that private Christian day schools would no longer enjoy tax exemption if they could not prove racial diversity. Angry letters quickly descended on Capitol Hill, and the IRS rescinded the policy. The die, however, had been cast.

A rising tide of evangelical activism—the Religious Roundtable, Christian Voice, and the work of scholars such as **Francis Schaeffer**—culminated in the creation of the Moral Majority in June 1979. Rev. Jerry Falwell, a Lynchburg, Virginia, pastor, articulated evangelical frustration and determination to act. Working with other Christian leaders such as Charles Stanley, Cal Thomas, D. James Kennedy, and **Tim LaHaye,** Falwell launched his organization also enjoying the support of tax revolt spokesman Howard Phillips, conservative

activist Paul Weyrich, and conservative direct-mail guru Richard Viguerie. This alliance coalesced around the candidacy of Ronald Reagan in 1980.

Sparking grassroots enthusiasm with "I Love America" rallies, Falwell's Moral Majority worked to encourage pastors to register new voters during church services and to become active in precinct politics. The Moral Majority built bridges to other socially conservative voters who in the past would have been shunned in the name of theological purity. These included Orthodox Jews, Mormons, and Roman Catholics. The organization promoted an agenda that included strong U.S. support for Israel and equally strong opposition to abortion rights and gay rights. Supporters also championed prayer in schools, the free-enterprise system, and national defense. Strongly supporting Reagan's candidacy and given a prominent place at the GOP convention, the Moral Majority also targeted high-profile Democratic senators running for reelection such as George McGovern, who suffered defeat on election day.

In many respects, the 1980 election represented the zenith of Moral Majority influence. While Falwell enjoyed access to the president and had a role in the 1984 Republican Convention, the Reagan White House paid little more than lip service to most of the group's agenda. Nevertheless, the Moral Majority continued its long-standing agenda and remained staunchly behind Reagan's pro-Israel stance and his militant anticommunism in Central America. Yet the intense media focus and criticism of the Moral Majority caused Falwell's Liberty University and his church to suffer a drastic decline in contributions, and he faced competition from other more charismatic leaders. Falwell announced in 1986 that the Moral Majority would become the Liberty Federation, but the move marked the effective end of the Moral Majority as a major player on the national political scene.

Bibliography. Falwell, Jerry. *Listen, America!* New York: Doubleday, 1980. Fowler, Robert Booth, and Allen D. Hertzke. *Religion and Politics in America.* Boulder, CO: Westview Press, 1995. Martin, William. *With God on Our Side: The Rise of the Religious Right in America.* New York: Broadway Books, 1996.

Mark Taylor Dalhouse

MORE, HANNAH (1745–1833). Active in movements to abolish slavery and establish Sunday Schools, More became a household name in many parts of Britain with a circle of friends and acquaintances that included such luminaries as Horace Walpole, **Thomas Babington,** Edmund Burke, and **William Wilberforce.** Her engagement with politics was far more than supportive or tangential. Her writings contributed to the formation of the emerging political and social culture of responsibility and respectability among the British middle classes.

Between 1758 and 1762, she and her four sisters opened a school for young ladies in Bristol. Here More taught for a number of years and also began to write. In 1777 she wrote the play *Percy,* and in the following decade underwent a religious conversion which propelled her increasingly into evangelical circles. She was now in the world of the sermons of Rev. John Newton and the agitation of such **abolitionists** as **William Wilberforce.** She supported the antislavery movement through her correspondence with Wilberforce and through her poetry.

On the eve of the French Revolution, she campaigned for Edmund Burke in Bristol. As the violence of that revolution escalated and Tom Paine published *The Rights of Man* and Mary Wollstonecraft *A Vindication of the Rights of Women,* Hannah More produced a series of pamphlets called the *Cheap Repository Tracts.* She cautioned that the upheaval in France could undermine the moral fibre of British society and political culture. She called on the middle and lower classes to buttress the established system through a return to frugality and morality. The popularity of these tracts—especially *The Shepherd of Salisbury Plain*—and More's writing generally reveal the widespread audience for political conservatism.

More's works outsold those of Jane Austen in her liftetime, and when she died she left £30,000 to be distributed mainly among charitable societies (Stott, xvii). Her two volumes of *Practical Piety* (1811) inspired such evangelical reformers as Scottish minister **Thomas Chalmers.**

Hannah More not only directly impacted British politics, but her life also foreshadowed the complexity of the direct and indirect roles in society and politics that Victorian middle class women would play (Stott, x-xi, 336; Demers, 132).

Bibliography. Demers, Patricia. *The World of Hannah More.* Lexington: University Press of Kentucky, 1996. Stott, Anne. *Hannah More—The First Victorian.* Oxford: Oxford University Press, 2003

Mary T. Furgol

MORO, ALDO (1916–1978). Five times Italy's prime minister, Moro was a leading figure in Italy's **Christian Democracy** during most of the twenty-year period preceding his violent death at the hands of the Marxist-Leninist Red Brigades in 1978. He had a highly self-conscious Catholic view of history, which he defined as an understanding of all human affairs as the mysterious working out of God's love in the world. He is one of the leading examples in the contemporary period of a Catholic intellectual in politics.

Moro was born in Maglie, Lecce. Although Catholic culture in this part of the south had long been in steep decline, his mother's devotion to the church permeated the middle-class Moro family home. A gifted student, he became a leader of Catholic youth groups. At the University of Bari, he studied law and continued to identify strongly with his Catholic faith while seeking an accommodation with Fascism. Such an accommodation was typical for young men of his background during the mid-1930s, when Benito Mussolini's regime stood at the peak of its popularity. Even then, though, Moro remained a Catholic first and foremost. Italian Catholics like him existed in an uneasy relationship with the Fascists, whose never-realized totalitarian vision required church subservience to the state.

From 1939 to 1942, Moro served as the national president of the *Federazione Universitaria Cattolica Italiana* (FUCI), the Italian Catholic University Federation. World War II, during which he was called to military service but saw no action, destroyed his hopes for Fascism. While teaching law at the University of Bari, he began to write articles about the need for Catholics to participate in Italy's reconstruction. At the same time he became active in the newly created Christian Democratic Party.

Married in 1945 and soon the father of a growing family, Moro after the war continued to teach and to write. In scholarly treatises and in articles for the progressive Catholic periodical *Studium,* which Moro also edited from 1946 to 1948, he exhorted the Italians to follow a morally uplifting conception of the law and politics. He spoke unabashedly of the spirit as the true guide in a world where unaided reason had been found wanting.

Moro's *Studium* editorials also chronicled his work as a Christian Democratic delegate to the Constituent Assembly of the Republic, where he distinguished himself as a spokesman for a pluralistic state and social justice. Like many other Catholics of his generation who abominated Fascism and viewed capitalism with suspicion as the primary cause of the Depression and all its attendant political ills, Moro turned to the Left. In so doing, he derived inspiration from **Jacques Maritain,** whose sympathy in *Humanisme intégrale* (1936) for a Marxist-Catholic dialogue served the Catholic Left as a point of departure in their exit from the Fascist era.

Distrustful of the centrist Christian Democratic leader, **Alcide De Gasperi,** Moro joined **Giuseppe Dossetti**'s leftist faction in the party. He never moved as far left as did Dossetti, who thought the Soviet Union a more vital society than the United States. Nevertheless, the public identified Moro with Dossetti's campaign to transform the party from merely an anticommunist force into a catalyst for social justice. De Gasperi's complete triumph in the party drove Dossetti out of politics in 1951 and, at the same time, marginalized Moro.

During the party secretaryship of **Amintore Fanfani** (1954–1959), the increasingly centrist Moro served as minister first of justice and then of public instruction. When Fanfani's centralizing ideas about the office of party secretary alienated influential Christian Democrats, the quiet and unassuming forty-three-year-old Moro seemed like an ideal replacement.

As secretary, Moro tried to mediate the disputes between the party's conservative and progressive factions. Though a very clear thinker and fully capable of saying exactly what he meant, as his early writings attest, he dealt with difficult party issues by camouflaging them in the woolly phrases that became his trademark in politics. The image that he subsequently acquired, as a verbose and dithering machine politician, does not accurately reflect his real skills and accomplishments as a leader in Italy's notoriously difficult democracy. He effectively espoused the cause of *aperturismo,* or the opening to the left, first to the Socialists in the 1960s and then to the Communists in the 1970s.

Throughout his years of power Moro understood the menacing implications of the country's labor unrest, student protest, and political violence. He especially feared the terrorists. By reaching a "historic compromise" with the Communists, he hoped to contain the country's emergency. On the very morning when the Communists would join in supporting the government, March 16, 1978, the Red Brigades abducted him after killing his five-man security guard. They hoped to plunge the government into a revolutionary crisis. Fifty-five days later they carried out their long-threatened death sentence, and ever since, the Moro murder case has generated conspiracy theories on an even more intense and widely believed scale in Italy than has the JFK assassination in the United States.

Bibliography. Drake, Richard. *The Aldo Moro Murder Case.* Cambridge, MA: Harvard University Press, 1995. Moro, Aldo. *Lezioni di filosofia del diritto tenute presso l'università di Bari: Il Diritto (1944–45), lo Stato (1946–47).* Bari, Italy: Cacucci, 1978. Moro, Renato. "La formazione giovanile di Aldo Moro." *Storia contemporanea* 4–5 (October 1983): 803–968.

Richard Drake

MOUNIER, EMMANUEL (1905–1945). The Catholic philosopher of personalism, journalist, and founder of the French monthly *Esprit,* Mounier achieved an advanced degree in philosophy at the Sorbonne in 1928. He undertook an intense study of **Charles Péguy,** the Catholic poet and socialist. Péguy's belief in the importance of putting philosophy into action inspired Mounier to found the journal *Esprit* in 1932. His list of distinguished collaborators included **Jacques Maritain,** Raymond Aron, and Nicholas Berdyaev, a Russian exile. In spite of their considerable diversity of viewpoints, they were all united in their commitment to the philosophy of personalism—Mounier's guiding star.

He set forth his mature reflections on this philosophy in *Personalism* (1950, translated into English in 1952). At the work's outset he identifies contemporary forces in the world tending toward depersonalization. In particular he singles out the advance of technology inasmuch as it tends to alienate persons from each other. In addition, capitalism and Marxism (formidable in France at the time) were anti-personalist insofar as they subordinated the individual person to the demands of production, the profit motive, or the historical process.

The philosophy of personalism he saw as a tract for his times. It centers on the dignity, rights, and needs of the concrete individual human being. It sees each person as a spiritual presence beyond time, space, or consciousness, a moral absolute, in effect, never an instrument. The individual person lives by a hierarchy of values freely chosen and assimilated, and by creative acts develops his or her individuality and vocation. Though embodied in the material world the person can transcend it through a spirit of detachment. The ethical, social, and political policies of a community were to be judged by how well they promote the development of each member. This communitarian dimension belonged to personalism since Mounier maintained that the fundamental drive of the human being is toward communication—not self-knowledge, originality, or individual affirmation. Modern bourgeois individualism is the antithesis of personalism. One must learn to move out of oneself to reach the other in self-giving love.

Mounier envisioned a society that would eliminate the primacy of the profit motive, uphold the priority of labor over capital and personal responsibility over organization, nurture cooperative endeavors, and further some socialization of industry. But at the end of his life, chastened by experience, he came to embrace a practical agnosticism as to which economic structure might be best suited to advance the personalist kingdom of God.

Esprit soon caught on among the French intellectuals who appreciated the novelty of a Catholic-dominated journal on the Left. It was fully involved in the great public debates over communism and fascism. With the outbreak of war and Nazi occupation, Mounier continued to publish *Esprit* with the permission of **Philippe Pétain**'s Vichy regime, and he even took part in its program of reeducating French youth. But his personalist approach did not fit well with the regime's ideology, and he was removed from the post and *Esprit* was banned. He was later arrested on suspicion of involvement in the Resistance and released for lack of evidence after he undertook a hunger strike. After the war, Mounier's efforts for a rapprochement with Marxism were rebuffed by Marxists suspicious of Catholics, while he in turn accused them of being impervious to new ideas. In the final analysis, Emmanuel Mounier stands as a herald of Pope **John XXIII**'s open church, a Catholic who assumed the nearly impossible task of uniting left-wing political activists and devout religious believers.

Bibliography. Bokenkotter, Thomas. *Church and Revolution.* New York: Doubleday, 1998. Mounier, Emmanuel. *Personalism.* Notre Dame, IN: University of Notre Dame Press, 1952.

Thomas Bokenkotter

MOUSKOS, MICHAEL [MAKARIOS III] (1913–1977). Mouskos, as Archbishop Makarios III of Cyprus (1950–1977), was the first president of the Cypriot Republic (1960–1977) and ethnarch. Makarios is arguably the most significant Cypriot political personality to emerge in the long history of the island. Educated in theology at the University of Athens, he was, for a time, a graduate student of theology in the United States. In 1938, the Cypriot Synod anointed Makarios a deacon of the Greek Orthodox Church. In 1950, he was elected archbishop of Cyprus.

As the spiritual leader of the Greek Cypriot community, Makarios represented the will of the overwhelming majority of people on the island. In 1950, Cyprus was a colony of the United Kingdom under the administration of a British-appointed governor. Roughly 80 percent of the island's inhabitants were ethnically Greek, the other 20 percent ethnically Turkish. The political goal of the Greek Cypriot community in the early postwar years was *enosis,* or Union, with the state of Greece.

As archbishop, Makarios campaigned incessantly to bring the Cyprus problem to the attention of the United Nations, emphasizing the right of all peoples to national self-determination. When the British proved unwilling to grant this right, Makarios surreptitiously authorized the use of force and organized the National Organization of Cypriot Fighters (the EOKA) under the command of Greek army colonel George Grivas. Escalating violence and political instability finally forced the British to grant Cyprus independence in August of 1960, and Makarios was elected the first president of the Cypriot Republic in a landslide victory.

The constitutional organization of the new Cypriot state was unique. Ethnic lines determined the division of power, with Greek Cypriots controlling the presidency and the majority of seats in Parliament, and Turkish Cypriots controlling the vice presidency and enjoying broad rights of veto. More significantly, three outside powers, according to the terms of the independence treaty, guaranteed the constitutional stability of the new state: Great Britain, Greece, and Turkey. Despite these innovations, it was obvious from the beginning that the Turkish Cypriot minority was not satisfied with its political status, apparently fearing that Makarios would still try to force enosis with Greece. In strictly functional terms, the Cypriot political system was defunct from its inception.

Makarios, nevertheless, tried to make the new state work and all but disavowed his aspirations for enosis. Few, however, were satisfied with the status quo. On the Turkish side, the insecurity of the Turkish Cypriot community eventually translated into a desire for double enosis, or the permanent division of the island between Greece and Turkey, a position that Turkey supported vigorously.

In 1967, a faction of the Greek military overthrew the democratically elected government of Greece and instituted a dictatorship. Gradually, the new Greek regime revived the idea of *enosis,* inspired by the dissatisfaction of many Greek Cypriots with the untenable situation on the island. By the early 1970s, these dissatisfied elements were logistically supported by the Greek dictatorship with both arms and money and coalesced under the leadership of Grivas, a convinced Unionist and hence an outright enemy of Makarios. Grivas proceeded to create a new organization, EOKA-B, to oppose the Makarios regime through violence.

Despite the death of Grivas in January 1974, the violence escalated. On July 15, 1974, an emboldened Greek government, motivated by the prospect of forcing immediate enosis, instigated a coup against Makarios by conspiring with EOKA-B and renegade units of Makarios's own Cypriot National Guard. Makarios fled for his life, and the government of Cyprus fell into the hands of Nick Sampson, Grivas's heir apparent. On July 20, Turkey, citing its status as guarantor power, invaded the island with overwhelming force, the ostensible purpose of the invasion to restore the constitutional order and protect the rights and lives of the Turkish Cypriot minority. In a series of successive offensives, Turkish forces seized 36 percent of the total territory of the island, a fact that led inevitably to a brutal population exchange between the Greek- and Turkish-controlled sectors of the island.

In December of 1974, Makarios returned from exile to his rightful position as president of Cyprus. His repeated attempts to engage the Turkish Cypriots in a dialogue to resolve the impasse proved fruitless, and the island remained divided into two armed camps. Archbishop Makarios died in 1977, as the president of a divided republic.

Bibliography. Mayes, Stanley. *Makarios: A Biography.* New York: St. Martin's Press, 1981. Vanezis, P.N. *Makarios: Pragmatism v. Idealism.* London: Abelard-Schuman, 1974.

Kyriakos Nalmpantis

MOUVEMENT REPUBLICAIN POPULAIRE. *See* Popular Republican Movement

MUMFORD, CATHERINE. *See* Booth, William and Catherine Mumford

MURRI, ROMOLO (1870–1944). A Catholic political activist, Murri was born in Italy's Marche region. After high school, he moved to Rome and earned a degree in theology at the Gregorian University. He was ordained a priest in February 1893, but that same year he began to take university courses from the Marxist philosopher Antonio Labriola. This experience pushed Murri into cultural and political activism.

During this period, Murri wrote in *La Vita Nuova*, a Roman journal of sociology. Murri hoped that the church would reassume its mission as a social guide through a new political party of Christian inspiration. Between 1897 and 1899, his thoughts show a marked evolution: he took a position at the Irish College of Rome and thus had the occasion to expand his knowledge with new cultural experiences. At this time, he also founded a new journal, *Cultura sociale*, in which he focused on two themes: the culture of the clergy and Italian political life. According to Murri, it was necessary to study the Socialist Party's organizational structure as an example of leadership from below with rules not imposed from above.

Murri imagined a Catholic party that would operate in the same manner but that would oppose the Socialists. He then founded numerous journals and promoted a library and some editorial groups, as well as the *Società Italiana di Cultura* (Italian Cultural Society). In 1900, Murri founded the first group of Christian Democrats in Italy; this group would officially take the Christian Democrat name at the Catholic Congress of Rome in 1900. For the next three years, Murri's *Democrazia Cristiana* developed throughout Italy, breaking the tradition of Catholic organizations not participating in politics. Pope **Leo XIII** responded to the *Democrazia Cristiana* with an encyclical, *Graves de communi,* which stated that the *Democrazia Cristiana* should only participate in social activities and avoid any political action.

In 1902, Murri received his first condemnation from the cardinal-vicar of Rome. A few years later, he intervened in the political debates that critiqued the Catholic movement and invited the Socialist leader Filippo Turati to think about possible alliances between Socialists and Catholics. In 1905, Murri founded the National Democratic League, a nondenominational party of Catholic inspiration. Murri acknowledged the religious authority of the church but affirmed its incompetence in nonreligious matters. After this declaration, Murri was forced to close *Cultura sociale* and received various warnings and censures until he was suspended *a divinis* in 1907. During this period, the Italian was in the middle of the crisis of modernism, which Pope **Pius X** condemned with his encyclical *Pascendi.* Even though Murri had declared himself independent of and even contrary to certain modernist positions, he too was condemned.

Murri was excommunicated in 1909 and forced to distance himself from Catholicism because of the Socialist and radical support that he received while a parliamentary candidate for the National Democratic League. The members of the league feared that Murri's presence would make it seem modernist even though the league itself was only a political group. The definitive break between Murri and the National Democratic League occurred in 1911. The next year Murri distanced himself completely from the church when in Rome he married the daughter of the president of the Norwegian Senate. While serving in Parliament, Murri joined the radical group and believed in the positive role of anticlericalism and was convinced of the necessity of a nonclerical Christianity. Disappointed in the church, Murri believed that the state could promote the civil renewal of society.

Murri was not reelected to Parliament in 1913 because of Catholic hostility. In 1915 he announced that he was in favor of Italy's entry into World War I, but in later years he dedicated himself, above all, to religious reflection. After various unofficial meetings with Vatican representatives, Murri was welcomed back to the Catholic Church in 1943. Murri's death in 1944 prevented his participation in the new *Democrazia Cristiana* (**Christian Democracy**), which assumed the name and initiatives of the group he founded.

Bibliography. Fontana, S. *Romolo Murri nella Storia politica e religiosa del suo tempo.* Rome: Cinque Lune, 1977. Guasco, M. *Il caso Murri dalla sospensione alla scomunica.* Urbino, Italy: Argalia, 1978. Guasco, M. *Romolo Murri e il modernismo.* Rome: Cinque Lune, 1968. Zoppi, S. *Dalla Rerum Novarum alla Democrazia Cristiana di Murri.* Bologna, Italy: Il Mulino, 1991.

Eliana Versace

N

NASH, WALTER (1882–1968). Nash was a leading figure in New Zealand politics for forty years. A Christian socialist, he was finance minister in the activist first Labour government (1935–1949) and later served three years as prime minister. Nash was born in Kidderminster, England, and as a young man worked for some years at Selly Oak, Birmingham. Here he was influenced by such Anglican socialists as **Charles Gore.** However, it was not until he immigrated to New Zealand in 1909 that Nash was confirmed and joined the Church of England Men's Society. He remained a member of this group throughout his life. Rarely interested in theological niceties, Nash regarded socialism as "applied Christianity" and applied a strong moral tone to his economic policies.

Nash joined the fledgling New Zealand Labour Party, entering the national executive in 1919. A relative moderate within the Labour Party, he took a particular interest in economic and international issues. He was elected to Parliament in 1929, representing the Hutt Valley, near Wellington, a seat he would hold until his death. In 1935 the Labour Party won a landslide election with a clear post-Depression mandate for change. Nash, as minister of finance, was a leading figure in the introduction of a social security system of targeted benefits, public works, and state housing. This moderate socialism remained a feature of New Zealand life for half a century. Given New Zealand's dependence on trade, Nash's twin interests in the economy and international affairs proved a strong combination. He spent considerable time on overseas missions, once spending sixteen straight months as a resident minister in the United States. Along with Prime Minister Peter Fraser, he supported the United Nations and was involved in the Bretton Woods Conference, which set up the International Monetary Fund.

With the eventual defeat of the Labour government in 1949 and the death soon after of Fraser, Nash became leader of the party. He found opposition difficult, responding poorly to the crucial 1951 waterfront dispute and becoming frustrated at the lack of a positive role. His chance came again with electoral success in 1957. Prime minister at seventy-five, Nash worked energetically (again, frequently overseas), but the issues were changing. Nash found himself out of step with some supporters over sporting contacts with South Africa. A currency crisis in 1958 led to an austere and hugely unpopular Black Budget, from which the government never recovered. Labour was defeated in 1960. Nash held on as leader but eventually bowed to pressure and resigned in 1963. He continued as a member of Parliament and was active in such causes as opposition to the Vietnam War.

Walter Nash was often pompous and could appear arrogant. This led to charges of hypocrisy. Yet the authenticity of his faith and its key role in his political motivation was never in doubt. In his last years he read the works of Teilhard de Chardin with approval. In a note to himself he once wrote, "A Christian does not merely record history—he makes it."

Bibliography. Oliver, William, and Claudia Orange, eds. *Dictionary of New Zealand Biography.* 5 vols. Auckland, NZ: Auckland University Press/Bridget Williams Books, 1990–2000. Sinclair, Keith. *Walter Nash.* Auckland, NZ: Auckland University Press, 1976.

Martin Sutherland

NATIONAL ACTION PARTY (MEXICO). Manuel Gómez Morín founded the *Partido Acción Nacional* (PAN) in 1939 to be an independent party promoting reform and a democratic political system. Gómez Morín opposed the existence of an "official" party, the Party of the Mexican Revolution (PRM), which later became the Party of the Institutionalized Revolution (PRI). Catholic activists, middle-class professionals, and entrepreneurs joined the new party. All felt alienated by the corporatist policies of the revolutionary regime and, particularly, the policies of President Lázaro Cárdenas (1934–1940), which privileged peasants and workers and incorporated socialist ideas into education.

Efraín González Luna, often called the second founder of the party, formulated PAN doctrine. Solidarity with the poor, subsidiarity, and the role of private enterprise are important to the party ideology, which is strongly influenced by Catholic social doctrine. Nonetheless, the PAN had a secular orientation in its early years. The period from 1949 until 1962 has been labeled one of "confessionalization." Leaders during that period reached political maturity as

Catholic activists, and some considered turning the party into a Christian Democratic party. However, party president (and committed Catholic) Adolfo Christlieb Ibarrola (1962–1968) led the party away from militant Catholicism. Christlieb also advocated electoral reform, which contributed to change in 1963 that allowed for minority representation in the federal Chamber of Deputies. Under his leadership and the influence of the Second Vatican Council, the party also began to promote social justice more strongly.

The party has often been called the "loyal opposition" because it was formed to oppose the PRI but has consistently participated in electoral politics despite fraud and corruption under PRI dominance. Some members disagreed with participation in elections, believing that the party's primary function was to educate the public and to serve as a public voice opposing the official party. This group also argued that participating in a fraudulent electoral system only served to legitimate it. Others, including Gómez Morín, supported electoral participation to publicize their political ideology and to demonstrate their intentions of becoming a significant political force. The participationists have generally prevailed, and the PAN has participated in municipal and federal elections since 1943. It won its first legislative seats in the Chamber of Deputies and its first municipal election in 1946. Despite these relatively early victories, the party's ability to control significant portions of the nation continued to be quite limited.

President José López Portillo enacted electoral reform in 1977 that opened additional political positions to opposition parties, and the PAN's electoral fortunes increased steadily from that time on, especially after the same president unilaterally nationalized the banking system in 1982. At that time, concerned businesspeople shifted their support to the PAN, the leading opposition party. In 1989, the PAN candidate won the governorship of Baja California. This was the first governor's seat not controlled by the PRI since the 1910 revolution. It was followed by more gubernatorial victories, and in 2000, PAN candidate Vicente Fox Quesada won the presidential elections.

Bibliography. Ard, Michael James. "Transforming Great Party Politics: The National Action Party and Its Role in Mexico's Democratic Transition." PhD diss., University of Virginia, 2001. Chand, Vikram K. *Mexico's Political Awakening.* Notre Dame, IN: University of Notre Dame Press, 2001. Loaeza, Soledad. *El Partido Acción Nacional: La larga marcha, 1939–1994.* Mexico City: Fondo de Cultura Económica, 1999. Mizrahi, Yemile. *From Martyrdom to Power: The Partido Acción Nacional in Mexico.* Notre Dame, IN: University of Notre Dame Press, 2003.

Lisa Edwards

NATIONAL AND FEDERAL COUNCIL OF CHURCHES (UNITED STATES). The Federal Council of Churches, and its successor, the National Council of Churches, are expressions of the twentieth century's movement toward organized conciliar ecumenism. Ecumenism captured the imagination of Christians who felt that the divisive, divided nature of the world's churches denied the Bible's injunction that they were made one through Jesus Christ. The term "ecumenism" refers to the movement to draw Christians together in an expression of that inherent unity. One manifestation of this includes helping churches make a joint Christian witness on social, economic, and political issues.

The Federal Council of Churches of Christ in America was formed in 1908 through the efforts of denominations active in promoting the **Social Gospel.** Thirty-three denominations became its first members. It served these churches as an advisory and organizational tool to unite their resources and voices behind issues of mutual concern. Reflecting Social Gospel interests, it focused first on economic

injustices within modern industry. It put the church's moral clout behind the rights of labor and investigated various strikes from 1910 into the 1940s. It championed shortened work hours, condemned child labor, took collections to aid families of striking workers, offered to help mediate disputes, and supported collective bargaining. Conservatives accused the Federal Council of being a communist sympathizer at a time when most Protestants associated unions with communism, immigrants, and Catholicism. However, President Franklin Roosevelt expressed gratitude for its support of his Wagner Act, which recognized unions' bargaining rights.

The Federal Council took a more popular position in its enthusiastic support for the First World War. Its General Wartime Commission in 1917 became a central organizing agency for cooperative Christian efforts to aid the war effort. Its subcommittees helped raise funds, distribute literature, assist the military chaplainry, pass information between government and churches, and plan for postwar peace. After the war, the council shared the nation's disillusionment with it. It advocated joining the League of Nations, creating a World Court, and signing the Pact of Paris (Kellogg-Briand), each of which it hoped would prevent another catastrophic war.

Reflecting popular sentiment, it opposed involvement in World War II until the Japanese attacked Pearl Harbor. It then endeavored to support the Allied fight against totalitarianism while resisting uncritical nationalism. It spoke out for preservation of civil liberties during wartime, including the rights of interned Japanese Americans and the religious freedom of conscientious objectors. It alerted Americans to the Nazi Holocaust in 1942, urging action to stop it and to grant asylum to Jewish refugees. The Federal Council also condemned racism as a violation against humankind's oneness under God. It created a Commission on International

Peace and Goodwill and a committee to study the bases of a just and durable peace. Under the directorship of John Foster Dulles, it crafted six pillars of peace and pressed for the creation of a United Nations. In fact, it helped draw ecumenical leaders into dialogue that helped shape the UN charter, including its commission on human rights.

After the **World Council of Churches** was formed in 1948, the Federal Council was rolled together with several other Christian agencies to create the National Council of Churches of Christ in the United States in 1950. While the National Council's work expanded far beyond the Federal Council's, the Federal Council's activist spirit was carried forward primarily within the National Council's Division of Christian Life and Work. (It would later be renamed the Division of Christian Life and Mission, then Division of Church and Society.)

In the 1950s, the council addressed the domestic issues of segregation, migrant work, and economic ethics. When accused of harboring communist sympathizers, it defended itself while attacking McCarthyite tactics and the suppression of dissent. On international affairs, it condemned the expensive arms race and reliance upon threats of massive retaliation, advocating instead peaceful negotiation to solve crises. In the 1960s, the council stepped more actively into the black freedom movement by participating in the 1963 March on Washington, creating the Delta Ministries in Mississippi, rallying key support for passage of the Civil Rights and Voting Rights Acts, and joining the Selma march. It also extended its migrant ministries to include support for **César Chávez** and striking farm workers.

The NCC's stands on international issues grew increasingly controversial. In 1965, it became one of the nation's first mainstream institutions to take a critical stand on the Vietnam War, a criticism that would sharpen each year. By the late 1960s, it was challenging the presuppositions and morality of the war, appealing for debate and action from laity, and supporting other antiwar groups like Clergy and Laymen Concerned about Vietnam, the Moratorium, Set the Date, and Negotiations Now! These actions, combined with its recommendation that the U.S. government recognize Red China and support its admittance to the United Nations, repelled more conservative laity. So, too, did its seeming tolerance of militant black leaders and support of Supreme Court rulings against prayer in the schools. As White House officials recognized that the council was losing sway with the masses, they ceased to grant it substantive visits to discuss policy. The Nixon administration even responded with harassment from the Internal Revenue Service.

With both its government and grassroots influence on the wane in the early 1970s, the council's budget also fell rapidly, followed by staff and program cuts. These were precipitated by similar cuts within its denominational members. On a steadily shrinking budget, the council continued to work in the 1970s on service projects to aid Vietnam veterans, seek amnesty for draft dodgers, support the American Indian Movement with medical and legal aid, and urge antiapartheid sanctions on South Africa. In the 1980s, it opposed President **Ronald Reagan**'s policies in Latin America and came under new attack from conservative groups. In more recent years, the council provided funds to rebuild burned churches and provide legal assistance to the father of Cuban refugee Elian Gonzales. It has moved increasingly into advocacy of a Christian environmental consciousness, while it continues to unite interfaith groups in efforts for economic justice. It was one of many religious voices that opposed the United States' preemptive war in Iraq in 2003. Clearly, efforts to speak truth to power on issues of peace and justice have connected the long history of the Federal and National Councils of Churches.

Bibliography. Findlay, James F., Jr. *Church People in the Struggle: The National Council of Churches and the Black Freedom Movement 1950–1970.* New York: Oxford University Press, 1993. Fones-Wolf, Elizabeth, and Ken Fones-Wolf. "Lending a Hand to Labor: James Myers and the Federal Council of Churches, 1926–1947." *Church History* 68 (1): 62–86. Gill, Jill K. "Peace Is Not the Absence of War But the Presence of Justice: The National Council of Churches' Reaction and Response to the Vietnam War, 1965–1972." PhD diss., University of Pennsylvania, 1996.

Jill K. Gill

NATIONAL CATHOLIC AGRARIAN FEDERATION [CONFEDERACIÓN NACIONAL-CATÓLICA AGRARIA— CNCA] (SPAIN). Established in 1917, the CNCA established a network of agrarian syndicates, rural savings banks, and cooperatives that spread throughout northern and eastern Spain. Strongly influenced by the Society of Jesus, the CNCA was a paternalist organization, tightly linked to the Jesuit-inspired **National Catholic Association of Propagandists** (ACNP).

Many landowners served on the governing committees of the CNCA, and in some areas, the entire landowning elite would be involved in the organization. Some historians have therefore seen the CNCA as a tool of the rich, and certainly it failed to make any real impact on the landless laborers of the latifundio south. Yet the CNCA was the only real success of social Catholicism, creating a formidable apparatus of agrarian defense among the peasantry of northern Spain. Among peasant proprietors, papal teaching on the sanctity of private property found a receptive audience. A commitment to the ideal that property had a social function found expression in some much-vaunted redistribution schemes. In 1920, 2,506 hectares were purchased by the CNCA in Ciudad Rodrigo and divided among 117 workers to create both a new community of small farms and a burden of debt that persisted for generations.

The CNCA also provided technical help, and the insurance schemes that were essential to survival in regions of long winters and hard frosts. The CNCA's bulletin had very little religious or ideological content but was crammed with technical information and advertisements for fertilizers. Catholic farmers proved remarkably loyal to the confederation, not least because its expertise and facilities enabled them to continue in their traditional way of life. Seasonal credit would not enrich them, but it could easily mean the difference between surviving on the land and uprooting to the cities.

During the Second Republic (1931–1936), this organizational network became a potent force in the creation of the **Spanish Confederation of Autonomous Right-Wing Groups** (CEDA), which mobilized first in the agrarian heartlands of Old Castile. The CNCA thus became part of the Catholic political option of the 1930s, a crucial part of CEDA's social base. During the civil war (1936–1939), the CNCA's heartlands largely coincided with the area held by the military rebels. It survived as an independent organization until 1942 but was gradually incorporated into the bureaucratic apparatus of **Francisco Franco**'s new corporate state.

Bibliography. Castillo, Juan José. *Propietarios muy pobres: Sobre la subordinación política del pequeño campesino.* Madrid: Servicio de Publicaciones Agrarios, 1979. Cuesta, Josefina. *Sindicalismo católico agrario en España, 1917–19.* Madrid: Narcea, 1978. Vincent, Mary. *Catholicism in the Second Spanish Republic: Religion and Politics in Salamanca, 1930–1936.* Oxford: Oxford University Press, 1996.

Mary Vincent

NATIONAL CATHOLIC ASSOCIATION OF PROPAGANDISTS [ASOCIACIÓN CATÓLICA NACIONAL DE PROPAGANDISTAS— ACNP] (SPAIN). The failure to create a modern Catholic political party in Spain under the Restoration (1875–1923) and **Miguel Primo de Rivera**'s dictatorship (1923–1930) encouraged the organization of several elite groups designed to lead the so-called Catholic masses when and if the establishment of such a party seemed possible. Of these groups none was more important than the National Catholic Association of Propagandists (*Asociación Católica Nacional de Propagandistas*). The ACNP's members played a critical role in directing Spanish Catholicism away from the historic divide separating Carlist integrists from those who accepted the necessity of working within the liberal state in existence until 1923. ACNP members were prominent in the organization of the short-lived *Partido Social Popular* in 1922, the first serious attempt among Spanish Catholics to create a modern political party.

Founded in 1909, the *Asociación Católica Nacional de Jóvenes Propagandistas,* as it was known until 1917, arose from the initiative of the Jesuit father Ángel Ayala, who believed that the Spanish Catholics needed to break away from the endemic dynastic quarrels of the past in favor of a modern approach to defending the church's interests within a society where anticlerical currents ran deep and new radical social movements, especially socialism and anarchism, were emerging. Spanish Catholicism, he believed, needed a modern elite of elites to direct the Catholic masses into effective action.

Ayala selected the first eighteen members of the organization from the ranks of a Jesuit religious association in Madrid. Young, talented and university educated, the *propagandistas* began their activities by participating in a series of distinctly modern public relations campaigns similar to those used by the political parties of the day. Although their objectives were not directly political at this time, the *propagandistas* urged Spanish Catholics to unify and modernize their organizational efforts. They supported, for example, the foundation of Catholic trade unions and Catholic agrarian syndicates. The *propagandistas* were, however, never numerous. The original eighteen grew to 145 by the mid-1920s and later under the Franco regime to about 500.

The key figure in the association's development was a young lawyer, **Ángel Herrera Oria** (1886–1968), who served as president between 1909 and 1935. In 1911, Herrera and a group of supporters acquired the Madrid daily, *El Debate,* which became for all practical purposes the vehicle for expressing the views of the *propagandistas.* Indeed, the ACNP's offices were located in the same building as the newspaper. The principal political objective of Herrera and the association between 1911 and 1930 was to prepare the way for the organization of a modern Catholic party, a goal blocked by the dominance of the Liberal and Conservative parties until 1923 and by the Primo de Rivera dictatorship until 1930, although Herrera and the ACNP sympathized with the regime's policies, albeit with some reservations.

The proclamation of the republic (1931) removed this block to political action. Herrera and the ACNP lay behind the organization of a new Catholic party, Acción Popular. Although it did poorly in the parliamentary elections of 1931, the AP's formation stimulated a two-year period of intense organizational activity in which ACNP members played a prominent role. Both at the national and local levels, the leadership of the AP and the ACNP were virtually interchangeable. The success of these organizing initiatives between 1931 and 1933 contributed to the establishment of the only mass Catholic party ever to have existed in Spain, the **Confederación Española de Derechas Autónomas (CEDA***)*, which became the largest party in parliament following the November 1933 elections. *Propagandistas* were prominent in the CEDA, but their influence was limited by the party's heterogeneous character. It was less a unified party than an alliance of right-wing Catholic groups with often contradictory opinions on policy. Whatever unity the CEDA possessed came from the determination of its constituent parts to undo much of the republic's legislation on such issues as education and social reform.

Herrera's decision to resign as editor of *El Debate* and from the ACNP in 1935 marked a certain decline of the organization's influence. The years of the civil war (1936–1939) saw it erode further, in part because **Francisco Franco**'s regime proved unsympathetic to an organization that had been willing to accept the republic, albeit with some ambiguity. The dictatorship refused, for example, to allow *El Debate* to reappear in spite of strenuous efforts by its supporters, many of them *propagandistas*. ACNP members occupied official positions under Franco and at various times attempted with little success to promote limited reform within the dictatorship. The organization became a lobby among many competing right-wing interest groups jostling for influence around the general. The original idea of an elite of elites preparing the Catholic masses for political action fell by the wayside.

Bibliography. Montero, Mercedes. *Historia de la Asociación Católica Nacional de Propagandistas: La construcción del Estado Confesional, 1936–1945.* Pamplona, Spain: Ediciones Universidad de Navarra, 1993. Ordovas, José Manuel. *Historia de la Asociación Católica Nacional de Propagandistas: De la Dictadura a la Segunda República, 1923–1936.* Pamplona, Spain: Ediciones Universidad de Navarra, 1993.

William J. Callahan

NATIONAL CATHOLIC LABOR CONFEDERATION [CONFEDERACIÓN NACIONAL CATÓLICA DEL TRABAJO— CNCT] (MEXICO). Late nineteenth-century Mexican Catholic activists, stimulated by

Pope **Leo XIII**'s *Rerum novarum,* began organizing among workers to counteract both the negative effects of capitalism and the anarchist, socialist, and communist movements that resulted. Catholic workers' circles were principally pious in nature and often included employers and supervisors, complying with church teachings opposing class warfare and encouraging cooperation. However, they also discussed working conditions and workers' rights and founded mutual aid societies, schools, libraries, and other facilities. Initially centered in specific parishes or factories, these circles began forming larger associations, such as the *Unión Católica de Obreros* (UCO, Catholic Worker's Union, 1907), which first proposed unionization in 1911. At the Second Diet of Zamora (1913), Alfredo Méndez Medina, SJ, presented ideas from European Catholic unions and committed to build a confederation.

Mexico's armed revolution (1910–1917) halted this organization, but it reemerged where it had been strongest, in central-western Mexico; thus, the Mexican Episcopate made Guadalajara the center of post-revolutionary Catholic worker organization. At the 1919 Guadalajara Regional Workers' Congress, representatives formed the Archdiocesan Confederation of Catholic Workers' Associations, which contacted workers' circles elsewhere to convoke assemblies. In 1920, the nationwide *Confederación Católica del Trabajo* (Catholic Worker's Confederation, CCT) was formed under the motto Justice and Charity.

Later that year, the Mexican Episcopate established the *Secretariado Social Mexicano* (**Mexican Social Secretariat**) in Mexico City, which supported Catholic labor organizing. As SSM director, Méndez Medina monitored Catholic worker and social organizations nationwide. Mexican Catholics also witnessed the growing strength and militancy of radical and state-affiliated workers' organizations like the

Confederación General de Trabajo (CGT, General Confederation of Workers) and the *Confederación Regional de Obreros Mexicanos* (CROM, Regional Confederation of Mexican Workers).

The CCT responded to Guadalajara locals' calls to organize a national Catholic workers' congress, which met in Guadalajara in October 1921 and in April 1922. At the 1921 congress, workers complained that even Catholic employers suppressed confessional workers' organizations, and they appealed to ecclesiastical leaders for a vehicle for stronger advocacy. Father José Toral Moreno brought the idea to the Mexican Episcopate, which approved the formation of a union. Representatives at the 1922 meeting formed the Confederación Nacional Catolica del Trabajo using the CCT's motto and emblem, but as an organization for workers only, recognizing their freedom to choose among unions, demands for better working conditions, and rights to negotiate and strike.

In 1922, the CNCT had about eighty thousand members; in contrast, the CROM had approximately 400,000 members, and the CGT about 15,000. The CNCT gained some ground in central and eastern Mexico and was favored by business associations like the *Cámara Nacional de Comercio de México* (National Chamber of Commerce) for its emphasis on cooperation. Anticlericals in and outside government attacked the CNCT, identifying it, like the church as a whole, as competition, and threatening to the Mexican state and social progress. Conflicts also erupted among workers as unions competed for membership and closed shops.

Catholics mobilized to resist the anticlerical legislation promoted by President Plutarco Elias Calles (1924–1928) in 1926, some calling for armed as well as peaceful resistance. CNCT membership fed into the *Unión Popular* (Popular Union), one of the key military organizations of the **Cristero** Rebellion (1926–1929). As part of the 1929 truce, ecclesiastical leaders promised that Catholics would obey governing laws. The Federal Labor Law of 1931 prohibited confessional unions and criminalized religious proselytization in workplaces.

Formal unionization of Catholic workers ceased, although the Acción Católica Mexicana (ACM, **Mexican Catholic Action**) sponsored workers' prayer, catechism, and other educational associations, in response to continuing radical organization and the ever-closer relations between the government and secular confederations like the CROM and the *Confederación de Trabajadores Mexicanos* (Confederation of Mexican Workers, CTM). A new generation of Catholic activists emerged with the relaxation of church-state tensions. The CNCT reemerged in Mexico City in the late 1930s, appealing to workers who, though pressured to join official unions, wished to meet in cooperative societies as Catholics. The SSM supported the nonsyndical CNCT, which continued as a "specialized" branch of the ACM until new worker organizations were created in the 1960s.

Bibliography. Adame Goddard, Jorge. *El pensamiento político y social de los católicos mexicanos, 1867–1914* Mexico City: Universidad Nacional Autónoma de México, 1981. Arrom, Silvia Marina. *The Women of Mexico City, 1790–1857.* Stanford, CA: Stanford University Press, 1985. Barquin y Ruíz, Andres. *Bernardo Bergöend, SJ.* Mexico City: Editorial Jus, 1968. Comisión de Formación de la Junta Nacional de la ACM. *La Acción Católica Mexicana Hoy* Mexico City: Junta Nacional de la ACM, 1993. Comisión Permanente de la Sexta Asamblea General de la CNCT, "Circular Núm. 2." Broadside. Mexico City, 5 February 1939. Curley, Robert. "Los laicos, la Democracia Cristiana y la Revolución mexicana, 1911–1926." *Signos históricos* 7 (January–June 2002): 149–70. Escontrilla Valdez, Hugo Armando. "El Secretariado Social Mexicano: Los orígenes de la autonomía, 1965–1973." MA thesis, Institución de Investigaciones Dr. Jose Maria Luis Mora, 2000. Lynch, John. "The Catholic Church in

Latin America, 1830–1930." In *The Cambridge History of Latin America,* ed. Leslie Bethell. Cambridge: Cambridge University Press, 1986. "La Unión de Damas Católicas Mexicanas en el XX Aniversario de su Fundación: 12 de septiembre de 1912." *Acción Femenina* 1 (1): 1–7. Ramírez, Manuel Ceballos. *El catolicismo social: Un tercero en discordia.* Mexico City: El Colegio de México, 1991. Ramírez, Manuel Ceballos. "El sindicalismo católico, 1919–1931." *Historia Mexicana* 35 (4): 621–73. Ramírez, Manuel Ceballos. "La encíclica *Rerum Novarum* y los trabajadores católicos en la ciudad de México (1891–1913)." *Historia Mexicana* 33 (1): 3–38. Velázquez, Manuel H. *El Primer Congreso Nacional Obrero en México.* Mexico City: Secretariado Social Mexicano, Sección CNCT, 1947.

Kristina A. Boylan

NATIONAL CATHOLIC PARTY [PARTIDO CATÓLICO NACIONAL—PCN] (MEXICO).

In 1870, Mexico's Liberal government banned conservative and Catholic political organizations because of their opposition in the Reform Wars and support for the French occupation and imperial rule of Mexico in the previous two decades. Inspired by papal encyclicals such as *Rerum novarum* (1891) and European Catholic associations, *fin de siècle* Mexican Catholics organized to counter political divisions, socioeconomic inequalities, and challenges to the church's social and moral authority. In 1904, members of the *Obra de Congresos Católicos* (Organization of Catholic Congresses) and the *Círculo Católico Poblano* (People's Catholic Circle) unsuccessfully approached President Porfirio Díaz (1876–1880, 1884–1911), proposing to form a moderate Catholic party.

The agenda of the Fourth Mexican Catholic Congress (1909) included another such proposal, but skeptical participants redirected the discussion to indigenous issues. The *Operarios Guadalupanos* (Guadalupan Workers, a Catholic labor association), however, sustained the idea and formed the *Unión Político-Social de los*

Catolicos Mexicanos (UPSCM, Social-Political Union of Mexican Catholics). Meanwhile, Mexico City lawyer Gabriel Fernández Somellera organized professionals into the *Círculo Católico Nacional* (CCN, National Catholic Circle). Though most members had not participated in the congresses, labor organizing, or charitable associations of the past decades, the CCN approached these groups proposing to form a political confederation to introduce religious influence into government as an alternative to abstaining and allowing radicals to dominate, or opting for rebellion.

In the 1910 electoral campaigns, some Catholics supported the National Porfirian Party and with it the status quo of the regime, which benefited socioeconomic elites and courted church leadership (albeit without reversing Liberal anticlerical laws). Though his religious and political inclinations seemed unorthodox, other Catholics supported Diaz's opponent Francisco I. Madero, a Coahuila businessman and lawyer who proposed political reform while not espousing anticlericalism. Díaz declared his own victory in the June elections. Fearing that Díaz might manipulate the forming of a Catholic party, archbishop of Mexico José Mora y del Río urged the CCN, the UPSCM, and other associations to convene.

In May 1911, Díaz resigned and left Mexico as Madero's movement grew stronger. At the concurrent convention, where the PCN was established formally and Fernández Somellera was elected its president, the central and contentious debate was whether to support Madero or Francisco León de la Barra, whom Díaz had designated interim president. The PCN supported Francisco I. Madero in the August 1911 elections, although his substitution of liberal Justo Pino Suárez as vice presidential candidate for León de la Barra widened the rift between progressives and conservatives. The PCN proved more capable of coordinating Catholics at the local and regional level, in great part by using the *Operarios Guadalupanos*' centers as campaign headquarters. Under its motto of God, Country, and Liberty, PCN candidates won four state governorships, several mayoralties of state capitals and key cities, and numerous municipal presidencies.

Initially, the PCN's strength indicated that it might endure in Mexico, but other Catholic leaders manifested their disapproval of the Madero government, and divisions within the party and the broader Catholic community combined to weaken it. General Victoriano Huerta dismissed PCN representatives and exiled Hernández Somellera when his 1913 coup d'état dissolved the Mexican Congress, but the indictment of Catholic involvement with and support of Huerta (some PCN politicians participated in the new government, like Eduardo Tamariz, Huerta's secretary of fine arts and education) followed Catholics thereafter and discredited their claims to be working patriotically for Mexico. Revolutionaries codified their distrust of Catholic political organizing in the constitution of 1917, Article 130 of which prohibits religiously oriented political parties.

Bibliography. Ceballos Ramírez, Manuel. *El catolicismo social: Un tercero en discordia.* Mexico City: El Colegio de México, 1991. "Documentación civil: Disposiciones Civiles que Atañen a los Católicos y que es muy Conveniente Conozcan y Recuerden los Eclesiásticos." *Christus* 1: (1): 37–41. Knight, Alan S. *The Mexican Revolution.* 2 vols. Cambridge: Cambridge University Press, 1986. MacGregor Gárate, Josefina. "Anticlericalismo constitucionalista." In *Relaciones Estado-Iglesia: Encuentros y Desencuentros,* ed. Patricia Galeana. Mexico City: Secretaría de Gobernación, 2001. *Mexicano: Esta es tu Constitución.* Mexico City: Cámara de Diputados del H. Congreso de la Unión, XLVII Legislatura, 1968. Schmitt, Karl. "Catholic Adjustment to the Secular State: The Case of Mexico, 1867–1911." *Catholic Historical Review* 48: (2): 182–204.

Kristina A. Boylan

NATIONAL CATHOLIC WAR/WELFARE CONFERENCE. The National Catholic Welfare Conference (NCWC) was organized initially as the National Catholic War Council in 1918. The NCWC replaced the War Council in 1919, and Father John Burke, CSP, was selected as general secretary. This new organization was designed to coordinate the church's national activities and to provide a forum for collective statements and action by the bishops. The NCWC remained in existence until 1966, when, following changes mandated by the Second Vatican Council, it was replaced by the National Conference of Catholic Bishops (NCCB) and the United States Catholic Conference (USCC). In 2001, the NCCB and NCWC were combined into the United States Conference of Catholic Bishops.

With the entry of the United States into World War I, the American Catholic hierarchy established the War Council in Washington, D.C., to coordinate church-supported services and relief efforts. Cardinal Gibbons of Baltimore had given his assurances to President **Woodrow Wilson** that Catholic resources would be mobilized in support of the war effort. The War Council was designed to accomplish this task and also to promote patriotism among American Catholics.

Prior to the NCWC, the church had no overarching national body. The bishops acted collectively only rarely, meeting together thirteen times between 1789 and 1919. Growth in the church's size and breadth of activity, along with the increasingly national focus of American life, made it necessary to establish institutional structures beyond the confines of the diocese.

The NCWC contained seven departments: Education, Press, Social Action, Legal, the National Council of Catholic Men, the National Council of Catholic Women, and Immigration and Youth. The most important and controversial of these was Social Action. This department was established to promote the teachings in Pope **Leo XIII**'s 1891 labor encyclical, *Rerum novarum,* and it quickly became the center of progressive Catholic thought on social and labor questions. Under the leadership of Rev. **John A. Ryan** (1920–1945), a professor at Catholic University, and his assistant, Rev. Raymond McGowan, the Social Action Department involved the church in debates about labor, industry, race, international affairs, rural life, and Communism. In 1919, the NCWC released the "Bishops' Program of Social Reconstruction," the church's first major statement on economics and social justice. Written by Ryan, the document gave the church's support to such ideas as the abolition of child labor, universal vocational training, a legal minimum wage, labor participation in management, insurance against unemployment and sickness, protection of the right to organize, public housing, and progressive taxation. Following Ryan's death, direction of the Social Action Department passed to McGowan (1945–1954) and then to Monsignor George Higgins (1954–1967). Until it was closed in 1968, the department remained at the center of progressive Catholic social action.

Bibliography. Slawson, Douglas J. *The Foundation and First Decade of the National Catholic Welfare Council.* Washington, DC: Catholic University of America Press, 1992. Williams, Michael. *American Catholics in the War: National Catholic War Council, 1917–1921.* New York: Macmillan, 1921.

Zachary R. Calo

NATIONAL COUNCIL OF CHURCHES IN THE PHILIPPINES. The National Council of Churches in the Philippines (NCCP) was organized in 1963 by the leaders of seven Protestant denominations to engender unity in preaching the Gospel. Today the NCCP comprises eleven member churches and ten affiliate organizations and, in addition to a national headquarters in Quezon City, has several regional offices. Although Protestants are a minority in the Philippines, representing approximately 9 percent of the population, within a decade after its founding the NCCP moved into national prominence for, first, its advocacy for the poor and oppressed and, second, its criticism of oppressive policies of the martial law regime of President Ferdinand E. Marcos.

Despite a military raid on the NCCP headquarters in 1974, resulting in the arrest of foreign missionaries and Filipino church leaders, the NCCP regularly issued statements against martial law abuses and established organizations for people's empowerment. The NCCP focused on grassroots participation and stimulating local initiative and offered a number of programs through its Commission on Development and Social Concerns. The NCCP also fostered programs to assist political prisoners and others abused by the Marcos regime. With the termination of martial law in 1981 and the ouster of President Marcos in 1986, the NCCP continued to speak out on political issues, worked with Catholic religious leaders to reestablish democracy, and expanded programs into new areas.

Throughout the late 1980s and 1990s, the NCCP denounced the attempted military coups against the government of President **Corazon Aquino,** opposed the extension of U.S.-Philippines military base agreements, and criticized the routine detention of political prisoners. The National Council worked to facilitate negotiated ends to the Muslim-Christian conflict in Mindanao and to the hostilities between the government and the Communist Party of the Philippines. The NCCP also established a number of new initiatives that focus on voter education, women's issues, environmental degradation, and the impact of globalization.

The NCCP remains an active voice in Philippine political, social, and religious life. The National Council regularly issues statements on a variety of issues that range from asking President Joseph Estrada to resign to opposition to the 2003 war in Iraq. The NCCP publishes a quarterly periodical, the *NCCP Newsmagazine,* an ecumenical journal titled *Tugon,* and other books, pamphlets, and papers dealing with issues of concern to Protestants.

Bibliography. Gowing, Peter G. *Islands under the Cross: The Story of the Church in the Philippines.* Manila, Philippines: National Council of Churches in the Philippines, 1967. Kwantes, Anne C., ed. *Chapters in Philippine Church History.* Manila, Philippines: OMF Literature, 2001. National Council of Churches in the Philippines. www.daga.dhs.org/nccp. Suarez, Oscar. *Protestantism and Authoritarian Politics: The Politics of Repression and the Future of Ecumenical Witness in the Philippines.* Quezon City, Philippines: New Day Publishers, 1999.

Robert L. Youngblood

NAUMANN, FRIEDRICH (1860–1919). Naumann blazed the trail in Germany for efforts to synthesize liberal Protestantism with political activism. The son of a Lutheran pastor, he studied theology at the universities of Leipzig and Erlangen, was ordained in 1886, and soon devoted himself to social work for the Inner Mission of the Evangelical Church in Frankfurt. He read the socialist classics and struggled in his first writings to articulate a vision of the kingdom of God, which Christians must strive to create on earth, as an alternative to the Marxist vision of the ideal future society.

Naumann also participated in the Evangelical Social Congress, founded in 1890, which brought together pastors, academics, and civil servants to discuss social problems. Most Lutheran theologians continued, however, to deny that any political or social program could be derived from the Bible, and in 1895 Kaiser Wilhelm II became so alarmed by the growth of Social Democracy that he issued strict orders as head of the Evangelical Church of Prussia that pastors should preach reverence for the existing social and political order. Dismayed by the near-universal compliance with these instructions, Naumann resigned from the pastorate in 1896 to devote himself to politics.

Naumann's first political initiative was the National Social League, designed to win workers away from Social Democracy by synthesizing enthusiastic support for trade unionism with patriotic values. The league caused furor within the Evangelical Workers' Clubs, where paternalistic employers exerted much influence, by urging all members to join a socialist trade union if they could not find an effective nonsocialist alternative. Naumann also urged workers to embrace the monarchy, however, and support the kaiser's quest for an overseas colonial empire as vital to the future prosperity of the nation. Many of his arguments were echoed by the Revisionist socialists, but Naumann underestimated the bonds that held the different factions of the Social Democratic Party together. In 1903 he dissolved the league and took up the more promising task of promoting coalescence among Germany's three rival parties of liberal democrats.

Naumann developed a penetrating analysis of the historic mistakes of liberals under Bismarck that had alienated workers and brought the rival groups together in 1910 in the Progressive People's Party, which supported British-style parliamentary government and expanded welfare programs. This party broke a major taboo in German politics by cooperating with the Social Democrats in the parliamentary elections of 1912. Naumann also cultivated ties with leaders of the left wing of the Catholic **Center Party,** and during the First World War he promoted ever-closer cooperation among Social, liberal, and Catholic democrats, laying the foundation for the coalition that founded the Weimar Republic in 1919. Naumann played a pivotal role in drafting the Weimar constitution and sought to anchor in it his ideas for transforming workers from the "subjects" of all-powerful management into "citizens" of industrial democracy. His sudden death shortly after his election as chair of the new German Democratic Party in July 1919 was a heavy blow to Germany's fledgling democracy.

Bibliography. Heuss, Theodor. *Friedrich Naumann: Der Mann, das Werk, die Zeit.* 2nd ed. Tübingen, Germany: 1948. Vom Bruch, Rüdiger, ed. *Friedrich Naumann in seiner Zeit.* Berlin: De Gruyter, 2000.

William Patch

NCUBE, PIUS (b. 1946). Ncube, the Catholic archbishop of Bulawayo, in Zimbabwe, from 1997 was the first and most outspoken member of the Catholic hierarchy in Zimbabwe to criticize the policy of farm invasions and associated political violence of president and fellow Catholic Robert Gabriel Mugabe and his ruling Zimbabwe African National Union-Patriotic Front (ZANU-PF). Because of his constant and unwavering opposition to Mugabe's policies, Ncube has endured constant harassment from the government's Central Intelligence Organization (CIO), including several death threats.

Pius Ncube was born in Gwanda, approximately 130 kilometers southeast of Bulawayo. He received his primary education at St. Patrick's School in Bulawayo and converted to Catholicism when he was fourteen years old. He attended the minor seminary in Gwelo (now Gweru) run by the Swiss Bethlehem Missionaries from 1963 to 1966, and the Major Seminary of Sts. Peter and Paul at Chishawasha under the Jesuits from 1967 to 1973, when he was ordained for the Catholic Archdiocese of Bulawayo.

During Zimbabwe's liberation war (1972–1979), Ncube was stationed at St. Joseph's Mission in Matopos District, approximately 170 kilometers south of Bulawayo, and later at Empandeni Mission, the oldest Catholic mission station in

Zimbabwe. At both mission stations he came into contact with and supported African nationalist guerrillas fighting against the Rhodesian Front regime of Ian Smith. Following Zimbabwe's independence in 1980, Ncube was among the first to help collect victim statements and disseminate information when the Zimbabwean army committed politically motivated atrocities in which several thousand people were killed across Matebeleland and the Midlands during the 1980s.

In 1997, Pope **John Paul II** appointed Ncube as the first African archbishop of Bulawayo. Following the defeat of the constitutional referendum of February 2000, Mugabe authorized the invasion of white-owned commercial farms by so-called liberation war veterans, who not only occupied the land but also violently intimidated the African farm workers as well as residents in rural areas and urban townships. In April, the first of several white farmers was killed. Shortly thereafter, Ncube issued a pastoral letter, "A Prayer of Hope for Zimbabwe: A Concern on the Present Situation in Zimbabwe," that criticized the government's policy of farm invasions and violent disregard for the rule of law. After the parliamentary elections in June, in which ZANU-PF failed to win any seats in any urban area or in the Matebeleland provinces, Mugabe held Archbishop Ncube personally responsible for the ruling party's electoral defeat in Matebeleland. Consequently, Ncube received death threats from the CIO and several pastors at rural Catholic mission stations in the Bulawayo archdiocese had to stand off war veterans intent on invading the missions.

In July 2000, a year after nationalist hero and former vice president Joshua Nkomo died, Nkomo's family invited Ncube to preside at the memorial mass. The president announced that he would not attend any event at which the archbishop was present. Nkomo's family, rather awkwardly, not only had to ask Ncube not to preside but further not to attend the service.

Although the Zimbabwe Catholic Bishops Conference has subsequently issued statements condemning the political violence, they were merely following the lead that Pius Ncube provided. Not until Robert Ndlovu, who—like Ncube and Nkomo—is from the minority Ndebele ethnic group, became archbishop of Harare in June 2004 has another individual Catholic bishop openly criticized Robert Mugabe and held him personally accountable for the ongoing political violence in Zimbabwe.

Bibliography. Creary, Nicholas. "Domesticating a Foreign Import? African Cultures and the Catholic Church at Jesuit missions in Zimbabwe, 1879–1980." PhD diss., Michigan State University, 2004. Meredith, Martin. *Our Votes, Our Guns: Robert Mugabe and the Tragedy of Zimbabwe.* New York: Public Affairs, 2003.

Nicholas M. Creary

NEA DEMOKRATIA. *See* New Democracy

NEUHAUS, RICHARD JOHN (B.1936). Neuhaus is a Catholic priest, theologian, and journalist most widely known as a defender of a more vigorous and prominent role for religion in American public life. Along with **Michael Novak** and George Weigel, he is one of the leading Catholic neoconservatives, or Whig Thomists, a group that has attempted to modernize the Catholic Church's positions on economic and political issues by defending capitalism, democracy, and cultural pluralism while also defending orthodox Catholic social teaching.

Neuhaus was born in 1936 in the Ottawa Valley of Canada, the son of a Missouri Synod Lutheran pastor. He was educated in Canada and the United States, receiving a graduate degree in theology from Concordia Theological Seminary in St. Louis, Missouri. Like other Catholic neoconservatives, including Novak, Neuhaus began his public career on the political Left. He was an outspoken opponent of American involvement in the Vietnam War and a cofounder of the antiwar group Clergy and Laymen Concerned about Vietnam. In his first notable publication, *Movement and Revolution,* which he edited with Peter Berger, a Lutheran sociologist with whom he has collaborated throughout his career, Neuhaus called for a moral and political revolution to bring down the American empire.

However, despite his own radical pronouncements, Neuhaus soon became disillusioned with the antiwar Left because of its anti-Americanism and, more importantly, because of its commitment to defending legalized abortion. He, along with Berger, began to focus on the alienating character of modern American life. In 1976, they published *To Empower People,* which analyzed the destruction of civil society in modern capitalist states by large impersonal bureaucratic structures. Neuhaus and Berger claimed that mediating structures, like the family and the local church, were being undermined by the nationalization of policy implementation by the courts and the public bureaucracies, and that instead of damaging these mediating institutions, government should do more to encourage their development and their involvement in policy making.

In 1984, Neuhaus published *The Naked Public Square,* which is his best-known and most influential book. In it, Neuhaus argued that contemporary secular liberalism was effectively banishing religious expression from the "public square." He suggested that this exclusion of religion from public policy debates had not only impoverished the public realm, but that it was also undermining the pluralism that is at the heart of the American political experience. Neuhaus called for the inclusion, not of subjective revealed religion, but of a rationalized or natural religious faith available to all reasonable people.

As part of his effort to reinject religious belief into American political discourse, Neuhaus founded the Center on Religion and Society and began publishing *This World,* a quarterly publication dealing with religion and political life. After a series of disputes in the late 1980s between traditionalist conservatives and neoconservatives over immigration and international issues in which he firmly sided with the neoconservatives, Neuhaus created the Institute on Religion and Public Life and began the publication of *First Things,* a monthly magazine concerned with religion and public policy.

In 1990, as Neuhaus was cementing his relationship with the neoconservatives, he converted to Catholicism. He justified his conversion not in terms of his dissatisfaction with the social and theological direction of contemporary Lutheranism, but instead as a logical consequence of his beliefs about ecclesiology, authority, and the successful reformation of the Catholic Church since the time of Luther.

Since allying himself with the neoconservatives, Neuhaus also has been an enthusiastic supporter of the global expansion of American economic, political, and cultural values and has consistently attempted to effect a synthesis of the American system with Catholic social teaching.

Bibliography. Dorrien, Gary. *The Neoconservative Mind: Politics, Culture, and the War of Ideology.* Philadelphia: Temple University Press, 1993. Rourke, Thomas R. *A Conscience as Large as the World: Yves R. Simon versus the Catholic Neoconservatives.* Lanham, MD: Rowman & Littlefield, 1997.

Kenneth B. McIntyre

NEVIN, JOHN WILLIAMSON (1803–1886). Born near Shippensburg, Pennsylvania, of Scotch-Irish descent, Nevin was nurtured in the tradition of Old School Presbyterianism. As a college professor and theologian, he became a sharp critic of the radical individualism that he believed had infected American evangelicalism and politics. As an antidote, he espoused a lifelong attention to the catechetical system as the pastoral way of Christianity and a guidepost for American political culture.

Nevin graduated with honors in 1817 from Union College in Schenectady, New York. He enrolled at Princeton Theological Seminary in 1823, where he encountered Reformed orthodoxy in both its pietistic and scholastic forms. Nevin's discomfort with the developing form of American religion and culture, however, led him into intensive study of German scholarship in history, philosophy, and theology. His growing knowledge of German language and scholarship brought him to the attention of the leadership of the German Reformed Church (in the United States), which managed a struggling college and theological seminary in the town of Mercersburg in Franklin County, Pennsylvania. Nevin joined the faculties of Marshall College and the seminary at Mercersburg in 1840. **Philip Schaff** joined Nevin at Mercersburg in 1844, and thus began the association of two seminal thinkers, whose work has been dubbed the Mercersburg Theology (or Movement). The ideas of John Williamson Nevin ran counter to the mainstream of American theology and American individualism. During the 1850s, he contemplated Catholicism and was in serious consultation with **Orestes Brownson** and other leaders of American Roman Catholicism. From 1866 to 1876 he served as president of Franklin and Marshall College in Lancaster.

Much of Nevin's theology was directed toward an understanding of the social and political circumstances of the mid-nineteenth century. Although his thought was based upon his study of the unbroken continuum of church history, it was often related to the crises of the times and the need to understand the unique responsibility of the emergent American Republic.

Nevin considered the United States to be a nation of "world-historical significance," part of a new era in formation. Here the European experience of nationhood was being transformed. Issues of human rights, self-government, social justice, race, and material well-being found in America a revolutionary mandate. The appropriate metaphor for American self-understanding was not the "city upon a hill," but the "theater for the world." Our public life was not a static destiny, but a drama of becoming. Here the revolutionary spirit is constituent in the inner life of virtue, which affirms the outer development of the nation.

Second, Nevin's understanding of Catholicism is that of a radical catholicity in which the incarnation is a public, mystical presence wherein universality is a wholeness challenging us to extend the limits of human nature, always radically rejecting any partial claim to universality. The role of Christian mission was not a collectivizing of individuals but the intensification of the perception of the incarnation in politics, art, and science. Catholicity extends not primarily to collectivity of "individuals separately considered," but intensively into the fabric of the culture. The universal is already present in wholeness, waiting to be actively perceived.

Third, for Nevin this notion of catholicity meant that there was a "divinity even in profane history." It was delusional for our intellectual life to seek to escape history. It was illegitimate for our religious life to affirm a history-less Christianity, in which individuals and rampant sectarianism seek to enjoy what **Ralph Waldo Emerson** called an "original relation to the universe." The sectarian impulse was as active in politics and culture as in religion. However, the incarnation has entered the organization of the world as a wholeness completing itself, "reaching forward as a single historical process."

Finally, Nevin gave deliberate attention to events like the Civil War, which was "the nation's second birth" and of world-historical significance. Nevin envisioned the war as eliminating old party issues that represented sectarianism. It was time to let the dead bury the dead. This observation relates to Nevin's opposition to the party system in politics as a subordination of public interest that impedes what the catholicity of the incarnation is making manifest in the "theater for the world."

Bibliography. Gerrish, Brian A. *Tradition and the Modern World: Reformed Theology in the Nineteenth Century.* Chicago: University of Chicago Press, 1978. Hewitt, Glenn R. *Regeneration and Morality: A Study of Charles Finney, Charles Hodge, John W. Nevin, and Horace Bushnell.* Brooklyn, NY: Carlson, 1991. Holifield, E. Brooks. *Theology in America.* New Haven, CT: Yale University Press, 2003. Nichols, James Hastings. *Romanticism in American Theology: Nevin and Schaff at Mercersburg.* Chicago: University of Chicago Press, 1961. Wentz, Richard E. *John Williamson Nevin: American Theologian.* New York: Oxford University Press, 1997. Yrigoyen, Charles, Jr., and George H. Bricker. *Catholic and Reformed: Selected Writings of John Williamson Nevin.* Pittsburgh: Pickwick Press, 1978.

Richard Wentz

NEW DEMOCRACY [NEA DEMOKRATIA] (GREECE). Created by **Constantine Karamanlis** in September 1974, this was a rejuvenated and liberalized version of his old party, which had ruled Greece for much of the period between the end of the civil war in 1949 and the military coup of 1967. It remains a major party in what since 1977 has been basically a two-party system, its main rival being the social democratic PASOK. New Democracy held power independently until October 1981, then as a partner in successive coalitions from June 1989 to April 1990, then in its own right again until October 1993. At other times, New Democracy has sat in opposition to PASOK governments.

The party's ideology has always been extremely vague, although consistently marked by devotion to traditional institutions and values. While its official policies have normally been moderate, the party has at different times tolerated—as members or allies—people nostalgic for monarchy or military dictatorship, or supporters of the Orthodox Church's more unrealistic claims.

Since 1974, the party has strongly supported the historic status of the Orthodox Church of Greece as the official church, one that claims at least the nominal support of a majority of the population. In 1975 the party insisted, against Karamanlis's preference, on a stipulation in the new constitution that the inculcation of the Christian (meaning Orthodox) faith remain an obligatory part of school curricula, although there was provision for children of other faiths to opt out of it. Muslim education was officially provided to a recognized minority in northeastern Greece under a treaty of 1923, but in 2000 New Democracy unsuccessfully opposed permission for a mosque for Muslims in the metropolis. In 1983, the party also challenged in vain the voluntary provision by the PASOK government for civil marriage. It was partially successful in 1987, however, in resisting this government's attempt to appropriate monastic property. New Democracy has also supported the church's massively organized protest, since 2000, against the government's omission of religion from state identity cards. This is a troublesome issue, because some members of New Democracy recognize the church's stance to be hopeless.

In their policy statements, New Democracy leaders have not usually emphasized religion, partly because religious issues cause some division among their supporters, and also because PASOK has not seriously challenged the church's status. But devotion to the church and its values is especially strong among most of the party at all levels.

Bibliography. Close, David H. *Greece since 1945.* London: Longman, 2002. Vasiliki, Georgiadou. "Secular State and Orthodox Church: Relations between Religion, Society and Politics during the Transition to Democracy." In *Society and Politics: Aspects of the Third Greek Republic, 1974–1994,* ed. C. Lyrintzis, I. Nikolakopoulos, and D. Sotiropoulos. Athens: Themelio, 1996.

David H. Close

NEWMAN, JOHN HENRY (1801–1890).

Newman, the leader of the Oxford movement and Britain's most famous nineteenth-century convert to Roman Catholicism, dedicated his life to resisting the Erastian and utilitarian tendency to turn religion into a useful tool of the state and to marginalize theological discussion. His most significant engagements with political culture were his defense of the prerogatives of the church against interference by the state, particularly in the area of education, and his explanation of the oft-confused relationship between liberty of conscience, the spiritual primacy of the pope, and civil allegiance in the wake of the declaration of papal infallibility.

Newman became vicar of St. Mary's and preacher for Oxford University in the midst of the controversies surrounding the repeal of the Test Acts, which enabled dissenters from the established Anglican Church to participate in public life (1828); Catholic Emancipation (1829); and the Reform Act of 1832, which liberalized representation in the British parliament. Following John Keble's criticism of the increasing secularization of the Church of England in his sermon "On the National Apostasy" on July 14, 1833, Newman began a series of sermons, published as *Tracts for the Times,* which launched a revival of Anglican interest in the Catholic doctrines of apostolic succession, the sacramental character of the church, and the importance of tradition (especially with reference to the early fathers) in establishing Christian teaching.

The culmination of these sermons came in *Tract 90,* in which Newman argued that the Church of England's creedal formulary, the Thirty-nine Articles, could be read as consistent with Roman Catholicism. When the Anglican bishop of Oxford condemned this position, Newman retired from St. Mary's and, after a year of secluded prayer and study, was received into the Roman Catholic Church in 1845. Newman's conversion to Rome, as the culmination of his participation in the Oxford movement, was the symbolic turning point of his life and his career as a public moralist, but he remained an important public voice for the rest of the century, receiving ordination in Rome, establishing the Oratory of St. Philip Neri in England, founding the Oratory School outside Birmingham, being caught up in a very public libel suit with an ex-monk, presiding over the ill-fated beginnings of a Catholic university in Dublin, engaging in public controversy with **Charles Kingsley** on the truth of Christianity, participating in the theological and ecclesiastical discussions surrounding the first Vatican Council and the declaration of the dogma of papal infallibility, and finally being made a cardinal by Pope **Leo XIII** in 1878. Meanwhile he laid before the public in exquisite prose full of imagination, dignity, wit, and irony the reasons for his acceptance of Rome, the interior windings of his personal religious journey, and his understanding of the place of Christianity in public life in his works, which include *An Essay on the Development of Christian Doctrine* (1845), his *Apologia Pro Vita Sua* (1864), *A Grammar of Assent* (1870), and *The Idea of a University* (1873).

Early in his career at Oxford, Newman developed a sense of Christianity as a social and sovereign organism distinct from the state, yet he resisted a strict separation between a political public sphere and a personal religious realm as institutionalizing a false dichotomy between reason and religion. The two incidents that most clearly reveal Newman's understanding of the place of religion in public life were his defense of the essential place of theology in the university in his *Idea of a University* and his careful explanation of the role of conscience as the recognition of natural law in reply of **William Gladstone**'s accusations of "Vaticanism" after the dogmatic definition of papal infallibility. As cardinal, Newman declared himself the "life-long enemy of liberalism" understood as "the doctrine that there is not truth in religion, but that one creed is as good as another," and at the same time he appealed in his apologetical writings to the common wisdom of humanity as something more trustworthy than the private judgment of the individual and contributed to a proper understanding of the role of the laity in the *sensus fidei* in the development of church doctrine. While Newman, always the Oxford scholar, was no democrat and often expressed suspicion of popular movements, the initial impulse to popularize the Oxford movement by publishing tracts continued to fuel his essentially hopeful struggle against the secularization of public life during his later years.

Bibliography. Ker, Ian. *John Henry Newman: A Biography.* Oxford: Oxford University Press, 1990. Ward, Wilfred P. *The Life of John Henry, Cardinal Newman.* London: Longmans, Green, 1912.

Susan Hanssen

NICARAGUAN COUNCIL OF EVANGELICAL CHURCHES. The Nicaraguan Council of Evangelical Churches (CEPAD) served as an active and vibrant force for social and political change throughout the Central American political conflicts of the 1970s and 1980s. Formed by a local Baptist minister as an outlet for earthquake relief in December of 1972, CEPAD's acronym originally signified *Comité de Emergencia Para Ayuda a los Damnificados* (the Emergency Committee for Aid to Victims). In the spring of 1973, CEPAD changed the *D* in its initials to stand for *desarollo* (development). In addition to continuing its role as an outlet for international aid, the CEPAD leadership began to organize community development programs in rural areas. These programs were run by regional committees of member pastors.

By the time of the 1979 overthrow of Nicaragua's corrupt Somoza dictatorship by the Sandinista National Liberation Front (FSLN), CEPAD had developed a majority coalition of Nicaragua's theologically diverse Protestant community. On October 5, 1979, CEPAD sponsored a national meeting of Protestant pastors, five hundred of whom signed a declaration thanking God for the liberation of Nicaragua and proclaiming evangelical support for the FSLN. The pastors requested recognition in the new government and passed along a request from their evangelical constituents for government sensitivity in dealing with Nicaragua's Protestant communities. For the Sandinistas, CEPAD was an obvious choice for serving as a liaison between the new government and Nicaragua's diverse Protestant population. CEPAD could claim to represent up to 90 percent of Nicaragua's Protestants, and the organization was already involved in development programs that corresponded with Sandinista goals.

CEPAD thus fulfilled a mediatory role between politically moderate evangelicals and the FSLN government. After an inflammatory anti-Protestant article that appeared in the official Sandinista press led to the appropriation of several church buildings in 1982, CEPAD representatives negotiated their return. The organization also obtained conscientious objector exemptions from a controversial draft law in 1983 and coordinated visits from eighty-five different North American Protestant groups to observe the political situation in Nicaragua in conjunction with the Witness for Peace movement. In 1985, CEPAD's founder and president received an appointment to the National Commission for the Protection and Promotion of Human Rights and subsequently served on the National Commission on Reconciliation. In the following year the group contributed to the process of drafting the new Nicaraguan constitution. CEPAD remained engaged with its evangelical roots, however, and a CEPAD General Assembly member and Sandinista congressman was instrumental in bringing internationally renowned evangelistic crusades to Nicaragua.

CEPAD's achievements stand as proof of the potential for Latin American Protestants to act in concert for social justice and development. The organization aligned itself with revolutionary and reform-oriented models of social change and worked with the Sandinista government to achieve substantial gains in terms of social programs and participation in the political process, without compromising its identity as an evangelical organization.

Bibliography. Dodson, Michael, and Laura O'Shaughnessy. *Nicaragua's Other Revolution: Religious Faith and Political Struggle.* Chapel Hill: University of North Carolina Press, 1990. Phillips, Katherine Amy. "Reconstruction and Reconciliation: The Protestant Church in Nicaragua." PhD diss., Vanderbilt University, 1985.

Barry Robinson

NIEBUHR, HELMUT RICHARD (1894–1962). Niebuhr's thought and ethical concerns were never limited to the theoretical or abstract, but grounded in the realities of the twentieth century. Niebuhr, younger brother to *Reinhold Niebuhr,* earned a bachelor of divinity at Yale Divinity School and a PhD at Yale. After ordination, he taught at Eden Theological Seminary and served as president of Elmhurst College before returning to Yale Divinity School to spend three decades on the faculty. His written work was carved out of days filled with teaching, family, and other demands on his time.

Niebuhr's theologically informed political outlook developed against the backdrop of the dramatic historical changes and the worldwide devastation of World War II. His work reflects a use of history, attention to context, and consideration of social reality that in many ways mirrors the development of liberation thought. Surveying the catastrophic damage of the war, Niebuhr saw the human drive to power as an attempt to claim the power of God. Yet Christ confronts humanity with sacrifice and self-emptying, culminating in the crucifixion. For Niebuhr, the "crucifixion" of the innocent in warfare forces recognition of how we allow values to become idols and demands the crucifixion of such values.

H. Richard Niebuhr's later thought developed along dual streams. One begins with his use of a typology of religious or ethical categories that he terms polytheism, henotheism, and radical monotheism. These terms were not originated by Niebuhr. In 1878 Julius Wellhausen, a German biblical scholar, used them to understand the development of Jewish conceptions of God in scripture and history. Wellhausen's biblical studies became widely accepted and well known to scholars working in religion or theological studies (Meissner, 107–9). Niebuhr, however, invested his own meaning in these terms in order to characterize types of faith.

Niebuhr viewed polytheism as belief scattered among competing loyalties. When different individuals or values compete for primacy in the belief system, one means of resolution is just to maintain a belief in multiple forms, the cafeteria-style so often bemoaned in both voters and faith communities. The polytheist is eager for the benefits that the placement of supreme value can bring, but not ready for commitment itself. Commitment to one might mean a loss of other opportunities that might potentially prove superior in providing benefits, but true faith cannot develop without commitment.

Niebuhr explained henotheism as a shift that permits commitment. Henotheism is a belief based in loyalty to a specific community, whether that community takes the form of family members, city-state, or political party. Still relevant today, it also comes in the form of unthinking nationalism promoting national political and military power as the primary virtue and source of value. Value and meaning in henotheism are made in terms of a closed society. Niebuhr's thoughts on henotheism may have been influenced, in part, by the work of Josiah Royce.

Perhaps the most important term to understand is the third, radical monotheism. Radical monotheism is belief in the underlying One beneath all other manifestations. For the Christian that One is Christ. The believer no longer believes in the value of the numerous principle "gods," or in the ultimate value of a closed society, regardless how loving or large. Radical monotheism sees the unity of God that underlies all created order and the Divine expressed in every order of Creation (Niebuhr, *Radical Monotheism,* 31–37). In radical monotheism, being and value are the same, a conception closely tied to Niebuhr's value theory.

The conflation of being and value is fundamental to Niebuhr's thought. Religious belief, according to Niebuhr, is closely related to valuation, to how one interprets and values God. At the core, Niebuhr's value theory is relational, based on the relationship between value and being. From the Creator's standpoint all that is, is good, and all that is has value. Humankind errs, however, when it substitutes loyalty to a particular community for loyalty to God. For Niebuhr, the love of God in radical monotheism demands pluralistic political and religious tolerance and rejects the intolerance that leads to destructive confrontations. As with Christ, our values must be challenged and subjected to crucifixion and resurrection, the only way to develop a true ethic of responsibility.

One can also understand Niebuhr's worldview as an evolutionary process consistent with the metaphor provided by Alfred North Whitehead. Whitehead suggests such a progression might just reflect "the transition from God the Void to God the Enemy, and from God the Enemy to God the Companion" (16). In Niebuhr's expression of this anthropological process, he saw challenges to dominant theological traditions stressing transcendent or sanctified suffering. A fully transcendent God could only be other, indifferent to extremes of human suffering. In the transition from God the Void to God the Enemy, God exists but is indifferent to my suffering. The challenge of theodicy, so pronounced after the horrors of the Holocaust, suggests that the conception of God must go beyond one of sheer transcendence. Resolution comes through the transition from God the Enemy to God the Companion. For Niebuhr, the transformation must be comprehended through divine revelation. Acceptance of revealed truth enables one to move from distrust to trust of God, a critical step in terms of ethics. Only when God becomes a loving companion do believers have an ethical imperative to do the work of God (*The Meaning of Revelation*, 129–37). Niebuhr explained this ethical imperative through three biblical metaphors for the relationship of the human to God—God as Creator, God as Governor, and God as Redeemer/Liberator (Fowler, 149). At the core of God's liberative and redemptive work is the Incarnation. Yet full Christian development means embracing not only Christ, but all three dimensions of God.

Bibliography. Fowler, James W. *To See the Kingdom: The Theological Vision of H. Richard Niebuhr.* Nashville, TN: Abingdon Press, 1974. Meissner, W. W. *Psychoanalysis and Religious Experience.* New Haven, CT: Yale University Press, 1984. Niebuhr, H. Richard. *The Meaning of Revelation.* New Haven, CT: Yale University, 1940. Niebuhr, H. Richard, *Radical Monotheism and Western Culture.* Louisville, KY: Westminster/ John Knox Press, 1993. Whitehead, Alfred North. *Religion in the Making.* Cleveland, OH: Meridian Books/World Publishing, 1960.

Lynn Bridgers

NIEBUHR, KARL REINHOLD (1892–1971). As a student at Elmhurst College, Eden Theological Seminary, and then Yale, Niebuhr absorbed the tenets of liberal theology and the **Social Gospel,** with their optimism for effecting transformation of the social order according to biblical morality. But thirteen years as an evangelical and Reformed pastor in Detroit, where his congregation's fortunes were at the mercy of the automotive industry, and then the ravages of World War I muted the hope that human society would ever reflect ethical ideals. Aware of neo-orthodoxy's renewed emphasis on human sin and shortcoming, Niebuhr labeled his emerging perspective Christian Realism. A powerful preacher, an internationally known lecturer, and a prolific writer, as a professor at New York City's Union Theological Seminary from 1928 until his retirement in 1960, Niebuhr was a major voice calling for the application of Christian ethics in politics and public life in the middle third of the twentieth century.

At the heart of Niebuhr's Christian Realism lay an appreciation for both human possibilities and human finitude, along with a stark awareness of the nature of power. Following biblical teaching, Niebuhr saw the exercise of freedom as essential to human being. Freedom endowed humans with visions for what might be as they sought to transform their potential into concrete reality, moving toward the ultimate telos, or end of creation itself. Yet too often humans forgot the limits inherent in being finite and also acted on the basis of self-interest, thwarting the principles of love and justice nurtured by biblical morality. As a Christian ethicist, Niebuhr claimed that God through Christ extended to humanity a gift of grace that made it possible to set aside self-interest and transcend egotism. On an individual level, humans could thus realize their potential to love one another.

But if humans had the potential for moral behavior, the situation was much more complex when it came to societies. Niebuhr knew that if power were necessary to restrain humans when they abandoned love, he then society's use of power rendered it virtually impossible for a nation, a people, to act consistently in a moral fashion. Collectivities could not manifest love in the same way that individuals might, but they could move toward justice. Simply put, for Niebuhr the whole was much more than the sum of its parts, for it developed an inertia of its own. On a social level, then, one could struggle only for proximate justice, but struggle one must if there was any hope in the ethical life. No social gain would transform the political order into the realm of God, the way earlier liberal thinkers anticipated, but each social gain, important though it was, would simply increase awareness of how much injustice remained and how short society fell from moral. Some saw Niebuhr's view here as a pessimism that overreacted against liberalism's optimism. Niebuhr saw it as more realistic, for it recognized not only the potential for making genuine gains through right use of power, but also the capacity for misuse of power in any human social achievement.

Niebuhr early articulated this approach in *Moral Man and Immoral Society* (1932); developed it in a more sophisticated theological fashion in his Gifford Lectures, published in two volumes as *The Nature and Destiny of Man* (1941, 1943); and continued to explore its implications in later works such as *The Children of Light and the Children of Darkness* (1944), *The Irony of American History* (1952), and *Man's Nature and His Communities* (1965). As a founding editor of *Christianity and Crisis,* Niebuhr used its pages to offer trenchant commentary on current political and social issues.

But Niebuhr was far more than an ethical theorist. His commitment to the struggle for a more just society, tempered by his awareness of human limitations, required active engagement in the public realm. After World War I, that activism began to take shape in Niebuhr's commitment to pacifism. Stunned by Hitler's demonic use of power, however, Niebuhr abandoned his pacifist posture and called for American support for the Allied cause in World War II. His suspicion of demonic use of power carried over into a distrust for Stalin's brand of communism. But it also required that Niebuhr challenge U.S. policies in Southeast Asia in the last years of his life. Critics saw an inconsistency in his posture, but Niebuhr did not. In each case, he argued that implementing justice demanded a particular action; even if the violence of war was reprehensible, it was more unjust not to stop Hitler, for example, than to use violent means to halt a worse injustice.

Niebuhr lived his realism in other ways. In 1930, he was an unsuccessful candidate for Congress, running as a Socialist. Later he became a strong supporter of most of Franklin Roosevelt's New Deal policies because he believed that they were in keeping with biblical notions of justice and equity. He also served in an advisory capacity to the U.S. Department of State during the Truman administration, urging officials to be aware of the dangers of power as well as the need to use it to advance justice. During the civil rights era, some activists criticized Niebuhr for being too moderate in his assessment of possible social gains for African Americans, while feminists questioned whether his understanding of power was rooted too much in male-oriented categories. If Niebuhr had his own limitations as a finite human being when it came to assessing particular social situations, however, his sense of how power operated in human society and his conviction that humans were indeed creatures, with all the shortcomings that term implies, fashioned in the image of God, with all the possibilities that phrase denotes, continue to influence Christian ethicists and politicians in the twenty-first century. But as a Christian thinker, Niebuhr would still insist that the full realization of human potential, individually and collectively, lies beyond the bounds of time and history.

Bibliography. Brown, Charles C. *Niebuhr and His Age: Reinhold Niebuhr's Prophetic Role and Legacy.* Rev. ed. Harrisburg, PA: Trinity Press International, 2002. Fox, Richard. *Reinhold Niebuhr: A Life.* San Francisco: Harper San Francisco, 1987. Stone, Ronald H. *Reinhold Niebuhr: Prophet to Politicians.* Nashville, TN: Abingdon Press, 1972. Warren, Heather A. *Theologians of a New World Order: Reinhold Niebuhr and the Christian Realists, 1920–1948.* New York: Oxford University Press, 1997.

Charles H. Lippy

NJEGOŠ, PETAR II PETROVIĆ (1811–1851).

Njegoš was prince-bishop of Montenegro (1830–1851) and a Serbian poet and philosopher. Throughout his reign, Njegoš subordinated his religious duties to his political and cultural program. Cultural nationalism and political independence movements, concepts introduced to the Balkans in the early nineteenth century, greatly inspired him. He became a leading proponent of liberating and uniting the Serbian people, willing even to concede his princely rights in exchange for union with Serbia. Although this did not occur, Njegoš successfully laid foundations for the political and cultural idea of Yugoslavism and at the same time introduced modern political concepts to Montenegro.

After the death of his uncle Peter I in 1830, Njegoš succeeded to the prince-bishopric at the age of nineteen. At that time, Montenegro was an autonomous principality in the predominately Ottoman Balkans. The bishop was the only central authority for numerous Montenegrin tribes, and Njegoš exploited this position to centralize power in the region. Influenced by visits to Russia and Austria, he implemented a rudimentary infrastructure for the Montenegrin state. He built roads and schools, developed the first printing press in Montenegro, organized a security force, and imposed taxes. When he died, his successor renounced the office of the bishop and became the first secular prince of Montenegro, a symbol of Njegoš's political success.

Despite his political achievements, Njegoš is best known for his writings, which drew on folklore, lyric poetry, and biblical stories. Prominent among his works are *The Ray of the Microcosm* (1845), a religious philosophical tome, and *The Mountain Wreath* (1846), a quintessential Serbian epic. His work blended Christian allegories with myths of Serbia and compared the Serbian struggle against the Ottoman Turks to the biblical struggle between heaven and hell. His religious views drew deeply from Montenegrin spiritual tradition and philosophy rather than Orthodox dogma.

Since his death, Njegoš has remained one of the foremost political and cultural fathers of modern Serbia and Montenegro. Various political factions in the late nineteenth and twentieth centuries—including nationalists, Yugoslavs, and Communists—adapted Njegoš's legacy and works to fit their programs. During the recent wars of Yugoslav succession, Serbian nationalists used Njegoš's work to historically justify Serbian aggression against Muslims in Bosnia.

Bibliography. Djilas, Milovan. *Njegoš: Poet, Prince, Bishop.* Trans. Michael B. Petrovich. New York: Harcourt, Brace & World, 1966.

Emily Greble Balic

NOCEDAL, CÁNDIDO (1821–1885). One of the chief voices in Spain's Catholic politics during the mid-nineteenth century, Nocedal was born at La Coruña. After having completed his university studies in law at Alcalá de Henares, Nocedal worked for a period of time in the tribunal courts of Madrid. He believed that social order and church interests should be promoted through politics and was first elected in 1843 to the Cortes (Spanish parliament), where he immediately showed his oratorical skills.

An outstanding representative of the so-called moderate party, in 1856 Nocedal was nominated minister of the interior in the cabinet of Ramón Narváez and soon drafted a law that restricted the press. Later, he slowly distanced himself from moderatism until, after the 1868 revolution, he began a relationship with traditionalism and Carlism. He made a famous speech (1865) against the recognition of the Kingdom of Italy because of its aggressions against the Holy See, and he published the antirevolutionary journal *La Costancia* (1867–1868). Following this, Nocedal became the central figure of a Spanish political Catholicism that leaned toward integralism and antimodernism.

In 1871, Nocedal offered his services to the Carlist pretender, Charles VII, an act that was rewarded with a profession of full faith, various jobs, and party leadership. Nocedal, nevertheless encountered some difficulties with the Carlists, particularly over rearmament. He distanced himself from the movement until 1871, when the new civil war broke out, first joining the legitimists and then the faction that supported the pretenders by the end of hostilities in 1875. Fully aware of the role of the press, Nocedal, with his son **Ramón** as editor, founded *El Siglo Futuro* (1875–1936), which guided the reorganization of the Carlist party and, as a lay publication beyond the hierarchy's control, became enormously popular, dwarfing the mainstream Catholic press, yet preferred by the lower clergy. Toward the end of his life, Nocedal also promoted two successful pilgrimages to Rome in 1876 and 1882.

Bibliography. Callahan, William. *The Catholic Church in Spain, 1875–1998*. Washington, DC: Catholic University of America Press, 2000.

Alfonso Botti

NOCEDAL, RAMÓN (1842–1907). Ramón Nocedal inherited from his father, **Cándido Nocedal,** his ideological and political views as well as his journalistic career. He graduated in law from Madrid in 1886 and wrote plays of little artistic value and scant success before entering the traditionalist Carlist party in 1871 and then becoming deputy in the Spanish parliament. With his father, he founded the immensely successful lay Catholic review *El Siglo Futuro* and was its principal promoter. From 1875 until his death, he directed it.

An integralist as well as a defender of religious unity and of the so-called Catholic thesis, he pitted himself against the vaguely compromising liberalist Catholics of Alejandro Pidal y Mon, who were called *mestizos* (according to the lexicon of the era, this meant "of impure blood," unlike the Catholics such as Nocedal who favored religious unity). From 1875 on, the bitter internal feud between Nocedal and Pidal's liberal Catholicism was so divisive it forced **Leo XIII** to compose his encyclical *Cum multa* (1882) and to allude to the fight in two others: *Immortale Dei* (1885) and *Sapientiae Christianae* (1890). Leo XIII's secretary of state, Cardinal **Rampolla,** intervened to quiet the situation but enjoyed little success.

Because of his intemperate attacks, which were eventually aimed even at Pope Leo, Nocedal provoked another split within the Carlists and founded the Integralist Party with the chief objective of legally molding society according to Catholic human rights principles and morals. Even **Pius X** had to intervene later in the division among Spanish Catholics in his encyclical *Inter Catholicos Hispaniae* (1906), although the Catholic Church never censured Nocedal for his doctrine. It believed, however, that his influence in politics weakened the Catholic united front against secularism and socialism; for this reason, the Jesuits campaigned against him and his party.

Bibliography. Nocedal, Rámon. *Obras de don Ramón Nocedal.* 19 vols. Madrid: de Fortanet, 1907–1928. Urigüen, B. *Origenes y evolución de la derecha española: El neo-catolicismo.* Madrid: Consejo Superior de la Investigaciones Científicas, 1986.

Alfonso Botti

NOVAK, MICHAEL (b. 1933). Novak is a Catholic polemicist best known for his attempt to synthesize modern Catholic social teaching with classical liberalism. He is one of the leading figures, along with **Richard John Neuhaus** and George Weigel, of a group of public intellectuals known alternatively as Catholic neoconservatives or Whig Thomists who have attempted to modernize the Catholic Church's positions on economic and political issues by defending capitalism, democracy, and cultural pluralism.

Novak was born in Johnston, Pennsylvania to an upwardly mobile working-class Catholic family of Slovakian heritage. He studied at Stonehill College, the Gregorian University in Rome, and Catholic University of America with the ultimate goal of entering the priesthood. However, his desire to have a family and his reluctance to live under the intellectual discipline of the church convinced him to abandon the priesthood in 1960.

Like many other Catholic neoconservatives, including Neuhaus, Novak began his public career as a man of the political Left. Novak's first books, including *The Open Church, Belief and Unbelief,* and *A*

Theology for Radical Politics, reflected his belief that the Catholic Church needed to open itself to modern radical developments in theology, economics, and politics. His twin commitments to political radicalism and theological modernism were weakened by his experience of student radicalism at SUNY-Old Westbury, where Novak had taken a job as dean of students in the late 1960s, and by his encounter with working-class Americans while working as a speechwriter for Sargent Shriver in the early 1970s.

His experiences with working-class Americans led to Novak's first notable literary success. *The Rise of Unmeltable Ethnics* was an extended critique of the myth of the so-called American melting pot. In it, Novak criticized the hegemony of WASP culture in America and celebrated ethnic pluralism. The negative reception of the book by his former liberal allies, along with the nomination and subsequent landslide defeat of George McGovern, convinced Novak that the Democratic Party and the social liberalism it represented were out of touch with mainstream America.

Novak's major contribution to Catholic intellectual and political life was the publication of *The Spirit of Democratic Capitalism,* which cemented his reputation as a leading figure among Catholic neoconservatives. In it, Novak argued that the Catholic Church's traditional hostility to democracy, capitalism, and pluralism were all misplaced. Novak insisted that each of these three institutions was mutually reinforcing and that each contributed to a fully realized freedom not only compatible with but essential to a mature Catholic Christianity. He rejected the criticisms of Christian socialists and liberation theologians that capitalism encourages selfishness and greed, claiming instead that capitalism supports democracy and promotes many of the virtues necessary to Christian life, including a concern for community, an enterprising and creative spirit, and a love of liberty. Novak extended his defense of capitalism in a series of articles critical of the American bishops' pastoral letter "Economic Justice for All," which faulted American capitalism for its promotion of inequality and social injustice.

Since the 1980s, Novak has been one of the most consistent defenders of neoconservative foreign policy goals. He was a persistent critic of the American bishops' pastoral letter on nuclear weapons and defended the traditional American reliance on nuclear deterrence as being consistent with the Catholic "just war" tradition. He has supported American-led democratization movements and was one of the most vocal supporters of the American invasion of Iraq in 2003, arguing both publicly and in an audience with Pope **John Paul II** that preventive war in an age of terrorism can and should be undertaken in the name of justice and that peace in the Middle East depends upon the institution of democratic capitalism there.

Bibliography. Allitt, Patrick. *Catholic Intellectuals and Conservative Politics in America, 1950–1985.* Ithaca, NY: Cornell University Press, 1993. Dorrien, Gary. *The Neoconservative Mind: Politics, Culture, and the War of Ideology.* Philadelphia: Temple University Press, 1993.

Kenneth B. McIntyre

O

O'CONNELL, DANIEL (1775–1847). Daniel O'Connell was the foremost Irish politician of his day and a hero of nineteenth-century nationalism. Working within the traditions of both his native culture and British constitutional government, O'Connell succeeded in creating a popular political organization that enlisted the support of thousands of ordinary Catholics in the movement for greater legal and political equality. He won election to a seat from County Clare in 1828, although Catholics were still barred from Parliament, and this event signaled an end to most legal discrimination and laid the foundations of an Irish party in the House of Commons. He was also an early advocate of religious freedom, and not only for Irish Catholics. Although O'Connell's achievements were limited by divisive conditions in Ireland, his tactics helped to demonstrate the possibility of liberal reform through moral force.

O'Connell was the eldest son among ten children in a family of minor Catholic landholders. His wealthy uncle took a particular interest in his education, and he was sent to seminary schools on the Continent. When his school was closed by the French Revolution, O'Connell returned to Ireland only an indifferent Catholic but already an opponent of political violence. Taking advantage of a recent change in the law, he enrolled to study for the bar, a decision that later equipped him to defend the rights of his fellow Irishmen in British courts. After a few years in London, he also became a deist and a fervent disciple of the English radical William Godwin. Yet O'Connell had no involvement in the Irish uprising of 1798 and privately lamented the atrocities committed by the rebels: "Oh Liberty, what horrors are committed in thy name!" (MacDonagh, *Hereditary Bondsman* 65).

O'Connell never entirely outgrew this youthful florid style, which served him well in public as an attorney and orator. Tall and striking in appearance, he dressed with flair and did not shrink from a challenge of honor; his wife's pleas against fighting a duel probably saved his life on at least one occasion. His voice was described as "leonine." Late in his career, attendance at the "monster meetings" where he spoke numbered up to half a million. O'Connell possessed the common touch, but he deliberately avoided the use of Gaelic, recognizing that English was the "medium of all modern communication." These traits, together with a driving ambition to achieve something great, account for his success. He married in 1802, and his wife, Mary, exerted a steadying influence in bringing him back to Catholic piety and overseeing their shaky domestic finances.

The Union of Ireland to the kingdom of Great Britain in 1801 was intended to be accompanied by broader civil and political rights for Catholic inhabitants, but the promise of emancipation was not fulfilled until much later, in 1829. O'Connell was among the first to denounce the union and took a leading role in organizing a Catholic committee to oppose it. His initial aim was to make Prime Minister Pitt carry out his promise to end legal disabilities against Catholics. This effort failed, and in the process O'Connell made some lifelong political enemies. Not only did he insult the young Tory politician Robert Peel, who came to despise him as a dangerous demagogue, but he also sided against Irish Catholics of the highest social rank, whom he accurately portrayed as willing to accept the British demand for "securities," including a veto over episcopal nominations, in exchange for granting Catholic rights. On the other hand, in his early thirties he already enjoyed a growing cult of personality, which reflected support for him among the Catholic populace, not only the minority who could vote, but the disenfranchised peasantry as well.

O'Connell seized the role of intermediary between the discontented Irish middle class and the British government at Westminster. Under his leadership, the Catholic Association functioned as a modern political organization, mobilizing voters and staging mass demonstrations. Sustained by the so-called Catholic rent, a subscription of one penny a month collected by sympathetic parish priests, its members defied their landlords' electoral influence. Once O'Connell had been admitted to Parliament and Catholic emancipation was secured, similar pressure was exerted to back up the demand for "Repeal." O'Connell's definition of this term remained usefully imprecise. On some occasions, his heated rhetoric seemed to threaten violent resistance—"I say they may trample me, but it will be my

Daniel O'Connell. Courtesy of the Library of Congress.

dead body they trample on, not the living man" (MacDonagh, *Emancipist* 222)—but at the same time he pursued legislative changes like land reform, extension of the franchise, and abolition of the Anglican tithe on Irish Catholics. In the end, more radical members of the association, the Young Ireland faction, blamed him for cooperating with the Whig administration during the 1830s and for peacefully abandoning a climactic monster meeting under pressure from the government. Even before O'Connell's death, the Repeal campaign faded under the impact of the Great Famine.

O'Connell was and has continued to be a controversial figure. His overarching commitment was to the principle of human liberty. He eloquently condemned American slavery at a time when many Irish emigrants held slaves, and he provided inspiration to romantic nationalists everywhere. The conservative Prince **Klemens von Metternich** was particularly alarmed at the popularity of his ideas among revolutionaries in the Austrian empire. Not surprisingly, O'Connell had an ambivalent relationship with the papacy, which feared that his activities would jeopardize the church's temporal influence. Although he couched his liberal reforms within the context of obedience to Christian doctrine, he also believed in a church that was itself independent of state control. When O'Connell died, while on pilgrimage to Rome, the pope eulogized him as "the great champion of the Church, the father of his country, the glory of the Christian world" (Nowlan and O'Connell, 105–6). But it is arguable that his cause was even wider than his Catholic identity would allow.

Bibliography. MacDonagh, Oliver. *The Emancipist: Daniel O'Connell 1830–1847.* New York: St. Martin's Press, 1989. MacDonagh, Oliver. *The Hereditary Bondsman: Daniel O'Connell, 1775–1829.* New York: St. Martin's Press, 1987. Nowlan, Kevin B., and Maurice R. O'Connell, eds. *Daniel O'Connell: Portrait of a Radical.* New York: Fordham University Press, 1985. O'Connell, Daniel. *Daniel O'Connell: His Early Life and Journal, 1795 to 1802.* Ed. Arthur Houston. London: Sir I. Pitman, 1906. O'Connell, Maurice R. *Daniel O'Connell: The Man and His Politics.* Dublin: Irish Academic Press, 1990.

John D. Ramsbottom

O'CONNOR, JOHN (1920–2000). O'Connor, the nation's leading Roman Catholic cleric during the 1980s and 1990s, rose from working-class Irish American roots to become a prince of the church. As archbishop of New York, he used the city's media to present a consistent Catholic perspective on the nation's social, political, and economic issues. O'Connor often created controversy when his soft-spoken but unshakeable convictions could not be reduced to soundbites.

O'Connor was born in 1920 to working-class second-generation Irish American parents in Philadelphia. He was ordained a Catholic priest in 1945. After two years of parish work, he became a navy chaplain. O'Connor served combat tours in Korea and Vietnam and eventually rose to the rank of admiral. After twenty-seven years he retired from the navy to become bishop of Scranton, Pennsylvania, in 1984. After only eight months, **John Paul II** surprisingly named O'Connor to replace Terrence Cardinal Cooke as archbishop of New York. O'Connor became a cardinal himself a year later. O'Connor's rapid ascendance coincided with the 1984 presidential election and illuminated emerging tensions in Roman Catholicism's close affiliation with the Democratic Party. While supportive of the Democrats' economic platform, O'Connor did not mince criticism of the party's defense of abortion rights. He singled out Mario Cuomo and Geraldine Ferraro, both Catholic New York Democrats, for refusing to support the church's antiabortion position.

O'Connor quickly and aggressively commanded New York's media to express unequivocally the church's views on anti-Semitism, sex, divorce, and euthanasia. With equal vigor he lauded the church's vision of economic justice for the working class and the poor. O'Connor never shied from any public conflict concerning these issues. Heated public exchanges in the New York, and thus national, media became standard fare during O'Connor's sixteen-year reign. Many opponents failed to grasp how O'Connor's Catholicism could support equally conservative social positions and liberal economic ones. Certainly no one doubted his loyalty to the Vatican. O'Connor expected the same from all American Catholics. His contradictory style continued until his death.

O'Connor worked tirelessly among New York's AIDS hospices but in 1995 refused to join a national initiative to reconcile the widening ideological distance between American Catholics. The archdiocese's priests feared him, but O'Connor also reserved one day a week for them to visit without appointment. Both supporters and opponents claimed his combative and proud demeanor matched perfectly that of his city.

Bibliography. Golway, Terry. *Full of Grace: An Oral Biography of John Cardinal O'Connor.* New York: Pocket Books, 2002. Hentoff, Nat. *John Cardinal O'Connor: At the Storm Center of a Changing American Catholic Church.* New York: Scribners, 1988.

Jeffrey Marlett

OGNEV, NIKOLAI VASIL'EVICH (1864– 1918). The son of a highly educated priest who was dismissed from the church school system in 1873 for "freethinking," Ognev was a prominent liberal clergyman and political activist with the Constitutional-Democratic Party (Kadets) in late imperial Russia.

He graduated in 1891 from the progressive Theological Academy of St. Petersburg. A priest from 1895 and archpriest from 1902, Ognev taught at church schools in his native Viatka Province. As superintendent of a church district, president of the district branch of the Viatka Diocesan Education Council and later clergy deputy in the Orlov city council, Ognev, like other educated and energetic priests of his generation, was trained in social activism and became an excellent orator.

After the outbreak of the 1905 revolution, Ognev organized meetings of clergy and laypeople in Viatka Province to discuss political questions such as the church's relations to the oppositionist "liberation movement" and the need for clergy to educate themselves and their parishioners about the electoral law of December 1905. Ognev associated himself early with Russia's main liberal party, the Kadets, organizing the local party committee and converting the meetings of peasant agricultural societies to forums of political discussion.

In 1906, the agricultural society Ognev himself headed joined the Kadets *in corpore* while he and the society's secretary were elected deputies to the first State Duma. Immensely popular with local clergy as a candid defender of their interests and a seasoned president of priests' assemblies and congresses, Ognev was considered a "notorious revolutionary propagandist" by the Viatka governor and police. In the Duma and at meetings of peasants from St. Petersburg Province, Ognev pronounced speeches against the death penalty and other government measures, founding his position on holy scripture. His demands on church reform, such as including laypeople in a hoped-for Church Council, assigning salaries to parish clergy, and electing prelates from among the white (married) clergy placed Ognev in disfavor with the local conservative Bishop Filaret.

Ognev's fate was sealed when he signed the June 1906 Vyborg Manifesto, which called on Russians to protest the dissolution of the first Duma by refusing to pay taxes and avoiding the military draft. In October 1906 the Holy Synod of the Russian Orthodox Church temporarily suspended Ognev from service. In 1907, although 331 parishioners sent a telegram to Prime Minister P.A. Stolypin supporting Ognev, he was exiled from Viatka Province and sentenced to three months' incarceration for "extremely harmful antigovernmental activity." Consequently the synod was forced to defrock Ognev, who was under constant police surveillance thereafter. From 1908 to 1912 he took on university studies in St. Petersburg and later worked as a sworn juror at the Viatka Circuit Court.

Remaining a loyal Kadet after the February revolution, Ognev became an assistant provincial commissar of the Provisional Government in May 1917. In June he was elected to the Viatka city council and in October–November he ran for the Constituent Assembly. In December 1917 a local Bolshevik committee arrested and incarcerated several representatives of the Provisional Government including Ognev, whom they executed in August 1918.

Bibliography. Ognev, Nikolai. *Na poroge reform tserkvi i dukhovenstva.* St. Petersburg: Levenshteina, 1907. Sudovikov, M.S. "N.V. Ognev -sviashchennik, politik, chelovek." In *Religiia i tserkov' v kul'turno-istoricheskom razvitii russkogo severa: Materialy mezhdunarodnoi nauchnoi konferentsii.* Kirov: Nauchnyi sovet RAN "Rol' religii v istorii." Departament Kul'tury i Iskusstva, Administratsiia Kirovskoi Oblasti & Viatskii Gos. Pedagogicheskii Universitet, 1996.

Argyrios K. Pisiotis

OSSICINI, ADRIANO (b. 1920). In his early years, Ossicini maintained contacts with key figures of the Catholic modernist movement such as **Romolo Murri** and Ernesto Buonaiuti, became an active young leader of **Italian Catholic Action,** and was among the founders of the so-called Christian Left in 1937.

Ossicini was born in Rome to a family of secular and antifascist Catholics, and his father was a close collaborator with **Luigi Sturzo** and a leader among **Italian Popular Party** Catholics, who gathered around the paper *Il Domani d'Italia* and rejected **Pope Pius XI**'s Concordat as a compromise with the Fascist regime. This group rejected Fascist ideology and resolved to take an active stand against it to counter the church's de facto support of Mussolini's regime. Subsequently, the group merged with others to constitute an extended network including young Catholic and communist students and workers.

Arrested along with many others and then released in late 1943 upon the demise of the Fascist regime, Ossicini took an active part in the underground anti-Nazi activity of the group that now identified itself as the Movement of Catholic Communists (*Movimento dei Cattolici Comunisti*). After the liberation of Rome (June 1944), the movement regrouped under the name Party of the Christian Left (*Partito della Sinistra Cristiana,* PSC). The motion for the dissolution of the PSC in December 1945 passed, notwithstanding Ossicini's opposition. He maintained that a "democratic party of Christians" could still provide an alternative to the formulated political unity of Catholics upon which the rise to power of the **Christian Democracy** rested with the decisive backing of the church.

For over twenty years Ossicini kept out of active politics while successfully pursuing an academic and professional career. At 26 he became full university professor in psychology and established his practice as a child psychiatrist. In response to Ferruccio Parri's 1967 appeal, he accepted a candidacy on the Independent Left slate. Parri, a most respected historic leader of the Action Party and of the antifascist Resistance, hoped thus to resurrect the third way as a means to depolarize Italian politics, which ultimately proved unsuccessful. Ossicini became a reference point for many Catholic personalities disillusioned with the Christian Democracy's power manipulation and was elected senator for the Independent Left for six consecutive terms (1968–1992). In 1996 he was elected to another term for the left-wing Ulivo coalition. In the Italian Senate he held the office of vice president for two terms, chaired the Commission on Education, and introduced significant bills in the field of health care, mental health, and mental health services for children. At the end of his final term in 1997 he returned to his academic activity and writing. He is professor emeritus of psychology at the University of Rome and is a member of many cultural and scientific bodies, including the National Commission of Bioethics, of which he is the honorary chair.

Bibliography. Malgeri, Francesco. *La sinistra cristiana (1937–1945).* Brescia, Italy: Morcelliana Editrice, 1982.

Margherita Repetto-Alaia

OTTAVIANI, ALFREDO (1890–1979). Born in Rome, Cardinal Ottaviani was one of the most powerful members of the Roman Curia (the administrative arm of the church) in the twentieth century. Known for his conservative and traditionalist orientation, Ottaviani's cardinal motto was *semper idem*—always and ever the same. Through his position in the Sacred Congregation of the Holy Office, Ottaviani exercised influence in virtually every matter that touched upon the doctrine, the structure, and the practices of modern-day Catholicism. Ever suspicious of liberal theologians and would-be reformers within the church, Ottaviani was a leading conservative spokesperson during the Second Vatican Council, and an outspoken anticommunist.

Ottaviani attended the Pontifical Roman Seminary and was ordained a priest in 1916. He also taught at various Roman pontifical universities before moving on to the Secretariat of State. He became assessor of the Holy Office in December 1935 and secretary in November 1959. The influence of the Holy Office allowed Ottaviani to emerge as one of a small handful of influential cardinals known in Vatican circles as "the Roman party." Some historians describe him as more of a jurist than a theologian. Ottaviani exhibited a legalistic and markedly "Roman" approach to the affairs of the Holy See. That is, he believed that supreme authority in the church resides with the bishop of Rome and with the juridical and hierarchical structure of the curia that surround the successor of St. Peter.

For Ottaviani, preserving the authority of the pope and the hierarchical structure of decision making allowed the church to carry out its providential mission as defender of the faith, and as the bearer of civilization. This was especially urgent in light of the rise of Soviet-style communism, which Ottaviani identified as the single greatest threat to the interests of the church and to all Western civilization. Ottaviani understood the church to be the bulwark against the spread of communism; fighting the spread of this atheistic and materialist doctrine became his overarching priority. Ottaviani saw communism and Catholicism as inescapably irreconcilable, a clash of civilizations between the church and the anti-church. Ottaviani's political struggle against communism inevitably spilled into matters of doctrine. In 1949, he ordered the excommunication of Catholics who joined Communist parties or openly supported them in any way.

Ottaviani believed that the church had to be engaged in politics. As he observed in 1956, if politics dared to touch the altar, how could the church not intervene to make sure the altar was not profaned? The church had the responsibility to be politically engaged in order to judge whether political leaders used their powers for the common good, which extended to the moral and spiritual well-being of society. He rejected those who wanted the church out of the political affairs of the state. As Ottaviani saw it, the church involved itself in politics in its providential role as teacher and guide of the people of God.

As a leading conservative in the Roman Curia, Ottaviani tried in vain to chart a traditionalist course for the work of the Second Vatican Council. With calls for reform in almost all areas of church life—from the role of the bishops to ecumenism, anti-Semitism, and liturgical reform—Ottaviani asked, "Are these fathers planning a revolution?" (Bokenkotter, 359)

While Vatican II was not the revolution Ottaviani had worried it might become, it did signal a fundamental shift in central aspects of church doctrine and structure. It also reflected the waning influence of Cardinal Ottaviani and the Roman party within an increasingly internationalized curia. Cardinal Ottaviani died in the Vatican City.

Bibliography. Bokenkotter, Thomas. *A Concise History of the Catholic Church.* New York: Doubleday, 1990. Riccardi, Andrea. *Il Potere del Papa da Pio XII a Giovanni Paolo II.* Bari-Rome, Italy: Laterza, 1993.

Robert A. Ventresca

OZANAM, ANTOINE-FRÉDÉRIC (1813–1853). The Milan-born Ozanam made his best-known and most important achievement early in his life during his studies at Paris (1831–1836), when he cofounded what later became known as the Society of St. Vincent de Paul (Société de Saint-Vincent de Paul), the so-called *conférence de charité,* on April 23, 1833,

After his time at university, Ozanam became a lawyer in Lyons (1836–1839) until he was called to a professorship of foreign languages at the Sorbonne in Paris in 1840. During his lifetime it was his academic career and publications concerning Dante, the early and medieval church, and the Christianization of Europe that gained him renown. Although those philosophical, theological, and historical studies still form the modern image of Ozanam, he is nowadays best remembered for his social ideas. They were not only expressed in the *conférence de charité* as a practical tool of Christian charity but had a theoretical foundation outlined in his writings as well.

He pleaded that the pope adopt a liberal policy (especially during and after the revolutionary events of 1848) and propagated Christian democracy as the true Christian vocation. His approach, revolutionary for the Catholicism of that time, was to denounce the old collaboration between throne and altar, which had lasted since the Christianization of Europe, and plead for a new union between the Catholic Church and the power of the people expressed in a democratic society. He was, however, not a Jacobin. The basis for Ozanam's thought was a belief that Providence forced history to go down the road of democracy. Nevertheless, his active engagement in politics betrayed his bourgeois sympathies, as he joined the National Guard to suppress the popular uprising in June 1848.

In the course of events he tried to mediate, but failed, when the archbishop of Paris was killed during a personal intervention to end the fighting. Politically Ozanam failed, as the socialists never accepted him as an honest reformer, and he was detested by many in his own bourgeois and Catholic circles. Although he cannot be considered a radical, he certainly was a revolutionary within the Catholic Church. His legacy was not only due to the charitable work of the Société de Saint-Vincent de Paul, but due also to the fact that Ozanam was the symbol for a more liberal, compassionate Catholicism. In a certain way Ozanam predicted some of the key ideas of the Second Vatican Council more than hundred years before it took place.

The most important legacy of Ozanam is without doubt the organization that he founded in 1833 with five companions as a conference for charity. It was transformed into the actual Société in 1835 and spread to Italy, Britain, and the United States in under ten years. Today it is a Catholic mass organization with a worldwide membership (up to 900,000 members by its own records) and is represented in every corner of France. In 1921 the *Union des Oeuvres Françaises de Saint-Vincent de Paul* was created to coordinate the local chapters. The beatification of Ozanam by Pope **John Paul II** in 1997 emphasized that he was as a forerunner of the lay engagement within the Catholic Church and an even more popular figure within French Catholicism.

Bibliography. Auge, Thomas. *Frederic Ozanam and His World.* Milwaukee, WI: Bruce, 1966 Cattanéo, Bernard. *Frédéric Ozanam le bienheureux.* Paris: Éditions du Cerf, 1997. Celier, Léonce. *Frédéric Ozanam.* Paris: Lethielleux, 1956. Chareire, Isabelle, ed. *Frédéric Ozanam: Actes du Colloque des 4 et 5 décembre 1998.* Paris: Bayard, 2001.

Oliver Benjamin Hemmerle

P

PADRE CÍCERO. *See* Batista, Cícero Romão

PAISLEY, IAN (b. 1926). Paisley has been the face of militant Protestantism and Unionism in Northern Ireland since the 1960s. Born in Ballymena, Antrim, he founded his own break-away church, known as the Free Presbyterian Church of Ulster, in 1951. Questions have been raised about the validity of his degrees and ordination, but he has had close links with the American fundamentalist Bob Jones University, which granted him an honorary degree in 1966. His religious opposition to Catholicism was linked to political fears of Catholics in Northern Ireland and their desire for unification with the Irish Republic.

The development of the civil rights movement and civil unrest that led to the Troubles in Northern Ireland led him into political life. He founded the break-away Democratic Unionist Party, a splinter party of the Ulster Unionist Party. It has successfully contested elections at the local and Northern Ireland levels as well as to the British parliament and the European Parliament. He was first elected to the British parliament in 1970. He was elected to the European Parliament in 1979, despite his opposition to the European Community, which he saw as a "popish plot." In the 2003 elections for the Northern Ireland Assembly, his party emerged as the majority party on the Unionist side. He has strongly opposed all moves toward reconciliation between the two communities in Northern Ireland and with the Irish Republic. He has denounced British prime ministers as fiercely as he has denounced Catholic priests and popes and Nationalist politicians and terrorists. He sees all of them as threats to the survival both of fundamentalist Protestantism and Northern Ireland.

Paisley has opposed all moves toward reconciliation, from the Sunningdale Agreement of 1975 to the Good Friday Agreement of 1999. He opposes power sharing with Catholics, whether this involves the Social Democratic and Labour Party (SDLP) or the more radical **Sinn Fein.** He refuses to participate in any discussions that involve the latter because of their association with the Irish Republican Army (IRA). Yet Paisley himself has not been above using the threat of violence and violent language to achieve his own ends.

Paisley has been a lightning rod in the ongoing conflict in Northern Ireland. He invokes strong feelings of loyalty among his followers, but even stronger feelings of anger and hatred among his opponents. His view of the contemporary world is rooted in the seventeenth-century religious values of evangelical Protestants, who believed their Calvinist doctrines were threatened by Catholicism and especially by the papacy. Such fears help produce language that thrills his followers, angers his opponents, and baffles outsiders.

Paisley's position of "No Surrender" on the Ulster Unionist link to Great Britain and opposition to any form of religious ecumenism sometimes seems at odds with his private self, of someone who seems to have good relationships with family and friends and even some of his political opponents, including former SDLP leader John Hume. He has the reputation of being a very good and capable MP who works hard for all his constituents, including Catholics.

Bibliography. Smyth, Clifford. *Ian Paisley: Voice of Protestant Ulster.* Edinburgh: Scottish Academic Press, 1988.

Gretchen M. MacMillan

PAPANDREOU, DEMETRIOS [DAMASKINOS] (1890–1949). Papandreou served as Greek Orthodox prelate, metropolitan of Corinth (1922–1938), archbishop of Athens (1941–1949), and regent of Greece (1944–1946). As Archbishop Damaskinos, he was the spiritual leader of Greece during the difficult years of Axis occupation and civil war.

Born in Dhorvitsia and educated as a lawyer at the University of Athens, Damaskinos was anointed a deacon of the Greek Orthodox Church by the Greek Holy Synod in 1917. His rise in the church hierarchy was meteoric, and within a year, the synod appointed him abbot of the Penteli Monastery in Athens. After a highly successful tenure as the metropolitan of Corinth, Damaskinos was elected archbishop of Athens in 1938, but the election was nullified for political reasons by the dictatorial Metaxas regime, and Damaskinos reentered the monastic life in protest.

In 1941, the Axis-controlled puppet government of General Tsolakoglou reinstated Damaskinos as archbishop of Athens. As the titular leader of the Greek Church, Damaskinos did much to surreptitiously aid Greek resistance to the Axis, while at the same time maintaining a delicate relationship with the occupying forces. Notified of the deportation of the Greek Jews of Thessaloníki in the early spring of 1943, Damaskinos undertook the risk of writing a letter of condemnation to the president of the puppet regime and to the Third Reich's administrator for Greece. In Athens, Damaskinos attempted to save the local Greek Jewish population by providing them with false identity papers and aiding them in finding covert means of escape from the city.

The withdrawal of Axis forces in October 1944 ushered in a period of civil strife in Greece, when local communist-led resistance forces clashed with British garrison troops, who were intent on supporting the establishment of an anticommunist coalition government. A bone of contention was whether postwar Greece would be a monarchy or a republic. Because of

Archbishop Damaskinos, 1945. © Time Life Pictures / Getty Images

his impeccable wartime reputation, Damaskinos was chosen by the exiled king to act as his regent until a plebiscite could occur. He fulfilled this duty ably and even briefly served as prime minister of Greece in October of 1945. The return of the monarchy in 1946 allowed Damaskinos to concentrate strictly on ecclesiastical duties until his death in 1949.

Bibliography. Venezis, Elias. *Archiepiskopos Damaskinos: Oi Chronoi tes Douleias.* Athens: Estia, 1981.

Kyriakos Nalmpantis

PARKER, THEODORE (1810–1860). A Unitarian clergyman in Boston, Parker may have been the greatest intellect ever to grace the American pulpit. Largely self-educated in his early years, Parker would become a graduate of Harvard University. During his life he mastered twenty languages and at his death his library, one of the finest in New England, numbered 20,000 volumes, spanning a wide variety of subjects.

Parker was an ecclesiastical and social reformer. For fifteen years he was the pastor of the Twenty-eighth Congregational Society in Boston, where three thousand people crowded the Music Hall every Sunday to hear a sermon from this brilliant and controversial preacher. Greatly influenced by transcendentalism, Parker's theology was based upon intuition, which he perceived to be the voice of God. Religious authority was not based upon the Bible, the church, or tradition, but upon conscience, which Parker labeled as higher law—higher than judicial law, ecclesiastical law, or even the United States Constitution. Though his congregation was considered Unitarian, most Unitarians in his era considered Parker heretical and would not associate or exchange pulpits with him. Though many transcendentalists, such as **Ralph Waldo Emerson,** left the church, Parker remained, hoping to reform the church

from within. Over time, Unitarianism became what Parker advocated, and he is generally credited with marking the emancipation of Unitarianism from all semblance of Christian orthodoxy.

Equally important with ecclesiastical reform was social reform. Nothing in society escaped Parker's scrutiny and critical judgment: poverty, ignorance, prostitution, capital punishment, those who paid low wages and high dividends, those who exacted exorbitant rents for wretched slum dwellings, lawyers who would defend the worst causes for the right price, judges who thought it a crime to be poor, and a criminal justice system that neither prevented crime nor reformed criminals. It was for slavery Parker reserved his harshest words, labeling it the "sum of all villainies." He castigated Daniel Webster, the popular Massachusetts senator, for his part in the passage of the Fugitive Slave Law. He helped in the formation of the Boston Vigilance Committee, which aided fugitive slaves to escape to safety. He denounced the Mexican War as a cruel conflict waged in the interests of expansionist slaveholders. He condemned his fellow clergymen for their timidity in taking a strong stand against the sin of slavery. For Parker, at the heart of almost every social evil was the inordinate desire for wealth—greed.

On May 10, 1860, three months shy of his fiftieth birthday, Parker died, apparently of tuberculosis, in Florence, Italy. He had gone to Europe in hopes of regaining his health. He is buried in the Protestant cemetery of Florence. In the fall of 1866, **Frederick Douglass** visited Parker's grave. Standing by the headstone, the former slave recalled "the many services rendered the cause of human freedom by [Parker], freedom not only from physical chains but the chains of superstition, those which not only galled the limbs and tore the flesh, but those which marred and wounded the human soul." Douglass remembered that Parker "had a voice for the slave; when nearly all the pulpits of the land were dumb."

Bibliography. Commager, Henry Steel. *Theodore Parker: Yankee Crusader.* Boston: Little Brown, 1936. Parker, Theodore. *Centenary Edition of the Works of Theodore Parker.* 15 vols. Boston: American Unitarian Association, 1907–1910.

David B. Chesebrough

PARKIN, GEORGE ROBERT (1846–1922). A Canadian educator and writer, Parkin was also, during the last twenty years of his life, the organizing secretary of the Rhodes Scholarship Trust. A widely known leader of the Imperial Federation Movement in Canada, as well as in Australia and other parts of the British Empire, he impressed all who met him with his everlasting energy and enthusiasm. His Anglican faith and his political beliefs were two sides of the same devotion; indeed, his religious fervor together with his passion for imperial unity unified the work he carried out as an educator and administrator.

Parkin strongly believed in the beneficial influence of Christianity in the world, the teachings of Christ being a universal solution to all problems, individual as well as national. Only such an influence could counterbalance modern individualism by implanting a sense of duty and service. Furthermore, for him the British Empire and the **Social Gospel** progressed hand in hand, for the former was the main vehicle of the latter, while, in turn, the member states of the empire would merely be feeble links if they were not politically purified by the Christian Social Gospel.

Parkin was an evolutionist who felt that the duty of the most advanced people was to help "backward" races to progress. Just as teachers instilled self-restraint, discipline, and scorn for debasing distractions into young men, so imperialism infused into less advanced nations a love for noble effort, sagacity, and broadmindedness, all virtues necessary to achieving

great spiritual ends. In this view, the Anglo-Saxon people were dedicated to addressing the higher problems of civilization, thus explaining why the British Empire was said to be a divine agency whose mission was to enhance the overall well-being of humanity.

Bibliography. Berger, Carl. *The Sense of Power: Studies in the Ideas of Canadian Imperialism, 1867–1914.* Toronto: University of Toronto Press, 1970.

Sylvie Lacombe

PARNELL, CHARLES STEWART (1846–1891). Parnell was an Anglo-Irish Protestant landlord from Wicklow who became the leader of Irish Catholic Ireland in the 1880s. Parnell first came to public attention following his election to the British parliament as MP for Meath in 1875. He engaged in several obstructionist activities in the British House of Commons in an attempt to engage the British government in the problems of Ireland. He became president of the **Land League** in 1879 and the following year was elected leader of the Irish Parliamentary Party (IPP). The 1885 general election resulted in the return of eighty-six IPP members of Parliament. The strength of the party in Parliament convinced British prime minister Sir **William Gladstone** to try to bring about home rule for Ireland. Although the bill failed in the British parliament, Parnell's dominance over Irish nationalist politics continued.

He began to lose influence in the late 1880s when he failed to support the Plan of Campaign, a continuation of the land agitation of the early 1880s. However, his fall from power came after he was named as correspondent in a divorce case brought by one of his own MPs, Willie O'Shea. Parnell's liaison with Katherine O'Shea had been known by some members of his party but had been kept secret from the public. Although initially Parnell's support in Ireland remained high, the divorce case made many supporters uncomfortable. It was, however, the pressure brought on Sir William Gladstone by his supporters among Methodists in Britain that would swing the Catholic hierarchy against him in Ireland. He was defeated in a vote on the leadership of the IPP in 1890. He died the following year from pneumonia.

While Parnell came from the Protestant landlord class and displayed no strong religious views of his own, he was able to create a strong nationalist-based political party built on Catholic support. The hierarchy might have been wary of his motives, but they were willing to give him support and to provide him with their backing. The degree to which he was able to use this depended on the issue. Moreover, this support sometimes conflicted with the support Parnell could expect from members of his own party and the people themselves. This is reflected in two major issues: the Plan of Campaign and the O'Shea divorce case.

The Plan of Campaign in the late 1880s was a continuation of the agrarian unrest associated with the Land League in the first years of the decade. It proved to be more violent and was associated with the civil unrest known as the boycott. The British government was able to persuade Pope **Leo XIII** to condemn the Plan of Campaign, which Parnell also opposed. The hierarchy did acquiesce in the Vatican's condemnation, but many Irish Catholic MPs who supported the agitation condemned the Vatican's interference. This was an area of public policy that did not fall under the unspoken agreement regarding areas that could be part of the bishops' purview, such as education and morality.

This was somewhat different in the fallout from the O'Shea divorce case. In this instance the moral authority of the bishops would have been brought into

Charles Parnell. Courtesy of the Library of Congress

question if they continued to support him following the O'Shea divorce case. This was particularly true after the Methodists in Great Britain threatened to withdraw their support from Gladstone if he continued to support Parnell. Many later nationalists and literary figures used this episode to indicate the lack of sympathy the Catholic hierarchy had for nationalism and independence. This was not entirely wrong, but what did bring the bishops and the MPs together on this issue arose from the Methodist opposition to Parnell. Whatever the bishops might have felt personally about the survival of Parnell as leader of Catholic Ireland, these feelings had to be put aside once the Methodist Church in Britain made clear their moral opposition to Parnell. For the members of the IPP, it was Gladstone's threat to withdraw his support for home rule that influenced the majority to withdraw their support for Parnell's leadership.

Bibliography. Larkin, Emmet. *The Roman Catholic Church in Ireland and the Fall of Parnell, 1888–1891.* Chapel Hill: University of North Carolina Press, 1979. Lyons, F. S. L. *Charles Stewart Parnell.* London: Collins, 1977.

Gretchen M. MacMillan

PARONETTO, SERGIO (1911–1945). After living in various Italian cities during his youth, Paronetto finally settled in Rome in 1932, when he enrolled at the Faculty of Political Science of the University of Rome. From a very early stage he displayed a profound interest and ability in the fields of financial and political economy, where he would contribute his most original and lasting ideas. After briefly working for the *Illustrazione Vaticana* magazine, he secured a position with the *Istituto di Ricostruzione Industriale* (IRI), the institute created by the Fascist state in the first months of 1933 in order to provide long-term government loans for industry.

During Paronetto's university years, he participated in the Catholic students' organization, the *Federazione Universitaria Cattolica Italiana* (FUCI), which was at the time led by the future **Paul VI**, Giovannni Battista Montini, and Igino Righetti. A close collaborator with the Montini-Righetti line—characterized by a sense of dialogue with the anxieties of modern men, a convinced support for the potentialities of the individual religious conscience, and the penetration of a Catholic intellectual elite in the structures of modern society—Paronetto was a fruitful witness in these delicate years, acting as national adviser for the federation and secretary of the association's journal, *Studium.* He also played a leading part (with Righetti) in the 1932 creation of the *Movimento Laureati,* an organization for Catholic alumni.

Paronetto formed part of the generation that matured under the "normality" of Fascist Italy or, as the historian Renzo De Felice has argued, the years of "consensus." In this respect, Paronetto was alien to the tradition of the pre-Fascist Catholic movement and, most notably, to the antifascist line adopted by some sectors of the former **Italian Popular Party** of Don **Luigi Sturzo.** As such, Paronetto was a warm enthusiast of state intervention in the economy as championed by the IRI, and the control of the economic forces in view of the general interest. Despite some reservations due to his Catholic formation, he embraced corporativism and the autarchic policies advanced by the regime.

During the 1930s the strong anticommunism espoused by the Catholic alumni led them to the support of **Francisco Franco**'s Nationalist forces in Spain. It is in this climate that one has to understand some antidemocratic stances taken by Paronetto and his praise for seemingly Catholic-authoritarian solutions, such as those found in **António Salazar**'s Portugal. Indeed, Paronetto vehemently condemned the diverse "human mystics" such as the "democratic ideology," in his opinion no less "satanic" and "totalitarian" than others, that he recognized in the French Popular Front.

Italy's alliance with Nazi Germany, the introduction of anti-Semitic legislation and, above all, the disastrous military defeats during the Second World War led many Catholics, and among them Paronetto, to lose any remote hope of a possible Christianization of the regime. He urged Catholics to adopt an active role in the destiny of the nation and, with admirable intellectual and moral honesty, proclaimed after the fall of Mussolini that few Italians could look upon their recent past without remorse.

In these new circumstances, he advocated a revolutionary role for the professions, their main goal being the enactment of social justice, which was uncompromising in its attack of the values of bourgeois capitalist society. It was a mentality far removed from the liberal democratic tradition that would lead to sharp contrasts with **Alcide De Gasperi**'s line in the nascent **Christian Democracy** (DC), albeit this did not preclude collaboration between the two. The high esteem De Gasperi held for Paronetto's competence in economic matters resulted in their cooperation in the composition of the *Idee ricostruttive della DC* (Reconstructive Ideas of the DC), a founding document of the party. Paronetto, nevertheless, refrained from a direct engagement in the newly formed Christian Democrat party.

It was undoubtedly the elaboration of the text *Per la comunità cristiana. Principi dell'ordinamento sociale*—better known as the Camaldoli Code—for which Paronetto is best known. Based on discussions that occurred in July 1943 at the Camaldoli monastery near Florence with other Catholic intellectuals, this text reflects the most enduring ideals espoused by Paronetto—social justice and the need of a fruitful state intervention. Above all, he wanted attention focused on concrete historical contingencies, and withdrawn from the temptation of simplistic and faddish recipes.

Significantly, Paronetto displayed a great independence from the social teachings of the church in this realm, opting instead for measuring socioeconomic issues on their own terms, albeit firmly rooted in a Christian conscience, in a personal spirituality that has come to be known as the "ascetic of the man of action," the title of a posthumous collection of his writings. Paronetto died prematurely in 1945 at the age of thirty-four.

Bibliography. Paronetto, Sergio. *Ascetica dell'uomo d'azione.* Rome: Studium, 1948. Paronetto Valier, M. L. *Sergio Paronetto: Libertà d'iniziativa e giustizia sociale.* Rome: Studium, 1991. Scaglia, G. B. "Pensoso uomo di azione." *Studium* 4 (1985): 423–40.

Jorge Dagnino

PARTI DEMOCRATE POPULAIRE. *See* Democratic Popular Party.

PARTIDO ACCIÓN NACIONAL (MEXICO). *See* National Action Party.

PARTIDO CATÓLICO NACIONAL (MEXICO). *See* National Catholic Party.

PARTIDO DEMÓCRATA CRISTIANO (CHILE). *See* Christian Democratic Party (Chile).

PARTIDO NACIONALISTA VASCO (SPAIN). *See* Basque Nationalist Party.

PARTIDO POPULAR (SPAIN). *See* Popular Party.

PARTI SOCIAL CHRÉTIEN (BELGIUM). *See* Christian Social Party.

PARTITO POPOLARE ITALIANO (ITALY). *See* Italian Popular Party.

PASCAL, PIERRE (1909–1990). Born at Mons-en-Baroeul (France), Pascal, the Catholic traditionalist polemicist and activist, was the son of Paul Pascal, the chemist who authored the twelve-volume *Treatise of Mineral Chemistry,* which was used as a university text for a considerable period of time.

As an adolescent, Pascal spent time in Japan, where he became familiar with Japanese culture and civilization. During the 1950s, he corresponded with the right-wing poet Yukio Mishima and gained entrance into the Academy of the Brush Forest through his poetry. Upon returning to France, Pascal studied literature and history at the Sorbonne in Paris and received a diploma from the School of Oriental Languages. It was while he attended this language school that Pascal learned Persian, which later gave him the opportunity to translate the quatrains of Omar Khayyân. Also during his studies, Pascal adhered to the **Action Française** and met **Charles Maurras,** of whom he remained a fervent disciple for the rest of his life.

Upon joining the French army, Pascal became an officer in the Foreign Legion. Following the 1934 February manifestations that endangered the French Republic, Pascal left his position and then devoted himself to literature and journalism. Also in 1934, Pascal founded *Eurydice,* a poetry review, and Trident Editions, which was a publisher of poetry (including works by himself, Maurras, and others).

During World War II, Pascal remained in Paris as an editor of various newspapers. Upon France's liberation, he was condemned to death in absentia for collaboration. Pascal took refuge in Rome, where he remained until his death, and worked as the chancellor of the Iran embassy to the Vatican as well as the librarian for the French Seminary in Rome. At the same time, he created a publishing house, Faithful Heart Editions, that published, in French, his poetic paraphrasing of the Apocalypse and the Book of Job. It also produced translated commentaries of Edgar Allan Poe and the poems of St. Theresa of Avila, in addition to publishing a translation in nine languages of the famous *Credo* of Pope **Paul VI** and a *Commemoration* of Padre Pio by Cardinal Lecaro. Pascal's work belongs to a now-defunct tradition of sacred poetry and civic poetry. He always looked to link his faithfulness to the nationalism of Charles Maurras and to the Catholic counterrevolutionary tradition.

As Vatican II (1962–1965) and the forces of liberalization confronted Catholics in the 1960s and 1970s, Pascal found himself closer to traditionalist Catholics and to Monsignor **Marcel Lefebvre.** While in Belgium in 1976, he published a long poem entitled *Discourse against the Abominations of the New Church.* Significantly, the work was prefaced by Cardinal **Mindszenty,** the prelate who took refuge in Rome upon exile from communist Hungary.

Bibliography. Chiron, Yves. *Pierre Pascal: A Biography.* Niherne, France: Éditions BCM, 2004.

Yves Chiron

PAUL VI [GIOVANNI BATTISTA MONTINI] (1897–1978). Giovanni Battista Montini was born in Concesio, near Brescia, Italy. His father, Giorgio, was well known in Lombard Catholic circles and became a leading member in the **Italian Popular Party** of Don **Luigi Sturzo.** From his mother, Giuditta, the young Montini took a passion for French culture, a love that accompanied him for the rest of his life.

After studies at the Brescia seminary, he was ordained in 1920 and sent shortly after to the Lombard College in Rome. In 1921 he began his studies at the Accademia dei Nubile Ecclesiatici, which trained diplomats of the Holy See. Prospects of a diplomatic career, however, left the young Montini cold. During his brief experience at the Warsaw nunciature in 1923, he lamented that "if Jesus was a carpenter, I suppose I can be an office boy."

Back in Rome, Montini was attached to the FUCI (Italian Federation of Catholic University Students), assuming its national spiritual direction in 1925. Despite Fascist pressures and centralizing and hierarchical demands from **Italian Catholic Action** and the Vatican, Montini and the new FUCI president, Igino Righetti, guided the federation on an intellectual and spiritual adventure informed by social and cultural obligations that accompanied a serious intellectual approach to life. A line not without elitist and aristocratic elements, it stressed social duty among young Catholic leaders beyond devotion. Montini also worked to shake Italian Catholics from their provincialism. In this, the FUCI promoted new foreign theological developments, especially from France and Germany and in the fields of ecclesiology and liturgy. The writings and ideas of Karl Adam,

Romano Guardini, and Yves Congar, among many other contemporary theologians, circulated widely, sometimes for the first time. Montini himself contributed with articles in the FUCI press, collaboration with the Brescian publisher Morcelliana, and translations of important French authors like **Jacques Maritain** and L. de Grandmaison. From this period came Montini's works, *Coscienza universitaria* (1930), *La via a Cristo* (1931) and *Introduzione allo studio di Cristo* (1934), all fundamental to his own development.

The Montini of this period, however, cannot be understood exclusively as an advocate of progressive Catholicism. Conservative and even reactionary elements surfaced in his promotion of **Pius IX**'s *Syllabus* or his translation of Maritain's antimodern *Trois reformateurs: Luther, Descartes, Rousseau*. Such tensions may have derived from his ambition to combine "doctrinal intransigence" with "practical tolerance" and been oriented by a sincere desire for dialogue with the modern world, a goal not without internal inconsistencies. In any case, Montini gave FUCI members a sense of identity, particularly as they approached culture, away from apologetic and defensive attitudes so common in interwar Italian Catholicism.

During these years Montini entered the Vatican's secretariat of state, a parallel job to his apostolate among the university students. In 1933, however, he left the FUCI, officially due to the pressures of work; although strong misgivings in some curia and Jesuit factions over his suspected (and unsubstantiated) modernist and protestant attitudes were probably more responsible.

Regarding Mussolini's regime, Montini displayed none of the philo-fascist attitudes that were so common elsewhere. His cool reception of the 1929 Lateran Accords was almost visceral and firmly anchored in his family's liberal democratic traditions. Although this prevented him

from embracing Fascism, it also hindered his comprehension of its appeal in an emerging mass society.

In the meantime, his career progressed at the secretariat of state. In 1937 he was promoted as substitute, and assigned to Ordinary Ecclesiastical Affairs. With the advent of **Pius XII** and the beginning of World War II, Montini played a crucial role at the newly created "Information Office" for refugees, POWs, and dispersed people. Between 1943 and 1945 he frequently intervened with German authorities in Italy to help victims of racial and police oppression. His old FUCI ties, moreover, blossomed into collaboration with future Christian Democrat leaders such as **Alcide De Gasperi,** Guido Gonella, and Giuseppe Spataro.

In 1952 Pope Pius appointed Montini and **Domenico Tardini,** together, as pro-secretary of state. However, the pontiff did not promote Montini to the purple, but instead to the See of Milan, where he exercised a dynamic apostolate among the immigrants and the poorest sectors of the city, addressing problems of modern urban life. In this he recognized the need for a new religious message capable of engaging with modern men.

In 1958 Montini's old friend Angelo Roncalli became Pope **John XXIII** and soon promoted him to the cardinalate. In turn, the new pontiff benefited from Montini's assistance in the preparations for the Second Vatican Council (1962–1965), where he promoted moderate reform, as alien to religious conservatism as it was to radical reformism. Montini maintained this approach after his election to the papacy in 1963, guiding the council's often-turbulent views toward much-needed consensuses. Paul's first encyclical, *Ecclesiam suam* (August 1964), vigorously underlined the necessity to engage the church in a serious and noncondemnatory dialogue with the world. The year 1964 also saw the promulgation of *Lumen* *gentium* and the ecumenical *Unitatis red-integratio.* Introducing liturgical reform, most notably sanctioning the use of vernacular languages as a means of promoting the active participation of the faithful and a clear role for the church in the modern world (in this sense the constitution *Gaudium et spes* is exemplary), Paul concluded the Council in 1965. He also transformed the Holy Office into the Congregation for the Doctrine of the Faith and abolished the Index of forbidden books. With the 1967 constitution *Regimini Ecclesiae universalis* he provided for much needed reform of the curia.

Application of the Council's reforms, however, proved to be a burden for the pope, who stood between conservatives and traditionalists, who often opposed their implementation, and so-called progressives, who favored more radical measures. As such, many of the pontiff's major pronouncements were coldly received, and a wide variety of interpretations emerged. Controversies developed over his *Populorum progressio* (1967) on issues of underdeveloped countries, his pronouncements in favor of ecclesiastical celibacy, and, perhaps above all, his encyclical on birth control *Humanae vitae* (1968).

Paul VI also inaugurated a new age by taking frequent trips, or, more precisely, pilgrimages abroad. From the Holy Land to India, through Africa and Hong Kong, Pope Montini delivered his message. In 1965 in New York at the UN, he spoke on the importance of peace, the reduction of armaments, and the much-needed assistance to underdeveloped countries.

In the delicate balance of cold war Europe, following Pope John's lead, Paul searched for contacts with Eastern Europe's communist regimes, thus arranging conventions with the governments of Yugoslavia, Poland, East Germany, Czechoslovakia, and Hungary, conventions that, despite heavy restrictions, assured juridical guarantees for the church in these countries.

Particularly painful for the pope in his last years was the increase of political violence in his native land, climaxed by the spring 1978 abduction and assassination of his close friend **Aldo Moro.** During the weeks of Moro's kidnapping Paul publicly begged for his release, offering himself as a hostage. After he received the fatal news, Paul VI presided over the funerals of the statesman.

Affected by a long-term illness, Paul VI died in the summer of 1978. His spiritual testament expressed his intimate belief in a "poor Church" dedicated to a humble apostolate and far removed from old triumphalisms.

Bibliography. AA.VV. *Paul VI et la modernité dans l'Église.* Rome: École Française de Rome, 1984. AA.VV. *Educazione, intelletuali e società in G.B. Montini-Paolo VI.* Brescia: Istituto Paolo VI, 1992. Acerbi, Antonio. *Paolo VI: Il papa che baciò la terra.* Milan: San Paolo, 1997. Hebblethwaite, Peter. *Paul VI: The First Modern Pope.* Mahwah, NJ: Paulist Press, 1993. Hera, E. de la. *La noche transfigurada: Biografía de Pablo VI.* Madrid: Biblioteca de Autores Cristianos, 2002.

Jorge Dagnino

PAVELIĆ, ANTE (1889–1959). One of Croatia's most controversial figures, Pavelić founded the fascist Ustaša organization and headed the collaborationist Independent State of Croatia (1941–1945). Pavelić dedicated his life to the fight for Croatian independence. His ideology combined extreme nationalism, fascism, clericalism, and Nazism, while his tactics included nationalist propaganda, terrorism, and mass violence. Debates surrounding Pavelić's dual historical role as champion of Croatian independence and perpetrator of genocide intensified with the collapse of Communist Yugoslavia and the foundation of the Republic of Croatia in 1991.

Educated as a lawyer, Pavelić entered politics as a member of the Croatian Party of Rights and served in the parliament of the Kingdom of Serbs, Croats, and Slovenes from September 1927 to January 1929. He consistently opposed state centralization. With the declaration of royal dictatorship in 1929, Pavelić fled to Italy. In 1930, he founded the revolutionary Croatian Liberation Movement, commonly called the Ustaša, which sought to create an independent Croatian state. He also established an Ustaša terrorist group, which organized training camps and participated in the assassination of Yugoslavia's King Alexander in 1934. His small network of supporters included clerical and right-wing Croatian movements that felt isolated and marginalized by the Yugoslav state. Throughout the 1930s, he received financial and ideological support from Benito Mussolini. As power shifted to Berlin, Pavelić courted Adolf Hitler and adapted the Ustaša program to include elements of Nazism.

Pavelić began his reign in April 1941, when Germany and Italy attacked Yugoslavia and established the puppet Independent State of Croatia. Appointed by Hitler and Mussolini as *Poglavnik,* authoritarian leader of Croatia, Pavelić directed state policies and ideology. His popularity surged after the declaration of Croatian independence but wavered when Germany and Italy pressured him to sign the Treaty of Rome on May 17, 1941, in which he gave part of Dalmatia, considered to be the cradle of Croatian civilization, to Italy. His popular base further declined under the impact of wartime deprivation, German and Italian occupation, and civil war.

Pavelić's legacy is linked to the Independent State of Croatia, which conducted one of the bloodiest genocide campaigns of World War II. Pavelić's government imposed race-based legislation, attempted to forcibly convert Orthodox Serbs to Catholicism, and deported and killed tens to hundreds of thousands of Serbs, Jews, Roma, and political opponents. As civil war erupted in Croatia, Pavelić focused his military and political resources against the Communist Partisans, whom he viewed as the greatest threat to Croatia.

The personal and political relationship between Pavelić and the Catholic Church, as well as the nature and extent of the church's awareness and support of his agenda, is widely debated. Officially, the Vatican did not recognize the wartime state. Some Croatian priests approved of or assisted Ustaša programs, while others condemned them, particularly practices of forced conversions and extermination camps. Pavelić allied himself to the Catholic Church and used it to legitimate and support fundamentalist policies. His politics, however, borrowed heavily from National Socialism, disregarding Catholic doctrine when convenient.

Pavelić remained in power until May 1945, when he fled Croatia during the German withdrawal from the Balkans. He escaped through Austria and Italy and eventually sought refuge in Argentina, where he organized an Ustaša exile organization. He was never prosecuted for his crimes against humanity. After an attempt on his life in 1957, he settled in **Franco**'s Spain, where he died in 1959.

Bibliography. Krizman, Bogdan. *Pavelić i Ustaše.* Zagreb, Croatia: Globus, 1978. Tomasevich, Jozo. *War and Revolution in Yugoslavia, 1941–1945: Occupation and Collaboration.* Stanford, CA: Stanford University Press, 2001.

Emily Greble Balic

PAYNE, DANIEL (1811–1893). Known as the patriarch of the African Methodist Episcopal (AME) Church, Payne served as bishop to that body for over forty years. Throughout the nineteenth-century struggle for African American liberation and rehabilitation, Payne persisted as a force of conservatism and stability.

Born to a free black father and Catawba Indian mother in Charleston, South Carolina, Payne was orphaned at ten. Free but financially incapacitated, he turned to carpentry, a trade that he continued until he was nineteen, when he decided to pursue education. His empathy for other black children similarly free but unschooled led to the opening of a school in Charleston, which he operated from 1829 to 1834. This experience inspired a lifelong devotion to the education of African Americans.

Payne left the South in 1834 to attend the Lutheran Theological Seminary at Gettysburg, Pennsylvania. Although ordained by the Franckean Lutheran Synod in 1837, Payne opted to join the African Methodist Episcopal Church in 1841. During his early career as a minister, he founded churches in East Troy; New York; Washington, D.C.; and Baltimore. At the same time, he gained a reputation as a voracious writer, becoming the official historian of the African Methodists. His vast corpus of documents provides a critical record of African American institutional activism in the nineteenth century.

When Payne was elected bishop in 1852, he was the first officer to have formal theological training. During his tenure, he fought against illiteracy among ministers. This educational fervor had a religious impetus. It was Payne's belief that in order to be redeemed, man must be free and educated. Only through education could man fully understand the Gospel message. As bishop, Payne propagated this idea, instituting education within the AME church ranks. When Wilberforce University in Ohio came up for sale, Payne led the purchase of it, becoming the president of the first African American institution of higher education, a position he held from 1863 to 1876.

Payne advocated institutional strength in all facets of African American life. Throughout his ministry, he discouraged African American folk religion, as he felt it overemphasized the exterior manifestations of the spirit, as opposed to the intellectual rejuvenations Payne thought

necessary to Christian conversion. He saw religious institutions as reliable structures for black self-determination. He encouraged asceticism, domestic stability, and financial independence through hard work. Upon Payne's death in 1893, the *Christian Recorder* compared him to Moses: "leader and teacher, he did for us what no other did or could."

Bibliography. Payne, Daniel. *Recollections of Seventy Years.* New York: Arno Press, 1968.

Kathryn Lofton

PEASANT AND SMALLHOLDERS PARTIES (HUNGARY). According to Hungarian political traditions, most peasant parties were called Smallholders parties. They generally represented the interests of the landowning, not the landless, peasantry. Although characterized by Christian agrarian orientation, these parties usually kept themselves apart from Christian Socialism. The first peasant party in Hungary was the Independent "Forty-eighter" Peasant Party, established in 1909 under the leadership of István Nagyatádi-Szabó (1909–1924). Following the collapse of Austria-Hungary, this party merged in 1919 with the Agricultural Party, founded earlier by large landowners. This resulted in the emergence of the National Smallholders and Agricultural Party (NSAP), which in 1922 fused with the newly established government-sponsored United Party. The Smallholders Party thus lost much of its political independence for a few years. In 1930 the Smallholders Party seceded from the United Party, merged with the Agrarian Party established by Gaszton Gaál (1926), and formed the Independent Smallholders, Agrarian, and Civic Party. Thereafter, this Smallholders Party assumed the role of a moderate opposition in the parliament, under the leadership of Gaszton Gaál (1930–1932), Tibor Eckhardt (1932–1941), and Endre Bajcsy-Zsilinszky (1941–1944).

During World War II, the Smallholders Party allied itself with the Socialist Democratic Party and pursued openly anti-Nazi policies. After Hungary's German occupation (March 19, 1944), members of the party became active in the anti-German underground. In December 1944 its leaders constituted a large portion of the Provisional National Government, established in Debrecen under the watchful eyes of the Soviet forces. At the end of the war, the Smallholders Party emerged as Hungary's largest and most popular political party. In the November 1945 elections it gained an absolute majority of 57 percent. Yet under the pressure of the Soviets, the party was forced to establish a coalition government with the participation of the communists, who gained some of the key ministries. Led by the Calvinist minister Zoltán Tildy (1945–1947), the Smallholders Party accepted the idea of the nationalization of the large estates, but it resisted the policy of the collectivization of small peasant plots. However, supported by the Soviet-dominated Inter-Allied Commission, the Communist Party infiltrated the Smallholders Party and purged it from its anticommunist leaders. In 1947 these leaders were either arrested or forced to flee to the West. The remaining crypto-communists, under the leadership of Lajos Dinnyés and István Dobi, gave power over to the Communist Party (1947) and then voted themselves out of existence (1949).

Reestablished in 1988, the Smallholders Party was never able to regain its former popularity. In May 1990, it joined the ruling coalition headed by the Hungarian Democratic Forum (HDF), but—under the erratic leadership of József Torgyán (after 1991)—it continued to be plagued by party factionalism. In 1994, following the fall of Hungary's first postcommunist government, the Smallholders Party went into opposition in the Hungarian parliament. It remained so right up to 2002, when it failed to gain 5 percent of the votes and thus lost its parliamentary representation. Parallel with the Smallholders Party, in 1939 a number of peasant-born intellectuals established the National Peasant Party (NPP) to represent the interests of the agricultural proletariat. Although active on the intellectual level, this party did not become active in politics until 1945, when it sent several dozen of its members to the Hungarian parliament. It participated in the postwar coalition government headed by the Smallholders Party, but it never went beyond being a minor party in the parliament. Like the Smallholders Pary, the NPP was infiltrated by the communists who purged it in 1947. It went out of existence in 1949. The Peasant Party reemerged momentarily as the Pet fi Party during the Hungarian Revolution of 1956, and then again in 1989, after the fall of communism. But it was never able to gain enough followers to gain membership in any of the postcommunist Hungarian parliaments.

Bibliography. Romsics, Ignác. *Hungary in the Twentieth Century.* Budapest: Corvina Press, 2000, chapters 3, 6, 8. Várdy, Steven Béla. *Historical Dictionary of Hungary.* Lanham, MD: Scarecrow Press, 1997.

Steven Béla Várdy

PÉGUY, CHARLES (1873–1914). Péguy, a Christian poet and editor of *Les cahiers de la quinzaine,* spent most of his life isolated from political circles and the established church, although his widely read writings carried significant weight in both.

Following a traditional Catholic upbringing, he became galvanized politically when the Dreyfus trial reopened in 1898. Passionately convinced that Alfred Dreyfus, a Jewish artillery officer in the French army, was innocent of treason, Péguy felt the necessity of declaring it. He joined a branch of the French Socialist Party but left when he found the party cared more for political maneuvering than for justice, truth, freedom of expression, and care for the downtrodden. Similarly, he distanced himself from the Catholic Church, which aligned itself with the establishment in condemning Dreyfus.

After his return to faith, however, Péguy consistently maintained that his political positions had always stemmed from Christian principles, and he continued to uphold what he believed true socialists and patriots stood for (see his *Notre jeunesse*), staunchly resisting overtures from such rightist movements as Action Française. Prevented by his marriage from returning to full communion with the church, Péguy nevertheless openly acknowledged his Christian commitment in the *Cahiers* and devoted himself to creating an impressive body of poetry exploring the Christian virtues, Joan of Arc, and other themes.

Although he remained independent of Left and Right, shortly after his death at the front early in World War I, both tendencies championed Péguy, with different aspects of his writings eventually becoming rallying points in World War II for both the Resistance and those who supported the Vichy government. Marginalized by his fierce polemics and his refusal to compromise in a world where he believed everything honorable degenerated into power politics, Péguy nevertheless emphasized Christian hope in his poetry.

Bibliography. Péguy, Charles. *The Portal of the Mystery of Hope.* Trans. David Louis Schindler, Jr. Grand Rapids, MI: William B. Eerdmans, 1996.

Joyce M. Hanks

PELLETIER, GÉRARD (1919–1997). Pelletier was president of the *Jeunesse Étudiante Catholique* (1940–1944), director of *Cité libre* (1950–1964), La Presse's editor in chief (1961–1962), minister and secretary of state in **Pierre Elliott Trudeau**'s liberal cabinet (1969–1975), Canadian ambassador to France, and senator. His commitments, inspired by his religious beliefs, helped define the social reforms of the sixties.

Cité libre is still regarded as the think tank of the Quiet Revolution (1960–1970) and the most influential magazine of the time. It was within its pages that the political opposition to the Union Nationale, based on the influential personalist philosophy, was most clearly elaborated.

On one hand, public policies had to be functional—not only rational but also democratic. A national health-care system, social security measures, and universal pension plans were all programs that had to be put in place. On the other hand, policies were to be unfolded and conducted to protect and serve each and every individual. The Charter of Rights and Freedom (1982) was the crowning achievement of this conviction. Ensuing from this perspective was Pelletier's continuous critique of nationalism, an ideology that, in his opinion, celebrated "race" at the expense of individual rights.

In 1965, Pelletier was elected to the House of Commons with Trudeau and **Jean Marchand**. When Trudeau became prime minister of Canada in 1968, Pelletier assumed considerable power within government. He supported numerous policies that transformed Canada's identity and political landscape. For example, the Official Languages Act, adopted in 1969, recognized both French and English as official languages and gave them equality of status in the federal institutions. A multicultural policy was adopted in 1971 and became law in 1982. Refusing the American melting pot model, Pelletier and Trudeau preferred to envision Canada as a "mosaic" composed of different ethnic groups. The racial, cultural, or religious backgrounds of ethnic groups were not an obstacle to national unity but a tribute to Canadian diversity. For this reason, people's distinct cultural diversity was to be fostered by the federal government instead of being melted in a single cultural mold.

At the same time this multicultural policy was implemented, Pelletier endorsed a nation-building policy that led to the Repatriation of the Constitution from London in 1982. The nationalization of Petro-Canada, the numerous encouragements to Canadian culture and symbols, and the distancing from American policies can be viewed as an integral part of this national self-consciousness.

Bibliography. Warren, Jean-Philippe. "Gérard Pelletier et Cité libre: La mystique personnaliste de la Révolution tranquille." *Société* 20 (21): 313–46.

Jean-Philippe Warren

PEOPLE'S UNION FOR A CATHOLIC GERMANY. Founded in November 1890 in the Rhenish industrial city of Mönchengladbach, the People's Union for a Catholic Germany (*Volksverein*) grew into the most successful Catholic association, which, at its peak on the eve of World War I, had over 800,000 members. **Ludwig Windthorst** created the association with the goal of constraining conservatives within his **Center Party** and the hope of maintaining Catholic workers' support for the Center Party after the fading of the *Kulturkampf* had removed an important incentive to vote for the party.

The Union was conceived in explicit opposition intentions of the conservative wing of the Center and the episcopate to found a Catholic counterpart to the Evangelical League. The founders of the *Volksverein* viewed the Social Democratic Party as a "powerful enemy" that threatened "the foundation of Christian society and civilization." They feared that Socialist "prophets of atheism clad in smocks" would woo Christian workers; therefore, it was necessary to provide protection against the dangers of Socialism. Education was seen as the best form of protection, and a potent tool for solving social ills. By 1898, the *Volksverein* was the leading organization of Catholic public education.

Besides offering lectures, study courses, pamphlets and books (through its own libraries) concerning political and social topics, the Union provided slide lectures and (later) "morally unobjectionable" films and distributed information on the cleanliness of food, clothes, and home. Some historians see this emphasis on social policies as an indication that the Center Party was prepared to break out of the Catholic ghetto.

A close relationship existed between the *Volksverein* and the Center. Although they both claimed to work independently of each other, they cooperated closely in creating Catholic organizations and furthering the political influence of the party. The Union also played a role in the conversion of the Center from a party of notables to a mass party. Success varied greatly from region to region. The Rhineland and Westphalia stand out as the most fertile ground for the Union's message. In time the success of the *Volksverein* was also noted abroad. Pope **Pius X** strongly recommended its organizational structure when the **Italian Catholic Action** was reorganized.

After 1918 the waning of the Catholic milieu, increasing competition from other Catholic associations, and the departure of important leaders as well as the establishment of formal Center Party membership led to a significant decline in membership and financial troubles. The final chapter was written by the Gestapo. On July 1, 1933, the offices of the *Volksverein* were closed and shortly afterwards (January 24, 1934) it was dissolved.

Bibliography. Heitzer, Horstwalter. *Der Volksverein für das katholische Deutschland im Kaiserreich 1890–1918.* Veröffentlichungen der Kommission für Zeitgeschichte 26. Mainz, Germany: Matthias-Grünewald-Verlag, 1979. Hürten, Heinz. *Kurze Geschichte des deutschen Katholizismus, 1800–1960.* Mainz, Germany: Matthias-Grünewald-Verlag, 1986. Ritter, Emil. *Die katholisch-soziale Bewegung Deutschlands* *im neunzehnten Jahrhundert und der Volks-verein.* Cologne, Germany: J. P. Bachem, 1954.

Thomas M. Bredohl

PERCY, ALAN IAN (1880–1930). Percy, the eighth Duke of Northumberland, was a major leader and publicist of the Die-hard movement in interwar British con-servatism. A rare representative of premillennialist fundamentalism in British Conservatism, his politics were strictly grounded in the theology of the Catholic Apostolic Church (the Irvingites), a small premillennialist and proto-Pentecostal group that had been formed in the 1830s.

Although he fought for the continued establishment of the Protestant faith, and for moral legislation, as a premillennialist, Northumberland believed that complete Christianization of society was impossible in the twentieth century and that Christians could only strengthen the few things that remained of older religio-political para-digms and structures. His conservatism was predicated on the assumption of grad-ual deterioration in all areas of temporal life, on a premillennialist resolve to defend the believed structural and ideational rem-nants of true Christianity, and on the expec-tation of a millennial kingdom of God.

Originally a career military officer, Northumberland's prominent public wit-ness to premillennialist Christian conserva-tism antedated his late 1918 accession to his dukedom. As a major advocate of pre–World War I military preparedness and uni-versal military training, and as a cofounder and early leader of the Boy Scout move-ment, he attempted to manufacture a citi-zenry disciplined by Christian and nationalist paradigms. After 1918, he tried to spread such paradigms through the Conservative party; through the publica-tion outlets that he controlled, the periodi-cals *Patriot* and *Morning Post,* and the Boswell Publishing Company; and with the means afforded by his dual membership in the Catholic Apostolic Church and the Church of England. In the latter he was the first vice-chairman of the House of Laity in the National Church Assembly and the president of the Marriage Defense Council, an all-Protestant pressure group formed to resist relaxations in divorce laws.

Northumberland's twenty-year fight for the retention of House of Lords preroga-tives, and his polemic against the sale of honors practiced by early twentieth-century British governments, were rooted in a theological affirmation of the divine institution and duties of the aristocracy. Likewise, his defense of British imperial-ism and the Unionist cause in Ireland rested on a belief in the Christian mission of the British Empire, and his passionate opposition to socialism flowed from the conviction that socialism was anti-Christian and counterbiblical. His frequent criticism of non-Orthodox Jewry and political, secu-lar Zionism was also based on Christian assumptions about the distinct premillen-nial roles of observant and nonobservant Jews. Frequently, this last plane of his wit-ness degenerated into various conspiracy theories that had recourse to anti-Semitic, anticommunist and anti-Masonic explana-tions of interwar de-Christianization and secularization.

Often seen as a proto-fascist, North-umberland's various causes were in fact prompted by the conservative public the-ology of the Catholic Apostolic Church. He tried to defend conservative Christian worldviews and structures in the context of a premillennial view of history.

Bibliography. Ruotsila, Markku. "The Catho-lic Apostolic Church in British Politics." *Jour-nal of Ecclesiastical History* 56 (1): 75–91. Ruotsila, Markku. "The Antisemitism of the 8th Duke of Northumberland's the *Patriot,* 1922–1930." *Journal of Contemporary History* 39 (January 2004): 71–92.

Markku Ruotsila

PERÓN, EVA (1919–1952). Perón, born María Eva Ibarguren, made the remarkable transformation from an obscure illegitimate child born in Los Toldos on the edge of the Argentine Pampas to become the most influential first lady in Latin American history. She died of cancer at thirty-three, but the image of "Santa Evita" continues to influence politics, culture, and religion in Argentina.

At age seventeen Eva moved to Buenos Aires to seek an acting career in radio and film. Her professional engagement brought her in contact with powerful admirers, among them Juan Perón, then a rising figure in Argentine politics. They were married before Perón became the president in 1946. His wife offered limitless support to implement his version of populist leadership, *Justicialismo,* a blend of democratic principles and authoritarianism.

As the first lady of Argentina, Eva supplied a popular and religious component to the Peronist political movement, tied intrinsically to the *descamisados*—the shirtless, the poor and working classes of Argentina. Relying on Catholicism and new welfare policies as her basis for political action, Evita presented herself as a devoted mother of the poor and as an ideal, faithful wife, willing to give all for the sake of others. On this basis, the Argentine public granted her a unique right from which to speak. She became an object of intense adoration, a saint-like figure, their Evita, dedicated and prepared to sacrifice her own life on their behalf.

The impact of Evita's political commitment went far beyond charismatic appearances: she founded her own charity foundation, controlled newspapers to shape public opinion, and was instrumental in the formation of the Peronist Women's Party. She won a significant

Maria Eva Duarte de Perón at a mass demonstration in Buenos Aires, 1940. © National Library of Vienna

legislative triumph in 1947, when a bill giving women the right to vote was approved. In the 1952 elections, Argentine women voted for the first time.

Sections of the political leadership and her followers encouraged her to seek the vice presidency in 1951. But when Evita was diagnosed with terminal cancer, her illness distracted from the controversy surrounding her political future. Holding on to her public life until the end, she died on July 26, 1952.

The national outpouring of grief that followed her death confirmed that her claim to political power in a country where politics was the domain of men was based on Evita's version of a charismatic moral and Christian leadership. Millions displayed their grief of having lost "Santa Evita," although the pope declined a 40,000-letter-strong petition for her canonization.

Bibliography. Fraser, Nicholas, and Marysa Navarro. *Evita: The Real Life of Eva Perón.* New York: W. W. Norton, 1996.

Jadwiga E. Pieper Mooney

PERRIN, HENRI (1914–1954). Born at Comimont in the Vosges Mountains, Perrin entered the seminary and studied theology during the years of a renewal for the French Christian community, a renewal that coincided with the years of the **Young Catholic Workers** (*Jeunesse Ouvrière Catholique,* JOC), of **Emmanuel Mounier** and *Esprit,* of **Francisque Gay** and his review, *Vie intellectuelle,* of the Catholic weekly, *Sept,* and of working-class hopes for Leon Blum's Popular Front government.

Perrin was ordained a priest before World War II as a member of the Society of Jesus, but it was during the war that he realized his true destiny. In 1943, he arrived in Germany as a worker and undercover chaplain to deported individuals through the *Aumônerie Générale des Prisonniers,* which organized assistance in the work camps through various parishes.

Priests like Perrin worked as intermediaries for this network. With the institution of forced labor, those in charge of the chaplains decided to send in several young priests disguised as workers. Perrin was among these priests and was sent to Leipzig, where he worked in junker workshops.

Before being discovered and sent back to France, Perrin was able to experience the life of a worker in these camps. His meetings with non-Christians, furthermore, inspired Perrin to practice evangelical counsel. While in the work camp, he organized the Groupe d'Amitié to serve fellow workers and create a form of life and communal sharing that showed disoriented and irreligious souls the way toward a Christian evangelical horizon. After his expulsion, he nevertheless returned to Germany between 1944 and 1945 as chaplain of the military corps of repatriation.

In 1947 he became a priest to the workers in Paris, which allowed him to continue with his ministry to the working classes. Before making his final vows, he left the Society of Jesus and immersed himself in the dual roles of militant worker and priest and actively participated in the long strikes of the early 1950s. At the end of 1953, the French bishops forbade priests ministering to workers to hold full-time industrial employment or belong to labor organizations and ordered them to reinsert themselves in a priestly community. This marked the end of an experience for Perrin that, beyond doing works of charity, had placed him in the heart of political struggle. He died in a motorcycle accident while undertaking his professional formation. His *Journal d'un prêtre ouvrier en Allemagne,* published in 1945, was immediately successful and translated into many languages.

Bibliography. Perrin, Henri. *Itintéraire d'Henri Perrin, prêtre ouvrier, 1914–1954.* Paris: Seuil, 1958. Perrin, Henri. *Priest and*

Worker: The Autobiography of Henri Perrin. Trans. Bernard Wall. New York: Macmillan, 1965.

Ilaria Biagioli

PÉTAIN, PHILIPPE (1856–1951). Born and raised in the church, Pétain was not a devout or even a seasonal Catholic, but circumstances led him to have an enormous impact on the church in France and on the way historians came to interpret its role in politics after 1945. Up until the outbreak of war in 1914, Pétain did not have a glittering career and was contemplating a quiet retirement, having reached the level of colonel in the French army. His involvement in the Great War changed everything, and he became a household name, the "Savior of Verdun." At war's end he was named marshal of France.

The interwar period saw Pétain assume various positions, including minister of war. He refused to stand for election himself because he considered his role in public life to be above politics but politicians of the Left and Right admired, even revered, him: dependable and incorruptible Pétain symbolized France itself. Nominated ambassador to Spain in 1939, Pétain returned to France in May 1940 as deputy premier after it had become obvious the Germans were overwhelming the French in their lightning invasion. Pétain's was the voice of pessimism and defeatism, and when he became premier (on the resignation of Paul Reynaud), he began negotiating an armistice that left many relieved and France divided into occupied and unoccupied zones. The National Assembly voted for the establishment of a new regime based in the spa town of Vichy with Pétain as its head (*chef d'état*) and premier. That Pétain himself was in large part responsible for the defensive mentality that had come to pervade military thinking and policy (best illustrated in the construction of the Maginot Line) may have had some bearing on his willingness to sign the armistice when others sought to continue resisting the Germans.

Shocked by the defeat, many in France spoke of the debacle as more than a military trouncing: it was a moral collapse, too. Unsurprisingly, people were responsive to the propaganda calling for a righting of the wrongs that had led to France's fall. As head of state, Pétain assumed a tone of sacrifice and repentance in his public utterances. He "gave France the gift of his person" in its hour of need and promised to lead the country out of the abyss. Guided by Pétain, the French would now see the error of their godless ways and atone for the sins of the Third Republic—individualism, secularism, even paid holidays—which were seen to be responsible for the humiliating defeat.

Pétain's popularity soared. Though his government embarked on the path of collaboration and assisted the enemy in many ways, from providing economic support and requisitioned French labor for German enterprises to helping the Nazi regime realize its goal of a "final solution" to the Jewish Question in Europe, many (including future resisters) dissociated Pétain himself from Vichy's cooperation with the Germans. With hindsight we can see that such was Pétain's prestige, and so reassuring was his public (military) presence that Catholics and non-Catholics alike, people on the left and right, invested his public statements with greater import than they merited. Indeed, it could be said that Vichy promoted a cult of personality, with immoderate expressions of support emanating from all quarters. A version of the Lord's Prayer incorporating Pétain's life and work, for example, circulated widely.

Vichy replaced Liberty, Equality, Fraternity with *Travail, Famille, Patrie* (Work, Family, Nation), and when Cardinal Gerlier of Lyon said "these three words are ours," he spoke the truth. Hence began the muddle that was Vichy and Pétain's religious or Christian project. Vichy initiated what became known as the National Revolution, the goal of which was moral and intellectual renewal and to reconnect French people with values and traditions the secular Third Republic neglected or, according to some, negated.

Vichy had much to recommend itself to Catholics. It promised to undo the discrimination against Catholic institutions that had come in the wake of the secularization of the state. For example it would subsidize Catholic schools and allow public school students the opportunity to receive religious instruction (off school premises) during school hours. Vichy also pledged to make families and mothers the center of national life, and though its natalist policies did not deviate significantly from those of the Third Republic, this aspect of national revolution rhetoric assumed a distinctly religious and spiritual tone. Cynics could not help but note it was odd that Pétain, the childless octogenarian who had married his partner, a divorcée, in a civil ceremony, heralded a regime of fecundity and spiritual renewal. Pétain had his marriage regularized in 1941, and he did attend Mass in Vichy.

The church's public, and in some quarters enthusiastic, official support for Pétain as head of the established government now generally overshadows the reservations the hierarchy expressed at the time. Church support for Vichy was not unconditional, as a series of carefully worded statements and directives clearly indicate. The church's phrase *loyalisme sans infeodation* neatly summarizes its position vis-à-vis the regime. The church's caution was evident in its efforts to separate itself from Vichy on the question of youth affairs, for example. The hierarchy supported the idea of "the unity of youth behind Pétain" but rejected outright the state monopoly of youth associations, which was the goal of some Vichy ideologues and which French Catholics compared to Nazi Germany's alarming youth policy.

The conflation of a series of benign and obviously positive proposals from the church's perspective with the more sinister anti-Semitic legislation of the Vichy regime has led to difficulties for historians assessing French religious responses to the war and occupation. How might one distinguish between support for what was morally unproblematic, and even good, from support for Vichy's political project for the entire period? After the initial relief with which they greeted Pétain, Catholics began to distance themselves from him and his regime, notably from mid-1942, when the extent of Vichy's anti-Semitism became clearer.

In 1945 Pétain was tried and condemned to death, but because of his age the sentence was commuted to life imprisonment. He died six years later, and while historians have debated the true nature of the Vichy regime and the extent of Pétain's responsibility for its crimes, it has been impossible for his supporters to rehabilitate him because it cannot be shown that he was unaware of the consequences of the worst elements of Vichy collaborationism. On the contrary, it seems he was closely involved with formulating the policies most injurious to France's reputation, including Vichy's anti-Semitic legislation.

Bibliography. Ferro, Marc. *Pétain.* Paris: Fayard, 1987. Griffiths, Richard, *Marshal Pétain.* London: Constable, 1970. Halls, W. D. *Politics, Society and Christianity in Vichy France.* Oxford: Berg, 1995.

Vesna Drapac

PETROV, GRIGORII SPIRIDONOVICH (1868–1925). Petrov was a Russian Orthodox priest and publicist who served as the leading proponent of the **Social Gospel** in Russia around the turn of the twentieth century.

Petrov was born in Iamburg, St. Petersburg Province. Although not from a clerical family, he was educated first at an Orthodox seminary and then at the St. Petersburg

Ecclesiastical Academy (1887–1891). In his second year there, he became one of the first student lecturers to teach for the Society for the Spread of Moral-Religious Enlightenment (SMRE), a citywide organization devoted to promoting Orthodox religious education to the lay public. Upon graduating, Petrov took clerical orders and was appointed to the church of the Mikhailovsky artillery school in St. Petersburg. He continued to teach for the SMRE and was elected to the society's governing council in 1894. Petrov served on the council until 1902 and worked for the organization until 1904.

During the 1890s, Petrov launched his career as a successful publicist. His first and most successful publication, *The Gospel as the Foundation of Life,* appeared in 1898. It went through seventeen editions by 1905. Through this work, Petrov presented his view that Christianity required believers to apply the literal teachings of Jesus to every aspect of their lives in order to transform society and begin building the kingdom of God on earth. Petrov's ideas were influenced by the American **Social Gospel** movement, as demonstrated by his 1903 Russian translation of **Charles Monroe Sheldon**'s 1896 book *In His Steps.* However, the new conceptions of pastorship and Christian social activism that had been developing in St. Petersburg since the reforms of the 1860s also influenced Petrov through his experiences at the academy and in the SMRE.

Petrov wrote many short works aimed at popular audiences that sought to inspire ordinary Russians to live more consciously religious lives. However, Petrov also won a following among the nobility. In the winter of 1903, he gave a series of public lectures based on his writings. The lectures were well attended by educated people but provoked criticism from conservatives in the church. As a result, in 1904 Petrov was dismissed from his position, declared ineligible for employment in St. Petersburg, and banned from public speaking.

Nevertheless, Petrov remained popular and continued his writings. He began to address himself to the intelligentsia. He became increasingly interested in Christian action as a collective, rather than an individual, undertaking. During the revolution of 1905, he became active politically through the newspaper *God's Truth,* which he founded in Moscow in 1906. In the elections for the First Duma, Petrov was elected as a deputy for the Constitutional Democrats.

Before Petrov could take up those duties, he was accused before church authorities of false teaching. Although he was exonerated, he was still placed under church discipline and confined to the Cheremenets monastery. Petrov's case aroused considerable public sympathy and demands for his release, but the sentence was upheld. Early in 1908, church authorities defrocked Petrov and banned him from Moscow and St. Petersburg for seven years and from public employment for twenty years.

Petrov became a journalist for the publication *The Word,* established by leaders from the 1904 liberationist movement. He continued to work as a journalist during the First World War, during which his son was killed. After the revolutions of 1917, he emigrated to Serbia and then, in 1922, to France. He died in Paris in 1925.

Bibliography. Hedda, Jennifer. "Good Shepherds: The St. Petersburg Pastorate and the Emergence of Social Activism in the Russian Orthodox Church, 1855–1917." PhD diss., Harvard University, 1998. Valliere, Paul. "Modes of Social Action in Russian Orthodoxy: The Case of Father Petrov's *Zateinik." Russian History* 4 (2): 142–58.

Jennifer Hedda

PIUS IX [GIOVANNI MARIA MASTAI-FERRETTI] (1792–1878). Born as Giovanni Maria Mastai-Ferretti, Pius was elected pope June 16, 1846, and died February 7, 1878, the longest-reigning pontificate in history. His reign witnessed the European political revolutions of 1848, the *Risorgimento* in Italy, and the proclamation of the Immaculate Conception of Mary (1854). Pius also presided over the calling of the first Vatican Council in 1869–1870 (which proclaimed papal infallibility), the collapse of the church's temporal power, and the papal "war" upon the modern era. During his last decade he had to confront the Italian seizure of Rome as well as Bismarck's *Kulturkampf* in the German Empire. He was the preeminent defender of church prerogatives in the ideological and political struggles of the mid-nineteenth century and shaped the character of the Catholic Church prior to the Second Vatican Council.

In 1803, the ninth child of Count Mastai-Ferreti was sent to school in Tuscany but returned home in 1809 following an epileptic seizure. Provided a dispensation for his illness by Pope **Pius VII,** he was ordained a priest in 1819. First assigned to the Roman orphanage of "Tata Giovanni," he remained there until 1823. Subsequently, he was dispatched on a diplomatic mission to Chile and Peru (1823–1825). In 1825, Pope Leo XII appointed him director of the Hospice of San Michele in Rome and, in 1827, as archbishop of Spoleto. In 1832, Pope **Gregory XVI** made him bishop of Imola, elevating him to the College of Cardinals in 1840.

Upon his assumption of the tiara, Mastai believed that the Papal States could be improved by an infusion of common sense. Following the guidelines of the Memorandum of the Powers of 1831, Pius proposed a series of administrative, economic, and political innovations. His July amnesty of political prisoners electrified Rome, Italy, and the world beyond. Extraordinary tribunals were abolished, the Roman ghetto was unlocked, railway lines were projected, and telegraph companies chartered. Word of his reforms was facilitated by a new press law that liberalized censorship and tolerated the expression of liberal and even nationalist sentiments. He brought forward a proposal for the creation of a council of state and a council of ministers, delighting liberals.

Conservatives remained skeptical, noting the dangers that nationalism and liberalism posed for the papacy. Pius hoped that the creation of a tariff league would coordinate economic activities and fulfill national concerns, while the consultative chamber would satisfy liberal sentiments. These concessions provoked a clamor for more, including the creation of a civic guard and the granting of a constitution. Although the pope granted both, the Romans demanded more, urging him to join in the first war of national liberation against Austria. His reluctance to do so, announced in an allocution in April 1848, provoked a revolution in Rome and his flight from the capital at the end of November 1848.

Restored to his state by the intervention of France, Austria, Spain, and Naples, the pope abandoned his earlier reformism. Following his return in 1850, Pius left political concerns to his secretary of state, **Giacomo Antonelli,** as he devoted himself to religious matters. In 1850, Pius reestablished the hierarchy in England and that of the Netherlands in 1853. During the course of his pontificate, the church erected new apostolic vicarates and prefectures. Pius encouraged seminarians to study in Rome and founded a French seminary there in 1853. In 1859, he inaugurated the North American College. His fervor to spread the faith led him to establish a special seminary for missionary priests. Religious scruples in 1858 led him to sanction the removal of the Jewish boy Edgardo Mortara, who was secretly baptized by a Christian domestic, from his parents in Bologna and subsequently raised as a Christian—provoking an international uproar.

The Franco-Piedmontese war of 1859 against Austria led to the loss of the greater part of the Papal State, which was incorporated into the Kingdom of Italy in 1861. Pius refused to recognize the development. In 1864 he issued his encyclical *Quanta cura* and an appended "Syllabus of Errors," which defended the temporal power, while condemning liberalism, nationalism, and the separation of church and state. He continued his centralization by convoking the Vatican Council (1869), which issued a declaration of Papal Infallibility on July 18, 1870—the year the Italian army seized Rome and ended the temporal power. Pius retreated into the Vatican declaring himself a prisoner therein, creating the so-called Roman Question, which was only resolved in 1929. Pio Nono's remaining years (1870–1878) were marked by conflict with the Italians over the Roman Question, and with Bismarck's Germany over church-state relations, the *Kulturkampf.* The cause for his beatification was opened in 1955 by **Pius XII,** and he was beatified by **John Paul II** in 2000. The controversy surrounding him resurfaced during his beatification in 2000.

Bibliography. *Atti del Sommo Pontefice Pio IX, Felicemente Regnante. Parte seconda che comprende I Motu-proprii, chirografi editti, notificazioni, ec. per lo stato pontificio.* 2 vols. Rome: Tipografia delle Belle Arti, 1857. Coppa, Frank J. *Pope Pius IX: Crusader in a Secular Age.* Boston: Twayne, 1979. Franciscis, Pasquale de, ed. *Discorsi del Sommo Pontefice Pio IX Pronunziati in Vaticano ai fedeli di Roma e dell'orbe dal principio della sua prigionia fino al presente.* Rome: Tipografia G. Aujrelj, 1872–1878. Martina, Giacomo. *Pio IX.* 3 vols. Vatican City: Tipografia Poliglotta Vaticana, 1974–1990. Serafini, Alberto. *Pio Nono. Giovanni Maria Mastai Ferretti dalla giovinezzza alla morte nei suoi scritti e discorsi editi e inediti.* Vol. 1. Vatican City: Tipografia Poliglotta Vaticana, 1958.

Frank J. Coppa

PIUS X [GIUSEPPE MELCHIORE SARTO] (1835–1914). Born of a peasant family in Riese, Treviso, Pope Pius X campaigned vigorously against modernism in the church during his reign and maintained a conservative posture toward the political world that ultimately diminished church influence on the world stage. He was educated in the diocesan seminary, was ordained in 1858, and served successively as curate then priest in country parishes. He was also chancellor of the diocese of Treviso, a cathedral canon, and spiritual director of its seminary.

Sarto was appointed bishop of Mantua in 1885 and then cardinal and patriarch of Venice in 1894. He was thus the first of three patriarchs of Venice to become pope in the twentieth century (the others were **John XXIII** and John Paul I) and was a classic product of that northern Italian Catholic milieu that was to provide a total of five popes before the end of the millennium.

Sarto was elected pope in 1903 after Puszyna of Cracow, an Austro-Hungarian cardinal, exercised a veto against Cardinal **Rampolla** on behalf of Emperor Franz Josef of Austria-Hungary. He won convincingly, but because of his natural humility it was only with some difficulty that he was persuaded to accept the papal throne, allegedly by the secretary of the conclave. This was typical of the man who was to be beatified in 1951 and canonized three years later, the first pope to become a saint for over three hundred years. But as pope, he ruled sternly and vigorously, belying the meekness and humility ascribed to him.

In contrast to **Leo XIII,** ever the aristocratic intellectual and diplomat, Pius X was the humble pastor, so much so that he has been nicknamed the "parish priest pope," and certainly his pontificate was marked by a commitment to pastoral ministry. He has been remembered for his encouragement of frequent communion for laypeople and early communion for children, as well as the restoration of Gregorian chant to a central place in church music. As a great reforming pope, he carried out a major overhaul of the training of priests, including the establishment of regional seminaries in Italy, the administration of the Roman Curia, and the setting up of a commission in 1907 to codify canon law.

He will be chiefly remembered, however, for his campaign against "modernism," encapsulated in his statements *Lamentabili* and *Pascendi* of 1907, which set in train a witch hunt against all clergy suspected of "modernist" opinions in theology, biblical exegesis, and church history. Supported by Msgr. Umberto Benigni and his *Sodalitium Painum,* Pius even sent apostolic visitors into the seminaries of such leading Italian prelates as Cardinal Maffi of Pisa, Cardinal Ferrari of Milan, and Archbishop Della Chiesa of Bologna (the future Pope **Benedict XV**). Fears of modernist contagion also induced Pius to oppose the reforming Christian democratic element in the Italian Catholic movement, leading him to dissolve the *Opera Dei Congressi* in 1904 and restructure it on centralized, hierarchically dependent lines.

Toward the Italian state, Pius X pursued a twin-track policy. On one hand, he repeated the protest for the loss of the Papal States, while on the other he encouraged good day-to-day relations with Italian authorities. When faced by the rise of a Marxian Socialist working-class movement, he permitted relaxations of the ban on Catholics from participating in parliamentary elections in order to prevent the victory of the Socialist Party. On social matters, Pius was inherently conservative and came close to condemning Catholic trade unionism toward the end of his reign.

His tenure was also marked by intransigent reaction against the anticlerical legislation of Émile Combes' government in France, which caused a bitter church-state dispute wherein Pius forbade any compromise over the *associations cultuelles,*

Pope Pius X. Courtesy of the Library of Congress

the means by which the French government sought to "lease back" church property. In 1905, after President Émile Loubet's visit to the Italian king in Rome, the diplomatic dispute led to a rupturing of relations with France. Church-state disputes in Portugal and Spain also plagued Pius's tenure.

By the end of his reign, thanks to his intransigent policies and those of his secretary of state, Cardinal **Merry Del Val,** the Vatican was diplomatically isolated as never before and appears to have been unable or unwilling to exercise any influence to prevent the First World War, which broke out just before his death.

Bibliography. Falconi, C. *The Popes in the Twentieth Century.* Trans. Muriel Gringrod. London: Weidenfeld & Nicolson, 1968. Levillain, P., ed. *The Papacy: An Encyclopedia.* Vol. 1. London: Routledge, 2002.

John F. Pollard

PIUS XI [ACHILLE RATTI] (1857–1939).
Pius XI promoted a Christian reconquest of the world to challenge the attractions of materialism and secularism. True peace would only return to the world when humanity turned once again to Jesus Christ. This central objective of the pontificate formed the substance of Pius XI's first encyclical, *Ubi Arcano Dei,* of December 1922 and informed his every action. During his reign, he concentrated on the importance of clerical education and also believed that the laity must help to permeate modern society with Christian values through the Catholic Action movement and its separate organizations for men, women, and youth.

Born in Lombardy, in northern Italy, Achille Ratti (Pius XI) was ordained a Catholic priest in 1879. He became prefect of Milan's Ambrosian Library in 1907, was transferred to the Vatican Library in 1911, and in 1914 was named prefect of that library. In 1918, Ratti was appointed apostolic visitor to Poland and, subsequently, first nuncio to the Polish Republic. There, he created the organizational structure of the Roman Catholic Church in the new Poland. The success of this mission ensured his 1921 appointment as archbishop of Milan. On the death of **Benedict XV,** Ratti was elected to succeed him as Pope Pius XI in February 1922.

With the destruction in 1918 of Austria-Hungary, the last great Catholic empire, the pope believed that the security of the church within the modern state system could only be guaranteed by negotiating concordats with individual states to protect the rights and independence of the clergy and the continued existence of Catholic Action. Since his message was being poorly received in France and Italy, Pius XI addressed both French and Italian issues in dramatic fashion in 1926. In that year, he publicly condemned the reactionary nationalism of **Charles Maurras's Action Française.** Pius also authorized

the opening of secret negotiations with Benito Mussolini's Fascist regime toward the settlement of the Roman Question in Italy. These negotiations resulted in the Lateran Agreements of 1929, which resolved the issue by the creation of the Vatican City State.

The conclusion of the Lateran Agreements brought the first phase of Pius's pontificate to a close. The second half was contingent upon the social and political upheaval of the Great Depression, when he feared that the ideological challenge of communism might find a ready response among the unemployed masses of Europe. To meet this threat, the Holy See launched an active campaign against Communist atheism in 1930.

The success of the Italian concordat, the fear of communism, and the culmination of long negotiations with the governments of Germany led to the conclusion of a concordat with that country in July 1933, barely six months after Adolf Hitler's National Socialists had come to power. The pope had been willing to sacrifice the Catholic German **Center Party** in return for promises of protection of the church in Germany. Pius XI soon found that Hitler's promises were worthless, and that the Nazis conducted an active persecution of the church in spite of the guarantees of the concordat.

Pius XI feared that the polarization of European society in the mid-1930s would only serve to drive more people into the Nazi fold, as he also feared that Mussolini, through a closer association with Hitler, would decide to emulate the Nazi persecution of the church within Italy. Once Hitler and Benito Mussolini had announced the creation of the Rome-Berlin Axis in late 1936, the pope sought to undermine the relationship by refusing to recognize the Spanish civil war, which teamed the two dictators against the forces of the Left, as an ideological crusade. Then, the pope established firmly the principles for which he stood and for which he expected Christians to stand. In March 1937, he released two encyclicals that denounced the totalitarians of left and right—*Divini redemptoris* against atheistic Communism, and *Mit brennender Sorge* against Nazism.

Pius XI publicly denounced Hitler and his acts in 1938. The pope despaired of the *Anschluss,* demonstrably left Rome on the eve of Hitler's visit to that city, and attacked Nazi racism. He warned Italians away from the German alliance and, more importantly, took a stand against Italian racism. Just before he died, he commissioned a new encyclical against racism and anti-Semitism.

The historical legacy of Pius XI lay in the manner in which he had developed and encouraged Catholic Action as a Christian institution in the increasingly intolerant, militarist, and authoritarian political cultures of the 1930s. With the defeat of the Axis in 1945, the new Christian democratic political leadership emerged from the Catholic Action movement. After 1945, European Christian Democracy stood as the vindication of Pius XI's commitment to a new infusion of Christian values into the secular world of the twentieth century.

Bibliography. Agostino, Marc. *Le Pape Pie XI et l'opinion (1922–1939).* Rome: École française de Rome, 1991. Binchy, D. A. *Church and State in Fascist Italy.* London: Oxford University Press, 1941. Kent, Peter C. *The Pope and the Duce: The International Impact of the Lateran Agreements.* London: Macmillan, 1981. Pollard, John F. *The Vatican and Italian Fascism, 1929–32: A Study in Conflict.* Cambridge: Cambridge University Press, 1985. Rhodes, Anthony. *The Vatican in the Age of the Dictators, 1922–1945.* London: Hodder & Stoughton, 1973.

Peter C. Kent

PIUS XII [EUGENIO PACELLI] (1876–1958). Pacelli (Pope Pius XII) was born a Roman in 1876. He was ordained priest in 1899 and began a career in the Vatican secretariat of state two years later. During the First World War, he rose to be undersecretary of state and worked on the codification of canon law. In 1917, he was named nuncio to Bavaria and, in 1920, nuncio to the German Republic. In 1929, he was made a cardinal and, in 1930, succeeded Cardinal **Gasparri** as Vatican secretary of state. Elected pope in March 1939, he chose the name of Pius XII out of dedication to his predecessor, **Pius XI.** He reigned for nineteen years, through war and cold war, until his death in October 1958.

From the beginning, Pacelli's experience was at the Roman heart of the church. His early career was in the curia, and through his work on the codification of canon law, he contributed to centralizing tendencies within the church. His intelligence and resourcefulness led to his appointment as papal representative in Bavaria.

His experience in Germany was an important part of his formation. With the 1918 disintegration of Austria-Hungary, the Holy See was bereft of its most important secular defender. It became necessary to deal directly with secular states, some of which were hostile to the goals of the Holy See. The contractual vehicle used to define these relationships was the concordat. It was Pacelli who regularized Vatican relationships with the German states by concluding concordats with Bavaria, Prussia, and Baden and by laying the groundwork for the concordat with Germany itself, eventually signed by the Hitler government in 1933.

Coupled with his exemplary service in Germany were two other formative experiences that marked the rest of his career. Pacelli developed a great empathy for Germany and the Germans, being himself influential in building and shaping the postwar German church. In his early years in Munich, Pacelli had experienced firsthand the Communist uprising of 1919, which he frequently cited in the future as his personal experience of the threat of atheist materialism to the teachings of the church.

His German career led to a cardinal's hat in 1929 and his selection as secretary of state in 1930. As secretary of state, Pacelli's role was indistinguishable from that of Pius XI, whose wishes he executed faithfully. He traveled extensively on behalf of the pope, including an important 1936 visit to the United States. He was the perceived heir apparent and, to no one's surprise, was elected pope on the death of Pius XI in 1939.

It was only with this election that the differences with his predecessor became apparent, in particular their different approaches to Nazi Germany. Where Pius XI had seen Nazism as a threat and had denounced German violations of the Concordat, Pius XII perceived communism as a greater threat and, consequently, adopted a more conciliatory approach to Berlin.

With the outbreak of war in 1939, Pius XII waited to be called as a mediator and, consequently, was reluctant to criticize either side, even after the Germans had destroyed Catholic Poland. The Vatican was willing to suspend its hostility to the Soviet Union once they joined the Grand Alliance in 1941. Nevertheless, Pius XII deplored the 1943 declaration of unconditional surrender, which negated his role as a potential mediator and guaranteed the collapse of central Europe and the extension of Soviet power after the war. During the latter half of the war, Pius sought to warn the Americans about the danger of a Soviet military advance into Eastern and Central Europe but was distraught to find President Roosevelt willing to appease Stalin in this area.

Pius XII was well informed about Nazi genocidal policies yet chose not to confront them, even remaining silent when Roman Jews were rounded up by the Germans in October 1943. He was compassionate yet did not feel that he could make a significant difference and, as a consequence, a response to the Holocaust was not as high a priority for him as his attempts to prevent the bombing of Rome.

With the end of the war, Pius XII sought to block a permanent Communist presence in Central Europe by advocating a reintegration of Christian Europe through conciliatory peace treaties with both Germany and Italy. These goals ran counter to the interests of both the USSR and the United States, who resolved their conflict in Europe by dividing the continent in 1947. Pius XII sought to sustain the church in Eastern Europe by calling for church resistance to the new Communist governments in that area. While some resisted, like Cardinal **Mindszenty** of Hungary, and some were conciliatory, like Cardinal **Wyszynski** of Poland, Soviet authorities arrested all senior church leaders in Eastern Europe after 1949 in spite of their previous positions.

In Western Europe, Pius XII had far greater influence with the emergence of Christian democracy, under the patronage of the church, in Italy, France, and West Germany. In these countries, Christian democracy formed a strong political center to work with American aid programs and the subsequent movement for European integration.

During the last years of his life, Pius XII remained an important icon of the cold war while, at the same time, resisting radical change within the church. Events in Hungary and Poland in 1956 were a cause for optimism, yet, in his last years, Pius XII was ever more in the control of conservative curial cardinals.

Bibliography. Falconi, Carlo. *The Popes in the Twentieth Century.* London: Weidenfeld & Nicolson, 1967. Kent, Peter C. *The Lonely Cold War of Pope Pius XII: The Roman Catholic Church and the Division of Europe, 1943–1950.*

Montreal: McGill-Queen's University Press, 2002. Phayer, Michael. *The Catholic Church and the Holocaust, 1930–1945.* Bloomington: Indiana University Press, 2000. Riccardi, Andrea, ed. *Pio XII.* Bari, Italy: Laterza, 1984. Sanchez, José M.. *Pius XII and the Holocaust: Understanding the Controversy.* Washington, DC: Catholic University of America Press, 2002.

Peter C. Kent

PLÁ Y DENIEL, ENRIQUE (1876–1968). Born to a wealthy family in Barcelona, Spain, Plá trained for the Catholic priesthood at the city's seminary, and the Gregorian University in Rome. Already distinguished as among the most able of his generation of clerics, Plá returned to Barcelona as a canon and seminary teacher before being appointed bishop of Avila in 1918. Highly active in Catholic social action in Barcelona, Plá brought great energy to his new see, where he consolidated a reputation for vigorously defending the rights of the church and resisting laicism through a combination of doctrinal conservatism and social Catholic activism.

As bishop of Salamanca in 1935, he achieved some fame (or notoriety) when he offered the episcopal palace to General **Franco,** who had made the city his temporary "capital." But Plá's identification with the Francoist cause was made most explicit in a careful and lengthy pastoral letter ("The Case of Spain") published on September 30, 1936. "The Two Cities" depicted Spain's civil war as between "two concepts of life": "heroism and martyrdom" against "communism and anarchy." Three weeks later, Cardinal **Gomá y Tomás** echoed Plá's words in a pastoral letter that referred to "a war . . . of one concept of life . . . of one civilization against another." Plá was thus instrumental in defining the civil war as a crusade. His support for the Nationalist cause never wavered.

On the day Franco became head of state, Plá congratulated him in anticipation of Spain's "glorious resurrection." As token of this resurgence, Plá played a prominent role in the mass acts of liturgy that characterized early Franco Spain. In 1940, on Gomá's death, he became archbishop of Toledo, winning a cardinal's hat in 1946. As primate, Plá defended both the moral and devotional certainties of national Catholicism and the church's autonomy against secular encroachments, not least from the fascist party, the Falange. The same stance led him to defend the increasingly radical Catholic workers' and youth organizations, though he never shared their political uncertainties. He resigned from the primatial see in 1966, after Vatican II had required bishops over seventy-five to retire.

Bibliography. Callahan, William J. *The Catholic Church in Spain, 1875–1998.* Washington, DC: Catholic University of America Press, 2000. Raguer, Hilari. *La pólvora y el incienso: La Iglesia y la Guerra Civil española, 1936–1939.* Barcelona: Península, 2001. Vincent, Mary. *Catholicism in the Second Spanish Republic: Religion and Politics in Salamanca, 1930–1936.* Oxford: Oxford University Press, 1996.

Mary Vincent

POBEDONOSTSEV, KONSTANTIN PETROVICH (1827–1907). The jurist, state official, and lay head of the Holy Synod of the Russian Orthodox Church (1880–1905), Pobedonostsev was a conservative writer on philosophical and literary subjects who served as a tutor and adviser in law and politics to Russian emperors. The youngest son of a Russian Orthodox priest and professor of Russian literature at Moscow University, he was educated at home and at St. Petersburg's Oldenburg School of Law (1841–1846) before service in various departments of the Senate (1847–1858).

As an author of books on the history of Russian civil law and institutions, he was invited to lecture at Moscow University (1859–1865). He taught law and politics to the sons of Alexander II (since 1861) and was an important collaborator to the 1864 reform of the Russian judicial system. In 1865 Pobedonostsev moved from Moscow to St. Petersburg and started to publish religious and moralistic books, mainly translations on a wide range of topics from the texts of St. Augustine to the sects in the United States, education of children, women in society, and universal suffrage.

Appointed to the Senate in 1868 and to the State Council in 1872, he became a member of the Commissions on People's Education (1875–1876) and on Prisons and Punishments (1877). In 1879, he took a seat on the council on prisons' affairs (1879). He finally served as the director general, or chief procurator, the lay head of the Holy Synod of the Russian Orthodox Church (1880–1905), a post that gave him immense power over domestic policy throughout the 1880s, not only in matters affecting religion, but also in education and censorship. Nevertheless, he exercised little authority in that post during the last fifteen years of his life.

Pobedonostsev denounced the eighteenth-century Enlightenment view of the perfectibility of man and society and therefore strongly supported paternalistic and authoritarian government. He considered each nation as rooted in the land, the family, and the national church and regarded the maintenance of order as the government's chief purpose. He sought, therefore, to defend Russia and the Russian Orthodox Church against all rival religious groups, such as the Old Believers, Baptists, Catholics, and Jews. He defended Russian rule and Russification over subject peoples and was largely responsible for the government's repressive policies toward religious and ethnic minorities. He promoted the rapid expansion of primary education in parish schools, seeking to keep each person in that station in life into which he or she had been born and to restrict higher education to the upper classes and exceptionally talented.

Deeply familiar with the great body of European and American literature and philosophy, Pobedonostsev struggled to curtail its influence in Russia, especially ideas concerning constitutional and democratic government. He strongly supported censorship and tight controls for other Russians. For his conservative positions, Pobedonostsev was nicknamed the "Grand Inquisitor."

Bibliography. Byrnes, R. F. *Pobedonostsev: His Life and Thought.* Bloomington: Indiana University Press, 1968. Simon, Gerhard. *Konstantin Petrovic Pobedonoscev und die Kirchenpolitik des Heiligen Synod, 1880–1905.* Göttingen, Germany: Vandenhoeck & Ruprecht, 1969.

Irina Novichenko

POPULAR PARTY [PARTIDO POPULAR] (SPAIN).

The Spanish Partido Popular (PP) was born from the reorganization of the Alianza Popular (AP), which was formed in 1977 from a confederation of smaller parties by Miguel Fraga Iribane, an ex-minister in **Francisco Franco**'s government. Launched to "spread the principles of Christian humanism," the AP had defined itself as a group of popular, interclass, conservative, liberal, reformist organizations of Christian persuasion.

In reality, the AP grouped together the various segments of Francoism, including many last-minute converts to democracy and the most conservative sections of Christian democracy that had attempted in vain to organize themselves outside Fraga's alliance. Most likely because of these origins, the AP was considered a rightist movement that, according to the democratic point of view, was not very trustworthy. The AP lost several elections beginning in 1977, such as when it was beaten by Adolfo Suárez and his Union of the Democratic Center (UCD) and then by Felipe González's Socialists (PSOE).

The AP recognized the need for a greater voting base as well as the problem of an aging leadership in the second half of the 1980s. At its Ninth Party Convention (Madrid, June 20–22, 1989), the AP transformed itself into the Partido Popular. At the Tenth Party Convention at Seville, Fraga ceded party leadership over to José Maria Anzar. Anzar had been a candidate in the 1989 elections and was once again in 1993. With him in charge, the PP tried to redefine itself as a party of the Right in Spanish politics. Its major victory in the 1996 elections and its win of an absolute majority in the 2000 elections opened a new era in recent Spanish history. The classic Right joined with modern professionals, who favored Catalan, Basque, and Gallegos nationalist parties, to give the PP most of its votes.

The PP also attracted the Spanish neonationalist vote. Inside the party, at least three political traditions worked together: liberalism, conservatism, and Catholicism shaped by both Christian democratic traditions, and others further to the right such as those affiliated with the Catholic lay apostolate, Opus Dei. The Christian tendencies of the party were sometimes unclear, however, and the party did not always enjoy a stable relationship with the Spanish Catholic hierarchy. The PP and the Catholic Church differed over the condemnation of Basque terrorism at the end of the 1990s, as well as over a document on the war against Iraq written by the Spanish Episcopal Conference.

Some PP leaders, furthermore, took unexpectedly secular positions in other matters. The PP, on the other hand, completely agreed with the desires and requests of the bishops as outlined in the *Ley orgánica de calidad de la Educación* (Organic Law on the Quality of Education) of 2002 regarding private schools and the teaching of the Catholic faith. The Madrid bombings of March 2003 brought down the Aznar government, which proved to be too quick in incorrectly blaming Basque separatists.

Bibliography. Baón, R. *Historia del partido Popular: Del franquismo a la refundación.* Madrid: Sapel, 2001.

Alfonso Botti

POPULAR REPUBLICAN MOVEMENT [MOUVEMENT RÉPUBLICAIN POPULAIRE] (FRANCE). Unlike the situation in the German Second Reich (1871–1918) where Bismarck's anti-Catholic policies produced in reaction the confessional **Center Party,** no Catholic political party of significance emerged during the French Third Republic (1871–1940), despite the equally anti-Catholic legislation of its leftist regimes. This seems due primarily to the support given by most practicing Catholics to parties advocating a restoration of the monarchy.

Following World War II, however, the Mouvement Républicain Populaire (MRP), a Christian Democratic party in all but name, developed as one of four major parties alongside the Communists, Socialists, and Radicals. **Georges Bidault,** François de Menthon, Pierre-Henri Teitgen, and **Maurice Schumann**—all leaders of the MRP—had been active in the Resistance and were appointed by General **Charles de Gaulle** as ministers in his first provisional government. Schumann was the first president of the MRP.

In the October 1945 parliamentary election, the MRP received 24 percent of the votes, having benefited from the bankruptcy of the traditional parties of the Right, which were seen as having collaborated with Vichy. In the June and November 1946 elections, the MRP won 28 percent and 26 percent of the popular vote respectively and 166 (27%) and 175 (28%) seats respectively in a National Assembly of 619 members. This showing made it the second-largest party in the Assembly, exceeded only by the Communist Party, with 187 seats (30.5%).

The MRP ran most strongly in the traditional Catholic and conservative regions of France: Brittany, the north, and Alsace-Lorraine. The 1944 enfranchisement of women also helped the MRP—one reason why the Left, which had controlled the Third Republic for seventy years, never extended the vote to women. A 1952 poll found that two-thirds of practicing Catholic women had voted MRP.

The MRP can be thought of as a centrist party, progressive on economic issues affecting workers, such as the issue of European integration; indeed, **Robert Schuman**, along with **Alcide De Gasperi** and **Konrad Adenauer,** can be seen as the triumvirate most responsible for the European Economic Community and ultimately the European Union of today. On the other hand, the MRP's attitude on social issues, the school question, and colonialism can be seen as more conservative, seeing in the latter issue a role for the missionary role of the church. Eventually the MRP divided—as did many French parties—over the issues of Algeria and Gaullism.

The rise of a Gaullist movement in 1958 deprived the MRP of its traditional base of Catholic support. In Charles de Gaulle, French Catholics got most of what they wanted: nationalism, social conservatism, an end to anticlerical legislation, and to boot, as president of the republic, a charismatic hero of the Resistance, a model Catholic layman, and a product of the Jesuits, and his pious wife as first lady.

As a last hurrah, Jean Lecanuet, who had become president of the MRP in 1963, opposed de Gaulle in the 1965 presidential election at the head of a new opposition party, *Centre Democrate*. He ran a creditable third-place race in the first round, polling 16 percent of the vote to de Gaulle's 45 percent and Mitterand's 32 percent.

The MRP disappeared as a formal party in late 1967, when its few remaining members of the Assembly joined the Gaullist Democratic Union for the Fifth Republic. It had lasted almost a quarter century.

Bibliography. Buchanan, Tom, and Martin Conway, eds. *Political Catholicism in Europe, 1918–1965*. Oxford: Clarendon Press, 1996. Hanley, David, ed. *Christian Democracy in Europe: A Comparative Perspective*. London: Pinter, 1996. Henig, Stanley, ed. *European Political Parties: A Handbook*. New York: Praeger, 1970.

William J. Parente

POWDERLY, TERENCE V. (1849–1924). Terence Vincent Powderly made his primary mark on American history as head of the Knights of Labor (1879–1893), the Gilded Age's largest labor union. An overlapping stint as mayor of Scranton, Pennsylvania, and several decades working in the federal bureaucracy comprised his other public occupations.

Powderly's religious convictions influenced in various and often subtle ways his conduct in office. Irish Catholic in upbringing, he dutifully practiced his faith throughout his mayoralty and most of his union career. Religion provided not only personal spiritual support but also, blended with practical imperatives and contemporary reform ideology, a rationale for his public life. Nevertheless, it also, for a while, jeopardized his success as a labor leader.

In the 1870s and 1880s, Powderly gradually developed his own version of applied Christianity. He kept over his office desk a depiction of the Crucifixion and later averred that, when he was vilified for his union work, he "could always look on the picture of the crucified Christ and find consolation in the thought that duty to fellow man called for agitation in their [*sic*] interests." (Powderly, 39) Indeed he frequently used Christological images in describing the mistreated working class and besieged labor leaders. Against prevailing mores he successfully promoted the admission of women and African Americans into his union, condemned clergymen who preached to laboring men passive acceptance of their lot, denounced the inequities of laissez-faire economics, and promoted workers' cooperatives as alternatives to wage dependency. As mayor he brought labor peace to Scranton, implemented a mildly progressive reform program, and, in his judicial capacity, treated defendants with compassion. Withal a man of unimpeachable personal integrity, he declined to use his public roles for inappropriate private gain.

On the other hand, Powderly had to mediate between his union and criticism of its secret character by certain Catholic bishops. Motivated by a combination of conviction and practicality, Powderly convinced the Knights to modify their secrecy requirements, opening the door to the organization's spectacular growth in the mid-1880s, and, through his lobbying of several key bishops (most notably Archbishop James Gibbons), helped forestall Vatican condemnation in 1887. The latter action played a role in eliciting the Catholic Church's ultimate support for unionism, although it also provoked nativist condemnation of Powderly as a tool of the pope.

Powderly, responding to criticism from Catholic (and some Protestant) sources, also moved decisively in the 1880s to disassociate his organization from radical socialism, anarchism, and violence. He, in fact, preferred settling labor disputes by negotiation rather than strikes. Though his ideological moderation pointed the way to the conservative unionism that would dominate America's future, the Knights continued to be tainted with extremism in the public perception, especially after the Haymarket Square riot of 1886, a factor in their precipitous decline thereafter.

In his post-Knights public career, Powderly, now a fervid Republican, won appointments in Washington, D.C., as commissioner of immigration (1897–1902) and chief of the Division of Information in the Bureau of Immigration (1907–1921). In those latter decades he drifted from the Catholic Church, joined the Masons in 1901, and subscribed to a generic nondenominational Christianity with a humanitarian emphasis. A moderate restrictionist and Americanizer, he energetically promoted policies to help newcomers find work and adapt successfully to American life without undermining the native workforce.

Terence Powderly died in Washington, D.C., and was buried with Masonic rites in Rock Creek Cemetery.

Bibliography. Browne, Henry J. *The Catholic Church and the Knights of Labor.* Washington, DC: Catholic University of America Press, 1949. Phelan, Craig. *Grand Master Workman: Terence Powderly and the Knights of Labor.* Westport, CT: Greenwood Press, 2000. Powderly, Terence V. *The Path I Trod: The Autobiography of Terence V. Powderly.* Ed. Harry J. Carman, Henry David, and Paul N. Guthrie. New York: Columbia University, 1940

Robert F. Hueston

PRIMO DE RIVERA, JOSÉ ANTONIO (1903–1936). The son of Spain's military dictator, **Miguel Primo de Rivera,** José Antonio founded a miniscule fascist party in 1933. The following year, Falange Española merged with another tiny fascist grouping, the JONS, to form Spain's only indigenous fascist party. Primo de Rivera soon emerged as the Falange's most significant political leader and its only elected parliamentary representative.

A man of great personal charm, José Antonio's poise and elegant appearance testified to his aristocratic upbringing. Many of the early Falangists shared this privileged background, often through personal connections to the Primo de Rivera family. Other adherents had greater ideological commitment. Throughout its existence, the

Falange included avowedly secular elements and was effectively bankrolled by Benito Mussolini's Fascist Italian government. However, the personal faith of Primo de Rivera and his fellow leader, Onésimo Redondo, ensured that the party was always officially Catholic. For Primo de Rivera, Catholicism was an essential component of both Spain's identity and its past (and supposedly future) imperial greatness.

The Falange's emphasis on violent confrontation also led to a growing number of party "martyrs," who were commemorated with distinctive liturgies involving, prayers, salutes, roll calls, and funeral orations. Jailed in March 1936 by the Republican authorities, Primo de Rivera directed his party from inside prison. Only after the Popular Front had won electoral power back from the Right did the Falange begin to attract large numbers of recruits, and during the civil war it finally became a mass party. By now, though, Primo de Rivera was dead, shot in Alicante prison on November 20, 1936.

News of Primo de Rivera's death was initially concealed by General **Franco,** who was looking to tame the Falange. He achieved this by creating a single party from the Falange and the Carlists. José Antonio became the first martyr of Francoism, and his name and image were incorporated into the iconography of the regime. After victory, his body was carried from Alicante to El Escorial in silent procession, on the shoulders of Falangist pallbearers. His name was painted on the outside walls of every church in Spain, heading a list of the Francoist dead, and schoolchildren memorized tracts of his often-opaque political writings.

One of Franco's most effective collaborators in creating a cult around Primo de Rivera was his sister Pilar (1907–1991). He had originally opposed the entry of women into the Falange, given the party's role as street fighters, but a women's section was soon established under Pilar's leadership.

After his execution; that of another brother, Fernando; and Redondo's death at the front, Pilar was left in a role she had never looked to play. A devout Catholic, she led the women's section until it was disbanded in 1977, overseeing the introduction of social service for unmarried women. Believing herself to be, as one Falangist intellectual put it, "the greatest and appropriate representative of her much missed brother," she adapted to social and political change in the 1960s and 1970s only by persuading herself that such changes were in accordance with José Antonio's cultural legacy.

Bibliography. Preston, Paul. *Comrades! Portraits from the Spanish Civil War.* London: HarperCollins, 1999. Primo de Rivera, José Antonio. *Selected Writings.* Ed. Hugh Thomas. London: Jonathan Cape, 1972. Primo de Rivera, Pilar. *Recuerdos de Una Vida.* Madrid: Dyrsa, 1983.

Mary Vincent

PRIMO DE RIVERA Y ORBANEJA, MIGUEL (1870–1930). Born in Jerez de la Frontiera (Cádiz) into a large, well-known family, Primo de Rivera was a Catholic traditionalist who became the dictator of Spain during the 1920s.

Uneven relations between church and state, however, distinguished his regime. He began a military career at a very young age (1884) and was promoted to the rank of captain in 1893 after having distinguished himself at Manila. Primo de Rivera then went to Cuba (1895) and to the Philippines (1897) as an assistant to his uncle, who was the captain general of the Spanish colony. In 1902 he married Casilda Sáez de Heredia, with whom he would have six children, including their firstborn, **José Antonio Primo de Rivera,** the founder of the Falange Española during the 1930s.

After having reenlisted several times and serving in Africa, Miguel Primo de Rivera became convinced that Spain should stop its colonial battles beyond the Straits of Gibraltar, and his career, up to that point rather promising, suffered repercussions for his having publicized such ideas. As commander of Barcelona, he continued to develop his idea of leading Spain to its regeneration according to pronational Spanish aspirations following the "disaster" of 1898, defeat at America's hands. The Catholic Church welcomed Primo de Rivera's coup d'état on September 23, 1923 and looked favorably on him as an ally, although his *Manifesto,* which accompanied the coup, contained no religious references, nor did he seem overly concerned by relations with the church. According to tradition, the Spanish are Catholics from birth but Primo de Rivera's policy was not particularly favorable to the Catholic Church, even though it had favorably welcomed his coup and supported his dictatorship until 1927–1928.

Primo de Rivera's dictatorship was initially a traditional military regime that was supposed to be temporary. With the creation of the *Unión Patriótica* (United Party), an economic and social policy that opposed workers' interests, and close relations with Benito Mussolini's Fascist regime, Primo de Rivera's dictatorship began to promote itself as a "new regime." The *Unión patriótica*'s motto was "Monarchy, Religion and Authority," and many Catholics flocked to it. The dictator, furthermore, favored Catholics in his administration. On frequent public occasions, Primo de Rivera himself provided ostentatious and perhaps theatrical shows of Catholic loyalty. His government's morality campaign, however, bore little fruit because of a reluctance to give it teeth with serious enforcement measures. The convocation of an assembly, moreover, to draft a new fundamental charter, accomplished little from the church's perspective.

Primo de Rivera also failed to deliver on greater state aid for the church, and he

Miguel Primo de Rivera y Orbaneja, 1928. © Getty

meddled in the choice of bishops, particularly in Catalonia. Only in education reform, via a purge of teachers and some benefits to the Catholic universities, did Primo de Rivera begin to satisfy clerical aspirations. By 1927–1928 the church began to distance itself from the regime, and, having lost his faith as well, King Alfonso XIII accepted Primo de Rivera's resignation in January 1930. He then went into exile in Paris, where he died a few weeks later.

Bibliography. Adagio, Carmelo. *Chiesa e nazione in Spagna: La dittatura di Primo de Rivera (1923–1930).* Milan: Unicopli, 2004. Ben Ami, Shlomo. *Fascism from Above: The Dictatorship of Primo de Rivera in Spain, 1923–1930.* Oxford: Oxford University Press, 1983. Gómez-Navarro, J.L. *El Régimen de Primo de Rivera. Reyes, dictaduras y dictadores.* Madrid: Cátedra, 1991.

Alfonso Botti

PROAÑO, LEONIDAS (1910–1988). A leading proponent of liberation theology in Ecuador, Proaño, known as the bishop of the Andes, ministered in the highland province of Chimborazo, where he championed the rights of the large Indian population living there. Proaño fought to improve the material as well as spiritual needs of his congregations by calling for medical services, allocation of land to peasants, an end to unfair labor practices, and better education.

As a native of Ecuador's central highlands, Proaño was well acquainted with the Indian customs, history, and sense of community. Therefore, he believed he was a better spokesperson for the indigenous peoples than the recently arrived Protestant missionaries from the United States. In addition, he established radio literacy programs and lay leadership schools. He also distributed church land holdings to the landless. In order to demonstrate the common touch of the church, he canceled plans for an expensive cathedral and adopted an impoverished personal lifestyle.

In 1976, he organized an international conference to highlight his approach to ministry. Convened with approval of the Vatican and Proaño's superiors in Ecuador, the meeting included seventeen archbishops from all over Latin America as well as other prominent theologians. However, Ecuador's ruling military government viewed Proaño's actions as seditious and arrested him and the conference participants. The incident was typical of the suspicion between the radical elements of the Catholic Church and military governments in Latin America in this period. In 1978, Proaño organized a coalition of Catholic and Protestant liberation theologians and labor organizations known as the Ecumenical Human Rights Commission of Ecuador to promote human rights and call attention to violations in Ecuador. Proaño was nominated for the Nobel Peace Prize in 1986. His efforts to promote human rights in Ecuador have been continued by Elsie Monge, a Maryknoll sister who now heads EHRCE.

Bibliography. Handelsman, Michael. *Culture and Customs of Ecuador.* Westport, CT: Greenwood Press, 2000.

George M. Lauderbaugh

PROHÁSZKA, OTTOKÁR (1858–1927). Bishop Ottokár Prohászka, along with **Sándor Canon Giesswein,** was the leading voice of Christian Socialism in Hungary in the early twentieth century. Born in what was formerly northern Hungary (now Slovakia) in the city of Nyitra (Nitra), Prohászka was educated in such centers of Hungarian Catholicism as Kalocsa and Esztergom, as well as in the Eternal City. Consecrated as a priest in Rome in 1881, three years later he was appointed a teacher of theology in Esztergom (Hungary's ecclesiastical center) and then in 1904 was named professor of dogmatics at the University of Budapest. He then became the bishop of Székesfehérvár (1905), a member of the Hungarian Academy (1909), president of the Christian National Unity Party (1919), and member of the Hungarian parliament (1920–1922).

Prohászka was both a powerful orator and a compelling writer. He advanced his ideas in the journals *Magyar Sion* (Hungarian Sion) and *Esztergom,* both of which he edited, as well as in such influential books as his *Diadalmas világnézet* (Triumphant World Ideology, 1903), *Modern katholicizmus* (Modern Catholicism, 1904), and *Az intellektualizmus túlhajtásai* (The Exaggerations of Intellectualism, 1911).

Prohászka targeted both atheistic communism and exploitive capitalism. As a champion of Christian Socialism, he spoke repeatedly for the rights of the peasants and the workers. His criticisms of the Catholic Church and its conservative hierarchy elicited the displeasure of the reactionary members of the religious establishment, including some of his fellow bishops. They accused him of communist sympathies, even as Hungary's Marxist intellectuals charged him with being a traditionalist chauvinist.

In his sociological works, Prohászka elaborated his views on human existence and historical evolution. He combined the official Catholic philosophy of neo-Thomism with the idealist and allegedly antirational ideas of Henri Bergson (1869–1941), who emphasized the unique role of "intuition," "mystical insight," and "spiritual comprehension" in the re-creation of history—as did the *Geistesgeschichte* philosophy of history of Wilhelm Dilthey (1834–1911). Repeated accusations by the conservative Right eventually resulted in the appearance of some of Prohászka's books on the Vatican Index of Forbidden Books.

In the midst of this struggle, Bishop Prohászka died at his pulpit while fighting for the implementation of progressive social ideas. His complete works were published in twenty-five volumes under the editorship of Antal Schütz (1928–1929).

Bibliography. Gergely, Jenö. *Prohászka Ottokár: "A napba öltözött ember"* [Ottokár Prohászka: "The Man Embraced by the Sun"]. Budapest: Gondolat Kiadó, 1994. Romsics, Ignác. *Hungary in the Twentieth Century.* Budapest: Corvina Press, 2000, chapters 1–2.

Steven Béla Várdy

R

RAGAZ, LEONHARD (1868–1945). Ragaz was the founding editor of the primary organ of Swiss Religious Socialism, *Neue Wege,* and along with Hermann Kutter was a central figure in the development of Swiss Religious Socialism, which reached its high point in the early twentieth century just prior to the First World War.

Born in the small Swiss village of Tamins in the vicinity of Chur, Ragaz was deeply affected by the communitarian and cooperative aspects of village life. His later understanding of Socialism was indelibly colored by this early experience. Ordained in 1890, Ragaz held a series of pastoral positions before receiving a call to the cathedral of Basel in 1902. In Basel, his engagement in social issues turned more decidedly toward the left, and by 1903 his identification with the workers movement was solidified through involvement in the Basel Bricklayers Strike.

In that same year he came into contact with the thought of **Christoph Blumhardt,** as mediated by Hermann Kutter. Kutter's 1903 *Sie müssen* marked the beginning of the Swiss Religious Socialist movement in earnest and gave decisive orientation to Ragaz's early thought. Though unbalanced, the work opened up a whole new world to Ragaz and introduced him to the theological interpretation of Socialism that he had been searching for: Socialism is a sign of the coming kingdom of God. Though Ragaz would later distance himself from Kutter (the two would unfortunately become representative figures for opposing groups within the Religious Socialist movement), the influence of Blumhardt would persist up to Ragaz's death in 1945, and Ragaz would play an important role in seeing Blumhardt's thought get a wide audience.

In 1906 Ragaz founded *Neue Wege,* through which Ragaz would shape the Religious Socialist vision, influence Socialist and Marxist party politics and give commentary on world events from a Religious Socialist perspective. In 1907, while at a conference in America, Ragaz met **Walter Rauschenbusch** and in 1908 was invited to become professor of practical theology at the University of Zurich, a position he would later resign (1921) to work in the slums of Zurich.

The First World War was a shock for Ragaz. In the face of the collapse of international Socialism he began to withdraw himself from Socialist Party politics, though he remained vigorously involved in the broader movement of Religious Socialism. Ragaz turned more toward pacifism, as he believed that the war was God's judgment on the nations. This new orientation also guided his earliest evaluation of fascism. As early as 1923, Ragaz recognized fascism as a brutal and growing menace, the core of which was fundamentally anti-Christian. In 1926 he published a full-scale analysis of fascism, and in 1930 he was the primary author of a warning put forth by the International Union of Religious Socialists on the danger of National Socialism. This was sharpened by a 1933 declaration that explicitly attacked the anti-Semitism of the Nazis. Though forbidden to publish his journal by the Swiss authorities, for fear it was too critical of the Nazis, Ragaz remained engaged by working with Jewish refugees, continuing his lively correspondence with Martin Buber (1878–1965), and writing on the so-called Jewish Question. His thought on Judaism and Christianity was ahead of its time.

Bibliography. Bock, Paul, ed. *Signs of the Kingdom: A Ragaz Reader.* Trans. Paul Bock. Grand Rapids, MI: William B. Eerdmans, 1984. Ward, W. R. *Theology, Sociology and Politics: The German Protestant Social Conscience, 1890- 1933.* Bern: Peter Lang, 1979.

Christian T. Collins Winn

RAMPOLLA DEL TINDARO, MARIANO (1843–1913). Mariano Rampolla del Tindaro was a cardinal and secretary of state who administered the Holy See's foreign affairs during the turn of the last century. He received ordination in Rome in 1866 and, after pursuing his studies there, graduated *doctor in utroque jure* in 1870. The whole of his priestly career was spent in the Roman Curia or as a papal representative abroad. After five years in the Congregation of Extraordinary Affairs, he spent another two at the Madrid nunciature. He was recalled to Rome as secretary for the Oriental rite churches in the Congregation of the Propagation of the Faith and then as secretary of the Congregation for Extraordinary Affairs (1880–1883), when he returned to Madrid as nuncio. There, he and his assistant Giacomo Della Chiesa (later **Benedict XV**) distinguished themselves for their unselfish service to the sick

and dying during the cholera epidemic. In March 1887 Rampolla was named cardinal and secretary of state to **Leo XIII** three months later. For the next sixteen years Leo and Rampolla pursued a policy of equidistance between France and Austria-Hungary, though with reservations toward the new German Reich, together with an attempt to repair relations with the czarist empire. As far as Italy was concerned, relations in the late 1880s and early 1890s were frequently difficult, prompting Leo to threaten to leave Rome on two occasions. Rampolla's interest in the plight of the southern Slav minorities within the Habsburg Empire earned him Franz Josef's veto on his candidature at the conclave that followed Leo's death in 1903. After the election of Giuseppe Cardinal Sarto as Pope **Pius X,** Rampolla was appointed secretary of the Holy Office and was clearly not in favor during Papa Sarto's pontificate. There is a sumptuous funerary monument to him in his titular church of Santa Maria in Trastevere.

Bibliography. Sinopoli di Giunta, G. Pietro. *Il cardinale Mariano Rampolla del Tindaro.* Rome: Tipografia Poliglotta Vaticana, 1923.

John F. Pollard

RAUSCHENBUSCH, WALTER (1861–1918). The son of a professor in Rochester Theological Seminary's German department, Rauschenbusch determined to become a pastor after having a personal conversion experience when he was eighteen. The family's German ties meant that Rauschenbusch received some of his formal education in the United States at Rochester and some in Germany. Consequently, he was deeply influenced by the liberal thinking of German theologians and scholars such as Albrecht Ritschl, Adolf von Harnack, and Julius Wellhausen. Following them, Rauschenbusch throughout his career as a pastor and seminary professor insisted that the biblical message centered on the ethical teachings of the

Hebrew prophets and the understanding of the kingdom of God proclaimed by Jesus in the New Testament Gospel accounts.

In 1886, Rauschenbusch became pastor of a German Baptist congregation on the edge of Manhattan's Hell's Kitchen area, one of the city's worst slums. The poverty and working conditions his parishioners confronted convinced him that there could be no individual salvation, the core of the evangelical stance, without social salvation or the application of biblical ethics to common life in very concrete ways. For him, there was no personal gospel without a "social gospel," the name attached to his viewpoint.

Rauschenbusch became involved in Henry George's unsuccessful 1886 New York City mayoral campaign as testimony to the need for social engagement, and he increasingly began to identify himself as a socialist, although not in a Marxist sense. For Rauschenbusch, a socialist was one who was committed to implementing Jesus's teachings about the kingdom in everyday life. Rauschenbusch's stance received confirmation through the Brotherhood of the Kingdom, a group of clergy and laity that began meeting in 1893 to consider how to remedy the socioeconomic evils accompanying rapid urbanization and industrialization through labor and business reform rooted in biblical ethics. About this time, Rauschenbusch began writing a manuscript called "Revolutionary Christianity," which remained unfinished and was finally published as *The Righteousness of the Kingdom* in 1968, a half century after his death.

Accepting appointment to the German department of Rochester Seminary in 1897 and then to the English faculty there as professor of church history in 1902, Rauschenbusch undertook writing and speaking engagements that allowed him to propound his **Social Gospel** ideas. His first major treatise, *Christianity and the Social Crisis* (1907), appeared while he was on sabbatical leave in Germany. Calling for just wages for factory workers and safe working conditions, Rauschenbusch also insisted that the Social Gospel required public ownership of such businesses as utilities that were essential to the commonwealth. Rauschenbusch's Social Gospel meant that all persons, because they were created in the image of God, had a natural right to adequate shelter, food, and clothing, without which the message of personal salvation was implausible. He therefore endorsed government regulation of business and industry, since those made rich at the expense of the working classes were unlikely to repent of their social sin of their own volition.

Rauschenbusch's work attracted a wide audience. It buttressed ideas being advocated by other religious thinkers like **Solomon Washington Gladden,** by economists like Richard Ely, and, in time, by many Progressive movement politicians like Theodore Roosevelt and **Woodrow Wilson.** Rauschenbusch became a major force on the lecture circuit, but he also brought his message to ordinary folk through a popular devotional work, *For God and the People: Prayers of the Social Awakening* (1910). He expanded his earlier arguments in *Christianizing the Social Order* (1912). His most sophisticated and most carefully reasoned argument came in *A Theology for the Social Gospel,* published in 1917 shortly before his death.

Rauschenbusch manifested a passion for social transformation. He was utterly convinced that humanity had the technical knowledge and resources to remake society into the kingdom of God on earth; only selfishness and sin stood in the way. When humanity finally etched biblical principles on every aspect of common life, the eschaton would arrive in all its fullness. But even before Rauschenbusch's voice was silenced by death from cancer, there were forces undermining the optimism and eschatological expectation of the Social Gospel. World War I impressed theologians and laity alike with the depth of human sin through the greed and violence of battle, as did calls for a new orthodoxy coming from theologians like **Karl Barth;** business and industrial leaders seemed unlikely to yield control of their wealth and resources to promote a vaguely defined common good. If the Social Gospel lost much of its force by the 1920s and failed to address adequately issues like race relations, the need to inform political and social life with the ethical teachings of scripture endured in the Christian Realism of **Reinhold Niebuhr,** John Bennett, and others, and in the theological support for the civil rights movement offered by **Martin Luther King, Jr.**

Bibliography. Hudson, Winthrop, ed. *Walter Rauschenbusch: Selected Writings.* New York: Paulist Press, 1984. Minus, Paul. *Walter Rauschenbusch: American Reformer.* New York: Macmillan, 1988. Sharpe, Dores R. *Walter Rauschenbusch.* New York: Macmillan, 1942.

Charles H. Lippy

REAGAN, RONALD (1911–2004). As a growing number of Americans sought religious answers to the cultural dislocation of the 1960s and 1970s, Ronald Reagan became their spokesman. Perhaps no other U.S. president has articulated the religious yearnings of a political constituency as powerfully as Reagan. Cultivating a message of moral certainty, religious renewal, and divinely sanctioned American internationalism, he legitimized the return of religion to American politics. The conservative evangelical tenets that he espoused became the framework for the Republican ideology that dominated the American political landscape in the late twentieth century.

Reagan's religious awakening followed his conversion to conservative politics. In his youth, he was nominally a member of the Disciples of Christ. He taught Sunday school classes, led Bible study sessions, and attended the denominational Eureka College, but his autobiography offers scant evidence of religious influences on his worldview. If Reagan avoided a life of dissipation in Hollywood, he did not escape scandal altogether, divorcing his first wife to marry Nancy Davis. His entanglement in the congressional purge of Hollywood communists—which saw Reagan testify before the House Un-American Activities Committee and defend the principle of democratic dissent—signaled his rejection of liberal politics as a smokescreen for subversive activity. Increasingly, Reagan echoed the central tenet of conservative politics: uninhibited individual freedom as the solution to the "creeping socialism" of the New Deal. His years as a spokesman for General Electric solidified the conservative philosophy that would guide his public life. Free markets, nongovernmental interference in the economy, vigorous anticommunism, and traditional morality became the central features of Reagan's worldview.

While Reagan accentuated the religious dimension of his political persona in the 1980s, he unveiled it in the tumultuous 1960s. Elected governor of California in 1966, he used his inaugural address to the state assembly to preview the religious themes that would continue throughout his public life. It also highlighted Reagan's dubious habit of extracting aphorisms from American public figures without demonstrating much understanding of the political and social context that influenced their pronouncements. Quoting Benjamin Franklin—a favorite in the Reagan arsenal—he declared the centrality of Christian ideals to American political life: "He who introduces into public office the principles of primitive Christianity will change the face of the world." More than this, the newly elected governor marveled at how "anyone could accept this delegated authority without asking God's help, and I pray that we who legislate and administer will be granted wisdom and strength beyond our own limited power, that with Divine guidance we can avoid easy expedients" (Freiling, 40).

Reagan gave concrete expression to his views in the form of support for prayer in public schools and, later, in his opposition to abortion. Important to note here is the theme of divine providence in the American experience. This notion of divine mission, of an American exceptionalism sanctioned by God reaching back to the Puritan conception of a new world redeeming the sins of a corrupt priest-ridden Europe, emerged strongly in Reagan's religious thought. According to Reagan, the American tradition was less the product of secular universalist ideals than of a religious covenant that placed the individual above the state. God granted Americans personal freedom and material abundance, and it was their responsibility to preserve against moral decay and government interference.

Ronald Reagan, 1981. Courtesy of the Library of Congress

Running for the Republican nomination in 1977, he announced that the party should "rediscover, reassert, and reapply America's spiritual heritage to our national affairs" (Freiling, 41). As president, Reagan blended the ideas of religious liberty, political freedom, and American exceptionalism into a potent ideological concoction that won him the support of conservative evangelicals.

His vision of America's providential mission was tied to his belief that its people had abrogated the religious contract that its earliest European settlers had made with God. Addressing the National Association of Evangelicals in 1983, Reagan denounced "modern-day secularism," which had repudiated the "tried and time-tested values upon which our very civilization is based." Despite the ascent of secular humanists, who had "taken upon themselves the job of superintending us by government rule and regulation," Reagan sensed "a great spiritual awakening in America, a renewal of the traditional values that have been the bedrock of America's goodness and greatness" (Boyer, 166). This narrative of spiritual election and decline played a prominent role in Reagan's effort to reclaim what he believed was the authentic tradition of American individualism and limited government from the agnostic, materialist ideals of contemporary liberals. The John Winthrop imagery of America as a "city on a hill," the beacon of liberty against Old World oppression, became a regular trope in his campaign to regenerate American patriotism. Reagan was convinced that Americans were "every bit as committed to that vision of a shining city on a hill as were those long-ago settlers" (Boyer, 22).

Throughout his political career, Reagan stressed the idea that the United States was engaged in a spiritual struggle, a "test of moral will and faith" (Freiling, 68). The conflict between the United States and the Soviet Union, no less than the conflict of moral traditionalists with secular liberals, was a contest between good and evil. In this conflict, Americans wielded rights to freedom and democracy granted by God, not simply the Constitution. They were obligated to protect those freedoms against moral relativism, government intrusion, and totalitarian despotism. What this suggests is that Reagan defined his religious views as a public and political figure. He did not leave a corpus of religious thought that would indicate any profound consideration of religious, theological, or moral questions prior to his presidency. Whether this suggests a cynical manipulation of religious imagery for political gain or a serious confrontation with moral issues that seemed peripheral before his presidency is a matter of historical debate. What we do know is that Reagan also addressed religious questions through *private* correspondence while serving as president. Evidently, his religious convictions were not simply for mass public consumption. Here is only one example: Responding to a minister who questioned Reagan's emphasis on the divinity of Jesus, Reagan wrote: "I realize, of course, that you are familiar with these words of Jesus [John 10, 'I am in the Father and the Father in me.'] These and other statements he made about himself, foreclose in my opinion, any question as to his divinity. It doesn't seem to me that he gave us any choice; either he was what he said he was or he was the world's greatest liar. It is impossible for me to believe a liar or a charlatan could have had the effect on mankind that he has had for 2000 years. We could ask, would even the greatest of liars carry his lie through the crucifixion, when a simple confession would have saved him?" Reagan added to his belief in the divinity of Christ a resolute belief in the inerrancy of the Bible, the sanctity of life, the timeless value of the Commandments, the existence of an afterlife, and the efficacy of prayer.

But it is as a public figure that his religious views had their greatest impact. Reagan often mixed sincere conviction with saccharine piety and moral self-righteousness, creating an image that appealed to conservative evangelicals and traditionalist Catholics alike. His vision of religious individualism comfortably fit a political ideology that championed market fundamentalism and government minimalism. While his policies often deviated from his rhetoric, Reagan helped restore conservative religiosity to American public life, accelerating what many commentators have described as the culture wars of the late twentieth and early twenty-first centuries.

Bibliography. Boyer, Paul ed. *Reagan as President: Contemporary Views of the Man, His Politics, and His Policies.* Chicago: Ivan R. Dee, 1990. Cannon, Lou. *President Reagan: The Role of a Lifetime.* New York: Simon & Schuster, 1991. Edel, Wilbur. *Defenders of the Faith: Religion and Politics from the Pilgrim Fathers to Ronald Reagan.* New York: Praeger, 1987. Freiling, Tom. *Reagan's God and Country: A President's Moral Compass: His Beliefs on God, Religious Freedom, the Sanctity of Life, and More.* Ann Arbor, MI: Servant Publications, 2000. Skinner, Kiron, Annelise Anderson, and Martin Anderson, eds. *Reagan: A Life in Letters.* New York: Free Press, 2003.

Michael Dennis

REED, RALPH (b. 1961). Reed is best known as an evangelical Protestant political operative who directed the Christian Coalition for eight years and built the organization into a significant political power especially supportive of the national Republican Party.

Reed, born in Portsmouth, Virginia, was introduced to politics as a junior high school student outside Miami, the host city of the 1972 Republican National Convention. After graduating from high school, Reed entered the University of Georgia, where he was elected chair of the school's College Republicans. He later achieved the same position in the statewide

College Republicans. A volunteer for **Ronald Reagan**'s presidential campaign in 1980, Reed was an intern in the U.S. Senate during the summer of 1981. He remained several months in Washington to work for the National College Republicans before returning to college in 1982. In 1983, he successfully campaigned for the position of executive director of the National College Republicans. He graduated from the University of Georgia with a degree in history. In 1984, he enrolled in Emory University in Atlanta to study American history and completed a doctorate in 1991.

Reed was a ruthless campaigner, often attacking the personalities and characters of his opponents. Early in his political career he was a heavy smoker and drinker. One evening in Washington in the summer of 1983, he observed a self-described pro-family congressman drinking heavily in the company of a woman who was not his wife and became disgusted with that type of lifestyle. Reed gave up smoking and drinking and sought new spiritual direction in an evangelical church. Reed's faith commitment did not change his political views much because he was already conservative, believing in smaller government, fewer taxes, tougher laws against crime and drugs, and policies to strengthen families. He believed less in the ability of government to legislative morality, but he did think that government should protect children and help families. While not changing his political philosophy, Reed's deeper Christian faith altered his political tactics. Prior to his spiritual transformation, Reed saw politics as a form of combat. Now, he no longer saw the need to do whatever it would take to win. In fact, he began to call his former enemies to try to bridge some of their differences. Many of the foes were taken aback at Reed's new outlook on politics.

In 1989, **Pat Robertson** hired Reed as the executive director of a new organization, the **Christian Coalition**. During his eight years at the Christian Coalition, the organization's budget grew from $200,000 to $27 million. Its membership base grew from two thousand to two million persons in two thousand local chapters. Despite his organizing success, some in the Religious Right criticized Reed for diverting attention away from purely social issues. He tried to broaden the coalition's agenda to include issues like congressional term limits, tax cuts, and "school choice." Under his leadership, the Christian Coalition played a significant role in the Republican takeover of Congress in 1994.

Reed stepped down as executive director of the Christian Coalition in 1997. He founded Century Strategies, a political consulting firm. Many candidates sought to employ the firm for their campaigns for Congress, state offices, and the presidency. In 2001, he was elected chairman of the Georgia Republican Party, raising concerns among some Republicans that he would tie the party closer to the Religious Right. Under his leadership, Republican candidates upset incumbent Democrats in the U.S. Senate and the Georgia governor's mansion. He resigned as chairman in 2003 to begin work on President **George W. Bush**'s reelection campaign in 2004.

Bibliography. Easton, Nina. *Gang of Five: Leaders at the Center of the Conservative Crusade.* New York: Simon & Schuster, 2000. Fowler, Robert Booth, Allen D. Hertzke, and Laura R. Olson. *Religion and Politics in America: Faith, Culture, and Strategic Choices.* 2nd ed. Boulder, CO: Westview Press, 1999. Reed, Ralph. *Active Faith: How Christians Are Changing the Soul of American Politics.* New York: Free Press, 1996.

John David Rausch, Jr.

REINYS, MEČISLOVAS (1884–1953). Mečislovas Reinys rose to prominence as the Catholic archbishop of Vilnius who in 1926, as minister of foreign affairs in the newly created nation of Lithuania, negotiated a nonaggression pact with the Soviet Union.

Reinys graduated from the St. Petersburg seminary and later (1916–1922) taught at Vilnius University. When Pope **Pius XI** reorganized the ecclesiastic divisions of independent Lithuania, Reinys assumed an important role (1926) as coadjutor bishop of Vilnius. In 1940 he was named auxiliary archbishop of Vilnius. Reinys was a noted critic of Nazism and published an essay denouncing Nazi racial ideology. He was also well known for his efforts to help Lithuanian Jews during the Second World War. At the end of the war, Reinys led rather delicate efforts to disband Lithuanian partisan cadres that drew their membership from the rural Catholic population.

As archbishop of Vilnius, Mečislovas Reinys was one of the most outspoken opponents of the Soviet State. Reinys resisted the effort to organize the church according to the *dvatsatka* model, in which parishes were to be run by a group of twenty laypersons who were then subject to government authority. Reinys also vociferously argued for the independence of Catholic seminary education, arguing that Soviet law did not permit interference in internal church affairs (Vardys, 69).

Reinys also argued that one of the charges brought against Nazi leaders at Nuremburg was that they had closed church educational institutions. By 1947 the Soviet authorities had incarcerated most of the Lithuanian bishops and in June of that year the KGB arrested Reinys on the charge that he was "an enemy of the people." He died in prison in 1953.

Bibliography. Vardys, V. Stanley. *The Catholic Church, Dissent and Nationality in Soviet Lithuania.* New York: Columbia University Press, 1978.

Mathew N. Schmalz

RENOVATIONIST UNION (RUSSIA). The Renovationist Union was established by a group of Russian Orthodox priests in St. Petersburg during the Revolution of 1905 to promote an activist interpretation of the Orthodox Church's role in society.

The Renovationist Union began to coalesce in the wake of the Bloody Sunday disaster. The St. Petersburg clergy were divided over whether to continue Father **Georgii Gapon**'s political activism or condemn it. Although most of the city's clergy cautioned against further action, about two dozen young priests expressed support for Gapon's work. They established the informal discussion group that became the core of the Renovationist Union.

In February 1905, the group met with the metropolitan of St. Petersburg, Antonii Vadkovskii. He approved the continuation of their private discussions. Encouraged, they decided to send him their ideas on the question of the church's relation to society. They sent their first essay in March. The metropolitan approved its publication in the church's official newspaper, the *Church Herald*, which attributed it to "the Group of Thirty-two Priests." In this essay, the Thirty-two called for a "renovation" of the church's spirit. They argued that the church should abandon its "ascetic" attitude toward worldly affairs and engage itself in all matters that concerned the Russian people, including issues of social and political reform. In order to make this spiritual renovation possible, they also advocated institutional reforms that would liberate the church from the government. A second article published in May explained their reform program further.

After a hiatus during the summer months, the group published a third article in October 1905, in which they took up the question of the clergy's role in the elected assembly, the Duma. Whereas many in the church believed the clergy should avoid politics, the Thirty-two argued the clergy had a vital role to play in educating the people about political issues, helping them understand the problems Russia faced, and explaining how the potential solutions accorded with Christian values. Shortly afterwards, the Thirty-two organized the Union of Zealots for Church Renovation. Clergy and laymen both participated; it included some famous individuals, such as Father **Grigorii Petrov**, Nikolai Berdiaev, and **Sergey Bulgakov.** The group dedicated itself to promoting discussion of the role of Christianity and the church in political life through its publications, the *Bellringer,* a monthly journal, and the weekly newspapers *Century* and *Church Renovation.* Over the course of 1906, the opinions expressed in these periodicals became more radical: the Renovationists criticized the timorous efforts at church reform, supported the Constitutional Democrats' demands for further political concessions, and endorsed popular demands for land reform and workers' rights.

Late in 1906, central church authorities began to reassert their authority over the parish clergy, focusing especially on the Renovationists. Censorship was restored, and troublemakers were silenced through fines, arrests, confinement, and defrocking. The Renovationist Union was disbanded in 1907, and their publications were shut down. The most prominent clerical leaders were transferred to the provinces, deprived of official positions, or dismissed from the clergy. Efforts to resist or protest proved futile: the parish clergy had no power against the bishops and the church courts, and their repression provoked little comment in the Duma or among the lay population.

The ideas were not entirely forgotten, however, and exerted a muted influence on some clerical publications in the inter-revolutionary years. After the first revolution of 1917, some former Renovationists joined the new Union of Democratic Clergy and Laity. This organization evolved into the Living Church, the members of which were often referred to as Renovationists. Some elements of the Living Church program were similar, but much had changed as well. In any case, the Living Church also fell victim to politics and was destroyed by the Soviet regime at the end of the 1920s.

Bibliography. Freeze, Gregory. "Counter-reformation in Russian Orthodoxy." *Slavic Review* 54 (2) : 305–39. Freeze, Gregory. "Subversive Piety: Religion and Political Crisis in Late Imperial Russia." *Journal of Modern History* 68 (1996): 308–50. Hedda, Jennifer. "Good Shepherds: The St. Petersburg Pastorate and the Emergence of Social Activism in the Russian Orthodox Church, 1855–1917." PhD diss., Harvard University, 1998. Roslof, Edward. *Red Priests: Renovationism, Russian Orthodoxy and Revolution, 1905–1946.* Bloomington: Indiana University Press, 2002.

Jennifer Hedda

REXIST MOVEMENT (BELGIUM). Rex was a Belgian social and political movement of the 1930s and 1940s that went through three distinct phases: Between 1931 and 1936, it was a publishing house and center for reform of the Belgian Catholic political party; From 1936 through 1940 in was a proto-fascist political party in Belgian electoral politics; And, finally, it became a collaborationist movement with the Nazi occupation of Belgium from 1940 to 1944.

Rex began in 1931 as a Catholic publishing house in the city of Louvain (Leuven in Dutch), directed by the twenty-five-year-old **Léon Degrelle.** Christus Rex (Christ the King) was the original name, but it was soon shortened in popular terminology, and later officially, to Rex. The cult of Christ the King had been encouraged by **Pius XI** in his 1925 encyclical *Quas primas,* and it was popular with many young Catholics in the interwar era who longed for a more deeply committed Catholic society that would replace the disorder of the post–World War I situation. Degrelle had been educated by Jesuits at a college in Namur, Belgium, and was deeply influenced by the monarchist French thinker

Charles Maurras and his journal, *L'Action Française*. The Rex publishing house, and the journal of the same name that appeared soon after, were originally seen as an arm of Catholic Action, the lay movement of Catholics encouraged by the Vatican in the interwar period.

Degrelle soon made Rex his instrument to call for a spiritual reformation of Belgian society. Immorality, materialism, and the weakening of family life were all to be changed. Enthusiastic young Catholics, many of them university students, gathered around the charismatic Degrelle. Publishing pamphlets and making speeches, Degrelle soon extended his call for reform to ending political corruption and combating Marxism. He even made a trip to Mexico to report on the persecution of the church by revolutionaries. Eventually, he attacked politicians in the Catholic Party, the country's largest, for their failures to fight the social problems of the Depression and demonstrate moral leadership. As a result of his attacks, Catholic Action and the church cut their ties with Rex in 1934.

Degrelle turned his organization into a movement fed by donations and in November 1935 disrupted a conference of the Catholic Party and thus broke his ties to the party. In anticipation of the elections of May 1936, Degrelle organized Rex as a political party. Rex's program was a potpourri of political attacks and vague moral idealism. The solution for parliamentary deadlock and corruption was "Sweep out the bastards!" Corrupt politicians were "banksters," a term coined by Degrelle. At the same time, one "Rexist principle" was "Without a moral revolution, there can be no revolution." Making as many as sixteen speeches in a single day, Degrelle transfixed Belgium with slashing criticism of opponents, vague calls to protect "healthy" economic sectors such as farming and shopkeeping from "financial capitalism," and pious, some-

times bizarre claims of morality. "Workers of all classes, unite!" was a typical slogan. Only Degrelle's personality held the movement together. One wit described him as "P. T. Barnum as Jesus Christ."

Given the traditional political loyalty of Belgian votes, Rex's winning 11.5 percent of the votes and 21 parliamentary seats out of 202 stunned the country. As a French-speaking movement in a bilingual country, Rex won few votes in Dutch-speaking Flanders. In French-speaking Belgium, Rex won one out of every six votes, mostly those of farmers, shopkeepers, and white-collar workers who had previously voted Catholic. In Parliament, however, Rex could achieve little. As the worst phase of the Depression began to lift, Degrelle had to satisfy his restless followers with action. In March 1937, Degrelle provoked a by-election in Brussels and stood as the Rex candidate for the parliamentary seat. The three established parties, Liberals, Catholics, and Socialists, all governing in coalition, joined forces behind one candidate, the moderate Catholic prime minister, Paul Van Zeeland. Even the Communists, following Popular Front tactics, supported Van Zeeland. Two days before the April election, Cardinal Van Roey, the archbishop of Malines (Mechelen), condemned Rex as "a danger to the country and the Church" and forbade Catholics from voting for Rex or even abstaining. Van Zeeland won 75 percent of the votes, Degrelle only 19 percent. Rex's support and donations soon dropped precipitously. In the elections in 1939, it won only 4.4 percent of the vote and elected four deputies.

When Germany conquered Belgium in May 1940, Rex received a new lease on life. Degrelle, after being arrested by Belgian authorities and nearly executed by the French during the invasion, tried to curry favor with German authorities. By 1941, he proclaimed his support for Nazism. The Germans never made Rex into a collaborationist regime such as that of Vichy France or Quisling in Norway. They did allow Rex to elect a large number of town councilors in French-speaking Belgium and to raise a Légion Wallonie to fight on the eastern front. The church, and almost all parts of the Belgian establishment, kept the movement at arm's length. Degrelle managed to escape Belgium in 1944 and lived out his life for decades in Spain.

Bibliography. Conway, Martin. *Collaboration in Belgium: Leon Degrelle and the Rexist Movement, 1940–1944.* New Haven, CT: Yale University Press, 1993. Laurent, Pierre-Henri. "Belgian Rexism and Léon Degrelle." In *International Fascism,* ed. George Mosse. Beverly Hills, CA: Sage, 1979. Wallef, Daniele. "The Composition of Christus Rex." In *Who Were the Fascists? Social Roots of European Fascism,* ed. Sten Ugelvik Larsen, Bernt Hagtvet, and Jan Petter Myklebust. Bergen, Norway: Universitetsforlaget, 1980.

Carl Strikwerda

ROBERTSON, MARION GORDON "PAT"

(b. 1930). One of the most controversial and polarizing figures in Christian politics is the Rev. Pat Robertson, a televangelist who entered national politics when he ran for president in 1988. Before entering politics, Robertson established himself as one of the most successful evangelical voices in the media.

Robertson was born to a family with links to Virginia's upper class. His father, A. Willis, was a U.S. congressman and senator. Pat spent his early years in a military prep school and entered Washington and Lee University upon graduation. Robertson interrupted his education to serve in the U.S. military during the Korean War conflict. Upon returning to the United States, Robertson completed his graduate studies at Yale Law School, but he never practiced law. Instead, Robertson found business to be a more attractive career and worked for W. R. Grace's South American manufacturing sector.

Though his father expected Pat to take the New York bar exam and follow him into politics, Robertson's business savvy and an emerging change in his spiritual life began to influence his career choices.

Robertson experienced a religious conversion in 1956 that compelled him into the ministry. He received a master of divinity degree from New York Seminary in 1959. Just one year later, Robertson founded the first Christian television station in the United States. The Christian Broadcasting Network (CBN) began operation from Virginia in 1960. This enterprise fueled both Robertson's business ventures and his religious ideas, all of which are closely tied to his political outlook. Today, CBN reaches 180 nations, broadcasting in seventy-one languages. There are over one million viewers for CBN's flagship show, the *700 Club*, which serves as part ministry, part political commentary, and part news program.

Another Robertson ministry is Operation Blessing, founded in 1978. This project offers humanitarian aid to distressed peoples around the world as well as operating a flying hospital, and its missions around the world also include evangelism. In the early 1980s, sensing a need to combat what Robertson perceived as the overt influence of liberal judiciaries on such issues as abortion, prayer in school, gay rights, and a host of court cases focusing on prayer in public settings, Robertson founded the American Center for Law and Justice, which was supposed to be the conservative alternative to the American Civil Liberties Union.

With the growth of CBN and Pat Robertson's business holdings, Robertson expanded his ministry to include opening a Christian liberal arts school called Regent University, which also has a school of journalism and a law school. The university, like most evangelical schools, serves as a place for like-minded students to receive instruction that supports their faith and, often, supports Robertson's political ideas. Other business ventures have not been as successful. He suffered financial setbacks because of some investments made with the profits of the 1997 sale of International Family Entertainment. Robertson made $19 million on the $1.5 billion transaction, while Regent received $148 million, and CBN garnered $136 million. Another $109 million went to Robertson's charitable trust. Financial losses from failed investments have since cost the trust an estimated $78 million.

Aside from the melding of religious and political ideas together in concrete institutions, Robertson's ability to stir supporters and detractors alike stems not only from his financial support to conservative causes, but also from his often incendiary comments. Some critics called his 1991 book, *New World Order,* anti-Semitic because they believed it fostered old discredited conspiracy theories about a Jewish cabal bent on world domination. Robertson caused more controversy in 2003 by suggesting that in light of State Department incompetence, the government branch deserved to be bombed. In that same year he also called on *700 Club* viewers to begin a prayer vigil for the U.S. Supreme Court, which he hoped would produce the retirement of three justices.

An undercurrent of Robertson's political ideology is the belief that evangelicals are marginalized in the United States and that without evangelicals in political power, there will be little to reverse what is perceived to be a forty-year slide into moral relativism and secular humanism.

In an attempt to make good on his religious fervor and political convictions, Robertson ran for president in 1988. His quest for the White House shocked the Republican Party establishment, who feared Robertson would siphon away evangelical voters, as well as opponents of the Religious Right who found the specter of a Robertson presidency unpalatable.

Robertson's campaign failed (although he did do well in the Washington primary), but it did make him a national figure and spurred interest in creating a national lobby for conservative evangelicals to air their issues. In 1989, Robertson founded the **Christian Coalition.**

The Christian Coalition was begun with a start-up grant from the Republican Senatorial Committee. The coalition's most successful years were under the leadership of **Ralph Reed** from 1989 to 1997. In 2001, Robertson resigned as president of the coalition to dedicate more time to his ministry.

Bibliography. Donovan, John B. *Pat Robertson: The Authorized Biography.* New York: Simon & Schuster, 1988. Foege, Alec. *The Empire That God Built: Inside Pat Robertson's Media Machine.* New York: Wiley, 1996. Roth, Daniel. "Pat Robertson's Quest for Eternal Life." *Fortune,* 10 June 2002. Slone, Christopher. "Robertson Shakes Up Empire." *Christianity Today,* 14 July 1997.

Arlene Sanchez Walsh

RODANO, FRANCO (1920–1983). Rodano was a political thinker close to the Italian Communist Party and simultaneously a convinced and practicing Catholic whose intellectual charisma and leadership touched a vast array of ordinary and extraordinary men and women from many sectors of the political and social spectrum.

An active antifascist as a young Catholic between 1937 and 1943, he was arrested and then released in the course of 1943 and took part in the underground resistance during the German occupation of Rome. His group, the Movement of Catholic Communists, evolved after the liberation of Rome (June 1944) into the Party of the Christian Left (*Partito della Sinistra Cristiana,* PSC) and dissolved in early 1945. That outcome was openly criticized by Palmiro Togliatti, leader of the Italian Communist Party (*Partito Comunista Italiano,* PCI), yet it reflected

Rodano's contrary view of a "party of Catholics" in favor of Catholics choosing their politics according to their best and honest judgment. Rodano made the "secular character" (*laicità*) of politics one of his strong tenets and expressed allegiance to the PCI after the Fifth Party Congress in January 1946 as the political form best suited to foster a "progressive and popular" democracy in Italy.

Neither a militant nor in a position of power after the immediate postwar era, he maintained strong connections with the Catholic world at large, including significant figures in the hierarchy, and with key political personalities within the PCI as well as within the **Christian Democracy** (*Democrazia Cristiana*, DC) and other government parties. His connection to Togliatti was influential from a distance, much as occurred later in mid-1970s, when the PCI leadership rested with Enrico Berlinguer.

In Rodano's view, the stalemate in Italian political life could only be broken by encounter between the two political traditions, catholic and socialist, respectively embodied albeit imperfectly in the two mass parties, the DC and the PCI. From the mid-1960s through early 1970s, with his quarterly review, *La Rivista Trimestrale,* Rodano fueled an intensely critical debate on the "affluent society" and on the inadequacy of Marxist revolutionary theories to deal with it both economically and politically. Later, from the mid-1970s, his attention understandably focused on the "historic compromise," wherein a governing arrangement would be reached between the DC and the PCI, a turning point that he cautioned should not be dismissed as a mere political maneuver. If his efforts were mainly directed to influence the strategy of the PCI and of Enrico Berlinguer, he also attracted a qualified following in those years in many sectors of the Catholic political world and even within the DC itself. When he died of heart failure, the prospects of an epochal change that he coveted had been effectively lost by the assassination of **Aldo Moro** in 1978 and by the turn taken in the subsequent two years by the DC and the PCI in their respective strategies.

Bibliography. Muste, Marcello. *Franco Rodano: Laicità, democrazia, società del superfluo.* Rome: Edizioni Studium, 2000.

Margherita Repetto-Alaia

ROMANO, ROSALEO "RUDY" (1940–1985). Romano was born in Manila to Gaudencio and Adelaida Romano. As a child, he was known to be popular among his classmates and was said to be exceptionally honest and hardworking in helping his parents run the family business (a dry goods store). Romano joined the Redemptorist Congregation in 1958 and was ordained a priest in 1964. Over the next decade (1967–1976), Father Rudy was immersed in missionary work in the Visayan Islands and Mindanao in the central and southern Philippines during the rise of the dictator Ferdinand Marcos (1972–1986). Coming from a sheltered childhood and the safe confines of the seminary, he encountered the poorest of the poor struggling to improve their circumstances. Father Rudy was involved in the everyday lives of tenant farmers and subsistence agriculturalists, a group of people that comprised 75 percent of the nation's impoverished population.

In 1978, Father Rudy Romano attended the Ateneo Summer Institute for Pastoral Counseling under Father Ruben Tanseco, a Jesuit, which forever changed his life as a Filipino Redemptorist priest. On his return to the Redemptorist Center in Cebu City, he saw no distinction between his priestly vocation and being a Filipino. He worked full-time for greater social justice. In 1979, Father Rudy helped to found the Visayas Ecumenical Movement for Justice and Peace together with Sister Margot Lloren, OSB, and Father Nemie Angus, OFM. Later, they were instrumental in founding the Philippine Council for Human Rights, an alliance of cause-oriented groups like **Task Force Detainees Philippines** and the Ecumenical Justice and Peace Desk. Aside from performing his duties as a priest, Father Rudy participated in protests, organized squatter communities, and got involved in every capacity for human rights. He worked through the heyday of the Marcos dictatorship, when the military had even taken over police activities. Although seriousness of purpose and a powerful idealism guided Romano, he was also known for his jovial sense of humor. His voice of political opposition made him a target of the Marcos regime, however, and on July 11, 1985, he "disappeared," presumably kidnapped by agents of the Military Intelligence Group (MIG) in Cebu. Romano's martyrdom has made him a powerful symbol of hope for the poor and oppressed in his native land.

Bibliography. Chan-Santos, Lilette. *Romano in the Philippines: The Life and Times of a Filipino Redemptorist Priest Desaparecido Who Was Abducted in Cebu in 1985.* Diliman, Quezon City, Philippines: Claretian Publications in cooperation with the Redemptorist Vice, Province of Cebu, 1995.

Kathleen Nadeau

ROMERO, OSCAR (1917–1980). On March 24, 1980, Archbishop Oscar Romero was assassinated while conducting the Eucharist. The murder followed months of death threats for his outspoken opposition to the murders of Salvadorans by members of military units.

Salvadoran Oscar Arnulfo Romero was born in Ciudad Barrios, ten miles from the Honduran border. On December 14, 1974, he was named bishop of Santiago de Maria, the diocese that included his hometown.

During two years as bishop, his political and theological convictions were in formation. His pastoral vicar recalled that he often quoted the documents of Vatican II but never quoted the more politicized documents of Medellin produced during the 1968 Latin American Bishops Conference. Romero began publication of *El Apóstol,* a weekly periodical of the diocese, offering his personal thought in a page called "The Pastor's Voice." Elevated to archbishop of Salvador in February of 1977, Romero was considered a compromise candidate, less offensive to landholders and the wealthy than his rival, Arturo Rivera Damas. Damas, auxiliary to the preceding archbishop, had been outspoken about official repression.

Three weeks after his installation, Romero's friend and fellow priest Otilio Grande was murdered with two parishioners. A month later another priest, Alfonso Navarro was murdered. An unprecedented wave of persecution of clerics followed. Between February 21 and May 14 of 1977, eight priests were expelled—five of them tortured before expulsion—two arrested, another detained and tortured, and ten exiled. Romero announced he would not attend any official acts until Grande's murderers were found and on July 1 declined to attend the inauguration of the president of El Salvador. His weekly radio program on the archdiocesan radio station became increasingly politicized, as Romero's sermons related scripture to the lived reality of the Salvadoran people, including a reading of all documented cases of abduction, assault, murder, or torture. Reactions escalated. Station equipment was bombed numerous times, along with the offices of the archdiocesan newspaper.

On March 9 a bomb was found in the Basilica of the Sacred Heart just before Romero was scheduled to preside. On March 23 Romero called on members of the armed forces to disobey orders to kill fellow Salvadorans. Romero's willingness to walk into the face of death consciously and publicly in defense of the Salvadoran people has earned him the titles of martyr and prophet. Two weeks before his death,

Romero rejected the title of martyr, saying it was undeserved. "But if God accepts the sacrifice of my life," he replied, "let my blood be a seed of freedom and the sign that hope will soon be reality. Let my death, if it is accepted by God, be for the liberation of my people and as a witness of hope in the future" (quoted in Brockman, 223).

Bibliography. Brockman, James R. *The Word Remains: A Life of Oscar Romero.* Maryknoll, NY: Orbis Books, 1982.

Lynn Bridgers

ROUPNEL, GASTON (1871–1946). With one foot in nineteenth-century philosophical traditions and the other in the social sciences of the 1920s and 1930s, Roupnel linked historical and geographical investigations to posit continuing relations between early and pre-Christian practices and modern agrarian regimes. This engagement with the spiritual dimension of the material universe reflected a resurgence of contemporary interest in the modalities of faith, intuition, and mysticism that existed in both the academic and popular worlds.

Roupnel grounded his scholarship on early twentieth-century French historical geography in a neo-romantic construction of nature with epistemological roots in a monist tradition. His *Histoire de la campagne française* (1932) depicted Nature—both transcendent and immanent—as providing both a symbolic location and physical manifestation of the cosmic synthesis between humankind and spirit. In a day when such analysis typically functioned within a moral discourse, Roupnel employed neo-romantic notions of regional identity to negotiate between the universal and emancipatory demands of neo-Kantian humanism and the vectors of historical contingency.

Roupnel's spiritual monism linked the natural and spiritual strains of European mystical traditions. While Roupnel resisted orthodox Catholic interpretations of divinity until his final years, this should not be interpreted to indicate that his prior pantheism represented anything other than a deeply personal and theological conception of God. Like Henri Bergson, Pierre Teilhard de Chardin, and Gaston Bachelard, Roupnel felt that mystical or intuitive modalities provide a direct and valid knowledge capable of synthesizing and harmonizing human experience with a universal logos. In his belief in the union of the immanent and transcendent aspects of divinity, Roupnel joined an awareness of the spatiotemporal unity of the infinite and eternal universe to a direct communication with a transcendent "absolute" in order to provide humanity with a vision of cosmic salvation. His reliance on the phenomenal aspects of time and space as subjectively experience placed him squarely in a discourse established by Henri Bergson and sustained by Gaston Bachelard.

Expressed through popular fiction (*Nono*, 1910; *Vieux Garain*, 1913; and *Hé vivant!* 1927), Roupnel's work offered a broadly conceived, historically informed, poetically rendered, and spiritually oriented interpretation of the relationship between humankind and the (preferably rural) environment to suggest a contemporary agenda. His scholarship addressed issues concerning contemporary gender roles, participatory politics, social justice, and sustainable economic development. Roupnel promoted a vision or idyll of agrarian society that was socially conservative, culturally provincial, politically progressive, economically stable, and spiritually informed.

From his provincial refuge at the University of Dijon, Roupnel achieved celebrity during his lifetime and ironically slipped into relative obscurity following his death.

Bibliography. Bachelard, Gaston. *L'Intuition de l'intant.* Paris: Stock, 1932. Roupnel, Gaston. *Histoire de la campagne française.* Paris: Plon, 1932. Roupnel, Gaston. "La vie de Notre Seigneur Jésus-Christ." *Pays de Bourgogne* 42 (1963): 777–87; 47 (1964): 47–53. Whalen,

Philip. *Gaston Roupnel: Âme paysanne et sciences humaines.* Dijon, France: Éditions Universitaires de Dijon, 2001.

Philip Whalen

RUETHER, ROSEMARY RADFORD (b. 1936). Ruether helped to create the movement known as feminist theology. Like many women in the second wave of feminism in the United States, Ruether was inspired by the civil rights movement to think about social change, to dream about a more just society, and to combine scholarship with political activism. Some feminists insist that Judaism and Christianity are hopelessly patriarchal, and they have criticized Ruether, a Catholic, for attempting to reform Christianity. While recognizing that religion has been a source for legitimizing women's oppression, Ruether doubts that a value-free secularism will liberate women from patriarchy. Drawing upon liberation theology, the Hebrew prophets, and critical studies, Ruether concludes that followers of Jesus have an obligation to transform unjust social systems into life-giving relationships. In her own words, "Feminist theology is not asserting unprecedented ideas; rather, it is rediscovering the prophetic context and content of the Biblical faith itself when it defines the prophetic-liberating tradition as norm" (Ruether, 31).

Ruether criticizes both liberal and radical feminists for failing to transform patriarchal culture. Liberal feminists, Ruether claims, focus upon individual attitudes and actions while ignoring the influence of the social systems (linguistic, religious, economic, and political) that shape individual attitudes and actions. Radical feminists, Ruether claims, encourage women to withdraw from what they consider to be a hopelessly patriarchal culture, fulfilling their expectations that the larger culture cannot be redeemed. For Ruether, every decision that we make ought to be understood as a moral and as a political issue: whether the language we use to talk about God/ess reinforces sexist stereotypes, whether the products we consume destroy the environment or exploit laborers, or whether U.S. foreign policy fosters inequality and terrorism. Although Ruether is best known as a feminist theologian, in over thirty books she has raised consciousness about a wide range of social problems, including anti-Semitism, the plight of the Palestinians, militarism, ecological destruction, and poverty.

Rosemary Radford Ruether has spent most of her career as the Georgia Harkness Professor of Theology at Garrett-Evangelical Theological Seminary, where she also served as a member of the graduate faculty at Northwestern University. In 2000 she accepted the position of Carpenter Professor of Feminist Theology at the Pacific School of Religion with a joint appointment in the Graduate Theological Union. She is a board member of the Friends of Sabeel and Catholics for a Free Choice. She also writes regularly for journals such as the *National Catholic Reporter* and *Sojourners.*

Bibliography. Ruether, Rosemary Radford. *Sexism and God-Talk: Toward a Feminist Theology.* Boston: Beacon Press, 1983.

Andrew D. Walsh

RUFFO, FABRIZIO (1744–1827). Cardinal Ruffo was one of the key European and Italian leaders of grassroots resistance to the French revolutionary (and Napoleonic) empire. Born of an aristocratic family at Castello di San Lucido, Calabria, in what was then the Bourbon Kingdom of Naples, Ruffo entered Catholic holy orders in 1768. He rose rapidly in papal service and received the cardinal's red hat in 1787. After the armies of revolutionary France invaded Naples and a Parthenopean Republic was proclaimed there in 1799, Ruffo fled to Sicily with the royal court. There, Ruffo pledged to King Ferdinand IV to launch a crusade against the usurpers back on the mainland. The cardinal, now vicar-general, returned to Calabria almost immediately with eight followers to arouse a holy war of the devout peasantry against the French and their Italian liberal supporters. His Christian Army of the Holy Faith (hence, the *Sanfedisti*) grew to seventeen thousand and quickly reconquered most of extreme southern Italy by the end of April. The cardinal and his forces victoriously entered Naples itself on June 13, 1799.

Seeking to end the bloodshed and reconcile his opponents, Ruffo promised full pardon to the defeated liberals. However, King Ferdinand, persuaded by his protector, Admiral Horatio Nelson, ignored the cardinal's promise and carried out a bloody repression, which unfairly blackened Ruffo's reputation in the eyes of contemporaries and many later historians. Disillusioned, Ruffo retired from politics, and when the French again conquered Naples in 1806, he refused to repeat his campaign of 1799. He died in Naples.

After 1815, many reactionary societies that organized to oppose liberalism and to support the concept of "throne and altar" were labeled *Sanfedisti*. Similar attempts at popular resistance to liberal threats, if less successful than Ruffo's, were made in the Papal States after the 1831 revolution and in Naples after Giuseppe Garibaldi's conquest in 1860.

Bibliography. Davis, John. "1799, the 'Sanfede' and the Crisis of the 'Ancient Regime' in Southern Italy." In *Society and Politics in the Age of the Risorgimento: Essays in Honour of Denis Mack Smith,* ed. John Davis and Paul Ginsborg. Cambridge: Cambridge University Press, 1991.

Alan J. Reinerman

RUÍZ-GIMÉNEZ, JOAQUÍN (b. 1913). Ruíz-Giménez was a political leader who became a leading advocate of Christian democratic principles during Spain's transition from **Francisco Franco**'s regime to democracy. He was profoundly influenced by his parents'

beliefs. His mother was devoutly Catholic; his father, then mayor of Madrid, combined faith with political liberalism.

As a student at Madrid's Complutense University during the Second Republic, Ruíz-Giménez became part of the circles around **Ángel Herrera,** joining the **National Catholic Association of Propagandists (ACNP).** He experienced the brutality of the civil war from both sides, first as a prisoner in the republican zone, then as a soldier in the Francoist army. As a result, Ruíz-Giménez acquired a profound Christian and humanitarian belief that the conflict should have been avoidable.

The commitment to dialogue that so marked his later political career thus dated from the 1930s. In 1948, he was named Spanish ambassador to the Holy See, negotiating the Concordat with the Vatican. This was signed in 1953, two years after Ruíz-Giménez left Rome to become Spain's minister of education. An outbreak of student unrest, however, led to his dismissal in 1956. Ruíz-Giménez's time in office had demonstrated the gulf between social rhetoric and educational policy in Franco's Spain, while his years in Rome had brought him into contact with Europe's Christian democratic mainstream. However, he only fully distanced himself from Franco's regime after Vatican II, which he attended as an observer.

In 1964, he withdrew from the Francoist parliament. The previous year, he had founded a journal, *Cuadernos para el diálogo,* which brought together various dissident currents, and became a seminal forum for the democratic opposition. This wholehearted embrace of political and intellectual pluralism characterized Ruíz-Giménez's stance during the transition to democracy (1975–1982). Though he was briefly put under arrest in November 1974, his work for the new democracy was essentially that of establishing dialogue and consensus. He forged close links with socialists and Social Democrats through *Cuadernos* and, as an ex-minister, also acted as an interlocutor with more liberal Francoists. His stature and influence remained, despite the failure of his political ambition to establish a Christian Democrat party in Spain. He contested the 1977 elections with the veteran politician **José María Gil Robles,** but their party failed to win a single seat. Cardinal **Tarancón**'s refusal to endorse confessional parties was a critical influence. Abandoning party politics, Ruíz-Giménez served as Spain's *defensor del pueblo* (ombudsman) from 1982 to 1986 and subsequently became president of the national branch of UNICEF.

Bibliography. *La fuerza del diágolo: Homenaje a Joaquín Ruíz-Giménez.* Madrid: Alianza, 1997. Ruíz-Giménez, Joaquín, ed. *Iglesia, estado y sociedad en España, 1930–82.* Madrid: Argos Vergara, 1984. Vilar, Sergio. *La oposición de la dictadura: Protagonistas de la España democrática.* Barcelona: Aymá, 1976.

Mary Vincent

RYAN, JOHN AUGUSTINE (1869–1945). Born in Vermilion, Minnesota, he died in St. Paul on September 16, 1945. Inspired by Pope **Leo XIII**'s encyclical on labor, *Rerum novarum* (1891), Ryan dedicated his academic and public life to the cause of social justice and the application of ethical principles to political and economic questions. By the early twentieth-century, Ryan had emerged as American Catholicism's leading advocate of progressive social action. His scholarship and broad public influence left a lasting influence on the shape of Catholic social thought in America.

Ryan entered St. Thomas Seminary (later St. Paul Seminary) in 1887 and was ordained a priest of the Catholic Church on June 4, 1898. After spending a summer as a parish priest, he proceeded to the Catholic University of America in Washington, D.C., to pursue graduate studies. He received a licentiate in moral theology in 1900. Ryan returned to St. Paul Seminary in the fall of 1902 as a professor. In 1906, he completed his doctoral dissertation, *A Living Wage: Its Ethical and Economic Aspects.* His dissertation was immediately published. It received widespread attention in the Catholic and non-Catholic press and quickly established his reputation as a leading Catholic social theorist.

Ryan joined the faculty at Catholic University in 1915. The most important scholarly achievement of his career came with the 1916 publication of *Distributive Justice.* Following *Distributive Justice,* Ryan's work became less scholarly, increasingly popularized, and more focused on political advocacy. In 1919 he wrote the *Bishops' Program of Social Reconstruction* for the National Catholic Welfare Conference. This widely read statement gave the church's support to a host of progressive reform measures, including minimum-wage legislation, unemployment insurance, public housing, progressive taxation, and greater rights for organized labor. The following year Ryan became director of the Social Action Department of the NCWC, a position he held until his death. Ryan used the Social Action Department to promote these reform ideas throughout the 1920s, during which time he also wrote extensively on prohibition, birth control, and church-state separation. His 1922 book *The State and the Church* attracted widespread attention for its controversial perspective on the relationship of Catholicism and liberalism.

Ryan's attention shifted almost exclusively to economic matters in the 1930s, and he became a vocal advocate of the Roosevelt administration and its New Deal programs. He corresponded with the president, delivered a national radio address in 1936 entitled "Roosevelt Safeguards America," and gave the benediction at the 1937 inauguration. Ryan was particularly enthusiastic about the National Recovery Act, which he believed embodied principles of Catholic social teaching. Pope Pius XI's encyclical *Quadragesimo anno* (1931) further bolstered Ryan's belief that the American economic order had to be fundamentally reconstructed.

Ryan had a marked influence not only on the development of progressive Catholic social thought, but in the harmonization of the Catholic and liberal traditions as well. He successfully brought Catholics into the broader American political conversation at a time when the church remained on the outside. His policies have been criticized for their reliance on legislation and the state, and his methodology has been criticized for its lack of theological richness or ecclesiological attentiveness, but his influence on a generation of Catholics is undeniable. Ryan's writings are now, perhaps unfortunately, examined largely for their historical importance.

Bibliography. Broderick, Francis L. *Right Reverend New Dealer: John A. Ryan.* New York: Macmillan, 1963. Ryan, John A. *Social Doctrine in Action: A Personal History.* New York: Harper, 1941.

Zachary R. Calo

RYDZYK, TADEUSZ (b. 1945). As the founder and director of Radio Maryja, Poland's largest Catholic broadcasting network, Father Rydzyk has become one of the most powerful public figures of the postcommunist era. He has used his radio station to propagate an intensely nationalist, right-wing Christian fundamentalism and has spread his influence to encompass a television station, several periodicals, and a political party.

Rydzyk's childhood was marked by hardship. His father died in the Dachau concentration camp during World War II, and his mother raised him and his four siblings on her own. He was trained at the Catholic Theological Academy in Warsaw and began work as a parish priest in 1971 (having joined the Redemptorist order). In 1986, he mysteriously disappeared while on a trip to West Germany, surfacing in Munich a half year later and remaining abroad until 1991. When he returned to Poland he launched Radio Maryja as a regional station in Toruń, but his popularity grew quickly, and in 1993 he received a license to broadcast nationally.

Initially Radio Maryja focused on devotional programming, but in 1995 Rydzyk entered the political fray with his vitriolic commentaries on the presidential elections of that year. His political prominence rose steadily during the late 1990s as he became a leading voice for those who were frustrated by the postcommunist transition, impoverished by the neoliberal economic policies of the day, and frightened by an uncertain future of European integration. Radio Maryja explains its listeners' problems by referring to anti-Polish and anti-Catholic conspiracies involving Jews, Freemasons, liberals, and communists, all of whom (Rydzyk informs his listeners) are working to undermine Polish independence and Christian values.

Rydzyk advocates an ultraconservative doctrine that repudiates most of the reforms of the post-Vatican II era and calls for a return to theological clarity, with high walls draw between orthodoxy and heresy. In 1997 a far-right political party, The League of Polish Families, was formed by a group of Rydzyk's supporters, and in 1998 the national newspaper *Nasz Dziennik* (Our Daily) was launched to further advance Radio Maryja's message. A TV station was added to this media network in 2003. The hierarchy of the Roman Catholic Church has repeatedly expressed reservations about the tone of Rydzyk's preaching, but because of the priest's enormous popularity they have been unwilling or unable to move firmly against him.

Bibliography. Duda, Sebastian. "Teologia Radia Maryja." *Tygodnik Powszechny,* 9 March 2003. Lizut, Mikołaj. "Jciec dyrektor i tajemnice rodziny." *Gazeta Wyborcza,* 25 November 2002. Rydzyk, Tadeusz. *Tak-tak, nie-nie: Z założycielem Radia Maryja rozmawia Stanisław Krajski.* Warsaw, Poland: Wydawnictwo Sióstr Loretanek, 2002.

Brian Porter

S

SABBAH, MICHEL (B.1933). The first Palestinian-born patriarch of the Latin Church of Jerusalem, Sabbah has been a consistent advocate of the Christian minority in the Holy Land and of nonviolent solutions to the region's political conflicts. Born in Nazareth in 1933 and ordained priest in 1955, he was a parish priest in Nazareth, Madaba (Jordan), and Beit Jala (West Bank). Later, Sabbah left for Beirut to complete his graduate studies in Arabic language and literature at the Jesuit-owned Université Saint Joseph.

Upon his return from Lebanon in 1967, and following the Israeli occupation of East Jerusalem, the West Bank, and the Gaza Strip, Sabbah left Jerusalem to teach Arabic and Islamic studies in Djibouti (East Africa). In 1980, Sabbah was appointed as president of Bethlehem University. Since he became the Latin patriarch of Jerusalem in 1987, Sabbah has been trying to maintain—in words and actions—a sense of hope for the dwindling Christian community in the Holy Land. In the last two decades of Palestinian history, Patriarch Sabbah played a prominent role in supporting his people's right to self-determination as well as acknowledging the Israelis need for security. During the two Palestinian intifada (uprising), Sabbah came out against occupation, favoring nonviolence instead. Such stands were perceived as controversial by the Israeli government and by Palestinian radical Islamist groups. Throughout his frequent visits to the United States and Western Europe, Sabbah has worked to promote a political balance that reduces misconceptions about the Holy Land, one that acknowledges Christian, Muslim, and Palestinian interests while at the same affirming that not all people of Arab origin are Muslim and that Palestinians are not all terrorists and suicide bombers. Lastly, Sabbah has undertaken many interfaith and ecumenical initiatives to keep the status of Jerusalem unaltered despite the expansion of Israeli settlements.

Bibliography. Irani, George E. *The Papacy and the Middle East: The Role of the Holy See in the Arab-Israeli Conflict, 1963–1984.* Notre Dame, IN: University of Notre Dame Press, 1986. Lorieux, Claude. *Chrétiens d'Orient en terres d´Islam.* Paris: Perrin, 2001.

George Emile Irani

SALAZAR, ANTÓNIO DE OLIVEIRA SALAZAR (1889–1970). The architect of Western Europe's most durable authoritarian regime, Salazar placed conservative Catholic values at the heart of his rule. Thanks to his political agility, Portugal emerged unscathed from the Second World War, by which time he enjoyed a reputation as a kind of philosopher king in international Catholic circles and indeed beyond. He kept Portugal isolated, however, and appeared unconcerned by crippling levels of poverty so that, by the time of the Second Vatican Council, his regime was an embarrassment to mainstream Catholics. His stubborn effort to maintain Portugal's African empire in the 1960s destabilized his regime and would bring a disastrous end to multiracial societies in Angola and Mozambique in the 1970s.

From a small-farming background in conservative northern Portugal, Salazar studied in a Catholic seminary from 1900 to 1908. He spent the next twenty years at Coimbra, Portugal's main university, first as a law student, then as a lecturer in political economy. He identified with, and became a driving force behind, the political resistance to the anticlerical republicans who tried to dominate Portugal from 1910 to 1926. Lay Catholics at Coimbra founded the Academic Center for Christian Democracy and a political party, the Portuguese Catholic Center. Salazar was elected to Parliament on its ticket in 1921, but he quickly resigned, appalled by the unruliness of competitive politics. He was already strongly influenced by the French reactionary **Charles Maurras** and by the latter's watchwords, Nation, Family, Authority, and Hierarchy. The republicans had been swept from power by inexperienced military officers by the time Salazar was asked to become minister of finance in 1928. Having insisted on extraordinary powers to avoid national bankruptcy, he was able to proclaim an "economic miracle" in 1930 as the rest of Europe was facing a disastrous economic slump. By 1932, he was prime minister, and he quickly established his mastery of a dictatorship that he rapidly civilianized. A new constitution in 1933 proclaimed Portugal a corporative state. Political parties and labor unions were abolished, but instead of ending class conflict, corporativism resulted in a redistribution of resources to the already privileged.

Salazar kept down opposition with the aid of a feared secret police. Nationalism, anticommunism, and hostility to liberal democracy were powerful impulses of his regime, known as the *Estado Novo* (New State). But Salazar's regime deviated in important respects from the classic fascist political model. His goal was depoliticization rather than mobilization of the population. Salazar refrained from setting up a party that would take over the machinery of the state and intervene at all levels of society. He warned about similarities between fascism and communism, especially their worship of the state and disdain for religion. Though Salazar's regime borrowed some of the trappings of fascism, it was a traditionalist and pro-clerical one; campaigns like the cult of the Virgin of Fatima had greater resonance than propaganda of the kind masterminded by Goebbels in Germany. The Catholic clergy were often a source of active support for the regime, especially in much of northern Portugal, where religious observance was high and where the regime's traditionalism was popular at least until the mid-1950s.

Salazar avoided all treaty obligations with Hitler and Mussolini for fear that Portugal might be destroyed on the altar of their ambitions. He kept out of the Second World War but was alarmed by the advance of Soviet power to the heart of Europe. This was mirrored by the rise of communism in the still anticlerical south of Portugal.

By 1945, Salazar, an austere, well-read, retiring figure, enjoyed respect even among European democratic leaders, and in 1949 Portugal was invited to become a founding member of NATO. But his refusal to liberalize the regime, and identification with a tiny rich elite of landowners and industrialists in a country with huge levels of poverty and illiteracy, made him appear a relic of the past by the 1960s. In 1958, stage-managed elections to Portugal's ceremonial presidency produced a popular opposition challenge from a dissident general, Humberto Delgado, who was later murdered by the secret police. In the early 1960s, Salazar came close to being overthrown by the army, where there was alarm at his determination to retain Portugal's vast and poorly governed empire in Africa.

With the second Vatican Council (1962–1965), Salazar lost the active backing of the papacy, but the Portuguese Catholic church continued to be a pillar of the regime. The costly and ruinous colonial war in Africa plunged Portugal into even deeper isolation. Salazar was incapacitated by a stroke in 1968, and he died in 1970 four years before the collapse of his regime. Given the lackluster democratic system that has emerged with the help of the European Union, Salazar remains a commanding and, in some quarters, increasingly respected figure in Portugal.

Bibliography. Duarte Silva, A. E. et al. *Salazar e o Salazarismo.* Lisbon, Portugal: Dom Quixote 1989. Gallagher, Tom. *Portugal: A Twentieth-Century Interpretation.* Manchester: Manchester University Press, 1983. Nogueira, Franco. *Salazar.* 6 vols. Coimbra, Portugal: Atlântida Editora, 1977–1985.

Tom Gallagher

SALIÈGE, JULES-GÉRAUD (1870–1956). Archbishop of Toulouse from 1929, and elevated to cardinal in 1946, Saliège is representative of the generation of French Catholics who viewed their country as "de-Christianized," in many respects Catholic in name only. As the first step in the re-evangelization of the nation, they sought a greater emphasis on personal faith and religious formation.

Inspired and guided by **Pius XI**'s teachings on Catholic Action, Saliège promoted the lay apostolate by endorsing the proliferation of specialized movements for men and women of all classes and from different professions. He especially supported the new Catholic Action groups directed toward young Catholics. Some of his co-religionists argued that action on the social terrain was tantamount to political activism, but Saliège argued forcefully against this misrepresentation of Catholic Action as a primarily political movement. He does not fit the mold of the stereotypical left-leaning "social Catholic" and argued that political engagement, like all Catholic activities in the worldly domain, had to be informed first by a firm grounding in Catholic faith and practice.

Nevertheless, like many of his contemporaries, Saliège was concerned about the excesses of capitalism and the negative effects on working people of the extreme individualism and gross inequalities the laissez-faire economy engendered. Much put out by what he perceived to be the continuing allegiance of a certain class of Catholics to the cause of the far Right and the condemned **Action Française** movement, Saliège was determined to fight its deleterious effects in his diocese. However, it would be wrong to label him simplistically as a "liberal." He deplored the attacks the local radical socialist press mounted against the church and adhered to orthodox Catholic teachings on matters social and spiritual. A good illustration of this is the fact that his devotion to the **Young Christian Workers** (Jeunesse Ouvrière Chrétienne, or JOC) did not translate into support for the worker-priest movement.

Saliège was alert to the dangers of Nazism in the 1930s and condemned its extreme nationalism and racism as inimical to Christian teaching on the inviolability and integrity of the human person. The French Catholic Church's apology for its silence during the Holocaust (delivered in September 1997) referred specifically to Saliège and his plea to Catholics on the eve of war to take heed of the teachings of Pius XI (on the spiritual connections between Judaism and Christianity).

After the defeat, Saliège expressed his loyalty to **Philippe Pétain** and did not deviate significantly from this stance in the first phase of occupation. Eventually, however, Saliège distanced himself from Pétain and many of Vichy's policies. He objected to its corporatist-leaning Labor Charter (*Charte du travail*) and voiced his support for the continued existence of Catholic trade unions. He was also highly critical of the forced requisition of French workers to Germany, believing this practice to be tantamount to deportation.

Saliège is best remembered and renowned for his strong stance against Vichy's anti-Semitic policies. In August 1942 and in defiance of the prefect's attempt to silence him, Saliège wrote a vigorous denunciation of the persecution of Jews in France. He required that this message be read from the pulpit in all the churches of his diocese. Together with other clerics and religious, he supported Christian underground organizations assisting Jews in flight as well as offering shelter of his own accord. He encouraged the adherents of the Catholic resistance movement, *Témoignage Chrétien,* and their organ, *Cahiers du témoignage Chrétien,* and shifted his allegiance from Pétain to **Charles de Gaulle.**

Saliège suffered ill health most of his life: a degenerative physical paralysis affected his mobility and, eventually, his speech. It is often remarked that though questioned on a number of occasions by German officials, 'Saliège was saved from arrest by his frailty. Saliège, rightly lionized after the liberation, came to symbolize the muscular strand of French Catholicism in opposition to the German occupation. The challenge remaining to historians is to identify how the less spectacular, seemingly quietist aspects of Catholic life and practice also had the capacity to mitigate the corrupting effects of occupation and collaboration.

Bibliography. Clément, Jean-Louis. *Monseigneur Saliège Archevêque de Toulouse 1929–1956.* Paris: Beachesne, 1994.

Vesna Drapac

SALVATION ARMY. The Salvation Army was founded in 1865 by **William and Catherine Booth** as a mission to England's urban working-class communities. In the 1880s, its evangelizing efforts reached into Europe, North America, and parts of the British Empire. In the 1890s, an extensive social service wing was established. By the early twentieth century it was best known as a provider of social services, but its evangelical mission remained at the core of its work.

Religion was associated by many Victorians with respect for the authority of the crown and government, particularly in Britain, where the monarch was also the head of the church. City dwellers were believed to be particularly prone to immorality because of the crowding, filth, and the temptations of commercial entertainment. Cities were also home to many Irish and Jewish immigrants, newcomers who were perceived as a particular threat to social stability. Various agencies strove to bring working-class people into the churches as a bulwark against social unrest. The Salvation Army was one part of that wider mission to the urban working class, but it also challenged political and religious conventions.

The organization began as a small home mission, and in 1879 it was reorganized into the Salvation Army, with William Booth as general. The name was intended to capture its aims as well as the dedication and obedience required of its members. Soldiers were members of the corps, or congregations. Officers were paid employees, including preachers, administrators, and social service workers. All members followed a hierarchy of command and a strict code of conduct. As general, William Booth controlled the

25

finances and all decisions. Many critics commented that his powers exceeded those of the pope. The use of a military structure and uniforms was regarded by some as an affront to the legitimate military and by others as unduly rigid. The Army employed sensational tactics. Street preaching, hymns based on music hall tunes, vivid stories of sin and salvation, and brass bands excited attention, drew audiences, and scandalized the established denominations.

The Army's claim of a woman's right to preach was among its most significant innovations. It recognized no difference between a man's or a woman's call to preach and allowed women full authority to preach and hold positions of authority. This degree of responsibility was matched in virtually no other denomination or voluntary organization at that time. The women who joined the Army were predominantly working class, and most had none of the qualifications usually required for ministry. Many clergy denounced the Army for permitting women to usurp authority, which, they believed, was expressly forbidden in scripture. Salvationists were associated with the wider women's rights movement through their work in woman' suffrage, rescue missions, and the social purity movement.

In 1890, William Booth published *In Darkest England and the Way Out*. The book marked an important shift in the Army's attitude toward poverty and its causes. It combined ideas of the social imperialists, anxious to use the empire to combat urban degeneration, and the Social Gospel movement, particularly the emphasis on rural solutions to urban ills. It reversed the dominant conviction of charity organizations that drunkenness and immorality caused poverty. Booth asserted that most unemployed wished to work and only needed to be guided into a better life. It was his goal to bring the clothing, food, and shelter of everyone up to the standard of those provided to the London cab horse.

The Army's social services grew very quickly to include a large number of full-time officers, a publication devoted to their activities, and a strong public presence. By the time of the 1909 Royal Commission on the Poor Law, some experts who addressed the committee advocated providing state subsidies to the Salvation Army to extend its social service work with the poor. During World War I, the Army offered assistance to refugees and those displaced by war and canteens for military men, where they first introduced doughnuts to many soldiers. These programs were well regarded. It offered similar services during World War II. In both wars, the Army offered services to all, regardless of nationality, but their programs were far more extensive in the Allied nations because of the Army's English origins and the difficulty of any religious organization operating independently under the Nazis. An enormous variety of people came into contact with the Army's services during the war, which greatly enhanced its public profile and support after 1945.

In 1999, the Salvation Army worked in over one hundred countries, and social service programs operated in more than 140 languages. It is among the world's largest providers of social services. Its unusual approach to Christian evangelism remains a challenge. In 2000, it was forbidden to operate in Moscow because it was regarded as a potential military threat, and only after a two-year court battle was it permitted to continue its work.

Bibliography. McKinley, Edward H. *Marching to Glory: The History of the Salvation Army in the United States, 1880–1992.* Grand Rapids, MI: William B. Eerdmans, 1995. Taiz, Lillian. *Hallelujah Lads and Lasses: Remaking the Salvation Army in America, 1880–1930.* Chapel Hill: University of North Carolina Press, 2001. Walker, Pamela J. *Pulling the Devil's Kingdom*

Down: The Salvation Army in Victorian Britain. Berkeley and Los Angeles: University of California Press, 2001.

Pamela J. Walker

SANDS, BOBBY (1954–1981). Revolutionary, member of the Irish Republican Army, and elected member of Parliament, Sands was born in 1954 in Rathcoole, a loyalist district in Belfast, Northern Ireland. He joined the Irish Republican Army in 1972.

Accounts written by fellow IRA members state that Sands had not expressed any overtly sectarian tendencies until his family was forced to move from the largely loyalist district where they lived. Sands was first arrested on an arms charge in 1973. Some six months after his release in 1976, he was arrested again after a bomb attack on a furniture warehouse. Sentenced to fourteen years' imprisonment in the H-Block of Long Kesh Prison, Sands agitated for political prisoner status for IRA members, who, as criminals according to British law, were required to wear prison uniforms.

Sands became a leader of the so-called blanket men protest, in which IRA prisoners wore blankets instead of prison uniforms, refused to bathe, and often smeared the walls of their cells with feces. On March 1, 1981, after an initial hunger strike in Long Kesh ended without any substantial concessions from the British government, Bobby Sands began a hunger strike, followed by Francis Hughes and eight other members of the "blanket men." During his hunger strike, Sands was elected a member of Parliament for Fermanagh/South Tyrone in a special by-election. He died on May 5, 1981, sixty-six days into the strike.

It is a complex question as to whether Bobby Sands and the IRA should be considered under the rubric of modern Christian politics. On one hand, their understanding of the status of ethnic Catholic identity in Northern Ireland was absolutely central to their justification of violence. On the other hand, the IRA drew much of the ideological substance of its political vision from elements of Irish nationalism and revolutionary Marxism. Sands's prison writings, however, are infused with subtle Catholic Christian themes, and most obviously the willingness to fast until death draws upon potent Catholic Christian understandings of sacrifice and atonement

Bibliography. Beresford, David. *Ten Men Dead: The Story of the 1981 Irish Hunger Strike.* New York: Atlantic Monthly Press, 1997. Sands, Bobby. *Writings from Prison.* Boulder, CO: Roberts Reinhert, 1987.

Mathew N. Schmalz

SANGNIER, MARC (1873–1950). Sangnier is a figure whose impact on twentieth-century French Catholicism has only recently been acknowledged. He was largely responsible for stimulating interest in social justice among Catholics at the turn of the century, for reconciling Catholicism with political involvement during the Third Republic, and for showing that it was possible to be both an opponent of war and a loyal supporter of France. Veteran, pacifist, deputy, publisher and above all *éveilleur,* Sangnier had a tremendous impact on the generation of French Catholics who helped shape France after 1945.

Sangnier is best remembered for his role in founding the Sillon. This organization, launched in 1894 while Sangnier was at the Collège Stanislas, was intended to bring together middle- and working-class youth, with the aim of promoting popular education and the democratic republic. Initially it enjoyed strong favor among the Catholic hierarchy, but support gradually vanished. Some questioned Sangnier's leadership style. Meanwhile, after the creation of the Le Plus Grand Sillon in 1906, Sangnier tended to be more ecumenical in his choice of collaborators and addressed political issues more frequently, which allowed the

Sillon's critics to characterize it as yet another manifestation of the modernism against which Rome moved with Pope **Pius X**'s encyclical, *Pascendi* (1907).

Pius X addressed the Sillon specifically in 1910. In his papal letter, *Notre Charge Apostolique,* he emphasized a number of doctrinal errors in Sillonist philosophy. He deliberately grouped his criticisms under the rubric "liberty, equality, fraternity" in order to emphasize the links between the ideas engendered by 1789 and the errors of Sangnier and his associates. He concluded by demanding that the Sillon be placed under direct ecclesiastical control. Claiming that he was *"catholique avant tout,"* Sangnier immediately complied, which earned him praise, even among some of his enemies.

Sangnier did not retire from action following this setback. In 1912 he launched the *Ligue de la Jeune République,* which occupied a position on the left of French Christian democracy. With the outbreak of war two years later, Sangnier was mobilized as a lieutenant in the Engineers. He was later chosen to deliver lectures to the troops to maintain morale and was entrusted with an important mission to the Vatican regarding peace feelers in 1916.

At war's end, Sangnier entered politics, serving as a deputy for the Bloc National from 1919 to 1924. Unfortunately, it was not an entirely happy experience. Sangnier's growing antipathy for war marked him out from among his peers. In the 1920s, he devoted a greater portion of his energy to antiwar activism. Sangnier organized the first postwar encounter between German and French democrats in 1921, and five years later, he hosted a large youth conference at Bierville, which was attended by more than six thousand young people from around the world.

In the 1930s—often mistakenly characterized as a period of retreat from politics—Sangnier devoted himself to antiwar activities such as the creation of the Volontaires de Paix (1928), the founding of the first French youth hostel (1929), and the launching of his new journal, *L'Éveil des Peuples* (1932). He was also one of the few Catholic leaders to enthusiastically embrace Leon Blum's Popular Front government in 1936. Sadly, his pacifist activities appeared futile when war broke out in 1940. Sangnier retreated to the family home in Treignac before returning to Paris and engaging his press on the boulevard Raspail in the publication of clandestine material. In 1943 he was arrested and sent to Fresnes but was released shortly afterward.

After the Second World War, Sangnier was selected by the organizers of the newly created confessional party, the **Popular Republican Movement** (*Mouvement Républicain Populaire*), as its honorary president. The emergence of this Catholic party and its acceptance of the republic represented vindication for a man who had always advocated acceptance of the republic.

In the final analysis, many of the movements founded by Sangnier failed to achieve their goals. His prime importance was less in his direct political impact than in his profound influence on a generation of French Catholics. His organizations—the Sillon most of all—were training grounds for many of the most influential Catholic leaders of the postwar era, including **Maurice Schumann** and **Georges Bidault.** And if Catholics in postwar France were reconciled to the existence of the republic, it was in no small part due to his efforts.

Bibliography. Barthélemy-Madaule, Madeleine. *Marc Sangnier, 1873–1950.* Paris: Éditions du Seuil, 1973. Caron, Jeanne. *Le Sillon et la Démocratie chrétienne.* Paris: Plon, 1966.

Peter Farrugia

SANTAMARIA, BARTHOLOMEW AUGUSTINE (1915–1998). Conservative Roman Catholic and social activist, Santamaria was also a principal anticommunist figure in

Australia during the cold war years. He was born in Brunswick, Victoria, the first of six children of Sicilian immigrants. Educated by the Irish Christian Brothers, he was accustomed to the Catholic intellectual tradition in the Campion Society, a group of young Catholic intellectuals.

Santamaria graduated from the University of Melbourne and almost immediately became a prominent intellectual within the Roman Catholic Church in Australia. He founded the *Catholic Worker* in 1936 and emerged in political debate as the defender of the Vatican and the Nationalist cause during the Spanish civil war. By the 1940s, Santamaria had found an ally in Archbishop **Daniel Mannix.** When Santamaria approached the archbishop with the worries about the incursion of Communism into the country, Mannix agreed to support the Catholic Social Studies Movement (CSSM), formed in 1941, and he sympathized with the activist's personal quest: to resist atheistic communism, a threat Santamaria laid out in *The Price of Freedom* (1964).

Initially, the movement was concerned with particular social justice issues such as the establishment of pastoral zones. In the early fifties, however, many of those who had joined the movement promised to improve the prospects of anticommunists in union elections. President of the National Civic Council and sentinel of the anti-left "industrial groups" on the labor front, Santamaria encouraged formation of the dissident Democratic Labor Party (DLP) in the 1950s in order to combat radical leftist influence in Australia. Following the lead of Pope Pius XI, Santamaria assumed the role of media-conscious promoter of Catholic principles in public life through his editorship of *News Weekly* and his popular television program, *Point of View.*

Throughout his life, Santamaria defended a traditionalist vision of the family, strongly opposed abortion and homosexuality, and advocated both the crucial importance of religious faith and a strong position for religious organizations in modern societies.

Bibliography. Ormonde, Paul. *The Movement.* Melbourne, Australia: Thomas Nelson, 1972. Santamaria, B.A. *Santamaria: A Memoir.* Melbourne, Australia: Oxford University Press, 1997.

Jérôme Dorvidal

SCELBA, MARIO (1901–1991). Scelba was vice-chair of the Italian **Christian Democracy** under **Alcide De Gasperi,** Italy's cold war minister of the interior twice (1947–1953, 1960–1961), and its prime minister in 1954–1955. Born in Caltagirone, Sicily, Scelba found early inspiration under the wing of Don **Luigi Sturzo,** whom he followed to Rome, where he joined the **Italian Popular Party** (*Partito Popolare Italiano,* PPI). After the Fascist regime disbanded the PPI and Sturzo fled the country, Scelba remained and worked as a lawyer in Rome, although he stayed close to Sturzo's chief aide, De Gasperi, who became a close friend.

During the Second World War, Scelba joined him and others to form "the nine," the nucleus of Christian Democratic leadership. As De Gasperi's protégé, Scelba formed part of the party's centrist wing although he is best remembered as a hardline cold war anticommunist and as a cultural and social conservative. When he was interior minister, Scelba organized the so-called *celere* squads of quick-response and rather brutal police, who dealt harshly with left-wing political and labor protesters, whom he considered enemies of democracy and the free economy. The most serious confrontation between the *celere* and such "enemies" occurred at Modena in January 1950 and left six dead and fifty-one wounded.

Scelba also considered it his personal mission to be a watchdog of Italy's Catholic culture and protect it from the secularization and relativism of the age. As interior minister and prime minister Scelba cracked down on evangelical Christian missionaries and their attempts to proselytize in Italy. He also employed police units to guard the nation's beaches from the bikini invasion and movie theaters from untoward displays of affection. Italy's leftist cultural elite derided Scelba after his famous declaration of war on them at the 1949 DC party congress in Venice, where he tagged them with the awkward term *culturame,* a word that entered the language as something of a joke. Like De Gasperi, Scelba believed in European union, and as prime minister he hosted the Messina Conference, which paved the way for the Common Market. He was elected president of the European Parliament in 1969.

Bibliography. Marino, Giuseppe Carlo. *La Repubblica della forza: Mario Scelba e le passioni del suo tempo.* Milan: Franco Angeli, 1995. Pizzinelli, Corrado. *Mario Scelba.* Milan: Longanesi, 1981. Scelba, Mario. *Mario Scelba, discorsi parlamentari.* 2 vols. Rome: Senato della Repubblica, 1996.

Roy P. Domenico

SCHAEFFER, FRANCIS AUGUST IV (1912–1984). Schaeffer, a missionary, writer, and one of the most influential evangelical apologists of the twentieth century, was born in Germantown, Pennsylvania. His parents possessed little formal education and denigrated book learning. Despite this, Schaeffer was precocious intellectually. Indifferent to religion as a child, he read through the Bible at age seventeen and was transformed by its message. By the time he graduated from high school, he believed that God was calling him into the ministry.

Schaeffer attended Hampden-Sydney College, graduating in 1935. At the same time, he married Edith Seville, the daughter of a missionary, who became his partner in ministry. After studying under J. Gresham Machen and Cornelius Van Til at Westminster Theological Seminary,

Schaeffer assisted in the formation of Faith Theological Seminary, from which he graduated in 1938.

After a decade of service in various Presbyterian churches, the Schaeffers headed to Switzerland in 1948 as missionaries for the Independent Board for Presbyterian Foreign Missions. Appalled by the intellectual and spiritual devastation of postwar Europe, they began to see fruit from their teaching after several years of frustrations. Spiritual seekers, particularly college students, came to their home with significant concerns and left with changed lives. As this ministry broadened, the Schaeffers formed their own independent mission in 1955, which they named L'Abri (shelter) Fellowship.

By the 1960s, Schaeffer developed an extended critique of modern culture that sought to turn individuals toward a distinctly biblical worldview. Thousands of people visited L'Abri over the next three decades to hear his teachings. Schaeffer's growing fame led to invitations by student groups in Europe, Britain, and America to deliver lectures on contemporary culture and biblical faith. In 1968, these lectures took book form in *The God Who Is There* and *Escape From Reason.* Schaeffer's major theme was that modern Western culture had abandoned the absolute truth of biblical revelation in favor of a synthetic and relative interpretation. The survey, which included many major philosophers, authors, and artists, evidenced a comprehensive analysis that was lacking in other evangelical apologetic efforts. Schaeffer held firmly to conservative Christian theology with his commitment to "fundamental" doctrines like biblical inerrancy, the deity of Christ, and the fallen nature of humanity. However, his insistence—born out of a deep concern for his listeners— that the Gospel of Christ was a saving message of truth and hope that must confront secular culture resonated deeply with the evangelical subculture. Over time, Schaeffer was revered as a kind of Christian guru to his followers, a role accentuated by his long hair and knickers.

In the 1970s, the Schaeffers left the administration of L'Abri to their family and assumed a ministry of lecturing and book writing. Significant volumes in the 1970s and 1980s included *Christian Manifesto* (1981), *The Great Evangelical Disaster* (1984), and *How Should We Then Live?* (1976) With the aid of C. Everett Koop, a doctor and later U.S. surgeon general, Schaeffer and his son Frank produced an influential film and book series in the late 1970s called *Whatever Happened to the Human Race?* In 1978, Schaeffer was diagnosed with lymphoma. Despite this, he maintained a rigorous traveling and lecturing schedule. After several remissions, he finally succumbed to cancer on May 15, 1984.

Schaeffer's bedrock conviction was that ideas have practical consequences. If Christians believe that the Bible contains absolute truth from God, knowing this truth should affect how they live. With his growing fame, Schaeffer spoke out more vociferously against the perceived inaction of the Christian community in the face of prevailing secular beliefs that degraded human worth and dignity. Schaeffer believed that an abandonment of biblical truth, through which individuals found ultimate worth as God's special creation, led inevitably to practices like abortion, infanticide, and euthanasia. Regarding abortion, no single individual probably did more to galvanize the evangelical subculture against the practice than Schaeffer, particularly through his *Whatever Happened to the Human Race?* series.

Although Schaeffer's popularity was undeniable, the scholarly community questioned the superficiality of his historical and philosophical analysis of modern intellectual culture. Some evangelicals were also troubled by Schaeffer's close association with the Religious Right, the aforementioned stance against abortion, and his unequivocal support of divisive doctrines like biblical inerrancy. All these issues received increasing emphasis in Schaeffer's later, increasingly strident, writings.

To criticize Schaeffer for a less-than-rigorous approach in his exposition misses the point of his work. Schaeffer never claimed to be an academician. Rather, it was as a pastoral figure that he preferred to be viewed. Despite his serious and often dour appearance, he cared for people and never saw himself more than a "country preacher"—one called by God to declare the truth of the Christian scriptures in love (Parkhurst, 28). Historians may see this analysis as overly self-deprecating. Certainly, his critique of twentieth-century culture greatly influenced the evangelical subculture, even if his analysis lacked the imprimatur of the academy. Even more significantly, Schaeffer was instrumental in popularizing and legitimizing the life of the mind for a generation of evangelicals, many of whom were the heirs of obscurantist Protestant fundamentalism.

Bibliography. Dennis, Lane T., ed. *Francis A. Schaeffer: Portraits of the Man and His Work.* Winchester, IL: Crossway Books, 1986. Parkhurst, Louis Jr. *Francis Schaeffer: The Man and His Message.* Wheaton, IL: Tyndale, 1986. Schaeffer, Edith. *The Tapestry: The Life and Times of Francis and Edith Schaeffer.* Waco, TX: Word Books, 1981. Schaeffer, Francis A. *The Complete Works of Francis A. Schaeffer: A Christian Worldview.* 2nd ed. 5 vols. Wheaton, IL: Crossway Press, 1982.

Robert H. Krapohl

SCHAEPMAN, HERMANN (1844–1903).

The Dutch politician and Roman Catholic priest Hermanus Johannes Aloysius Maria (Hermann) Schaepman was born in Tubbergen, the son of the mayor of Tubbergen and Hellendoorn. In a state dominated by Protestants, Schaepman gave Catholicism a significant place at the political table.

Between 1856 and 1858 Schaepman attended Oldenzaal's secondary school and entered the Small Seminary of Culemborg in August 1858. In October 1863 he began to study theology at the Great Seminary for Roman Catholic Priests in Rijsenburg, from which he graduated in 1867 with excellent marks. Afterwards he took his doctoral degree in Rome (theology) and Leuven (philosophy). Ordained a priest in 1867, Schaepman was subsequently appointed bishop's secretary by the archbishop of Utrecht. In 1870, he was called as university teacher to Rijsenburg's Great Seminary and at the same time took over the office as archbishopric's second secretary.

Schaepman's first steps in politics date from this time, beginning with reviews. In the early 1870s, he became political editor of *De Tijd*, editor of the monthly *De Wachter* (later *Onze Wachter*), and court editor for *De Tijd*. Beginning in 1884, moreover, he wrote for the Catholic Frisian paper *Ons Norden* and in 1886 for the daily *Het Centrum*. From 1890 he led *De Katholiek*, the most important Dutch Catholic paper. In 1893 Schaepman became the archbishopric's chairman of the Association of Catholic Employees but also a member of the State's Committee for the Employee's Insurance. He was the first priest to be elected for the district of Breda for the Dutch lower house in July 1880. Schaepman sat for Breda until 1888; for Wijk until 1891; and, from then until his death, for Amelo.

Because of his success, Schaepman quickly became noted for parliamentary work. He was a member of all key committees, particularly the Central Committee as of 1897, and was chairman of various further committees. Schaepman mainly engaged in the sectors of health, justice, traffic (building of railroads), and colonization. Besides the social aims of his politics, Schaepman's greatest importance was in the building of a powerful political Catholicism within a Protestant-Reformed dominated state. Schaepman contributed considerably to this, for example with his platform of 1896, which led to the *Algemeene Bond van RK-kiesverenigingendie,* founded one year after Schaepman's death. From this association of Catholic electors came the Dutch Catholic political party, the RKSP, in 1926. He was also able to cooperate with **Abraham Kuyper** and his protestant **Anti-Revolutionary Party.**

Schaepman left a voluminous amount of literary, theological, and journalistic works that he published, often under the pseudonyms Corvinus, De Doktor, E.L.C., or De Rijsenburgse Professor. Pope **Leo XIII** appointed him apostolic prelate in 1901 and protonotary apostolic in 1902. In 1886 he was decorated with the fourth-class knight's *Orde Van de Gouden Leeuw van het Huis van Nassau* and in 1887 he became a knight of the *Orde van de Nederlandse Leeuw.* Many places and buildings, furthermore, were named in his honor. Schaepman died in Rome.

Bibliography. Bornewasser, J. A. *Curiale appreciates van der priester-politicus Schaepman.* Amsterdam: Noord-Hollandsche Uitg. Mij., 1986.

Helmut Rönz

SCHAFF, PHILIP (1819–1893). Born into poverty and obscurity in Coire (Chur), the capital of the Canton de Grisons, in Switzerland, Philip Schaff reminisced (sometime between 1871 and 1890): "I am a Swiss by birth, a German by education, an American by adoption." This statement measures well the character of his view of history, his theology, and his sociopolitical concerns as an American. "Restraint of individual freedom, regard for law and custom, self-government and discipline," he wrote in the same memoir, "are indispensable to the permanency and prosperity of a

Republic." As importantly, he continued, "I doubt whether we could maintain our liberty for six months, without our Christianity, our churches, our Bible and our Sabbath" (Penzel, 15).

The maintenance of liberty lay upon the heart of Schaff's theological and historical endeavors for half a century. Educated at the universities of Tubingen, Halle, and Berlin, he came to the United States in 1843 to join the faculty of the German Reformed theological seminary at Mercersburg, Pennsylvania. When Schaff delivered his inaugural lecture in Reading, Pennsylvania, in October of 1844, entitled "The Principle of Protestantism" (published in 1845), his ideas ran counter to the denominational sentiments of an Americanizing church under the influence of revivalistic evangelicalism and the anti-Catholicism of a transplanted Reformed scholasticism. Schaff was accused of heresy but was exonerated in both 1845 and 1846.

Along with **John Williamson Nevin,** his colleague at Mercersburg, he became an advocate of an evangelical (read Protestant) Catholicism that stressed the history of the church as an unbroken continuum from apostolic times. His scholarly vocation became increasingly historical as he sought to sort out the issues in the development of this continuum. In preparation for a visit to Germany in 1854, he authored what is still one of the most insightful analyses of American religion and culture: *America: A Sketch of the Political, Social, and Religious Character of the United States of North America* (1855).

Having been "adopted" by America, Schaff sought to understand what was happening in the American stage of church history—the unbroken continuum of Christianity. Under the influence of thinkers like Georg Hegel and Friedrich Schelling, Schaff's reading of history took a romantic and idealistic turn. His vision of the future perceived a Johannine (Gospel of John) age of love—an age of

evangelical Catholicism wherein the best of Catholicism and Protestantism would flow synthetically into a new order of the ages. This consummation was to take place in America., "the grave of all European nationalities" and all European churches and sects, the grave of Protestantism and Romanism. But it was to be a "Phoenix grave" from which new life would rise. "America, without earning it, has appropriated the civilization and church-history of two thousand years, as an inheritance" and has already begun to profit from that bequest (Schaff, 51, 210).

Although Schaff merits the respect of the scholarly communities for his pioneering work in church history (he was a founder of the American Society of Church History), his public and political theology deserves careful attention. First, he considered the "motley sampler" of American religion to be unsatisfactory and temporary. An ecumenical unity was in the making that would provide the foundation for the moral and metaphysical order of the Republic.

For Schaff, the moral and cultural effects of Christianity were very evident in America. Presidents attend public worship, and statesmen favor religious responsibility and devotion—they understand Christianity to be the fundament of America's revolutionary character. The central stream of American life was nurtured by the Reformation, which fashioned a culture of dissent and vision—"the ideal part, the heart's blood." There was an organizing talent, a firmness of purpose, and a capacity for improvement—all visible in the churches and the voluntary reform societies, and benevolently offered to the political welfare.

Schaff was convinced that Christianity alone, if it advanced to the stage of an evangelical Catholicism, was the powerful corrective to a "bottomless materialism" that also threatened the future of the Republic. There had been a democratic leveling of social distinctions, so that average intelligence, average morality, and average piety could lead to a populism of uninformed and quietistic citizenship.

America, however, was safe from violent revolution. Partly as a result of English heritage, the American revolution had been markedly different from European revolutions since 1789. Religious freedom, in the context of frontier circumstances, was fashioning a uniquely American character. Americans understood freedom to be "a rational, moral self-determination" that worked "hand in hand with law, order, and authority" (Schaff, 37). These characteristics had their roots in the history of Christianity.

Bibliography. Schaff, Philip. *America: A Sketch of Its Political, Social, and Religious Character.* Cambridge, MA: Belknap Press, 1961. Schaff, Philip. *Philip Schaff: Historian and Ambassador of the Universal Church.* Ed. Klaus Penzel. Macon, GA: Mercer University Press, 1991. Shriver, George. *Philip Schaff: Christian Scholar and Ecumenical Prophet.* Macon, GA: Mercer University Press, 1987. Yrigoyen, Charles, Jr., and George H. Bricker. *Reformed and Catholic. Selected Historical and Theological Writings of Philip Schaff.* Pittsburgh: Pickwick Press, 1979.

Richard Wentz

SCHLAFLY, PHYLLIS (b. 1924). Schlafly is a devout Catholic and mother of six who led a movement to block ratification of the equal rights amendment. She also founded the pro-family organization Eagle Forum.

Born Phyllis Stewart in St. Louis, Missouri, she graduated first in her Catholic school class and was awarded a scholarship to Maryville College of the Sacred Heart. After one year at Maryville, she transferred to Washington University in St. Louis. While attending Washington University during World War II, she worked nights at the St. Louis Ordnance Plant test firing ammunition. She graduated Phi Beta Kappa from Washington in 1944. Stewart

received a master's degree in government from Radcliffe College in 1945.

Deciding against a career in academia, Stewart traveled to Washington to work for several members of Congress before returning to St. Louis. There she managed the successful campaign of a Republican candidate for Congress. In 1946, she took a job as a researcher at a bank in St. Louis, continuing her activities in the Republican Party as a hobby. The newsletter she wrote for the bank attracted the attention of Fred Schlafly, a conservative attorney in Alton, Illinois. They were married on October 20, 1949. Mrs. Schlafly quit her job at the bank and moved to Alton to become a homemaker. The couple had six children.

Phyllis's marriage to Schlafly changed her life and directed her into the political activities for which she would become famous. She told acquaintances that marriage freed her from a life as a "working girl." It also strengthened her Catholic faith. Fred Schlafly was a devout Catholic and an ardent crusader against communism. He influenced his wife to become more devout and instilled in her an even greater faith in the free-enterprise system. Observers noted that Phyllis Schlafly's speeches against the equal rights amendment tied the issue closely to her religious outlook. Religion also permeated her newspaper columns, largely influenced by Mr. Schlafly's piety (Felsenthal, 110). Her critique of the women's movement and feminism, *The Power of the Positive Woman* (1977), also included a nondenominational attack on secular humanism. Fred Schlafly died in 1993.

In Alton, Schlafly continued her role in the community and expanded her political activities. She made an unsuccessful bid for Congress in 1952. She played a role in every Republican National Convention from 1952 through 2000. In 1964, she wrote her first book, *A Choice Not An Echo,* in which she advocated

Arizona Republican senator Barry Goldwater for the Republican presidential nomination in 1964. She wrote numerous other books, primarily advancing conservative ideological positions on defense policy and nuclear strategy.

Schlafly was elected first vice president of the National Federation of Republican Women in 1965. In 1967, she was unsuccessful in her bid for the presidency of that organization, losing to a more liberal candidate by a narrow margin. In 1970, she was defeated in a second bid for Congress.

In the February 1972 issue of the *Phyllis Schlafly Report,* she began her campaign against the equal rights amendment. She founded Stop ERA later that year, and the Eagle Forum in 1975. Both organizations were created to defeat the amendment using sophisticated grassroots organizing techniques. As the leader of Stop ERA, Schlafly testified in thirty state legislatures, causing the rapid succession of ratification votes to slow down. The equal rights amendment was defeated in 1982.

After Schlafly was criticized by an Illinois legislator for testifying before the Illinois House without a law degree, she decided to enter law school. Over her husband's initial objections, Schlafly attended Washington University Law School, earning her law degree in 1978. She continued her political activities and writing after her victory in defeating the ERA.

Bibliography. Critchlow, Donald T. *Phyllis Schlafly and Grassroots Conservatism: A Woman's Crusade.* Princeton: Princeton University Press, 2005. Felsenthal, Carol. *The Sweetheart of the Silent Majority: The Biography of Phyllis Schlafly.* Garden City, NY: Doubleday, 1981. Oldfield, Duane M. *The Right and the Righteous: The Christian Right Confronts the Republican Party.* Lanham, MD: Rowman & Littlefield, 1996. Schlafly, Phyllis. *The Power of the Positive Woman.* New Rochelle, NY: Arlington House, 1977.

John David Rausch, Jr.

SCHLEIERMACHER, FRIEDRICH DANIEL ERNST (1768–1834). Born in Breslau, Schleiermacher was descended from a Prussian family of pastors and, on his father's wish, entered the Pädagogium Niesky, a Moravian Brüdergemeine seminary. Because of religious doubts, he left the institution in 1787 and enrolled at the University of Halle, which had developed into an academic center of the Enlightenment. Here, Schleiermacher made a critical study of the writings of Christian Wolff and Emanuel Kant. After work as a private tutor and a curate, in 1796, he obtained his first independent position as a hospital chaplain at the Berlin Charité. He frequented the Berlin salons, where he came into close contact with the philosophical-literary movement of early romanticism. In these circles, he also met Friedrich Schlegel, whom he befriended and with whom he shared an apartment at times.

In 1799, Schleiermacher achieved fame with his study *Über die Religion: Reden an die Gebildeten unter ihren Verächtern* (On Religion: Speeches to Its Cultured Despisers). Out of the self-awareness and sense of mission of the romantic circles, he sought to recover the autonomy of religion—between the orthodox dogmatic belief on one hand, and the enlightenment's moral theory of religion on the other. The autonomous religious dimension of reality, according to Schleiermacher, was accessible only to feeling paired with contemplation. Religion, according to him, was "sense and taste of the infinite," an independent entity opposite art and science, but indispensable for both. With these theses, he became the "church-father of the nineteenth century," for he anchored Christian religion in the concept of education, turning it into a cultural necessity.

On the other hand, religion lost its transcendent content and remained completely at the borders of humanity. By assigning religion to the subjective feeling of the infinite, Schleiermacher introduced the thought of modern subjectivism into theology. This access no longer takes seriously the objective claim of truth of religion and was therefore a nuisance for **Karl Barth** and the theology of the Word of God in the 1920s. However, for Schleiermacher's contemporary theologians, his romantic version of a pure religion rooted in feeling represented a coup from the dogmatic and intellectual distress in which Christianity found itself at the turn of the nineteenth century.

In 1802 Schleiermacher was promoted to pastor of the community of the small town of Stolp in Pomerania. There, he found time for more studies: the *Grundlinien einer Kritik der bisherigen Sittenlehre* (Essentials of a Criticism of Traditional Ethics, 1803), the first volumes of his translation of Plato's works, and two considerations on the "Nature of the Protestant Church" (*Das protestantische Kirchenwesen*, 1804). In 1804, Schleiermacher was called to the University of Halle as an associate professor and Reformed university preacher, where he dealt, among other things, with exegetic studies. After Halle was occupied by Napoleon's troops in 1806 and annexed to the new kingdom of Westphalia, this Prussian patriot resettled to Berlin. There, he lived for three years as a private scholar and was then given a parish at the Trinity Church in 1809 and a professorship at the new University of Berlin in 1810. Sympathetic to the Prussian reformers, he collaborated in the reform of the university and published literary works during the wars of liberation against the French. During the Restoration, however, after police examinations and interrogations, he was considered untrustworthy politically, and his sermons were subjected to surveillance. In Berlin, Schleiermacher taught at the schools of theology and of philosophy. Of his scientific works, besides the "Speeches," it was the *Kurze Darstellung des theologischen Studiums* (Brief Outline of Theology as a Field of Study, 1811–1830) and his two-volume dogmatics entitled *Der christliche Glaube nach den Grundsätzen der evangelischen Kirche im Zusammenhange dargestellt* (The Christian Faith in Outline [According to the Principles of the Protestant Church], 1821–1822), which enjoyed a permanent reputation. The latter work is conceived as "union dogmatism." Schleiermacher denied the church-separating meaning of the controversial topics existing between Lutheran and Reformed teaching and also engaged himself for the formation of a United Protestant Church of Prussia in 1817—which, however, should not originate on command of the king but through the insight of the believers. In the correcting addition to the "Speeches," he defines the nature of religion in his dogmatics as follows: "Piety, which is the basis of all church communities, when viewed alone, is neither knowledge nor action, but a certainty of feeling or of immediate self-awareness." Schleiermacher understands Christianity as the highest monotheistic step of religion. Dogmatism does not determine what is to be believed but expresses and represents the experience of belief.

Bibliography. Nowak, Kurt. *Schleiermacher. Leben, Werk und Wirkung.* Göttingen, Germany: Vandenhoeck & Ruprecht, 2001. Schleiermacher, Friedrich Daniel Ernst. *Brief Outline of Theology as a Field of Study.* Trans. Terrence N. Tice. Lewiston, NY: Mellen, 1990. Schleiermacher, Friedrich Daniel Ernst. *The Christian Faith.* Ed. H. R. Mackintosh and J. S. Stewart. Edinburgh, Scotland: T. & T. Clark, 1999. Schleiermacher, Friedrich Daniel Ernst. *Kritische Gesamtausgabe.* Ed. Hans-Joachim Birkner, Hermann Fischer, et al. Berlin: Walter de Gruyter, 1980. Schleiermacher, Friedrich Daniel Ernst. *On Religion: Speeches to Its Cultured Despisers.* Trans. Richard Crouter. Cambridge: Cambridge University Press, 1996.

Gerhard Besier

SCHMITT, CARL (1888–1985). Schmitt was one of the most controversial German Catholic political thinkers of the twentieth century. He began his career with his *Habilitation* at the University of Strassburg during World War I. After the war, he earned appointments as professor of public and constitutional law at the universities of Greifswald, Cologne, and Berlin. During the years of the Weimar Republic, he became one of the foremost critics of parliamentary government, which often led him to be miscategorized as a conservative revolutionary. During the National Socialist period, Schmitt first opportunistically supported the regime but then found himself marginalized as the regime radicalized. After 1945, Schmitt's teaching career ended when he refused denazification, but he was able to continue publishing until his death in 1985 at the age of ninety-seven.

Schmitt's work is difficult to categorize. He called for an authoritarian state that embodied principles of justice and righteousness. The individual is called upon to serve the state. While bound up in the German tradition of the strong state, Schmitt was able to combine an admiration for the Catholic Church's ability to represent both a rule-bound institution and a higher ideal with a call for a leader, or *führer,* who represents the general will. For Schmitt, that general will could never be the result of a majority opinion; right could only be based on absolute principles tested against the most extreme cases. Thus, Schmitt rejected both romanticism and liberalism. Instead, he viewed politics as a fierce conflict between friend and foe, between whom no compromise was possible.

Schmitt rejected parliamentary government not only because of its reliance on compromise, but also because he considered it the object of industrial and social interest groups that were not truly representative of the people. For Schmitt,

the führer state, in which the leader enjoyed direct legitimacy, was truly democratic.

Schmitt's work must be understood in context, and not only through the lens of his servile cooperation with the National Socialists. Raised a Catholic during the late Kulturkampf period, Schmitt fiercely rejected the protestant anti-Catholic critique of the institutional church mounted by such leading protestant theologians as Adolf von Harnack. Even though Schmitt himself was excommunicated after a civil divorce, he remained committed to the Catholic Church as an ideal. Another experience that left a deep impression on Schmitt was the revolutionary unrest he experienced in Munich at the end of the First World War. These two events together left Schmitt with a deep-seated desire for order and authority in government. In fact, at the end of the Weimar Republic, Schmitt actively sought to maintain President Paul von Hindenburg's rule by decree against the appointment of Hitler as chancellor. Only after Hitler's appointment did Schmitt begin to publish pro-Nazi and anti-Semitic works. In these, however, he compromised his scholarly integrity, and thus most scholars today focus on his earlier work.

Bibliography. Bendersky, Joseph W. *Carl Schmitt: Theorist for the Reich.* Princeton, NJ: Princeton University Press, 1983. Schmitt, Carl. *The Concept of the Political.* Trans. George Schwab. Chicago: University of Chicago Press, 1996.

Martin Menke

SCHMUCKER, SAMUEL (1799–1873). Schmucker was a Lutheran pastor and theologian who struggled on behalf of a Lutheranism at once American and loyal to its confessional roots in the sixteenth century. In this capacity he was a pastor, professor, and ecumenist, and president of the General Synod of the Evangelical Lutheran Church.

The 1830s and 1840s in American history were a time in which new religious and political perceptions were being shaped to accommodate the expectations of a republic not yet a half-century old. American denominations were coming to terms with disestablishment and trying to preserve their inherited traditions. They aspired to unity in a society that seemed to be raging toward what many thought to be barbarism, exemplified by unsettled conditions on an expanding frontier. What was to guarantee the moral welfare and provide the institutional foundations for reform and social order?

Perhaps no Protestant tradition faced this dilemma with more trepidation than American Lutheranism, and Schmucker assumed pivotal importance in negotiating this difficult passage. He had studied at the University of Pennsylvania and, like many of his contemporaries, had undergone a subjective conversion experience as revivalist evangelicalism began to press American religious sentiments into the service of the common man and woman. In 1818, Schmucker enrolled at Princeton Theological Seminary, the preeminent theological school of the times, and a bastion of Reformed orthodoxy. At Princeton he pursued his education alongside **Charles Hodge** and Archibald Alexander.

Although Schmucker espoused the somewhat exclusionary confessionalism of the Augsburg Confession, he was a Pietist in the heritage of Henry Melchior Muhlenberg (1711–1787). When he founded the Lutheran seminary at Gettysburg, Pennsylvania, in 1826, he thought of it as an American Halle. As the seminary's first professor of theology, Schmucker sought to fashion a practical approach to theology, a system of doctrine that would accord with the democratic spirit of the people without succumbing to the subjectivism of revivalist Christianity.

Schmucker's *Popular Theology,* published in several editions beginning in 1834, was "Designed Chiefly for Private Christians and Theological Students" and demonstrates his desire to make Lutheranism democratic and responsive to the uniqueness of the American experiment. In his *Fraternal Appeal to the American Church* (1838), he revealed a nativist support for an alliance of American Protestantism in the face of the emerging strength of Roman Catholicism and the need to keep American Christianity grounded in its sixteenth-century roots.

Much of American theology in the first half of the nineteenth century may be understood as political because it was concerned to address and interpret the American polis as it sought to find moral and social sanctions in a fragmentary society without the venerable presuppositions of religious establishment. Schmucker supported the work of the "benevolent empire" of interlocking voluntary associations intended to provide for the reform and stabilization of a "westering" America. He opposed the Anabaptist interdiction of civil duties as well as the perfectionism of evangelicals who wished to create an ideal society through a process of collective individual conversions.

For Schmucker, legitimate political enactments were good works of God, and civil responsibility was of divine order. In this sense he represented the Lutheran doctrine of two kingdoms (this world and the kingdom of God), both under divine appointment. The church could advocate but not agitate. Schmucker could advocate the manumission of slaves yet support the work of the American Colonization Society, knowing that it could not remove slavery from the nation. The work of Christ *redeems the human family* by establishing here a kingdom not "of this world." The marks of Christ's kingdom are present in, but not identified with, the political order. Schmucker's "American Lutheranism" was

as much concerned with the moral and religious welfare of the whole American community as with the preservation of a pristine sixteenth-century Lutheranism.
Bibliography. Holifield, E. Brooks. *Theology in America.* New Haven, CT: Yale University Press, 2003. Schmucker, Samuel S. *Fraternal Appeal to the American Churches.* Ed. Frederick K. Wentz. Philadelphia: Fortress Press, 1965. Tappert, Theodore, ed. *Lutheran Confessional Theology in America, 1840–1880.* New York: Oxford University Press, 1972.

Richard Wentz

SCHÖNERER, GEORG VON (1842–1921). Schönerer was an Austrian politician, a member of the Reichsrat (1873–1888 and 1897–1907), and an anti-Semitic figure who exerted great influence on the Christian social movement. His father was an Austrian engineer and pioneer of Austrian railway building. In 1869, after studies at several agricultural colleges, he took over his father's property at Rosenau (Waldviertel, Lower Austria), turning it into a model estate.

He used his wealth to finance the building of some two hundred fire departments and two dozen public libraries. This and his promotion of traditional culture made him a revered regional figure. Schönerer joined the Progressive Party (*Fortschrittspartei*) and was elected to the Reichsrat for the Waldviertel in 1873. There he gained notoriety by criticizing the railway monopoly of the Rothschilds and grew increasingly critical of his own party and its liberalism. Gradually, Schönerer transformed himself from an idealistic radical democrat to a radical populist demagogue.

Taking an anti-Habsburg stance, he advocated the creation of a Greater Germany under Prussian leadership and vehemently opposed the occupation of Bosnia-Herzegovina. In his programmatic statements of 1879 (*Mein Programm*) and 1882 (*Linzer Programm*), Schönerer elaborated

on his pan-German views and demanded universal franchise as well as social and welfare legislation. Employing the modern agitator's techniques, Schönerer presented himself as a patriot and champion of the people. During the 1880s, the tenor of his pronouncements became increasingly anti-Semitic. In his newspapers (*Deutsche Worte,* 1881, and *Unverfälschte Deutsche Worte,* 1883) and fiery speeches he condemned Russian Jewish immigrants as a wave of "unproductive and alien elements." Without consulting the coauthors of the *Linzer Programm,* he added an Aryan clause, arguing that it was essential to remove Jewish influence from public life.

After a violent attack on the offices of the *Neue Wiener Tageblatt* in 1888, Schönerer was sentenced to four months in prison and stripped of his political mandate and his hereditary title. He again became a member of the Reichsrat in 1897, this time without much influence. His opposition to the Catholic Church and to what he perceived as pro-Slavic sentiments among the clergy made him a pioneer of the *Los von Rom* movement, which urged conversion to Protestantism, and in 1900, Schönerer himself converted. However, when he founded the Pan-German Union (*Alldeutsche Vereinigung*) in 1901 his political star was already waning.

Despite his anti-Catholicism, many of his followers joined the United Christian Alliance or drifted into the heavily Catholic Christian social movement. The main consequence of his political agitation was the growth of anti-Semitism in Austrian political discourse and his influence on **Karl Lueger** and the young Adolf Hitler. Nazi philosophy was informed by Schönerer's anti-Semitism; Hitler adopted the title "führer" and the Nazi salute from his Vienna idol.

Bibliography. Hamann, Brigitte. *Hitlers Wien: Lehrjahre eines Diktators.* Munich: Piper, 1996. Rumpler, Helmut. *Österreichische Geschichte, 1804–1914: Eine Chance für Mitteleuropa;*

bürgerliche Emanzipation und Staatsverfall in der Habsburgermonarchie. Vienna: Ueber-reuter, 1997. Whiteside, Andrew G. *The Social-ism of Fools: Georg Ritter von Schönerer and Austrian Pan-Germanism.* Berkeley and Los Angeles: University of California Press, 1975.

Thomas M. Bredohl

SCHOUTEN, JAN (1883–1963). Schouten was a major leader of the Calvinist politi-cal party known as the **Anti-Revolutionary Party** (ARP) in the Netherlands before and after World War II. Organized by **Abraham Kuyper** in 1879, the ARP joined the **Christian Democratic Appeal** party in 1980.

From humble circumstances, Schouten, a devout evangelical believer, rose in busi-ness to become a bank director and politi-cian. In 1918 he was elected to Parliament, where he served until 1956, except for during the war years, which he spent in the Resistance and in the Mathausen con-centration camp. He served as chair of the ARP delegation twice (1933–1940 and 1945–1956). Working closely with ARP leader **Hendrikus Colijn,** Schouten served as acting party leader while Colijn was premier (1933–1939) and party leader in his own right (1946–1955).

During the Depression, Schouten helped to shape many of Colijn's moder-ate policies of fighting unemployment, promoting public works projects, and using social insurance—similar to the Hoover-Roosevelt programs in America. When the German occupation of the coun-try started in May 1940, Schouten was quicker than Colijn to realize that the ARP had to join the underground resistance. Soon, however, Colijn led the ARP under-ground. The result was the resistance paper *Trouw.* After Colijn and Schouten were arrested, **J.A.H.J.S. Bruins Slot** became the leader of the Trouw group.

"I have not changed my mind," Schouten remarked when he returned from the German camp in 1945. This remark was in opposition to the secularist Breakthrough proposal to scrap the old confessional/worldview parties for pragmatic ones. The Breakthrough failed, and the old parties came to life again, including the ARP, which held up Christian moral principles. Schouten refused to recognize Indonesia's right to independence, and the ARP stayed out of the government from 1945 to 1952 in protest.

The ARP leader strongly endorsed the European Union movement in the coal and steel community proposal of Robert Schuman in 1950. He wanted a free mar-ket that would bring prosperity to Western Europe and prevent the spread of commu-nism. Likewise, a strong commitment to NATO would keep his country secure in the Western alliance. At the same time the ARP leader accepted the welfare state only temporarily.

Bibliography. Langley, M. R. "Starting Over: The ARP, 1943–1956." *Christian Renewal,* 11 March 2002.

McKendree R. Langley

SCHUMAN, JEAN BAPTISTE NICOLAS ROBERT (1886–1963). A devout Roman Catholic and native of the Franco-German borderlands, Schuman built a political career in France that spanned more than three decades (1919–1963) and included eight months as prime minister in the Fourth Republic. He is most remembered, however, for his role as France's minister for foreign affairs over an almost unbro-ken period of four and a half years (1948–1953), during which time he helped to inaugurate a process of Franco-German reconciliation and transnational integra-tion in Europe.

Like his counterparts in West Germany (**Konrad Adenauer**) and Italy (**Alcide De Gasperi**), Schuman understood his "Europeanism" to be both the product and the expression of his Catholic world-view and binational upbringing in one of Europe's borderland regions, where frontiers were impermanent, languages mixed, and nations overlapped.

Born in Luxembourg but raised in Lorraine (whence his parents had emigrated following the German annexation of 1871), Schuman studied at several German universities before returning to his hometown of Metz in 1912 to practice law. Although conscripted into the German army as a noncombatant during the First World War, Schuman's experience of the conflict seems to have strengthened his binational outlook and his belief in the Christian foundations of European civilization. At war's end, and with the return of Lorraine to France, Schuman was elected in 1919 to the Chamber of Deputies as a member of the *Union Républicaine Lorraine,* a component of the conservative, nationalist, and Catholic *Fédération Républicaine.* Though initially preoccupied with the defense of Catholic educational prerogatives in Lorraine, Schuman—with his concern for social peace and international conciliation, and his instinctive moderation—was increasingly drawn to the **Popular Democratic Party** (*Parti Démocrate Populaire,* PDP), a party of Christian democracy that drew upon the traditions of social Catholicism but had no presence in Lorraine. A member of the PDP from 1932 onwards, Schuman was notable for his measured criticism of the weaknesses of the parliamentary system of the Third Republic. Named to the Paul Reynaud government of 1940 as undersecretary of state for refugees, Schuman voted full powers to Marshal **Philippe Pétain** later that year but almost immediately quit the marshal's government and returned to Metz. Imprisoned and then placed under house arrest by the German occupation authorities, Schuman escaped to southern France, where he took refuge in religious houses following the German military occupation of the Vichy zone in November 1942.

Following the personal intervention of **Charles de Gaulle** in the summer of 1945, Schuman was able to resume his participation in public life notwithstanding his support for Pétain in 1940. He joined the **Popular Republican Movement** (*Mouvement Républicaine Populaire*), a new Christian democratic party with links to both the interwar PDP and the wartime resistance, and represented the Moselle department in the National Assembly from 1945 to 1958. It was under the coalition governments of the Fourth Republic, of which governments the MRP was almost always a member, that Schuman achieved high office. As minister of finance (1946–1947), his policies aimed at deflation and balanced budgets, and as prime minister (1947–1948), his government weathered a strike wave that threatened to paralyze the nation.

It was as minister of foreign affairs from 1948 to 1953, however, that Schuman left his greatest mark on France and Europe. In the space of a few years, Schuman introduced programs and policies that, taken together, amounted to a fundamental reorientation of French foreign policy. Schuman's Catholic anticommunism led him to speak out strongly in favor of close relations with the United States through French participation in the European Recovery Program and French membership in NATO.

Aware that the United Kingdom and the United States would not support French plans to permanently hobble West Germany, Schuman instead proposed that Franco-German relations be stitched back together within a European cloth. Along with Jean Monnet, Schuman developed a plan for economic integration in Western Europe through the pooling of coal and steel. He deftly shepherded the project through the cabinet in spring 1950 and defended it against the attacks of parliamentary opponents until the National Assembly's lukewarm acceptance of the plan at the end of 1951. Accepted by six West European governments (those of Belgium, France, Italy, Luxembourg, Italy, and West Germany) in April 1951, Schuman's proposal for a European Coal and Steel Community (ECSC) placed the Franco-German relationship at the heart of a new model for transnational integration in Western Europe. Popular enthusiasm in France for the ECSC was virtually absent. Nor was this the last time that government elites would push through a "European" policy against a backdrop of public apathy and relative ignorance.

In any case, by 1953 the peculiar constellation of circumstances that allowed for Schuman's foreign policy innovations seemed already to be passing; and indeed it was his very Europeanism that led to Schuman's departure from the foreign ministry that year in the face of determined Gaullist opposition to the Pleven Plan (which Schuman supported) for the creation of a European Defense Community.

Bibliography. Eldin, Grégoire, et al. *L'Europe de Robert Schuman.* Paris: Presses de l'Université Paris-Sorbonne, 2001. Lejeune, René. *Robert Schuman, père de l'Europe, 1886–1963.* Paris: Fayard, 1999. Poidevin, Raymond. *Robert Schuman, homme d'État, 1886–1963.* Paris: Imprimerie nationale, 1986.

Ramesh J. Rajballie

SCHUMANN, MAURICE JACQUES (1911– 1998). For much of his life, Schumann was a public figure of considerable prominence in France. His seven decades of professional life as, variously, a journalist, politician, and writer were informed by his Catholicism, his Europeanism, and his Gaullism. He developed a particular interest and expertise in foreign affairs— serving in a number of governments under the Fourth and Fifth Republics—while at the same time achieving success as a writer of fiction and nonfiction alike.

Born in Paris into a family of practicing Jews, Schumann converted to Catholicism in his teens, moving in social Catholic and Christian democrat circles in the 1930s, where he developed his humanistic and progressive Catholic worldview. His job as a foreign correspondent for a Paris-based news agency placed him in London in 1940, where he gained renown as the voice of **Charles de Gaulle**'s Free French organization on BBC radio. At the liberation, he cofounded the Christian democratic **Popular Republican Movement** (*Mouvement Républicain Populaire,* MRP), serving as party president from 1945 to 1949. First elected in 1945 as an MRP deputy from the Nord department (which he represented until 1968), Schumann's governmental posts included several assignments as a junior minister for foreign affairs between 1951 and 1954 and four years (1969–1973) as minister for foreign affairs, during which time he worked to maintain Franco-German reconciliation as the keystone of France's European policy.

Schumann's political career under the Fourth and Fifth Republics illustrated the often-difficult relationship between the Gaullist and "European" wings of French Christian democracy, which was shaken and divided by de Gaulle's resignation from government in 1946, and his evident hostility toward European integration in the 1950s and 1960s. While always viewing himself as a loyal Gaullist, Schumann on two occasions (in 1962 under de Gaulle, and in 1973 under Georges Pompidou) resigned from government in response to presidential expressions of hostility toward European integration; and while the MRP had ceased to exist by the mid-1960s, Schumann did not join a Gaullist party (the *Union des Démocrates pour la République*) until 1974.

Schumann spent his later years as a lifetime member of the Senate and, from 1974, an elected member of the Académie Française. He was a productive writer and active participant in public affairs almost to the very end of his life, as well as an unwavering advocate of both the progressive and humanist Catholicism of his youth and the Europeanism of post-1945 Christian democracy.

Bibliography. Rimbaud, Christiane. *Maurice Schumann: Sa voix, son visage.* Paris: Odile Jacob, 2000.

Ramesh J. Rajballie

SCHUSCHNIGG, KURT VON (1897–1977). The Christian Social chancellor of Austria, Schuschnigg was born in Riva del Garda in Austria-Hungary (now Italy). A student at the Jesuit high school Stella Matutina in Feldkirch, Vorarlberg, when war broke out with Italy, he reported for duty as a volunteer at the front on July 1, 1915. From November 1918 until August of 1919 he was a prisoner of war in Italy. Upon his return to Austria, he studied at the University of Innsbruck and earned his doctorate in law in October 1921.

Schuschnigg became a disciple of Austria's Jesuit chancellor, **Ignatz Seipel,** and joined the **Christian Social Party.** As such, he served as a deputy in the Austrian parliament (Nationalrat) from 1927 until 1934. While in that capacity, he founded the *Ostmärkische Sturmscharen,* a Christian paramilitary unit. In 1932, chancellor **Engelbert Dollfuss** appointed him as a minister of justice and then minister of education. With the assassination of Dollfuss by the Nazis in 1934, Schuschnigg became chancellor (as well as secretary of defense, education [until May 1936], and agriculture), and he continued Dollfuss' authoritarian rule. Schuschnigg advocated corporatist principles, supported the dethroned Austro-Hungarian Hapsburg dynasty, and was no friend of democracy.

In 1936 he eliminated the paramilitary but anticlerical Heimwehr and replaced it with his pro-Catholic and anti-Marxist Fatherland Front (*Vaterländische Front*). He tried to keep Austria independent from Germany and promoted the concept of Austria as a second, and independent, German state. In this he initially followed Dollfuss's line of close cooperation with Fascist Italy, although this policy ended in failure. He tried to placate the Germans by signing the *Juliabkommen* agreement of 1936 that amnestied Nazis and admitted two of them into his cabinet. He offered further concessions to Hitler at the Berchtesgaden meeting on February 12, 1938. Shortly after, however, under heavy German pressure to capitulate, Schuschnigg scheduled a referendum on Austria's independence for March 13. Two days after this announcement, Hitler's forces crossed the Austrian border that joined the nation to the German Reich. Schuschnigg was arrested and imprisoned at the Dachau concentration camp until the end of the Second World War.

In 1947 Schuschnigg settled in the United States and taught law at St. Louis University from 1948 until 1967, when he returned to Austria. Ten years later he died in the Tyrolean village of Mutters.

Bibliography. Hopfgartner, Anton. *Kurt Schuschnigg: Ein Mann gegen Hitler.* Graz, Austria: Styria, 1989. Schuschnigg, Kurt von. *The Brutal Takeover: The Austrian Ex-Chancellor's Account of the Anschluss of Austria by Hitler.* New York: Atheneum, 1971. Streitle, Peter. *Die Rolle Kurt von Schuschniggs im Österreichischen Abwehrkampf gegen den Nationalsozialismus (1934–1936).* Munich: Tuduv-Verlagsgesellschaft, 1988.

Jürgen Nautz

SCHUSTER, ALFREDO ILDEFONSO (1880–1954). Schuster was born in Rome, became a monk in 1899 at age nineteen, and was ordained priest in 1904. In 1918, he became the abbot of his monastery and in 1929 was made archbishop of Milan and a cardinal, positions he held until his death. Although he was an early enthusiast for Benito Mussolini's regime, he distanced himself from Fascism during World War II to become a wartime mediator in Italy and a humanitarian voice that extended support to Jews fleeing Nazi Germany.

Cardinal Schuster has been referred to by one of his successors as "the cardinal of prayer." He was also a strong advocate of Mussolini's Fascist regime and the Lateran Agreements. In 1930, he claimed that "Catholic Italy and even the Pope himself, have blessed Fascism" (Pollard, 60), only to have his remarks publicly repudiated by **Pius XI.** Following Italy's invasion of Abyssinia in 1935, Schuster instructed religious establishments in his diocese to contribute their silver and gold to the national war effort. He was again corrected by the pope through the *Osservatore Romano,* which indicated that free-will offerings to the national cause were acceptable, but not the contribution of church property. His early support for Fascism faded as Italy strengthened its ties with Nazi Germany.

Schuster was really put to the test between 1943 and 1945, once the Germans had occupied northern Italy and propped up Mussolini's Social Republic. By virtue of his position, Schuster found himself a central mediator between the Germans, the Fascists, the Anglo-Americans, and the forces of the Resistance, represented by the CLNAI (*Comitati della liberazione nazionale, alt'italia*), with its headquarters in Milan. Schuster tried to protect his people from brutal German retaliations and, at the same time, to prevent a popular uprising, which he believed would only benefit the Communists. While his wartime mediations were not particularly successful, there was no doubt about his humanity. Not only did he do everything that he could to relieve suffering during the war, but he also gave the full support of his diocese to protect and rescue Jews fleeing from the German roundup.

After the war, along with Pope **Pius XII,** Schuster was concerned about the danger of Communism in Italy. During the 1948 election campaign, he forbade the sacrament of confession in his diocese to all Communists and other opponents of Catholicism.

Appropriate to his monastic formation, Cardinal Schuster was out of his element in the politics of peacetime. Yet during the Second World War, he demonstrated his humanity and his inner resources in the complex period between 1943 and 1945.

Bibliography. Binchy, D. A. *Church and State in Fascist Italy.* London: Oxford University Press, 1941. Pollard, John F. *The Vatican and Italian Fascism, 1929–32: A Study in Conflict.* Cambridge: Cambridge University Press, 1985. Zuccotti, Susan. *Under His Very Windows: The Vatican and the Holocaust in Italy.* New Haven, CT: Yale University Press, 2000.

Peter C. Kent

SCOTT, SIR RICHARD WILLIAM (1825–1913). Scott is considered the "father of the separate school system of Ontario." In 1857 he was elected a member of the legislative assembly (MLA) for Bytown (now Ottawa), Upper Canada (now Ontario). To this position he brought experience as a lawyer and a former councilor, then mayor for Bytown. Raised as a Catholic in nearby Prescott, he brought to the legislature religious convictions that inspired him to work for a legally secure basis for Roman Catholic separate schools.

Fully state-supported separate schools do not exist in the United States or in many other provinces of Canada. They came into existence in 1841 because of the united legislature of Canada East (now Quebec) and Canada West. Exactly half the members, mostly French Catholic, represented Canada East and advocated state-supported Catholic schools. The attitude of Canada West MLAs to separate school legislation varied from mere toleration to strong opposition. Thus, when Scott arrived in the legislature, separate school boards existed but were burdened by legislative impediments. Scott set about to correct this situation.

In March 1860, he submitted a private member's separate school bill to the legislative assembly. The progress of Scott's bill was slow and contentious. It was late in the session, and his party's leader required him to withdraw the bill. Needing the support of his party members in Canada East, he agreed to let Scott's bill come before the legislature again. In April 1861, Scott reintroduced his bill; it died on the order paper. In April 1862, Scott again brought forward his bill. Encountering prolonged debate and opposition from the Canada West members, the bill could not reach a second reading before the summer recess.

By then there was a high degree of urgency in the minds of Scott and the bishops. Negotiations were ongoing to form a confederation of the provinces to create Canada. Education was to be a provincial matter. Consequently, the Catholics of Upper Canada would no longer have the French Catholic MLAs to support their schools. The following year, 1863, Scott submitted his bill once more. This time it progressed within days to final reading, since the Canada East MLAs dealt with it when, not coincidentally, many of the Upper Canadian members were absent.

In 1867, the British North America Act created the federal government of Canada and the provincial governments. Section 93(1) of the act states, "Nothing in any such [provincial] Law shall prejudicially affect any Right or Privilege with respect to Denominational Schools which any Class of Persons [separate school supporters] have by Law in the Province at the Union." This legislation permanently guaranteed all the separate school rights contained in the Scott Act of 1863. Catholic parents have the right to form a separate school board, elect trustees, build a separate school, collect taxes, and receive a per-pupil government grant equal to that for public schools. Separate school supporters in Ontario owe a great debt to Scott for the financially secure existence and for the constitutional protection of their schools.

Bibliography. Clarke, Brian P. "Scott, Sir Richard William." In *Dictionary of Canadian Biography,* ed. George W. Brown, David M. Hayne, and Frances G. Halpenny. Vol. 8. Toronto: University of Toronto Press, 1976. Power, Michael. *A Promise Fulfilled: Highlights in the Political History of Catholic Separate Schools in Ontario.* Toronto: Ontario Catholic School Trustees' Association, 2002. Walker, Franklin A. *Catholic Education and Politics in Upper Canada.* Toronto: Federation of Catholic Education Association. 1955.

Robert Thomas Dixon

SECRETARIADO SOCIAL MEXICANO. *See* Mexican Social Secretariat

SEGURA Y SÁENZ, PEDRO (1880–1957). Cardinal Segura was archbishop of Toledo, primate of Spain, and president of the Committee of Metropolitans representing the country's archbishops at the time of the Second Republic's proclamation (April 14, 1931).

He had not been an overtly political bishop in his previous appointments as bishop of Coria (1920–1927) and archbishop of Burgos (1927–1928). He was no admirer of the dictatorship of General **Miguel Primo de Rivera** (1923–1930), in spite of the regime's pro-clerical policy. But his attachment to the monarchy, particularly to King Alfonso XIII, to whom he owed his ecclesiastical ascent, and his deep ideological hostility to liberalism and democracy surfaced soon after the republic's establishment. In a narrow sense, he followed the example of his episcopal colleagues by urging the faithful to accept the new regime, although he was among the last to do so. But in a pastoral letter of May 1, 1931, the cardinal went beyond his fellow bishops by praising Alfonso XIII and the monarchy for having been "always respectful of the Church's rights." He also criticized measures already being taken by the provisional republican government to end the church's historic privileges.

The pastoral letter created a storm of controversy. Republican opinion fastened on Segura as a symbol of clerical intransigence. After official pressure was brought to bear on the papal nuncio, the cardinal was forced into exile, although under the cover of a face-saving formula. But his surreptitious return a short time later provoked a tough government response. The cardinal was arrested and again expelled from the country. His return and the frenzied reaction it provoked among republicans came at an inopportune time. They threatened to throw a roadblock into negotiations between the hierarchy, now under the leadership of Cardinal Francisco Vidal y Barraquer, archbishop of Tarragona, and the government for a modus vivendi between church and state. The cabinet, pressured on all sides by its supporters, believed that it could not continue negotiations unless Segura were removed as archbishop of Toledo. Vidal y Barraquer and the Vatican accepted the necessity of Segura's resignation. The reluctant cardinal had no choice but to agree, although his resignation did little to advance the negotiated settlement that the Vatican and the hierarchy had in mind.

Segura spent the next six years in Rome until **Francisco Franco** approved his appointment as archbishop of Seville in 1937. The cardinal proved as much a thorn in the side of the regime as he had been of the republic. Segura sympathized, of course, with a government based on antidemocratic values. But he was a resolute clerical conservative who viewed the totalitarian pretensions of the regime and its quasi-fascist party, the Falange, with the deepest suspicion.

Between 1938 and 1940, he angered the party by refusing to allow fascist symbols to be painted on the exterior walls of churches and irritated the authorities by publishing **Pope Pius XI**'s condemnation of Nazi Germany, *Mit brennender Sorge,* in his diocesan bulletin. Nor did he win friends in Madrid by condemning the suppression of Catholic student associations, which were to be absorbed in a new fascist organization. These were more than pinpricks to official sensibilities. Franco was indignant at his conduct and seriously considered removing him as archbishop, although he did not do so, fearing that an unpleasant comparison would be made between such an action and Segura's expulsion and removal from office under the republic.

Segura continued to vex the regime until his repeated attacks on Protestantism in Spain during the late 1940s and early 1950s became an embarrassment to a government seeking to negotiate a treaty with the United States. The Vatican too had tired of his authoritarian and idiosyncratic ways. Both cooperated in 1954 to remove Segura as effective administrator of the Seville archdiocese through the appointment of a coadjutor archbishop with full powers. Segura had the dubious distinction of being forced out of two archbishoprics by two very different regimes and with the Vatican's cooperation in each case.

Bibliography. Garriga, Ramón. *El Cardenal Segura y el Nacional-Catolicismo.* Barcelona: Editorial Planeta, 1977. Gil Delgado, Francisco. *Pedro Segura: Un cardenal de fronteras.* Madrid: Biblioteca de Autores Cristianos, 2001.

William J. Callahan

SEIPEL, IGNATZ (1876–1932). In the last days of World War I, the Roman Catholic priest Ignatz Seipel served as minister of social affairs in the last Hapsburg cabinet under Heinrich Lammasch. From 1919 to 1920, Seipel was a member of the Constituent National Assembly of the new Austrian Republic, and from 1920 until 1932 he served in the Austrian parliament (Nationalrat). As leader of Austria's **Christian**

Social Party from 1921 to 1929, he became chancellor in 1922. He was hurt seriously by an assassination attempt in 1924 and ended his first period in office that year. He served his second turn as head of the government from 1926 to 1929. Finally, he became Chancellor Karl Vaugoin's secretary of state in 1930.

Ignaz Seipel was born the son of a cabdriver (*Fiaker*) in Vienna. He studied theology at the University of Vienna and was ordained to the priesthood in 1899. He later became a professor of moral theology at the University of Salzburg, transferring to the University of Vienna in 1917. In 1921, Seipel became a prelate. In addition to his political activities, he penned a number of publications.

Seipel's first cabinet, a Christian Socialist and Social Democrat (SDAP) coalition, succeeded in the fight against hyperinflation and in the rehabilitation of the state budget by 1922. The Geneva Protocols secured a League of Nations loan in the amount of 650 million gold crowns for Austria (Economic Reconstruction). The Austrian shilling became the new legal tender, a currency so stable that, up to the German *Anschluss* of 1938, it was known as the "Alpine dollar."

Seipel pushed an antisocialist policy in his second term. He merged the Christian Socialist Landbund and the Pan-Germans in a conservative bloc, the Burgerblock, which, conceived as an anti-Marxist front, would fight social democracy. Toward this end, after 1927 he also supported the right-wing militia, the Heimwehr. Such strategy earned Seipel the epithet "prelate without mercy" on the part of the Social Democrats. In contrast to Socialist and liberal economic systems, Seipel promoted a corporate order, although he never implemented it. He died in Pernitz in Lower Austria.

Bibliography. Birk, Bernhard. *Dr. Ignaz Seipel: Ein Österreichisches und europäisches Schicksal.* Regensburg, Germany: Manz, 1932.

Reimann, Viktor. *Zu gross für Österreich: Seipeil und Bauer im Kampf um die Erste Republik.* Vienna: Molden, 1968. Rennhofer, Friedrich. *Ignaz Seipel: Mensch und Staatsmann. Eine biographische Dokumentation.* Vienna: Bühlau, 1978. Von Klemperer, Klemons. *Ignaz Seipel: Christian Statesman in a Time of Crisis.* Princeton, NJ: Princeton University Press, 1972.

Jürgen Nautz

SEYMOUR, WILLIAM (1870–1922). An African American minister, Seymour provided the symbolic genesis of the U.S. Pentecostal movement when he hosted the Asuza Street Revivals at a storefront church in 1906 Los Angeles. Seymour's advocacy of individual spiritual salvation, a rigid moral code, and the futility of worldly change all became central facets of Pentecostalism.

The son of freed slaves, Seymour was born in Centerville, Louisiana, to a large family. The death of his father left the family in poverty, and Seymour was unable to receive any formal education; instead, he began an itinerant lifestyle in the quest for work and spiritual sustenance. Over a fifteen-year period he lived in Memphis, Indianapolis, Columbus, and Cincinnati, working as a waiter and traveling salesman. In 1900, while in Cincinnati, Seymour came into contact with the Holiness movement. Baptized Catholic, Seymour had attended Baptist and Methodist churches during his travels but found professional inspiration in the experience of sanctification. Proponents of the Holiness revivals advocated sanctification as a second moment of empowerment by the Holy Spirit (following the salvific experience of being born again) necessary to complete for conversion. Seymour embraced this theology and became an itinerant Holiness preacher.

Seymour followed his calling to Houston, Texas, where he became the minister at Evening Light Saints Church.

He attended Charles Parham's Bible Institute in 1905, where he learned of the new movement that centered speaking in tongues as definitive evidence that a believer had received baptism in the Holy Spirit. Seymour did not adopt Parham's Pentecostal theology wholesale, as he held to the importance of sanctification (which Parham did not) and the necessity of ritual enthusiasm (which Parham decried).

Finally, Seymour disagreed with Parham's lenience toward divorce and racial discrimination against nonwhites. Still, Seymour borrowed Parham's Pentecostal vision and transplanted it to a tiny African American Holiness mission in Los Angeles. On April 9, 1906, speaking in tongues overwhelmed the congregants at this Asuza Street mission. Thousands of blacks, whites, Mexicans, and Asian immigrants attended the subsequent revivals held there, which included prayers and hymns alongside the widely reported healings and incidents of speaking in tongues.

By 1909, the Asuza Street Revival waned, and the mission became exclusively black as white Pentecostals formed denominational splinters. The failure of racial integration affirmed Seymour's theological antipathy for social and political change; he, like most Pentecostals, believed there is no reformation save the reformation of the individual spirit. This message, along with the movement that spawned it, continues to this day.

Bibliography. Martin, Larry. *The Life and Ministry of William J. Seymour and a History of the Asuza Street Revival.* Joplin, MO: Christian Life Books, 1999.

Kathryn Lofton

SHARPTON, ALFRED CHARLES, JR. (b. 1954). Through relentless self-promotion and inflammatory protest tactics, Sharpton emerged in the 1980s as an aggressive political voice for urban African Americans. With an emphasis on social equality, judicial reform, and governmen-

tal overhaul, Sharpton pursued several positions of elected office, including a 2004 bid for the presidency.

Born and raised in Brooklyn, New York, Al Sharpton began preaching at the age of four. At nine, he was ordained and licensed as a Pentecostal reverend by the Bishop Frederick Douglass Washington. Although Sharpton would eventually convert to Baptist affiliation, his career as a minister and agitator has been marked by the sermonic flair and millennial ferocity of American Pentecostalism. Indeed, in his youth he was renowned for his fiery exhortations on the reforming power of the Holy Spirit and the revolutionary ideals modeled by Jesus Christ. At the 1964 New York World's Fair, Sharpton was billed as "the Wonder-Boy Preacher." Throughout Sharpton's early years, he lived in middle-class comfort in Queens, New York, touring in the summer as a revival preacher and boycotting cafeteria food during the school term. Following his parents' separation, Sharpton and his mother moved to a housing project. This financial descent encouraged Sharpton's preaching and personal ambition and thrust him into the tutelage of such paternal mentors as Bishop Washington, Democratic congressman (and Harlem Baptist minister) Adam Clayton Powell, and civil rights organizer **Jesse Jackson.** Sharpton's youthful precocity and protest instinct impressed Jackson, who appointed Sharpton as youth director of his Operation Breadbasket, an organization devoted to the distribution of food to underserved communities, in 1969.

While serving at the New York branch of Operation Breadbasket, Sharpton attended two years at Brooklyn College (1973–1975). However, the majority of Sharpton's educational experience came at the foot of his mentors and through his own independent reading of works such as the writings of Protestant theologian **Paul Tillich.** Sharpton had little interest, however, in the abstractions of intellectual discourse, choosing instead to pursue the pragmatic mechanics of promotion, protest, and publicity. In this vein, Sharpton left Brooklyn College to be a tour manager for the soul singer James Brown, a job he held until 1980. Although Sharpton was immersed in the music industry, he remained committed to issues of social justice. In 1971, he founded the National Youth Movement, an organization focused on the reduction of drug usage and creation of positive programming for impoverished youth. Seven years later he ran for a New York State senate spot, initiating his foray into public candidacy.

Not until the 1980s did Sharpton gain national attention as an agitator and key African American leader in New York City. With his jogging suits and straightened hair, Sharpton cut an unusual figure in the political landscape. Whereas his elementary schoolmates once taunted him with the moniker "Booker T. Bellbottoms" for his espousal of nonviolence and integration, Sharpton now pursued equality with an aggressive edge. In 1986, he launched a series of large-scale protests in Howard Beach after a black man was hit and killed by a car while fleeing a white mob. In 1987, Sharpton acted as advisor for Tawana Brawley, a black teenager who claimed she was raped by white police officers before being left to die in a garbage bin. Although her claims were eventually proved to be untrue, Sharpton ardently defended Brawley's accusations. In 1991, Sharpton led marches through Crown Heights, Brooklyn, after a Hasidic Jew killed a young black child in a traffic accident. Throughout these legal quagmires and protest efforts, Sharpton proclaimed himself the primary protector of African American judicial equality. However, in his pursuit of justice, Sharpton frequently fell prey to slander and prejudice, accusing prominent public officials of racism, while frequently deploying anti-Semitic and violent discourse to underscore his deep frustration with white bureaucracy. Sharpton's elaborate protest machine thus provided a mechanism for agitation and irritation that produced the images and sound bites requisite for the multimedia age. In his analysis of Sharpton's tactics, historian Clarence Taylor describes Sharpton as possessing a typical "patriarchal black preacher's style," wherein "what he says is not as important as how he says it" (Taylor, 127).

By the 1990s, Sharpton began to moderate his racial ire and magnify his statesmanship. In 1992 and 1994, he was a candidate for the U.S. Senate from New York, and in 1997 he ran for mayor of New York City. Although he has never won an elected office, his campaigns have provided a critical platform for Sharpton's moral vision and political fervor. A proponent of black capitalism and entrepreneurship, Sharpton has never fit easy political categorization, endorsing Republican senator Alfonse D'Amato in 1986, then campaigning against him in 1992. Critics cite such political waffling, alongside Sharpton's ruthless self-promotion and anti-Semitism, as evidence that he is merely an agitator without consequence. However, to his supporters, Sharpton is a unique voice of genuine outrage, focused on the persistent poverty and disenfranchisement of American minorities. During his campaign for the presidency in 2004, Sharpton spoke consistently and passionately about the need for full employment, adequate housing for the poor, and reform of the criminal justice system in America. In a nation continuing to suffer the effects of deindustrialization and the class striation of racial oppression, Al Sharpton provides an articulate voice of Christian discontent and social revolution.

Bibliography. Bowden, Mark. "Pompadour with a Monkey Wrench." *New Republic,* July–August 2004, 88–106. Taylor, Clarence. "'A Natural Born Leader': The Politics of the Reverend Al Sharpton." *Black Religious Intellectuals: The*

Fight for Equality from Jim Crow to the Twenty-first Century. New York: Routledge, 2002.

Kathryn Lofton

SHELDON, CHARLES MONROE (1857–1946). A popular author and parish pastor, Sheldon championed a conservative strand of social Christianity that stressed the Christian's responsibility in politics and to society but primarily promoted individual compassion and morality, not systemic change. Born in Wellsville, New York, in 1857, the young Sheldon moved frequently until, at age twelve, his family settled in the Dakota Territory, where his father, a Congregational minister seeking a healthier climate, had moved to homestead and do mission work. At twenty, Charles went back east to school, first to Phillips Academy, then Brown University, and finally Andover Theological Seminary. After completing seminary, Sheldon served a church in Waterbury, Vermont, for a year and then became pastor of Central Church, a Congregational church in Topeka, Kansas, where he remained, with a brief interruption, until he retired in 1919. As pastor there, Sheldon balanced pastoral ministry, social research and reform, and writing.

He published hundreds of articles, poems, and hymns and more than fifty books, some first tried out on his congregation. One series of talks became *In His Steps* (published in 1896), which sold millions, perhaps tens of millions, of copies. The story of a congregation that pledged always to ask "What would Jesus do?" the novel at once revealed middle-class fears of the modern city and promoted a middle-class activism, rooted in a traditional Christian faith, that combined concern for workers and slum dwellers with a call for personal morality, especially temperance. The book reflected both Sheldon's commitment to the Christian's responsibility to society and the vagueness of his definition of that involvement.

He himself rarely endorsed systemic change and instead urged individual compassion and morality. He found partisan politics distasteful, although he did campaign for William Allen White for governor in 1924 after he took a stand against the **Ku Klux Klan.** Sheldon also served briefly as police commissioner in Topeka and on a commission to study Kansas's penitentiary, but his major foray into politics came in the campaign for prohibition. He spoke in favor of it in England and the United States, perhaps most importantly as part of the so-called Flying Squadron, touring the country in the final battle for the Eighteenth Amendment.

Sheldon retired from Central Church for good in 1919 but continued to write. He took no part in the fundamentalist-modernist controversy of the 1920s and expected it would soon be forgotten. Throughout his career he expressed little interest in theological discussions. Sheldon defined his own understanding of the faith in very simple terms: "Love to God and man." Sheldon died in 1946 and is best known for *In His Steps,* which remains in print and popular among Christian conservatives.

Bibliography. Miller, Timothy. *Following In His Steps: A Biography of Charles M. Sheldon.* Knoxville: University of Tennessee Press, 1987

Gaines M. Foster

SHENOUDA III [NAZEER GAYED] (b. 1923). Since becoming patriarch in 1971, Shenouda has made growth and ecumenical outreach the focal point of his leadership of the Coptic Orthodox Church, the largest Christian denomination in the Middle East, numbering between five and a half to six million followers. Born Nazeer Gayed in Asiut (Upper Egypt), he completed his studies at the University of Cairo and at the Coptic Theological Seminary. Following a period of monastic life in a monastery in the western desert of Egypt (1956–1962), he was ordained bishop and took the name of Bishop Shenouda.

In November 1971, Pope Shenouda III was installed as the 117th pope of Alexandria and patriarch of the See of Saint Mark. Given the sometimes-precarious status of the Coptic Christian community in Egypt, Shenouda focused on the survival of his community. Sometimes this led to a clash with Egyptian authorities. Under President Sadat, following acts of vandalism by Islamist radical groups against Coptic businesses and churches, Shenouda protested and Sadat exiled him. Sadat´s successor, Hosni Mubarak, decreed the return of Pope Shenouda after forty months away from his community.

Shenouda has strived to foster better relations between Muslims and Christians in Egypt. Pope Shenouda was very instrumental in expanding his church's presence worldwide, especially in countries that have large Coptic diaspora communities (Canada, the United States, and Australia). Shenouda was also very committed to ecumenical relationships with other Oriental Orthodox churches and Protestant denominations. In May 1973, he visited Pope **Paul VI** in Rome.

Under his patriarchate, the Coptic Orthodox Church has become a full member of the World Council of Churches, the Middle East Council of Churches, the National Council of Churches in Christ in the United States, the Canadian Council of Churches, and the Australian Council of Churches. In May 2000 he established the first ecumenical office in the Coptic Orthodox Archdiocese of North America. He is the author of more than one hundred books.

Bibliography. Betts, Robert B. *Christians in the Arab East: A Political Study.* Atlanta, GA: John Knox Press, 1978. Horner, Norman A. *A Guide to Christian Churches in the Middle East.* Elkhart, IN: Mennonite Board of Missions, 1989.

George Emile Irani

SHEPTYTSKY, ANDREI (1865–1944). Sheptytsky was a Greek Catholic metropolitan archbishop whose tenure in western Ukraine spanned numerous political contexts—Austria-Hungary, Russian occupation during World War I, interwar Poland, and World War II occupations by the USSR and Nazi Germany. An outstanding church leader for forty-five years, Sheptytsky shunned partisan politics but promoted human and cultural rights on local and international stages.

With a Polish Roman Catholic upbringing, Sheptytsky completed studies in law before undertaking theological and priestly formation as a Basilian monk in the Eastern rite, Ukrainian tradition of his paternal ancestors. Ordained in 1892, he proved a talented teacher, novice master, and editor. Consecrated bishop in 1899, the following year he took the helm of the Greek Catholic Church as metropolitan archbishop.

As a bishop in Catholic Austria, Sheptytsky served in both the local parliament of Galicia and in the House of Lords in Vienna. He advocated cultural and educational rights, pushing for a more equitable electoral law and the creation of a Ukrainian university. But when Ukrainian frustrations with Polish dominance led to the assassination of Polish viceroy Andrzej Potocki in 1908, Sheptytsky condemned the act and its popularization.

Following the Russian occupation of Galicia (1914), Sheptytsky was arrested and exiled after he referred in a sermon to the Russian Orthodox Church as a "state church." Although he had previously faced ambivalence and even opposition from Ukrainian society, on his return from exile in 1917 Sheptytsky was given a hero's welcome, which defined his social authority for the remainder of his life.

At the war's end, Sheptytsky faced especially complex challenges. Arrested and interned by a Polish government cognizant of his support for Ukrainian independence and doubtful of his loyalty, he promised not to fan anger over the decision of the Council of Ambassadors (Paris, 1923), which turned

Ukrainian territories over to Poland. Sheptytsky protested, however, when the Warsaw government enacted policies viewed as threats to Ukrainian culture and rights—enforcement of the Polish language and the suppression of Ukrainian, discrimination in schools, violent "pacification" (1930), and the destruction of Orthodox churches (1938). He likewise condemned violence as contrary to Christianity, whether it was nationalist terror against the Polish state, or Stalinist genocidal famine in Soviet Ukraine (1932–1933).

In the autumn of 1939, the Soviets invaded western Ukraine and began a twenty-two month occupation. Official atheism threatened the life of the church to the core. Despite the beginnings of religious persecution, the metropolitan held fast to a strong prophetic witness for the Christian community under adversity.

Sheptytsky shared the initial optimism— the Soviet rout was seen as a godsend, and Ukrainian autonomy was anxiously awaited. But soon the contrary intentions of German rule became clear. Sheptytsky deplored the political reality and condemned the moral chaos of genocide. He saved Jews and assisted escapes through a network of monasteries. The scholarly study of Sheptytsky and his political activity has benefited from access to post-Soviet archives. Soviet and other critiques are giving way to sound documentation and to a more complete historical record.

Nazi Germany's invasion in the summer of 1941 initiated a three-year occupation.
Bibliography. Krawchuk, Andrii. *Christian Social Ethics in Ukraine: The Legacy of Andrei Sheptytsky.* Edmonton-Ottawa-Toronto: Canadian Institute of Ukrainian Studies Press, 1997.
Andrii Krawchuk

SILVA HENRIQUEZ, RAÚL (1907–1999).
A Chilean human rights campaigner, Silva Henriquez was born in Talca and ordained a priest of the Catholic Church's Salesian order in 1938. He became a bishop of Valparaiso in 1959, and a cardinal in 1962, and was the archbishop of Santiago from 1961 until 1983. Silva Henriquez shaped Chilean national life in key periods of transition and crisis from Christian Democratic over Socialist leadership to the Pinochet dictatorship. Since his death in 1999, he has been best remembered for his moral courage and unwavering opposition to the unprecedented violence institutionalized by the military regime that seized power in 1973.

Silva Henriquez's activist position for human rights was inspired by the progressive Vatican II church program set in motion under Pope **John XXIII** in the 1960s. It outlined the church's responsibility to promote social advancement for the poor, landless, and underprivileged. Accordingly, Silva Henriquez advocated land reforms, supported unions, and promoted decent housing in poor areas. His lasting contributions to human rights in Chile were most pronounced in his work as archbishop of Santiago, when he founded and directed the Vicariate of Solidarity, an institution to defend the rights of thousands of persecuted Chileans who were tortured or "disappeared" during the years of military dictatorship.

In the aftermath of the 1973 military coup, the Santiago Archbishop first helped create the multidenominational Peace Committee, aimed at protecting human rights and aiding individuals seeking asylum from Augusto Pinochet's military regime. When pressured by Pinochet to terminate the Peace Committee in 1974, Silva Henriquez acquiesced but transformed it into an official part of the Catholic Church, the Vicariate of Solidarity. Throughout the course of the seventeen-year dictatorship he appealed to the armed forces for restraint based on the church's belief in the sanctity of human life. With the vicariate, he took an active role in providing moral opposition and a protective umbrella for organized resistance groups.

The collected testimonials in the vicariate's archive became key data to document and prosecute human rights abuses.

In the 1980s, when the regime could no longer suppress public protests, Silva Henriquez joined the opposition in its call for an end to violence and a return to constitutionality. His progressive leadership shaped the way in which the Chilean Catholic Church contributed to the transition to democracy after the dictatorship was voted out of office in 1988. The church hierarchy's progressivism, led by Silva Henriquez, helped strengthen the Chilean church's national influence and the scope of its authority in contemporary Chile.

Bibliography. Smith, Brian H. *The Church and Politics in Chile: Challenges to Modern Catholicism.* Princeton, NJ: Princeton University Press, 1982.

Jadwiga E. Pieper Mooney

SIN, JAIME (1928–2005). In 1974, Sin was appointed archbishop of Manila, the largest archdiocese in the Philippines, and in 1976, he was elevated to the College of Cardinals by Pope **Paul VI.** Considered a moderate within the Philippine Catholic hierarchy, Cardinal Sin enunciated a policy of "critical collaboration" toward the martial law regime of President Ferdinand E. Marcos, signaling he would cooperate with the government where possible but reserved the right to criticize. As reports of government and military abuses increased during martial law (1972–1981), Cardinal Sin's comments about Marcos and the regime became increasingly trenchant, particularly after the 1983 assassination of Benigno Aquino, Jr., Marcos's chief political rival.

In 1986, Cardinal Sin became internationally prominent for opposing Marcos's attempt to manipulate his reelection as president and for calling on Filipinos in greater Manila to surround two military bases along Epifanio de los Santos Boulevard (EDSA) in support of a military revolt against Marcos by his minister of defense, Juan Ponce Enrile, and vice

Cardinal Jaime Sin ordains three priests in the Santa Cruz Church, Manila, 1995. © Abbas / Magnum Photos

chief of staff, Fidel V. Ramos (president, 1992–1998). Thousands of citizens responded to Sin's call, forcing Marcos into exile in Hawaii, where he died in 1989. Benigno Aquino's widow, **Corazon Aquino,** was inaugurated president (1986–1992).

From the ouster of Marcos to the end of his life, despite reports that the Vatican ordered him in 1986 to decrease his political involvements, Cardinal Sin maintained a high profile in Philippine politics. He remained close to Aquino throughout her presidency and in 1990 characterized his relationship with the Aquino government as one of "Critical Solidarity." In contrast to his support of Aquino, he not only opposed the election of Fidel Ramos, a Protestant, as president, but also clashed with Ramos on government family planning policy and on proposals to amend the 1987 constitution. Cardinal Sin also opposed the election of Joseph E. Estrada as president (1998–2001) and in October 2000 called for Estrada's resignation, saying he had "lost the moral ascendancy to govern" after accusations surfaced that the president had received more than $11 million in illegal gambling payoffs. Just as with President Aquino, Cardinal Sin supported the presidency of Gloria Macapagal-Arroyo (2001–) and called on Filipinos to protect the "president and the legitimate government" in response to a mutiny of a small group of officers and soldiers in July 2003.

Cardinal Sin has been at the forefront of Catholic Church officials speaking out against graft and corruption in Philippine politics, supporting groups engaged in election education and reform, and challenging the electorate to vote on the basis of issues. Upon turning seventy-five on August 31, 2003, Cardinal Sin tendered his resignation as archbishop of Manila.

Bibliography. Bautista, Felix B. *Cardinal Sin and the Miracle of Asia.* Manila, Philippines: Vera-Reyes, 1987. Felipe, Virgilio T.J. Suerte. *Cardinal Sin and the February Revolution.* Manila, Philippines: TJ Publications, 1987.

Robert L. Youngblood

SINN FEIN (IRELAND). Sinn Fein, which means "Ourselves Alone," was originally founded in 1905 by an Irish Catholic journalist named Arthur Griffith. Like all radical Irish nationalist groups, it was Catholic in culture. Griffith was a constitutionalist who argued for MPs to abstain from Parliament in support of Irish economic self-reliance, and as a nonviolent response to British rule. This last form of protest was not for religious or ethical reasons, but because it would give them a practical and political advantage in their fight against British rule

The Sinn Fein Party in Northern Ireland is called Provisional Sinn Fein and is the fourth party to bear this name since 1905. The Sinn Fein Party founded by Griffith was given credit by the British for the 1916 Easter Rising. It was reconstituted in 1917 as the Second Sinn Fein Party. While it remained an abstentionist party, it accepted the use of force and was linked from this point onwards with the Irish Volunteers, or the Irish Republican Army (IRA). The party split in 1922 over the treaty with the British, and a rump survived in the period after a further split in 1926. The party after this date found its major support among a few surviving intractable nationalists committed to a republic.

The term "nationalist" in Ireland from the late nineteenth century is linked to Catholicism. Since 1922 it has been more specifically associated with the minority Catholic population in Northern Ireland. When the Catholic civil rights movement in Northern Ireland led to violence, the IRA and Sinn Fein emerged as radical supporters of the Catholic or nationalist population.

The party's strength among the Catholic population remained low in the 1970s but gained momentum in the aftermath of a series of hunger strikes by IRA prisoners, which resulted in ten deaths. One of the

Sinn Fein leader, Gerry Adams attends Mass in the cemetery on the Day of the Assumption (August 15), Tory Island. © Martine Franck / Magnum Photos

hunger strikers, **Bobby Sands,** was elected to the British parliament before his death in 1981. Sinn Fein candidates since then have been elected to the British parliament (they abstained from taking their seats), to local councils, and to the Northern Ireland Assembly, in Stormont. They did take part in these latter groups and have been seen as effective community leaders.

In the 2003 elections to the Northern Ireland Assembly, they emerged as the largest political party on the nationalist/ Catholic side. It is difficult to define Sinn Fein as a Catholic political party in terms of adherence to a platform of Catholic moral values. At the same time there have been links between Sinn Fein and individual members of the clergy, but this has been more often linked to the commitment by individual members of the clergy to Irish nationalism and unification of the island under one republican government than to clerical control.

On what type of government they would support and what its relationship would be to Catholic moral values if unification did occur, the party's platform is vague. The party and its supporters are often more cultural than spiritual Catholics even if they make extensive use of Catholic symbolism. For example the IRA/Sinn Fein prisoners in the British prisons in Northern Ireland would collectively say the Rosary, but in Gaelic.

Bibliography. Coogan, T. P. *Ireland in the Twentieth Century.* London: Hutchinson, 2003. Feeney, Brian. *Sinn Fein: A Hundred Turbulent Years.* Madison: University of Wisconsin Press, 2003. O'Brien, Brendan. *The Long War: The Ira and Sinn Fein.* 2nd ed. New York: Syracuse University Press, 1999.

Gretchen M. MacMillan

SMITH, ALFRED EMANUEL, JR. (1873– 1944). Smith was one of the most popular and successful political leaders of the early twentieth century. As a lifelong member of the Democratic Party, he served in the New York State Assembly from 1904 to 1915, and as governor of New York from 1919 to 1921, and again, from 1923 to 1929. He also ran for the Democratic nomination for the presidency in 1924, 1928, and 1932 and won his party's endorsement in 1928.

This 1928 campaign against Republican Herbert Hoover is one of the most controversial and important events in American history, because it best exemplifies the influence of religion on voting behavior. Millions of Americans voted for Smith because he was Roman Catholic, while millions more voted against him because of his faith. Smith has come to symbolize the dangers of religious bigotry and intolerance in American society. His political career also marked the emergence of the "new immigrant" groups of the late nineteenth century—mostly Catholic, Orthodox, or Jewish in religion—into prominence in American politics. Throughout his life, Smith was renowned as an advocate for non-Protestant America and immigrants in general, and also for his religious tolerance.

Smith was born in the Fourth Ward of New York City, known as the Bowery, an impoverished area where more than one-half of the people were foreign born. He was of mixed Italian-German-Irish ancestry but identified thoroughly with his Irish Catholic heritage because of the influence of his pious mother. As a state assemblyman and governor, Smith supported Progressive causes, such as legislation to protect the health and safety of factory workers, which reflected his belief in Catholic social teachings. Pope **Leo XII** had revolutionized Catholic political doctrine in his 1891 encyclical, *Rerum novarum,* calling for Catholics to use government to mitigate the harsh features of industrial capitalism. Although Smith was never well versed in theology, he was a devout Catholic who followed the moral teachings of his church with exemplary rigor.

Smith's 1928 campaign for the presidency ended in disastrous defeat for the Democratic Party. Smith had secured the nomination because of his charismatic personality, his knowledge of public issues, and his demonstrated administrative skills as governor. Democrats had severely underestimated, however, the obstacles that would face the first Roman Catholic nominee of a major political party. Throughout the campaign, Smith faced a barrage of anti-Catholic attacks. This rhetoric has led historians to conclude that opposition to a Catholic president was the primary cause of Smith's defeat. Statistical analysis of voting returns tends to reinforce this evaluation. Protestant opposition to Smith was especially pronounced among Methodists, Southern Baptists, and the Disciples of Christ. The arguments against a Catholic president had existed at least since the mid-nineteenth century and ranged from sophisticated political reasoning to shameless propaganda and hysteria. Many Americans feared that the authoritarian and hierarchical nature of the Catholic Church would undermine democracy and legal equality in the United States. Others believed that the papacy would exercise an inappropriate influence over policy if Smith were president. Traditional emotional arguments included inciting fear and suspicion of allegedly corrupt and immoral Catholic clergy and the belief that Smith and the papacy intended to outlaw public education in America. Many Protestants opposed Smith not because he was Catholic, but because he was opposed to the prohibition of alcohol. Many Americans considered the outlawing of alcohol to be the moral foundation of society during the 1920s. Smith's candidacy drew hundreds of thousands of Catholic, Orthodox, and Jewish Americans into the Democratic Party and helped prepare the way for the election of Franklin D. Roosevelt in 1932. These Americans accepted Smith as a defender of moral government, religious toleration, and immigrant cultures.

Bibliography. Finan, Christopher M. *Alfred E. Smith: The Happy Warrior.* New York: Hill & Wang, 2002. Slayton, Robert A. *Empire Statesman: The Rise and Redemption of Al Smith.* New York: Free Press, 2001.

Michael S. Fitzgerald

SMITH, FRANK (1854–1940). Smith was one of the founders of the British Labour Party, a pioneer in the Christian settlement movement, and an early leader of the **Salvation Army.** Sometimes called the "St. Francis of the labor movement," he was unique among his peers in the depth of his mystical affirmation of human fellowship as the only proper basis for social life and organization.

Born in 1854, privately educated, and comfortably middle class, Smith had been managing his own furniture-making company when through the Chelsea Mission he came into contact with the emerging Salvation Army. Within years, he was commissioner in charge of all Salvation Army operations in the United States, and upon his return to Britain it was he who suggested that henceforth the organization combine evangelism with social relief work. The result, of which Smith was named the first leader, was the Social Wing of the Salvation Army. Under its auspices, Smith helped **William Booth** write the influential expose of Victorian inner-city squalor, *In Darkest England and the Way Out* (1890), and he drafted a Salvation Army program for systematic social improvement through such innovations as organized labor exchanges, food distribution networks, cooperative workshops and farms, and colonial emigration schemes. Feeling constrained in implementing this program and increasingly attracted to the secular labor movement, Smith decided in 1890 to leave the Salvation Army and enter politics.

Smith was a founding member of the Independent Labour Party in 1893 and an early Fabian Society activist. He contested twelve parliamentary seats for Labour before being elected MP in 1929. By that time, he had already made his mark as a leader in the municipal Labour party in London, having served on the London County Council for much of the period 1892–1913 and having helped to make Labour the council's predominating power for decades to come.

An early supporter of parliamentary socialism, throughout his career Smith sought to dispel the popular perception of the socialist movement as irreligious in nature. As a keen spiritualist, an experimenter in a range of psychic phenomena, and a critic of formal theology and church hierarchy, Smith was convinced that the divinity was inwardly present in every person, no matter what his or her religion, and that spiritual growth was but the actualization of this inner divinity through ethical social action. In all his activities and especially through his lay preaching for the Brotherhood Movement, Smith witnessed to this vision, which, in his view, was exemplified also in the Labour party's political program.

Smith died in 1940 without leaving a legacy of legislation or a body of systematic political writings. His unique contribution was his exceptionally deep mystical religious witness to social cooperation, which underlined the central role that ethical religious concepts played in the working-class politics of late nineteenth- and early twentieth-century Britain.

Bibliography. Bellamy, Joyce M., and John Saville, eds. *Dictionary of Labour Biography.* Vol. 9. London: Macmillan, 1993. Champness, E. I. *Frank Smith, MP: Pioneer and Modern Mystic.* London: Whitefriars Press, 1943.

Markku Ruotsila

SMITH, GERALD LYMAN KENNETH (1898–1976). Smith, one of America's most popular racist and anti-Semitic speakers from the 1930s to the mid-1970s, was born in Pardeeville, Wisconsin, the son of a fundamentalist Protestant minister. Smith first attended a one-room schoolhouse. That sentimental image, coupled with his simple and austere Christian faith, remained with Smith. He demonstrated an inexhaustible industriousness, working his way through Valparaiso University in two and a half years. He began preaching to tiny fundamentalist congregations while still a college student. After graduating in 1918 he quickly ascended to larger and larger pulpits in Indiana.

While present during the **Ku Klux Klan**'s control of the Hoosier state, Smith apparently never joined the hooded order. In these early years Smith embodied the fundamentalist Protestant wariness of the political order's worldliness. Smith instead focused his energy on strengthening weak churches by increasing membership and raising money. Still, Smith's political career grew out of his ministerial activities.

Called in 1929 by a church in Shreveport, Louisiana, Smith soon met the state's mercurial populist governor and U.S. senator, Huey P. Long. The governor enchanted Smith, and he quickly exchanged the ministry for politics. Long hired Smith to advance his so-called Share the Wealth program. Smith spoke enthusiastically across the state, comparing Long to Jesus. Long's assassination in 1935 left Smith emotionally devastated and unemployed. He hoped to inherit Long's legacy by garnering Dr. Francis Townsend's popular Old Age Revolving Pensions plan. Smith also connected with Fr. **Charles Coughlin,** the nationally known Catholic "radio priest." Smith, Townsend, and Coughlin realized their shared antipathy toward the New Deal. They formed a hastily conceived third-party presidential campaign in 1936. Coughlin provided the most followers but as a priest could not run for office. William Lemke, a Catholic congressman from North Dakota, was chosen to represent the National Union Party. Nevertheless,

Smith remained the star attraction at political rallies. He regularly spoke for hours, until he was hoarse and drenched with sweat. Smith tirelessly insisted that working Americans, much like Jesus, had been betrayed by money and special interests. Feeling upstaged, Coughlin occasionally tried to compete but only emphasized Smith's superior showmanship. The actual candidate, Lemke, exhibited the poorest oratorical skills, and Smith himself often ridiculed Lemke's disheveled appearance. The National Union ticket received fewer than a million votes nationwide as Roosevelt claimed his second term.

After the election Smith broke with Coughlin and began an independent speaking tour to stir up his national following. Despite traveling day and night to crisscross the country, Smith failed to turn his large and raucous audiences into a cohesive movement. He fared better in 1942, when he made a concerted run for Michigan's open U.S. Senate seat. In the wake of that electoral defeat, Smith openly blamed Jewish conspirators. He soon cast Jews and African Americans (whose pursuit of integration Jews had instigated) as the greatest threat to the American nation. The Red menace that occupied so many other Americans, Smith felt, was a façade for Jewish subterfuge. He asserted (falsely) that a Jew had assassinated Huey Long, and he blamed the New Deal's failures on Jewish business interests. In 1946, Smith founded the Christian Nationalist Crusade in St. Louis to defend the nation from this subversion. Smith toured relentlessly to garner support from veterans, Protestant Christians, and rural and suburban Americans. His publication, *The Cross and the Flag,* carried the same message. Smith moved around between Southern California and Tulsa, Oklahoma, during the 1950s. He viewed the civil rights movement as further Jewish meddling with white Christian America. Smith's emphasis on Christian nationalism inspired several leaders of Christian Identity, such as Wesley Swift, who claimed that white Euro-Americans were the true descendents of biblical Israel. Smith's spiritual primitivism had no room for even that sort of theological innovation. He instead insisted on a marriage of simple biblical faith and feverish patriotic nationalism.

Attempting to withdraw completely from an integrating nation, Smith moved to Eureka Springs, Arkansas, in 1964. He contributed to the revitalization of the Ozark resort town by developing several "Sacred Projects." In 1966 he dedicated the Christ of the Ozarks, a seventy-foot-tall white statue of Jesus. Set in cruciform shape atop a mountain overlooking Eureka Springs, the statue's face resembled Smith himself. In 1968 he debuted *The Passion Play*, a summertime outdoor theater production, which, not surprisingly, laid the blame for Jesus's crucifixion squarely on Jewish shoulders. The pageant became the nation's largest outdoor theater event. Other projects included a "Christ Only" art museum and a Bible museum. These projects did not bear the baldly racist and anti-Semitic sentiments of his earlier career. Nonetheless Smith never backed away from those beliefs. His mercurial career of linking bigotry and Christianity ended in relative quiet with his death in 1976.

Bibliography. Brinkley, Alan. *Voices of Protest: Huey Long, Father Coughlin, and the Great Depression.* New York: Alfred A. Knopf, 1982. Jeansonne, Glen. *Gerald L. K. Smith: Minister of Hate.* 1988. Baton Rouge: Louisiana State University Press, 1997. Ribuffo, Leo. *The Old Christian Right: The Protestant Far Right from the Great Depression to the Cold War.* Philadelphia: Temple University Press, 1983.

Jeffrey Marlett

SMITH, GERRIT (1797–1874). Among the most renowned abolitionists and philanthropists of the nineteenth century,

Smith devoted his life and most of his great wealth to the cause of equal rights for all men and women. From 1838 until the Civil War, he passionately pursued the immediate abolition of every sin. To this end, Smith (along with close friend John Brown) was virtually unique among white reformers in his efforts to destroy class and racial barriers and to identify with blacks. Only after his participation in **John Brown**'s Harpers Ferry raid in 1859 did Smith retreat to more conservative reform measures.

Born into wealth in Utica, New York, Smith moved in 1806 with his parents, Peter and Elizabeth Livingston Smith, to Peterboro, a village they founded in Madison County. Growing up in a region powerfully shaped by the evangelical fervor of the Second Great Awakening, young patriarch Smith aspired to professional training until the death of his young wife and parents left him burdened with family business responsibilities in Peterboro.

In 1823 he married Ann Carroll Fitzhugh Smith, a cousin of George Fitzhugh and a fervent evangelical. She fueled her husband's religious zeal and helped spawn his vision of a broad sacralization of the world. He soon became an avid temperance reformer, and in 1827 he joined the American Colonization Society, whose efforts to colonize blacks in Africa represented for him the most effective way to achieve social justice. His abandonment of colonization for immediate abolition in 1837, however, reflected a fundamental shift in his values. He became a self-described "outsider" and "fanatic," affirming his spiritual instincts and passions of the "heart." His belief in the colonization movement's hierarchical social principles crumbled in the face of financial hardship during the Panic of 1837, the deaths of two children, and his growing reliance on "sacred self-sovereignty."

Smith's religious vision defined the Golden Rule as empathy, and he continually sought to identify with the black struggle. "To recognize in every man my brother— ay, another self" was his wish, and he often described his efforts "to make myself a colored man." He helped turn Madison County into the most fervent abolition county in the country, with Peterboro becoming a model of interracial harmony. In 1846, he gave to each of some three thousand poor New York blacks roughly fifty acres of land in the Adirondacks as a path to political power, economic self-sufficiency, and triumph over racism. He befriended black leaders throughout the North, and one black abolition paper even called Smith a "colored man."

Smith, together with New York's black leaders, lost faith in peaceful abolition schemes in light of the Fugitive Slave Act of 1850. Smith helped found the Liberty Party in 1840, which interpreted the Constitution as an antislavery document, and in 1852 he was elected to Congress on an abolition platform. Following passage of the Kansas-Nebraska Act in 1854, however, Smith resigned his House seat and became a revolutionary. He began to see himself as a prophet and accepted blood atonement as a necessary means for vanquishing the forces of evil. He donated over $16,000 to support antislavery emigrants to Kansas and became a lead conspirator in John Brown's 1859 attack on the Harpers Ferry arsenal.

Smith's guilt over lives lost at Harpers Ferry led to a brief emotional collapse. Recovery in 1860 led to a profound transformation as he rejected his identification with blacks as a misguided "black dream," a dark path leading to violence. His short story "The Ruinous Visit to Monkeyville" confirmed Smith's disillusionment with radicalism and a retreat to moderate reform.

Although nominated for president on a Radical Abolition ticket in 1860, Smith supported **Abraham Lincoln** and believed that a lower tariff and compensated emancipation might restore the Union without bloodshed. The war, however, convinced Smith that Confederacy and slavery had to be ruthlessly crushed. Through his support of Lincoln and his financial commitment to the war effort and relief Smith shed his radical image and elevated his public standing.

Although Smith supported black participation in the war as a pragmatic measure and continued to press for equal rights, he had also become convinced that blacks were an inferior race with dark and violent propensities who must be convinced to colonize outside the United States. During Reconstruction, he adopted moderation and urged leniency toward Confederate leaders.

Not surprisingly, Smith's declension from his perfectionist vision and close identification with blacks in the 1840s and 1850s earned harsh criticism from black leaders. Still, his early defense of equal rights prompted Henry Highland Garnet to call Smith perhaps "the most affectionately remembered and loved" of the early abolitionist leaders.

Bibliography. Harlow, Ralph Volney. *Gerrit Smith: Philanthropist and Reformer.* New York: Henry Holt, 1939. Stauffer, John. *The Black Hearts of Men: Radical Abolitionists and the Transformation of Race.* Cambridge, MA: Harvard University Press, 2002.

John Stauffer

SMITH, HANNAH WHITALL (1832–1911). Religious author, lay preacher, and social reformer, Smith was known during her lifetime as a Bible teacher and author of more than twenty books and pamphlets about the Christian life. Several of her works have remained in print and are widely available, most notably *The Christian's Secret of a Happy Life* (1875). In the mid-1870s, Smith joined the Woman's Christian Temperance Union (WCTU), continuing her religious work under its auspices. In the mid-1870s, Smith met **Frances Willard,** future president of the **Woman's Christian Temperance Union** (WCTU), and they formed a life-long friendship. Shortly thereafter, Smith became an officer in the national WCTU. After she moved to England in 1888, she held several positions in the British Women's Temperance Association (BWTA). Drawn into women's rights through her involvement in the temperance movement, Smith began speaking for women's suffrage in 1881.

Born a birthright Quaker in Philadelphia, Pennsylvania, Smith was deeply influenced by the Society of Friends, although she was estranged from the faith for decades. Her parents, John Mickle Whitall and Mary Tatum Whitall, could trace their Quaker heritage back to colonial America. Hannah Whitall attended a Quaker girls' school in Philadelphia until 1849, and, in November 1851, she married Robert Pearsall Smith, another birthright Quaker. Together the couple had seven children, but only Mary (1864–1945), Lloyd Logan (1865–1946), and Alice (Alys) (1867–1951) survived to adulthood.

Influenced by internal conflict in the Society of Friends and the Revival of 1857–1858, Smith left the Quakers in 1859. After she moved to Millville, New Jersey, in 1864, Smith attended Methodist prayer meetings and was instantly attracted to their teachings. She was drawn to the 1860s Holiness movement and became a Bible teacher at prayer and camp meetings. In 1874, Robert Pearsall Smith organized a number of Holiness camp meetings in England, where Hannah led popular Bible readings. Plain spoken and witty, Smith drew large audiences. She wrote as well as she spoke, and two books written in the mid-1870s established her reputation as a Christian author. *Frank: The Record of a Happy Life* (1873), described how her son Frank met the challenges to a modern boy's Christian development before his death at age seventeen. *The Christian's Secret of a Happy Life* (1875) was a collection of articles written

for her husband's *The Christian's Pathway of Power* (1873–1875).

Hannah Whitall Smith's social reform activities began in the 1870s and continued in the United States and England until the end of the nineteenth century, when she retired from public life. In 1886, Smith reconciled with the Society of Friends and joined the Baltimore Yearly Meeting. She continued writing into her seventies and died in England in 1911.

Bibliography. Meneghel, Meg A. "Becoming a 'Heretic': Hannah Whitall Smith, Quakerism, and the Nineteenth-Century Holiness Movement." PhD diss., Indiana University, Bloomington, 2000. Strachey, Barbara [Barbara Strachey Halpern]. *Remarkable Relations: The Story of the Pearsall Smith Women.* London: Gollancz, 1980.

Meg Meneghel MacDonald

SMITH, JAMES MCCUNE (1813–1865). Smith, a black abolitionist and physician, was born the son of slaves in New York City. All that is known of his parents is that his mother was, in his words, "a self-emancipated bond-woman." His own liberty came on July 4, 1827, when the Emancipation Act of the state of New York officially freed its remaining slaves.

Smith graduated with honors from the African Free School, but his race prevented admission to Columbia College and Geneva, New York, medical schools. With assistance from the black minister Peter Williams, Jr., he entered the University of Glasgow, Scotland in 1832, returning to America in 1837 as the first professionally trained black physician in the country. He set up practice in Manhattan as a surgeon and general practitioner for both blacks and whites and became the staff physician for the New York Colored Orphan Asylum.

It was as a radical abolitionist and reformer, however, that Smith built his national reputation. While **William Lloyd Garrison** and the American Anti-Slavery Society sought to convince slaveholders to renounce the sin of slavery and emancipate their slaves, Smith moved gradually toward political abolitionism and ultimately supported violent intervention to end slavery. He affiliated with the Liberty Party in the late 1840s, and when its successor, the Radical Abolition Party, nominated him for New York secretary of state in 1857, he became the first African American in the country to run for a political office.

The driving force behind Smith's reform vision and sustained hope for equality was his supreme "confidence in God, that firm reliance in the saving power of the Redeemer's Love." Much like other radical **abolitionists** such as **Frederick Douglass** and **Gerrit Smith,** he viewed the abolition movement and the Civil War in millennialist terms; slavery and black oppression were the most egregious of a plethora of sins ranging from tobacco and alcohol to apathy and laziness that needed to be abolished in order to pave the way for a sacred society governed by "Bible Politics," as he envisioned God's eventual reign on earth. He strove to follow his savior's example by embracing the doctrine of "equal love to all mankind" and at the same time remaining humble before him. He likened himself to "a coral insect . . . loving to work beneath the tide in a superstructure, that some day when the labourer is long dead and forgotten, may rear itself above the waves and afford rest and habitation for the creatures of his Good, Good Father of All."

Smith's writing gave force and direction to the black abolitionist movement. He contributed frequently to the *Weekly Anglo-African* and the *Anglo African Magazine,* as well as *Frederick Douglass' Paper* under the pseudonym "Communipaw," an Indian name that referred to a charmed and honored settlement in Jersey City, New Jersey, where blacks had played an important historic role. He also wrote the introduction to Douglass's 1855 autobiography, *My Bondage and My Freedom.* Douglass considered Smith the "foremost" black leader who had influenced his reform vision.

Smith sought black liberation primarily through education, self-help, citizenship, and active resistance to racism. He opposed white attempts to colonize blacks in Liberia and elsewhere and criticized black nationalists who encouraged emigration to Haiti and West Africa rather than continuing to fight for citizenship and equal rights. He defended integration but also encouraged blacks to establish their own presses, initiatives, and organizations. "It is emphatically our battle," he wrote in 1855. "Others may aid and assist if they will, but the moving power rests with us."

His embrace of black self-reliance in the late 1840s paralleled his departure from Garrisonian doctrines and the American Anti-Slavery Society, which largely ignored black oppression in the North—even among abolitionists—by focusing on the evils of slavery in the South. Emphasizing black education in particular, he called the schoolhouse the "great caste abolisher" and vowed to "fling whatever I have into the cause of colored children, that they may be better and more thoroughly taught than their parents are."

The racist belief in innate black inferiority was for Smith utterly inconsistent with his understanding of Christianity and the most insidious obstacle to equality. In 1846, he became despondent over the racial "hate deeper than I had imagined" among the vast majority of whites. Fourteen years later, he continued to lament that "our white countrymen do not know us" and that "they are strangers to our characters, ignorant of our capacity, oblivious to our history." He hoped his own distinguished career and writings would serve as both a role model for uneducated blacks and as a powerful rebuttal against racist attacks. And as a black physician, he was uniquely suited to combat the pseudo-scientific theories of innate black inferiority. In two important and brilliantly argued essays—"Civilization" (1844) and "On the Fourteenth Query of Thomas Jefferson's Notes on Virginia" (1859)—he incorporated his extensive knowledge of biology and anatomy to directly refute scientific arguments of innate black inferiority.

Bibliography. Blight, David W. "In Search of Learning, Liberty, and Self Definition: James McCune Smith and the Ordeal of the Antebellum Black Intellectual." *Afro-Americans in New York Life and History* 9 (July 1985): 7–25. Dain, Bruce. *A Hideous Monster of the Mind: American Race Theory in the Early Republic.* Cambridge, MA: Harvard University Press, 2003. Rael, Patrick. *Black Identity and Black Protest in the Antebellum North.* Chapel Hill: University of North Carolina Press, 2002. Stauffer, John. *The Black Hearts of Men: Radical Abolitionists and the Transformation of Race.* Cambridge, MA: Harvard University Press, 2002.

John Stauffer

SMITH, JOSEPH (1805–1844). Born in Vermont in 1805, Smith rose from modest material circumstances and an orthodox Protestant upbringing to become the founder of the Church of Jesus Christ of Latter-day Saints—the Mormons. Following a spiritual encounter in 1823, Smith claimed a new prophetic insight into God's plans for humanity, which resulted in the Book of Mormon (1830).

Smith and his followers promised a restored full revelation of Jesus Christ and a new earthly kingdom—a New Zion— with the United States as the physical focal point of God's divine plan. Although Smith expected Mormons to receive full constitutional protection, the Saints' radical doctrinal and cultural departures from mainstream orthodox Christianity, especially the Southern variety, facilitated suspicion and persecution. Throughout his life, he sought political means to ensure the safety and prosperity of the Mormons, but that involvement brought almost constant controversy. Smith alone was hauled into court over forty times (almost always acquitted) and faced an almost constant barrage of physical threats that culminated in his assassination in 1844.

Smith accepted the Constitution as a divinely ordained document and assumed its pivotal role in protecting the Mormon community. He also taught the importance of being subject to law and political authority. Indeed, Smith saw himself as the greatest champion of the Constitution the United States had. Yet his powerful religious vision enforced a sharp separation between Mormon believers and the "gentiles" outside the faith and included both strong antislavery sentiment and a welcoming posture toward Native Americans (understood to be one of the lost tribes of Israel). Moreover, the Saints' internal policies included a strict leadership hierarchy that gave Smith—the Prophet—substantial power in virtually all decisions. For example, the practice of block voting—church leaders identifying the best candidate and then instructing members to support him—angered frontier residents, who resented such a quest for political clout. Similarly, Smith employed vote trading, especially in Illinois. Often in need of political favors in order to escape arrest and extradition to hostile prosecutors in Missouri, Smith would make deals with prominent state politicians, pledging the church's vote in exchange for various forms of help.

Growing numbers, **abolitionist** credentials, and a strident sense of political and religious mission proved a recipe for conflict—especially when Smith decided to settle his flock in the slave state of Missouri. Ensuing tensions left homes burned, crops and property destroyed, and people and families mobbed and killed. With his appeals to state leaders for protection rejected, Smith determined to defend the Saints' rights. As bands of armed men plundered Mormon settlements, the Saints retaliated with equal fervor in the so-called Mormon War (1838). Believing church leaders culpable for the violence, Governor Lilburn Boggs issued his famous extermination order against the Mormons. Faced with legally sanctioned violence, Smith and his followers escaped to found Nauvoo, Illinois, in 1839.

His petitions to President Martin Van Buren for political redress and material restitution denied, Smith remained confident that political structures could still provide security. Nauvoo became Illinois' third-largest city within three years, and Smith devised a charter for its governance unprecedented for its time. It would bestow broad powers upon the city council and provided for a military organization, the Nauvoo Legion. Controversy followed the Legion, as it was independently commanded by Smith and not subordinate to the Illinois National Guard. A strong municipal court helped Smith evade extradition several times. Critics insisted that Smith's plans would make Nauvoo an independent state within Illinois. Since both the Democrats and Whigs curried Mormon favor in 1840, however, the act incorporating the city of Nauvoo easily passed. State legislators failed to see potential for the charter to spark conflict.

As expanding numbers gave Mormons local political predominance, Smith told Illinois politicians that they would support candidates who defended liberty. When presidential candidates in 1843 virtually ignored his appeals for justice regarding the Missouri depredations, he decided to run for the presidency himself in 1844 on a platform that called for a smaller congress, abolition of slavery, a national banking system, territorial expansion, and broad federal power to protect citizens and secure individual liberty.

Troubles in Nauvoo, however, ended Smith's plans, as disputes raged between the Nauvoo Mormons and Hancock County government and county residents increasingly interested seeing Smith extradited to Missouri. Smith nevertheless continued to direct town business, and as mayor he acted swiftly to curb opposition. In June 1844, he moved to dispense with a newspaper created by his enemies. In the resulting melee of writs, arrests, threats, and rumors, Governor Thomas Ford ordered Smith to Carthage. Ensuing events included illegal imprisonment in the Carthage jail, Governor Ford's disarming of the Nauvoo Legion, and then his departure for Nauvoo. On June 27, 1844, Joseph and his brother Hyrum were dragged from jail and killed.

Although some Mormons elected to stay in the east, **Brigham Young** led most of them westward to the shores of the Great Salt Lake in 1846. In 1976, the state of Missouri formally rescinded Boggs's extermination order and apologized for its abusive actions.

Bibliography. Andrus, Hyrum L. *Doctrines of the Kingdom.* Salt Lake City, UT: Bookcraft, 1973. Barrett, Ivan J. *Joseph Smith and the Restoration.* Provo, UT: Brigham Young University Press, 1973. Bushman, Richard Lyman. *Joseph Smith: Rough Stone Rolling.* New York: Knopf, 2005. Flanders, Robert Bruce. *Nauvoo: Kingdom on the Mississippi.* Urbana: University of Illinois Press, 1975. Gibbons, Francis M. *Joseph Smith, Martyr, Prophet of God.* Salt Lake City, UT: Deseret Book Company, 1977. LeSueur, Stephen C. *The 1838 Mormon War in Missouri.* Columbia: University of Missouri Press, 1987. Ludlow, Daniel H. *Encyclopedia of Mormonism.* 4 vols. New York: Macmillan, 1992. Smith, Joseph, et. al. *The Book of Mormon: The Doctrine and Covenants. The Pearl of Great Price.* Salt Lake City, UT: Church of Jesus Christ of Latter-day Saints, 1981.

Roy L. Tanner

SOCIAL GOSPEL (UNITED STATES). The social Christianity movement that became known as the Social Gospel started in the 1870s and, by the first decade of the twentieth century, had changed the face of Protestantism in the United States. A response to the social implications of industrialization and urbanization, the Social Gospel emerged as middle-class Protestants began to look beyond personal salvation and to work for the salvation of society as a whole. Without denying the importance of individual spiritual growth, many Protestant clergy and laypersons realized that when people suffered from poverty and inequity, religion's sphere of influence must include the material realm as well. These social Christians no longer anticipated the kingdom of heaven as a personal future reward but, instead, hoped to bring it about on earth through education and legislation. Sharing many goals with contemporary secular movements— populism, socialism, labor, and progressivism—the Social Gospel pervaded the reforms of the Progressive Era, which live on today in national social welfare programs and our modern social conscience.

The Social Gospel was never identified with a unified organization; even the term "social gospel," first used in the 1880s, did not identify a movement until the early 1900s. Proponents of the Social Gospel included conservatives, liberals, evangelicals, and Christian socialists, all of whom intermingled across a multitude of educational, religious, and social service organizations. Overall, social gospelers shared two basic objectives: educating middle-class and wealthy American Protestants about the economic inequities that caused contemporary social problems, and inspiring them to solve those problems by providing fair wages and decent living conditions. Christian socialists went further, opposing capitalism itself. They could not envisage a Christian nation that was not socialistic or a socialist state that was not based on Christian principles.

By the turn of the twentieth century, many Protestant denominations in the United States had incorporated social concerns into their teachings. Furthermore, the interpretation of Christian duty was no longer the exclusive prerogative of the clergy but was also undertaken by laymen and women. At the height of the Social Gospel's influence in the 1910s, the results of its efforts in the secular world became evident as the U.S. government increasingly assumed new responsibility for the social welfare of its citizens.

At the heart of the Social Gospel was a profound criticism of predominantly Protestant thought, launched by clergy and congregants who felt that the meaning of "true Christianity" had been obscured. Social gospelers sought to replace passive worship with an active living out of the gospel message. They believed that charity, meted out to the "deserving poor," should be replaced by the social justice due to all sufferers. Discarding the prevalent view that sin was the cause of poverty, social gospelers taught that poverty resulted from an unjust economic structure. Thus the wealthy and middle class were morally responsible for ameliorating the adverse conditions that they themselves had created. This sense of the interdependence of society led social gospelers to oppose the Gilded Age's spirit of competition, and to advocate cooperation and a sense of brotherhood. The Social Gospel's motto, based on Matthew 7:12 and Luke 6:31, was the Golden Rule: "Do unto others as you would have others do unto you."

The cornerstone of the American Social Gospel came from England, where, in the 1840s, Anglican priest **John Frederick Denison Maurice** (1805–1872) and others, recognizing problems resulting from industrialization, urbanization, and rural poverty, had promulgated a spirit of brotherhood and social service that they called Christian Socialism. Interest in Maurice's teachings revived in the 1870s as a new generation of clergy and laypersons in England and North America began gained personal experience of the dire situation of the poor and the wage laborer. Meanwhile, in the American seminaries, liberal theology and new courses in the social sciences prepared future clergymen to address issues of modern life. Recent German biblical criticism emphasized the social teachings of the historical Jesus. The theological concept of immanence, which located God within all of nature and society, engendered the essential Social Gospel ideal of a kingdom of heaven on earth. In addition, many clergymen, fearing that their congregations were disillusioned with organized religion, hoped to retain their dwindling flocks by speaking to their worldly concerns.

To social gospelers, Jesus Christ was the first sociologist—and, as Christian socialists believed, the first socialist. In particular, Jesus's example of service and self-sacrifice took on new meaning as American Protestants considered their own comfortable circumstances. But their Gospel went beyond the Bible; in addition to the works of Maurice, it was informed by secular or quasi-religious literature and thinkers. Most influential were Henry George's *Progress and Poverty* (1879) and Edward Bellamy's *Looking Backward* (1887), the social writing of John Ruskin (1819–1900) and Leo Tolstoy (1828–1910), and the life of Italian radical **Giuseppe Mazzini** (1805–1872). Social gospelers also adopted methods from sociology and economics, illustrating their arguments with statistics and surveys.

The strength of the Social Gospel was its dynamic representatives, who spoke, wrote, and organized to promote social justice within a Christian context. In the United States, the Episcopal Church (with its Anglican roots) and the Congregational Church were the first denominations to produce advocates for social Christianity, but others soon followed. Most of the influential social gospelers came from the Northeast and Midwest, although the movement had adherents—both black and white—in the South as well.

Important clerical figures included Episcopalians Frederic Dan Huntington (1819–1904) and **William Dwight Porter Bliss** (1856–1926); Congregationalists **Washington Gladden** (1836–1918), George Herron (1862–1925), Josiah Strong (1847–1916), and **Charles Sheldon** (1857–1946); Baptists **Walter Rauschenbusch** (1861–1918) and Shailer Mathews (1863–1941); African Methodist Episcopal (AME) Reverdy Ransom (1861–1959); Presbyterian Charles Stelzle (1869–1941); Methodist Harry Ward (1873–1966); and Unitarian Francis Peabody (1847–1936). Among prominent lay advocates were Episcopalians Richard Ely (1854–1943), economist, and Vida Scudder (1861–1954), labor activist and settlement founder; and Methodist **Frances Willard** (1839–1898), president of the **Woman's Christian Temperance Union** (WCTU).

Through the efforts of these spokespersons, Protestants of all ages were educated about the social interpretation of the Bible. Gladden's and Herron's sermons, and Willard's speeches, were delivered before large audiences or read in published form. Nonfiction books like Rauschenbusch's *Christianity and the Social Crisis* (1907) sold briskly, and fiction such as Sheldon's best-selling *In His Steps* (1897) created a new literary genre of Social Gospel novels. Hymns—such as Frank Mason North's "Where Cross the Crowded Ways of Life" (1903)—Sunday school lessons, serial publications, and home-study curricula poured from social gospelers' pens.

Religious or ecumenical Social Gospel organizations sprang up across the nation. Many were ephemeral and local, although some attained national influence. Some sought out and included non-Protestant members. The interdenominational Brotherhood of the Kingdom mobilized the clergy; Men and Religion Forward targeted men and boys. The Church Association for the Advancement of the Interests of Labor (CAIL), an organization of Episcopalian clergy and laity, focused on labor issues. Christian socialists, including Bliss, Herron, Scudder, and Willard, affiliated with mainstream Social Gospel groups as well as the Society of Christian Socialists or the Christian Socialist Fellowship (CSF). A small band of Christian socialists also formed the Christian Commonwealth, a short-lived (1896–1900) utopian community in Georgia.

Numerous lay social service organizations, many of them run by women, built on the traditions of voluntary societies and home missions. Participants in the deaconess movement, the YM and YWCA (Young Men's and Young Women's Christian Associations), and the social settlements supplied a range of services—medical, child care, legal, vocational—to poor urban neighborhoods. The explicitly religious counterpart of the settlement house was the institutional church, which stayed open all week to provide educational and recreational services to the community.

Social gospelers' diligent efforts to create a culture of social service inevitably—and intentionally—affected the political culture as well. Some groups lobbied for specific legislation, for example, the WCTU for prohibition and woman suffrage. Aside from Toledo mayor Samuel "Golden Rule" Jones (1846–1904), however, few social gospelers were politicians. Nor did they try to establish their own political party; in fact, the lack of cohesion in the movement was reflected in the 1912 presidential election: while CSF members voted for Eugene Debs, other social gospelers divided their endorsements between Democrat **Woodrow Wilson** and Progressive Theodore Roosevelt.

But the Social Gospel had a definite political agenda. By creating an enlightened electorate, its advocates hoped to instill a social conscience in all levels of government. While Protestant social gospelers could perceive their goal as promoting Christian principles, the separation of church and state in the United States

ensured that their endorsement of government-sponsored social services had no religious connotation. Social gospelers pursued their agenda in the political realm by joining forces with secular groups that were working toward the same reforms, including labor legislation, pension plans, woman suffrage, and antilynching laws. Hoping to eliminate corruption and to attract honest men back to politics, they also supported such "good government" reforms as direct legislation, the initiative, and the referendum. While few Christian socialists were Socialist Party (SP) members, they shared the SP's goals of economic equality, national ownership of industry, and unionization. Ultimately, the combined forces of the Social Gospel and Progressivism made social welfare a legitimate function of government.

The most significant result of the Social Gospel was a changed worldview for many American Protestants. In some areas of the country, the Protestant Church was accepted as an agent of social as well as spiritual betterment—a role codified in such documents as the 1908 Social Creed of the Churches, endorsed by thirty-three denominations belonging to the Federal Council of Churches (itself a Social Gospel innovation).

But the Social Gospel also had negative repercussions on the Protestant Church. The most serious was that the church's' offer of social services without a spiritual commitment contributed to the increasing secularization of society—an outcome that social gospelers deplored. And the inevitable consequence of the government assuming responsibility for social welfare was that people no longer needed to turn to the church for those services.

Critics charged that the Social Gospel was idealistic, unrealistic, and simplistic; that its focus on making life more comfortable for more people only encouraged worldliness and materialism; and that, given the middle-class status of most social

Christians, it was an attempt to retain social control of the poor and working class. Further, to the dismay of the Christian socialists, the Social Gospel was often manifested merely as traditional charity, not social justice.

There had always been opposition to the Social Gospel from Protestants who did not accept liberal theology. Others feared that ministers who actively pursued worldly reforms were creating a godless society. By the 1920s, postwar disillusionment and the Red Scare had their effects on the Social Gospel and Christian socialism. Protestant fundamentalism was growing in the United States, offering a literal interpretation of the Bible and a return to a transcendent view of the kingdom of heaven. The Social Gospel's impact also diminished as its principles became incorporated into religious and secular policy; with the New Deal, it faded away as a significant movement.

However, the legacy of the Social Gospel was a powerful one. Its message of social interdependence resulted in an acceptance, on the part of both individuals and the government, of responsibility for the salvation of society. The men and women, clergy and laity, who taught and preached, ran the settlements, and lobbied for fair pay and good government instilled in Americans a social conscience that is reflected in such modern social and political impulses as the civil rights movement. Dr. **Martin Luther King**, Jr., acknowledged the Social Gospel's impact when he wrote of his "conviction ever since reading Rauschenbusch that any religion which professes to be concerned about the souls of men and is not concerned about the social and economic conditions that scar the soul is a spiritually moribund religion" (King, 91).

Bibliography. Dombrowski, James. *The Early Days of Christian Socialism in America.* New York: Columbia University Press, 1936. Edwards, Wendy J. Deichman, and Carolyn DeSwarte Gifford, eds. *Gender and the Social Gospel.* Urbana: University of Illinois Press, 2003. Gorrell, Donald K. *The Age of Social Responsibility: The Social Gospel in the Progressive Era, 1900–1920.* Macon, GA: Mercer University Press, 1988. Hopkins, Charles Howard. *The Rise of the Social Gospel in American Protestantism, 1865–1915.* New Haven, CT: Yale University Press, 1940. King, Martin Luther, Jr. *Stride toward Freedom.* New York: Harper & Row, 1958. White, Ronald C., Jr. *Liberty and Justice for All: Racial Reform and the Social Gospel, 1877–1925.* New York: Harper & Row, 1990; Louisville, KY: Westminster John Knox Press, 2002.

Janet C. Olson

SÖLLE, DOROTHEE (b. 1929). Sölle is a German theologian, poet, and activist for peace, human rights, and environmental justice. She was born in Cologne, Germany, and came of age in the aftermath of World War II. She studied philosophy, literature, and theology at Cologne, Freiburg, and Göttingen and has held professorships in Europe and the United States. From 1975 to 1987, she was professor of systematic theology at Union Theological Seminary in New York. Sölle's poetry and theological work have been widely published. Her early writings, along with the work of Johann Baptist Metz and **Jürgen Moltmann,** helped to redefine political theology in the context of post-World War II Europe. She eventually aligned herself with liberation theology as articulated by contemporary Latin American and feminist theologians.

From the publication in 1965 of her first book, *Stellvertretung* (translated into English as *Christ the Representative*), Sölle's work has asked how Christians can speak of God after Auschwitz. She insists that theology, particularly German theology, cannot be the same after Auschwitz, and she finds it impossible to believe in a God who had the power to stop the Holocaust but chose not to do so. The omnipotent God of classical theology is dead to Sölle, who instead envisions God as interdependent and in need of our help. Her central concern is peace, which she broadly construes to include social justice and environmental issues, as well as disarmament. Her analyses of social structures rely heavily on Marxist theory, and she identifies herself as a "radical-democratic socialist." Sölle's theological work speaks strongly against militarism, fascism, consumerism, and capitalism.

Fundamental to Sölle's work is her conviction that theology and spirituality cannot be divorced from politics. She also believes that true piety unites the mystical and revolutionary spirit. From 1968 to 1972, Sölle participated in the Cologne-based Political Evensong, which combined political activity with liturgical practice. The group's services focused on issues such as the Vietnam War and included both prayer and a call to action. Sölle's continuing engagement in political movements extends from antiwar protests to specific human rights issues and ecological concerns. In addition to her involvement in the global peace movement, she has helped to bring attention to human rights violations, particularly in Latin America and South Africa. Sölle lives in Hamburg with her husband, Fulbert Steffensky.

Bibliography. Sölle, Dorothee. *Against the Wind: Memoir of a Radical Christian.* Trans. Barbara Rumscheidt and Martin Rumscheidt. Minneapolis, MN: Fortress Press, 1999.

Susan J. Hubert

SOMERVILLE, HENRY (1889–1953). A Catholic journalist, advocate of the social teachings of the Roman Catholic Church and the rights of working people, Somerville became the Catholic equivalent of the Protestant social gospelers in the mid-twentieth-century Canada. As the longest-serving editor of the *Catholic Register* weekly newspaper—the voice of English-speaking Catholics in Canada—Somerville used both his newspaper columns and his lecture tours in Canada and the United States to fight for minimum wages, decent housing for the working class, the right of workers to organize unions, and the necessity of lay Catholics to educate themselves so they could participate fully in public life.

Henry Somerville was born in Leeds, England, the second of twelve children in a poverty-stricken working-class family. Although he had to leave school at age thirteen to work in a factory, he continued his education on his own, eventually obtaining a diploma in social science from Ruskin College at Oxford. His studies focused on history, economics, and the social teachings of the church, particularly Pope **Leo XIII**'s famed social encyclical *Rerum novarum* of 1891. He became convinced that the Catholic Church could be a champion of the working class if it zealously applied its social teachings to the plight of workers, thus fighting off challenges for their loyalty from communism and socialism. He became an advocate of social studies clubs, in which Catholic laypeople could learn how to apply their own beliefs to the challenges created by the Industrial Revolution.

Somerville's adult life was marked by numerous transatlantic voyages between England and Canada. During the First World War and the 1920s, he worked mainly as a journalist, filing articles to the *Catholic Register* and the *Toronto Star.* As editor of the *Register* from 1933 until his death, he strived to help Canadians overcome their suspicions of socialism and persuaded the Catholic hierarchy to abandon their overt hostility to left-wing political parties, such as the fledgling Cooperative Commonwealth Federation, an early Canadian labor party.

Having settled down in Toronto, he and his wife Margaret (née Cooper) raised five children. During his lifetime, Somerville was awarded two papal honors—the Cross

Pro Ecclesia et Pontifice in 1937 from Pope **Pius XI** and the Knight Commander of St. Gregory by Pope **Pius XII** in 1947.
Bibliography. Sinasac, Joseph. *Fateful Passages: The Life of Henry Somerville, Catholic Journalist.* Ottawa, ON: Novalis, 2003.

Joseph Sinasac

SOUTHERN CHRISTIAN LEADERSHIP CONFERENCE (UNITED STATES). Martin Luther King, Jr., Ralph Abernathy, Fred Shuttlesworth, Bayard Rustin, and others established the Southern Christian Leadership Conference (SCLC) in 1957 with the expressed goal of redeeming the "soul of America." The SCLC hoped to achieve this goal by coordinating nonviolent protests and by utilizing the power and influence of Southern African American churches to put the struggle for black civil rights in moral terms.

The driving philosophy of SCLC proceeded directly from King's belief that each human being possessed a natural identification with every other human being. This interconnectedness dictated that all persons possessed a moral responsibility for one another. **Walter Rauschenbusch**'s Social Gospel imperative of reconstructing society into a moral Christian commonwealth, Thoreau's insistence that one honest man could morally regenerate society, and Ghandi's principles of nonviolent resistance, rounded out King's philosophy and guided the formation and function of SCLC.

Unlike organizations such as the National Association for the Advancement of Colored People (NAACP) and the Student Nonviolent Coordinating Committee (SNCC), the SCLC did not solicit individual membership but coordinated the activities of local organizations, trained communities in the philosophy of Christian nonviolence, operated citizenship schools, and assisted in registering black voters. The SCLC's coordinating position and its connection with black churches provided a degree of flexibility that proved invaluable in mobilizing the loosely structured African American constituency during the 1960s. It was the linkage of morality and politics, directed by King's philosophy of nonviolent resistance, which guided the SCLC through its participation in sit-ins, voter registration campaigns, Freedom Rides, and antipoverty programs.

In November 1961, SCLC joined the SNCC-led nonviolent campaign against segregation already underway in Albany, Georgia. Although this campaign proved unsuccessful, King understood that the Albany movement failed largely because it attacked segregation as a whole rather than one distinct aspect of it. This lesson guided SCLC's strategy in Birmingham, Alabama, in 1963 when it instituted Project C, aimed at desegregating just downtown Birmingham. This strategy, along with the violence initiated by police chief Eugene "Bull" Connor and the national media attention that violence attracted, resulted in a desegregation settlement and set the stage for the 1964 Civil Rights Act. Also in 1963, SCLC played a pivotal role in organizing the March on Washington, which included more than 200,000 participants and King's famous "I have a dream" speech delivered from the steps of the Lincoln Memorial. In 1964, SCLC joined the Congress of Racial Equality (CORE) in a voter registration campaign in the South. In 1965, SCLC launched a voting rights campaign in Selma, Alabama, and, in March of that year, organized with SNCC a fifty-mile march from Selma to Montgomery. Although the march produced the landmark Voting Rights Act of 1965, it also produced tensions between SNCC and SCLC. SNCC members accused King of working a compromise with Governor George Wallace and criticized SCLC for being too moderate and for not responding to the more militant voices crying black power.

SCLC responded to this criticism by directing its moral politics toward the more radical goal of economic justice. Believing that poverty was the root cause of inner-city violence, SCLC launched Operation Breadbasket in 1967. This campaign organized black consumer boycotts in Northern cities, most notably Chicago, to press for jobs and encouraged the formation of black businesses. SCLC also began planning the Poor People's Campaign, aimed at securing employment, housing, and income for impoverished African Americans through federal legislation. Although Operation Breadbasket proved marginally successful under Jesse Jackson's leadership, the Poor People's Campaign never materialized. After King's assassination in 1968, **Ralph Abernathy** assumed leadership of the SCLC and organized another march on Washington that brought between 50,000 and 100,000 people to Washington to protest against economic injustice.

A decline in SCLC's influence and effectiveness accompanied the organization's shift to economic radicalism. Although Operation Breadbasket and the Poor People's Campaign were designated national campaigns, they were largely directed at the situation of African Americans in Northern urban ghettoes. As SCLC moved north, it nearly abandoned the church-centered, grassroots strength it possessed in its Southern black constituency. As such, many believed it also abandoned its moral and religious principles in its apparent acquiescence to the calls for black power. Moreover, the shift to economic radicalism alienated much of the organization's white liberal support.

King's death precipitated further decline in SCLC as the organization received fewer contributions and experienced dissent over Abernathy's leadership. In the late 1970s, Joseph Lowery revitalized SCLC by expanding the organization's scope beyond traditional civil rights activities. The SCLC continues its form of moral politics as it seeks to redeem "the soul of America" through effecting policy. Programs at the turn of the twenty-first century include Campaign for Tobacco-Free Kids, Martin Luther King Schools Program, National Youth Voter Registration Campaign, Anti-Death Penalty, and Racial Profile Hearings.

Bibliography. Fairclough, Adam. *To Redeem the Soul of America: The Southern Christian Leadership Conference and Martin Luther King, Jr.* Athens: University of Georgia Press, 1987. Garrow, David J. *Bearing the Cross: Martin Luther King, Jr., and the Southern Christian Leadership Conference.* New York: W. Morrow, 1986. Peake, Thomas R. *Keeping the Dream Alive: A History of the Southern Christian Leadership Conference from King to the Nineteen-Eighties.* New York: Peter Lang, 1987.

William L. Glankler

SPANISH CONFEDERATION OF AUTONOMOUS RIGHT-WING GROUPS (CONFEDERACIÓN ESPAÑOLA DE DERECHAS AUTÓNOMAS—CEDA). Formally established in February 1933, the CEDA developed from an "organization of social defense"—Popular Action (Acción Popular, AP)—which was set up as an immediate response to the coming of the Second Spanish Republic in April 1931. Initially a vehicle for those who had campaigned for the monarchy in the April elections, AP soon developed into Spain's first mass Catholic political party.

Under the leadership of **José María Gil Robles** and the direction of **Ángel Herrera Oria,** the new party was defined as "accidentalist," respecting the republic's constitution and legal authority. Just how far CEDA really accepted democracy is a matter of debate. Some historians regard its accidentalness simply as a tactic, a means of using the electoral process to redefine the republic as an authoritarian, confessional state.

In terms of method, CEDA was a modern political party that employed the full machinery of liberal politics, organizing electoral rolls, using agents and volunteers, and staffing campaign offices. Such an accommodation with liberalism was not to the taste of all CEDA allies, particularly not the Carlists. The political program espoused by what was essentially a broad alliance of the Catholic Right was based around the defense of landed property, religion, and public order. Much of the initial mobilization was based on the Catholic agrarian networks established by the **CNCA,** and the rapid polarization of politics between 1931 and 1936 saw the CEDA achieve real electoral success, notably among the peasant proprietors and agrarian middle classes of northern and central Spain.

Constituted as a federation of local groups, which retained considerable autonomy, CEDA mobilized new constituencies of voters. Women were widely seen as a 'natural' source of support for the Catholic Right. Their sudden entry into politics after 1931 gave credence to the CEDA's female orators' claim that they had come out of the home "in defense of the home." Women's sections ran campaigns against divorce, civil marriage, and, above all, the republic's secularizing legislation. As they were also usually involved in catechesis and charity work, they bridged the familiar world of philanthropy and the new world of politics. Drawing on established traditions of voluntary work also enabled the CEDA to develop a substantial pool of female labor to build up voting registers and help get the vote out on polling day.

Women voted for the first time in November 1933, when the Left was defeated, though CEDA failed to win a parliamentary majority. A period of power sharing with the Radical Party followed, though suspicion of CEDA's intentions on the part of the Left was so great that, in 1934, the appointment of three CEDA ministers—including Gil Robles as minister of war—became the pretext for an insurrectionary general strike led by the Socialist Party. Focused on the mining region of Asturias, the uprising was a fiasco and was fiercely repressed. All Socialist Party offices were closed, and its leaders detained without trial. However, in the wake of the uprising, concern for the dispossessed led the CEDA minister for agriculture, Manuel Giménez Fernández, to introduce proposals for agrarian reform. As a professor of canon law, Giménez Fernández was guided by papal teaching and Catholic social principles. However, his moderate proposals for redistribution, which included a limited right to buy for long-standing tenants, split the increasingly uneasy coalition that made up the CEDA. In the face of intransigent opposition, Giménez Fernández resigned.

The only section of the CEDA that supported the agrarian reform proposals unequivocally was the youth movement (JAP). The only party section to be organized centrally, the increasingly radical JAP adopted khaki shirts and a fascist-style salute. It staged huge rallies at historic sites such as El Escorial, fostered an increasingly intemperate leader cult around Gil Robles, and established networks of "civil defense." The JAP was highly visible during the February 1936 elections, guarding campaign meetings and escorting voters to the polls. Defeat by the Popular Front left the JAP, which had been convinced of outright victory, in a state of disarray, like the wider CEDA. All were agreed that the new government would be disastrous for Spain, but the failure of the accidentalness tactic to win power through the ballot box left them without a strategy. In spring 1936, Giménez Fernández and Luis Lucía, leader of Derecha Regional Valenciana (Valencian Christian Party), attempted to strengthen centrist links with Catholic Republicans and even some moderate Socialists. But many more *cedistas* turned to conspiracy and threw in their lot with the military plotters or, in the case of the JAP, the fascist Falange.

The CEDA's formal existence came to an end in April 1937, when Franco merged the Falange and the Carlists to form a single party and declared all other political organizations to be illegal. After the civil war, some *cedistas* became active in the moderate opposition to Franco, notably Gil Robles and Giménez Fernández, both of whom led small Christian democrat parties. But more collaborated with the regime, particularly in its early years, providing a generation of local officials and administrators for Franco's new state. Some historians have seen the CEDA as a prototypical Christian democrat initiative, but most see this label as applicable only to those convinced republicans around Lucía and Giménez Fernández, at least during the 1930s.

Bibliography. Montero, José Ramón. *La CEDA: El catolicismo social y politico en la Segunda República.* Madrid: Revista de Trabajo, 1977. Preston, Paul. *The Coming of the Spanish Civil War.* 2nd ed. London: Routledge, 1994. Tusell, Javier, and Calvo, José. *Giménez Fernández: Precursor de la democracia española.* Seville, Spain: Mondadori, 1990. Vincent, Mary. *Catholicism in the Second Spanish Republic: Religion and Politics in Salamanca, 1930–1936.* Oxford: Oxford University Press, 1996.

Mary Vincent

SPELLMAN, FRANCIS JOSEPH (1889–1967). Cardinal Spellman personified the cultural and political power acquired by the Roman Catholic Church in the United States during the twentieth century. He served as New York's Roman Catholic archbishop from 1939 until his death in 1967. He also served as Catholic archbishop for the American military. Spellman consorted regularly with popes and presidents. He enjoyed national prominence for his patriotism and anticommunism. His reputation as the unsurpassed power broker of Catholicism's East Coast establishment diminished only when his support for the Vietnam War estranged him from most younger Catholics.

The preeminent "prince of the Church," Spellman was born in Whitman, Massachusetts. After graduating from Fordham University in 1911, Spellman attended the North American College in Rome in 1916. He was ordained that year and returned to parish work in the Boston archdiocese. Appointed chancellor of the archdiocese in 1922, Spellman rarely enjoyed his relationship with his archbishop, the intransigent William Cardinal O'Connell. Spellman's contacts in Rome helped him survive O'Connell's frequent insults. Spellman enjoyed the confidence of Pope **Pius XI,** who appointed him Boston's auxiliary bishop (with right of succession) in 1932. In 1931 Spellman had helped smuggle Pius XI's antifascist encyclical *Non abbiamo bisogno* out of Rome. In 1939 **Pius XII** appointed him archbishop of New York as well as vicar of the American military. These moves made Spellman the Catholic spiritual leader of the nation's largest city as well as all Catholics serving in the nation's armed forces. Spellman became a cardinal in 1946.

Spellman did not shy away from his duties. He quickly became the most prominent Catholic priest associated with national politics. Throughout World War II and the Korean and Vietnam wars he traveled widely to visit the American troops. Spellman aggressively used his public image to defend Catholic social and political interests. He intervened regularly in New York City politics. In 1949, Eleanor Roosevelt and Spellman sparred publicly over granting federal aid to parish schools. When Roosevelt opposed, Spellman accused her of anti-Catholicism. During the 1950s Spellman zealously supported Senator Joseph McCarthy and Roy Cohn. Spellman also developed an intense interest in the career of South Vietnamese leader **Ngo Dinh Diem.** He supported without question the escalating Vietnam War.

The intensity of the antiwar movement surprised and dismayed Spellman. He easily equated American patriotism in the cold war with Christian duty. While quite attuned to the needs of Puerto Rican immigrants in New York, he could not understand the civil rights movement's prophetic activism. He did not sympathize with the labor movement. In 1949, for example, he ordered seminary students to break a grave diggers' strike. Known for a functional, if not profoundly mystical, faith, Spellman coined the familiar phrase "Pray as if everything depends on God. Act as if everything depends on man." Despite his thorough conservatism, he often deflected criticism away from other Catholics. He single-handedly renovated and expanded the prestigious St. Joseph Seminary in Yonkers, New York. Spellman patronized the Catholic Theological Society of America from its origins in 1946. He brought John Courtney Murray, SJ, to the Second Vatican Council (1962–1965) as a theological advisor. Murray later authored the Council's revolutionary declaration endorsing religious freedom. This legacy of extending the American presence in Catholicism, while simultaneously expanding Catholicism in America, suitably describes Spellman's life. He died in 1967, disillusioned with the counterculture's vehement rejection of values he defended so vigorously.

Bibliography. Cooney, John. *The American Pope: The Life and Times of Francis Cardinal Spellman.* New York: Times Books, 1984. Fogarty, Gerald. "Francis Cardinal Spellman: American and Roman." In *Patterns of Episcopal Leadership*, ed. Gerald Fogarty. Bicentennial History of the Catholic Church in America. New York: Macmillan, 1989. Shelley, Thomas J. "Francis Cardinal Spellman and his seminary at Dunwoodie." *Catholic Historical Review* 80 (1994): 282–99.

Jeffrey Marlett

SPIEGEL ZUM DESENBERG UND CANSTEIN, FERDINAND AUGUST VON (1764–1835).

Count Spiegel, the archbishop of Cologne, Germany, from 1824 until 1835, was born in Westphalia. He descended from thirteenth-century nobles, the barons Spiegel zum Desenberg, and was the fifth child of the Cologne privy councillor baron Theodor Hermann von Spiegel zum Desenberg and his second wife, Adolphine Franziska von Landsberg zu Erwitte.

After his mother died in 1777, followed by his father two years later, Ferdinand August and his older brother Max were sent to the noble convent school at Fulda, were he studied theology, philosophy, and law until 1783. In 1779 he received his tonsure in Fulda and continued his studies in law and economics at Münster from 1783 to 1785. Already in May 1783 he was appointed canon for the first time. He became a deacon in 1796 and was ordained in 1799 with a position second only to the bishop. In August 1802 Prussian forces occupied Münster on the basis of the 1801 Peace of Lunéville, and Spiegel lost his state offices. He worked with the new rulers, however, particularly since he hoped for an office within the state administration.

He was appointed bishop of Münster in 1813 by Napoleon but with the arrest of Pope Pius VII, papal confirmation could not be effected, and so the legal chapter vicar, Klemens August von Droste-Vischering, agreed only after the French prefect's demand to admit Spiegel as second chapter vicar. After the end of French rule, Spiegel's contacts to Berlin and especially with the reformers Karl von Hardenberg and Karl vom Stein were useful for him. Early in 1803, he had taken the lead of the university's commission, hoping for the office of minister for culture, education, and church affairs. He took part in the Congress of Vienna, where together with Ignatz Wessenberg and in accordance with the Prussian king **Friedrich Wilhelm III,** he spoke for an independent national church under German control. In recognition of his efforts he was made a count in 1816 and a consul of state in 1817.

During the following upheavals over the German bishoprics, Spiegel turned into a fighter for the church's freedom. During the reorganization of the Prussian bishoprics, he was appointed subdelegate of the executor of the papal bull *De salute animarum,* the Ermland's Bishop Josef von Hohenzollern, in 1824. Fearful of conflicts with Berlin, he refused offers to become bishop of Breslau and, for a while, even of Cologne. In 1823, however, Spiegel agreed to the Cologne archbishopric and was appointed by Pope Leo XII the following year. Spiegel embarked on an ambitious reform program to reorganize the see's pastoral structures, the education of priests, the church's authorities, the chapter, and the order's life. He maintained close contact with state authorities, who now got to know him as an inconvenient and principled cleric. On the other hand, in his wish to keep good relations with the Prussian state, he occasionally forgot Catholic interests in other Prussian regions. At the 1834 Berlin Convention, for example, on the problem of mixed marriages, Spiegel appeased the state and granted priests wide latitude and so made allowances in contradiction to Roman doctrine. Pope **Gregory XVI,** therefore, refused to give his consent to the agreement.

Before the quarrel over mixed marriages could ignite the church's first big conflict with the Prussian state, however, Spiegel died in Cologne. He doubtless belongs to the German Catholic Church's most important figures of the first half of the nineteenth century. Spiegel was buried in the archbishops' crypt of the Cologne Cathedral.

Bibliography. Lipgens, Walter. *Ferdinand August Graf Spiegel und das Verhältnis von Kirche und Staat 1789–1835.* Münster: Aschendorff, 1965.

Andrea Rönz

STANTON, ELIZABETH CADY (1815–1902). Stanton was one of the foremost political activists of the nineteenth century.

Active in many social reform movements, including temperance and antislavery, she is best known as one of the founders of an organized woman's rights movement. From its inception in 1848 until the 1880s, Stanton worked ceaselessly on behalf of women's legal and political rights. Always progressive, Stanton became increasingly radical and outspoken with age. When the National American Woman's Suffrage Association (NAWSA) was formed in 1890 in a merger between Stanton's and **Susan B. Anthony**'s National Woman Suffrage Association (NWSA) and the more conservative American Woman Suffrage Association (AWSA), Stanton was named president. By that time, however, she had become frustrated with the slow progress of the movement and with the increasingly conservative attitude of the new generation of suffrage leaders. She spent her final years writing her autobiography, *Eighty Years and More* (1898), and a critique of the Bible, published as *The Woman's Bible* in two volumes (1895 and 1898).

Elizabeth Cady Stanton grew up in Johnstown, New York, one of six surviving children born to Daniel Cady (1773–1859) and Margaret Livingston Cady (1785–1871). Stanton's parents were well-respected members of the community. Her father was a lawyer who also served as a state assemblyman, member of Congress, and state supreme court justice. Her mother was the daughter of Colonel James Livingston, a Revolutionary war hero. Stanton received a first-rate education for a woman of her day at the Johnstown Academy and **Emma Willard**'s Troy Female Seminary, where she finished her schooling in 1833.

In 1839, Elizabeth Cady fell in love with Henry Brewster Stanton, an antislavery lecturer ten years her senior. They married in May 1840 and left almost immediately for London and the World's Anti-Slavery Convention. In London, Elizabeth Cady Stanton met many American antislavery activists, including the Quaker Lucretia Mott, a delegate from the Pennsylvania Anti-Slavery Society. On the first day of the convention, the male delegates voted not to recognize the female representatives. After watching the proceedings from the gallery, Stanton and Mott resolved to hold a convention on women's rights in the United States.

On her return to the United States, however, Stanton became occupied with her growing family. She bore seven children between 1842 and 1859. She had three small boys by 1848, when Stanton, Mott, and others convened the first Woman's Rights Convention in Seneca Fall, New York. Throughout her career, Stanton juggled family obligations with speaking and writing commitments.

In 1851, Stanton formed a lasting partnership with another New York reformer, Susan B. Anthony. Both women were dissatisfied with the secondary role that women reformers played in the temperance and antislavery movements. By the mid-1850s, Stanton and Anthony were focusing on women's rights to political and legal equality. It was not until 1869, in reaction to the Fifteenth Amendment's failure to extend suffrage based on gender, that they created the NWSA, an organization devoted exclusively to women's rights.

Both women remained committed to the cause of women's enfranchisement, but Stanton's social reform interests continued to broaden. During the 1870s, she traveled the United States as a lyceum lecturer. In the 1880s, Stanton retired from the lecture circuit and began several ambitious writing projects. The first of these was *The History of Woman Suffrage,* edited by Stanton, Anthony, and Matilda Joslyn Gage. A collection of letters, documents, and reminiscences, *The History of Woman Suffrage* grew to encompass six volumes, although Stanton only collaborated on the first three.

In the mid-1880s, Stanton wrote her memoirs and her magnum opus, *The Woman's Bible.* In both works, she argued that Christianity had a stifling effect on women's lives. Stanton's *Bible,* a collection of commentaries on biblical passages written by Stanton and a committee of sympathetic feminists, was not well-received. In 1896, NAWSA denounced the first volume from the platform of their national convention. Stanton's credibility and historical reputation were eclipsed by that of her friend and colleague Susan B. Anthony. When Stanton died in October, 1902, she no longer occupied a central position in the folklore of the movement that she had helped bring to life.

Bibliography. Gordon, Ann D., ed. *The Selected Papers of Elizabeth Cady Stanton and Susan B. Anthony.* 3 vols. New Brunswick, NJ: Rutgers University Press, 1997–2003. Kern, Kathi. *Mrs. Stanton's Bible.* Ithaca, NY: Cornell University Press, 2001.

Meg Meneghel MacDonald

STEPINAC, ALOJZIJE (1898–1960). Stepinac served as Catholic archbishop of Zagreb during the 1941–1945 pro-German Croatian state and was appointed cardinal in 1953. As archbishop, Stepinac strove to regenerate Catholic culture, renegotiate a traditional division of influence between church and state, and redirect his clergy away from politics.

As a fervent Croat, he strove to see his nation independent and revitalized. Although his Catholic program prevailed over his nationalist one, both led him to ally himself with fascists and to oppose Communists. Within the context of Yugoslav history—rent by Croat/Catholic-Serb/Orthodox conflict, genocide, world war, and revolution—Stepinac is a contradictory figure, symbolizing both Catholic/Croat complicity in fascist crimes and Catholic/Croat resistance to totalitarianism.

Ascending to office in 1937, Stepinac was an especially young, ascetic, and puritanical archbishop; interactions with totalitarianism, however, defined his career. In 1941, when Adolf Hitler created a puppet Croatian state and installed Croatian fascists (the Ustaša) in power, Stepinac endorsed the state as a national triumph. His satisfaction likely grew when the Ustaša issued fundamentalist and anti-Orthodox decrees, thus confirming them as allies in the church's campaign against liberals, Freemasons, Communists, schismatics, and Jews.

But as the Ustaša pursued racial persecution and genocide (slaughtering, forcibly converting, or deporting hundreds of thousands of Serbs, but also Jews and Roma), Stepinac privately intervened with the regime. He did not vigorously criticize their policies in public, however, until spring 1943, when he began to preach stirring denunciations of racism, ultranationalism, and violence. While he did not explicitly condemn Ustaša genocide, he quietly protected several thousand persecuted individuals. He then courageously defied the postwar Communist regime, which convicted him of collaboration after a politically manipulated 1946 trial. He spent the rest of his life in prison or under house arrest. Despite ongoing controversy over his character and wartime activities, he was beatified in 1998.

Bibliography. Alexander, Stella. *The Triple Myth: A Life of Archbishop Alojzije Stepinac.* Boulder, CO: East European Monographs, 1987.

James Mace Ward

STOECKER, ADOLF (1835–1909). Stoecker was one of the chief voices in Germany's religious politics before the First World War. Born in Halberstadt, the son of a blacksmith-turned-constable, from 1853 to 1859 Stoecker studied Protestant theology in Halle and Berlin while he worked as a tutor in the Neumark area and, later, for Count Lambsdorff in Riga. In 1863, he became a parish rector in rural Seggerde (Altmark) and in 1866 took a

position as pastor in the industrial parish of Hamersleben (Magdeburger Börde).

After heavy disputes, he left this parish in 1871 and, due to the patriotic articles he had published in the *Neue Evangelische Kirchenzeitung,* found work as military chaplain in Metz (Lorraine), where he established a German Protestant community. He was soon called to Berlin to preach at the cathedral and in the Hohenzollern court. Stoecker's special interest was *Volksmission* (people's mission) and the so-called Social Question. In 1877, he took over the direction of the Berlin Town Mission. The same year, with national economist Adolph Wagner and pastor Rudolf Todt, who had social reform ambitions, he founded the *Central-Verein für Socialreform auf religiöser und konstitutionell-monarchischer Grundlage* (Central Association for Social Reform Based on Religious and Constitutional Monarchic Grounds).

The *Central-Verein*'s main publication was the *Staats-Socialist: Wochenschrift für Socialreform* (*State Socialist: Weekly Publication for Social Reform*). Stoecker, however, intended to create a more ambitious political countermovement to social democracy, not a debating club. Thus in 1878 he founded the anti-social democratic *Christlich-soziale Arbeiterpartei* (Christian Social Workers' Party) and left the *Central-Verein,* which existed until 1881. Stoecker nevertheless remained editor of the *Staats-Socialist.* But his new party, which had 3,000 members at the most, had no chances at the parliamentary elections (*Reichtagswahlen*) of July 1878. Thus Stoecker joined the *Deutschkonservative Partei* (German Conservative Party) and was elected as a conservative to the Prussian chamber.

After the inception of the *Gesetz gegen die gemeingefährlichen Bestrebungen der Sozialdemokratie* (Law Against the Endeavors of Social Democracy Dangerous to Public Safety), known as the

Sozialistengesetz (Socialist Law), of October 1878, the Prussian church administration expressed reservations of church ministers who engaged in political activity, a monition aimed in part at Stoecker. He then turned away from working-class politics and focused more on the economically pressed lower-middle classes. Consequently, he deleted the expression "workers" from his party's name, renamed it *Christlich-soziale Partei* (Christian Social Party) instead, and introduced it as an independent group into the Deutschkonservative Partei.

Reflecting the sentiments existing in the milieu he now represented, Stoecker launched a massive anti-Semitic campaign. He reinforced anti-Semitic bias existing in the lower-middle classes and defined Jewish citizens as the main culprits responsible for social hardships in German society. Jewish money and Jewish media, he said, impelled "mammonization and atheism, depravation and de-Christianization, [and] political dissolution." He formed political alliances with anti-Semitic parties and the League of Anti-Semites and agitated to spread anti-Semitic ideas throughout German Protestantism. In 1890, Stoecker had to give up his position as a court preacher and dedicated himself to the Reichstag seat that he held, as a conservative from 1881 to 1893 and from 1898 to 1908.

Furthermore, he developed considerable effectiveness as a preacher and people's missionary (*Volksmissionar*), and he still exerted influence in the Centralausschuss für Innere Mission (Central Committee for People's Mission). In 1890 he founded the *Evangelisch-sozialer Kongress* (Protestant Social Congress) with renowned liberal theologians. After heavy disputes with them, he left the Kongress in 1896 and founded a conservative rival organization in 1897, the *Freie Kirchlich-soziale Konferenz* (Free Ecclesiastical Social Conference). With his anti-social

democratic, anti-Semitic, and antimodernist ideology, Stoecker contributed considerably to the polarization of German society before and after World War I.

Bibliography. Rogge, Joachim, and Gerhard Ruhbach, eds. *Die Geschichte der Evangelischen Kirche der Union.* Vol. 2. Leipzig, Germany: Evangelische Verlagsanstalt, 1994.

Gerhard Besier

STOKER, HENDRIK GERHARDUS (1899–1993). Stoker's philosophical work powerfully influenced the debates over political options and alternatives in South Africa. The Afrikaner Calvinist philosopher and educator was born in Johannesburg of Dutch parents. His family shared the suffering of Afrikaner concentration camp experiences during the Anglo-Boer War, a familial experience that deeply affected Stoker and no doubt fueled his family's anti-imperialist outlook. After the war, and the enforced British Anglicization educational policies, his parents sent him to the German School in Johannesburg.

He completed his schooling in 1916 at the Gymnasium at Potchefstroom, where he was deeply influenced by Calvinism. In 1919 he was granted his degree by the University of South Africa, followed in 1921 by an MA first class in philosophy. Studying under Max Scheler of the Free University, he earned his doctorate, focusing on the subject of conscience, in 1924.

Returning to South Africa, in 1930 he was appointed professor of philosophy and psychology at Potchefstroom University and taught courses deeply influenced by Calvinist thought. When invited to address the Dutch Reformed Stellenbosch *Calvinistiese Studentebond,* his suggestion that all three of the Dutch Reformed student movements be unified led to the formation of the joint Federation of Calvinist Student Societies (FCSV).

Stoker strongly identified with Afrikaner nationalism and actively supported the establishment of public holidays such as

Kruger's Day and the Day of the Covenant and actively participated in the 1938 Centennial of the Great Trek. Viewing Prime Minister General Jan Christian Smut's holistic understanding of human society as a threat to Afrikaans culture, he joined the ultranationalist movement the *Ossewabrandwag.* Charges (false) that he was pro-German, indeed pro-Nazi, led to his internment during the Second World War in the Koffiefontein camp. Here, he set up an informal Calvinist extension school by providing lecture series to inmates in Calvinism, political philosophy, and theology, an effort nicknamed "the University of Koffiefontein." Its most famous graduate was John Vorster, later nationalist prime minister of South Africa.

While Stoker never wrote a systematic work, he is survived by a number of books and scores of articles and pamphlets, which most unfortunately have not been translated from German, Dutch, or Afrikaans. His basic ontological and epistemological theory is set out in his *Die Wysbegeerte van die Skeppingsidee: Die Grondbeginsels van 'n Kalvinistiese Wysbegeerte* (1933) and other works on Calvinism and the doctrine of the law-spheres. Stoker defends a creationist basis for philosophy. Thus within God's creation there are different modalities, degrees, and values, each of which possesses both sovereignty and universality in its own sphere. In *Stryd om die Ordes* (Struggle around the Orders) Stoker contrasts communism, liberal democracy, and Nazism with his alternative, a Calvinist politics based on creation sphere ordering.

He retired as professor at Potchefstroom in 1964 and took a position from 1969 to 1972 at the Rand Afrikaans University in Johannesburg. During this period, he devoted himself to the examination of the bases of law.

Bibliography. Stoker, H. G. *Das Gewissen.* Bonn, Germany: Cohen, 1925. Stoker, H. G. *Die Stryd om die Ordes.* Pretoria, South Africa: Caxton, 1941. Stoker, H. G. *Die Wysbegeerte van die Skeppingsidee: Die Grondbeginsels van 'n Kalvinistiese Wysbegeerte.* Pretoria, South Africa: J. H. De Bussy, 1933. Stoker, H. G. *Koers in die Krisis.* 3 vols. Stellenbosch: Pro Ecclesia Drukkery, 1935, 1940, 1941. Stoker, H. G. *Oorsprong en Rigting.* 2 vols. Cape Town, South Africa: Tafelberg Uitgewers, 1967, 1970.

Iain S. Maclean

STOWE, HARRIET BEECHER (1811– 1896). Harriet Elizabeth was the seventh child in revivalist **Lyman Beecher** and Roxana Foote Beecher's auspicious brood, which included domestic reformer **Catharine** and eminent pulpit luminary **Henry Ward.** Harriet's upbringing mingled her own questing nature and the earnest New England Calvinism of her father with memories of her mother, who died when Harriet was four but whose gentle piety continued to inspire her children. These influences led Harriet to write in support of social reform grounded in God's sovereign justice, most notably on behalf of abolition. After the success of that cause, Stowe expressed her social concern through writings that explored the politics of the home and their implications for the nation.

Born in Litchfield, Connecticut, Harriet experienced a first conversion in 1825. She moved with her father and his second wife to Cincinnati, Ohio, in 1832, where he presided over Lane Theological Seminary. Harriet married Lane's professor of biblical literature, Calvin Stowe, in January 1836. In September of that year, she gave birth to twin daughters. Five more children would come; three children would survive her. She moved with Calvin and her children to Brunswick, Maine, in 1850, when he accepted a position at Bowdoin College. They would move again, in 1852, to Andover Theological Seminary in Massachusetts.

Harriet began to explore a public literary identity in Cincinnati, publishing stories and a geography textbook. A visit to a Kentucky plantation and her reading of antislavery literature strengthened her sense of slavery's injustice. In 1836, Stowe wrote to the *Cincinnati Journal and Luminary,* over which brother Henry Ward had temporary charge. Writing as "Franklin," and at least as fervently in support of free speech and liberty of conscience as against slavery, Stowe bemoaned the fate of antislavery partisans who suffered abuse at the hands of proslavery mobs.

Stowe experienced a second conversion in 1843, overwhelmed by the suicide of her brother George and her own inadequacy in caring for a newborn daughter. Through this conversion came her sense that God redeemed, indeed favored, those who suffered. The Fugitive Slave Law of 1850 outraged this sensibility. Having already published several stories in the antislavery *National Era,* Stowe intimated to its editor that a vision had inspired her to write an extended story against slavery, to last through three or four issues. That

Harriet Beecher Stowe. Courtesy of the Library of Congress

story became *Uncle Tom's Cabin; or, Life among the Lowly,* which ran from June 5, 1851, until April 1, 1852. John P. Jewett then published the serial as a book in 1852. It sold 300,000 copies in its first year of publication.

The Fugitive Slave Act served as the immediate occasion for the appearance of *Uncle Tom's Cabin.* But in answering that unjust law, Stowe also acted upon other impulses. In portraying slavery's destruction of family relationships, she drew on her sadness over the 1849 cholera death of her infant son: "It was at *his* dying bed, and at *his* grave, that I learnt what a poor slave mother may feel when her child is torn away from her" (quoted in Hedrick, *Life,* 193). In addition, her 1843 conversion confirmed in her the redemptive value of suffering, even the suffering of slaves. By rendering clear pictures of their agonies, Stowe might hasten the slaves' liberation and the nation's redemption. She wrote, then, out of a sense of prophetic ambition that looked for a sovereign God to set right the nation—and through the nation, the world. She knew that the inherently unjust system of slavery should end, must end. God would act through the transformative triumph of redemptive love enacted by Christ but modeled in Stowe's novel by the book's many heroic mother characters, and of course by Tom and Eva.

In response to the firestorm of protest the book ignited among slavery's defenders, Stowe published in 1853 *A Key to Uncle Tom's Cabin,* a compendium of slave-culture artifacts—legal decisions, advertisements for escaped slaves, slave and owner testimony, and official church declarations. Stowe had collected many of these documents after the novel's publication. She would draw on these resources again in her 1856 novel, *Dred: A Tale of the Great Dismal Swamp.*

In 1854, on the eve of the passage of the Kansas-Nebraska Act, which gutted the Missouri Compromise, Stowe published in the antislavery *Independent* "An Appeal to Women of the Free States of America, on the Present Crisis in Our Country." She exhorted American women, free from "the stronger sex's" lust for power, to exercise their "deeper" and "more immoveable knowledge, in those holier feelings, which are peculiar to womanhood," to protect all families, black and white, from the scourge of slavery. The United States, she claimed, disappointed the democratic hopes of the world in continuing and indeed extending slavery. Stowe recommended that women educate themselves and others about the true nature of the slave system, petition Congress, and pray for guidance from the "Almighty Guardian and Ruler of nations" (Hedrick, *Reader*, 455, 456).

In Stowe's response to subsequent unrest in Kansas, the novel *Dred*, the title character answered Uncle Tom's Christ-like suffering with the prophetic fury of rebellion. Although Stowe did not recommend rebellion, the novel showed the logical result of an evil system that suppressed the better instincts of all those, white and black, entangled in it.

Stowe continued to write on the slavery question up to and during the Civil War. Responding to President **Abraham Lincoln**'s declaration that preserving the Union, rather than abolishing slavery, motivated his political actions, Stowe published "Will You Take a Pilot?" in the *Independent* in 1862. Reasoning from Jesus's declaration of his partisanship with the downtrodden, Stowe indicted Lincoln's expediency. Stowe declared that Lincoln would have spoken better to have said, "I shall do less for the Union whenever it would hurt the cause of the slave, and more when I believe it would help the cause of the slave" (Hedrick, *Reader*, 472). Lincoln did appear, however, in Stowe's celebration of the North's victory over Southern slave-holding morality, *Men of Our Times*, published in 1868.

After Emancipation and the conclusion of the war, Stowe turned her literary attention in part to women's proper role in society. The postwar atmosphere increasingly crackled with questions about women's rights, women's literary voice, and the sexual double standard. These issues coalesced for Stowe in her publication in the *Atlantic Monthly* of "The True Story of Lady Byron's Life" (1869). Upending conventional wisdom about the storied pair, Stowe set the Christ-like suffering of Lady Byron against the tyranny and incestuous infidelity of her husband. The full force of public disapproval descended upon Stowe for her immodesty, yet she expanded the article into a book, *Lady Byron Vindicated* (1870).

Stowe objected to the double standard that bound women to unworthy men. She also objected, however, to those in the women's rights movement, such as the radical Victoria Woodhull, who advocated the abolition of marriage altogether. Stowe's was a measured feminism, and after *Lady Byron*, she engaged the issue of women's rights primarily through domestic fiction that revered marriage and Christian domesticity. In these later novels, as in all of her writing, Stowe persuaded her audience by using the language and logic of popular conventions to transform the culture within which those conventions operated. Her faith in the virtues of domesticity and republicanism were at once confirmed and challenged by her Christian faith, which considered seriously both the "kindness and severity" of God.

Bibliography. Adams, John R. *Harriet Beecher Stowe.* New York: Twayne, 1963. Hedrick, Joan. *Harriet Beecher Stowe: A Life.* New York: Oxford University Press, 1994. Hedrick, Joan, ed. *The Oxford Harriet Beecher Stowe Reader.* New York: Oxford University Press, 1999. Stowe, Calvin Ellis. *Life of Harriet Beecher Stowe, Compiled from Her Letters and Journals.* Boston: Houghton, Mifflin, 1889. Wilson, Forrest. *Crusader in Crinoline: The Life of Harriet Beecher Stowe.* Philadelphia: J. B. Lippincott, 1941.

Anne Blue Wills

STRAUSS, FRANZ JOSEF (1915–1988).
Strauss was one of the founding fathers of
the **Christian Social Union** (CSU) in 1945
and was elected to the Bundestag (Federal
Parliament of West Germany) in 1949. The
son of a Munich butcher, Franz Josef
Strauss studied at the University of Munich
and passed his examination in classics with
intentions of becoming a teacher. In the
Second World War, he was drafted and
became an officer.

After the war, he became federal minister for various portfolios under Chancellor
Konrad Adenauer and also served as federal minister of defense for several years.
In this position he was responsible for the
fast and efficient rearmament of West
Germany after the Second World War, and
he vehemently demanded nuclear weapons for the German army. He was forced
to resign in 1962 when it became known
that he had induced police raids on an
opposition news magazine without legal
reasons (the so-called Spiegel affair).
Nevertheless he later became minister of
finances in Kurt Georg Kiesinger's government (1966–1969). In the early 1970s,
Strauss strongly and ideologically opposed
the treaties normalizing relations between
West and East Germany, the USSR, and
other Eastern European States, the
Ostpolitik of Social Democratic chancellor Willy Brandt. In 1978 Strauss was
elected premier of the German state of
Bavaria. Nominated by the **Christian
Democratic Union** and the Christian
Social Union, in 1980 Strauss lost the federal election to Helmut Schmidt. He
remained premier of Bavaria until his
death in 1988. In the United States he
received honorary doctorates from half a
dozen universities.

Conservative but open to modern
Bavarian industrial interests, Strauss helped
to transform rural Bavaria into one of the
leading high-tech regions of the world. He
was famous for his eloquence, and his slogan "freedom instead of socialism" against

Brandt in the 1970s is a well-known example of his brilliant polemics. Strauss was
also successful in organizing the CSU and
led it to a majority of almost two-thirds in
Bavaria for decades. He sometimes surprised even political allies with unexpected
turns such as the first official visit of a leading West German politician to the People's
Republic of China in 1975 and the arrangement of a billion-mark loan to the German
Democratic Republic in 1983. Already during his lifetime rumors arose regarding corruption and a system of illegal financial
transactions in favor of his election campaigns, accusations that continued to
plague his reputation (and that of one of
his two sons) after his death.

In the German collective memory Franz
Josef Strauss holds a unique position as
an intelligent but often impetuous
Bavarian fighter against communism and
socialism.

Bibliography. Bickerich, Wolfgang. *Franz
Josef Strauß—ein Mensch in seinen Wider-
sprüchen: Die Biographie,* Düsseldorf, Germany: Econ, 1996. Siebenmorgen, Peter. *Franz
Josef Strauss,* Munich: Deutsche Verlagsanstalt,
2002. Strauss, Franz Josef. *Die Erinnerungen.*
4th ed. Berlin: Siedler, 1989.

Bernd Leupold

STRONG, JOSIAH (1847–1916). Ordained a Congregationalist minister in
1871, Strong was an evangelical and social
gospel reformer best known for his most
influential book, *Our Country* (1885).
Following its publication, he was invited to
serve as General Secretary of the Evangelical
Alliance for the United States. He resigned
this position in 1898 to found and serve as
president of the American Institute of
Social Service until his death in 1916.

Strong's *Our Country* was a rewriting of
a Congregationalist home missionary tract,
designed to provide both a rationale and
motivation for supporting home missions.
Strong's unapologetic statement of missionary ideology had both nationalistic

and imperialistic overtones. Merging religious and political objectives, it reasserted the Puritan vision of a Christian America in the then popular language of manifest destiny. Strong fused the American Puritan idea of national "chosenness" with a religious and political interpretation of social Darwinism. He argued that the American "Anglo-Saxon," conditional upon faithfulness to the divine will, was destined to carry "spiritual Christianity" and "civil liberty" to the world. Though this view was widely embraced when first published, posthumously it has earned Strong severe criticism as a racist and imperialist.

Strong believed Christian faith must be applied to all of life and acted upon in concrete, socially transformative ways that included political activity. His most explicitly political book, *Expansion, Under New World-Conditions* (1900), called for an end to U.S. isolationism which, Strong argued, had become nothing more than a dangerous illusion. Changing world conditions required crucial leadership from America as the most powerful Christian nation.

In this spirit, in 1909, he embarked upon a pilgrimage to establish Institutes for Social Service throughout the world, starting in South America. His two final books, *Our World: The New World-Life* (1914) and *Our World: The New World-Religion* (1915), served as a sequel to the missionary ideology put forth in *Our Country* thirty years earlier. These volumes called for a global, applied Christianity that would finally result in the long awaited establishment of the Kingdom of God on earth.

Bibliography. Edwards, Wendy J. Deichmann. "Manifest Destiny, the Social Gospel and the Coming Kingdom: Josiah Strong's Program of Global Reform, 1885–1916." *Perspectives on the Social Gospel: Papers from the Inaugural Social Gospel Conference at Colgate Rochester Divinity School*, edited by Christopher H. Evans, 81-116. (Lewiston, N.Y.: The Edwin Mellen Press, 1999). Reed, James Eldin. "American Foreign Policy, The Politics of Missions and Josiah Strong," *Church History* 41 (June 1972): 230–45.

Wendy J. Deichmann Edwards

STROSSMAYER, JOSIP JURAI (1815–1905). Bishop Strossmayer was the foremost clerical proponent of South Slav unity during the nineteenth century. He advocated the idea of a South Slav entity under Catholic and Croatian leadership. A forceful personality at the First Vatican Council, Strossmayer also challenged the papal claim of infallibility in matters of faith and in 1872 was the last bishop to finally concede to the pontiff. During his lifetime, he succeeded in achieving neither of his pet issues but established a reputation as a fighter for Croatian rights in Hungary and did more than any clergyman to promote the idea of Croat, Serb, and Slovene unity.

Born of modest parentage, Strossmayer obtained his religious education in Djakovo, Pest, and Vienna. After becoming a priest in 1838, he earned a doctorate in theology in 1842, writing his dissertation on the topic of church unity. After a post as an assistant minister in Petrovaradin (1840–1842), he lectured at the Djakovo seminary (1842–1847) and, upon moving to the Austrian capital in 1847, served as a court chaplain and taught canon law at the University of Vienna. His career culminated with his consecration as bishop of Djajokovo, in Slavonia (Croatia) in November 1849. Prior to Austrian annexation, his diocese included Bosnia and Herzogovina as well as Serbia (1851–1896).

Bishop Strossmayer devoted his life to the reconciliation of Croats and Serbs. Prior to the Austro-Hungarian *Ausgleich* (Compromise) of 1867, he fought for Catholic-Orthodox unity based on the use of the Old Church Slavonic in the liturgy. In his diocese, Strossmayer built a neo-Gothic cathedral in Djakovo. He arranged for the education and missionary work of

Franciscans in Bosnia, and he supported the schooling of Balkan priests at the College of St. Jerome in Rome.

Strossmayer was also the leading political advocate of a federalist solution to the nationality problem before the *Ausgleich*. Active in the Croatian National Party, Strossmayer opposed Habsburg absolutism and sought a compromise with the Magyars in negotiating the *Nagodba*, the constitutional agreement on the position of Croatia in the monarchy. In so doing, he contributed to the creation of an autonomous Croatia within the Hungarian kingdom after 1867. Although he maintained secret exchanges with Prince Mihailo of Serbia, he never realized his dream of Yugoslav unity, s Serbia acquired its independence from the Ottoman Empire. Even though he was willing to compromise, the Serbs rejected his proposals for unity under Croatian leadership. His frustration led to his departure from politics in the latter years of his life.

While not achieving his lofty political goals, Bishop Strossmayer used his leverage in cultural matters to promote South Slav unity. In Zagreb, he established and funded a South Slav academy (1868) and university (1874). He generously contributed financial support for the publication of historical documents supporting South Slav unity. An avid collector of art, his gifts formed the basis for the creation of a national art museum.

Bibliography. Bukowski, James B. "Bishop Strossmayer's Political Career, 1860–1873." PhD diss., Indiana University, 1972. Kann, Robert. *A History of the Habsburg Empire 1526–1918*. Berkeley and Los Angeles: University of California Press, 1974. Krokar, James. "Strossmayer, Bishop Josip Juraj (1815–1905)." In *Encyclopedia of Eastern Europe*, ed. Richard Frucht. New York: Garland, 2000. Slovak, Charles J., III, "J.J. Strossmayer as a Balkan Bishop." *Balkan Studies* 18 (1977): 121–44.

Michael J. Kopanic, Jr.

STURZO, LUIGI (1871–1959). A Sicilian priest and political activist, Sturzo founded the **Italian Popular Party** (Partito Popolare Italiano, PPI) and, following its demise in 1925, became a leading adversary of Benito Mussolini's Italian Fascist state.

During Sturzo's youth and in the wake of Italian unification, lay activities of the Catholic community centered around the *Opera dei Congressi*, inaugurated in 1874. These congresses were instrumental in organizing and supporting the peasantry through the creation of rural banks and agricultural cooperatives and thereby helping them cope with the policies of the liberal state. Generally speaking, the church hierarchy tended to cooperate with the agencies of the state, while the lower clergy, working closely with the peasants, were active supporters of the lower classes and opponents of the government of the day. In 1891, Pope **Leo XIII** defined Catholic social policy in his encyclical *Rerum novarum*, calling for class cooperation mediated by the church, and justifying the work of the clergy with the lower classes.

Born in Caltagirone, Sicily, the young Sturzo became interested and active in developing the church's political and social influence, especially in relation to the Italian South. He was ordained priest in 1894 and studied at the Gregorian University in Rome, receiving his degree in 1898. His formation occurred in the aftermath of *Rerum novarum*, in the tensions of social repression in the 1890s. As a result, he helped to found a rural bank and an agricultural cooperative in Caltagirone in 1897.

The repressions of the 1890s and the rise of Socialism raised the question of whether Catholics should take an active role in politics. The Christian democrats within the *Opera dei Congressi* were divided on this issue. The radical extremists were opposed to Catholic voting, lest Catholic conservatives would thereby be enabled to lend their support to the existing government. A more moderate group, supported by Luigi Sturzo, was willing to promote a political party to run in local and national elections. Within the *Opera dei Congressi,* however, the Christian democrats were opposed and outnumbered by conservatives, who believed the proper role for the *Congressi* was as a vehicle for the papal will. The matter was ultimately resolved by Pope **Pius X** in 1904, when he abolished the *Opera dei Congressi* and decreed that there would be no Catholic political party in Italy. At the same time, he relaxed the ban on Catholic voting, so that Catholics might endorse those parties that supported the church.

Sturzo concentrated on his work in Caltagirone for the next decade. In 1905, he was elected mayor of the town, a position he held until 1920. He favored local autonomy within the state and was generally critical of the policies of the liberal Giolitti government. He did support the Libyan War of 1911, however, as a means to open new markets for the south, and in 1915, he supported Italian intervention in World War I because he hoped that the war would destroy liberal Italy and bring much-needed social reform.

Pius X reorganized the Catholic movement in 1905 by creating four new lay organizations in place of the *Opera dei Congressi.* In 1914, **Benedict XV** named Sturzo secretary-general of one of these organizations, the *Unione Popolare,* but in 1915, these organizations were brought together under the umbrella organization of **Italian Catholic Action** (*Azione Cattolica Italiana*).

By the end of the war, recognizing that the participation of the clergy in support of the national war effort had changed the public attitude toward the church, Sturzo and a number of his colleagues felt that the time had come to create a secular broad-based political party founded on Catholic social principles. This party was to be autonomous of the church hierarchy and would promote the family, local autonomy, the right to work, freedom for the church, proportional representation, and voting rights for women. When Benedict XV did not oppose the initiative, the Italian Popular Party was founded on January 18, 1919. Don Luigi Sturzo was named secretary of the party.

While it had been Sturzo's original intention to have the PPI function as a political pressure group, its success in the first elections under proportional representation in November 1919 meant that it was immediately faced with the prospect of forming electoral alliances with either the traditional liberal political leadership or with the newly emergent Socialist Party. Sturzo asserted the autonomy of the party and refused all alliances, with the result that it proved impossible to secure stable government in postwar Italy. Moreover, in refusing political alliances, Sturzo disappointed the Vatican and the conservatives in his party, who feared the rise of Socialism and wanted the PPI to join a broad antisocialist coalition. Benedict XV was also disappointed that Sturzo and the PPI would not give priority to a settlement of the Roman Question. In fact, the existence of this autonomous Catholic party created new difficulties for the Vatican in its negotiations with the Italian government.

Sturzo's difficulties were compounded in 1922 by the election of a new pope and the rise of Mussolini's Fascists. Pope **Pius XI,** elected in February 1922, recognized that the PPI was going to be of little help in his determination to settle the Roman Question. He sought instead to build a strong Catholic movement around *Azione Cattolica Italiana,* which could then be used as a significant political lever in his dealings with the Fascists. Sturzo also had to contend with those members of the PPI who wanted the party to ally itself with the Fascists.

In 1923, Mussolini's government introduced the Acerbo Election Act, designed to change proportional representation to favor of government electoral slates. Sturzo opposed the act and all collaboration with the Fascists, while the Fascists threatened that PPI opposition to the act would have a serious impact on future relations with the Vatican. Pius XI was uninterested in supporting the PPI and, following official hints in the Catholic press that Sturzo was proving to be an embarrassment to the Vatican, he tendered his resignation as party secretary in July 1923. When the vote was taken on the Acerbo Election Act, the bulk of the PPI abstained, but some members of the party deserted the leadership to vote for the bill, were expelled from the party, and thereafter joined the Fascists.

Sturzo remained active in the party until 1924, when continuous attacks by the Fascists indicated that his safety could not be guaranteed in Italy. He moved to London in October of that year, just before Mussolini began to implement the Fascist dictatorship. The last congress of the PPI was held in June 1925, and by 1926, the

PPI ceased to exist in Italy. In exile, Sturzo continued his antifascist campaign through his journalistic activities. When Italy entered the war in 1940, he moved to the United States, returning to Italy in 1946. After the war, he did not return to political activity but worked as a journalist until his death in 1959. He was made a senator in 1952.

Bibliography. Molony, John N. *The Emergence of Political Catholicism in Italy: Partito Popolare, 1919–1926*. London: Croom Helm, 1977 Pollard, John F. *The Unknown Pope: Benedict XV (1914–1922) and the Pursuit of Peace*. London: Geoffrey Chapman, 1999. Webster, Richard A. *The Cross and the Fasces: Christian Democracy and Fascism in Italy.* Stanford, CA: Stanford University Press, 1960.

Peter C. Kent

SUNDAY, WILLIAM ASHLEY "BILLY" (1862–1935). Sunday was born in Story County, in central Iowa. After a childhood plagued by poverty, and a disrupted family life, Sunday, in the 1880s, became a

William Sunday. Courtesy of the Library of Congress

popular professional baseball player for clubs in Chicago, Pittsburgh, and Philadelphia. A religious conversion in 1886 eventually led Sunday to abandon professional sports for religious service. In the 1890s, he worked first as an associate secretary for the Chicago YMCA, then as an advance man for revivalist J. Wilbur Chapman, and finally as head of his own evangelistic ministry.

From 1896 to 1935, Sunday toured the nation, preaching a dramatic but conventional version of the Gospel. The sophisticated organization of his ministry, his businesslike financial methods, his skillful use of the press, and his association with some of the best-known men of his day lent to his ministry an aura of modernity. Yet the essence of his theology and social message was informed by the evangelical Republican values of his youth in Iowa.

Contemporary admirers sometimes saw Sunday as a force for social change, noting a diminution of crime, vice, and political corruption, as well as a general improvement in the moral tenor of their communities in the wake of his revivals. The evangelist believed his primary mission was to preach the Gospel, but he too thought his message had important implications for solving the problems of an urbanizing, industrializing nation. There is, however, little evidence that Sunday grasped the complexities and inequities of the new urban industrial order. He attacked moral evils such as trafficking in alcohol, prostitution, gambling, and the erosion of the American Sabbath, all of which seemed accentuated by the rise of the city. He sometimes called for justice for laborers, occasionally expressed appreciation for the immigrant, and now and then condemned lynching and other forms of racial violence. Still, he never recognized the systemic injustices inherent in American capitalism, never really appreciated cultural diversity, and never challenged the racial mores of late nineteenth- and early twentieth-century America.

During the 1910s, at the zenith of his success, the perception of Sunday as a proponent of reform was derived largely from the fact that he was an ardent champion of prohibition. The success of his ministry was, in part, linked to the growing popularity of the crusade against "demon rum." Politicians, civic leaders, and reformers who might otherwise have declined to embrace Sunday's ministry recognized his usefulness as an ally in the campaign against alcohol and supported his revivals.

By the 1920s, Sunday's ministry had lost much of its appeal, and he struggled for relevance in a changing America. The revivalist did not question the Republican policies on which Coolidge's prosperity rested. Indeed, he railed against any dissent from economic, political, or cultural norms. In the late twenties, he directed much of his vitriolic rhetoric against those striving for repeal of prohibition. As the nation sank into the Great Depression, he failed to see the need for innovative action to cope with it. He opposed the New Deal of Franklin Roosevelt, believing its policies too radical and intrusive.

Billy Sunday was widely admired in conservative Christian circles as both an evangelist and a positive influence upon society. In retrospect, however, his impact on the fundamental social and political issues of his day appears to have been minimal.

Bibliography. Dorsett, Lyle W. *Billy Sunday and the Redemption of Urban America.* Grand Rapids, MI: William B. Eerdmans, 1991. Martin, Robert F. *Hero of the Heartland: Billy Sunday and the Transformation of American Society, 1862–1935.* Bloomington: Indiana University Press, 2002.

Robert F. Martin

T

TAPARELLI D'AZEGLIO, LUIGI (1793–1862). A leading second-generation reactionary thinker who succeeded figures such as **Joseph de Maistre,** Taparelli d'Azeglio was born in Piedmont to an aristocratic family of Turin. His father, Cesare, had been one of the founders of the brief but influential reactionary Catholic society, the Catholic Friendships (*Amicizie Cattoliche*). At twenty the son entered the priesthood and took the name Luigi (he had been baptized Prospero).

In 1814 he went to Rome with his father, who had been named the Sardinian ambassador to the papacy. There, Luigi was among the first to join the Jesuits when that society was revived by **Pope Pius VII,** and from 1824 until 1829 he served as rector of (what became known as) the Gregorian University. Taparelli d'Azeglio soon made a name for himself in conservative circles with his carefully argued defense of the existing social and political order against the challenge of liberalism.

Among his many works, the most important were *Saggio teoretico di diritto naturale* (1840*),* which played an important role in the revival of Thomistic philosophy in the Catholic Church, and *Esame critico degli ordini rappresentativi nella società moderna* (1854), an eloquent critique of liberal parliamentary government. From 1833 until 1848, Taparelli d'Azeglio taught in Palermo but was expelled after he supported Sicilian autonomy demands against the Kingdom of the Two Sicilies. In 1850 he relocated to Naples, where he assisted Carlo Maria Curci in the foundation of the Jesuit journal *Civiltà cattolica,* which became a major force in the defense of Catholicism and the papacy against liberalism. He remained its guiding spirit and an effective spokesman for its ideals until his death in 1862.

Bibliography. Connolly, M. "A Pioneer Catholic Sociologist: Luigi Taparelli, SI, 1793–1862." *Irish Jesuit Directory and Yearbook* 20 (1947): 167–76. Di Rosa, Luigi. *Luigi Taparelli, l'altro d'Azeglio.* Milan: Cisalpino, 1993.

Alan J. Reinerman

TAPPAN, ARTHUR (1786–1865) AND LEWIS (1788–1873). The sons of Benjamin and Sarah Homes Tappan of Northampton, Massachusetts, Arthur and Lewis Tappan spent their adult lives as well-respected entrepreneurs and evangelical reformers. Best remembered for their work as **abolitionists,** including Lewis's two-year involvement on the famed *Amistad* case, the Tappans were also entrepreneurs and innovators of their day who developed the concept of credit reporting, a practice that forever changed American business practices.

They were raised in a religious household that placed a premium on moral and social codes of behavior. Influenced by the likes of men such as **Charles Grandison Finney,** the famed revivalist preacher, they began their careers in reform focusing on issues of temperance and the use of tobacco. Echoing the business practices of such religious groups as the Quakers, the Tappans, more than any of their evangelical contemporaries, were able to blend entrepreneurialism with religious conviction in shaping the mission of creating a "benevolent empire" by Protestant evangelicals during the antebellum period.

Aspiring young men, the Tappans learned the principles of business from their father, Benjamin, who owned a gold and silversmith business for twenty years. He eventually entered the dry goods business under the firm Tappan and Fowle—later titled Tappan and Whitney. With Arthur working in the silk trade business in New York City, the younger Lewis decided to join the business world serving as a clerk in nearby Boston. Not long after, and with the encouragement of his brother, Lewis joined Arthur in the silk trade industry. There, the two began publishing the New York *Journal of Commerce* in 1827. A work that displayed their evangelical sensibilities, they refused to print advertisements by businesses, such as taverns and theaters, they deemed to be of ill repute.

More than a decade later, the Tappans had established a reputation for hard-money and frugal lending practices which led to the founding of the Tappan Mercantile Agency in 1841. This firm served as the first commercial credit-rating service in the United States—later becoming Dun and Bradstreet. Deeply informed by biblical admonitions against immoral borrowing and lending practices, the brothers' firm quickly became a success among creditors, with 280 clients and branch offices in Baltimore, Boston, and Philadelphia. The

Tappans were now prepared to lend their business savvy, evangelical aspirations, and financial backing to the cause of immediate abolition.

Believing the nation to be steeped in the sinful practice of chattel slavery, the brothers applied a Christian theological canon centering on notions of divine retribution, sin, human depravity, and final judgment to formulate their understanding of the institution. Moved by his reading of **William Lloyd Garrison**'s piece "Baltimore Jail," Arthur paid the hundred-dollar fee to free Garrison. Although often overlooked and perhaps unrealized at the time, this gesture bound the cause of immediate abolition to evangelical Christianity for several years to come.

Garrison's uncompromising stand against the colonization movement, which sought to free and then remove slaves from American soil, inspired many evangelical reformers, including the Tappans, to decree colonization as sinful. Garrison's growing constituency led to the founding in 1832 of such groups as the Massachusetts Anti-Slavery Society, which proved to be widely influential.

The following year, former colonization representatives Lewis Tappan (Arthur stayed at home for the journey), William Lloyd Garrison, and **Gerrit Smith** met in Philadelphia to form the American Anti-Slavery Society. Although the Tappans' contribution to the ideological framework and rhetoric of immediate abolition was negligible, their financial backing and tireless work were substantial. For many in these groups, their "call" to reform was rooted in the theological conviction that Christianity "forb[ade] the doing of evil that good may come."

In these efforts the brothers displayed sympathy toward African Americans that far outstripped that of most of their contemporaries and became leading spokesmen in numerous public debates. Like other prominent figures of the cause, they suffered public ridicule and remained targets of violence by proslavery men. In the wake of riots in New York City in 1834, for example, local newspapers blamed "Tappanists" for inviting public animus and creating forums for violence.

The successful blending of Garrisonian abolitionism with Protestant evangelicalism was short lived, however. By 1834, Garrison complained to other leaders that he was doing the work of antislavery entirely alone. The New Englander's criticism portended two problems that would plague the movement. Hardened by their associations with the business world, the Tappans were pragmatists who moved cautiously in areas of reform. While more conservative in their approach to reform than Garrison's Massachusetts following, the American Anti-Slavery Society also lacked the charismatic leadership to galvanize adherents in the cause of reform.

Divisions between Garrisonians and evangelical reformers were exacerbated in 1836, the result of a literary polemic between Garrison and the prominent New England divine, **Lyman Beecher.** Suspicious of Garrison's religious sincerity and use of scriptural argument, Beecher persuaded Congregational clerics in Connecticut and Massachusetts to exclude individuals with questionable views from their pulpits. In addition, that summer he addressed the Presbyterian General Assembly to encourage its members from holding any discussion concerning slavery. Garrison interpreted these moves as a direct affront to abolition and an indication of the spiritual void found within Northern churches. These differences came to a head when well-respected evangelical abolitionists and clerical leaders within the Massachusetts Anti-Slavery Society, including Henry B. Stanton, Elizur Wright, Jr., and Charles T. Torrey, challenged Garrison on his assertions of religious orthodoxy and helped to fracture the movement.

Like many evangelicals, the Tappans were cautious about endorsing violence for the cause. They were equally suspicious of what they perceived to be Garrison's willingness to sacrifice social and political expediency for what many considered his obtuse moral absolutism. With the election of Abigail Kelley Foster, a nonresistant feminist, to the executive business committee of the American Anti-Slavery Society, Lewis Tappan led evangelicals out of the organization to found the American and Foreign Anti-Slavery Society in 1840. The move had a profound effect by forever dividing the cause of antislavery in the United States.

The new antislavery organization met with mixed success. Taking the cause of abolition to the nation's denominations, the society helped to fracture denominational ties and created new forums for applying their abolitionist sentiment. By 1842, Wesleyan Methodists formally severed ties with the Methodist Episcopal Church, and four years later, a body of "Free Presbyterians" formed. Evangelical antislavery sentiment also encouraged the formation of the American Baptist Free Mission Society in 1845. Although these organizations provided thousands of churchgoing activists a forum to exercise their religious convictions, their insistence that the ultimate success of the cause lay "mainly on the blessings of the Almighty" at times hampered their attempts for meaningful societal change.

At the same time, events precipitated changes in the Tappans' more conservative approach to the antislavery cause. After the passage of the Fugitive Slave Law in 1850, Arthur and Lewis declared their willingness to disobey the law of the land in order to secure the freedom of African Americans. To combat what the Tappans perceived was a new moral evil, they began to contribute substantially, both financially and through personal efforts, to the cause of the Underground Railroad.

At the outset of the Civil War, Lewis committed to financing the *Independent,* an abolitionist newspaper whose owner faced temporary bankruptcy upon the loss of the silk trade from the South. This act saved the publication, which became a forceful voice in shaping Northern perspectives on emancipation. Secondly, he championed the policy of the American Missionary Association regarding the freed blacks in the South. Tappan urged the administration to emancipate blacks on Southern soil. He then appealed to Union commanders, including General Benjamin Butler, to allow the organization to send missionaries to areas of Union army occupation to work with contrabands and freemen.

The abolitionist cause took a physical toll on the Tappans. Following Arthur's death in 1865 and passage of the Thirteenth Amendment, which ended slavery, Lewis turned his reform efforts to a heavy indictment of the materialism of his age in a work entitled *Is It Right to Be Rich?* The work sounded a familiar refrain, criticizing the greed of a new industrial order, including a renewed distrust of credit and paper money. Prior to his death, Lewis also completed a biography of his brother.

Bibliography. Strong, Douglas M. *Perfectionist Politics: Abolitionism and the Religious Tensions of American Democracy.* Syracuse, NY: Syracuse University Press, 1999. Tappan, Lewis. *The Life of Arthur Tappan.* New York: Hurd and Houghton, 1870. Wyatt-Brown, Bertram. *Lewis Tappan and the Evangelical War Against Slavery.* Cleveland, OH: Press of Case Western Reserve University, 1969.

Kent A. McConnell

TARANCÓN, VINCENTE ENRIQUE Y (1907–1994). During Spain's struggle to replace **Francisco Franco**'s government with pluralistic democracy in the 1970s, Tarancón led the Catholic Church's struggle to remain a powerful and independent social and moral force in the nation.

Born in Burriana (Castellón), Spain, to a small farming family, Vincente Tarancón's decision to enter the Catholic priesthood was fostered by the example of his uncle, also a priest. His education at the diocesan seminary and the pontifical university in Valencia was conventional. Unusually for a Spanish bishop of the period, however, Tarancón served as both parish priest and rural dean before becoming bishop of Solsona in 1945.

During the era of the Second Republic (1931–1936), he spent three years working in Madrid with Catholic Action, returning to parish work before and during the civil war (1936–1939). Tarancón drew on his experience of violently divided communities during his later career. This is evident in his mildly dissident pastorals of the 1950s, in his work as archbishop of Oviedo (1964), and in his leadership of the Spanish church throughout the death throes of Francoism and the transition to democracy.

As archbishop of Toledo (1969), cardinal primate (1969), and then archbishop of Madrid (1971), Tarancón was Rome's candidate to lead Spain through the changes inspired by Vatican II. Relations between Franco and Pope **Paul VI** were notoriously difficult, and an intractable minority within the Spanish Church remained overtly hostile to the Council. Moving Tarancón to Madrid placed a skillful ecclesiastical diplomat at the heart of secular politics and gave him real authority over the Spanish church. In 1971 he used this authority to convene a national assembly of bishops and priests, which asked forgiveness for not having been "true ministers of reconciliation" during "a war between brothers" (Blázquez, 200). This statement gave Tarancón moral authority among left-wing politicians while his own commitment to defending the church's interests avoided overt schism within it.

The cardinal's political skills and firm belief in hierarchical authority brought a united church through the uncertain process of transition to a pluralist democracy. By 1978, with Catholicism affirmed as "the religion of the majority of Spaniards" in the new constitution, the Spanish church was, as Tarancón had wanted, unencumbered by the establishment of a defined Catholic political option, and free to speak out on moral and social issues. Tarancón's aspiration for a renewed Catholic identity for Spain, however, was not realized.

Bibliography. Blázquez, Feliciano. *La traición de los clerigos en la España de Franco.* Madrid: Trotta, 1991. Callahan, William J. *The Catholic Church in Spain, 1875–1998.* Washington DC: Catholic University of America Press, 2000. Enrique y Tarancón, Vicente. *Recuerdos de Juventud.* Barcelona: Grijalbo, 1984. Lannon, Frances. *Privilege, Persecution, and Prophecy: The Catholic Church in Spain, 1875–1975.* Oxford: Oxford University Press, 1987. Ruíz-Giménez, Joaquín, ed. *Iglesia, Estado y Sociedad en España, 1930–82.* Madrid: Argos Vergara, 1984.

Mary Vincent

TARDINI, DOMENICO (1888–1961). As a member of the Vatican secretariat of state under three successive pontiffs, Cardinal Tardini was a central figure of twentieth-century papal diplomacy. Perhaps no one knew the inner workings of Vatican diplomacy and the Roman Curia better than Tardini, who pursued a practical approach to preserving and promoting the interests of the Holy See.

Domenico Tardini was born in Rome. His rise through the diplomatic ranks began when he became a substitute of the secretary of state in 1935. Along with Giovanni Battista Montini (the future Pope **Paul VI**), Tardini served as deputy to the cardinal secretary of state, Luigi Maglione, under Pope **Pius XII.** Together, they were the nerve center of papal diplomacy during the crisis years of the Second World War. After the war, Tardini continued to work closely with Pius XII, serving as pro-secretary of state in

the last four years of Pacelli's pontificate. As such, Tardini was one of a small handful of people with insight into the character of this controversial pontiff and his actions during the Second World War.

Tardini was known for his short temper and colorful criticism of the papal diplomatic corps, toward which he harbored serious doubts. Tardini regularly marked the dispatches of papal representatives with comments such as "Imbecile!" On one occasion, he complained aloud, "People always say the diplomacy of the Holy See is the first in the world. If ours is the first, I'd like to see the second" (Alvarez, 270).

Tardini was pivotal in the reorientation of the papacy after the Second World War. He convinced a skeptical Pius XII that the wisest course for the Holy See was to support the **Christian Democracy** and other antifascist parties as a way of promoting Italy's peaceful transition to democracy after Mussolini. At the same time, Tardini reasoned that the Holy See's primary objective in the nascent cold war should be to stop the spread of Soviet Communism into Eastern and Western Europe.

The French intellectual **Jacques Maritain** observed that Tardini was a positivist and a realist at heart, conservative in temperament and in politics, and someone not easily swayed by rhetoric or idealism (Riccardi, 50). He reflected the dominant strain of Vatican diplomacy that saw its role in formalistic and legalistic rather than idealistic terms. For Tardini this entailed working for concrete guarantees from the states of Europe for the protection of basic religious liberties of Catholics.

After Pius XII's death, Tardini reluctantly agreed to serve as **John XXIII**'s secretary of state, a position he occupied until his death in July 1961. Relations between the two men were often strained. This was evident when John convoked the Second Vatican Council. As the individual responsible for the preparations of the Council, Tardini balanced the pope's ambitious vision for the Council against his own conservative instincts. He worried that the historic deliberations could get out of hand and take the church into uncharted territory. Yet, as John XXIII readily admitted, without Tardini's collaboration, the Council may never have happened.

Witty, irascible, and impulsive, yet pragmatic, Domenico Tardini symbolized a generation of papal diplomats whose pastoral function played itself out in the annals of political power. Recognizing that the days of the confessional state were long gone, Tardini strove to adapt the Holy See to the political and social realities of a changing world.

Bibliography. Alvarez, David. *Spies in the Vatican: Espionage and Intrigue from Napoleon to the Holocaust.* Lawrence: University Press of Kansas, 2002. Riccardi, Andrea. *Il Potere del Papa da Pio XII a Giovanni Paolo II.* Bari-Rome, Italy: Laterza, 1993.

Robert A. Ventresca

TASK FORCE DETAINEES PHILIPPINES. In response to an increasing number of human rights violations following the declaration of martial law in 1972 by former president Ferdinand E. Marcos (1965–1986), the Association of Major Religious Superiors of the Philippines (AMRSP) organized Task Force Detainees Philippines (TFDP) to monitor and report abuses by the police, military, and other government agencies.

Beginning as a small group of clergy, laypersons, and student volunteers, TFDP grew into a nationwide organization with a national headquarters in Manila, fourteen regional centers, and a full-time workforce of 284 by 1994. Between 1983 and the present, TFDP has helped establish a number of other human rights NGOs, including the Ecumenical Movement for Justice and Peace (EMJP), the *Kapisanan para sa Pagpapalaya ng mga Detenidong Pulitikal* (KAPATID), the *Samahan ng mga Ex-Detainees Laban sa Detensyon at para sa Amnestiya* (SELDA), the Philippine Alliance of Human Rights Advocates (PAHRA), and Families of Victims of Involuntary Disappearance (FIND). TFDP works with these and other groups on a number of human rights issues affecting the Philippines and the world.

Although disrupted by internal problems in 1995 resulting from a rump group's attempted takeover, TFDP remains at the forefront of human rights monitoring organizations. Not only does TFDP continue to monitor human rights abuses such as illegal arrests, detentions, and extrajudicial killings, but it has expanded its mission since the fall of the Marcos regime to include other activities. After 1986, TFDP initiated the Educational Assistance Program for children of human rights victims, and in 1996, during the administration of Fidel V. Ramos (1992–1998), TFDP began focusing on socioeconomic and cultural issues arising from the conversion of lands in the name of economic development that resulted in demolitions and the displacement of residents lacking the resources to resist.

TFDP publishes a quarterly journal, the *Philippine Human Rights Update.*

Bibliography. Dimaranan, Mariani. *Mariani: A Woman of a Kind.* Compiled and edited by Sr. Marie Teresita Bravo. Quezon City, Philippines: Task Force Detainees of the Philippines, 2001. McCoy, Alfred W. *Priests on Trial.* New York: Penguin, 1984. Task Force Detainees of the Philippines. 2004. www.tfdp.org.

Robert L. Youngblood

TEMPLE, WILLIAM (1881–1944). One of the most important British church leaders of the twentieth century, Temple was the son of an archbishop of Canterbury who came himself to hold the same office in the Church of England. Never primarily a theologian, and too aristocratic for traditional pastoral work, throughout his more than thirty years of public life, Temple concentrated on popularizing radical Christian social thought.

Born in 1881, Temple grew up and was educated in secure and privileged surroundings, but from the beginning of his clerical career he came to question some of the basic tenets of traditional Christian theology and social practice. He could not accept traditional views on the literal inspiration of the Bible, nor the socially quietist orientation of the Anglican Church of his formative years. Instead, he chose to align himself with the clerical and political Left that concerned itself with social improvement, not theological contention. From 1904 a fellow of Balliol College, Oxford, he became an early activist and later longserving president of the Workers' Educational Alliance, a group of university teachers and labor activists working for the spreading of advanced social theory. In 1918, he joined the Labor party, having come to regard it as the best vehicle for creating a more just and "Christian" social order. Also in 1918, Temple inspired the writing of *Christianity and Industrial Problems,* a major wartime manifesto by the socialistically inclined clergy of the Church of England, and two years later he founded the journal *Pilgrim* to further popularize like ideas.

In 1919, Temple was appointed canon of Westminster; in 1921, bishop of Manchester; in 1929, archbishop of York; and in 1942, archbishop of Canterbury. While holding these powerful offices, he continued his witness for Christian socialism. In 1924, he helped to pave the way for the interdenominational Christian Conference on Political and Economic Cooperation (COPEC), which under his chairmanship issued ambitious Christian socialist plans for strengthening the powers of the state. In the mid 1920s, Temple was active in the Standing Committee of the Christian Churches on the Coal Dispute,

which tried to mediate in a particularly bitter industrial dispute, and in 1941 he organized the Malvern Conference, where Anglican and labor activists devised further legislative reform programs for after the Second World War.

As primate, Temple's inspirational radio addresses were much listened to during the difficult years of the Second World War. He defended the war on a Christian basis and appealed for aid to the Jews, but Temple also caused some controversy when he refused to condemn the massive Allied bombings of German cities.

While in his later years Temple became more conservative in some of his views, it always remained his calling to lead in educating Anglicans about the putative social aspects of the Christian message. It was in this work that Temple left his most abiding mark on British Christianity.

Bibliography. Iremonger, F. A. *William Temple, Archbishop of Canterbury: His Life and Letters.* London: Oxford University Press, 1948. Kent, John, *William Temple: Church, State and Society in Britain, 1880–1950.* Cambridge: Cambridge University Press, 1992.

Markku Ruotsila

TEUSCH, CHRISTINE (1888–1968). A German Christian democratic politician, Teusch was born in the industrial Cologne quarter of Ehrenfeld of a well-known Catholic family of merchants. She trained to be senior school teacher and taught from 1910 and 1913 in Neuss and afterwards in Cologne. She engaged early on in politics, at first in Catholic associations and societies.

During World War I, she became chairperson of the Catholic Society of Woman Teachers for the Cologne district, an office she held until 1917, when she was conscripted and took over the management of a branch office for woman's work at the military administration at Essen. Later in the war she became secretary of the new woman's department in the Cologne central office of the General Association of Christian Labor Unions. Elected for the Weimar constituent assembly in 1919, she was not only the youngest (thirty-one years old) but also one of the few female members of parliament. Teusch belonged to the Reichstag as a member of the **Center Party** (*Zentrum*) from 1920 until 1933. In 1925 she was made recording clerk in the Reichstag's presidency. She also served as vice-chair of the *Zentrum*'s parliamentary committee for social politics.

From 1923 until 1965 she headed the Catholic Society for the Protection of Young Girls. As was usual for female teachers and politicians at that time, Teusch did not marry but lived together with her twin sister, Käthe, who ran the household. The accession in 1933 of the National Socialists under Adolf Hitler meant the suspension of Teusch's political work. She returned to Cologne as a primary school teacher and took premature retirement for health reasons in 1936. During National Socialist rule she continued to keep contact with her friends from the Christian Labor Union movement and took part in a Catholic resistance group, the so-called Cologne Circle, which included the Labor Union secretary Nikolaus Gross, who was murdered by the Nazis and recently beatified.

After the downfall of the Hitler regime, Teusch joined the newly founded **Christian Democratic Union** (CDU) and was appointed to Cologne's town council and to the advisory province council of North Rhine. In 1946 she was elected to the board of the CDU within the British zone of occupation. In 1947, she became a member of Parliament of North Rhine-Westphalia and its politico-cultural committee. Despite some protests, some of which came from members of her own party and from the churches, North Rhine-Westphalia's prime minister Karl Arnold appointed Teusch as minister of culture, education, and church affairs. After the Social Democratic politician Martha Fuchs,

Teusch became the second woman in the new democratic Germany to assume a ministerial office. Based on Christian values and tradition, Teusch set as her goal the education and cultivation of a free democratic spirit. She considered parent's rights and freedom of conscience fundamental ideas. Another priority was the development of educational opportunities for the lower strata. Beyond that, Teusch had great influence on the formulation of North Rhine-Westphalia's politico-cultural and church-political principles. Her university politics have been labeled a "page of glory in the history of Germany's recovery."

Teusch remained minister of culture, education, and church affairs until 1954, and in 1953 she headed the federal republic's influential Conference of Ministers of Culture. She was one of the founders and promoters of the German People's Institution for Studies, the German Academic Exchange Service, and the Society of German Science at the European College in Bruges. When she had to retire in 1954, she was (in her own words) "cut to the quick."

Teusch remained as a member of North Rhine-Westphalia's parliament until 1966 and was an active figure on many cultural, charitable, and ecclesiastical committees. In 1956, she became the first woman decorated with the federal republic's highest order, the Great Distinguished Service Cross with Star and Shoulder Ribbon. She died in Cologne.

Bibliography. Eich, Klaus-Peter. *Schulpolitik in Nordrhein-Westfalen, 1945–1954.* Dusseldorf, Germany: Schwann, 1987.

Helmut Rönz

THOMAS, NORMAN MATTOON (1884–1968). A former Presbyterian pastor, Thomas was a leading public activist, pacifist, and six-time presidential candidate for the Socialist Party. His convictions, influenced by the **Social Gospel** movement, Marxist writings, and anarchism, crystallized into a secularized version of Christian moral perfectionism tempered by American pragmatism and practicability. Although he resigned from the Presbyterian Church after his mother died in 1931, he never renounced Christianity, referring to himself as an agnostic. Thomas never claimed to be an atheist, and toward the end of his life, he asked for a Christian burial instead of a socialist funeral. "I am not an orthodox Christian," he said, "but the Christian tradition is so much a part of our life, of my life, and Christ is to me so commanding a figure who so released all that I care most for that I feel justified in asserting Christian service which should not play up personal immortality" (Swanberg, 407).

Son of a Presbyterian minister, Thomas was born in Marion, Ohio. He studied political science under **Woodrow Wilson** at Princeton University. After graduating in 1905, he volunteered for social work in New York City before enrolling at Union Theological Seminar to study theology. Ordained in 1911, Thomas became a pastor of the East Harlem Presbyterian Church in New York City. Amid public debate over America's entry into World War I, Thomas wrote a letter to the press advocating a pacifist stance, a position that led to a forced resignation from his pastorate. Afterwards, he joined Abraham Muste, Scott Nearing, and Oswald Garrison Villard to form the Fellowship of Reconciliation (FOR). With Crystal Eastman and Roger Baldwin, he established the National Civil Liberties Bureau (NCLB), and in 1920 he worked with **Jane Addams,** Elizabeth Gurley Flynn, and Upton Sinclair to establish the American Civil Liberties Union (ACLU). Joining the Socialist Party in 1918, Thomas also ran as the socialist candidate for the governorship of New York in 1924. As the socialist presidential candidate between 1928 and 1948, he personally won the respect of the American establishment but presided over the decline of the Socialist Party.

Besides his socialist views, Thomas was an ardent supporter of pacifism, as advocated in *The Conscientious Objector in America* (1923). His other public activities included work as associated editor of the *Nation* (1921–1922), co-director of the League of Industrial Democracy (1922–1937), and founder of Southern Tenant Farmers Union (STFU). With Burton K. Wheeler and Charles A. Lindbergh, he helped form the America First Committee (AFC). During World War II, Thomas opposed the internment of Japanese Americans and afterwards denounced rearmament and the development of the cold war. His support for much of Roosevelt's New Deal legislation, especially Social Security, led to support for the civil rights movement and strong stands against poverty, racism, and the Vietnam War during the 1960s. His best known works are *A Socialist Faith* (1951), *The Test of Freedom* (1954), *Socialism Re-examined* (1963), and *Is Conscience a Crime?* (1927)

Bibliography. Duran, James C. *Norman Thomas.* New York: Twayne, 1974. Johnpoll, Bernard K. *Pacifists' Progress: Norman Thomas and the Decline of American Socialism.* Westport, CT: Greenwood Press, 1987. Seidler, Murray B. *Norman Thomas: Respectable Rebel.* Syracuse, NY: Syracuse University Press, 1967. Swanburg, W.A. *Norman Thomas: The Last Idealist.* New York: Charles Scribners' Sons, 1976.

Lee Trepanier

THORNTON, HENRY (1760–1815). Thornton was a London banker and evangelical who took a leading part in the varied activities of the so-called **Clapham Sect** during the later eighteenth and early nineteenth centuries. Born into a successful merchant family, Thornton was educated privately and eventually became the chief partner in his cousin's banking firm. But his main interest and religious calling lay in promoting the Gospel and the cause of evangelical reform through political and personal contacts with fellow members of the English social elite. First returned to the House of Commons in 1786, he was reelected continuously until 1812 and supported his close friend **William Wilberforce,** especially in the successful campaign to abolish the slave trade. He corresponded with the most prominent evangelicals of his day, notably Mrs. **Hannah More,** and together they founded the *Christian Observer,* a monthly journal to which he contributed over eighty articles. He also wrote *An Enquiry into the Paper Credit* (1802), a work prompted by the Bank of England's wartime crisis and still held in high regard by modern economists.

Like all evangelicals, Thornton was an Anglican, disparaging High Church rationalism but equally avoiding any identification with Methodist "enthusiasm." In his view, all people, rich or poor, would be better served by conversion to serious Christianity than by any kind of social engineering. He helped to found or administer dozens of missionary and reform projects, including the Society for the Relief of Poor Pious Clergymen and the British and Foreign Bible Society. The scheme that consumed much of his energy was the Sierra Leone Company (1791), which he hoped would demonstrate the progress of "civilization" in Africa by reviving the fortunes of the colony there. The original settlement of black freedmen and women, founded in 1787 by loyalist refugees from Canada, had collapsed from the effects of mismanagement and local hostility. After being elected chairman on account of his financial acumen, Thornton devoted himself tirelessly to the work of raising funds, organizing the government, and sending out more settlers. At the start, he noted, the business of the company drove everything else from his mind; eventually he served as a director for over thirty years. In 1808, Sierra Leone became a crown colony, although Thornton had not achieved the goal of demonstrating that it could be self-sufficient.

Thornton's intensely personal and self-critical faith undergirded his efforts in the wider world, and his belief in the natural weakness of humankind made him a political conservative. He deplored the influence of "modern" writers like Voltaire, Rousseau, Paine, and Godwin and regretted the effects of excessive democracy in revolutionary France. In Parliament during the 1810s, however, he maintained an independent stance and was more interested in curbing government corruption than in promoting the war against Napoleon. A reserved temperament and a capacity to see all sides of an issue kept him from allowing even his religious convictions free rein in the House of Commons: "It seems a difficult question to say how far we who know ourselves to be a minority and differ as such should press our own system on the legislature" (quoted in Meacham, 72). According to a later evangelical biographer, Thornton was "affectionate but passionless . . . a lover of mankind but not an enthusiast in the cause of our common humanity" (Thornton, 34). An incident in 1812 certainly suggests his lack of interest in redemptive projects of human design: while listening to Robert Owen outline his plans for transforming New Lanark, he and Wilberforce fell asleep.

Bibliography. Meacham, Standish. *Henry Thornton of Clapham, 1760–1815.* Cambridge MA: Harvard University Press, 1964. Thornton, Henry. *An Enquiry into the Nature and Effects of the Paper Credit of Great Britain.* Edited with an introduction by F. A. von Hayek. New York: A. M. Kelly, 1965.

John D. Ramsbottom

THORNWELL, JAMES HENLEY (1812–1862). A native of South Carolina, Thornwell was noted in his state and throughout the South as a preacher, educator, editor, and ardent defender of slavery and secession. In 1831 he, graduated at the top of his class from South Carolina

College, where he openly opposed the religious liberalism of the college president. After a dramatic religious conversion in 1832, he soon resolved to be a minister.

In 1834, he briefly journeyed to the North, where he attended Andover Theological Seminary and Harvard. Finding both schools far too liberal, he returned to South Carolina before the year was over. From 1835 to 1838 he pastored churches in South Carolina. In 1838 Thornwell accepted a position as a professor of philosophy at his alma mater, South Carolina College. After a year he returned to the pastoral ministry, but in 1841 he went back to the college, serving as its president from 1852 to 1855. In 1855, he became a professor of theology at Columbia Theological Seminary, a position he held until his death from consumption in 1862.

In the early years of his career, he believed that slavery was a civil issue and not a concern of the church. After 1831, however, when Northern **abolitionists** began to proclaim that slavery was immoral, Thornwell joined with many Southern preachers in responding to the charge and became an ardent defender of the "peculiar institution." Thornwell delivered a sermon in 1850 that is often referred to as the classical religious defense of slavery—"The Rights and the Duties of Masters." The sermon addressed an even wider issue. "The parties in this conflict," Thornwell argued, "are not merely abolitionists and slaveholders—they are atheists, socials, communists . . . on one side, and friends of order and regulated freedom on the other."

In 1847, Thornwell became the founding editor of the *Southern Presbyterian Review*. The journal became a popular vehicle for the dissemination of his religious, political, and social views. Often referred to as the "[John C.] Calhoun of the Church," he became a leading influence in the organization of the Presbyterian

Church in the Confederate States of America. Until the election of **Abraham Lincoln** to the presidency, Thornwell strongly opposed the idea of political secession and was alarmed at what he perceived as South Carolina's willingness to go it alone if necessary. Within two weeks following the election, however, he became a vigorous champion of secession and, shortly after, an advocate of war. In January of 1861 Thornwell published "The State of the Country," a widely circulated and influential treatise articulating and defending the Southern point of view. In 1862, six weeks before his death, Thornwell issued a pamphlet for Confederate soldiers, "Our Danger and Our Duty," in which he warned what would happen should the South lose the war. Her homes would be pillaged, her cities destroyed, her men hanged, and her women would become "the prey of brutal lust." The noble and glorious Southern way of life would be forever gone.

Bibliography. Thornwell, James Henley. *The Collected Writings of J. H. Thornwell.* Ed. J. B. Adger and J. L. Girardeau. 4 vols. Richmond, VA: Presbyterian Committee of Publication, 1871–1873.

David B. Chesebrough

THREE-SELF MOVEMENT (CHINA). The term "three-self," originally coined by Rufus Anderson of the American Board of Commissioners for Foreign Mission and Henry Venn of the Church Missionary Society in the nineteenth century, describes a mission policy that organized native Christians in Africa and Asia into self-supporting, self-governing, and self-propagating churches. After the Communist Revolution of 1949, the Chinese government replaced the "Three-Self" slogan with the Three-Self Patriotic Movement (*sanzi aiguo yundong*) in order to legitimatize the state takeover of the Protestant Church.

Politically, the Three-Self Patriotic Movement was a mass organization along the Communist Party's united front policy. In

1949, Y. T. Wu (Wu Yuzong), the general secretary for publications of the Young Men's Christian Association (YMCA), acted as a middleman between the Chinese Communist Party and National Christian Council, urging church leaders to support the Communist movement. In July 1950, Wu drafted "The Christian Manifesto," a statement about Chinese Christians' loyalty to the Communist state, and declared the beginning of the Three-Self Movement. The movement proclaimed to be concerned with indigenization and ecclesiastical autonomy, calling on the Chinese Protestant Church to sever the institutional ties with foreign missions, and with foreigners in general.

In the midst of the Korean War, the Preparatory Committee of the Oppose America and Aid Korea Three-Self Reform Movement of the Christian Church was founded to conduct denunciation campaigns against Western missionaries and Chinese church leaders. After a series of denunciations, the first National Christian Conference sponsored by the Preparatory Committee was held in the summer of 1954. Wu was elected chairman and assigned to take charge of the Three-Self Patriotic Movement. The officials of the Bureau of Religious Affairs served as "advisors" to the movement. Within less than a decade, the Three-Self Patriotic Movement ended the missionary era in China and marked the beginning of the Communist state intrusion into church affairs.

Bibliography. Wickeri, Philip L. *Seeking the Common Ground: Protestant Christianity, the Three-Self Movement, and China's United Front.* Maryknoll, NY: Orbis Books, 1988.

Joseph Tse-Hei Lee

TIKHOMIROV, LEV ALEXANDROVICH (1852–1923). Born in Gelendzhik, Russia, Tikhomirov was a philosopher, a specialist in public law, and a conservative political and religious publicist whose thought evolved from Marxism to monarchism and finally to Orthodox theology.

After studies at the gymnasium in Kerch, the Crimea, he entered the medical faculty of Moscow University (1870) where, as a *narodnik* influenced by the ideas of N. V. Chajkovskij, he took part in revolutionary activity. He was arrested in 1873 and detained in Petropavlovsk Fortress, St. Petersburg, and other prisons until 1878, when he was released into the probation custody of his father. He subsequently married Ekaterina Dmitrievna Sergeeva (1880), edited newspapers, and composed literature for the liberal and democratic press.

In 1882 Tikhomirov emigrated to Switzerland, then to France, where, with P. L. Lavrov, he published *Vestnik Narodnoj Voli* (A Bulletin of People's Will) and participated in discussions on the theory and tactics of revolutionary struggle. By the mid-1880s, however, political, religious, and moral doubts led the atheist to return to the Orthodox Church, which he embraced for the rest of his life. He surprised his comrades-in-arms when he submitted an application to Czar **Alexander III** for a pardon. He wrote a pamphlet—"Why I Ceased to be a Revolutionary"—in 1888 and was pardoned the following year. He first moved to Novorossijsk under police surveillance (1890), then to Moscow (1892), where he wrote for official newspapers. His subsequent publications—*Statehood and Religion* (1903), *Individual, Society and Church* (1903), *Christianity and Politics* (1906), *State, Freedom and Christianity* (1912), and others—discussed the links between politics and Christianity.

The government frequently relied on Tikhomirov as an expert on revolutionary and labor movements. He later served as a member of the Council of the Interior Ministry (1906) and as chief editor of the *Moscow Gazette* (1909–1912). In 1913 he abandoned political and public activity and left Moscow for Sergiev Posad, one of the most important centers of Russian

Orthodoxy. There, in solitude, he wrote his memoirs, *Teni proshlogo* (The Shadows of the Past), and started his *Religious and Philosophical Grounds of History,* which went unpublished until 1997. While he developed views on Orthodoxy, he never created a complete theological system. As a politician he admitted his failure, but it was as a Christian in politics that he preferred most to be remembered.
Bibliography. Burin, S.N. *Sud'by bezvestnye: S. Nechaev, L. Tikhomirov, V. Zasulich.* Moscow: Institute of General History, 1994.

Irina Novichenko

TIKHVINSKII, FEDOR VASIL'EVICH (1867–?). Born in northeastern Russia in the family of a highly educated Orthodox priest, Father Fedor Tikhvinskii was the most eloquent clerical critic of the czarist autocracy as a deputy to the second State Duma (1906–1907) from Viatka Province. To church conservatives, Tikhvinskii was a synonym for all dissident clergymen. Together with two other clerical deputies, Tikhvinskii, who was a member of the nonpartisan but populist Peasant Union, joined the leftist party of the Trudoviki.

In a fiery speech in March 1907 Tikhvinskii denounced field courts-martial and capital punishment as contrary to Christ's teachings. He charged that people who were executed for participation in the 1905 revolution were innocent, unlike Russia's leaders, who should be executed for being "responsible for the conditions that provoked unrest" and other crimes. Already immensely popular with peasants, Tikhvinski became famous across Russia, and his portrait was hung in shops when he replied to Prime Minister P. A. Stolypin's accusation that the Duma demanded "hands up" from the government: "We do not demand from our government 'hands up,' we demand 'conscience up.'" Tikhvinskii spoke for the peasants on labor and private property. In a Duma speech he

declared that they had the right to the land just as they had a right to water and air. In another speech Tikhvinskii voiced the warning of liberals that the uncontrolled bureaucracy was usurping imperial authority and separating the czar from the people: "How I wish I could fly on a magic carpet and with the cap of invisibility to the foot of the throne and say, 'Your Majesty, your main enemy, the main enemy of the people, is the irresponsible ministry.'"

In May 1907, Tikhvinskii, four other clerical deputies, and the entire Duma Left absented themselves during a vote expressing joy at the failure of an assassination attempt on Czar Nicholas II. Tikhvinskii refused both choices presented to him by St. Petersburg Metropolitan Antonii (Vadkovskii), to leave oppositionist parties or the priesthood, and was consequently suspended from service by the Holy Synod of the Russian Orthodox Church. After an ecclesiastical trial that signaled the church conservatives' counterattack on a burgeoning clerical movement that combined church reform with political emancipation, Tikhvinskii was defrocked. He vanished after the 1917 revolutions.
Bibliography. Curtiss, John Shelton. *Church and State in Russia: The Last Years of the Empire, 1900–1917.* New York: Octagon Books, 1965.

Argyrios K. Pisiotis

TILLICH, PAUL (1886–1965). Paul Tillich was a German Protestant theologian who immigrated to the United States in 1933 and spent the remainder of his life teaching at Union Seminary in New York, Harvard, and the University of Chicago. The move was precipitated by his suspension from the University of Frankfurt by the Nazi regime in retaliation for his public defense of Jewish colleagues and his involvement in political circles that had opposed Hitler.

Tillich's political awakening came during World War I while he was serving as a chaplain to German troops at the western front, where he endured some of the worst battles of the war. He learned during these years that one of the great temptations of human beings is to conflate nationalism with the purposes of God and that the brunt of war is felt disproportionately by the working class—not by those who make war and profit from it. As the war ended, returning soldiers were bitter toward both the kaiser, whose abdication they demanded, and toward the German churches, which had fully supported the regime's pursuit of the war. Alongside other German citizens, many of them bolted from their churches and rushed to embrace the wave of Marxist-inclined labor movements that were coordinating uprisings across the country. Tillich reached the conclusion that at this historical moment God was speaking more directly through these movements—even the ones that identified themselves as enemies of religion—than through his own church.

After the war, Tillich taught at the University of Berlin, where he commiserated with a group of Christian and Jewish intellectuals who formed what they called the "*kairos* circle." They adopted the biblical word *kairos* to describe their efforts because it referred to auspicious moments in history when the eternal breaks into ordinary time, opening up new ways of life. They believed they were in the maelstrom of one of those moments. Convinced that capitalism bore a significant share of the blame for the war, they began to explore socialist alternatives. There was a prophetic demand for justice in socialism that they appreciated, but the Bolshevism that was gaining recruits in postwar Germany was to be rejected for its naive and dangerously utopian ambitions. Instead, the *kairos* circle sought a socialist restructuring of the German political order that was moderated by a more sober view of the human condition, taking seriously the ever-present enticements of

the "demonic" to spoil every advance of justice.

In a book that he wrote in 1925 reflecting his thinking of the *kairos* period (*The Religious Situation*), Tillich granted that while capitalism had achieved something important (he credited it with breaking apart the stultifying heteronomy of the medieval social order and giving rise to the modern notion of the individual), the pendulum of its atomizing effects had swung too far and was responsible for introducing an alienating rootlessness to Western culture. He praised Leo Tolstoy and Karl Marx for providing a worthy prophetic critique that affirmed his concerns.

In 1929, Tillich joined the faculty at the University of Frankfurt. In the four years he was there, he supervised Theodor Adorno's dissertation and helped Max Horkheimer establish the Frankfurt Institute of Social Research. The Frankfurt Institute, under the leadership of Horkheimer and Adorno, became one of the dominant think tanks of left-leaning, neo-Marxist political and cultural theory in the twentieth century. It was transplanted to New York City in the 1930s, a casualty of Nazi anti-Semitism, which allowed Tillich to retain his contact with this circle of friends. The book that reflects the ideas that matured in Tillich as a result of their mutual influence is *The Socialist Decision* (1932). In the book he argues that political conservatism and progressivism both have religious roots. Conservatives order their political thinking around myths of origin, believing that it was in the time of the beginnings that society had things right and that history is one long story of decline from those noble beginnings. Politics, for them, is all about restoring the social order to its original purity. Progressives, on the other hand, order their political thinking around visions of justice, which they are convinced none of our predecessors has ever achieved. Conservatives, in other words, favor the garden of

Eden, while progressives prefer the New Jerusalem.

During World War II, from his home in New York, Tillich wrote more than one hundred radio addresses, which were broadcast into Germany by the Voice of America. In these addresses, he encouraged the German people to recognize the viciousness of the path their government had chosen; instructed them on the nature of true prophetic liberation, which can be found in the Bible; and divulged to them the extent of Hitler's campaign to exterminate the Jews.

In the two decades after World War II, Tillich confessed to becoming more politically quiescent. The difficulty of being a foreign-born citizen in a country with lingering resentments toward his homeland was one obstacle. But he also reached the judgment during the cold war that the *kairotic* moment for the West had passed, and the time was not ripe for political transformation. The political climate, he determined, was such that small cadres of ideological and economic leaders held such power that they were untouchable by any grassroots activity. These were the decades of what he came to call "the sacred void," a time that was to be endured and not prematurely injected with solutions that had not been adequately considered.

Bibliography. Stone, Ronald H. *Paul Tillich's Radical Social Thought.* Atlanta, GA: John Knox Press, 1980. Tillich, Paul. *Love, Power, and Justice.* London: Oxford University Press, 1954. Tillich, Paul. *Political Expectations.* Ed. James Luther Adams. New York: Harper & Row, 1971. Tillich, Paul. *The Religious Situation.* Trans. H. Richard Niebuhr. New York: Henry Holt, 1932. Tillich, Paul. *The Socialist Decision.* Trans. Franklin Sherman. New York: Harper & Row, 1977.

Kelton Cobb

TISCHNER, JÓZEF (1931–2000). Not only was Tischner one of the foremost Catholic philosophers of the post-WWII era in Poland, but as an essayist and a preacher he may have done more than any other single individual to set the ethical tone of the nation's anticommunist opposition during the last decade of communist rule. Although his identification with the more "open" or "modern" wing of the Catholic Church would generate some controversy toward the end of his life, he was widely considered in the 1980s to be the chaplain of the Solidarity movement. Tischner grew up in the mountains of southern Poland, where both his parents served as village schoolteachers. In 1950 he entered a seminary in Krakow to prepare for the priesthood while simultaneously pursuing a degree in theology and philosophy at Jagiellonian University. He was ordained in 1955, after which he continued his studies at the Catholic Theological Academy in Warsaw (1955–1957) and once again at Jagiellonian University. He obtained is doctorate in philosophy from the latter institution in 1963, with a dissertation on the phenomenology of Edmund Husserl. In his long career as an author, he produced everything from scholarly volumes to newspaper essays (mainly in the Catholic weekly *Tygodnik Powszechny* [Universal Weekly]) and covered themes ranging across the fields of philosophy, theology, politics, theater, ethics, and social theory. Among his most important texts were *The Polish Form of Dialogue* (1980), *The Ethics of Solidarity* (1981), *A Philosophy of Drama* (1990), *The Unfortunate Gift of Freedom* (1993), *Confessions of a Revolutionary* (1993), *How to Live* (1997), and *A Priest Led Astray* (1999). All his works were marked by a deep grounding in contemporary philosophy, both Christian and secular. Although a harsh critic of Marxist theory and the practices of the socialist regimes of Eastern Europe, he became one of the foremost advocates within Poland for a dialogue between Catholics and communists, and he did much to propagate a greater openness to the modern world (particularly twentieth-century philosophical trends) within the Polish church. Most his work revolved around the relationship between public life and personal morality. From the rise of the Solidarity movement through the negotiated surrender of power by the communists in 1989, and into the contentious political climate of the 1990s, Tischner was a consistent advocate for dialogue and compromise, which he defended not as a mere tactical option but as a fundamental ethical stance. According to Tischner, Christian politics ought to be focused not so much on specific legislative accomplishments or institutional forms, but on a political process rooted in openness, negotiation, social solidarity, and a stance of compassionate understanding toward one's opponents.

Bibliography. Bonowicz, Wojciech. *Tischner.* Krakow, Poland: Znak, 2001. Michnik, Adam, Józef Tischner, and Jacek Żakowski. *Między Panem a Plebanem.* Krakow, Poland: Znak, 1995.

Brian Porter

TISO, JOSEF (1887–1947). Tiso was a Roman Catholic priest, president of the 1939–1945 pro-German Slovak state, and perhaps Slovakia's most controversial historical figure. Executed for treason, collaboration, and crimes against humanity, Tiso is nonetheless still promoted by nationalists as a Slovak martyr and prospective saint. While his politics drew on papal encyclicals, Austrian and Slovak Christian thinkers, and natural law, his most controversial policies followed Aquinas's argument of the "lesser evil." Because Tiso defined evil according to how it affected Slovaks first, his actions consequently often mocked the spirit and teachings of Christianity.

Tiso devoted the first half of his life to the church, and the second to Slovak nationalism. Apparently assimilated to Hungarian culture, he was a rising clerical star before 1918. With the breakup of Austria-Hungary and the creation of Czechoslovakia, however, he publicly embraced Slovak identity and politics, wedding himself for life to **Hlinka**'s Slovak People's Party. In 1927–1929 he represented the party as Czechoslovak minister of health and later served as the party's ideologist. In 1938 he led the party in exploiting the Munich Agreement to gain Slovak autonomy. Although apparently content with this victory, Tiso drifted toward separatism under pressure from domestic instability, party radicals, and Adolf Hitler's imperial designs. After Prague sacked him in March 1939 as Slovak prime minister, he and his parliament accepted Hitler's demand to declare independence.

Though enjoying some domestic autonomy, Tiso's one-party authoritarian state was subordinate to Germany. Tiso initially divided his attention between state building and checking the power of party radicals. After the 1940 defeat of France, Hitler made the radicals his protégés, and Slovak politics more closely imitated Nazism. Tiso outflanked the radicals in 1942 after consolidating support among party conservatives, co-opting fascist rhetoric, and importing the führer principle into party structures. A growing German desire for stability in Slovakia especially solidified his authority, which went unchallenged until the 1944 Slovak National Uprising. Denouncing the revolt as foreign, Tiso helped the Germans to suppress it.

Tiso's involvement in the Holocaust is especially controversial. A strong anti-Semite, Tiso oversaw the passage of legislation defining Jews according to confession and limiting their employment in the free professions. After 1940, the anti-Semitic initiative passed to the radicals, whose harsher approach was exemplified by a switch to racially based persecution. As the church never embraced National Socialist racial doctrine, this created a crisis of legitimacy, which Tiso's conservatives tried to resolve by empowering him to protect select racially defined Jews, such as converts. In 1942, the regime deported around 58,000 Jews, almost all of whom perished. While his apologists credit Tiso with saving up to 40,000 Jews from a similar fate, he in fact protected only around 1,000 such individuals, most of whom had excellent Christian credentials. He also sanctioned the deportations through law and public statement. When the Germans with Slovak assistance deported around 13,500 more Jews in 1944–1945, he showed virtually no concern for the deportees, instead blaming them for supporting the uprising.

Postwar Communists manipulated Tiso's 1946–1947 trial, thus discrediting it for many Slovaks. Both domestic and international opposition, however, defeated a postcommunist attempt to rehabilitate him.

Bibliography. Kamenec, Ivan. *Tragédia politika, kňaza a človeka: Dr. Jozef Tiso 1887–1947.* Bratislava, Slovakia: Archa, 1998. Ward, James Mace. "'People Who Deserve It': Jozef Tiso and the Presidential Exemption." *Nationalities Papers* 30 (4): 571–601.

James Mace Ward

TIWARI, YISU DAS (1911–1997). Indian Christian convert, theologian, and social activist, Tiwari was born into a Brahmin family influenced by the Arya Samaj reformer Dayannand Saraswati. Tiwari converted to Christianity after an intensive reading of St. John's Gospel and the writings of the missionary C. F. Andrews. Tiwari was baptized in January 1935 and chose the name Yisu Das (Slave of Jesus). After his conversion, he became a wandering ascetic (*sadhu*) dedicated to Christ and made a decision to become a member of Mahatma Gandhi's ashram at Wardha.

Following Gandhi's example, Yisu Das performed tasks specifically prohibited by his Brahmin upbringing, such as cleaning latrines and sweeping. Like many of Gandhi's followers, Yisu Das took a vow to always

uphold the Truth (*satya*), and he exclusively wore clothes of homespun (*khadi*) fabric. Yisu Das also opened a night school for Untouchables and worked for the abolition of child marriage and bonded labor.

After moving from Gandhi's ashram, Yisu Das received a master's degree in Hindi and Sanskrit and in 1947 was ordained by the Union of Baptist Conferences of North India. He taught at Serempore University and Bishop's College and received a doctoral degree in divinity (*honorius causa*) from Serempore University in 1995, two years before his death. Yisu Das completed a revised translation of the New Testament in Hindi and wrote extensive commentaries on John's Gospel. Yisu Das's interpretation of the Bible and Christianity owed much to his Hindu nondualist (*advaitin*) upbringing, for he liberally used Vedantic terms in his Hindi translations of Christian scripture.

The influence of Gandhi also definitively shaped Yisu Das's articulation of his Christian identity, for he revered the philosophy of the Upanishads and rejected what he considered to be dangerously narrow understandings of Christianity as the only way to God. In the final decades of his life, Yisu Das became a prominent proponent of an Indian Christian vision that rejected communalism in favor of interreligious dialogue and cooperation in the building of Indian nationhood.

Bibliography. Tiwari, Ravi, *Yisu Das: Witness of a Convert.* New Delhi: Indian Society for Promoting Christian Knowledge, 2000.

Mathew N. Schmalz

TOCQUEVILLE, ALEXIS DE (1805–1859). Tocqueville's two-volume *Democracy in America* (1835, 1840) remains the most enduring, comprehensive, and influential commentary on American democratic culture.

The French aristocrat, politician, historian, and social theorist was born to a Norman noble family. Several of his close relatives had been executed by the guillotine during the French Revolution, a fate his own parents barely escaped. Convinced by what he saw in France that aristocratic control of government was a thing of the past, in 1831 Tocqueville set out for the United States with his friend Gustav de Beaumont, ostensibly to study the American prison system and suggest reforms for France. He also developed another goal, perhaps stronger in his mind: to examine American government and political culture at every level and in all areas. Despite the efforts of European leaders at the Congress of Vienna in (1814–1815) to forestall popular empowerment and preserve the continent's political status quo, Tocqueville viewed political transformation as inevitable. Representative democracy in America, he believed, could provide a useful window onto the political future of Europe as well. His examination led to an eloquent, forward-looking, and influential treatise on both American government and democratic culture in general. After his return to France, he became involved in French politics and continued to write until his death in 1856.

During his early years Tocqueville studied his family's Catholicism and a priest, Abbé Lesueur, directed his education. He was very close to his teacher and was firm in his religious study and beliefs. Around the age of fifteen, however, Tocqueville experienced a crisis of faith that transformed him from a devout Catholic into a disillusioned one. From this point on, the precise nature of his religious convictions is elusive, but it is certain that for all of his skepticism of the church's theology and ritual, Tocqueville never abandoned the moral and ethical teachings of Christianity. Indeed, they became a key facet of his social and political theorizing in *Democracy in America*. Although he published volume one of his promising but unfinished *The Old Regime and the Revolution*

just before his death, *Democracy* remains the key to understanding Christianity's role in his political thought.

Certainly Tocqueville's personal religious doubts never led him to diminish religion's role in democratic culture. Although unsure at times of his own faith, he believed strongly that every person needed solid spiritual moorings in order to achieve complete liberty. Paradoxically, he also saw religion as a means of preserving social order. No doubt he had inherited his father's anxiety over the power of the masses. Christianity instilled in the people common moral and ethical beliefs, creating both morally sound and orderly citizens. Individuals needed religion for their eternal souls; society needed it for stability.

The United States he traveled through was dominated by Christianity and seemed to him far more religious than the nations of Europe. He believed, however, that American religious fervor was encouraged more by Christianity's practical and social benefits than because of the typical believer's deep personal conviction or transcendent theological concerns. But even in this detached study of a country dominated by Protestant groups, he defended Catholicism's compatibility with the emerging democratic culture. Catholics, he wrote, "constitute the most republican and democratic class in the United States" (Tocqueville, 332).

Americans so easily confounded liberty and Christianity, Tocqueville insisted, that they found it virtually impossible to separate the two. Christianity was especially strong among American women, who utilized their moral influence in the home to sustain a Christian foundation for American mores. This surprised Tocqueville, as he felt that the American penchant for material gain was inconsistent with Christian teachings, which discouraged an attachment to worldly goods. He found that the opposite had occurred: American self-interest actually encouraged Americans to practice Christianity.

Recalling the logic of Pascal's wager, he saw American religious commitments as motivated by their brains as much as their hearts. They were concerned with heavenly goods just as they were earthly ones, and with constitutional guarantees of religious freedom, they had much to gain and nothing to lose through their spiritual allegiance. Consequently, Christianity could be integrated easily with American democratic principles precisely because it had no institutional ties to the political establishment, a trap that in Europe had led Christianity to be "buried, as it were, beneath the debris" of crumbling states (Tocqueville, 347). Ministers could speak boldly of a salutary connection between Christian faith and the personal freedom and public order that Americans regarded as essential to their private pursuits of material happiness.

Bibliography. Tocqueville, Alexis de. *Democracy in America.* Trans. Arthur Goldhammer. New York: Library of America, 2004. Goldstein, Doris S. "The Religious Beliefs of Alexis De Tocqueville." *French Historical Studies* (Autumn 1960): 379–93. Siedentop, Larry. *Tocqueville.* Oxford: Oxford University Press, 1994. Wach, Joachim. "The Role of Religion in the Social Philosophy of Alexis De Tocqueville." *Journal of the History of Ideas* 7 (January 1946): 74–90. Wolin, Sheldon S. *Tocqueville between Two Worlds.* Princeton, NJ: Princeton University Press, 2001.

Matthew A. Magruder

TONIOLO, GIUSEPPE (1845–1918). Born in Treviso, near Venice, Toniolo was a scholar, university lecturer, activist, and leading ideologue of the Italian Catholic Social movement. His research and teaching interests spanned a wide spectrum— history, sociology, philosophy, and political economy. During the course of his career, he developed a wide network of contacts with Catholic thinkers and activists in Belgium, France, and Germany.

Toniolo taught at the universities of Padua and Modena and, from 1878 until his death, at Pisa. In 1879 he initiated the study of Catholic Social principles as an alternative to both liberalism and Socialism. In 1889 he established the *Unione Cattolica per gli Studi Sociali* and in 1893 founded the *Rivista Internazionale per gli Studi Sociali ed ausiliarie,* all with the support of **Leo XIII** and Cardinal **Rampolla.**

Much influenced by his historical studies of medieval Christian society, he put social ethics at the heart of his analysis of the economic and social order in his various programs and other writings for social reform.

Toniolo's most important publication, the Milan "Program of Catholics Faced by Socialism" of 1894, stressed the dignity of labor; the need to encourage wider property owning, especially of the land; the provision of technical instruction for small farmers; social housing; and workers' participation in the profits of business. He also underlined the importance of cheap credit and supporting small Catholic banks—the *casse di risparmio* and the *banche popolari.* Though Toniolo was effectively the founder of the Christian Democracy movement in Italy, his ideas did not entirely fit with those of the Christian Democratic "young Turks" at the turn of the century, especially with regard to **Romolo Murri.** In consequence, Toniolo's efforts to mediate between Murri and his followers, on one hand, and the "old guard" in the *Opera dei Congressi* failed. When **Pius X** dissolved the Opera in 1904, Toniolo was involved in drawing up new statutes for the Catholic movement that created three replacement organizations for the *Opera,* the *Unione Popolare, Unione Economico-Sociale,* and *Unione Elettorale,* and served as president of the first for four years.

Toniolo also contributed to plans for a Catholic Institute for the Study of International law (1916) and for the Milan

Catholic University of the Sacred Heart (1923). A process for his beatification was opened in 1951.

Bibliography. Traniello, Francesco and Giorgio Campanini, eds. *Dizionario Storico del Movimento Cattolico in Italia: 1860–1980.* 2 vols. Casale Monferrato, Italy: Marietti, 1982.

John F. Pollard

TORRES, CAMILO (1929–1966). Born in Santa Fé de Bogotá, Colombia, to a well-established family, Torres became a priest, intellectual, and *guerillero* who urged Christians to follow what he saw as a moral and ethical necessity to support revolutionary change for the sake of social justice. He was killed in revolutionary action in 1966 and is remembered as a martyr in the struggle of the Latin American poor, and as a cleric who articulated an emerging split of the Catholic Church at the time.

Torres graduated with honors in Colombia and began to study law. Shortly thereafter he entered the diocesan seminary in Bogotá and was ordained into the Catholic priesthood in 1954. Subsequently, he studied sociology at the University of Louvain, Belgium, and addressed questions of equal resource distribution in his analytical writing.

Torres witnessed Latin American development challenges in a period when some Christians began to raise questions over the theological significance of social revolution, concerns also reflected in many of the documents of the Second Vatican Council (1962–1965). Returning to Colombia, he established the United Front, a group that linked peasants, workers, and the urban poor. The Front's popularity grew, but increased political repression and the imprisonment of some members of the Front contributed to the progressive radicalization of Torres.

In 1965, Torres carried his ideals from his leadership of the Front to an emerging guerilla movement, the National Liberation Army (ELN). In a letter to the Colombian people, he confirmed that he had joined the ELN as a combatant. Rupture with the church became inevitable, and the church leadership ordered his laicization. Having joined the struggle for liberation as a scholar, a politician, a revolutionary, and, in his own view, always as a priest, he fell in his first combat in 1966.

Bibliography. Broderick, Walter. *Camilo Torres: A Biography of the Priest-Guerillero.* New York: Doubleday, 1975.

Jadwiga E. Pieper Mooney

TROELTSCH, ERNST (1865–1923). Ernst Troeltsch was a German Protestant theologian who taught at the universities of Heidelberg (1894–1915) and Berlin (1915–1923). He was an heir to the Protestant modernist tradition of **Friedrich Schleiermacher** and a close associate of sociologist Max Weber.

During his years in Heidelberg, Troeltsch was a typical academic mandarin, accepting various duties of public service in the local government as he was writing and teaching on the theology faculty. His years at Heidelberg culminated in the publication of the *Social Teachings of the Christian Churches* (1912), in which he argued that Christianity did not begin as a social movement but as a religious one. The early church existed to promote what it believed to be a new revelation about God's will in relation to humanity and to encourage new forms of devotion and worship. Troeltsch held the view that this movement first took root among the lower classes, that it gestated there for several centuries, absorbing their working-class aspirations, and that it eventually spread to wider circles of Roman society. Troeltsch depicted early Christianity as a cluster of ideas that only came to influence the social order as a secondary effect. Jesus was not a political revolutionary, but the preacher of the kingdom of God, foretelling a time when God would rule the earth and warning all who would listen to get ready.

Getting ready was a matter of accepting that God peers deeply into the inner lives of human beings and finds them wanting, and that believers are to learn to conform their wills to God's will, which is a will guided by moral purpose. This message, Troeltsch claimed, quietly did its work in relatively insulated communities, forming the self-understanding of people over several generations. Then, when the ancient world began to disintegrate, this uniquely formed Christian community was "able to step in and fill the vacant space with its own ideas and its own sentiment" (Troeltsch, *Social Teachings*, 48).

With the outbreak of World War I in 1914, Troeltsch began writing furiously to defend what he believed were legitimate "war aims" for Germany. Troeltsch was never as uncritically supportive of the war as the vast majority of German intellectuals, and he publicly opposed the calls to annex Belgium and parts of Russia that many others supported. What he did find worth defending through war was the distinctive German understanding of freedom. He contended that with France attempting to force its "scientific view of liberty" on everyone, and Britain seeking to dominate the moral order of the world through what it took to be its superior legal institutions, Germany had to be the lone defender of the romantic idea that freedom is found in each nation's cultivation of its own collective spirit. When multiple nations struggle to develop unique "spiritual powers" in concert with their own histories, languages, and climates, he argued, it is as if we catch a glimpse in a mirror of the complex creativity of God. "The great national cultures all have their advantages and their drawbacks," he wrote, "and the earth has room for them all" (Troeltsch, "The Spirit," 88). Any alternative leads the world to mediocrity and shallowness.

With his move to Berlin in 1915, Troeltsch gained a closer look into the political forces that were driving the German war effort. He came to believe that the war was more about weak politicians and an opportunistic officers' corps than it was about the noble idea of freedom. When the war was over and Germany collapsed, Troeltsch accepted it as the judgment of God and sought for lessons it contained. He began writing a column for a periodical, *Der Kunstwart,* where he noted the grievances of the veterans of the war, most of whom had been drawn from the working class, and surveyed the harsh conditions of the factories to which they returned. He heard their demands for a more equitable division of labor and distribution of goods. During the crucial months when Germany submitted to the stipulation of the armistice that it install a representative government, Troeltsch wrote long columns about democracy, aristocracy, bolshevism, and socialism, scrutinizing the options and various combinations that should be considered.

As a reformer, Troeltsch was an incrementalist and an advocate of compromise. He argued in both his scholarly and popular writing that lasting political change had to grow organically even in times of catastrophic change, and that the order that is built must be a mixture of the old and the new. His own compromise in these early years of the Weimar Republic was to concede that the standardizing Anglo-French models of universal rights and cosmopolitanism could be incorporated into the German political culture and serve alongside the more homegrown ideal of collective personality.

Bibliography. Troeltsch, Ernst. "Socialism." Trans. Dennis F. McCann. *Journal of Religious Ethics* 4 (1): 159–80. Troeltsch, Ernst. *The Social Teachings of the Christian Churches.* Trans. Olive Wyon. Chicago: University of Chicago Press, 1931. Troeltsch, Ernst. "The Spirit of German *Kultur.*" In *Modern Germany in Relation to the Great War,* ed. William Whitelock. New York: Mitchell Kennerley, 1916.

Kelton Cobb

TRUDEAU, PIERRE ELLIOTT (1919–2000). Trudeau, the fifteenth prime minister of Canada, was born in Montreal to Charles-Emile Trudeau and Grace Elliott, a privileged family that provided him with position and identity. Both Anglophone and Francophone, Trudeau carried within him—in his very bone and marrow, as it were—the quintessential tensions and contradictions that defined Catholic life in the very Catholic province of Quebec in the early part of the twentieth century. Trudeau was educated at the elite Jean-de-Brébeuf College in Montreal. He secured a law degree from the University of Montreal in 1943 and a graduate degree in political economy from Harvard in 1945. He then went on for a year at the École Science Politique in Paris and then a year at the London School of Economics. These varied sojourns at elite institutions provided Trudeau a pedigreed educational background that matched his lineage and style.

A deeply committed Roman Catholic, Trudeau, both as a political thinker and as a member of Parliament, was not unaccustomed to occasional collisions—even substantive—with ecclesiastical authorities. He was a strong believer in the freedom of the individual, and of the supreme importance of personal conscience, and remained ever fearful of the dread specter of collectivity and authoritarianism. After all, he had tasted it directly in his own life as a Catholic in the Quebec of Maurice Duplessis. The Asbestos Strike of 1948 galvanized Trudeau's opposition to what he perceived as the dangerous alliance of church and state.

In 1950, Trudeau cofounded *Cité Libre*, an impressive publication of progressive lay Catholic insight, and served as a lawyer, professor, and for a short time privy council advisor until his election as leader of the Liberal Party of Canada and as prime minister. Trudeau was prime minister for the period of 1968 to 1979 and then from 1980 to 1984. Under his leadership the country had its divorce and homosexuality legislation radically overhauled, saw the implementation of the War Measures Act in 1970 following the October Crisis, and struggled with the Wage and Price Controls of 1975. Trudeau struggled to hold the country together during a series of separatist challenges emanating from Quebec following the election of the Parti Québécois in 1976.

Although there was great national debate over the wisdom of some of his economic initiatives, on the legal and philosophical front Trudeau won the hearts and minds of the nation. He was responsible for the Canadian Charter of Rights and Freedoms as well as the repatriation of the Constitution Act in 1982. He also appointed the first female Speaker of the House in 1980 and the first female governor-general in 1984 (in fact, it was the same woman, the distinguished *L'Action Catholique* notable, Mme. Jeanne Sauvé).

If Trudeau was a progressive in Catholic matters—as was evidenced with his *Cité Libre* undertakings and his resistance to the Duplessis government—he was far from enthusiastic for many of the center-left positions of the Canadian Catholic episcopate on matters of social policy. In fact, Trudeau had very little stomach for the social initiatives of the Canadian episcopate—particularly as they involved a sharp critique of his own government's fiscal policies—and when his friend Gerald Emmett Cardinal Carter of Toronto publicly distanced himself from the 1983 "Ethical Reflections on the Economic Crisis" (a document issuing from the Social Affairs Commission of the Canadian Conference of Catholic Bishops), Trudeau mused aloud and for the clear benefit of the media, "The fox is now among the chickens".

Trudeau delighted in the cut and thrust of Catholic intellectual life. After all, the Jesuit child knew the value of first sources, the importance of languages, the Jesuit love of the syllogism, the centrality of *eloquentia perfecta* in the making of a Christian gentlemen, and the intellectual allure of the Jesuit model to do all things, and explore all things, for the greater glory of God—*ad majoram dei gloriam*. In addition, of course, there is that wellspring of French Catholic intellectual life—the personalist school—with philosophers **Emmanuel Mounier** and Gabriel Marcel, and the non-Gallic Lublin School of Philosophy. This is Trudeau the Catholic thinker.

In addition, for most of his life, Trudeau sought out confessors, confidantes, interlocutors, and intellectuals from within the Dominican order. Louis-Marie Regis, Benôit Lacroix, and Gilles-Dominique Mailhot were just a few of the Canadian Dominicans who were close to him.

The intellectual appeal of the Dominicans, and the methodological rigor of the Jesuits, needed some counterbalancing, and I believe that that could be found in the Benedictine tradition, with its sweet savoring of the word and mystery in *lectio divina* and its plenitude of graces, its natural rhythms of mind, body, and spirit. Trudeau frequently chose St. Benôit du Lac for his retreats—a community of the Solesmes tradition—as well as for meditating and attending the Hours and Eucharist at Montreal's Benedictine community with some regularity.

Catholics in Canada are greatly divided, however, over the impact and direction his private religious ideas and deep devotional life had on his policies. For those inclined to celebrate the progressive social insights found in the philosophical tradition of personalism and Maritain's integral humanism, Trudeau was a Catholic politician well situated in an established philosophical tradition. For others, his vigorous defense of individual rights, his strong personal commitment to human freedom in all its personal and social dimensions, and his overt liberalization of Canadian laws on matters pertaining to sexual morality have gone a long way to define him as a "cultural" rather than committed Catholic. Such a judgment, in my view, seriously misses the mark.

Bibliography. Cohen, Andrew, and J. E. Granatstein, eds. *Trudeau's Shadow.* Toronto: Random House. 1998. English, John, Richard Gwyn, and P. Whitney Lackenbauer, eds. *The Hidden Pierre Elliott Trudeau.* Ottawa, ON: Novalis, 2004. Graham, Ron, ed. *The Essential Trudeau.* Toronto: McClelland & Stewart, 1998.

Michael W. Higgins

TRUFANOFF, SERGEI MIKHAILOVICH [ILIODOR] (1880–1952). A religious and political orator and writer from the Don Cossack region, Trufanoff, known as the priest-monk Iliodor, was the most notorious case of extremist right-wing activism by an Orthodox clergyman in imperial Russia.

In his memoirs, Iliodor emphasized the poverty of his childhood, which allegedly made him a populist maverick fighting the bureaucratic autocracy. "The fire," he wrote, "of protest against falsity and injustice in every possible form began to consume my soul." After graduating with honors from the St. Petersburg Theological Academy in 1905, he took monastic vows and taught at the city's seminary, provoking progressive-minded seminarians to boycott his classes. In 1906, the conservative Russian Assembly invited Iliodor to address rightist deputies to the first Duma. However, Iliodor proved to be a rightist populist rather than an unthinking champion of autocracy. At the Third All-Russian Congress of Russian People held in Kiev in March 1907, Iliodor announced his vision of a peasant communal society with no provision for private property, annoying the landed nobility that sponsored the congress.

Iliodor converted the Pochaev monastery in Volynia to a rightist propaganda center, publishing the *Pochaev Leaflet* and millions of brochures. His fiery speeches attacked leftists and Jews as well as the entrepreneurial elite, officialdom, and church hierarchy, prompting the Holy Synod, the members of which Iliodor criticized as complacent, rich-living, slothful individuals, to forbid his publicist activity in 1907. Pressured by the synod, Bishop **Antonii Khrapovitskii** of Volynia ousted Iliodor, who found refuge in Saratov under the protection of Bishop Germogen (**Georgii Dolganov**) in 1908.

Iliodor's ambition found an outlet in the construction of his own monastery in Tsaritsyn, where he organized mass meetings spreading hatred against revolutionaries, Jews, the liberal intelligentsia, capitalists, landowners, bureaucrats, and all who opposed him. Venomous sermons spared no social group, government institution, or person except Czar Nicholas II. His publication *Thunder and Lightning* incited political violence and supported peasant chimeras such as equal land distribution. A true demagogue, Iliodor employed antics such as chopping off the head of a makeshift dragon representing the Left, which appealed to the ethnic Russian peasantry, whose interests he claimed to champion. Rumors that he was the illegitimate brother of the czar or that he performed healing miracles attested to his popularity in Tsaritsyn. In 1911, when he went on a pilgrimage to Sarov through the Volga cities, masses of his adherents committed street violence. At the same time, Iliodor's maverick activity and youthful energy was discussed in plays and vaudeville shows, intriguing elite audiences.

His high-society connections and association with Rasputin, whom he renounced later in a caustic attack entitled *The Holy Devil*, allowed Iliodor to evade punishment by government authorities and the synod, including repeated attempts to arrest and imprison him, to forbid him to officiate and

to publish, to exile him to Minsk Province, and to confine him in a monastery. Finally, in January 1912 he was confined in the Forishchev Monastery in Vladimir Province, where he wrote to the synod, expressing repentance and asking forgiveness of Jews but repudiating the Orthodox Church. The synod defrocked Iliodor, whereupon most of his adherents abandoned him.

He went to Norway in 1914 and later to New York, where he published his memoirs after the October Revolution. Returning to Russia, he headed his own alternative to the Orthodox Church, benefiting from Bolshevik attempts to divide Orthodoxy by sponsoring the **Renovationist Union.** After the 1920s, he lost all importance and died unknown in Moscow.

Bibliography. Geekie, John M. "The Church and Politics in the Reign of Nicholas II." PhD diss., University of East Anglia, 1976. Rawson, Don C. *Russian Rightists and the Revolution of 1905.* Cambridge: Cambridge University Press, 1995. Trufanoff, Sergei M. *The Mad Monk of Russia, Iliodor: Life, Memoirs, and Confessions of Sergei Michailovich Trufanoff (Iliodor).* New York: Century, 1918.

Argyrios K. Pisiotis

TRUTH, SOJOURNER (c. 1797–1883). African American evangelist, abolitionist, civil rights activist, women's rights advocate, and social reformer, Truth (whose given name was Isabella) was born a slave in Ulster County, New York. After the state of New York abolished slavery in 1827, she went to New York City and worked as a domestic for several years. In 1843, she changed her name to Sojourner Truth and spent the remainder of her life as an activist for racial justice, women's rights, and various social reforms. Although she never learned to read or write, she lectured widely and was renowned for her extraordinary oratorical ability.

Truth's religious convictions fueled her commitment to civil rights and progressive reform. Shortly after she obtained her freedom, Isabella had a vision of Jesus and a profound experience of God's omnipresence. Her religious conversion culminated in 1843, at which time she changed her name to Sojourner Truth because she felt divinely inspired to travel the country and proclaim the truth to the American people. She was convinced that God had called her to profess her faith and to make people aware of their sins. Truth's religious beliefs and personal experience confirmed that slavery was the principal sin of the United States, and she had no doubt that God was on the side of the **abolitionists**.

Throughout her life, Truth associated with both heterodox and traditional religious groups. Between the time of her conversion and her call to preach, Truth attended Methodist churches and was also involved with the messianic commune of Matthias and Millerite Second Adventism. Following her break with the Millerites,

Sojourner Truth. Courtesy of the Library of Congress

she sought out spiritual communities that were committed to social reform. In 1843, she joined the utopian Northampton Association and remained in Massachusetts after the dissolution of the association. She eventually moved to Michigan to live in a community of Progressive Friends near Battle Creek.

In 1850, she published the first edition of the *Narrative of Sojourner Truth,* which focuses on her religious experiences and the evils of slavery. The book was sold at abolitionist and women's rights meetings, and the proceeds constituted Truth's main source of income. The following year, Truth addressed a woman's rights convention at Akron, Ohio, and delivered what later became known as her "Ain't I a woman?" speech. Recent scholarship, however, has cast doubt on whether Truth's address actually included the famous rhetorical question that is now so closely associated with her.

After emancipation, Truth's activities focused on relief efforts for former slaves, and she was appointed to work for the Freedmen's Bureau immediately following the Civil War. While she was employed by Freedman's Hospital, Truth initiated legal action that resulted in the integration of streetcars in Washington, D.C. During the last years of her life, she campaigned for the allocation of land in Kansas to former slaves. She died at her home in Battle Creek, Michigan, on November 26, 1883.

Bibliography. Painter, Nell Irvin. *Sojourner Truth: A Life, A Symbol.* New York: W. W. Norton, 1996.

Susan J. Hubert

TURNER, NAT (d. 1831). Born into slavery in Southampton County, Virginia, Turner led one of the bloodiest and most notorious slave rebellions of the antebellum period.

As the slave of Benjamin Turner, Nat escaped in 1821, only to return voluntarily. Turner was then sold to Thomas

Moore, who held him for eight years until selling him to Joseph Travis. Soon after returning to bondage, Turner reportedly became deeply religious. Baptized in 1825 by his white overseer, Turner led a life of asceticism and dabbled in messianic speculation. He soon became an exhorter and lay preacher heard by both whites and blacks. Identifying himself as a type of modern-day Moses, he believed he had been called to lead African Americans out of bondage.

Turner was also said to have been greatly influenced by astrological speculation, which led him to choose the date of August 21, 1831, to launch his rebellion. Joining forces with approximately sixty other men, Turner and his following went on a killing spree, which ended with the deaths of approximately fifty-five white Virginians. Joseph Travis and his family were the first targets of Turner's insurrection. Local militia and federal troops were called in quickly to put down the uprising, which also resulted in the deaths of approximately a hundred blacks. Although most of the group was killed or captured within a day of their revolt, Turner remained at large for more than a month. Captured on October 30, 1831, he was jailed in Jerusalem, Virginia, where he was tried, pronounced guilty, and executed on November 11, 1831.

Memories of the former slave brought terror to some, and cause for celebration among others. Shaken by yet another insurrection, this time taking place just seventy miles from the state capital, Virginia along with other Southern states passed stringent laws relating to the education and public assembly of slaves. Fearing the possibility of a general servile war, Southerners placed much of the blame for the insurrection on Northern **abolitionists,** whom they said encouraged violence with little regard for civil or divine laws. In the North, word of Turner's rebellion was received with a range of sentiment. **Harriet Beecher Stowe**'s novel *Dred* was one among many works by Northerners who immortalized Turner's life and efforts. Even more popular was William Styron's work *Nat Turner's Confessions.*

The impact of Turner's revolt was profound and reveals some of the apparent contradictions of the period in American religious life. Whereas prior to the insurrection many white slaveholders feared the implications of Christianizing slaves, afterwards religion was seen and employed as a means of social control. Following the rebellion, antislavery sentiment in Southern churches declined precipitously, laws were written to curb the influence of black preachers, and slaves were encouraged to be given oral rather than written instruction in the faith. At the same time, a reform campaign was started among Protestant evangelicals calling for the more humane treatment of slaves by their owners. A similar campaign urged slaveholders to be sensitive to the spiritual needs of slaves and to treat them as their spiritual and moral "children."

Bibliography. Foner, Eric. *Nat Turner.* Englewood Cliffs, NJ: Prentice Hall, 1971. Greenberg, Kenneth S., ed. *Nat Turner: A Slave Rebellion in History and Memory.* New York: Oxford University Press, 2003. Johnson, F. Roy. *The Nat Turner Slave Insurrection.* Murfreesboro, NC: Johnson, 1966.

Kent A. McConnell

TUROWICZ, JERZY (1912–1999). Never in Poland—and rarely in any other country—has a magazine been as influential as *Tygodnik Powszechny* (Universal Weekly), which Turowicz edited from its founding in 1945 until his death in 1999. This Roman Catholic periodical was the only independent magazine in the entire East Bloc, and Turowicz utilized this small space of relative freedom to cultivate a vibrant Christian culture within an extremely hostile political environment.

Turowicz lived his entire life in Krakow, steeped in an intelligentsia milieu (his father was a judge, and his siblings included a mathematician, a philosopher, two priests, an accountant, and a judge). While still a teenager, in 1930 he joined a Catholic lay group called Rebirth (*Odrodzenia*), which strove to construct a more open, less nationalistic alternative to the forms of Catholicism then dominant in Poland. From this period Turowicz became interested in the personalism of **Jacques Maritain** and **Emmanuel Mounier,** which would profoundly shape his approach to both faith and politics. During World War II Turowicz worked in the underground press, and on March 24, 1945 (even before the final capitulation of the Nazis), he participated in the founding of the magazine with which he would be so closely identified for the next half century.

Tygodnik Powszechny, which was loosely affiliated with the Archdiocese of Krakow, faced enormous pressures as the Soviet-backed Communist Party solidified its rule in Poland, and by the late 1940s the publication was subjected to harsh censorship. Nonetheless, it was not shut down—perhaps so that the authorities could sustain some tenuous claim that they respected press and religious freedom, perhaps because they wanted to cultivate the magazine's more progressive Catholic circle as a counterbalance to the conservative church hierarchy. Only Turowicz's refusal to publish an obituary for Joseph Stalin in 1953 led to a brief takeover of the paper by a communist-sponsored editorial board, but the original staff was allowed to return when Poland's own Stalinists fell from power three years later.

Tygodnik Powszechny was never able to openly oppose the communist regime, and in fact Turowicz and his colleagues sincerely believed that it was better to try to accomplish whatever they could within the system rather than boycott public life.

The magazine reported extensively about intellectual and spiritual trends among Christians inside and outside of Poland, giving particularly enthusiastic coverage to the reforms of Vatican Council II. The cultural and social commentary of the magazine constantly pushed the limits of the censorship, and Turowicz's masterful Aesopian prose often transcended those limits. At the same time, Turowicz frequently provoked angry responses from the episcopate because of his openness to a wide variety of Catholic (and non-Catholic) approaches to doctrinal, social, cultural, and political issues.

After the fall of communism in 1989, *Tygodnik Powszechny* had to compete with a multitude of Catholic media outlets, and while Turowicz remained an extraordinarily influential figure among Poland's intelligentsia (religious and secular alike), his magazine has been unable to compete in terms of circulation with more conservative and nationalistic Catholic publications.

Bibliography. Jarocki, Robert. *Czterdzieści pić lat w opozycji: o ludziach "Tygodnika Powszechnego."* Krakow, Poland: Wydawnictwo Literackie, 1990. Turowicz, Jerzy. *Bilet do raju.* Krakow, Poland: Znak, 1999.

Brian Porter

TUTU, DESMOND MPILO (b. 1931). Tutu is archbishop emeritus of Cape Town, a Nobel Peace Prize winner, and past chairman of the South African Truth and Reconciliation Commission.

Born in Klerksdorp, Western Transvaal, South Africa, in humble circumstances, Tutu was early influenced by the Anglican priest Trevor Huddleston of Sophiatown. Graduating from the Johannesburg Bantu High School, he initially followed in his father's footsteps, gaining a teaching qualification at the Pretoria Bantu Normal College and pursuing a bachelor of arts degree at the University of South Africa. After several years of teaching, Tutu entered the ministry of the Anglican Church (Church of the Province of Southern Africa), receiving his ordination in 1961.

Furthering his studies in London, he received the bachelor of divinity and master of theology degrees before returning to South Africa in 1967 to teach at the Federal Theological Seminary in Alice and to serve as the chaplain at the University of Fort Hare. In 1970, he became lecturer in the Department of Theology at the University of Botswana, and then he proceeded to England to become associate director of the Theological Education Fund of the World Council of Churches. In 1975, he became the first black dean of St. Mary's Cathedral in Johannesburg, and then he was appointed the bishop of Lesotho.

The civil unrest sparked by the 1976 black student protests in Soweto was critical in persuading Tutu to return to South Africa and to become general secretary of the South African Council of Churches from 1978 to 1985. This ecumenical and public role, in a country where much of the political debate was conducted in theological and ethical terms, gave Tutu much prominence. Tutu's public voice was amplified by a deep conviction that the God-given dignity and humanity of all races mandated justice for all those oppressed by South Africa's apartheid policies. Striking in his approach was his commitment to treating the oppressors as likewise human. For such efforts, he received the Nobel Peace Prize in 1984 and a year later accepted his appointment as bishop of Johannesburg. In 1986, he became the archbishop of Cape Town.

In a political culture where most black opposition was illegal and subject to internal exile (banning orders), Tutu (and the so-called English churches) became "the voice of the voiceless," proclaiming basic civic liberties such as equal justice, the removal of the hated internal passports (pass books), the ending of deportation to "homelands," and the legalization of black opposition parties. In 1990, the Afrikaner-dominated National Party lifted the banning orders on many political parties,

Archbishop Desmond Tutu gives the morning service in St. George's Cathedral, Cape Town, 2003. © Ian Berry / Magnum Photos

including the African National Congress. Shortly thereafter, they released its leader, Nelson Mandela, who spent his first night of freedom in the archbishop's residence.

In 1995, Mandela, then state president, appointed Tutu chair of the South African Truth and Reconciliation Commission, which he led and served with distinction, courage, and compassion under continual and worldwide media attention. He submitted the commission's report to the state president in 1998.

Throughout his career, his work, whether ecclesiastical or political (he views both as parts of his pastoral calling), has been governed by his belief in the basic humanity and interrelatedness of all peoples. His approach fuses African relational thought with Christian conceptions of community in a philosophy of "Ubuntu," or holistic intercommunion of all. As a result, Tutu has received many honors for his continuing efforts at reconciling divisions across racial, economic, and political lines. He is chancellor of the University of the Western Cape, and recipient of the highest South African civil award, the Order for Meritorious Service. He has also received the Archbishop of Canterbury's Award for Outstanding Service to the Anglican Communion; the Prix d'Athene; and the **Martin Luther King, Jr.,** Non-Violent Peace Prize. He is the recipient of honorary doctorates from his alma mater, the University of South Africa, and from the universities of Cape Town, Witswaterrand, Aberdeen, Columbia, Emory, Harvard, Kent, Oxford, and Ruhr. He retired as archbishop of Cape Town in 1996, subsequently serving as a distinguished visiting professor of theology at the Candler School of Theology of Emory University in Atlanta, Georgia.

Bibliography. Battle, Michael. *Reconciliation: The Ubuntu Theology of Desmond Tutu.* Cleveland, OH: Pilgrim Press, 1997. Tutu, Desmond. *Crying in the Wilderness: The Struggle for Justice in South Africa.* Grand Rapids, MI: William B. Eerdmans, 1982. Tutu, Desmond. *No Future Without Forgiveness.* Johannesburg, South Africa: Rider, 1999.

Iain S. Maclean

U

UKRAINIAN CATHOLIC POLITICAL PARTIES. In 1896, a group of Ukrainian Catholic populists in Austrian Galicia led by the historian and pedagogue Oleksander Barvins'kyi (1847–1926) founded the Catholic Ruthenian People's Union (CRPU). Pro-monarchy but opposed to Polish domination, the CRPU advocated the official use of Ukrainian in administration, courts, and schools, and an autonomous Ukrainian crownland.

Greek Catholic metropolitan Sylvester Sembratovych was a supporter. Its organ, the daily *L'viv* (1897–1914), covered sociopolitical affairs, sought equality for Ukrainians through cooperation with Polish parties and an anti-Russophile stance, and promoted ties with Ukrainians in the Russian Empire. In 1897, six members were elected to the Austrian parliament. Together with other Slavic representatives, they formed a Slavic Christian National Club. Unable to elect any members to Vienna in 1907, the CRPU reorganized in 1911 into a new formation, the Christian Social Party (CSP), led by Oleksander Barvins'kyi. Dedicated to Christian principles in social policy, the CSP advocated language and national rights, and the establishment of a Ukrainian university. Exclusively Catholic, the party comprised mostly teachers and priests. Criticized for clericalism and conservatism, and for advancing Polish-Ukrainian cooperation against Russophiles, the CSP never enjoyed widespread support. In 1914, it withdrew from politics and in the 1920s dissolved itself.

Barvins'kyi's political and religious track record preceded the CRPU. In the 1880s, he had worked out a populist political program and in 1890–1894, with Metropolitan Sembratovych and others, he represented the Ukrainian side in an attempt to win Polish support for Ukrainian rights, within a program of mutually beneficial development. The initiative (dubbed the New Era) failed, but Barvins'kyi remained committed to Ukrainian-Polish cooperation in politics. First elected to the Viennese parliament in 1891, he would continue to serve until 1907. He also served in Galicia's school council (1889–1918) and in its diet (1894–1904).

In interwar Poland, some former CSP members created the Ukrainian Catholic People's Party (1930). Based in Stanyslaviv and supported by Ukrainian Catholic Bishop Hryhorii Khomyshyn, the party was loyal to Poland but worked for Ukrainian autonomy and opposed atheism and Freemasonry. It published the newspaper *Nova Zoria,* edited by Osyp Nazaruk

(1883–1940), an organizer of the party with monarchist convictions.

In interwar Czech Transcarpathia, Ukrainian Catholic political activists founded the Christian People's Party (1924–1938). It published the weekly *Svoboda* (Liberty, 1925–1938) and cooperated with the Czech Catholic Party of Monsignor J. Sramek. A founding member, and its president, was the Greek Catholic priest **Avhustyn Voloshyn** (1874–1945), who represented it in the Czech parliament (1925–1929).

Bibliography. Kost' Levyts'kyi. *Istoriia Politychnoi Dumky Halyts'kykh Ukraintsiv, 1848–1914.* L'viv, Ukraine: Drukarnia Oo. Vasyliian u Zhovkvi, 1926.

Andrii Krawchuk

ULSTER UNIONISTS (NORTHERN IRELAND). The Ulster Unionists are Scots Presbyterians who originally settled in the area now known as Northern Ireland in the seventeenth century. Encouraged by the English Stuart monarchy, which was committed to consolidating its control of Ireland, the settlers took lands occupied by Irish Catholics. They combined a strong sense of community and faith with a frontier mentality to resist the opposition of the dispossessed Irish Catholic population.

A siege mentality, developed over the next two centuries among these Scots Presbyterians, was reinforced in the nineteenth century by rapid industrialization of the area. Organizations such as the Orange Lodge and inspiration derived from periodic religious revivalism helped to sustain a coherent Protestant community. At the same time, increased democratization expanded the voting and civil rights of Catholics, whom they saw as a threat to their freedom. This was only strengthened when Catholic demands for home rule or internal self-government in the late nineteenth century meant that they might well be a minority governed by a majority population made up of Catholics. They became known as Unionists because of their support for continuing the union with Great Britain.

The resolution to this conflict came with the 1920 Government of Ireland Act, which partitioned the island into two areas of twenty-six counties (the modern Irish Republic) and six counties (Northern Ireland). This was reinforced in the 1921 Anglo-Irish Treaty. The Protestant Unionist majority of Northern Ireland was able to ensure their dominance over the next half century before the demand for equal rights by Catholics in the 1960s resulted in the Troubles and renewed militancy and threats to British control.

The Presbyterianism of the Ulster Unionists was and is strongly evangelical and fundamentalist. Its fear of the Catholic population is based not only in what is often described as racial (ethnic) differences but also religious anxieties. At the same time, the Unionist population is not a monolith any more than is the nationalist or Catholic population. Unionists have divided their support among several groups, with the Ulster Unionist Party vying with the more hard-line Democratic Unionist Party for dominance in recent years. The DUP eclipsed the Ulster Unionists in the 2005 general election, winning nine seats in the parliament of the United Kingdom and affirming its position as the largest unionist party.

While the Ulster Unionist Party has become recently more moderate even as the Democratic Unionist Party has become more militant, both unionist groups see their dominance of the region as both economically and politically essential to their religious and ethnic survival. It is a religious doctrine that is strongly rooted in the Protestant radicalism of the seventeenth century and still envisages the Catholic Church's institutions and leadership as both a religious and political threat. Ironically, the views that many hold on contemporary moral issues such as divorce and abortion are similar to those held by their Catholic neighbors. Moreover, while they demonstrate an enormous fear of the power that members of the Catholic clergy exercise over the Catholic laity, Protestant unionists have always had a number of ministers within their active political leadership.

In 1998, the Belfast Agreement established a framework for devolution or shared local governance in Northern Ireland between nationalists and unionists based upon democratic elections, demilitarization, and the establishment of a Northern Ireland Assembly. To date, the Assembly has been plagued by suspensions as unionists led by the DUP continue to dispute the nationalist Catholic **Sinn Fein** party's claims to power sharing and political legitimacy.

Bibliography. Boyce, D. G., and Alan O'Day, eds. *Defenders of the Union: British and Irish Unionism 1800–1999.* London: Routledge, 2001.

Gretchen M. MacMillan

UNION OF SELF-DETERMINATION (ARMENIA). The Union of Self-Determination is the larger of Armenia's two Christian Democratic parties, the other being the Christian Democratic Union of Armenia, which is a member of the Christian Democratic International. Like its smaller co-ideologist, the party currently does not have representation inside the Armenian parliament. It has served mainly as the electoral vehicle of Paruyr Hayrikyan, its founder and leader. Aside from indicating a belief in the relevance of Christian principles for informing political decision making, the party is not ideological. Its leader and founder, however, remains a very popular politician. In 1998, he was appointed human rights advisor to Armenian president Robert Kocharian.

The popularity of Paruyr Hayrikyan stems from his immense personal sacrifices during Soviet times. As a Soviet-era human rights activist, he spent eighteen years in Soviet prisons, and despite his party's weakness, he earned a second-place finish in the 1996 presidential elections with about 15 percent of the vote in a field of seven candidates. It would not be an exaggeration to classify Hayrikyan as an Armenian Mandela.

Born in 1949, he was first arrested in 1969 and sentenced to four years in prison. A year after he was released, he was arrested again and sentenced to a longer prison term. Throughout his political career as a Soviet human rights activist, he took the traditional Christian opposition to violence and arms very seriously and made it a centerpiece of his political work. Hayrikyan organized the Armenian National Liberation Party, an opposition party under the Soviets, which was the forerunner of the Union of Self-Determination. During the Glasnost period, he produced the Armenian form of the journal *Glasnost* and used it to raise issues like human rights, ecology, and democratization. As a result of his activities, he was again arrested in 1988, an act met with protests from the Armenian population as well as from Soviet expatriate liberal opposition figures. Overall, the political movement personified by Paruyr Hayrikyan can be characterized by a search for an alternative to Communism as an organizing principle to life.

The Union of Self-Determination still exists as an extra-parliamentary party. It is probably best characterized as a classic post-independence party that rose out of informal groups concerned with specific issues like ecology, human rights, and in this case the relevance of Christianity in today's world. While not everyone agrees with Hayrikyan's politics, there is wide consensus that his personality and sacrifice are rare and admirable.

Bibliography. Grigorian, Mark. "Armenia's 1996 Presidential Election Coverage in the Media." *Caucasian Regional Studies* 2, no. 1 (1997), http://poli.vub.ac.be/publi/crs/eng/0201–02.htm. Organization of Security and Cooperation in Europe, Office of Democratic Institutions and Human Rights. *Parliamentary Elections 1999: Final Report.* www.ifes.am/library/pdf/oscereport.pdf (accessed January 2004). Yarim-Agaev, Yuri, et al. "An Armenian in Prison." *New York Review of Books,* July 1988. www.nybooks.com/articles/4369 (accessed January 2004).

Jack V. Kalpakian

UPADHYAY, BRAHMABANDHAB (1831–1907). Indian Catholic convert, theologian, and revolutionary, Brahmabandhab Upadhyay was born Bhawani Charan Banerji in 1831 to an orthodox Brahmin family in the Indian state of Bengal. In his youth he was described as one of the most brilliant members of the Brahmo Samaj, an influential Hindu reform movement, and was a close friend of Naren Dutt, who later became Swami Vivekananda. In 1891, he converted to Christianity and joined the Roman Catholic Church, taking the name Brahmabandhab, meaning "friend of Brahman." He donned the ochre robe and proclaimed himself a Catholic *sannyasi* (renunciant). He worked for the establishment of a Catholic monastic order and throughout his life remained concerned with how Christianity could shed its eurocentric strictures and become truly Indian.

Upadhyay began his effort to reconcile Catholicism with Indian culture by attempting to establish the Vedas, the central Hindu religious texts, as an Indian Old Testament. Upadhyay argued that the idea of a supreme being undergirded the Vedas and Hinduism itself. Upadhyay characterized the Christian Trinity as *sat-cit-annanda:* Truth, Consciousness, and Bliss. Upadhyay understood God as Truth (*sat*) with Christ as *cit,* or divine consciousness, proceeding from God. The Holy Spirit constituted the bliss (*annanda*) that proceeds from the union of the Father and Son, of Truth and Consciousness. For Upadhyay, the Veda and Vedanta provided a philosophic and social grounding necessary if Christianity were ever to take firm root on Indian soil. To this end, Upadhyay understood the cultural and social preservation of the Vedas and caste as central to his philosophical and political arguments as well as his Indian Catholic identity.

While Upadhyay always resented British influence in India, his writings became especially polemical when he assumed the editorship of the Bengali periodical *Sandhya.* With a circulation of nearly 7,000 copies a day in Calcutta, *Sandhya* was at the forefront of intellectual resistance to British rule. Upadhyay penned bitterly sarcastic essays lampooning the *phirangi* (foreign) British. But it was for an article in which he seemed to advocate violent resistance to British rule that led him to be charged with sedition. While in detention in 1907, Upadhyay died from complications related to tetanus.

Bibliography. Amindanda, Brahmachari Rewachand. *The Blade: Life and Work of Brahmabandhab Upadhyay.* Calcutta: Roy, 1945. Lipner, Julius. *Brahmabandhab Upadhyay: The Life and Thought of a Revolutionary.* Delhi: Oxford University Press, 1999.

Mathew N. Schmalz

V

VANIER, GEORGES-PHILEAS, (1888–1967) AND PAULINE NÉE ARCHER (1898–1991). Soldier, diplomat, and governor-general of Canada (1959–1967), Georges was born in Montreal, as was Pauline. They were married there in 1921. He was a much-decorated hero of the Great War on the verge of a brilliant career in the diplomatic corps. She was a lively, outgoing young woman with high religious ideals.

As a diplomat, Georges represented Canada in Geneva and in London until 1939, when he became minister to France and in 1943 minister to all allied governments in exile. He returned to Paris in 1944 as ambassador and in 1959 became governor-general, the senior representative of the Crown in Canada. Pauline supported him in all these moves, keeping her Christian faith at the forefront of her social responsibilities.

On Good Friday, April 15, 1938, while attending a Three Hours Mediation with Pauline in a London church, Georges underwent an intense spiritual experience. Overcome by the intensity of God's love, he resolved to attend Mass every day, a promise he kept until the last day of his life. Despite the many obligations of their very-draining public lives, the Vaniers also decided to set aside a half-hour for daily meditation. For the Vaniers, everyday matters of business blended easily with profound truths of the spirit, giving them a deep sensitivity to the needs of others and influencing their diplomatic and political actions.

In the Paris of 1939 and in the Algiers of 1943, when Georges' concern was to find new homes for refugees in Canada, Pauline's care was to provide immediate aid and sustenance for them, often in the couple's own quarters. After the liberation in 1944, she helped to strengthen Georges' influence with the French government by becoming, in her Canadian Red Cross uniform, a daily presence greeting the trains of returning prisoners and orphaned children of French deportees.

As governor-general, Georges Vanier made prayer and spiritual values one of his themes of office. "I believe we must shape our lives on moral standards," he said in an address to the Canadian Club in Vancouver in 1960. "Let us begin to associate prayer with power, faith with fire, charity with clear, swift action." He established a chapel at Rideau Hall, his official residence, where he and Pauline continued to attend daily Mass. While ambassador in Paris in 1944, his deep religious convictions had led him to take a strong stand with the Canadian and French governments on caring for Jewish refugees and on dealing with French clergy who had been too friendly with the

Pétain regime. His strong beliefs led him to oppose the death penalty. As governor-general, he intervened convincingly with the prime minister, and as a result, not a single capital sentence was carried out after 1962. He had, in effect, abolished capital punishment.

Vanier's years in office were turbulent ones in Canadian politics, but his obvious concern for the poor, the problems of youth, and the conditions of modern family life set him outside the fray and won for him and Pauline the admiration and affection of the country. In 1964, he summoned to Rideau Hall some 350 scholars and experts for a conference on the family. This led to the founding later of the Vanier Institute of the Family, which has continued to help parents in need of counsel and to promote among all Canadians a greater appreciation for family life. The institute is perhaps the Vaniers' main legacy.

After the governor-general's death, Pauline moved back to France to support her son Jean at L'Arche, near Paris, headquarters of the worldwide movement he had founded in 1964 to care for the mentally disadvantaged. There, her small home again became a refuge for the needy.

Georges and Pauline Vanier are remembered as exemplary Christians whose extraordinary achievements in the service of others was a genuine expression of their generous life of prayer. In the 1990s the Diocese of Ottawa officially took the first steps to prepare the case for their beatification.

Bibliography. Speaight, Robert. *Vanier: Soldier, Diplomat, and Governor General.* Toronto: Collins, 1970. Cowley, Deborah, and George Cowley. *One Woman's Journey: A Portrait of Pauline Vanier.* Ottawa: Novalis, 1992.

Jacques Monet

VANONI, EZIO (1903–1956). One of postwar Italian **Christian Democracy**'s leading economics experts, Vanoni was born in Morbegno, a Lombard village in the Alps. He turned to law studies at the University of Pavia, from which he graduated in 1925 with a thesis on the interpretation and nature of tax legislation. During his university years he had been active in politics in the form of a hybrid non-Marxist socialism. In 1927 and 1928 he undertook further studies at the Catholic University of Milan, where, more importantly, his politics matured, turning to the Catholic social traditions.

In 1928, thanks to a Rockefeller scholarship, he left for Germany, where he remained for the next two years. This proved to be a fruitful intellectual experience, and upon his return to Italy, he held chairs at the universities of Cagliari, Pavia, and Rome. In 1937 he published perhaps his most important work, *Elementi di diritto tributario* (Elements of Tax Law).

Besides his academic endeavours, Ezio Vanoni played an important political role in post-Fascist Italy. He participated in the elaboration of the Camaldoli Code, which exerted a notable impact on the policies of Italian **Christian Democracy,** most notably those parts devoted to the economic role of the public sector. In September 1943, after Italy's first post-Fascist government collapsed and the nation succumbed to Allied invasion in the south and German occupation in the north, Vanoni joined the Resistance within the Christian Democrat ranks.

He was elected to the Constituent Assembly in 1946 and was part of the Commission of Seventy-five, the most important of the proceedings. As a result of the Christian Democrat party's electoral triumph in 1948, Ezio Vanoni took a senate seat, which he held for the rest of his life.

Vanoni served as minister of finance under **Alcide De Gasperi** and Giuseppe Pella between 1948 and January 1954 when he assumed the budget ministry. He concluded as ad interim minister of the treasury from January 1956 until his death.

These positions gave him the opportunity to elaborate and implement his economic plans such as an ambitious reform of the tax system. In this regard, his most important achievement was the promulgation of the law of January 1951, commonly known as the Vanoni law, which reinstated obligation in the declaration of revenues. Above all, the legislation aimed at the technical and organizational modernization of the tax system, combined with a new type of relationship and a closer collaboration between the citizen and tax collection.

At the DC's fifth party congress in 1954, Vanoni announced what became known as the Vanoni Plan, perhaps the first attempt in the history of the peninsula at formulating a unitary national economic policy based on Keynesian premises. A convinced critic of the liberal approach to the economy and skeptic of the supposed natural adjustments of the economic order, he denounced the structural deficiencies of the Italian system, most notably the sharp regional differences and high unemployment levels. As such, the plan, rather optimistically, launched the project of full employment to be realized within ten years, under stable monetary levels. Public investments were boosted in such key areas as agriculture and public works. At a political level, it was intended to offer a realistic alternative to Communist models of development. Sharply criticised by many sectors, the plan lost much of its momentum after Vanoni's untimely death in 1956.

Bibliography. Magliulo, Antonio. *Ezio Vanoni: La giustizia sociale nell'economia di mercato.* Rome: Studium, 1991. Saraceno, Pasquale. *Gli Anni dello schema Vanoni (1953–1959).* Milan: Giuffré, 1982.

Jorge Dagnino

VÁSQUEZ DE MELLA, JUAN (1861–1928). Born in Cangas de Onís (Asturias) to a middle-class family, Vásquez de Mella's early religious education and traditional family values shaped his identity. He received his law degree from the University of Santiago de Compostela. His love for Spain's history blended with his impressive oratorical abilities to send him in 1893 to the Cortes as a deputy, where he earned the reputation as an eloquent spokesman for Carlist, Catholic, and monarchical causes. He resigned in 1916, however, after his Germanophilia during the First World War provoked the split in the Carlist movement. His fondness for Germany represented his deep anti-English sentiments, a result of sixteenth-century Britain's rise to power at Spain's expense.

Through Vásquez de Mella's articles in the press, his reflections entered the political discourse. His name became famous through the pages of the Carlist newspaper *El Correo Español* and later through his own journal, *El Pensamiento Español,* which he founded in 1919. He was most active as a propagandist during Carlism's "lean years" after the pretender Carlos VII left Spain in 1876, vowing to return someday; and through his writings Vásquez de Mella has been credited with keeping the Carlist vision alive in Spain.

Along with economic crisis as a result of the unsettled political situation, during these years Spain lost Cuba and the Philippines, the last remains of her empire overseas, to the United States (1898). It was then that in both Spain and the rest of Europe a tendency toward atheistic positivism emerged, compounded in Spain with a confrontation between Krausism and neo-scholastic Catholic philosophy. Catholics also faced the challenge of modernism. In this climate Vásquez de Mella strove to encourage the faith of his country, trying to defend a tradition as an inspiration for new life.

Unselfish and lacking political and financial ambitions, and respected even by his enemies, Vásquez de Mella slowly retired from political life in the first decades of the new century. He died in 1928, a man noted for his richly humanistic and historic contributions (both sacred and political) to Spain's culture. His intellectual maturity achieved its climax in his 1926 *Filosofia al la Eucaristia,* the publication of which coincided with the International Eucharistic Congress in Chicago. Four other volumes of his complete works are dedicated to philosophy, theology, and apologetics.

Bibliography. Cathey, Boyd D. "Juan Vazquez de Mella and the Transformation of Spanish Carlism." In *Spanish Carlism and Polish Nationalism,* ed. Marek Jan Chodakiewicz and John Radzilowski. Charlottesville, VA: Leopolis Press, 2003.

Fernando Murillo Rubiera

VAUSSARD, MAURICE (1888–1978). A Catholic journalist, polemicist, and historian, Vaussard received his diploma in Italian studies at Pisa, where he met **Giuseppe Toniolo** and first encountered Social Catholicism. After returning to Paris, he married Madeline Drouet, a writer who concentrated on the history of spirituality and then became his active collaborator.

Following his marriage, he collaborated with the *Revue des jeunes* and served as the assistant director of the French Institute of Milan during World War I. Also during the war, he was asked by Cardinal **Baudrillart** to participate in the *Comité Française de Propagande à l'Étranger* in an attempt to win the neutral Italians over to the French cause. After World War I, he continued his activities as a publicist and in 1923 launched an inquiry in *Les lettres* on nationalism that involved historians, jurists, theologians, and Catholic journalists throughout all of Europe. Nationalist doctrine divided Catholics in such a way that some denounced it as a rebirth of pagan ideas, while others, especially those who sympathized with the **Action Française**, found themselves drawn to its core values.

Vaussard published various articles against the Action française in which he refuted the ideas of his friend **Jacques Maritain.** A militant in international intellectual organizations for the promotion of peace, he created a strong network among the Catholic intellectuals of Europe. In 1925 Vaussard founded the *Bulletin Catholique International* (BCI) and made it the center of his antinational and pacifist activities through the use of a skilled team of associates. Vaussard advocated the supernationalization of the Catholic Church during the French nationalist rebirth. The BCI had a strong influence in educating French Catholics on international themes as well as in Catholic unity. The BCI was forced to close and was absorbed by *L'Univers* of abbot Paul Catrice for a variety of reasons; including the changing political climates, Hitler's rise to power, rearmament, and Europe's possible entry into a new war. Furthermore, the journal's promotion of ideas, such as a possible revision of the Treaty of Versailles or a U.S. intervention in Mexico to stop religious persecution there, had sometimes been too controversial for the opinion of the French Catholic media.

A prolific writer, Vaussard collaborated with various Catholic journals, from *Correspondant* to *La vie catholique,* working, as did his friend Don **Luigi Sturzo,** to show the ambiguities and evils of fascism. Vaussard's positions were most likely the reason why he failed to receive an honorary degree from the Catholic University of the Sacred Heart of Milan in 1929. In the 1930s, Vaussard worked as a history professor at the École des Roches and then director of the Collège de Normandie. From 1945 on, he was editor of *Le monde.* At the beginning of the 1960s, he directed the first course on the history of nationalism at the École Pratique des Hautes Études.

Bibliography. Biagioli, Ilaria. "Maurice Vaussard, un cristiano contro l'eresia' nazionalista." In *Cattolicesimo e totalitarismo: Chiese e culture religiose tra le due guerre mondiali (Italia, Spagna, Francia),* ed. Daniele Menozzi and Renato Moro. Brescia, Italy: Morcelliana,

2004. Serra, Enrico, ed. *Luigi Sturzo: Maurice Vaussard, Carteggio 1917–1958.* Rome: Cangemi Editore, 1999.

Ilaria Biagioli

VERONESE, VITTORINO (1910–1986). Among twentieth-century Italy's most versatile and ecumenically minded Catholic intellectuals and activists, Veronese was born in Vicenza in the Veneto region and graduated with a degree in law from the University of Padua. During the early interwar period he fell under the sway of Giovanni Battista Montini, the future **Paul VI,** after the two met within the ranks of the *Federazione Universitaria Cattolici Italiani* (FUCI).

In 1939 Montini invited Veronese, then twenty-nine years old, to Rome to assume the general secretaryship of the *Movimento Laureati* (Catholic University Graduates' Association) affiliated with **Italian Catholic Action.** During the war years, Veronese assumed responsibility for the educational and organizational initiatives of the *Istituto Cattolica di Attivita Sociale* (ICAS), as well as directing the Catholic review *Studium,* and the publishing house of the same name. Between 1944 and 1946, he assisted in the establishment of the *Associazione Cattolica Lavoratori Italiani* (ACLI), Italy's future Catholic trade union association. Veronese's influence within Italian Catholic circles culminated in his tenure (1946–1952) as the first lay general president of Italian Catholic Action.

Precipitously removed from that office by Pope **Pius XII** in favor of a longstanding Catholic Action rival—the forceful, highly conservative Lombard physician **Luigi Gedda**—Veronese shifted his energies over the ensuing decade to the international stage. In October 1951 he coordinated the First World Congress for the Apostolate of the Laity, bringing to Rome over a thousand delegates from seventy-four countries. Citing the success of this event, Pius named Veronese secretary of a new body,

the *Comitato Permanente per i Congressi Internazionali dell'Apostolato dei Laici* (Permanent Committee for International Congresses of the Lay Apostolate, or COPECIAL). The ecumenical synergy of persons, ideas, and projects that Veronese catalyzed in this office over the next six years impressed many international observers. In October of 1958, he was named director general of UNESCO, a post that took him to Paris for the next three years.

The sentimental apogee of Veronese's public career, in his own estimation ("an honor worthy of a lifetime"), was his selection by Paul VI as a lay auditor to the Vatican II Council. During the council's second session in 1963, Veronese, along with Frenchman Jean Guitton, was invited to address the entire council gathered at St. Peter's. Having resumed residence in Rome in 1961, Veronese also served as president of the Bank of Rome until his retirement in 1976. Ever the Catholic activist, he continued to volunteer his energies in charitable initiatives and in the international peace movement. He was nominated a member of the Pontifical Commission for Justice and Peace in 1967.

Characteristic of Veronese's leadership was his gift for fostering dialogue between adherents of diverse religious and political persuasions. He believed that the church could best contribute to the regeneration of post-Fascist Italy by working pastorally, from the bottom up, and not (as in the past) "formally intervening as an *instrumentum regni.*" Like his mentor Montini, he believed that lay organizations such as Catholic Action could complement but should not preempt the political vocation of the **Christian Democracy.** More broadly, Veronese understood the global promotion of democracy and human dignity to be ongoing causes that Catholics were called to serve, but the outcomes of which could not be guaranteed by human agency.

Bibliography.*Vittorino Veronese dal dopoguerra al Concilio: Un laico nella Chiesa e nel* *mondo. Atti del Convegno di studi promosso da l'Istituto Internazionale J. Maritain, l'Istituto Luigi Sturzo e l'Istituto Paulo VI a Roma, 7–8 maggio 1993.* Rome: A.V.E., 1994.

Steven White

VEUILLOT, LOUIS (1813–1883). Veuillot always described himself as a writer (and indeed he is celebrated for his novels, poetry, and mastery of the French language), but he is best known as the irrepressible editor for some forty years of the Catholic newspaper *L'Univers.* "Catholic-before-all," Veuillot was interested in politics primarily as it affected Catholicism. At a time when neuralgic religious issues troubled French political life, Veuillot's contribution to modern Christian politics was that of a talented layman fighting for what he saw as Catholic truth and the rights of the church.

Born in the provinces to poor parents, Veuillot was largely self-educated. Leaving primary school at thirteen, he was apprenticed to a law office in Paris. Fortuitously, the lawyer's brother was a famous poet, and the law office was the gathering place for writers, who soon discovered and encouraged the young Veuillot's literary talent. At seventeen he was editing a newspaper in Rouen, and then shortly after, another in Périgueux. Back in Paris by 1836, Veuillot wrote on politics and culture for a number of newspapers and attracted the attention of François Guizot, an influential political figure. From 1839 to 1843, Guizot arranged for Veuillot to draw a salary from the ministry of the interior in positions with light duties—in effect subsidizing the young writer.

The major turning point in Veuillot's life was a visit in 1838 to Rome, where he was converted from being a nominal Christian to become an enthusiastic ultramontane Catholic. On his return to Paris, Veuillot threw himself into a controversy over freedom of education, a political battle in which a Catholic party sought to free Catholic schools from the domination of

Louis Veuillot. © Roger Viollet / Getty Images

the government's university. By 1843, Veuillot had given up his government salary and won the editorship of the *Univers,* a small and floundering Catholic newspaper. Under Veuillot's direction, the paper became an important force in French religious and political life, popular especially with the country's parish clergy.

A combative journalist who relished a good fight, Veuillot never hesitated to challenge both political and religious authorities as well as other newspapers. In his bitter disputes with "Gallican" bishops (including successive archbishops of Paris), he was supported by Pope **Pius IX,** who often received him in audiences in Rome and called him his "dear Louis." Courted early on by Emperor Napoleon III, Veuillot accorded him support as long as it appeared that the Second Empire favored the church but then turned against the emperor when the latter decided to assist the movement for Italian unification, thereby threatening the Papal States. When *Univers* published the pope's encyclical protesting French actions, the government suspended the paper for some years (1860–1867).

Veuillot's greatest influence came during the First Vatican Council (1869–70), when he championed the passage of the declaration of papal infallibility.

Bibliography. Brown, Marvin L., Jr. *Louis Veuillot: French Ultramontane Catholic Journalist and Layman, 1813–1883.* Durham, North Carolina: Moore, 1977. Pierrard, Pierre. *Louis Veuillot.* Paris: Beauchesne Éditeur, 1998.

Richard A. Lebrun

VOLKSVEREIN. *See* People's Union for a Catholic Germany

VOLOSHYN, AVHUSTYN (1874–1945). Ukrainian Greek Catholic priest, promoter of Transcarpathian self-determination and president of independent Carpatho-Ukraine. After completing theological studies, Voloshyn was ordained in 1897, and pursued further studies in education. He served as professor (1900–1917) and director (1917–1938) of the Teacher's Seminary in Uzhhorod. In pre-World War I Hungarian Transcarpathia, Voloshyn was one of a small group of populists who organized Ukrainian resistance to the culturally oppressive policy of Magyarization. From 1899 onwards, in the face of Hungarian and Russophile obstruction, Voloshyn and his Ukrainophile colleagues published religious and literary books as well as newspapers in the vernacular of the majority Ukrainian population.

With the post-World War I incorporation of Transcarpathia into Czechoslovakia, Voloshyn's cultural activism extended into the political sphere. Voloshyn was the first president of the Central Ruthenian People's Council (CRPC), a political organization of Ukrainians in Transcarpathia. In May 1919, the CRPC adopted a resolution on the autonomy of Transcarpathia and union with Czechoslovakia. In interwar Czechoslovakia, the Party functioned as a coalition of non-communist Ukrainian groups.

In 1920, along with the Greek Catholic Reverend Victor Zheltvai (1890–1974) and A. Tovt, Voloshyn co-founded the populist Ruthenian Agrarian Party (RAP). The RAP's organ, *Rus'ka nyva* (1920–1924), advocated the unification of Ukrainian territories, autonomy for Transcarpathia and the Presov region, and the official use of the Transcarpathian dialect.

The RAP was succeeded by a new political formation, the Christian People's Party (CPP) in Uzhhorod, (1924–1938). Voloshyn was a founder of the CPP, serving as its president, representing it as an elected member of the Czech parliament (1925–1929) and editing its weekly newspaper *Svoboda* ("Liberty", 1925–1938). Among other things, the paper reported on life in the USSR—from the early Ukrainianization policy to subsequent repressions, genocidal famine and Stalinist terror.

In 1938, the CPP reorganized itself as the Central Ukrainian People's Council which played a key role in achieving autonomy for Carpatho-Ukraine. On October 26 of that year, on the heels of the Munich Conference, the president of a weakened Czech state granted autonomy to Transcarpathia and shortly thereafter appointed Voloshyn premier. The Voloshyn government enacted Ukrainianizing reforms in education, publishing and administration. In the elections of February, 1939, Ukrainophiles received the support of 86% of voters, and Voloshyn subsequently became president of independent Carpatho-Ukraine. The Hungarian seizure of Transcarpathia (14 March, 1939) put an end to that project. Voloshyn retired to Prague, teaching at the Ukrainian Free University and serving for a time as its rector. At the end of World War II, in May 1945, he was arrested by the Soviet secret police and deported to the USSR, where he died that same year.

Bibliography. Bednarzhova, Tetiana E. *Avhustyn Voloshyn: derzhavnyi diiach, pedoboh, myslytel.* L'viv: Osnova, 1995.

Andrii Krawchuk

W

WALLIS, JIM (b. 1948). Wallis is one of the most renowned American progressive evangelical political activists in the late twentieth and early twenty-first centuries. He is the editor of *Sojourners* magazine and convener of Call to Renewal, a national federation of churches and faith-based organizations from across the theological and political spectrum working to overcome poverty. He is a leading activist and Christian commentator on ethics and public life.

A self-professed "white" evangelical minister, Wallis was raised in a Midwestern Republican family. While living in an African American community in Detroit, the young Wallis observed police brutality against African Americans and developed a righteous indignation at racial discrimination and profiling. These experiences helped to make him more conscious of the scourge of racism, viewing race as a top priority in his construction of social justice. Wallis's thinking was further radicalized through the peace movement in the 1960s.

The founding of the Sojourners movement produced a critical alternative to mainstream American evangelicalism. The original name of *Sojourners* was the *Post-American,* indicating its criticism of American foreign policy as reflected in the Vietnam War and other police actions on the international scene. Debates about Christian identity and social ethics, vital to the early Sojourners outreach, even attracted the attention of non-evangelicals, including John Howard Yoder, William Stringfellow, and **Daniel Berrigan.** Their struggle to revitalize a nineteenth-century Christian radicalism embodied in the **abolitionist** movement has led some scholars like Donald W. Dayton to interpret *Sojourners* as "post-evangelical" or a new expression North American Christian radicalism.

In the 1970s the Sojourners community provided a communitarian alterative to establishment political culture; however, through the decades, Jim Wallis has led the movement toward a more aggressive advocacy for policy changes in the government. Wallis's many books on faith and public life have heightened the visibility of *Sojourners.* In *God's Politics: Why the Right Gets It Wrong and the Left Doesn't Get It* (2005), Jim Wallis calls progressive justice activists back to religion, adding to his traditional call to evangelicals their historic commitment to social justice. Wallis sees the privatization of faith embodied in this fundamentalist anti-political separatism as "the great heresy of twentieth century evangelicalism." During the early twentieth century and particularly in the 1920s, evangelicalism was transformed by a number of cultural and theological factors and lost its commitment to social justice. The factors leading to a privatized faith included fundamentalist separatism, premillennial dispensational eschatology, and a focus on personal morality instead of public justice.

Wallis points to two alternative political strategies in contemporary evangelical political life: the power politics of the Religious Right and the countercultural campaign for justice in the spirit of the civil rights movement. Wallis passionately opts for the latter, arguing that the Religious Right has been to accepting of a "theology of war" and a Manichean understanding of the United States' global war on terror.

Aligning himself with Dr. **Martin Luther King**'s legacy, Wallis pointedly critiques the failure of **Jerry Falwell**'s **Moral Majority** and **Pat Robertson**'s **Christian Coalition**: "The Religious Right went wrong by forgetting its religious and moral roots and going for political power; the civil rights movement was proven right in operating out of its spiritual strength and letting its political influence flow from its moral influence." The thesis of *God's Politics* is that belief in the personal God of the Christian faith demands socially transformative public action conceived as prophetic worship of the triune God. Critical to this radical evangelical public theology is the building of ecumenical coalitions.

For four decades Wallis has shared his vision for a progressive evangelical social movement in the United States. He has spoken at hundreds of events, and his columns have appeared in the *New York Times, Washington Post, Los Angeles Times,* and other major newspapers. Following the terrorist attack on the World Trade Center in 2001, Wallis and *Sojourners* worked on a six-point plan as an alternative to war with Iraq but failed to gain an audience with the Bush administration (British Prime Minister Tony Blair and his minister Claire Short did meet with the delegation).

While seeing the biblical story of Exodus as a primary political narrative, Wallis emphasizes the role of the church in America as sojourners in the wilderness, in contrast to the Religious Right, which often assigns peculiar spiritual significance to the United States.

Bibliography. Dayton, Donald W. *Discovering an Evangelical Heritage.* Peabody, MA: Hendricks, 1976. Gutterman, David S. *Prophetic Politics: Christian Social Movements and American Democracy.* Ithaca, NY: Cornell University, 2005. Wallis, Jim. *God's Politics: Why the Right Gets It Wrong and the Left Doesn't Get It.* New York: Harper San Francisco, 2005.

Peter G. Heltzel

WEBER, HELENE (1881–1962). Weber was a leading figure in the German **Center Party** (*Zentrum*) and then in the **Christian Democratic Union** (CDU), particularly in the field of women's issues.

Born in Elberfeld, she finished her examinations in 1900 and began her career as a primary school teacher in Aachen and in Elberfeld. In 1905 she began to study language and literature and then worked at secondary schools in Bonn and Cologne. At the start of World War I, she took part in the foundation of the Social Women's School of the German Association of Catholic Women and led it until 1916. After the war she worked at the Prussian Ministry for Public Relief in Berlin and took charge of it in 1920. In 1919, Weber, chairwoman of *Zentrum* Women's Association, represented the party in the national assembly. From 1921 to 1924 she was a member of the Prussian parliament, and from 1924 until 1933 she served as a member of the German Reichstag. She declared herself an enemy of the Versailles peace treaty, which for her was an unbridgeable obstacle to the reconciliation of the belligerent nations. She also opposed any compromise over the penal code section that dealt with criminal abortion.

Weber was mainly engaged in social political questions, especially those on women's education, youth welfare, and family law. In 1933, she declared herself against the Enabling Act, which Adolf Hitler used to establish his dictatorship, but on March 23 voted for it because of party discipline. Suspended from her government role, she afterwards engaged in charity work. Immediately after World War II, Weber joined the newly founded CDU and became a member of North Rhine-Westphalia's parliament. In 1948–1949 she belonged to the parliamentary council and, from 1949 until her death, to the German Bundestag. She was also a member of the Catholic Women's Association and since 1952 chairwoman of the German Welfare Service for Mothers in Need of a Rest. Weber died in Bonn.

Bibliography. Prégardier, Elizabeth, and Anne Mohr. *Helene Weber (1881–1962): Ernte eines Lebens.* Annweiler/Essen, Germany: Plöger, 1991.

Andrea Rönz

WEST, CORNEL (b. 1953). A prominent American scholar and public intellectual, West is best known for his works on race, religion, and politics in America. An American Book Award recipient, West serves as cochair for the National Parenting Organization's Task Force on Parent Empowerment and has been a longtime member of the Democratic Socialists of America. He also participated in President Clinton's National Conversation on Race and was a senior advisor to 2000 Democratic presidential candidate Bill Bradley and 2004 Democratic presidential candidate **Al Sharpton.** In several books, such as *The American Evasion of Philosophy* (1989), West has tried to incorporate Marxist analysis into the different strands of American thought and practice, ranging from black religious congregations to university-trained philosophers like John Dewey, in his critique of American society.

Born on June 2, 1953, in Tulsa, Oklahoma, West was active in civil rights demonstrations, having been influenced by the works and examples of Malcolm X, the Black Panther Party, and **James Cone.** He graduated from Harvard in 1973 and completed his doctorate at Princeton in 1980. His dissertation, published as *The Ethical Dimensions of Marxist Thought* (1991), incorporates Marxist analysis into the prophetic tradition of the African American Baptist Church. This theme is explored again in his book *Prophesy Deliverance!* (1982). Between 1977 and 1987, West taught at both Union Theological Seminary and Yale Divinity School. In 1988, he was director of African American Studies and a professor of religion at Princeton University, where he stayed until 1993, when he joined the W.E.B. Du Bois Institute for Afro-American Research at Harvard University. While at Harvard, West coauthored two books with Henry Louis Gates, Jr.—*The Future of Race* (1996) and *The African-American Century* (2000)—before returning to Princeton University in 2002 after a public dispute with Harvard president Larry Summers about the amount of time West was spending in political activity.

The book that brought public prominence to West was *Race Matters* (1993). In this work, West examines an array of controversial topics such as black-Jewish relations, the Clarence Thomas confirmation hearings, and the black conservative movement. In this work, West criticizes both conservatives and liberals for their dependence upon the capitalist economy to provide solutions to social, cultural, and political problems and advocates a restructuring of economic relations on a socialist model. Later, with Rabbi Michael Lerner, West explored black-Jewish relations in *Jews and Blacks* (1995). Here, West is unwilling to repudiate Louis Farrakhan's anti-Semitism, although in *Race Matters* he does criticize black leadership for not condemning the 1991 murder of Yankel Rosenbaum. More recently, West has returned to his earlier theme of prophetic criticism in *Democracy Matters* (2004). Placing himself in the African American prophetic tradition, West draws upon American cultural, political, and religious thought to criticize the United States' free-market economy, foreign policy, and Christian fundamentalism, equating the last with Islamic fundamentalism.

Bibliography. Cowan, Rosemary. *Cornel West: The Politics of Redemption.* Cambridge: Polity, 2003. Johnson, Clarence Sholé. *Cornel West and Philosophy.* New York: Routledge, 2002. Wood, Mark David. *Cornel West and the Politics of Prophetic Pragmatism.* Champagne: University of Illinois Press, 2000. Yancy, George, ed. *Cornel West: A Critical Reader.* Oxford: Blackwell, 2001.

Lee Trepanier

WILBERFORCE, WILLIAM (1759–1833). A member of Parliament and an abolitionist, Wilberforce was born in Hull, England, into a High Church Anglican family. Although his businessman father died when William was only nine, a substantial estate was left behind, and in short order William became sole heir. His first publication at age fourteen was a letter to the editor of the local *Yorkshire Gazette* condemning slavery—a harbinger of his future vocation.

He attended St. John's College at Cambridge, where his work was undistinguished, but he had the good fortune to make the acquaintance of William Pitt the Younger, future prime minister of England (1783–1801, 1804–1806). Wilberforce, eschewing a career in the family business, was determined on politics and

the House of Commons. At age twenty-one, he presented himself to the voters of Hull in 1780 and, spending nearly nine thousand pounds, easily out-polled two opponents. In Parliament, Wilberforce along with Burke and Pitt opposed Lord North's war against the Americans. By 1784 Wilberforce was elected as one of the MPs from Yorkshire, England's largest county.

At this time, Wilberforce began adhering to the evangelical wing of the Church of England. In his youth, under the influence of relatives, he had become something of a Methodist, but his mother had put an end to this. Now through the influence of Milner and Newton, he left High Church Anglicanism and became both more puritanical and more zealous in pursuit of what today we would call social justice issues. Throughout his life, his philanthropy toward the poor and missionary activity was exceptional.

He supported Pitt in the latter's bill on Catholic emancipation and the related question of Ireland—though evangelicals had less love of Catholicism than did the Church of England. Wilberforce founded the Proclamation Society, later known as the Society for the Suppression of Vice—basically an anti-pornography organization—of which George III was a patron. In 1787 at age twenty-nine, Wilberforce took up the parliamentary cause that was to be his enduring legacy: the suppression of the slave trade. In this crusade, his eloquence and the justice of his cause were his greatest weapons; the financial interests of the business community in England's port cities—Bristol and Liverpool chiefly—and Caribbean possessions grown wealthy on the trade were his greatest opponents. Prime Minster Pitt himself asked Wilberforce to introduce the motion in Commons for Britain to end the slave trade. The bill had to be a private one since many in Pitt's own Cabinet and the king himself opposed such a measure for both narrow financial reasons and the complications it would cause in foreign relations with the French and Spanish governments; thus a coalition approach was deemed necessary.

On May 12, 1789, Wilberforce, in a stirring three-hour address, proposed anew the motion to end the slave trade. Edmund Burke himself lauded its "Grecian eloquence." John Wesley on his deathbed applauded the bill and the speech. Charles James Fox as well as the prime minister, as a member of Commons rather than as head of government, spoke in support of the bill. On April 20, 1791, after delays of over two years and after a debate lasting to past three in the morning, Commons rejected the Wilberforce bill 163–88.

In 1797 his book *Practical Christianity* was a tremendous success and heightened his prestige among the public. Finally in 1807 the abolition bill was passed by both houses of Parliament. Follow-up legislation was passed to ensure the suppression of the slave trade in foreign countries. In 1808 the United States Congress ended the importation of slaves.

Wilberforce and his supporters now turned to the task of freeing those already enslaved prior to the bill's 1807 passage and therefore not covered by its terms. This struggle was to last until 1823, when a month after his death, the bill to abolish slavery throughout the British Empire was finally passed. Wilberforce was buried with great honor at Westminster Abbey. Wilberforce University, an African Methodist Episcopal institution in Ohio, is named in his honor, as is the town in which it is located.

Bibliography. Belmonte, Kevin. *Hero for Humanity: A Biography of William Wilberforce.* Colorado Springs, CO: Navpress, 2002. Piper, John. *The Roots of Endurance.* Wheaton, IL: Crossway Books, 2002. Wilberforce, William. *A Practical View of Christianity.* Peabody, MA: Hendrickson, 1996.

William J. Parente

WILLARD, EMMA HART (1787–1870). Willard pioneered education for young women in the United States as a teacher, founder of Troy Female Seminary, author, and educational theorist. She believed that the republic's survival would be ensured through the education of American women—the nation's mothers and, increasingly, its teachers. Willard developed a rigorous curriculum that required Bible study and integrated God into all subjects (Lutz, 96). Protestantism's traditional emphasis on individual conscience, literacy, and simplicity underpinned her educational program.

Emma Hart was born in Berlin, Connecticut, into the large family of Revolutionary War veteran Captain Samuel Hart and his second wife, Lydia Hinsdale Hart. During Emma's youth, girls attended school only in the summer and focused on rote learning and "ornamental" subjects. Yet encouraged by her father, Emma distinguished herself at the village school and then at a nearby academy. Beginning in

William Wilberforce. Courtesy of the Perry-Casteñeda Library

1804, Emma took a series of teaching positions in these schools then taught briefly in 1807 in Massachusetts. By late 1807, she had moved to Middlebury Academy for girls in Vermont. She married Dr. John Willard, marshal of the District of Vermont, in 1809. She left teaching but continued to study on her own. The Willards' only child, John Hart Willard, was born September 28, 1810.

Their home's proximity to Middlebury College—and her exposure to its curriculum through Dr. Willard's nephew, a student there—impressed upon Willard the insufficient higher educational opportunities available to girls. When in 1814 financial problems struck, Emma opened Middlebury Female Seminary, a college-level boarding school. She campaigned relentlessly for governmental support. New York's governor invited her to speak to the state legislature. Somewhat reluctantly in light of prevailing strictures on women's public speech, Willard addressed several members of that assembly. In 1819, she published *An Address to the Public, Particularly to the Members of the Legislature of New-York, Proposing a Plan for Improving Female Education.*

The *Plan* explained the flaws in girls' education and offered correctives. Female education failed because it set men's "approbation" as women's "highest object." She wrote that for any Christian, "the will of God … is the only standard of perfection" (quoted in Lutz, 31). Educated women in full command of their God-given rational powers could train virtuous Christian sons to defend the fledgling American republic.

Confident that her appeals would bring financial support, Willard moved her seminary in 1819 to Waterford, New York. Yet funding did not come. The enterprising city of Troy, New York, however, raised the funds on its own. In September 1821, Willard opened the Troy Female Seminary.

The seminary trained a generation of teachers for schools throughout the growing nation and built an international reputation. The students used many textbooks written by Willard herself, including *A System of Universal Geography* (1822; coauthored) and *Republic of America* (1828; revised as *History of the United States*). She insisted that students learn through understanding, not memorization.

Willard adhered strictly throughout her life, ideologically if not practically, to ideas of the "woman's sphere" that would dominate elite culture through the nineteenth century. She influenced and enjoyed the support of Sarah Josepha Hale, editor of *Godey's Ladies Book,* and **Catharine Beecher,** educator and author. She forbade her students from engaging in public political debates and expressed dismay at the activism of former students such as **Elizabeth Cady Stanton.**

She retired from Troy Female Seminary in 1838, when her son and his wife, Willard's former pupil and assistant, took over. Dr. Willard had died in 1825. Willard married again late in 1838, but the unhappy match lasted only nine months. Ashamed of this failure, she spent the next five years working in Connecticut. In 1844, the marriage legally dissolved, she returned to Troy and lived on the seminary campus, writing, advising students and graduates, and touring the South and West to survey educational practices. In 1895, Troy Female Seminary became the Emma Willard School.

Bibliography. Goodsell, Willystine, ed. *Pioneers of Women's Education in the United States: Emma Willard, Catherine [sic] Beecher, Mary Lyon.* New York: McGraw-Hill, 1931. Lutz, Alma. *Emma Willard: Pioneer Educator of American Women.* Boston: Beacon Press, 1964.

Anne Blue Wills

WILLARD, FRANCES ELIZABETH CAROLINE (1839–1898). Willard, president of the **Woman's Christian Temperance Union** (WCTU, 1879–1898), was born in western New York on September 28, 1839. She spent much of her childhood and adolescence on a farm in southeastern Wisconsin. The Willards and their neighbors were transplanted Yankees, vitally interested in education, local and national politics, temperance reform, and the antislavery movement. Like many evangelical Protestants of their era, her parents believed that their religious faith must be demonstrated through ethical behavior, in particular by responsible civic and political citizenship in the young American republic. This belief became Willard's guiding principle throughout her life.

When the Willard family moved to Evanston, Illinois, in the late 1850s, they entered an exciting political milieu focused on **Abraham Lincoln**'s Republican presidential bid. Willard was vitally interested in this lively political scene and disturbed that her sex disqualified her from voting. Her support for women's rights deepened during her twenties, and by 1868 she had decided that her vocation was to champion "the cause of woman." At first, she sought to carry out this intent by educating young women, but in 1874 she turned her attention to the growing movement of women advocating temperance. At the founding convention of the WCTU, she was elected national corresponding secretary with the duty of organizing local Unions throughout the country. In 1879 she was chosen president of the WCTU. Her election represented the victory of the liberal wing of the organization, which advocated "Home Protection," a slogan she devised to signify that women would use their voting power to legislate prohibition of the sale of liquor.

As leader of the rapidly growing WCTU, Willard sought to broaden its reform program beyond temperance to include all aspects of women's rights. She understood her organization, above all, as a powerful vehicle for women's self-development, one that would train American women for responsible participation in the public life of their country. Under her direction, the WCTU became a powerful pressure group, bringing its increasing influence to bear on political parties and government at all levels, as well as on other civic and cultural institutions, in pursuit of social betterment. Willard encouraged WCTU leaders and membership to work toward a variety of goals, from legislation curbing the liquor industry to raising the age of consent for girls, from scientific temperance instruction in public and Sunday schools to the placement of police matrons in courts and prisons. Her WCTU presidency provided her with a powerful national "pulpit" from which she could inspire her audience, one that reached far beyond her WCTU constituency. Willard was adept at creating alliances with other organizations and individuals who espoused reform goals similar to hers, from women's rights leaders **Susan B. Anthony** and Mary Livermore to Prohibition Party politicians.

In the late 1880s, Willard turned her attention, as did many other early **Social Gospel** figures, to the pressing problems of urban industrialization, especially the growing inequities between rich and poor. She saw this as an issue that demanded justice, not charity—the usual way to address poverty during the nineteenth century. In a stunning reversal, she also rejected the traditional explanation that intemperance caused poverty, insisting that poverty often was a cause of intemperance. Willard supported the developing labor movement, particularly **Terence Powderly** and the Knights of Labor, and supported many of labor's demands for improving the situation of workers, especially women and children. After studying various alternatives to what she viewed as an increasingly unjust capitalist system, she declared herself a Christian socialist, drawing her understanding of socialism from the British Fabians and such American thinkers as Edward Bellamy, Henry George, and Henry Demarest Lloyd.

During the 1890s, Willard gave an increasing amount of time and energy to the international dimension of her organization. She became president of the World's WCTU in 1891 and directed efforts to create a network of women reformers stretching around the globe. Working in the British Isles for several years with Isabel (Lady Henry) Somerset, president of the British Woman's Temperance Association, Willard encouraged British temperance reformers to broaden their interests to women's rights and other issues, as the American organization had. She continued to support temperance measures, appearing on the platform with clergy and members of Parliament who pushed for prohibitory legislation. Yet she and Isabel Somerset began to investigate other ways to address excessive drinking, initiating a live-in treatment center for women inebriates similar to facilities being established in the United States. Willard was slowly coming to believe that legislation alone would not be sufficient to eliminate drunkenness; she began to place more emphasis on education for prevention and on rehabilitation.

By the mid-1890s, Willard had become ill with pernicious anemia, then a fatal disease. Lacking her former energy, she curtailed her rigorous speaking schedule and embarked on a program of exercise and diet to regain her health. But she grew steadily weaker over several years; she died on February 17, 1898. Hundreds of thousands across the country and throughout the world mourned the loss of their "Uncrowned Queen," who had successfully built the WCTU into the largest women's organization of the time and linked American women with an international sisterhood of reform.

Bibliography. Bordin, Ruth. *Frances Willard: A Biography.* Chapel Hill: University of North Carolina Press, 1986. Earhart Dillon, Mary. *Frances Willard: From Prayers to Politics.* Chicago: University of Chicago Press, 1944. Gifford, Carolyn DeSwarte. *"Writing out My Heart": Selections from the Journal of Frances E. Willard, 1855–96.* Urbana: University of Illinois Press, 1995. Slagell, Amy Rose. *"A Good Woman Speaking Well: the Oratory of Frances E. Willard."* PhD diss., University of Wisconsin–Madison, 1992. Willard, Frances E. *Glimpses of Fifty Years: The Autobiography of an American Woman.* Boston: Geo. Smith for the Woman's Temperance Publishing Association, 1889.

Carolyn DeSwarte Gifford

WILLEBRANDS, JOHANNES GERARDUS MARIA (1909–2006). A former archbishop of Utrecht and cardinal of the Roman Catholic Church, Willebrands has been a leading ecumenical voice in the Netherlands, encouraging wider Catholic involvement in Dutch society and resisting the "confessional separatism" that had long characterized Catholicism's attitude to the broader culture.

Born in Bovenkarspel, Willebrands was ordained in 1934. After being ordained titular bishop of Mauriana, he was appointed president of the Roman Curia in 1969 and elevated to cardinal in 1975. As president of the St. Willibrord Association for ecumenical work in the Netherlands, Willebrands organized the Catholic Conference for Ecumenical Questions, an international organization that maintained ties with the **World Council of Churches** and brought theologians together to reflect upon ecumenical questions.

Because of his work in ecumenism, Willebrands was appointed to head the Secretariat for Promoting Christian Unity, and his specific attention to the needs of interchurch families was highly praised. He also devoted his attention to making possible Eucharistic sharing among interchurch marriage partners. This ecumenical concern also characterized Willebrands's work as archbishop of Utrecht. Willebrands was noted for a collegial approach to church governance that included laity and cordial relationships with Protestant churches. In spite of his close connections to the Roman Curia, Willebrands at times opposed certain Vatican initiatives and most publicly resisted Rome's insistence that married ex-priests be removed from theological teaching positions.

Willebrands's name was prominently listed among leading *papabile* during the 1978 papal elections. After the election of **John Paul II,** Willebrands continued his work as head of the Secretariat for Promoting Christian Unity, later renamed the Pontifical Council for Promoting Christian Unity. Willebrands was one of the key mediators in 1980 to heal the conservative-liberal split between Dutch bishops during a special synod of bishops for the Netherlands. Willebrands also publicly defended John Paul II's meeting with Yasir Arafat in 1982 and had a significant role in removing a Carmelite convent from the precincts of Auschwitz in 1989.

His work for the Vatican continued even after he was succeeded by Edward Cardinal Cassidy as head of the Pontifical Council for Promoting Christian Unity. Most notably, Willebrands traveled to the Soviet Union in 1990 as the Vatican's official emissary to discuss the status of the Ukrainian Catholic Church.

Bibliography. Briggs, Kenneth. "Vatican Aid Defends Pope's Meeting with Arafat." *New York Times,* 24 October 1982. Coleman, John A. *The Evolution of Dutch Catholicism, 1958–1974.* Berkeley and Los Angeles: University of California Press, 1978. Simons, Marlise. "Vatican Strongly Urges Removal of Convent at Site of Auschwitz." *New York Times,* 20 September 1989.

Mathew N. Schmalz

WILSON, WOODROW (1856–1924). Religion and politics have been closely entwined in the lives of American presidents, and perhaps none more conspicu-

ously than Wilson. A Southern Presbyterian and a conservative evangelical, Wilson combined moral certainty and experiential Protestantism in a political worldview suffused with religious meaning.

Born in 1856 in Staunton, Virginia, Wilson inhabited a home defined by his father's religious sensibilities. Joseph Ruggles Wilson, a minister who helped establish the denomination's secessionist branch in 1861, inculcated his son in the Southern Presbyterian tradition, which drew heavily upon the covenant theology of Calvinism. Covenant theology proposed that God and humanity were bound together by covenants of grace and nature, grace providing forgiveness in return for obedience to divine precepts, and nature dictating moral law in the manner of a constitution governing worldly political institutions. The elder Wilson made the covenant tradition the foundation of his insistence on obedience to moral law. It also organized his thinking about the responsibilities of a Christian in the modern world, the nature of history and Protestant election, and the harmony between slavery and natural law. A devoted and admiring son, Woodrow Wilson absorbed these ideas from a father who closely supervised his intellectual development.

The covenant theology encouraged Wilson to see the world as an arena of moral struggle and himself as a Christian militant. In 1876 while he was a student at Princeton, Wilson described the cosmic contest this way: "The field of battle is the world. From the abodes of righteousness advances the host of God's people under the leadership of Christ. Immediately behind the great Captain of Salvation come the veteran regiments of the soldiers of the cross. . . [who] girt about with truth, their breast plates of righteousness beneath the bright rays of their Master's love, each one grasping the sword of the spirit" (quoted in Dennis, 65). The covenant tradition imbued Wilson with a sense of moral righteousness in his struggles against the corporate trusts, against insufficiently liberal revolutionaries in Mexico, and against the forces of international aggression that Wilson believed had compelled the United States to take up the sword. The Presbyterian covenant tradition gave him not only a propensity for inflexible moral categories but also the belief that moral convictions required social action.

Beyond moralism and the call to action, the Presbyterian covenant tradition instilled in Wilson a strong preference for order and cohesion over atomistic individualism. One of the principle ways that Wilson manifested this influence was through his penchant for covenants and constitutions. As a student looking toward graduation from Princeton, Wilson forged a solemn covenant with his friend Charlie Talcott to "school all our powers and passions for the work of establishing the principles we held in common" and to "acquire knowledge that we might have power" (Mulder, 229). Debating societies provided Wilson an opportunity to express his constitutional proclivities. Yet *Congressional Government,* his 1885 critique of government paralysis, encapsulated his belief that political order could be achieved by synthesizing competing interests through debate and cabinet-style government.

As Wilson cultivated his lifelong interest in government administration, he also expressed the covenant principles inherited from his Southern Presbyterian tradition. In "The Modern Democratic State," he postulated an organic conception of society that harmonized individual self-interest and corporate needs. He stressed the idea that democracy found its vitality and cohesion in moral principles. As president of Princeton, he applied the covenant theology by emphasizing the organic character of the university bound together by

Woodrow Wilson at the Versailles Treaty negotiations in Paris. Courtesy of the National Archives and Records Administration

common principles and discerning leaders. He sought to reform the university along these lines, promoting egalitarian reform of the college's elitist eating clubs.

Wilson's moral convictions influenced his approach to domestic politics, but they made a lasting impression on American foreign relations. By casting international relations in a moral framework of mutual responsibilities and legal obligations, Wilson fired the imagination of liberals throughout the West. The language of collective security and national self-determination reflected his covenant predilections and offered an alternative to the national chauvinism that lay behind the First World War. It offered an international version of the Progressive movement, which had carried overtones of national regeneration through moral reform. Wilsonian internationalism would survive not only through the League of Nations and its successor, the United Nations, but through the political leaders and commentators who identified American national interests with international law, free markets, and the extension of liberal democracy abroad. But if he offered hope to Europeans traumatized by war, he also alienated European leaders unaccustomed to moral idealism. Led by Republican "reservationists" like Henry Cabot Lodge, Congress balked at Wilson's "covenant" of collective security, which opponents believed would threaten national sovereignty and involve the United States in remote and costly wars. Through the struggle over ratification of the Treaty of Versailles, Wilson mirrored the efforts of **abolitionists** and temperance advocates to transform the United States according to a vision of national greatness anchored in religious precepts. His strenuous cross-country campaign on behalf of the treaty and the league echoed the camp revivalists of the nineteenth century. But Wilson's political evangelicalism was ill suited to a country exhausted by war and unwilling to reassemble the fragmented nineteenth-century evangelical consensus.

Bibliography. Bragdon, Henry Wilkinson. *Woodrow Wilson: The Academic Years.* Cambridge, MA: Belknap Press of Harvard University Press, 1967. Dennis, Michael. "The Southern Evangelicalism of Woodrow Wilson." *Fides et Historia* 33 (Winter–Spring 2001): 57–72. Mulder, John M. "'A Gospel of Order:' Woodrow Wilson's Religion and Politics." In *The Wilson Era: Essays in Honor of Arthur S. Link,* ed. John Milton Cooper, Jr., and Charles E. Neu. Arlington Heights, IL: Harland Davidson, 1991. Mulder, John M. *Woodrow Wilson: The Years of Preparation.* Princeton, NJ: Princeton University Press, 1978.

Michael Dennis

WIRTH, JOSEF (1879–1956). Josef Wirth was one of the most enigmatic German politicians of the twentieth century. He was fiercely principled, but his principles often led him to decisions that seemed shortsighted and pragmatic. Wirth can be characterized by three traits: his pride in being German, his commitment to a republican form of democratic government, and his Catholicism. Unlike many of his contemporaries, Wirth saw no contradictions among these commitments.

In 1921–1922, Wirth served as chancellor of the young Weimar Republic. Later, he served as minister for the occupied territories and as minister of the interior. He emigrated during the National Socialist period, first to France and then to Switzerland. After the war, Wirth returned to Germany, were he became involved in inter-German politics until his death in 1956.

For Wirth, the state was "a moral community of the people" and "a Christian democracy with social welfare concerns." It was the purpose of the state to protect the less fortunate and also to protect the church. Those opposed to democracy or even to parliamentary government, Wirth believed, were unacceptable political opponents who should not call themselves Christian. In this, Wirth was ahead of his times. All were called upon to serve the state as it fulfilled its Christian mission. Wirth's ideal Christian state did not exclude Jews or others. Rather, it was guided by social goals that were Christian in nature. In fact, while in exile, Wirth urged the Vatican to condemn anti-Semitism and racism.

Wirth was an observant Catholic whose political home was in the German **Center Party.** Becoming chancellor, however, was not a sign of his popularity, but rather of his expendability during a time of crisis. In spring 1921, the defeated Germany faced an Allied ultimatum over the total sum of war reparations. The Allies had already occupied important German towns along the Rhine to prove their serious intentions. As chancellor, Wirth inaugurated *Erfüllungspolitik,* fulfillment policy. The

German government would accept the unacceptable terms in order to preserve Germany. By failing to meet the terms, despite its best efforts, Germany would prove the terms unfeasible. By fall 1922, Germany's increasingly desperate position led to Wirth's replacement with a cabinet of business leaders who continued Wirth's policies until the French occupation of the Ruhr industrial era and Germany's economic collapse under hyperinflation.

During his chancellorship and beyond, Wirth demanded that Catholics commit themselves wholeheartedly to democracy and to a republican form of government. Unlike Weimar politicians, including Catholics, Wirth did not simply support the republic until something better came along. He opposed those within his own party who were increasingly willing to cooperate with the right-wing parties. By the end of the republic, his principled defense of republican democracy as well as his quick temper left him fairly isolated, even within his own party.

In foreign policy, Wirth personally was a nationalist, but he pursued a pragmatic policy on which Gustav Stresemann could build his rapprochement with France. At Rapallo, Wirth negotiated a treaty with the Soviet Union to guarantee Germany diplomatic freedom. In 1940, he was among the few Germans who recognized that peace would not be possible if Germany insisted on her territorial gains since 1937.

As an emigrant, Wirth sought ties to other exile groups but found few who were interested in his ideas. After the war, he returned to western Germany. Antipathy between Wirth and **Adenauer** prevented his return to political prominence. Instead, in the 1950s, Wirth became actively involved in efforts to undo the cold war partition of Germany. While many in the West saw him as a tool of Eastern Bloc communism, Wirth saw himself carrying out a Christian mission and considered Adenauer's alliance with the West a great obstacle to peace.

Wirth's death in 1956 drew little national attention, but he is now considered one of the most principled, if not particularly successful, German Catholic political leaders of the twentieth century.

Bibliography. Hörster-Philipps, Ulrike. *Joseph Wirth, 1879–1956: Eine politische Biographie.* Paderborn, Germany: Ferdinand Schöningh, 1998. Küppers, Heinrich. *Joseph Wirth: Parlamentarier, Minister und Kanzler der Weimarer Republik.* Historische Mitteilungen der Ranke Gesellschaft 27. Stuttgart, Germany: Franz Steiner, 1997.

Martin Menke

WOMAN'S CHRISTIAN TEMPERANCE UNION (UNITED STATES). The Woman's Christian Temperance Union (WCTU) was founded in November 1874 in Cleveland, Ohio. Over one hundred women, many of whom had participated in the women's temperance crusade of 1873–1874, gathered to create a permanent national temperance organization whose leadership and membership would be exclusively female and whose agenda would focus on the disastrous results of male drunkenness for women and children. Convention delegates elected Annie Turner Wittenmyer president of the newly formed WCTU, and **Frances E. Willard** corresponding secretary. Together they began to orchestrate a sustained effort against the powerful liquor industry under the banner "For God and Home and Native Land."

Women had become increasingly active in temperance reform during the middle decades of the nineteenth century but were usually foot soldiers in a war led by men. As political and legislative action became more important than individual moral suasion, women's role in temperance reform shrank. They could pray, plead, and petition but could not vote. Much of their work against liquor dealers and saloon keepers was temporary, subject to reversal in political and judicial processes over which they had no real power.

From its earliest days the WCTU sought more political influence, at first through the familiar method of petitioning at local, state, and national levels. But several leaders, including Willard, quickly began to push for woman suffrage in order to help win legislative prohibition. Willard was elected national WCTU president in 1879, signaling a triumph for the liberal wing of the organization that championed "Home Protection"—the vote for women as their most effective weapon in the fight against drunkenness.

During Willard's long presidency (1879–1898), she encouraged the organization to broaden its reform vision beyond temperance to encompass women's rights and the aims of the rising labor movement. Under the rubric "Do Everything," the WCTU pursued six areas of work—education, evangelism, social outreach, organizational extension, legal work, and prevention—that remain the focus of the organization's efforts today. In order to carry out her ambitious reform goals, Willard built a strong leadership of department superintendents who oversaw all the various aspects of the activities undertaken by WCT local and state unions. WCTU leaders molded their constituency into a powerful and efficient pressure group, lobbying for myriad local, state, and national reforms. Under WCTU auspices, thousands of women learned about how the U.S. political system worked and how to make it responsive to their aims.

The organization became a "school" for civic participation, producing generations of highly skilled reformers who advanced the causes of prohibition and woman suffrage. Beginning in 1880, it pioneered efforts to achieve constitutional prohibition in individual states through statewide referendums. During the 1880s and early 1890s, Willard persuaded the WCTU to engage actively in third-party politics, first aligning with the Prohibition Party to urge its adoption of a woman-suffrage platform

plank, and, then, participating in an unsuccessful attempt to create a coalition reform party with labor, populist, and prohibition leaders. By 1900, the organization had achieved a number of goals that included securing scientific temperance instruction in many of the nation's public and Sunday schools; raising the age of consent in almost every state; and, in concert with other women's rights, civic, and labor organizations, bringing about improvements in working and living conditions in towns and cities throughout the United States.

The WCTU grew rapidly during its first quarter-century and by 1900 boasted nearly two 200,000 members spread throughout the country, making it the largest women's organization of that time. Although its membership was predominately white, middle class, and evangelical Protestant, it claimed a number of working-class and African American women as well. Realizing early on the importance of recruiting the next generation of reformers, the WCTU founded groups for children and youth, which grew swiftly to several hundred thousand members. The organization also expanded internationally with the formation of the World's WCTU in the mid-1880s. For the next several decades, World's WCTU missionaries traveled the globe organizing unions and encouraging women to work for prohibition of the global trade in alcohol, opium, and other narcotics. They also championed women's educational and political emancipation and their protection from sexual oppression. By the 1920s, the World's WCTU had 766,000 members, with branches in forty nations.

During president Lillian M. N. Stevens' tenure (1898–1914), the WCTU increasingly focused on the struggle for national prohibition. Working with longtime legislative superintendent Margaret Dye Ellis, a skilled lobbyist headquartered in the WCTU's Washington, D.C., office, Stevens, and her presidential successor, Anna Adams Gordon (1914–1925), presented Congress with massive petitions calling for a national prohibition amendment. They also persuaded sympathetic members of the House and Senate to shepherd many other WCTU-sponsored bills aimed at curbing the liquor traffic through Congress. At the same time, the organization continued to support campaigns for state and local prohibition laws and ordinances. The WCTU cooperated with the Anti-Saloon League in the final push toward passage of the Eighteenth (National Prohibition) Amendment in 1919.

Elated by the achievement of its longtime goals of prohibition and woman suffrage (Nineteenth Amendment, passed 1920), the WCTU embarked on an ambitious membership and fundraising drive, aiming for a million members and a million dollars by 1924, the year of the organization's fiftieth anniversary. The money raised would support the work of the Americanization, Scientific Temperance Instruction, and Child Welfare departments, areas on which Gordon wished the WCTU to focus during the 1920s. Although these goals were not met, the WCTU's membership did reach a peak of nearly 500,000 in 1924 and collected a substantial sum of money. Spurred on by the successful struggle for prohibition in the United States, the WCTU also encouraged the World's WCTU toward its goal of global prohibition of alcohol and narcotics. At the same time, the WCTU maintained a steady pressure on government at all levels to enforce national prohibition.

As support for repeal of the Eighteenth Amendment grew during the 1920s and early 1930s, the WCTU fought to retain national prohibition, supporting "dry" candidates and "dry" planks in party platforms, and attempted to counter the work for repeal by the influential Women's Organization for National Prohibition Reform. After repeal in 1933, the WCTU began to lose its prestige and power, and membership steadily declined, dwindling to around seven thousand members by 1997. As its political activities shrank from a pre-prohibition high level, the organization stressed its goal of education for abstinence, developing presentations through a variety of media, including movies, film strips, videotapes, and radio programming, in addition to its large output of printed materials begun in the late 1870s.

The WCTU still retains its strategy of influencing the American political system. In 1997–1998, for example, one of its goals was the distribution of an educational packet about marijuana to each state legislator, in the face of discussion about possible legalization of the drug. The WCTU has changed over the course of its 125-year history from an organization in the vanguard of Progressivism to one that now locates itself in the camp of Christian conservatism. And it has lost most of the political influence it once wielded. Yet its warnings about the dangers of substance abuse still remain relevant in contemporary American society.

Bibliography. Blocker, Jack S., Jr. *American Temperance Movements: Cycles of Reform.* Boston: Twayne, 1989. Bordin, Ruth. *Woman and Temperance: The Quest for Power and Liberty, 1873–1900.* Philadelphia: Temple University Press, 1981. Gordon, Elizabeth Putnam. *Women Torch-Bearers: The Story of the Woman's Christian Temperance Union.* Evanston, IL: National Woman's Christian Temperance Union, 1924. Tyrell, Ian. *Woman's World, Woman's Empire: The Woman's Christian Temperance Union in International Perspective, 1880–1930.* Chapel Hill: University of North Carolina Press, 1991. Woman's Christian Temperance Union. *The Temperance and Prohibition Papers.* Microfilm edition. Ann Arbor: University of Michigan, 1977.

Carolyn DeSwarte Gifford

WOODSWORTH, JAMES SHAVER (1874–1942).

Woodsworth was a famous social reformer and an uncompromising pacifist revered by a whole generation of Canadians who reckoned him the "conscience of Canada."

His life was steadfastly dedicated to serving the poor and establishing the kingdom of God on earth, although the means he chose to achieve such noble goals substantially changed during his lifetime.

His early endeavor to bring about social justice was first shaped by his Methodist ministry. Soon, however, this denominational framework proved to be irrelevant for, as superintendent of a city mission, he worked amongst immigrant Canadians living in deteriorating slum conditions. Many key elements were lacking, including a healthy urban environment, community organization, and a compulsory educational system, all beyond the reach of any church mission. Woodsworth came to see that his ultimate task was to close the gap between rich and poor, native and alien. He thus increasingly favored a lay plan of intervention, intellectually veering from biblical knowledge toward sociology and social-work theory.

If, as he believed, prosperity was reflected in the social and moral welfare of the people, then social initiatives must be broad in scope and involve the whole community. Otherwise, the most important needs would not be met. After leaving the church for good in 1918, he then embraced pure political action. He became involved in and was arrested at the Winnipeg General Strike (1919) while acting as editor of the strikers' newspaper. Two years later, he was elected a Labour member of Parliament, a seat he held until his death. In the early 1930s, he was a founding member of a party of the Left in Canada—the Co-Operative Commonwealth Federation, later renamed the New Democratic Party.

Bibliography. Mills, Allen. *Fool for Christ: The Political Thought of J. S. Woodsworth.* Toronto: University of Toronto Press, 1991.

Sylvie Lacombe

WOODWARD, MICHAEL (1932–1973). Woodward is an important example of a Catholic priest who became involved in the world of the poor and in Chilean politics due to his Christian convictions. Born in Chile of a British father and Chilean mother, he was educated at the Benedictine school at Downside, England, and later studied engineering at King's College London. He trained for the priesthood in the Catholic Church in Chile, entering the Santiago Seminary in 1954. Ordained as a priest for the Valparaiso Archdiocese in 1961, he spent two years at the Institut Superieur de Catechétique, part of the Institut Catholique in Paris.

On his return, Woodward served as chaplain to youth groups, the Student Catholic Action, and the Movement of Catholic Professionals. In 1966, he moved to the parish of Peña Blanca, an hour from Valparaiso, where he was appointed priest-in-charge. His pastoral activities included the traditional dispensing of the sacraments, but he also introduced new catechetical methods that included home visits, helping local residents to build their homes, and general concern for community work.

After a short stay in Europe, Woodward returned to Chile as a worker priest and lived in Cerro Placeres, a working-class area of Valparaiso. In 1969, he accepted employment at the Las Habas shipyard, where he operated a lathe. He shared his wages with the poor and became a member of a left-wing political party (MAPU) and the **Christians for Socialism** Movement.

After the Chilean military coup, he was arrested at his house in Cerro Placeres and tortured by navy personnel at the training ship *Esmeralda*. He was falsely accused of possessing arms in order to kill armed forces personnel. He died of multiple injuries caused by severe beatings and systematic torture. He was interred in a pauper's grave at the Cemetery of Playa Ancha, where the bodies of those who had not been identified were buried.

Bibliography. Aguilar, Mario I. *A Social History of the Catholic Church in Chile.* Vol. 1: *The First Period of the Pinochet Government 1973–1980.* Lewiston, NY: Edwin Mellen, 2004. Crouzet, Edward. *Blood on the Esmeralda: The Life and Death of Father Michael Woodward.* Stratton-on-the-Fosse, UK: Downside Books, 2002.

Mario I. Aguilar

WORCESTER, SAMUEL (1798–1859). Minister and translator for the Cherokees, Worcester became famous for his part in the Supreme Court decision *Worcester v. Georgia.* Raised in Vermont, his father a minister, Samuel graduated from the University of Vermont in 1819 and then entered Andover Theological Seminary. After graduating in 1823, he went to Boston to work for the American Board of Commissioners for Foreign Missions (ABCFM); there, **Jeremiah Evarts** urged him to work with Cherokees. On August 25, 1825, slightly more than a month after marrying Ann Orr, Worcester was ordained at the Park Street Church in Boston. Six days later, the couple left for the Brainerd boarding school in Tennessee near the Georgia border. Cherokees gathered to welcome them named Worcester *A-tse-nu-sti,* "messenger."

By 1827, A-tse-nu-sti had established a printing press that could use English and Sequoyan letters. Unlike most missionaries, he saw the potential for the Cherokees to quickly become literate using their own language. Worcester published hymnals, religious tracts, and almanacs in Sequoyan and English and began translating the Bible from Greek into Cherokee. He hired as an assistant Elias Boudinot, the prominent son of a Cherokee chief, and the two became very close. In 1828, he moved to New Echota, where he helped Boudinot start the *Cherokee Phoenix,* which featured articles in both Sequoyan and English.

As Georgia sought to force out the Indians, Worcester became involved in Cherokee resistance. When a group went to Washington, D.C., in March 1830 to lobby against Georgian laws, Worcester wrote (at the ABCFM's request) a long account that detailed their tribe's progress. After the ABCFM voted to oppose removal, Worcester gathered missionaries from all denominations working with Cherokees to discuss the threat. On December 22, all but the Methodist signed a resolution condemning removal. That same day, Georgia's legislature declared that the missionaries could stay only if they obtained a permit from the governor. This law would elevate Worcester to martyrdom.

In *Cherokee Nation v. Georgia,* in March 1831, Chief Justice John Marshall rejected the tribe's challenge of that state's laws but showed sympathy for federal sovereignty over Indian relations. The ABCFM therefore encouraged Worcester to disobey the Georgian law, which, if he were jailed, would enable him (as a Vermont citizen) to sue in federal courts. On March 12, 1831, Worcester was arrested. He was tried along with eleven others on September 16 and quickly found guilty. Only Worcester and Elizur Butler refused to leave the state or take an oath to Georgia and were sentenced to four years at hard labor. In February 1832, their case came before the Supreme Court, and, on March 3, Marshall rejected Georgia's claims of sovereignty over the Cherokees.

But over the next nine months, politics and the Nullification crisis led many who had supported Cherokee resistance to advise the missionaries to seek a pardon. On December 7, Worcester and Butler decided to halt further appeals and five weeks later were released from jail. Worcester ceased to oppose removal; in fact, he urged Boudinot to work for a good removal agreement. In April 1835, the Worcesters headed west, leading many to accuse him of desertion. Eight months later, some Cherokee leaders, including Boudinot, signed the Treaty of New Echota, agreeing to sell the tribe's land. Within a year, Boudinot and several others were killed as traitors.

By December 1836, Worcester had reestablished his printing press, school, and church at Park Hill, near Tahlequah, in Cherokee territory. By his death, the mission had become one of the largest institutions in Indian Territory.

Bibliography. Dale, Edward E. "Worcester, Samuel Austin." In *Dictionary of American Biography,* vol. 10. New York: Scribner, 1995. McLoughlin, William G. *Cherokees and Missionaries, 1789–1839.* New Haven, CT: Yale University Press, 1984.

Daniel R. Mandell

WORLD COUNCIL OF CHURCHES. The World Council of Churches (WCC) unites 340 Protestant and Orthodox churches, denominations, and fellowships in 120 countries to pursue Christian aims and advance ecumenism. Since its founding in 1948, the WCC has antagonized conservatives by refusing to proselytize, by accepting delegations from communist nations, by opposing weapons of mass destruction, and by providing funds to violent liberation movements.

The WCC emerged as a response to World War I. Protestant religious leaders, horrified by the enormous human carnage of the war and ashamed of their inability to prevent such destruction, decided to form a global organization that would hold the world together through the teachings of Jesus Christ. The Catholic and Orthodox Churches, suspicious of this new concept of ecumenism, refused to cooperate. Evangelical Christian denominations, such as the Southern Baptist Convention, also declined to participate on the grounds that their interest lay in gaining converts and not in supporting ecumenical apostasy.

The steady march of nations toward a second world war gave renewed impetus to the ecumenical movement. On May 12, 1938, eighty Christian leaders representing 130 branches assembled at Utrecht to adopt a provisional constitution for an organization dedicated to improving international relations through the cooperation of all Christian churches. A few months later in July 1939, the embryonic WCC issued a statement declaring that the force of arms would lead only to evil. The leaders of the German Christians, supportive of Adolf Hitler's plan to build an empire, attacked the WCC as an effort to stand above the nations of the world. When Europe went to war in 1939, the WCC entered a holding pattern.

With the end of war, the WCC boxed Bibles for delivery to war-torn areas; offered medical, clothing, and food aid; and rebuilt churches. Orthodox leaders in Eastern Europe were the main beneficiaries of construction aid and this assistance prompted them to participate in the official formation of the WCC at Amsterdam in August 1948. The Catholic Church sent no official observers and refused to allow any priests to attend. The 147 churches from forty-four countries that did participate at the 1948 WCC Assembly charged that the horrors through which the world had just lived testified in part to the failures of the churches to promote peace and justice. Having witnessed the failure of the League of Nations to prevent war, the church leaders did not believe that politicians alone could steer the world away from future sins. To these organizers, the WCC would play an absolutely essential role in developing a worldwide sense of community. Shortly after Amsterdam, the WCC joined the newly formed United Nations (UN) as one of the largest nongovernmental organizations within that body.

As the cold war heated up, the WCC responded both to the increased threat of world destruction and the continued menace of nationalism. At its second assembly in 1954 in Evanston, Illinois, the WCC called for the prohibition of all weapons of mass destruction and the sharp reduction of all other armaments. It asked for international inspection and control of weapons, with the inspectors presumably drawn from the UN. The council also sought assurances from nations that no country would engage in or support aggressive or subversive acts in other countries. In the climate of the 1950s, such a stance in support of internationalism drew the ire of conservatives who feared losing national sovereignty and retained a deep suspicion of UN motives Anticommunists also supported aggressive measures against communists and angrily charged the WCC with working with Moscow.

As time passed, Western influence within the organization faded as churches and theologians from Africa, Asia, and Latin American increasingly dominated the ecumenical movement. These new members led the WCC in 1969 to establish the controversial Program to Combat Racism (PCR) targeting governments or multinational corporations that provide economic support to racism. In 1978, PCR gave a grant to the Patriotic Front of Zimbabwe, which was then engaged in an armed struggle to overthrow the white minority government of Rhodesia. In protest, both the Salvation Army and the Presbyterian Church of Ireland withdrew from the WCC.

Liberation theology, another controversial teaching, has also found support within the WCC. In 1975, the WCC declared that churches should develop activities to make the oppressed, including women, aware of their oppression so that they may change society. By the 1980s, it had launched attacks upon capitalism and imperialism for laying the foundations of oppression. In 1983, the council charged that governments had begun using the notion of national security to justify repression and foreign intervention. As always, it encouraged its membership to lobby for an end to such sinful practices.

The WCC is the most visible ecumenical movement of the twentieth century. By taking a public stand on controversial political issues, it has prompted many churches to reevaluate their commitment to establishing a global community of all Christians.

Bibliography. Koshy, Ninan. *Churches in the World of Nations: International Politics and the Mission and Ministry of the Church.* Geneva: World Council of Churches, 1994. Macy, Paul Griswold. *If It Be of God: The Story of the World Council of Churches.* St. Louis, MO: Bethany Press, 1960. Marty, Martin E. *Modern American Religion: Under God Indivisible, 1941–1960.* Chicago: University of Chicago Press, 1996.

Caryn E. Neumann

Y

YAT-SEN, SUN (1866–1925). Revolutionary leader and founder of the Chinese Nationalist Party (*Guomindang*), Sun is known as the father of the nation after the 1911 revolution that toppled the Qing dynasty.

Sun's upbringing made him a product of maritime China, the southeast coast of China with a long history of overseas migrations and exposure to foreign ideas. Born into a Cantonese peasant family in Xianshan County, Guangdong Province, only forty miles north of the Portuguese colony of Macao, he grew up in Hawaii and studied at Christian mission schools there. Later, he went to Hong Kong for medical training and was baptized there in 1884 by Charles Hager, an American Congregationalist missionary.

Convinced of China's need for change after her defeat by Japan in 1895, Sun became an anti-Manchu activist. Forced into exile upon an abortive insurrection in Canton, he emerged as an international figure after the Chinese Legation briefly imprisoned him in 1896. For nearly a decade, he relied on an extensive network of Chinese Christians, secret societies, radical students, and Overseas Chinese communities for support. In 1905, Sun presided over the umbrella organization known as the Revolutionary Alliance (*Tongmenghui*) in Tokyo, forerunner of the *Guomindang*. After the collapse of the Qing dynasty in 1911, Sun was the ideal candidate for the president of the Republic of China, but he resigned in favor of Yuan Shikai as the first president.

Throughout the 1910s and 1920s, Sun fought against warlord factions in northern China in an attempt to unite the country. Without much support from the West, Sun accepted the Soviet Union's offer of help and launched a united-front alliance with the Chinese Communist Party in 1923. He also reorganized the *Guomindang* based on the Leninist model and established the Whampoa Military Academy to train officers for a party army. After he died in 1925, leadership of the *Guomindang* was passed to Chiang Kai-shek.

One of Sun's influential writings, *The Three People's Principles* (Nationalism, Democracy, and People's Livelihood), revealed a Westernized frame of mind. Apart from calling for economic modernization, he proposed a three-stage transition from military rule through party tutelage to constitutional democracy and drafted a five-power constitution with the checks and balances of Western democracies by adding censorial and examination branches. Neither of these political schemes nor *The Three People's Principles* became an ideological guide for the *Guomindang* after his death. Sun's legacy

Sun Yat-Sen. Courtesy of the Perry-Casteñeda Library

Andrew Young. Courtesy of the Library of Congress

was to personify popular struggle against foreign imperialism, warlords, and bureaucrats in early twentieth-century China.

Bibliography. Chen, Stephen, and Robert Payne. *Sun Yat-Sen: A Portrait.* Phoenix, AZ: Simon Publications, 2001. Bergère, Marie-Claire. *Sun Yat-Sen.* Stanford, CA: Stanford University Press, 1998.

Joseph Tse-Hei Lee

YOUNG, ANDREW (b. 1932). Minister, international businessman, human rights activist, and politician, Young has given his lifetime in service to the uplift of oppressed peoples. His success in the political arena has provided a continuing reminder of the problems posed during the civil rights movement.

Raised in a middle-class black family, Young frequently cites Luke 12:48 ("From everyone to whom much has been given, much will be required") as a guiding principle in his life. He attended Howard University with the goal of following his father into dentistry yet decided instead to pursue the ministry. Graduating from Hartford Theological Seminary in 1955, he became pastor of several churches throughout the rural South. For several years, he served as a staff member for the National Council of Churches in New York City. In 1961, he joined the **Southern Christian Leadership Conference** (SCLC) as a top aide to **Martin Luther King, Jr.** Following the passage of the Civil Rights Act of 1964, Young was made executive director of the SCLC, working primarily behind the scenes as a financial manager and organizing bureaucrat.

Young continued to work at the SCLC until 1970, when he decided to move out from behind the scenes and into the political spotlight. He fervently believed that pervasive minority poverty marred the American dream, and that through government intervention financial disparities could begin to be resolved. He was elected to three terms in the U.S. House of Representatives from the Fifth Congressional District of Georgia (1972–1978), during which time he advocated welfare programs and an end to the war in Vietnam. In 1977, President **Jimmy Carter** named him ambassador to the United Nations, a position he was forced to resign in 1979 after it became widely known that he had met with a representative of the Palestine Liberation Organization (PLO). Young then returned to Atlanta, where he served two terms as mayor (1981–1989). Shortly thereafter, Young returned to his international interests when President Bill Clinton appointed him chairman of the Southern Africa Enterprise Development Fund, a $100 million fund to provide equity to businesses in eleven African countries. Over the last ten years, Young has attempted to reiterate the necessity of creative market strategies to assist third-world nations. Young continues his labors on behalf of the disinherited as chairman of the Atlanta-based GoodWorks International, a consulting group that aids corporations in the growing global economy.

Bibliography. Young, Andrew. *An Easy Burden: The Civil Rights Movement and the Transformation of America.* New York: HarperCollins, 1998.

Kathryn Lofton

YOUNG, BRIGHAM (1801–1877). President and prophet of the Church of Jesus Christ of Latter-day Saints (1847–1877), Young assumed leadership of the church at a critical moment, following **Joseph Smith**'s murder in 1844. He subsequently led the Mormons in their exodus to the Utah Territory, becoming in the process a lightning rod for national political controversy as he sought to establish a New Zion in the West, as well as political legitimacy and freedom from persecution for the Saints.

Born in Vermont, Young converted to Methodism in the 1820s before being attracted to Smith's new revelations, published as the Book of Mormon in 1830. He accepted Mormon baptism in 1832 and became an avid missionary for the church. In the face of determined anti-Mormon hostility in Missouri—culminating in the infamous "extermination order" of Governor Lilburn Boggs—Young helped orchestrate the relocation of the Saints to Nauvoo, Illinois. Following Smith's assassination in 1844, Young decided to put substantial geographic distance between the faithful and the religious and political persecution that had marked their lives in the east. Confronted by the repealing of the Nauvoo City charter and the unwillingness and inability of the Illinois state government to offer sufficient aid and protection, he organized and led the evacuation of thousands of Saints, first to Iowa, and then in 1847 on to the Great Salt Lake basin, where he hoped to achieve both political power and autonomy. This exodus marked Young as a man of vision and leadership.

Young claimed the region as a divinely ordained gathering place for believers, the center of a New Zion that would become the focal point of God's planned destiny for humanity. Sheer numbers, disciplined by well-defined, hierarchical institutional structures, assured that the Mormons could exert enormous influence on the political development of the Salt Lake region and, following the Mexican-American War, the newly formed Utah Territory. As president of the Quorum of the Twelve Apostles, Young took the lead in making policy for the church. This position committed Young to seeking both the spiritual and temporal welfare of the Saints and brought him into frequent confrontation with the American political culture of his time.

Once in the valley of the Great Salt Lake, the Saints organized a provisional government, with Young as governor. An energetic and industrious colonizer, he initiated the establishment and oversaw the expansion of some 350 Mormon communities throughout the Great Basin. Congress granted territorial status in 1850 and appointed Young governor of the new Territory of Utah, initiating an eight-year period that concentrated political and ecclesiastical authority under his leadership. Soon friction arose between the governor and non-Mormon federally appointed territorial officers, who, in 1856, communicated to Washington a number of inflammatory reports against the Saints, their main criticism centering on the joining of civil and religious authority in the hands of one man. Young considered this mixing of power a positive good, not a violation of constitutional freedoms. In an 1855 discourse to church leaders, he explained that "The Priesthood assists me to honor, preserve, . . . and understand the welfare of the Government I am acting for." Logically, Young found it difficult to secure federal officers with whom he could work well. Upon hearing that he would not be reappointed territorial governor in 1857, he wrote to Utah's territorial representative in Congress, John Bernhisel, excoriating the actions of "infernal, dirty, sneaking, rotten-hearted, pot-house politicians."

On August 29, 1852, the church first announced publicly the doctrine of plural marriage. By 1856, anti-polygamy resolutions began to appear in Congress as the church's policies emerged as a national political issue and the new Republican Party spoke out against the "twin relics of barbarism—Polygamy and Slavery." President Buchanan appointed Alfred Cumming to replace Young as governor and sent along with him a large military force. Not having been notified of the change, and fearing the worst, Young declared that the Mormons were compelled to actively resist government encroachments. On September 15, 1857, he declared martial law in Utah Territory

and forbade the entry of armed forces. Adding to tensions was a clash at Mountain Meadows in Utah between Mormons, together with a group of Paiute natives, and a wagon party of 120 emigrants headed west. The latter were almost completely destroyed, and the precise details of and responsibility for the tragedy remain clouded in controversy. Young was exonerated, but John D. Lee, a Mormon settler present at Mountain Meadows, was executed two decades later. This standoff between Young and the U.S. government, the so-called Mormon War that never materialized, was finally resolved in 1858, allowing Governor Cumming to assume his office.

In 1862, the first successful anti-Mormon legislation was passed in Congress. It levied penalties against plural marriage and disincorporated the church. Nevertheless, under Young's direction, the church continued to expand. Denied statehood for a third time, the people of Utah in 1862 drafted a constitution for the state of Deseret and elected Brigham Young as governor. This "ghost governorship" continued until his death in 1877.

From 1866 on, Young had to deal with intensified judicial and political crusades against the church in the form of a series of anti-polygamy bills from Congress. On October 5, 1869, Vice President Schuyler Colfax visited Utah and spoke out against polygamy. John Taylor, one of the twelve apostles of the church, responded under Brigham's direction through a series of letters that "detailed the weaknesses and abuses of Utah's federal appointees— 'petty lords of misrule'" and reasserted the fundamental rights of the Mormon people.

Various federally appointed judges, particularly James B. McKean, proved especially fervent in their efforts to topple Young's presidency and destroy plural marriage. In 1875 in a divorce case, McKean ordered the aging president of the church to pay court fees and alimony to a former wife. He refused, pending an appeal. Nevertheless, he was found in contempt and sent to prison for a day. Five days later President Ulysses S. Grant removed McKean from office.

For non-Mormons—the "gentile" population, as the Saints called them—Young was a man bent on establishing a theocracy utterly inconsistent with American constitutional principles. Mormons, however, hailed him as a "Lion of the Lord," a leader who for thirty years defended the Mormon way of life from government abuses. Death spared him the even more severe battles of subsequent years. Mormons ultimately disavowed the practice of polygamy and accepted political arrangements that finally gave Utah statehood in 1896.

Bibliography. Allen, James B., and Glen M. Leonard. *The Story of the Latter-day Saints.* Salt Lake City, UT: Deseret Book Company, 1976. Arrington, Leonard J. *Brigham Young: American Moses.* Urbana: University of Illinois Press, 1986. Ludlow, Daniel H. *Encyclopedia of Mormonism.* 4 vols. New York: Macmillan, 1992. Melville, J. Keith. "Theory and Practice of Church and State during the Brigham Young Era." *BYU Studies* 3 (Autumn 1960): 33–55.

Roy L. Tanner

YOUNG CHRISTIAN WORKERS (JEUNESSE OUVRIÈRE CHRÉTIENNE, JOC).

The Jeunesse Ouvrière Chrétienne, or Young Christian Workers, is an international Catholic movement of young workers founded by Father Cardijn of Belgium in 1925 in an effort to bridge the gulf between the Catholic Church and an increasingly secularized working class. Begun at a moment of intense Catholic concern over socialist and communist influence among workers and extensive political attention to youth across Europe, the JOC quickly became an international movement, appearing in France in 1927 and Quebec in the early 1930s. The JOC differed from earlier social Catholic initiatives by targeting only young workers and by assigning them the central role in the effort to evangelize the working class.

Under the supervision of movement chaplains and following the "see, judge, act" method devised by Cardijn, movement militants, who are known as *Jocists,* endeavored to bring Catholic religious, social, and moral teachings to their fellow young workers. They emphasized young workers' spiritual worth and human dignity, providing social services and leisure activities, and defending youth interests at the workplace and in the public sphere. The 1930s proved the high point of JOC influence; by the end of the decade, the JOC, along with its sister organization, the JOCF, was the largest movement of working-class youth in France.

The French JOC's relationship to working-class politics was fraught with tension, and the movement's stance toward political action and, more particularly, the parties and trade unions affiliated with the Marxist left, evolved throughout the twentieth century. During the 1920s and 1930s, individual *Jocists* were expressly forbidden from participating in politics, and this was most closely enforced with regard to cooperative action with the Socialist or Communist parties and their affiliated organizations.

During the politically and ideologically charged Popular Front period of the mid-1930s, the JOC leadership attempted to carve out a distinct, nonpolitical position. Asserting that the movement was outside and above politics, JOC leaders argued that they were preparing a spiritual revolution, one that eschewed violence and class struggle. Although the JOC leadership took a cautious stance toward the massive strike movement of May–June 1936, male and female militants participated in the factory occupations, struggling to defend both the rights of young workers and the Catholic trade union confederation, the CFTC, which had only a small presence in industrial workplaces.

The political, social, economic, and religious developments of the post-1940 period altered the French movement's relationship to politics, especially more traditional forms of working-class politics. During the war, the conscription of young male workers for labor service in Germany led some JOC militants into Resistance networks, where they worked alongside youth from a range of political and trade union backgrounds. The postwar decades witnessed a gradual embrace of increased cooperation with parties and trade unions on the left, even as the JOC worked to maintain its distinctive role as a nonpolitical Catholic movement of young workers. Retaining its commitment to the defense of young workers, the JOC expanded its prewar practice of investigating the living and working conditions of France's working youth, focusing increased attention on immigrant young workers in the 1950s and 1960s. By the end of the 1960s, however, the JOC had aligned itself with parties and unions on the left. In 1976, the JOC leadership announced its rejection of capitalism and capitalist society and its support for a new kind of socialist society.

Bibliography. Pierrard, Pierre, Michel Launay, and Rolande Trempé. *La JOC: Regards d'historiens.* Paris: Les éditions ouvrières, 1984. Whitney, Susan B. "Gender, Class and Generation in Interwar French Catholicism: The Case of the Jeunesse Ouvrière Chrétienne Féminine." *Journal of Family History* 26 (October 2001): 480–507.

Susan B. Whitney

Z

ZACCAGNINI, BEGNINO (1912–1989). A pediatrician by training, Zaccagnini engaged in partisan action in Italy as a Catholic representative with the clandestine Committee of National Liberation during World War II. He succeeded in involving many local priests who offered their churches and rectories for his underground activities. His leadership in **Italian Catholic Action** and **Christian Democracy** (Democrazia Cristiana, DC) helped sustain Christian influence in postwar Italy as multiple parties competed for power and ideological influence.

Born in Faenza in the Italian province of Ravenna into a middle-class family, he spent his childhood in Veneto because of his father's work with the Italian State Railroads. Eventually returning to Emilia-Romagna and enrolling at the University of Bologna, he received his degree in pediatric medicine in 1936.

As a medical officer, he was sent with Italian troops during World War II to Yugoslavia and was captured and imprisoned by the Germans after the fall of Benito Mussolini's Fascist regime. Escaping from the train that was taking him to Germany, he returned to Ravenna in October 1943 and joined the Committee of National Liberation. The partisan Zaccagnini, who assumed the name Tommaso Moro (in honor of the great English saint and philosopher Thomas More), participated in the Garibaldi Brigade, which was led by the communists and was an important common experience that defended shared values.

During the first postwar elections, Zaccagnini, encouraged by the bishop of Ravenna, was elected to the ranks of the Christian Democracy after having been active in Italian Catholic Action. The party represented for him the ideal continuation of the collaboration among differing political forces in which he had taken part during the Resistance. After entering the government, he eventually became undersecretary in the Department of Labor and Social Welfare during **Amintore Fanfani**'s second ministry (July 1958–February 1959). As minister of labor, he was sensible to Catholic reform and egalitarianism and tried to change the popular consensus to consolidate democracy through a law on collective bargaining and another on the welfare of workers.

During Fanfani's third term from February 1959 to March 1960, Zaccagnini was nominated minister of public works and, under his direction, the development of a construction grant for the state through the creation of regulatory plans by the various communes against speculation and the construction of lower-cost housing was favored.

Zaccagnini, served as president of the DC parliamentary faction from 1962 until 1968, a particularly intense time during which Prime Minister **Aldo Moro** engineered the so-called opening to the Left, which brought the Socialists into the governing coalition. In 1968, Zaccagnini became the vice president of the Italian Chamber of Deputies, demonstrating a great capacity for mediation. He kept this position until 1975, when, following the defeat of the DC after the divorce referendum, Fanfani handed party leadership to Zaccagnini on a provisionary basis. At the DC congress in March 1976, a majority confirmed Zaccagnini over his challenger, Arnaldo Forlani.

The years of Zaccagnini's leadership signaled the renewal of the Christian Democracy's image through the policy of teamwork with all political parties, including the Communists. The DC, however, could not accept the Communist proposal of a "historic compromise" and maintained a policy of national solidarity to guide the country through the period of economic crisis and increasing terrorism. Moro authored this policy and remained an important DC leader before his kidnapping by the Red Brigades on March 16, 1978. Moro's imprisonment marked the most difficult period for the DC and especially for Zaccagnini, who was his close friend. The party held firm and refused to negotiate with Moro's kidnappers, who killed him on May 19.

Moro's death signaled the end of the party's national solidarity policy. Zaccagnini continued his battle to reinvigorate his party based on Moro's beliefs, but the party's National Council, pushed by a union of centrists and trade unionists, replaced him in 1980 with Flaminio Piccoli as party chair. In 1983, following a long period in the Chamber, Zaccagnini was elected senator and was reelected in 1987, continuing his focus on contemporary society, and sensitive to the initiatives of solidarity and to the church's magisterium.

In October 1989, while speaking to the young people of Ravenna, Zaccagnini affirmed his belief that democracy would win over Communism. Unfortunately, he did not live to see the fall of the Berlin Wall in 1989.

Bibliography. De Mita, C. *Tre generazioni per un grande partito di popolo.* Rome: EBE, 1989. Belci, C. *Zaccagnini.* Brescia, Italy: Morcelliana, 1990. Zaccagnini, B. *La politica del confronto: Relazioni al Consiglio Nazionale D.C. 1975–1978.* Rome: DC-SPES, 1979.

Eliana Versace

ZENTRUM (GERMANY). *See* Center Party

Selected Bibliography

General and Global

Berger, Peter L., et al. *The Desecularization of the World: Resurgent Religion and World Politics.* Grand Rapids, MI: William B. Eerdmans, 1999.

Bruce, Steve. *Religion and Modernization: Sociologists and Historians Debate the Secularization Thesis.* Oxford: Clarendon Press, 1992.

Corrin, Jay P. *Catholic Intellectuals and the Challenge of Democracy.* Notre Dame, IN: University of Notre Dame, 2002.

Djupe, Paul A., and Laura R. Olson. *Encyclopedia of American Religion and Politics.* New York: Facts on File, 2003.

Encyclopedia of Politics and Religion. New York: Routledge, 1998.

Hanson, Eric O. *The Catholic Church in World Politics.* Princeton, NJ: Princeton University Press, 1987.

Haynes, Jeff. *Religion in Third World Politics.* Boulder, CO: Lynne Rienner, 1994.

Ivereigh, Austen, ed. *The Politics of Religion in an Age of Revival.* London: Institute of Latin American Studies, 2000.

Misner, P. *Social Catholicism in Europe: From the Onset of Industrialization to the First World War.* New York: Crossroad Books, 1991.

Norris, Pippa, Ronald Inglehart, David C. Leege, and Kenneth D. Wald, eds. *Secular: Religion and Politics Worldwide.* Cambridge: Cambridge University Press, 2004.

Rémond, Rene. *Religion and Society in Modern Europe.* Oxford: Blackwell, 1999.

Rhodes, Anthony. *The Power of Rome in the Twentieth Century: The Vatican in the Age of Liberal Democracies, 1877–1922.* New York: F. Watts, 1983.

Rhodes, Anthony. *The Vatican in the Age of the Dictators, 1922–1925.* New York: Holt, Rinehart and Winston, 1973.

Stehle, Hansjakob. *Eastern Politics of the Vatican, 1917–1979.* Athens: Ohio University Press, 1981.

Wallace, Lilian Parker, *Leo XIII and the Rise of Socialism.* Durham, NC: Duke University Press, 1966.

Warner, Carolyn M. *Confessions of an Interest Group, The Catholic Church and Political Parties in Europe.* Princeton, NJ: Princeton University Press, 2000.

West, John G., Iain Maclean, and Jeffrey D. Schultz, eds. *Encyclopedia of Religion in American Politics.* Westport, CT: Oryx Press, 1998.

Whyte, J. M. *Catholics in Western Democracies: A Study in Political Behavior.* Dublin: Gill & Macmillan, 1981.

Wolff, Richard J., and Jörg K. Hoensch. *Catholics, the State, and the European Radical Right.* Boulder, CO: Atlantic Research and Publications, 1987.

Wuthnow, Robert, ed. *Encyclopedia of Politics and Religion.* Washington, DC: Congressional Quarterly, 1998.

United States and Canada

Bellah, Robert N., et al. *The Good Society.* New York: Knopf, 1991.

Bellah, Robert N., et al. *Habits of the Heart.* Berkeley and Los Angeles: University of California Press, 1985

Carter, Stephen L. *The Culture of Disbelief.* New York: Basic Books, 1993.

Carwardine, Richard. *Evangelicals and Politics in Antebellum America.* New Haven, CT: Yale University Press, 1993.

Corbett, Michael. *Politics and Religion in the United States.* New York: Garland, 1998.

Craig, Robert H. *Religion and Radical Politics: An Alternative Christian Tradition in the United States.* Philadelphia: Temple University Press, 1995.

Dreisbach, Daniel L. *Thomas Jefferson and the Wall of Separation between Church and State.* New York: New York University Press, 2002.

Ellwood, Robert S. *The Fifties Spiritual Marketplace: American Religion in a Decade of Conflict,* New Brunswick, NJ: Rutgers University Press, 1997.

Green, John, Mark Rozell, and William Clyde Wilcox, eds. *The Christian Right in American Politics: Marching Toward the Millennium.* Washington, DC: Georgetown University Press, 2003.

Gutterman, David S. *Prophetic Politics: Christian Social Movements and American Democracy.* Ithaca, NY: Cornell University Press, 2005.

Hanley, Mark Y. *Beyond a Christian Commonwealth: The Protestant Quarrel with the American Republic: 1830–1860.* Chapel Hill: University of North Carolina Press, 1994

Heclo, Hugh, and Wilfred McClay. *Refurnishing the Public Square: Religion and Public Policy in Twentieth-Century America.* Washington, DC: Woodrow Wilson Center/Johns Hopkins University Press, 2003.

Lambert, Frank. *The Founding Fathers and the Place of Religion in America.* Princeton, NJ: Princeton University Press, 2003.

Lasch, Christopher. *The Revolt of the Elites and the Betrayal of Democracy.* New York: W. W. Norton, 1995.

Lyon, David and Marguerite Van Die, eds., *Rethinking Church, State, and Modernity: Canada between Europe and America.* Toronto: University of Toronto Press, 2000.

Marsden, George M. *The Soul of the American University.* New York: Oxford University Press, 1994.

Martin, William. *With God on Our Side: The Rise of the Religious Right in America.* New York: Broadway Books, 1996.

Marty, Martin E. *Politics, Religion, and the Common Good.* San Francisco: Jossey-Bass, 2000.

Marty, Martin E. *Religion and Republic.* Boston: Beacon Press, 1987.

Menendez, Albert J. *Church and State in Canada.* Amherst, NY: Prometheus Books, 1996.

Noll, Mark A. *America's God: From Jonathan Edwards to Abraham Lincoln.* New York: Oxford University Press, 2002.

Noll, Mark A. *Religion and American Politics: From the Colonial Period to the 1980s.* New York: Oxford University Press, 1989 and

Phillips, Kevin P. *The Cousins' Wars: Religion, Politics, and the Triumph of Anglo-America.* New York: Basic Books, 1999.

Sassi, Jonathan D. *A Republic of Righteousness: The Public Christianity of the Post-revolutionary New England Clergy.* New York: Oxford University Press, 2001.

Van Die, Marguerite, ed. *Religion and Public Life in Canada: Historical and Comparative Perspectives.* Toronto: University of Toronto Press, 2001.

Wald, Kenneth D. *Religion and Politics in the United States.* 4th ed. New York: Rowman & Littlefield, 2003.

West, John G., Jr. *The Politics of Revelation and Reason: Civic Life in the New Nation.* Lawrence: University Press of Kansas, 1996.

Woods, Thomas E. *The Church Confronts Modernity,* New York: Columbia University Press, 2004.

Latin America

Ai Camp, Roderic. *Crossing Swords: Politics and Religion in Mexico.* New York: Oxford University Press, 1997.

Cleary, Edward L., and Timothy J. Steigena, eds. *Resurgent Voices in Latin America: Indigenous Peoples, Political Mobilization, and Religious Change.* New Brunswick, NJ: Rutgers University Press, 2004.

Freston, Paul. *Evangelicals and Politics in Asia, Africa and Latin America.* Cambridge: Cambridge University Press, 2001.

Gill, Anthony. *Rendering unto Caesar: The Catholic Church and the State in Latin America.* Chicago: University of Chicago Press, 1998.

Levine, Daniel H. *Religion and Politics in Latin America: The Catholic Church in Venezuela and Colombia.* Princeton, NJ: Princeton University Press, 1981.

Lynch, Edward. *Latin America's Christian Democratic Parties: A Political Economy.* Westport, CT: Praeger, 1993.

Lynch, Edward. *Religion and Politics in Latin America.* Westport, CT: Praeger, 1991.

Mainwaring, Scott, and Scully Timothy R., eds. *Christian Democracy in Latin America: Electoral Competition and Regime Conflicts.* Stanford, CA: Stanford University Press, 2003.

Penyak, Lee M., and Walter J. Petry, eds. *Religion in Latin America: A Documentary History.* Maryknoll, NY: Orbis, 2006.

Smith, Bryan H. *Religious Politics in Latin America, Pentecostal vs. Catholic.* Notre Dame, IN: University of Notre Dame Press, 1998.

Eastern Hemisphere

Alexander, Stella. *Church and State in Yugoslavia since 1945.* Cambridge: Cambridge University Press, 1979.

Blinkhorn, Martin. *Carlism and Crisis in Spain, 1931–1939.* Cambridge: Cambridge University Press, 1975.

Boyer, J. W. *Political Radicalism in Late Imperial Vienna: Origins of the Christian Social Movement, 1848–1897.* Chicago: University of Chicago Press, 1981.

Brassloff, Audrey. *Religion and Politics in Spain: The Spanish Church in Transition, 1962–1996.* London: Macmillan, 1998.

Brown, Richard. *Church and State in Modern Britain 1700–1850.* New York: Routledge, 1991.

Buchanan, Tom, and Martin Conway. *Political Catholicism in Europe, 1918–1965.* Oxford: Clarendon Press, 1996.

Callahan, William, *The Catholic Church in Spain, 1875–1998.* Washington, DC: Catholic University of America, 2000.

Cary, Noel. *The Path to Christian Democracy, German Catholics and the Party System from Windthorst to Adenauer.* Cambridge, MA: Harvard University Press, 1996.

Clark, Christopher, and Wolfram Kaiser, eds. *Culture Wars: Secular-Catholic Conflict in Nineteenth Century Europe.* Cambridge: Cambridge University Press, 2003.

Dansette, Adrien. *Religious History of Modern France.* Freiburg, Germany: Herder, 1961.

Einaudi, Mario, and François Goguel. *Christian Democracy in Italy and France.* Notre Dame, IN: University of Notre Dame Press, 1952.

Evans, Ellen L. *The Cross and the Ballot: Catholic Political Parties in Germany, Switzerland, Austria, Belgium, and the Netherlands, 1785–1985.* Boston: Humanities Press, 1999.

Evans, Ellen L. *The German Center Party 1870–1933: A Study in Political Catholicism.* Carbondale: Southern Illinois University Press, 1981.

Fogarty, Michael. *Christian Democracy in Western Europe 1820–1953.* London: Routledge & Paul, 1957.

Hanley, David, ed. *Christian Democracy in Europe: A Comparative Perspective.* London: Pinter, 1996.

Hempton, David. *Religion and Political Culture in Britain and Ireland: From the Glorious Revolution to the Decline of Empire.* New York: Cambridge University Press, 1996.

Kaiser, Wolfram, and Helmut Wohnout, eds. *Political Catholicism in Europe, 1918–1945.* New York: Routledge, 2004.

Kalyvas, Stathis N. *The Rise of Christian Democracy in Europe.* Ithaca, NY: Cornell University Press, 1996.

Kselman, Thomas, and Joseph A. Buttigieg, eds. *European Christian Democracy: Historical Legacies and Comparative Perspectives.* Notre Dame, IN: University of Notre Dame Press, 2003.

Jemolo, Arturo Carlo. *Church and State in Italy, 1850–1950.* Oxford: Blackwell, 1960.

Lannon, Frances. *Privilege, Persecution and Prophecy: The Catholic Religion in Spain, 1875–1975.* Oxford: Oxford University Press, 1975.

Leonardi, Robert, and Douglas Wertman. *Italian Christian Democracy: The Politics of Dominance.* London: Macmillan, 1989.

Levy, Guenter. *The Catholic Church and Nazi Germany.* New York: McGraw-Hill, 1964.

Molony, John. *The Emergence of Political Catholicism in Italy: Partito Popolare 1919–1926.* Totowa, NJ: Rowman & Littlefield, 1977.

Murray, Patrick. *Oracles of God: The Roman Catholic Church and Irish Politics, 1922–37.* Dublin: University College Dublin Press, 2000.

Nicholls, David. *Church and State in Britain since 1820.* New York: Humanities Press, 1967.

Pridham, G. *Christian Democracy in Western Germany: The CDU/CSU in Government and Opposition, 1945–1976.* London: Croom Helm, 1977.

Ramet, Pedro, ed. *Eastern Christianity and Politics in the Twentieth Century.* Durham, NC: Duke University Press, 1988.

Ramet, Sabrina, and Donald W. Treadgold, eds. *Render unto Caesar: The Religious Sphere in World Politics.* Washington, DC: American University Press, 1995.

Ravitch, Norman. *The Catholic Church and the French Nation, 1589–1989.* London: Routledge, 1990.

Spotts, Frederic. *The Churches and Politics in Germany.* Middletown, CT: Wesleyan University Press, 1973.

Stehlin, Stuart. *Weimar and the Vatican, 1919–1933.* Princeton, NJ: Princeton University Press, 1983.

Webster, Richard. *The Cross and the Fasces, Christian Democracy and Fascism in Italy.* Stanford, CA: Stanford University Press, 1960.

Index

About the Editors and the Contributors

EDITORS

ROY P. DOMENICO is professor of history at the University of Scranton in Pennsylvania. His book *Italian Fascists on Trial, 1943–1948* was the recipient of the 1992 Marraro Prize in Italian History.

    Christian Democracy (Democrazia Cristiana)
    European Peoples' Party
    Italian Catholic Action (Azione Cattolica Italiana)
    Giorgio La Pira
    Mario Scelba

MARK Y. HANLEY is professor of history at Truman State University in Missouri. He is the author of *Beyond a Christian Commonwealth: The Protestant Quarrel with the American Republic, 1830–1860* (1994).

    Robert Neely Bellah
    John Brown
    Orestes Augustus Brownson
    Catharine Esther Beecher
    George Walker Bush
    Horace Bushnell
    Charles Grandison Finney
    Abraham Lincoln

CONTRIBUTORS

MARIO I. AGUILAR is director of the Centre for the Study of Religion and Politics at St. Mary's College, University of St. Andrews in Scotland. He is the author of a four-volume work, *A Social History of the Catholic Church in Chile* (2005).

    Christian Left Party (Izquierda Cristiana)
    Christians for Socialism (Cristianos por el Socialismo)
    Michael Woodward

ANTHONY D. ANDREASSI is a member of the department of history at Regis High School in New York City. His research focuses on American Catholic history.

    Joseph Bernadin
    John England

TIMOTHY BAYCROFT is senior lecturer in French history at the University of Sheffield in the United Kingdom. He is the author of *Culture, Identity and Nationalism: French Flanders in the Nineteenth and Twentieth Centuries* (2004) and *Nationalism in Europe 1789–1945* (1998).

Christian Social Party (Parti Social Chrétien)
Adolphe Daens
Jules Auguste Lemire
Achille Liénart

GERHARD BESIER is director of the Hannah Arendt Institute for Research on Totalitarianism in Dresden, Germany. He is the author of *Religion, Nation, Kultur: Die Geschichte der christlichen Kirchen in den gesellschaftlichen Umbrüchen des 19. Jahrhunderts* (1992) and *Der Heilige Stuhl und Hitler-Deutschland: Die Faszination des Totalitaeren* (2004).

Marc Boegner
Leopold and Ernst Ludwig von Gerlach
Wilfred Monod
Friedrich Daniel Ernst Schleiermacher
Adolf Stoecker

ILARIA BIAGIOLI is attachée de recherché at École Pratique des Hautes Études in Paris. She is the author of *La patria in pericolo: L'uso politico del nemico interno in Francia fra Otto e Novecento* in *Storia e problemi contemporanei* (2004) and coeditor (with A. Botti and R. Cerrato) of *Romolo Murri e i murrismi in Italia e in Europa cent'anni dopo* (2004).

Madeleine Delbrêl
Stanislas Fumet
Francisque Gay
Henri Perrin
Maurice Vaussard

THOMAS BOKENKOTTER is a freelance writer, Catholic historian, and priest in the Archdiocese of Cincinnati. He is the author of *A Concise History of the Catholic Church* (1990) and *Church and Revolution: Catholics in the Struggle of Democracy and Social Justice* (1998).

Albert De Mun
Félix Antoine Philibert Dupanloup
John XXIII
Jean Baptiste Henri Lacordaire
Félicité Robert de Lamennaise
Charles Humbert René La Tour du Pin
Charles René Forbes Montalembert
Emmanuele Mounier

FRANK BÖSCH is junior professor of history at Historisches Institut, Ruhr–Universität Bochum in Germany. He is the author of *Die Adenauer-CDU: Gründung, Aufstieg und Krise einer Erfolgspartei, 1945–1969* (2001).

Christian Democratic Union (Christlich-Demokratische Union)
Ludwig Erhard

ALFONSO BOTTI teaches European and contemporary history at the University of Urbino. He is the author of *La questione basca: Dalle origini allo scioglimento di Batasuna* (2003).

Basque Nationalist Party (Partido Nacionalista Vasco)
José Bergamin y Gutiérrez
Alfonso Comín
Juan Donoso Cortés
Cándido Nocedal
Ramón Nocedal
Popular Party (Partido Popular)
Miguel Primo de Rivera y Orbaneja

KRISTINA A. BOYLAN is assistant professor of history at SUNY–Institute of Technology in Utica. She is the author of "Gendering the Faith and Altering the Nation: The Unión Femenina Católica Mexicana and Women's Revolutionary and Religious Experiences (1917–1940)" in *Engendering Revolution* (forthcoming).

Catholic Action (Acción Católica Mexicana)
Mexican Social Secretariat (Secretariado Social Mexicano)
National Catholic Labor Confederation (Confederación Nacional Católica de Trabajo)
National Catholic Party (Partido Católico Nacional)

THOMAS M. BREDOHL is associate professor of history at the University of Regina (Canada). He is the author of *Class and Religious Identity: The Rhenish Center Party in Wilhelmine Germany* (2000).

Otto Dibelius
People's Union for a Catholic Germany
Georg von Schönerer

LYNN BRIDGERS is assistant professor of pastoral ministries and religious education and coordinator of graduate programs at St. Thomas University in Florida. She is the author of *Contemporary Varieties of Religious Experience: James's Classic Study in Light of Resiliency, Temperament and Trauma* (2005) and *The American Religious Experience: A Concise History* (2006).

Helmut Richard Niebuhr
Oscar Romero

GÜNTER BUCHSTAB is head of the Department of Reference and Research Services at the Archive of Christian Democratic Policy at the Konrad Adenauer Foundation in Sankt Augustin, Germany. He is coeditor of the journal *Historisch-Politische Mitteilungen.*

Konrad Adenauer

WILLIAM J. CALLAHAN is professor of history (emeritus) at the University of Toronto. He is the author of *The Catholic Church in Spain, 1875–1998* (2000).

Isidro Gomá y Tomás
The Historics
National Catholic Association of Propagandists
Pedro Segura y Sáenz

ZACHARY R. CALO is a doctoral candidate in history at the University of Pennsylvania and a doctoral student in religious studies at the University of Virginia. He is the author of "The Indispensable Basis of Democracy: American Catholicism, the Church-State Debate, and the Soul of American Liberalism, 1920–1929" in *Virginia Law Review* (2005).

Catholic Worker Movement
National Catholic War/Welfare Conference
John Augustine Ryan

JEAN-YVES CAMUS is a political scientist at the Centre Européen de Recherche sur le Racisme et l'Antisémitisme (CERA) in Paris. He is the author of *Les Extremisms en Europe* (1998).

Bernard Antony
Jean-Louis Arfel
Marcel Lefebvre

EDWARD J. CAPESTANY is professor of philosophy (emeritus) at the University of Scranton in Pennsylvania. He is the author of *Filosofia politica* (1976).

Jaime Luciano Balmes
Marcelino Menendez y Pelayo

DOUGLAS W. CARLSON is associate dean of multicultural and off-campus programs and professor of history at Northwestern College in Iowa. He is the author of "'Drinks He to His Own Undoing,' Temperance Ideology in the Deep South," in the *Journal of the Early Republic* (1998).

American Temperance Societies

PETER E. CARR is a retired archaeologist and independent scholar who resides in Palm Coast, Florida. His research interests include Cuban history, and he is the author of *Cuban Census Records of the 16th, 17th, and 18th Centuries* (2004).

Juan José Diaz de Espada y Fernandez de Landa

RICHARD J. CARWARDINE is Rhodes Professor of American History at St. Catherine's College, University of Oxford. He is the author of *Evangelicals and Politics in Antebellum America* (1993) and *Lincoln: A Life of Purpose and Power* (2006).

Abolitionists
Henry Ward Beecher
Charles Hodge

ANTONIO CAZORLA SANCHEZ is assistant professor of history at Champlain College, Trent University (in Ontario, Canada. His is the author of *Las Politicas de la Victoria: La consolidacion del Nuevo Estado Franquista, 1938–1953* (2000).

Francisco Franco
Ángel Hererra Oria
Claudio Lopez Bru

KAY CHADWICK is senior lecturer in French at the University of Liverpool (United Kingdom). She is the author of *Alphonse de Châteaubriant: Catholic Collaborator* (2002).

Alphonse de Châteaubriant
Philippe Henriot

The late DAVID B. CHESEBROUGH was professor of history at Illinois State University in Bloomington-Normal. He is the author of *Frederick Douglass: Oratory from Slavery* (1998), *Theodore Parker: Orator of Superior Ideas* (1999), and *Phillips Brooks: Pulpit Eloquence* (2001).

Phillips Brooks
William Lloyd Garrison
Elijah Parish Lovejoy
Theodore Parker
James Henley Thornwell

YVES CHIRON is a professor of history at the École Sainte-Michel in Niherne, France. He is the author of *Pierre Pascal: A Biography* (2004).

Pierre Pascal

DAVID H. CLOSE is senior lecturer in history (retired with academic status) at Flinders University of South Australia in Adelaide. He is the author of *Greece since 1945: Politics, Economy and Society* (2002).

Constantine Karamanlis
New Democracy (Nea Demokratia)

KELTON COBB is professor of theology and ethics at Hartford Seminary in Connecticut. He is the author of *The Blackwell Guide to Theology and Popular Culture* (2005).

Paul Tillich
Ernst Troeltsch

CHRISTIAN T. COLLINS WINN is assistant professor of biblical and theological studies at Bethel University (Minnesota). His research focuses on the theology and ethics of Karl Barth, religious socialism, and the history and theology of Pietism.

Karl Barth
Christoph Friedrich Blumhardt
Leonhard Ragaz

FRANK J. COPPA is professor of history at St. John's University in Queens, New York. He is the author of *The Modern Papacy Since 1789* (1998) and *The Papacy Confronts the Modern World* (2003).

Giacomo Antonelli
Pius IX

RICHARD FRANCIS CRANE is professor of history at Greensboro College in North Carolina. He is the author of "La Croix and the Swastika: The Ambiguities of Catholic Responses to the Fall of France" in *Catholic Historical Review* (2004) and *A French Conscience in Prague: Louis Eugene Faucher and the Abandonment of Czechoslovakia* (1996).

Georges Bernanos
Paul Claudel
Jacques Maritain

NICHOLAS M. CREARY is assistant professor of history at Marquette University in Milwaukee, Wisconsin. His research focuses on African history and religion in Africa, especially Christianity, the Catholic Church, and adaptations thereof to African cultures.

John Chilembwe
Denis Eugene Hurley
Pius Ncube

JORGE DAGNINO is a doctoral candidate in history at the University of Oxford. His research focuses on modern Italian history.

Sergio Paronetto
Paul VI
Ezio Vanoni

MARK TAYLOR DALHOUSE is director of the Office of Active Citizenship and Service at Vanderbilt University in Nashville, Tennessee. He is the author of *An Island in the Lake of Fire: Bob Jones University and Separatist Fundamentalism* (1996).

Jerry Falwell
Robert "Bob" Jones
Moral Majority

WENDY J. DEICHMANN EDWARDS is Vice President for Academic Affairs and Associate Professor of History and Theology at United Theological Seminary in Ohio.

Josiah Strong

MICHAEL DENNIS is associate professor of history at Acadia University in Nova Scotia, Canada. He is the author of *Luther P. Jackson and a Life for Civil Rights: Lessons in Progress: State Universities and Progressivism in the New South* (2004).

William F. Buckley
Francis J. Haas
Ronald Reagan
Woodrow Wilson

ROBERT THOMAS DIXON is adjunct professor of history, especially the history of Catholic education, at St. Augustine's Seminary, University of Toronto. He is the author of *Catholic Education and Politics in Ontario, 1965–2001* (2003).

Sir Richard William Scott

JÉRÔME DORVIDAL is lecturer in history at the Université de la Réunion in France. His research interests include the Eastern Pacific region, Australia, the cold war, and pacifism.

Alfred Walter Averill
Ormond Edward Burton
Frank John Hartley
Daniel Mannix
Farnham Edward Maynard
Bartholomew Augustine Santamaria

RICHARD DRAKE is professor of history at the University of Montana, Missoula. He is the author of *The Aldo Moro Murder Case* (1995) and *Apostles and Agitators: Italy's Marxist Revolutionary Tradition* (2003).

Don Lorenzo Milani
Aldo Moro

VESNA DRAPAC is a senior lecturer in history and politics at the University of Adelaide, Australia. She is the author of *War and Religion: Catholics in the Churches of Occupied Paris* (1998).

Henri Marie Alfred Baudrillart
Philippe Pétain
Jules-Géraud Saliège

LISA EDWARDS is an assistant professor of history at the University of Massachusetts at Lowell. Her research focuses on the nineteenth- and twentieth-century Catholic Church in Latin America.

Christian Democratic Party (Partido Demócrata Cristiano)
Eduardo Frei Montalva
National Action Party

PETER FARRUGIA is assistant professor of contemporary studies at Wilfrid Laurier University in Ontario. He is the editor *The River of History: Trans-National and Trans-Disciplinary Perspectives on the Immanence of the Past* (2005).

Democratic Popular Party (Parti Democrate Populaire)
Marc Sangnier

TERENCE J. FAY is a Jesuit priest and a faculty member in church history at the Toronto School of Theology for St. Augustine's Seminary, University of Toronto. He is the author of *A History of Canadian Catholics: Gallicanism, Romanism, and Canadianism* (2002).

Thomas Louis Connolly
Thomas D'Arcy McGee

JAMES RAMON FELAK is associate professor of history at the University of Washington in Seattle. He is the author of *At the Price of the Republic: Hlinka's Slovak People's Party, 1929–1938* (1994).

Andrej Hlinka
John Paul II

JAMES T. FISHER is professor of theology and codirector of the Curran Center for American Catholic Studies at Fordham University in New York. He is the author of *Communion of Immigrants: A History of Catholics in America* (2002).

Daniel and Philip Berrigan
Dorothy Day
Ngo Dinh Diem

MICHAEL S. FITZGERALD is associate professor of history at Franciscan University of Steubenville in Ohio. He is the author of "'Nature Unsubdued': Diplomacy, Expansion and the American Military Buildup of 1815–1816" in *Mid-America: An Historical Review* (1995).

William Jennings Bryan
Alfred Emanuel Smith, Jr.

GAINES M. FOSTER is T. Harry Williams Professor of History at Louisiana State University, Baton Rouge. He is the author of *Moral Reconstruction: Christian Lobbyists and the Federal Legislation of Morality, 1865–1920* (2002).

Charles Monroe Sheldon

MARY T. FURGOL is director of the Montgomery Scholars and chair of the history and political science department at Montgomery College in Rockville, Maryland. Her research focuses on early nineteenth-century poor relief in Scotland and the United States.

Thomas Chalmers
Hannah More

TOM GALLAGHER is chair of ethnic peace and conflict at the University of Bradford in Great Britain. He is the author of *The Balkans in the New Millennium: In the Shadow of Peace and War* (2005).

Manuel Gonçalves Cerejeira
Iuliu Hossu
Iron Guard
Justinian Marina
António de Oliveira Salazar

CAROLYN DESWARTE GIFFORD is a research associate in gender studies at Northwestern University in Evanston, Illinois. She is the editor of *"Writing Out My Heart": Selections from the Journal of Frances E. Willard, 1855–1896* (1995).

Frances Elizabeth Caroline Willard
Woman's Christian Temperance Union

JILL K. GILL is associate professor of history at Boise State University in Idaho. Her research focuses on twentieth-century American religious history with emphasis on Christian liberalism (or the "religious left") and sociopolitical issues post-1945.

Martin Luther King, Jr.
National and Federal Council of Churches

WILLIAM L. GLANKLER is a processing archivist for the Missouri State Archives in St. Louis and a doctoral candidate in history at St. Louis University. His research explores the use of historical narrative by African Americans as an important component of their social protest thought during the late nineteenth and early twentieth centuries.

Marcus Mosiah Garvey
Jesse Louis Jackson
Southern Christian Leadership Conference

LEN GOUGEON is professor of American literature and distinguished university fellow at the University of Scranton in Pennsylvania. He is the author of *Virtue's Hero: Emerson, Antislavery, and Reform* (1990) and *Emerson and Eros: The Making of a Cultural Hero* (2006).

Ralph Waldo Emerson

EMILY GREBLE BALIC is a doctoral candidate in history at Stanford University in California. Her research focuses on Eastern European history.

Petar II Petrović-Njegoš
Ante Pavelić

GERALD MICHAEL GREENFIELD is associate provost and professor of history at the University of Wisconsin–Parkside. He is the author of *The Realities of Images: Imperial Brazil and the Great Drought* (2001).

Cícero Romão Batista
Antônio Conselheiro

JOYCE M. HANKS is professor of French at the University of Scranton in Pennsylvania. She is the author of *Jacques Ellul: An Annotated Bibliography of Primary Works* (2000).

Jacques Ellul
Charles Péguy

SUSAN E. HANSSEN is assistant professor of history at the University of Dallas. She is the author of "Chesterton's Reputation as a Roman Catholic Convert in the Twentieth Century" in *Chesterton Review* (2005).

Robert Browning
Cecil Chesterton
Christopher Dawson
Henry Edward Manning
Charles Frederick Gurney Masterman

JENNIFER HEDDA is associate professor of history at Simpson College in Indianola, Iowa. Her research focuses on social-religious thought and political action in the Russian Orthodox Church during the nineteenth and twentieth centuries.

Georgii Apollonovich Gapon

Grigorii Spiridonovich Petrov
Renovationist Union

PETER G. HELTZEL is assistant professor of theology at New York Theological Seminary. With Bruce Ellis Benson, he is the coeditor of *Evangelicals and Empire* (forthcoming).

Jürgen Moltmann
Jim Wallis

OLIVER BENJAMIN HEMMERLE is a professor in the Faculty of Social Sciences at the University of Mannheim in Germany. He studies radical movements in France and the United States and is the author of *Der arme Teufel: eine Transatlantische zeitschrift zwischen Arbeiterbewegung und bildungsbürgerlich em Kulturtransfer um 1900* (2002).

Philippe Joseph Benjamin Buchez
Empress Eugénie
Frédéric-Antoine Ozanam

MICHAEL W. HIGGINS is professor of English and religious studies and president and vice chancellor of St. Jerome's University. He is the coauthor of *Power and Peril: the Catholic Church at the Crossroads* (2002).

Jean Marchand
Pierre Elliott Trudeau

PONTUS HIORT is an instructor and doctoral candidate at Northern Illinois University in DeKalb. His research focuses on nineteenth-century German history with an emphasis on construction of religious, social, cultural, and political identities.

Karl Bachem
Matthias Erzberger
Hermann von Mallinckrodt

SUSAN J. HUBERT has taught English, women's studies, and history at Western Michigan University and is a consultant on the staff of the Frederick Douglass Papers Project (Indiana University-Purdue University at Indianapolis). She is the author of *Questions of Power: The Politics of Women's Madness Narratives* (2002).

Richard Allen
Timothy Dwight
Dorothee Sölle
Sojourner Truth

ROBERT F. HUESTON is associate professor of history at the University of Scranton in Pennsylvania. He is the author of *The Catholic Press and Nativism, 1840–1860* (1976).

Terence V. Powderly

GEORGE EMILE IRANI is senior project manager for Africa and the Middle East at the Toledo International Center for Peace in Madrid. He is the author of *The*

Papacy and the Middle East: The Role of the Holy See in the Arab-Israeli Conflict (1989).

Mar Rouphael Bidawid
Paul Meouchi
Michel Sabbah
Shenouda III (Nazeer Gayed)

WILLIAM ISSEL is professor of history at San Francisco State University. He is the author of *Social Change in the United States* (1987).

Joseph Lawrence Alioto
Hugh Aloysius Donohoe

FRANK JEHLE is university chaplain (emeritus) at the University of St. Gallen in Switzerland. He is the author of *Ever Against the Stream: The Politics of Karl Barth, 1906–1968* (2002) and *Emil Brunner, 1889–1966* (2006).

Emil Brunner

JACK V. KALPAKIAN is assistant professor of international studies at Al Akhawayn University in Ifrane, Morocco. He is the author of *Identity, Conflict and Cooperation in International River Basins* (2004).

Bachir Gemayel
Pierre Gemayel
Mkrtich Khrimian
Union of Self-Determination

PETER C. KENT is professor of history (emeritus) at the University of New Brunswick in Canada. He is the author of *The Lonely Cold War of Pope Pius XII* (2002).

Pius IX
Pius XII
Alfredo Ildefonso Schuster
Luigi Sturzo

JOSEPH M. KNIPPENBERG is professor of politics and associate provost for student achievement at Oglethorpe University in Georgia. He is the author of "Religion and the Limits of Liberal Pluralism" in *Democracy and Its Friendly Critics: Tocqueville and Political Life Today* (2004).

Stephen L. Carter

RICHARD A. KOFFARNUS is professor of church history, theology, and philosophy at Central Christian College of the Bible in Moberly, Missouri. His recent research has focused on the relationship between religion and political culture in the early American Republic.

Alexander Campbell
William Ellery Channing

MICHAEL J. KOPANIC, JR., is assistant professor of history at St. Francis University of Pennsylvania in Loretto. He is editor and translator of *Konstantin čulen's*

Slovaks in America (2006) and *Anton Spiesz's Illustrated Slovak History* (2005).

Štefan Furdek
Pavol Petor Gojdič
Andrew G. Grutka
Ján Chryzostom Korec
Josip Juraj Strossmayer

DAVID T. KOYZIS is professor of political science at Redeemer University College in Ontario, Canada. He is the author of *Political Visions and Illusions: A Survey and Christian Critique of Contemporary Ideologies* (2003).

Center for Public Justice
Russell Kirk

ROBERT H. KRAPOHL is university librarian and adjunct professor at Trinity International University in Deerfield, Illinois. He is coauthor (with Charles Lippy) of *The Evangelicals: A Historical, Thematic, and Biographical Guide* 1999).

William John Bennett
James Earl "Jimmy" Carter, Jr.
James C. Dobson, Jr.
Francis August Schaeffer IV

ANDRII KRAWCHUK is president, vice chancellor, and professor of Christian ethics at the University of Sudbury in Ontario, Canada. He is the author of *Christian Social Ethics in Ukraine: The Legacy of Andrei Sheptytsky* (1997).

Brotherhood of Saints Cyril and Methodius
Andrei Sheptytsky
Ukrainian Catholic Political Parties
Avhustyn Voloshyn

PAUL KUBRICHT is professor of history and political science at LeTourneau University in Longview, Texas. He is the author of "Soviet Expansion into Eastern Europe, 1945–1952: U.S. Policy Confronts the Issue of Religious Freedom" in *Fides et Historia* (2002).

Czechoslovak People's Party (československá Strana Lidová)
Josef Lukl Hromádka

SYLVIE LACOMBE is professor of sociology at the Université Laval in Quebec. She is the author of *La rencontre de deux peuples élus: Comparaison des ambitions nationale et impériale au Canada entre 1896 et 1920* (2002).

Henri Bourassa
Lionel Groulx
George Robert Parkin
James Shaver Woodsworth

The late MCKENDREE R. LANGLEY was adjunct professor of history at Eastern University in St. Davids, Pennsylvania, and at Esperanza College in Philadelphia.

He is the author of *The Practice of Political Spirituality: Episodes from the Public Career of Abraham Kuyper 1879–1918* (1984).

Anti-Revolutionary Party
J.A.H.J.S. Bruins Slot
Hendrikus Colijn
Guillaume Groen van Prinsterer
Jan Schouten

GEORGE M. LAUDERBAUGH is assistant professor of history at Jacksonville State University in Florida.

Catholic Political Parties
Gabriel Garcia Moreno
Leonidas Proaño

RICHARD A. LEBRUN is professor of history (emeritus) at the University of Manitoba in Canada. He is the author of *Joseph de Maistre: An Intellectual Militant* (1988) and editor of *Joseph de Maistre's Life, Thought, and Influence: Selected Studies* (2001).

Louis de Bonald
François-René de Chateaubriand
Joseph de Maistre
Louis Veuillot

JOSEPH TSE-HEI LEE is associate professor of history at Pace University in New York. He is the author of *The Bible and the Gun: Christianity in South China, 1860–1900* (2003).

Xiuquan Hong
Three-Self Movement
Sun Yat-sen

BERND LEUPOLD is a member of the Faculty of Cultural Studies at the University of Bayreuth in Bavaria, Germany. He is the author of *"Weder anglophil noch anglophob": Grossbritannien im politischen Denken von Konrad Adenauer* (1997).

Christian Social Union (Christlich-Soziale Union in Bayern)
Deutsche Christen (German Christians)
Helmut Kohl
Franz Josef Strauss

CHRISTIANE LIERMANN is research executive at Centro Italo-Tedesco Villa Vigoni in Menaggio (Como) Italy. She is the author of *Rosminis politische Philosophie der zivilen Gesellschaft* (2004).

Cesare Balbo
Alessandro Manzoni
Antonio Rosmini

CHARLES H. LIPPY is LeRoy A. Martin Distinguished Professor of Religious Studies at the University of Tennessee in Chattanooga. He is the author of *Do Real*

Men Pray? Images of the Christian Man and Male Spirituality in White Protestant America (2005) and coeditor (with Samuel S. Hill) of *Encyclopedia of Religion in the South* (2005).

Karl Reinhold Niebuhr
Walter Rauschenbusch

KATHRYN LOFTON is assistant professor of religious studies at Indiana University in Bloomington. She is the author of "The Preacher Paradigm: Biographical Promotions and the Modern-Made Evangelist, 1886–1931," in *Religion and American Culture: A Journal of Interpretation* (2006).

Ralph Abernathy
Jane Addams
Fannie Lou Hamer
Daniel Payne
William Seymour
Alfred Charles Sharpton, Jr.
Andrew Young

STEFANO LUCONI is professor of history of North America in the Department of Political Science at the University of Florence in Italy. He is the author of *La "Diplomazia Parallela": Il Regime Fascista e la Mobilitazione Politica Degli Italo-Americani* (2000) and (with Guido Tintori) *L'ombra Lunga del Fascio: Canali di Propaganda Fascista per gli "Italiani d'America"* (2004).

Davide Albertario
Giulio Andreotti
Giuseppe Dossetti
Primo Mazzolari

MEG MENEGHEL MACDONALD is a counselor for student services at the Office of Minority Affairs at the University of Washington in Seattle. She is the author of "'Dear Mother': Ray Strachey's Role in Feminism and the League of Nations as Seen from the Lilly Library," in *Women in the Milieu of Leonard and Virginia Woolf: Peace, Politics, and Education* (1998).

Susan Brownell Anthony
Elizabeth Cady Stanton
Hannah Whitall Smith

KATHLEEN M. MACKENZIE is an archivist at St. Francis Xavier University in Antigonish, Nova Scotia. Her research interests focus on Catholic history in Nova Scotia, and she is the editor of *Antigonish Diocese Priests & Bishops, 1786–1925 by Rev. A. A. Johnston* (1994).

John Cameron
Moses Michael Coady
Colin Francis MacKinnon

IAIN S. MACLEAN is associate professor of Western religious thought at James Madison University in Harrisonburg, Virginia.

Leonardo Boff
Abraham Kuyper
Daniel François Malan
Hendrik Gerhardus Stoker
Desmond Mpilo Tutu

GRETCHEN M. MACMILLAN is associate professor in the Department of Political Science at the University of Calgary in Alberta, Canada. Her research interests include Irish history and politics, the European Union, and American politics.

Eamon de Valera
Fianna Fail
Fine Gael
Land League
Ian Paisley
Charles Stewart Parnell
Sinn Fein
Ulster Unionists

JOHN T. S. MADELEY is lecturer in government at the London School of Economics and Political Science. He is the editor of *Religion and Politics* (2003) and coeditor (with Z. Enyedi) of *Church and State In Contemporary Europe: The Chimera of Neutrality* (2003).

Christian Democrats (Denmark)
Christian Democrats (Finland)
Christian Democrats (Sweden)
Christian People's Party
Nicolai Frederik Severin Grundtvig

MATTHEW A. MAGRUDER is a graduate student in history at Purdue University. His research focuses on antebellum American political culture.

Alexis de Tocqueville

DANIEL R. MANDELL is associate professor of history at Truman State University in Missouri. He is the author of *Behind the Frontier: Indians in Eighteenth-Century Eastern Massachusetts* (1996).

William Apess
Jeremiah Evarts
Samuel Worcester

JEFFREY MARLETT is associate professor of religious studies at the College of Saint Rose in Albany, New York. He is the author of *Saving the Heartland: Catholic Missionaries in Rural America, 1920–1960* (2002).

Charles Coughlin
James E. Groppi
John O'Connor

Gerald Lyman Kenneth Smith
Francis Joseph Spellman

ROBERT F. MARTIN is professor and head of the Department of History at the University of Northern Iowa in Cedar Falls. He is the author of *Hero of the Heartland: Billy Sunday and the Transformation of American Society, 1862–1935* (2002) and *Howard Kester and the Struggle for Social Justice in the South, 1904–77* (1991).

Russell Herman Conwell
Solomon Washington Gladden
William Ashley "Billy" Sunday

WILLIAM MARTIN is Harry and Hazel Chavanne Professor of Religion and Public Policy (emeritus) at Rice University in Houston, Texas. He is the author of "With God on Their Side: Religion and American Foreign Policy" in *Refurnishing the Public Square: Religion and Public Policy in Twentieth-Century America* (2003).

William Franklin "Billy" Graham, Jr.

EFHARIS MASCHA completed her doctoral degree at the University of Essex in the United Kingdom. Her research interests include political ideologies, Italian fascism, popular culture, and political satire.

Giuseppe Dalla Torre
Giuseppe Donati
Giovanni Guareschi

KENT A. MCCONNELL is visiting assistant professor of history at Wake Forest University in Winston-Salem, North Carolina. He is the author of "'Betwixt and Between': Topographies of Memory and Identity in American Catholicism" in *Vale of Tears: New Essays on Religion and Reconstruction* (2005).

Ku Klux Klan
Arthur and Lewis Tappan
Nat Turner

KENNETH B. MCINTYRE is assistant professor of political science at Campbellsville University in Kentucky. He is the author of *The Limits of Political Theory* (2004).

Herbert Butterfield
Richard John Neuhaus
Michael Novak

ROHAN MCWILLIAM is senior lecturer in history at Anglia Ruskin University in the United Kingdom. He is the author of *Popular Politics in Nineteenth-Century England* (1998).

John Emerich Edward Dalberg Acton
William Ewart Gladstone

MARTIN MENKE is associate professor and director of the Social Studies Program at Rivier College in Nashua, New Hampshire. He is the author of "Thy Will Be Done:' Nationalism and Faith in German Catholicism" in *Catholic Historical Review* (2005).

Dietrich Bonhoeffer
Center Party (Deutsche Zentrumspartei)
Jakob Kaiser
Carl Schmitt
Josef Wirth

JACQUES MONET is professor of historical theology (emeritus) and former president of Regis College at the University of Toronto. He has published widely on Catholic history and the monarchy in Canada and is currently director of the Canadian Institute of Jesuit Studies.

Sir Wilfred Laurier
Paul-Emile Léger
Georges-Phileas and Pauline Née Archer Vanier

RUDOLF MORSEY is professor of modern history at Deutsche Hochschule für Verwaltungswissenschaften Speyer. He is the author of *Görres-Gesellschaft und NS-Diktatur: Die Geschichte der Görres-Gesellschaft 1932/33 bis zum Verbot 1941* (2002).

Michael Faulhaber
Josef Frings

PATRICIA A. MULVEY is professor of history at Bluefield State College in West Virginia. She is the author of "Festas and Funerals: Funerary Politics in Colonial Brazil" in the *Journal of Plantation Studies* (1999).

Diogo Antonio Feijó

KATHLEEN NADEAU is associate professor of anthropology at California State University, San Bernadino. She is the author of *Liberation Theology in the Philippines, Faith in a Revolution* (2002).

Corazon Aquino
Basic Ecclesial Community
Rosaleo "Rudy" Romano

KYRIAKOS NALMPANTIS is instructor of history at the University of Pennsylvania in Edinboro. His research focuses on modern Greek and Balkan history.

Stylianos Karavaggelis (Germanos)

Michael Mouskos (Makarios III)
Demetrios Papandreous (Damaskinos)

JÜRGEN NAUTZ is assistant professor of economic history at the University of Vienna. He is the author of *Taxes and Civil Society* (2005).

Christian Social Party (Christlichsozialen Partei)

Kurt von Schuschnigg
Ignaz Seipel

CARYN E. NEUMANN is a lecturer in history at Ohio State University in Newark. She is the author of "Escaping the Christian Mystique: Church Women United and the Development of Christian Feminism" in *Feminist Coalitions: Historical Perspectives on Second-Wave Feminism in the United States* (2006).

Mary Jane McLeod Bethune
Church Women United
World Council of Churches

W. BRIAN NEWSOME is assistant professor of history at Alfred University in New York. He is the author of "The Apartment Referendum of 1959: Toward Participatory Architectural and Urban Planning in Postwar France" in *French Historical Studies* (2005).

Jeanne Aubert-Picard
Paul-Henry Chombart de Lauwe

IRINA NOVICHENKO is senior researcher at the Institute of General History Russian Academy of Sciences, and head of the Moscow Office of the International Institute of Social History. She is the author of *Charles Kingsley and English Christian Socialism in the Middle of the 19th Century* (2001).

Sergey Nikolaevich Bulgakov
Christian Socialist Workers and Peasants Party
Charles Kingsley
John Frederick Denison Maurice
Konstantin Petrovich Pobedonostsev
Lev Alexandrovich Tikhomirov

CHRISTOPHER OLDSTONE-MOORE is a lecturer of history at Wright State University in Dayton, Ohio. He is the author of *Hugh Price Hughes: Founder of a New Methodism; Conscience of a New Nonconformity* (1999).

Hugh Price Hughes

JANET C. OLSON is assistant university archivist at Northwestern University in Evanston, Illinois. She is the author of "In His Steps: A Social Gospel Novel" in *Religions of the United States in Practice* (2002).

Herbert Seely Bigelow
William Dwight Porter Bliss
Social Gospel

WILLIAM J. PARENTE is professor of political science at the University of Scranton in Pennsylvania. His research focuses on comparative politics.

Georges Bidault
Charles de Gaulle
Popular Republican Movement (Mouvement Republicain Populaire)
William Wilberforce

WILLIAM PATCH is professor of history at Washington and Lee University in Lexington, Virginia. He is the author of *Christian Trade Unions in the Weimar Republic, 1918–1933* (1985) and *Heinrich Bruning and the Dissolution of the Weimar Republic* (1998).

Heinrich Brüning
Ludwig Kaas
League of Christian Trade Unions of Germany
Friedrich Naumann

LEE M. PENYAK is associate professor of history and director of Latin American Studies at the University of Scranton in Pennsylvania. He recently completed a manuscript on haciendas in San Luis Potosí.

Cristeros Movement
Miguel Hidalgo

JADWIGA E. PIEPER MOONEY is assistant professor of history at the University of Arizona in Tucson. Her research interests include Chile, southern Cone, health, gender equity, reproductive rights, and comparative history.

Frei Betto
Emilio Máspero
María Celia Frutos de Meyer
Evita Peron
Raúl Silva Henriquez
Camilo Torres

ARGYRIOS K. PISIOTIS is senior desk officer at the European Commission in Brussels, Belgium. He is the author of *French and German, Greek and Turk: "Hereditary Enmity," U.S. Hegemony and the Limits of Integration* (1995).

Georgii Efremovich Dolganov (Germogen)
Vasilii Seymonovich Georgievskii (Evlogii)
Aleksei Khrapovitskii (Antonii)
Nikolai Vasil'evich Ognev
Fedor Vasil'evich Tikhvinskii
Sergei Mikhailovich Trufanoff (Iliodor)

JOHN F. POLLARD is a fellow in history at Trinity Hall College, University of Cambridge. He is the author of *Money and the Rise of the Modern Papacy: Financing the Vatican, 1850–1950* (2005).

Benedict XV
Italian Popular Party (Partito Popolare Italiano)
Filippo Meda
Raphael Merry Del Val
Pius X
Mariano Rampolla Del Tindaro
Giuseppe Toniolo

BRIAN PORTER is associate professor of history at the University of Michigan, Ann Arbor. He is the author of *When Nationalism Began to Hate: Imagining Modern Politics in 19th Century Poland* (2001).

August Hlond
Wojciech Korfanty
Tadeusz Rydzyk
Józef Tischner
Jerzy Turowicz

RAMESH J. RAJBALLIE is a doctoral candidate at the University of Oxford and lecturer in history at John Cabot University in Rome, Italy. His research focuses on twentieth-century France and political Catholicism.

Action Française
Leo XIII
Jean Baptiste Nicolas Robert Schuman
Maurice Jacques Schumann

JOHN D. RAMSBOTTOM is a lecturer in the Department of History at the University of Illinois at Urbana-Champaign. His research focuses on British social and religious history from 1500 to 1850.

Clapham Sect
Thomas Babington Macaulay
Daniel O'Connell
Henry Thornton

JOHN DAVID RAUSCH, JR., is associate professor of political science at West Texas A&M University. He is coeditor (with Rick Farmer and John Green) of *The Test of Time: Coping with Legislative Term Limits* (2003).

Gary L. Bauer
Tim LaHaye
Ralph Reed
Phyllis Schlafly

NORMAN RAVITCH is professor of history (emeritus) at the University of California, Riverside. He is the author of *The Catholic Church and the French Nation, 1589–1989* (1990).

Edouard Drumont
Charles Maurras

ALAN J. REINERMAN is professor of history at Boston College in Chestnut Hill, Massachusetts. He is the author of *Revolution and Reaction, 1830–1838* (1989), volume 2 of *Au tria and the Papacy in the Age of Metternich, 1809–1848*.

Gregory XVI
Fabrizio Ruffo
Luigi Taparelli d'Azeglio

MARGHERITA REPETTO-ALAIA is an associate at the Institute of European Studies, University of British Columbia. She is the coauthor of *UDI, Laboratorio di politica delle donne* (1998).

Armida Barelli
Adriano Ossicini
Franco Rodano

BARRY ROBINSON is assistant professor of history at Samford University in Birmingham, Alabama. His research focuses on Latin American society and culture.

Ernesto Martinez Cardenal
Nicaraguan Council of Evangelical Churches

ANDREA RÖNZ is *Stadtarchivarin* at Stadtarchiv Linz am Rhein in Germany. She is the author of *Zur Geschichte des Hospitals St. Martin in Linz am Rhein* (2004).

Hermann Ehlers
Friedrich Wilhelm IV
Johann Joseph Görres
Adolph Kolping
Ferdinand August von Spiegel zum Desenberg und Canstein
Helene Weber

HELMUT RÖNZ is *Wissenschaftlicher Referent* at Landschaftlicher Rheinland Amt für Rheinische Landeskunde Abteilung Stadtgeschichte in Bonn, Germany. He is the author of *Der Weltklerus der Diözese Trier von der Säkularisation bis zum Ersten Weltkrieg* (2006).

Christian Democratic Appeal (Christen Democratisch Appèl)
Friedrich Wilhelm III
Clemens August von Galen
Rudolphus "Ruud" Franciscus Marie Lubbers
Wilhelm Marx
Hermann Schaepman
Christine Teusch

CHRISTIAN ROY is a historian and member of the faculties of theology and philosophy at Université Laval in Quebec. He is the author of *Alexandre Marc et la jeune Europe 1904–1934: L'Ordre Nouveau aux origines du personnalisme* (1999).

Raymond De Becker
Léon Degrelle
George Grant

FERNANDO MURILLO RUBIERA is professor of international law at the Universidad Complutense School of Law in Madrid.

Gonzalo Fernandez de la Mora
Eugenio Vegas Latapié
Juan Vásquez de Mella

MARKKU RUOTSILA is adjunct associate professor of history at the University of Tampere in Tampere, Finland. He is the author of *British and American Anticommunism before the Cold War* (2001), *Churchill and Finland: A Study in*

Anticommunism and Geopolitics (2005), and *John Spargo and American Socialism* (2006).

Hilaire Pierre Belloc
Gilbert Keith Chesterton
Charles Gore
Henry Scott Holland
William Joynson-Hicks
Alan Ian Percy
Frank Smith
William Temple

ARLENE SANCHEZ WALSH is an associate professor in the Haggard School of Theology at Azusa Pacific University in Azusa, California. She is the author of *Latino Pentecostal Identity: Evangelical Faith, Society and the Self* (2003).

Christian Coalition
Marion Gordon "Pat" Robertson

ROLAND SARTI is professor of history (emeritus) at the University of Massachusetts, Amherst. He is the author of *Giuseppe Mazzini: La poitica come religione civile* (1997) and *Italy: A Reference Guide from the Renaissance to the Present* (2004).

Vincenzo Gioberti
Giuseppe Mazzini

JONATHAN D. SASSI is associate professor of history at the College of Staten Island, CUNY. He is the author of *A Republic of Righteousness: The Public Christianity of the Post-revolutionary New England Clergy* (2001).

Lyman Beecher
Theodore Frelinghuysen
John Leland

MATHEW N. SCHMALZ is associate professor of religious studies at the College of the Holy Cross in Worcester, Massachusetts. His research interests include world Catholicism, South Asian studies, and modern religious movements.

Wihelmus Bekkers
César Chávez
Josemaría Escrivá de Balaguer y Albá
Michael Fu Tieshan
Stephen Kim Sou-hwan
Ignatius Pin-Mei Kung (Gong)
Pierre-Guillame-Frédéric Le Play
Mečislovas Reinys
Bobby Sands
Yisu Das Tiwari
Brahmabandhab Upadhyay
Johannes Gerardus Maria Willebrands

THOMAS J. SHELLEY is a priest of the Archdiocese of New York and is professor of historical theology at Fordham University in New York. His most recent book is *Greenwich Village Catholics* (2003).

John Joseph Hughes
John Ireland

JOSEPH SINASAC is publisher and editor of the *Catholic Register* in Toronto. He is the author of *Fateful Passages: The Life of Henry Somerville, Catholic Journalist* (2003).

Henry Somerville

RODERICK STACKELBERG is professor of history (emeritus) at Gonzaga University in Spokane, Washington. He is the author of *From Völkisch Ideology to National Socialism* (1981) and *Hitler's Germany: Origins, Interpretations, Legacies* (1999).

Houston Stewart Chamberlain

JOHN STAUFFER is professor of English, African, and African American studies at Harvard University. He is the author of *The Black Hearts of Men: Radical Abolitionists and the Transformation of Race* (2002).

Frederick Douglass
Gerrit Smith
James McCune Smith

JOHN STRICKLAND is a lecturer at Seattle University.

Alexander I
Alexander III
Black Hundreds
Klemens von Metternich

CARL STRIKWERDA is dean of the Faculty of Arts and Sciences and professor of history at the College of William and Mary in Williamsburg, Virginia. He is the author of *A House Divided: Catholics, Socialists, and Flemish Nationalists in Nineteenth Century Belgium* (1997).

Belgian Christian Labor Movement
Malines Congress
Rexist Movement

MARTIN SUTHERLAND is dean of Tyndale-Carey Graduate School in Auckland, New Zealand. He is the author of *Peace Toleration and Decay: The Ecclesiology of Later Stuart Dissent* (2003).

John Kendrick Archer
John Ross Marshall
Walter Nash

ROY L. TANNER is professor of Spanish at Truman State University in Missouri. He is the author of *The Humor of Irony and Satire in the Tradiciones peruanas of Ricardo Palma* (1986).

Joseph Smith
Brigham Young

GREGOR THUSWALDNER is assistant professor of German at Gordon College in Wenham, Massachusetts. He is the coeditor (with Olaf Berwald) of *Gott ist untot: Religion und Ästhetik in deutscher und österreichischer Kultur des 20. Jahrhunderts* (forthcoming).

Engelbert Dollfuss
Franz Grillparzer
Friedrich Heer
Bernhard Lichtenberg
Karl Lueger

FRANCESCO TRANIELLO is chair of contemporary history at the University of Turin in Italy. He is the author of *Cattolicesimo conciliatorista: Religione e cultura nella tradizione rosminiana lombardo-piemontese (1825–1870)* (1970) and is the director of the quarterly historical review *Contemporanea* in Bologna.

Cesare Balbo

LEE TREPANIER is assistant professor of political science at Saginaw Valley State University in University Center, Michigan. He is the author of "Nationalism and Religion in Post-Soviet Russian Civil Society: An Inquiry into the 1997 Law 'On Freedom of Conscience'" in *Civil Society and the Search for Justice in Russia* (2002).

Patrick Joseph Buchanan, Jr.
Martin E. Marty
Norman Mattoon Thomas
Cornel West

STEVEN BÉLA VÁRDY is McAnulty Distinguished Professor of European History at Duquesne University in Pittsburgh, Pennsylvania. His research focuses on Hungarian and East Central European social and intellectual history and the history of immigration and ethnic life in America.

Christian Socialism
Christian Socialist Parties
Sándor Giesswein
Jósef Mindszenty
Peasant and Smallholders Parties
Ottokár Prohászka

ROBERT A. VENTRESCA is associate professor of history at King's University College at the University of Western Ontario in Canada. He is the author of *From Fascism to Democracy: Culture and Politics in the Italian Election of 1948* (2004).

Ercole Consalvi
Pietro Gasparri
Giovanni Gronchi
Alfredo Ottaviani
Domenico Tardini

ELIANA VERSACE is a professor of contemporary history at the Catholic University of Milan. Her research focuses on the Catholic Church and Christian democratic politics in Italy.

Communion and Liberation (Comunione e Liberazione)
Amintore Fanfani
Luigi Gedda
Romolo Murri
Benigno Zaccagnini

MARY VINCENT is senior lecturer in history at the University of Sheffield in the United Kingdom. She is the author of *Catholicism in the Second Spanish Republic: Religion and Politics in Salamanca, 1930–36* (1996).

José María Gil Robles y Quiñones
National Catholic Agrarian Federation (CNCA)
Enrique Plá y Deniel
José Antonio Primo de Rivera
Joaquín Ruíz-Giménez
Spanish Confederation of Autonomous Right-Wing Groups (CEDA)
Vicente Enrique Y. Tarancón

PAMELA J. WALKER is professor of history at Carleton University in Ottawa, Canada. She is the author of *Pulling the Devil's Kingdom Down: The Salvation Army in Victorian Britain* (2001) and coeditor (with Beverly Mayne Kienzle) of *Women Preachers and Prophets Through Two Millennia of Christianity* (1998).

William and Catherine Booth
Salvation Army

ANDREW D. WALSH is assistant professor of religion and philosophy at Culver-Stockton College in Canton, Missouri. He is the author of *Religion, Economics and Public Policy: Ironies, Tragedies and Absurdities of the Contemporary Culture Wars* (2000).

James Cone
Gustavo Gutiérrez
Rosemary Radford Ruether

JAMES MACE WARD is a doctoral candidate in history at Stanford University in California. His research focuses on Eastern Europe.

Alojzije Stepinac
Josef Tiso

JEAN-PHILIPPE WARREN is professor of sociology at Concordia University in Montreal. He is the author of *L'engagement sociologique: La tradition sociologique du Québec francophone* (2003) and *Un supplément d'âme: Les intentions primordiales de Fernand Dumont* (1998).

Fernand Dumont
Georges-Henri Lévesque
Gérard Pelletier

RICHARD WENTZ is professor of religious studies (emeritus) and founder of the Department of Religious Studies at Arizona State University in Tempe. He is the author of *John Williamson Nevin, American Theologian* (1996).

John Williamson Nevin
Philip Schaff
Samuel Schmucker

PHILIP WHALEN is assistant professor of history at Coastal Carolina University in Conway, South Carolina. He is the author of "'Food Palaces Built of Sausages [and] Great Ships of Lamb Chops': The Gastronomical Fair of Dijon as Consuming Spectacle" in *The Business of Tourism: The Production and Consumption of Experience* (2006).

Paul Desjardins
Gaston Roupnel

STEVEN F. WHITE is Morrison Professor of International Studies at Mount Saint Mary's University in Emmitsburg, Maryland. He is the author of "Christian Democracy or Pacellian Populism? Rival Forms of Post-war Italian Political Catholicism" in *European Christian Democracy: Historical Legacies and Comparative Perspectives* (2003) and *Progressive Renaissance: The United States and the Reconstruction of Italian Education, 1943–1962* (1991).

Alcide De Gasperi
Agostino Gemelli
Vittorino Veronese

SUSAN B. WHITNEY is assistant professor of history at Carleton University in Ottawa, Canada. Her research focuses on twentieth-century French history.

French Confederation of Christian Workers (CFTC)
Young Christian Workers (Jeunesse Ouvrière Chrétienne)

ANNE BLUE WILLS is assistant professor of history at Davidson College in North Carolina. She is the author of "Pilgrims and Progress: How Magazines Made Thanksgiving" in *Church History: Studies in Christianity and Culture* (2003).

Sarah Moore and Angelina Emily Grimké
Harriet Beecher Stowe
Emma Hart Willard

LIA YOKA is lecturer in art history at Aristotle University of Thessaloníki in Greece. Her research focuses on nineteenth- and twentieth-century intellectual and cultural history and modern art.

Apostolos Makrakis

ROBERT L. YOUNGBLOOD is professor of political science at Arizona State University in Tempe. He is the author of *Marcos Against the Church: Economic Development and Political Repression in the Philippines* (1991).

Catholic Bishops' Conference of the Philippines Commission
National Council of Churches in the Philippines
Jaime Sin
Task Force Detainees Philippines